An Honest Enemy

Mary and George Crook, circa 1880s. Courtesy of Mark Kasal.

An Honest Enemy

**George Crook
and the Struggle for Indian Rights**

Paul Magid

University of Oklahoma Press : Norman

Publication of this book is made possible through the generosity of Edith Kinney Gaylord.

Library of Congress Cataloging-in-Publication Data

Names: Magid, Paul, 1940– author.
Title: An honest enemy : George Crook and the struggle for Indian rights / Paul Magid.
Other titles: George Crook and the struggle for Indian rights
Description: Norman : University of Oklahoma Press, [2020] | Includes bibliographical references and index. | Summary: "The third and final biography of George Crook's life and involvement in the Indian wars, his campaigns against the Chiricahua Apaches and their leader Geronimo, his struggle to reconcile fulfilling his duties as a soldier and his humanitarian values, and his metamorphosis from Indian fighter to outspoken advocate of Indian rights."—Provided by publisher.
Identifiers: LCCN 2019049799 | ISBN 978-0-8061-6500-4 (hardcover)
Subjects: LCSH: Crook, George, 1829–1890. | Indians of North America—Wars—1866–1895. | Indians of North America—Government relations—1869–1934. | Generals—United States—Biography. | United States. Army—Biography.
Classification: LCC E467.1.C86 M344 2020 | DDC 355.0092 [B]—dc23
LC record available at https://lccn.loc.gov/2019049799

The paper in this book meets the guidelines for permanence and durability of the Committee on Production Guidelines for Book Longevity of the Council on Library Resources, Inc. ∞

1 2 3 4 5 6 7 8 9 10

*To Cynthia Riggs, whose unflagging enthusiasm, support,
and generosity on behalf of aspiring Vineyard writers has meant
so much to those of us privileged to know her over the years.*

Contents

List of Illustrations   ix
Acknowledgments   xi

Introduction   3
 1 It Is an Outrage   7
 2 Blood on the Snow   18
 3 I Am a Man   47
 4 The Ponca Commission   77
 5 Crook House   89
 6 Cowboys and Indians   97
 7 Investing in the Future   112
 8 Return to Apacheria   123
 9 There Is Not Now a Hostile Apache in Arizona   144
10 Preparations for a Campaign   161
11 Into the Sierra Madre   181
12 Geronimo—Hunter and Prey   196
13 Fire in My Rear   219
14 Settling Down the Chiricahuas   230
15 Move to Turkey Creek   242
16 More Fire from the Rear   255
17 Breakout   276
18 Pursuit into Mexico   293
19 A Tragic Loss   316

20 Cañon de los Embudos   327
21 Too Wedded to My Views   342
22 Changing of the Guard   353
23 Campaigning for Indian Rights   372
24 Omaha Sojourn   400
25 Chicago   414
26 The Sioux Commission   422
27 End of Days   445
28 Summing Up   463

Notes   467
Bibliography   527
Index   539

List of Illustrations

FIGURES

Mary and George Crook, circa 1880s   *frontispiece*
Thomas Henry Tibbles   49
Standing Bear, Ponca Chief   58
Crook House, Omaha, as it appears today   91
Lieutenant Walter Scribner Schuyler, circa 1880   115
Lieutenant General Philip H. Sheridan   121
Crook, accompanied by his White Mountain Scout Alchesay   124
Captain Emmet Crawford   153
Britton Davis as a West Point cadet   154
Lieutenant Charles Gatewood, circa 1880   155
Mickey Free, scout and interpreter   163
Geronimo and Naiche   171
Chatto   172
Chihuahua   173
Major General Nelson A. Miles   311
Surrender talks at Cañon de los Embudos, Mexico   336
Herbert Welsh, founder of the Indian Rights Association,
    circa 1880   378
Fall hunt, taken at Fort Washaki, circa 1886–87   403
Lieutenant Lyman W. V. Kennon, Crook's aide, circa 1885   407

The Sioux commissioners at the outset of their visit to the
    Sioux agencies, 1889   432
Crook Crest, Oakland, Maryland, as it appears today   457
Crook's gravesite, Arlington National Cemetery   459

MAPS

Routes followed by Northern Cheyennes and Poncas, 1879   45
Department of the Platte showing locations of Bannock and
    Ute conflicts, 1878–79   98
Arizona, New Mexico, and Old Mexico locations, Geronimo
    campaigns, 1883–86   182
Lakota reservations at time of Sioux commission visit, 1889   423

Acknowledgments

In 2001 when I set out on my maiden journey into the world of historical writing, I had no clear idea of where it would take me or how long it would last. Not long after I began work on the Crook project, David Everett, the director of the writing program at Johns Hopkins's Krieger School where I was then enrolled, assured me that before I reached my final destination, I would find myself on many unanticipated detours. Neither of us remotely contemplated that it would take eighteen years and three volumes to complete. But looking back, for me, the time and effort were well spent. The work has given me great personal satisfaction, earned me new friendships, exposed me to new places and a world of knowledge, and rewarded me with a greater understanding of the human cost of America's westward expansion. It has also driven home the truth that writing history may be an individual pursuit, but it is by no means a solo endeavor.

Of those who helped me along the path, I must first acknowledge my indebtedness to my publisher, University of Oklahoma Press and its former editor-in-chief, Charles Rankin, and Robert Clark, former acquisitions editor of the Arthur H. Clark Company (an OU Press imprint). They have patiently endured the fumbling and misapprehensions of a first-time author and, with editorial guidance from Steve Baker, led and supported me through the myriad of steps that precede publication. Regarding the actual production of the final manuscript for this book, I would be remiss in not thanking my copyeditor, Leslie

Tingle, who is responsible for removing dangles and straightening out the footnotes and bibliography.

In my two previous books, I acknowledged my indebtedness to many people and institutions whose contributions were essential to my research, plowing important ground before I ever set foot on it. Several, like Robert Utley, Jerome Greene, Neil Mangum, and Paul Hedren, are noted veterans of the National Park Service, while others, like Paul Hutton, have university affiliations. Some are authors who have independently produced important works simply by dint of hard work and love of their subject with little support or expectation of remuneration. While I wrote this latest work, a number of the most accomplished western historians have sadly passed from the scene, including Thomas Buecker, Ed Sweeney, John McDermott, and Douglas McChristian. The importance of their contributions to my work, particularly those of Ed Sweeney, is evident from the frequency with which they are cited in my endnotes.

I also want to gratefully acknowledge the contributions of Ms. Cindy Hadsen and her fellow board members at the Douglas County Historical Society, who organized my visit to Omaha's Crook House. Thanks to their efforts, I had a delightful weekend in Omaha and learned much valuable information about the building's history and construction that I incorporated into the chapter on that venerable structure.

My books would have been incomplete without the original documents and photos carefully collected, preserved, and identified by the personnel of historical societies and museums. In the case of *An Honest Enemy,* I used materials provided by the Nebraska State Historical Society, Sharlot Hall Museum, the Arizona Historical Society, the U.S. Army Heritage and Educational Center at Carlisle Barracks, and, of course, the National Archives.

A special note of thanks goes to Mark Kasal, who was unstinting in his generosity in allowing me to use photos from his bottomless collection without charge in both this book and the previous volume; and to Tom Jonas, who produced the fine maps so necessary to an understanding of my story.

At home on Martha's Vineyard, far from research facilities and publisher, I have relied heavily on my own West Tisbury Free Public Library, whose facilities and dedication to service far outstrip those of far larger towns and cities, and to my Sunday writers' group. The latter is an ongoing weekly gathering of writers from all walks of life united by their dedication to improving their own and one another's works. Their friendship, support, and willingness to serve as a sounding board for my writings over the past several years have been of immeasurable assistance in keeping me on track and focused, a necessity in any project of such duration.

Finally, I must thank my family for their endurance over the past eighteen years. My wife and children have had to put up with George Crook far longer than any of us expected, a guest who came for dinner.

An Honest Enemy

Introduction

The winter of 1877–78 on the high plains was so exceptionally mild that it would be remembered by some as the winter without winter. The *Monthly Weather Review* for February 1878 reported prairie fires and grass greening in Dakota at a time when the region normally lay under a deep blanket of snow.[1] Such fair weather would ordinarily have drawn the nomadic tribes out on to the prairies to fatten their ponies and hunt fresh game. Yet the most dominant among them, the Lakotas and their Cheyenne and Arapaho allies, remained cloistered in villages along the White and Niobrara Rivers, distant from white habitation and under the army's watchful eye. Defeated, divided, and impoverished after two years of war, they no longer presented a threat to travelers or to the settlements, ranches, and homesteads that had now begun to sprout across the landscape like mushrooms after a rainstorm. That fall and early winter, during the trek of the Sioux nation from the Nebraska agencies to their new homes in the Dakota Territory, many of the so-called Northern Sioux, the last to surrender, had fled north to join Sitting Bull in the Grand Mother's land across the border. These chiefs and their followers, still angered by the killing of Crazy Horse and restless under the unaccustomed constraints of reservation life, might have posed a real problem for the army. But now, camped with Sitting Bull's followers in the Wood Mountain region of the Northwest Territories, they remained quiescent, closely supervised by Canada's North-West Mounted Police. So, for the moment, peace prevailed in the Department of the Platte.[2]

Almost twenty-five years of unremitting warfare—nine in the Pacific Northwest, four in the crucible of the Civil War, and a decade campaigning across the Great Basin, the southwestern desert, and the Great Plains—had left their indelible mark on George Crook. The war against the Sioux had been particularly daunting, both mentally and physically. Prior to encountering them, his career had been auspicious. An understanding of Indian habits and culture almost unrivaled in the military service, a dogged style of campaigning, and his enthusiastic embrace of life in the field had brought him success and renown as an Indian fighter and rapid advancement to the rank of brigadier general. But his reputation following the war with the Sioux nation was clouded by a stalemate on the Rosebud, by allegations that his dawdling at Goose Creek had contributed to Custer's defeat at the Little Big Horn, and by the ensuing frustrating and fruitless misery of the so-called Starvation March. Instead of the accolades to which he had become accustomed, he found himself the target of intense public criticism.[3] Private and reticent by nature, he had been unwilling, and perhaps unable, to draw on the strength of others to relieve his inner burdens. So he bore alone the vilification of sniping journalists, impatient superiors, and competitive fellow officers.

But now the Sioux had surrendered, thanks to a peace initiative in which he had played a prominent role, ending the war and with it much of the criticism that had dogged him. With renewed confidence he looked forward to the coming year as a time of peace, bringing with it, perhaps, the opportunity to enjoy the meager prerogatives afforded a military commander on the frontier and, for the first time in several years, the uninterrupted attentions of his wife, Mary.

The recent conflict had been equally difficult for her. Though comfortably ensconced in the quarters that served as the Omaha residence for the general and his family, during the past several years Mary had suffered repeated, prolonged separations from her husband. During these periods the only news she received of his whereabouts and welfare often came from press reports that routinely described him as engaged in mortal combat with a foe frighteningly described as "savage," "ruthless," and "bloodthirsty." The general, uncommunicative by nature and increasingly moody and tense as the war dragged on, had probably not been the best of companions, even on those rare occasions when he had been at home. To relieve the tension and escape the harsh western winters, Mary had formed the habit of visiting her family home in Oakland, Maryland, during the bleakest months of the year. But now, with the war over, her life had returned to some semblance of normalcy. Her sister had come to visit her in Omaha, and Mary remained by her husband's side, at least for the holidays, enjoying such festivities as the town offered and, on New Year's Day, hosting an open house at the general's residence.[4]

Though uninterested in ladies' socials, George, too, undoubtedly craved the opportunity for a little recreation, perhaps something he and Mary could enjoy together. So when a letter arrived in mid-December from J. J. Dickey, superintendent of the Omaha office of the Atlantic & Pacific Telephone Company, he was delighted. Mr. Dickey had written to say that he had received a set of Mr. Bell's new telephones, which he hoped to introduce to the people of Omaha and points west. Would General Crook and his friends and fellow officers be interested in a demonstration of the instrument at the general's residence? If so, Mr. Dickey proposed to run a wire from Crook's home at the corner of Eighteenth Street and Davenport to Omaha Barracks, a distance of some three or four miles, and demonstrate the instrument's ability to relay communications between the two points. Crook enthusiastically agreed, and on the evening of January 3, Mr. Dickey arrived and set up his equipment as promised. There followed a three-hour performance during which the musical notes of a clarinet, violin, cornet, and piano were transmitted by wire from the barracks to the transfixed audience at Crook's home. Then, to the amusement of his fellow officers and their wives, the general picked up the receiver and bantered briefly in the Crow language with his friend Captain Andrew Burt of the Ninth Infantry at the barracks. The program concluded with the clear, ringing notes of a bugle call.[5]

But even as the general's guests marveled at the sounds of the regimental bugle issuing from the strange new instrument, ominous rumblings from the western reaches of the Department of the Platte vied for their host's attention. An article on the front page of the Christmas Day edition of the *Omaha Republican* had certainly caught his eye. Beneath an unusually restrained headline—"Probability that the Bannocks Will Cause Trouble the Coming Spring"—was the tale of the murder of a white settler at Ross Fork in Idaho Territory. A Bannock warrior stood accused, and the army had demanded his surrender. Though the tribe has agreed to deliver the culprit, many doubted that it would. Portentously, the *Republican* concluded, "They are well armed, well mounted and insolent. It is thought they will make trouble in the spring."[6]

That such unrest could occur among members of a tribe that had been confined to a reservation for well over a decade reinforced Crook's growing conviction that the government's reservation policies would not solve the so-called Indian problem. Perhaps of greater import, these latest troubles would appear to have aroused something deep in the general's core that eroded the inhibitions that had heretofore limited his responses to government mismanagement of Indian affairs to internal military communications. Henceforth, deeply stirred by the mistreatment of the tribes, he would gradually emerge, publicly and sometimes behind the scenes, as a prominent figure in the struggle for Indian rights. His metamorphosis from an Indian fighter to an outspoken advocate for the welfare of his former enemy dominated the final chapters of his life and, as such, is the subject of this, the third and final volume of his biography.

CHAPTER ONE

It Is an Outrage

The Bannocks had garnered a few headlines in the West during that mild winter. For Crook's superior, General Philip Sheridan, commander of the Military Division of the Missouri, and others in the army, the primary threat to peace and order on the frontier was Sitting Bull, lurking just across the Canadian border. Sheridan declared to reporters that, should the "hostiles . . . venture away from the border and attempt a reoccupation of their old stamping grounds south of the Yellowstone, the troops will endeavor to give them a warm reception." To that end, he ordered Crook to mass his soldiers north of the Black Hills that spring.[1] But when spring arrived, it was the Bannocks, not the Sioux, who would occupy Crook's attention.

The Bannocks shared a reservation with their cousins, the Shoshones, at Ross Fork, near Fort Hall in southern Idaho, on the western edge of Crook's department. They were a small but warlike tribe, steeped in the buffalo-hunting horse culture of the Plains Indians, who had maintained a checkered relationship with the white man, marked by periods of warfare interspersed with acts of generosity and cooperation. Their proximity to the immigrant trails to Oregon and California tempted them to raid wagon trains for plunder and offered them the opportunity to sharpen their combat skills. Their aggressiveness increased over time, spurred by anger at the whites for their indiscriminate slaughter of the game the Bannocks relied on for food.[2] Whites retaliated in kind, committing outrages, one officer wrote, "that the heart would shudder to record."[3]

The accelerating cycle of violence precipitated military intervention, culminating in a decisive defeat for the tribe and their Shoshone allies in January 1863.[4] Shocked by the army's fighting skills and brutality, the Bannocks, following the lead of a prominent Shoshone chief, Washakie, signed a treaty agreeing to share a reservation in the Fort Hall region with a portion of the Shoshone tribe. That decision placed the tribe within Crook's jurisdiction when the reservation was transferred from the Department of Columbia to his Department of the Platte in June 1875.[5] The treaty ceded to the tribes a fairly large area and included access to the Camas Prairie, a valley adjacent to the reservation. There, each year, the bands traditionally harvested the root of the camas lily that, ground into flour, formed a vital part of their diet.[6] In addition, the Bannocks received the right to continue to take the buffalo and other game on adjacent lands "unoccupied by the United States" and were to receive rations to supplement the declining take of their annual hunts.[7]

Over the next several years the government consistently failed to provide adequate supplies and the promised rations, but the Bannocks warded off starvation by hunting and gathering the camas roots from the prairie. During this period they ceased all hostilities against the whites, channeling their love of warfare into service with the army as scouts.[8] Under their chief, Buffalo Horn, they earned Crook's esteem for their loyalty and courage at the Rosebud as well as that of Colonel Nelson A. Miles for their service against the Cheyenne.[9]

During the 1870s, though outwardly adhering to the 1868 treaty and dutifully serving the army, beneath the surface the Bannocks' resentment toward the whites smoldered as hunger continued to stalk the tribe. Settlers killed off their game while their other major resource, the camas root, came under siege by farmers, who drove their livestock on to the prairie in the spring to fatten them on the starchy tubers.[10]

Confined by the army to their reservation during the Nez Perce conflict in the summer of 1877, they were deprived of even these meager resources. Forced to rely entirely on government rations, hardly plentiful under the best of circumstances and now further diminished by corruption and a stingy Congress, they could longer fulfill their basic nutritional needs. By that winter at Fort Hall, the Bannocks faced starvation, their hunger pangs sharpened by their perception that the

Shoshone on the same reservation were receiving more than they did.[11] Yet still their tribesmen volunteered to scout for the army against the Nez Perce under General Oliver O. Howard, who gladly accepted their services on Crook's recommendation. By all accounts, they proved loyal and effective.[12]

In August 1877, as the Nez Perce War ground to a close, a Bannock, believing that a white man had raped his sister, shot and seriously wounded two teamsters, precipitating a cycle of events that would turn the tribe's frustration and anger into open rebellion. The tribesman's subsequent arrest moved a warrior named Tambiago to retaliate by killing an innocent settler, the event chronicled in the paper that Crook had read on Christmas Day.[13] This second murder not only alarmed whites in the area, but when, in turn, Tambiago was apprehended, it sent shockwaves of discontent through the Fort Hall Bannocks, about 150 warriors and their dependents.[14]

The unrest prompted the local Indian agent, William Danilson, to request military intervention. Captain A. H. Bainbridge, commanding officer at nearby Fort Hall, reported to Crook in late November that the Bannocks seemed, indeed, "disposed to be troublesome." But after the tribe agreed to arrest Tambiago and turn him over to the agent, Bainbridge was satisfied that matters were under control and returned to his post some fifteen miles away, leaving a handful of men to keep an eye on things.[15]

Unfortunately, the situation continued to deteriorate. The Bannocks failed to keep their promise to arrest Tambiago and were behaving in what Bainbridge described as a "threatening and impudent manner." He now forecast an imminent outbreak, probably by summer at the latest, in which two to three hundred related Bannocks living at the Lemhi and Wind River agencies might well participate. Against such an eventuality, he requested reinforcements.[16] Crook responded by sending Colonel John E. Smith and a company of infantry from Fort Douglas, Utah, to reinforce the beleaguered captain.

Smith proved to be a poor choice, as he regarded the Bannocks as inherently hostile and in need of a forceful response.[17] He arrived at Fort Hall in mid-December, just as the reservation's warriors, both Bannocks and Shoshones, were gathering to receive pay due them for service in the Nez Perce War. Taking advantage of the moment, Smith announced that until the Bannocks surrendered the murderer, he would withhold their pay and stop their rations. If that proved insufficient, he threated to make war on them. While their chiefs sought to placate the colonel, aroused warriors moved about the agency brandishing their weapons and muttering dire threats against all whites in the vicinity. With only a single company of infantry and unable to rely on the Fort Hall Shoshones, who wanted no part in the matter, Smith wired Crook for additional reinforcements—at least two companies of cavalry. Based on Smith's analysis, the general, with Sheridan's enthusiastic endorsement, complied.[18]

In the interim Tambiago was apprehended without incident, but Colonel Smith believed that a show of force was still required. With his reinforcements on hand, on January 12 he asked permission to surround the culprit's village and confiscate their ponies and firearms to cow the tribe into quiescence.[19] While Crook may have doubted the wisdom of Smith's proposal, he was not in the habit of second-guessing his officers on the spot. Sidestepping the issue, he ordered the colonel to use his own judgment in the matter.[20] Smith justifiably interpreted this as approval and executed his plan. The Bannocks, overawed, surrendered without a fight, and the colonel confiscated their ponies and their guns, an unimpressive collection of obsolete muzzleloaders. Smith also took fifty warriors captive, but he quickly released them, with the exception of several of Tambiago's immediate relatives.[21]

Smith's actions proved significant, though hardly in the manner he had anticipated. Rather than deter future hostilities, the seizures only increased the tribe's restiveness, a circumstance that Smith and his subordinates strangely failed to grasp. Settlers in the vicinity, however, were less oblivious. While the officers, anxious to return to their post in Utah, reported the Indians as generally peaceful and unthreatening, fearful frontier farmers and ranchers petitioned Agent Danilson to request that the troops remain in the area.[22] The agent, perceiving that much of the tribe's hostility was directed at him as the source of their inadequate rations, forwarded their petition to Washington with his hearty approval.

Disturbed by the conflicting descriptions of the situation and wishing to resolve the matter without violence, Crook dispatched Colonel William B. Royall, now inspector general of the Department of the Platte, to the Fort Hall Agency in early March to personally investigate. Though Royall and Crook had crossed swords on occasion during the Sioux War, Crook evidently had faith in the colonel's instincts where Indians were concerned.[23] After a brief investigation Royall reported that he agreed with the officers at the post that the Bannocks were "friendly and peaceable." But in an apparent contradiction, he also wrote that the tribe had become "very much opposed to their agent, Mr. Danilson," to such an extent that his life was, indeed, threatened.[24]

To Crook, Royall's contradictory conclusions only muddled the situation further. Fearing that matters were about to spiral out of control, he decided to personally intercede. Accompanied by his aides, Lieutenants John G. Bourke and Walter S. Schuyler, he set out for the Ross Fork agency. The journey proved arduous, occupying the better part of six days in wintery weather and harsh conditions and at one point requiring that the officers travel on an open railway car strapped to chairs.[25] En route Crook encountered Colonel John G. Gibbon, traveling east to Washington. At dinner that evening the two officers discussed the recent war against the Nez Perce and agreed that the conflict was "an unjustifiable outrage upon the red men, due to [the government's] aggressive and untruthful behavior towards those poor people." These policies, the two generals unhappily predicted, would "be repeated with every tribe until the whole race shall become extinct."[26]

Arriving at Ross Fork about noon on April 2, Crook summoned Tokio, the principle chief of the Bannocks, and other tribal leaders for a parlay. In the presence of Captain Bainbridge and Agent Danilson, he asked Tokio how the tribe was getting along. The chief allowed that "everything is all right and quiet." A skeptical Crook received this response without comment. Instead, he gruffly reminded the Indians of the fate met by the Nez Perces as the result of their uprising, a rather surprising statement in view of his recent discussions with General Gibbon.[27]

He then turned to the immediate cause of the current discontent, Smith's seizure of their ponies and government's failure to compensate the tribe for them. This issue had been hanging fire since January, as the War and Interior departments squabbled over who was responsible for the sale of the ponies and the purchase of cattle for the Indians with the proceeds.[28] That an intense bureaucratic rivalry between the departments had delayed resolution of the issue was incomprehensible to the Bannocks.[29] Oblivious to Washington's turf wars, they understood only that the government had arbitrarily taken their ponies, and they had received nothing in return.

Crook, who at this point probably deeply regretted his decision to allow Smith to carry out the seizures in the first place, frankly admitted that taking the ponies as punishment had been a mistake and promised to recommend their return. His gesture was well received by the tribesmen who responded with assurances of friendship and peace. Then, sensing that Crook seemed sympathetic to their interests, they brought forward their most critical concern: their inadequate rations, on which they were now completely dependent. These were, they told the general, barely sufficient to provide food for four days out of every seven, leaving them to go hungry for the rest of the week. They only asked for a modest increase in their rations equal to the amount received by the Sioux and other tribes. Crook could not have missed the irony in the chiefs' request, a pointed reminder that the Sioux who had fought against the soldiers in the recent war were being treated better than the Bannocks, who had aided the government.[30]

Crook could not make a definitive commitment to the chiefs with respect to rations. This issue, as well as the matter of the confiscated firearms, also a source of concern, was beyond his immediate authority to resolve, and he was not in the habit of making promises on which he could not guarantee delivery. Yet he saw their resolution as critical to the prevention of future unrest. Consequently, the next day in a wire to Sheridan he made a strong case on the Bannocks' behalf. Characterizing Tambiago's crime as "an individual act and not one with which any portion of the tribe sympathized," he declared that it had been wrong to punish an entire people for the disaffection of a few. Regarding the seizure of the ponies, he argued that it had been counterproductive. The tribe had hidden most of its war ponies, ridding themselves of mostly old horses good only for farming. They had played a similar game with their firearms, surrendering "old-fashioned pieces of very little account except for shooting small game." Convinced that the threat of war had been much exaggerated, Crook now urged that both ponies and the guns be returned to the tribe. Failure to do so, he concluded, would serve no purpose and would only "be dwelt upon as a grievance." He concluded with a warning. An outbreak might still occur if the matter of rations remained unaddressed. To that end, he urged that food supplies be increased immediately to the more life-sustaining levels currently provided to the Sioux and Crows.[31]

Crook's pressing appeal received mixed reactions. Sheridan quickly approved the return of the ponies but summarily rejected the idea of returning the tribe's firearms—a decision that, in view of later events, probably spared Crook and the War Department a great deal of embarrassment. With respect to the question of rations, that, as Crook knew, was a matter beyond the purview of the military. Management of the reservations was now in the hands of the Department of the Interior. Nevertheless, Sheridan was sufficiently impressed by his general's arguments to forward Crook's recommendation to the Interior Department with his own endorsement, pointing out that current appropriations had been "fixed upon when the Indians could take part in the chase and supply themselves to some extent with game," a resource no longer available to them.[32] The Interior Department's response, that they had insufficient funds to increase the allotted rations, insured that events would move rapidly toward fulfillment of Crook's prediction.

Fighting erupted at the end of May during the Fort Hall and Lemhi Bannocks' annual pilgrimage to the Camas Prairie to dig for camas bulbs, now desperately needed to supplement their food supply. When the tribesmen arrived on the prairie, they found cowboys grazing a large herd of cattle and horses where the Indians' traditionally harvested the bulbs. A firefight erupted and two of the drovers were seriously wounded. Assuming that the army would hold the entire band, about 150 men and their families, accountable, their leader, Buffalo Horn, called on his people to take to the warpath.[33] The Lemhis declined and returned to their reservation, anxious to avoid a confrontation. But the Fort Hall band fled west across the Snake River, out of Crook's department and into the military Department of Columbia, then under General Howard's command. There they allied themselves with the Paiutes and Umatillas at the Malheur Reservation, who had similar grievances, and the allies went to war against the whites.

Responsibility for suppressing the outbreak fell to Howard and then to Colonel Nelson Appleton Miles when some of the Bannocks followed the Nez Perce trail into his Montana district. Crook's task was limited to positioning troops at Fort Hall to block the insurgents from carrying the fight into Nebraska and Wyoming, thus removing him from an active role in the conflict he had sought to prevent.

Though the number of Indians involved in the uprising eventually swelled to about two thousand warriors, the war was fought in a series of relatively small engagements. Buffalo Horn was killed early in the fighting, depriving the Bannocks of his expertise in military tactics.[34] Leadership then passed to Chief Egan of the Paiutes. Egan was himself murdered in mid-July by his Umatilla allies for the $1,000 reward the army had placed on his head. During August and September the remnants of Egan's now-leaderless forces were defeated piecemeal in a series of skirmishes. Abandoning the field and seeking refuge in their home reservations, they were hunted down by the government and imprisoned at various military posts throughout the northwest.[35]

After Egan's death, as the war wound down, Crook visited the Ross Fork agency to assess the extent to which the tribes under his jurisdiction had participated in the uprising. He later claimed that the Bannocks and Shoshones who had remained on the reservation had continued farming during the conflict and were "anxious to keep the peace." He estimated that only 150 warriors had actually left the agency to participate in the fighting.[36] His calculations appear so far off that he probably intentionally undercounted the number of warriors to deter Sheridan from punishing the entire tribe for the acts of a relative few.[37]

The mistreatment of the Bannocks touched Crook deeply, perhaps more so because it came hard on the heels of the injustice of the forced removal of the Sioux to the Missouri River reservations.[38] Previously he had confined his critiques of government Indian policies to official channels, explaining his reasons in a letter to his friend Rutherford B. Hayes in 1871. While he considered it proper to criticize government policies in official communiqués, he wrote to Hayes, he felt it "an impropriety" to do so publicly.[39] As his objections were confined to official reports and correspondence with his superiors, his protests were similar to those lodged by a number of his contemporaries. Ranald S. Mackenzie, John Pope, and, on occasion, even Nelson Miles had expressed their dissatisfaction with certain aspects of the government's Indian policy in military communiqués. But with war against the Bannocks heating up, Crook's emotions led him on a different a path, one that would eventually align him with the eastern reformers from whom he had previously maintained a safe distance. Publicly and with great feeling he expressed his views to a journalist, a decision that, for a career officer, held some risk.

In June of 1878 he was interviewed by Thomas Henry Tibbles, an assistant editor of the *Omaha Herald* with definite reformist views. In the course of the interview Tibbles suggested that it was a hard thing for soldiers to be asked to kill Indians when the fault lay with thieving Indian agents, a remark obviously intended to elicit a reaction from the general. And it did. "That is not the hardest thing," Crook responded heatedly. "A harder thing is to be forced to kill Indians when they are clearly in the right." The normally phlegmatic veteran then went on to passionately exclaim, "I do not wonder, and you will not either, that when these Indians see their wives and children starving, and their last source of supplies cut off, they go to war. And then we are sent out there to kill them. It is an outrage. . . . Our treatment of the Indians is an outrage." His remarks were widely disseminated and were repub- lished in the influential and widely read *Army and Navy Journal*.[40]

Some would say that Crook was emboldened by his relationship with Hayes, recently elected president. However, it is likely that he regarded his outburst as simply a reflection of the thoughts of many in the military hierarchy. Army officers in general had always held a dim view of placing the management of Indian affairs on the reservation under civilian control. They believed that corruption and mismanage- ment by Interior Department appointees, particularly in the area of rationing, was one of the major causes of Indian unrest. Crook had personally witnessed the problem firsthand in Apacheria and again on the Platte. The issue would remain a major point of contention during the latter half of the nineteenth century. While his interview may have raised eyebrows in the War Department, particularly given Sherman's well-known dislike of the press, Crook likely believed that publicly airing his views on the Bannock War was well within the bounds of acceptable military opinion. In fact, he seems to have been so comfort- able with his sentiments that he reiterated and expanded them in his annual report to the secretary of war for the year 1878.

Of the outbreak he wrote:

> It was a matter of surprise to no one acquainted with the facts.
> . . . The great wonder is that so many have remained on the
> reservation. With the Bannocks and the Shoshone our Indian
> policy has resolved itself into a question of warpath or star-
> vation, and being merely human, many of them will always

choose the former alternative. . . . They cannot hunt for subsistence, as the influx of immigration is each day adding to
the cordon of settlements about them; and if for any purpose
they leave their agency it is only by the merest accident in the
world that they can avoid a conflict of some kind with the
whites.

These savages know nothing and can be made to understand
nothing of such things as the "failure of an appropriation" or
the cumbersome and dilatory complications of administrative
"red tape"; they only know that we have promised faithfully to
feed and clothe them and teach them to earn their own living,
and they insist upon our living up to our contract, or they will,
if driven to the war-path, wreak a vengeance upon the unprotected ranchmen and miners near them.[41]

It was around the time that the Bannocks moved their fight out of the
Department of the Platte and Crook was interviewed by the *Omaha
Herald,* that Azor Nickerson, the general's loyal aide for the past decade,
applied for a transfer. His decision cannot have surprised Crook, though
he must have deeply regretted it. Nickerson's health, always precarious
as the result of wounds received during the Civil War, had further
deteriorated following his years of difficult and physically demanding
campaigning. In addition to concerns about his health, he had been
a captain for quite some time and now longed for advancement into
the senior ranks of the military. He consequently sought Crook's support for assignment to a desk job with the army's Office of the Adjutant General in Washington, where he thought promotion would be
more likely than in the field. Crook responded generously, interceding
with President Hayes on his aide's behalf. Aware that Hayes might be
far too busy to pay personal attention to a routine recommendation,
Crook enlisted the help of Mrs. Hayes in gaining his old friend's ear.
In a personal letter to her, penned at the height of the Bannock crisis,
he wrote, "Both [Nickerson's] wounds and his service speak his cause
much more eloquently than I can." Under the circumstances, would
she use her good offices to arrange a private interview for Nickerson
with the president?[42]Through Mrs. Hayes intercession, a meeting was
arranged that resulted in a bond between the president and the captain
that soon bore fruit. Nickerson was promoted to major and appointed

adjutant general of the Department of the Columbia, headquartered in Portland and conveniently close to his wife's family in San Francisco. Crook marked Nickerson's departure from the Platte with a general order that handsomely complimented his aide's character and service and congratulated him on his promotion.[43]

That fall, at Nickerson's request, the general again wrote the White House, an initiative that resulted in Nickerson's appointment as assistant adjutant general of the army. In that letter Crook again lauded him for his "conspicuous and meritorious service."[44] Two years later, when Nickerson's relations with the adjutant general became strained, Crook intervened once more, this time helping him to secure a position in the office of the chief signal officer.[45]

But then Nickerson's private life began to unravel in ways that earned him the opprobrium of the army and ultimately ended his relationship with General Crook. After the death of his first wife, Nickerson had remarried and had a daughter. In the early 1880s he began an affair with his second wife's dressmaker. To rid himself of that wife in order to marry his new lover, he concocted a discreditable scheme that involved sending his wife and daughter to Europe and then suing for divorce, claiming desertion. Instead, his wife returned to the States and countersued to annul the marriage, claiming that Nickerson's charges against her were fraudulent. The case scandalized military authorities and led to an investigation and a decision to court-martial Nickerson for conduct unbecoming an officer. Nickerson fled to Canada and only returned after he had cut a deal with the army to resign his commission in lieu of prosecution. The officer's conduct so alienated Crook that he severed all ties with him. His disappointment in his former aide subsequently led him to publicly accuse Nickerson of neglect of duty at the Rosebud, a dereliction that he claimed was partially responsible for the poor outcome of the battle. This accusation was completely without foundation, but there is no record that Crook ever apologized or retracted it. The incident serves to illustrate what Joseph C. Porter, John Bourke's accomplished biographer, perhaps too mildly characterized as the general's occasional insensitivity to those most devoted to him.[46] For his part Nickerson spent the rest of his days striving to clear his reputation and have his name restored to the rolls of retired officers. He succeeded but died a week before the army agreed to do so, and thus never knew of it.[47]

CHAPTER TWO

Blood on the Snow

As the hot, dry summer of 1878 faded into fall on the northern plains and peace returned to his department, Crook decided that the moment was opportune to visit the family farm in Taylorville, Ohio, to celebrate his upcoming fiftieth birthday. While in the East, he also planned to attend a reunion of the Society of the Army of West Virginia, which included veterans of his beloved Civil War regiment, the Thirty-Sixth Ohio Volunteer Infantry. Mary preceded him east, staying with her family in Oakland, Maryland, where he planned to join her toward the end of his leave. As he was about to depart the Taylorville homestead, in an unusual burst of sentimentality he confessed to his brothers that he would be unable to return any time soon. "The fact is," he told them, "it is easier for me to stay away from here than to get away if I come here. It hurts less."[1] The old soldiers' reunion sounded a happier note. His former comrades in arms received their old commander with great enthusiasm, electing him president of their association and warmly applauding his call for reconciliation with the former Confederacy.[2]

Following the reunion he joined Mary in Oakland. While there he received a telegram from Webb Hayes, the president's son. The young man was eager to accompany the general on a hunt that fall. Crook was delighted. During the war he had established a close relationship with the future president, who had served as a regimental commander in Crook's Army of West Virginia.[3] The two men remained close in the postwar years, and the Crooks visited the Hayes at their family home in Fremont, Ohio, whenever the their duties allowed. The Hayes children, and Webb in particular, became surrogate children for the Crooks, who, though childless, had a great fondness for young people. Webb responded with something akin to hero worship for the general. Now twenty-four or twenty-five years old, he was not, as one might expect, the spoiled scion of a powerful political figure, but, according to John Bourke, who had occasion to travel with him, a thoroughly likeable, modest, and forthright young man.[4]

Crook responded to Webb's telegram by inviting him on an expedition into the mountains of Wyoming.[5] The hunt, planned for the fall of 1878, would inaugurate an annual tradition of such expeditions that would continue for the next twelve years, ending only with the general's death. Webb and the general would be accompanied by an assortment of other friends and acquaintances, together with the general's military aides, favorite scouts, and packers who handled the mule trains that carried their supplies, forage, and game slaughtered along the way.

While the size of these expeditions might convey the impression of grand safaris, they bore little relationship to the lavish excursions that wealthy hunters engaged in during the latter years of the nineteenth century. Although soldiers and civilian packers performed most of the heavy work, the campsites were primitive affairs, usually pitched in trackless mountain wilderness cleared for the purpose. The terrain was difficult and the weather often cold and stormy. The food was primarily the fish and game the hunters bagged during the day, and usually the hunters skinned and dressed their own kills.

Sheridan, at one time Crook's closest friend in the military, had carefully planned similar expeditions to cultivate his connections in business and politics.[6] In contrast, Crook had no apparent agenda other than the opportunity to spend time relaxing with close friends and enjoying his favorite pastime—hunting, fishing, and tramping through the wilderness. His experience and woodcraft ensured his companions the selection of excellent campsites and good hunting. His relish for the kill and the sheer numbers of animals slaughtered during these annual events might appall today's more conservation-minded hunters, but in Crook's day there was nothing unusual in his attitude. And, unlike many hunters of the period, he made some effort to control the amount of game taken. His friend and hunting companion John Collins reported that the general made a habit of asking his guests to limit their shooting to animals of trophy size and to kill no more than the expedition needed for food, though it seems both he and they frequently ignored this injunction.[7]

The planning for the fall hunt of 1878 was conducted in a tense atmosphere due to events that were unfolding several hundred miles to the south. On September 9 the Northern Cheyenne, under the leadership of their chiefs Dull Knife and Little Wolf, bolted their reservation at Darlington in Indian Territory and embarked on an odyssey that they hoped would return them to their homeland in the Yellowstone country. On September 14, already aware of the outbreak, Crook wrote Webb about the proposed hunt, cautioning the young man that the Big Horn Mountains, his first choice, but formerly a favored Cheyenne hunting ground, would now be too dangerous a locale for their planned excursion. Rather than abandon the hunt altogether, he speculated that they might look for game in the Medicine Bow range in southern Wyoming.[8]

Crook might have foreseen the flight of the Northern Cheyennes, or Tsitsistas (the Called Out People), as they referred to themselves, from the Darlington reserve. They had vigorously opposed General Sheridan's decision the previous April to relocate them to Indian Territory to join the southern branch of their once-united tribe. Crook had supported their position, aware that the hot, malarial southern plains would be ill-suited to a people used to the dry, high climate of their mountain homeland and knowing that they had little desire to live among their southern cousins.[9] As an alternative, he was said to have suggested that they be allowed to remain in the Department of the Platte with either the Shoshones or the Oglalas, pending the ultimate resolution of their fate.[10] But the Interior Department and Sheridan overruled him and had insisted on their immediate removal to the south. So Crook, on orders from his superiors, had little choice but to convince the tribe to accept their resettlement at Darlington.[11] Sheridan would claim subsequently that the movement of the Tsitsistas to the Southern Cheyenne reservation was "a purely voluntary act upon their part, and upon their own application." In an Orwellian rewrite of history, he would explain that they had decided to join their southern cousins because they no longer wished to live among the Sioux, who had angered them by their lack of hospitality when the Tsitsistas had come to them for succor after General Ranald Mackenzie had destroyed their village.[12]

What Crook said to convince the Tsitsistas to accept exile in the south has become a matter of controversy. Their chiefs afterwards claimed, and probably believed, that Crook had promised them that if they remained at Darlington on a trial basis for one year, they could return north if dissatisfied with life in Indian Territory.[13] Other than statements from the Tsitsistas, there is no record that Crook made such a commitment. Knowing the premium he placed on not lying to the Indians, it seems unlikely that he would have given such specific assurances, as he had no authority to guarantee that they would be honored. Both he and Mackenzie, also present at the council with the Cheyenne leaders, later denied making the promise, attributing the misunderstanding, if that is what it was, to poor translation.[14] But Crook may well have remained silent when the Cheyennes said that they would go to Indian Territory on a trial basis, perhaps intending that they should believe he was in accord with the idea. Allowing the chiefs to interpret his silence as assent would not have been beyond him.

In February 1880 Crook provided his version of the relevant meetings with the Northern Cheyennes in a letter to the chairman of the Senate select committee set up to look into the tribe's flight. He made no mention of a promise to allow the tribe to return north after one year. Rather, he described how at the time the Interior Department had declared its intention to remove all of the Indians at the Red Cloud agency to the Missouri. As the Northern Cheyennes adamantly opposed such a move, Crook said, "upon being consulted, the Interior Dep't consented to letting these Northern Cheyennes go to Indian Territory if they so desired." He then presented the tribe with the choice of either accompanying the Sioux to the Missouri or joining the Southern Cheyennes in Indian Territory. "I was careful not to advise them in any particular, as I knew nothing about that country and preferred to let them form conclusions among themselves." Admitting there was disagreement among them, he noted that they "had many councils . . . before coming to tell me that they had decided to go."[15]

During the year the Northern Cheyenne spent at Darlington, hunger stalked the agency. A parsimonious Congress had appropriated insufficient funds to purchase rations for the tribes in Indian Territory, assuming that they would be able to meet the remainder of their requirements through their annual buffalo hunts. As the southern buffalo herds had been wiped out by white buffalo hunters, the Cheyennes were unable to acquire sufficient meat to supplement their rations. Two years of unsuccessful hunts precipitated such an acute food shortage that the Cheyennes were driven "to eat the flesh taken from horses that had died from disease or natural causes."[16]

Malnourished and residing in a climate of unaccustomed heat and humidity, the northerners soon succumbed to a host of diseases to which their systems had no natural immunity.[17] Starvation, disease, and a growing rancorous relationship with their southern cousins, many of whom viewed the presence of the northerners as a drain on already scarce resources, worked misery on the Tsitsistas and divided the band. A portion of the tribe, led by Dull Knife, Wild Hog, Old Crow, and Little Wolf, believing that only death awaited them if they remained at Darlington, chose to head north and seek sanctuary at the Red Cloud agency with their former allies, the Lakotas, unaware that these bands had already been moved further north to the Missouri River.[18]

On September 9 about three hundred of the northerners—including sixty adult warriors, thirty old men and boys, and the remainder women and children—stole away in the night.[19] Before departing the young warriors were reported to have sung, "We are sick and dying here and no one will speak our names when we are gone. We will go north at all hazards and if we die in battle, our names will be remembered and cherished by all our people."[20]

The army's reaction was swift but ineffective. Troops from General Pope's Department of the Missouri quickly caught up with the fleeing Cheyennes, but to their embarrassment the outnumbered and outgunned tribesmen, commanded by their canny war chief, Little Wolf, eluded their grasp.[21]

Sheridan viewed the breakout as catastrophic. He wired Crook that if the Northern Cheyennes succeeded in reaching their homeland, "it will endanger the peace of the North-West as well as materially affect for a while the whole Indian reservation system of the government." Recognizing that insufficient rations, a leading cause of the outbreak, was a problem "common to nearly all the agencies and reservations," he worried that the army's "inability to capture or destroy this small body will be interpreted as a sign of weakness which may bring about results at other places." Accordingly, he directed Crook to "spare no means at your command to kill or capture the band of Cheyennes now on its way north."[22]

Crook had not needed Sheridan's wire to alert him of his responsibilities. He had recognized immediately that the failure of Pope's troops to intercept the Cheyennes meant that the Indians would soon arrive in his department. Alert to this possibility, he wired Major Thomas T. Thornburgh, commander at Fort Steele, to move his troops to Sidney Barracks on the Union Pacific rail line in far western Nebraska, the most likely point at which the Tsitsistas would enter territory under his jurisdiction. To give Thornburgh's troops mobility, a special train was readied at Sidney to carry the troops and their horses west or east along the line to interdict the Indians wherever they attempted to cross.[23]

On September 21, two days after receiving Sheridan's dire warning, Crook boarded a Union Pacific train west to Sidney Barracks, accompanied by his aides, Bourke and Schuyler, and Webb Hayes and John Collins, who had come to Omaha in anticipation of the fall hunt. Clearly he undertook the journey to review and finalize preparations underway to intercept the Tsitsistas, but the presence of Hayes and Collins in his party indicated that he probably still had plans for the hunt.[24]

Arriving at Sidney on September 22, he found Thornburgh's force in a poor state of readiness. Many of his better troops had been widely disbursed about the northern part of his department pursuing the last remnants of the rebellious Bannocks. Those soldiers who had assembled at Sidney Barracks were what Bourke called "the scrapings" of the department, detachments representing bits and pieces of companies from several different infantry regiments and cavalry units.[25] In Bourke's professional judgment, which undoubtedly reflected Crook's, individually these men may have been good soldiers, but as a force they lacked the cohesion provided by long-term service as a unit.[26] Another shortcoming, pointed out by Sheridan in a telegram to Pope on September 18, was that they were nearly all infantry, hardly a match for a body of warriors reputed to be the best horsemen on the plains.[27] To this concern Crook added his own: the force lacked scouts and trackers to gather intelligence on the Cheyennes' whereabouts. In their absence he had to settle for a distinctly less reliable resource, telegraph operators and citizens in the vicinity who were asked to keep an eye out for the Indians.[28]

Crook also had to deal with another issue that white residents in the area found profoundly disturbing. Five days before his arrival, a band of 186 Northern Cheyennes under Little Chief arrived unexpectedly at Sidney Barracks from the north. Escorted by a small detachment of Seventh Cavalry troopers, their numbers included 40 armed warriors who had surrendered with their families to Colonel Miles months before on the Tongue River and who subsequently had served as scouts against the Sioux and Nez Perce.[29] Miles had allowed them to remain with him when Dull Knife's people had been transported south. Sheridan had overruled the colonel's decision, believing that permitting them to remain in the north would create a dangerous precedent, and belatedly ordered them sent to join the rest of the northerners in Indian Territory. In compliance with this decision, Little Chief's band was en route southward at the same time that Dull Knife's people were headed north into Nebraska. Though under guard as virtual prisoners of war, the warriors had been permitted to retain their guns and ponies so they could hunt during their passage to Indian Territory.[30] Afraid that on hearing of Dull Knife's flight the band might be tempted to join him, the army had sequestered the band in a camp about a mile outside the town of Sidney. Crook now rode out to the camp to assess the situation and, if necessary, intervene to avert trouble.

Little Chief immediately apprised Crook that his people were aware of the outbreak and its causes and consequently knew of the terrible conditions that awaited them in Indian Territory. While his followers were anxious about the welfare of their fellow tribesmen, among whom they had many friends and relatives, he declared that they had no plans to resist their own removal or join Dull Knife and Little Wolf. Perhaps aware of Crook's concern for Indian welfare, the chief pointed out the impoverished condition of his people and implored him to provide increased rations and blankets to ward off starvation and winter cold. At the same time, he wanted reassurance that the army would keep its promise to allow his warriors to retain their ponies and arms and asked for additional ammunition to enable them to hunt game on the way south. Bluntly, he concluded, "We are not fools. We have our senses; but we are going down there because we have to. That is all I have to say." Interestingly, Bourke recorded in his diary that during this conversation Little Chief had referenced a meeting with Sheridan in Chicago and had quoted the latter as saying that if the band could not get along "with those fool Southern Cheyennes," they could return and get their "own country back." Bourke did not mention whether Crook responded, though one suspects that he greeted this surprising news with his habitual silence.[31]

What Crook did say to the chief, according to Bourke's account, shaded the truth more than a little, probably out of concern that the band might yet decide to join Dull Knife and his warriors. After reassuring Little Chief that he (Crook) had hunted in the south that past winter and to him it looked like "good country," he offered what appears to have been a completely fabricated explanation of why Dull Knife's people had left Darlington. It was his understanding, he said, that "those people (Cheyennes) down there left because you didn't come in sooner. They became impatient and came as much to meet you as anything else." How he learned this, he did not say. He then allowed that Sheridan's order sending the band south was motivated by a desire to get all of the Northern Cheyennes in one place together, which though true on its face was far from the whole story. He concluded, "When this matter is settled, if those Indians [i.e., the refugee Cheyennes] go back, you can go on down; if those Indians are allowed to go to Red Cloud [agency] I'll ask to have you sent to join them." Crook omitted any mention of Sheridan's determination not to allow the Tsitsistas to remain in the north under any circumstances or of his order to kill or return them to Indian Territory. Having placated the band with half-truths and a sprinkling of lies and omissions, he counseled them that they were to remain at Sidney until the present crisis had been resolved, in order to avoid any chance that they might encounter Dull Knife's band and "get [themselves] into trouble."[32] This last, at least, had the ring of truth to it.

On September 23, satisfied that Little Chief's band now presented no threat and that Thornburgh's deployments were the best possible under the circumstances, Crook left Bourke in Sidney to monitor the situation and entrained for Fort Fred Steele in Wyoming Territory, coincidentally adjacent to the Medicine Bow range, with his aide, Walter Schuyler, and Webb Hayes.[33] His movements from there were undocumented. Historian Charles Robinson asserts that the general returned to Omaha to oversee operations against the Cheyenne from the vantage of his headquarters.[34] However, evidence points in another direction—that, now satisfied that defense of his department was in good hands and unwilling to forgo the hunt and disappoint his friends, he embarked on his expedition into the Medicine Bow Range. Not only was Fort Fred Steele a convenient departure point for such a hunt, but subsequent correspondence between Sheridan and Crook's headquarters confirms that the general was absent from Omaha for some weeks following his departure from Sidney, leaving another officer in charge in his stead.

On October 4, twelve days after Crook's departure for Fort Fred Steele, Dull Knife's band, having driven off their pursuers in four separate engagements, evaded Thornburgh's troops and crossed the Union Pacific line from Kansas into Nebraska near Ogalalla, about one hundred miles east of Sidney Barracks.[35] Before leaving Kansas a number of young Cheyenne warriors broke away from the band and unleashed a series of particularly brutal raids against settlers in the northwest part of the state along Beaver and Sappa Creeks, formerly a traditional Cheyenne hunting ground.[36] Just why the Cheyennes carried out these savage depredations has been the subject of much speculation.[37] In total, they resulted in the death of ten drovers and twenty-one settlers, many of whom were unarmed, and the rape of twenty-five women and children, the youngest of whom was only eight years old.[38] It is equally noteworthy that upon the band's arrival in Nebraska, the depredations ceased entirely.

Even as Sheridan learned that the Cheyennes had entered the Department of the Platte, he also received word that Lakota warriors had left their agency on the White River and were "burning the country in all directions." His information was correct, but the Lakotas' actions were entirely unrelated to the Cheyenne outbreak.[39] Nevertheless, Sheridan envisioned a general uprising among the Sioux in sympathy with their Cheyenne allies.[40] Impelled by images of thousands of painted Sioux and Cheyenne warriors wreaking havoc across the Great Plains, a thousand-fold replication of the Cheyenne depredations in Kansas, the lieutenant general fired off a flurry of anxious telegrams. In one to Sherman, he warned of impending disaster, blaming the entire fiasco on the Interior Department's mismanagement of Indian affairs.[41] In another to Colonel Robert Williams, acting commander at Crook's Omaha headquarters, he evinced growing irritation at Crook's absence from his post during this crisis. "I think," he wrote, "it would be well to inform General Crook of the crossing of the Cheyennes and that the

Red Cloud Indians are in a complete state of insubordination and no one can tell what might happen and that it would be well for him to return to his headquarters."[42] Crook got the message. While he did not share Sheridan's sense of urgency, he most definitely caught his commander's tone of suppressed annoyance. In less than a week, he was back in Omaha.

Likely, Crook had another reason for his hasty return to Nebraska. Seemingly oblivious to the Cheyenne crisis, a group of congressmen arrived in Omaha to hold hearings on the perennial quarrel over whether the military or the Interior Department should manage the Indian reservations. Possibly spurred by Crook's public comments on the Bannock outbreak, the legislators were particularly interested in his views. While their timing could have been better, the issue they raised had been debated since 1848, when jurisdiction over Indian affairs had been transferred from military to civilian control. It became particularly heated following the Civil War, receded somewhat during the period of Grant's peace policy, and flared anew in early 1876 as part of the battle over Reconstruction. At that time, scandals within the Indian Bureau and corruption-induced unrest on the Sioux Reservation handed the Democrats an opportunity to embarrass the Republican administration. They seized it by introducing a bill to transfer control of the reservations to the military. The bill passed in the House but died in the Senate's Republican-dominated Committee on Indian Affairs.[43] The issue refused to go away and had been reignited by the Bannock uprising and the Cheyenne outbreak, giving each side reason to criticize the other. Public feuding between Secretary of the Interior Carl Schurz (backed by Ezra Hayt, his Indian commissioner) and Generals Sherman and Sheridan further stirred the pot.[44] In typical bureaucratic fashion, in June 1878 Congress created a special committee to study the question. Hence the committee's presence in Omaha at the height of the Cheyenne crisis.

The congressmen convened on October 10 and, before calling General Crook, took testimony from several junior officers who had actually managed the Lakota agencies during the recent Sioux conflict. Based on their experiences, the officers viewed the military as much better-equipped to manage Indian affairs than the civilian agents of the Indian Bureau. Then Crook testified, supporting his subordinates and airing opinions that he had voiced previously, both in military communiqués and more recently in the newspaper.[45] His comments are germane as they outlined a philosophy of Indian management that he would soon be given an opportunity to implement.

As one might expect, Crook was more circumspect in his testimony before Congress than he had been in his internal dispatches. Rather than taking aim at corrupt Indian agents, as he was wont to do to his War Department superiors, he chose a less abrasive line of attack. Describing the reservation as a ship with two captains, one military and one civilian, he noted that while the civilian agent had administrative authority, he lacked power to enforce his decisions and thus could not command respect, an essential component, he believed, in managing Indian affairs. Enforcement authority lay uniquely with the army. That authority, together with the experience its officers had acquired in recent years, made the military the only logical choice to run the reservations.

The committee seemed favorably impressed and asked him what policies the army would establish if placed in charge of the reservations, a question that afforded Crook an opportunity to expound on his philosophy of Indian management. He responded with a degree of specificity that indicated he had given the matter much thought. His ultimate goal, he said, was the assimilation of the Indian into white society. In his opinion, tribal (communal) ownership of reservation lands discouraged the individual initiative needed to achieve assimilation and success in the American capitalist culture. To counter what he regarded as the iniquitous influence of tribalism, he favored a concept then current in the Indian reform community: divesting the tribes of their ownership of the land and conferring title instead to individual tribesmen. Not for the first time, he allowed that the reservation Indian, if provided with his own land, would be eager to develop it. That, in turn, would cause his "tribal nature" to wither away, facilitating his absorption into Euro-American culture. He could not have foreseen that a decade later he would play an important role in implementing Indian land reform legislation based on these ideas with devastating results for Native Americans.

The committee then turned to the subject of misconduct by Indian agents, perhaps hoping to elicit from Crook examples that they could use to justify the transfer of control over Indian affairs to the military. Crook seems to have misinterpreted the congressmen's rationale behind the line of questioning. Thinking that they meant to hold him responsible for the Cheyenne breakout, perhaps because he felt guilty about his role in banishing the tribe to Indian Territory, he launched into an entirely new exclamation of why, in his view, the tribe was sent to Darlington and the reasons for their subsequent breakout. Absolving himself of responsibility, he said that when the Cheyennes had been at Camp Robinson in 1877, he had given them the choice as to where to go.[46] They had elected to go to Indian Territory, where they had expected Colonel Mackenzie to look after them. When Mackenzie was transferred to Texas, they were angry, blaming him for deserting them. That perceived desertion, Crook said, together with their belief that if they returned to the Platte, he (Crook) would take care of them, motivated their flight.

To cap off his performance, Crook amazed the committee by announcing that though he heartily endorsed the transfer of authority to the military as best for the country, he personally hoped that it would not happen. Why? the bemused senators inquired. If the transfer were accomplished, he replied, he thought that he would be asked to play some role in the future administration of Indian affairs. In a moment of unrehearsed sincerity, he declared that he did not want it. "I have had enough of the Indians," he said.[47] One can imagine the committee's confusion at this remark. Uncertain of how to proceed, they adjourned for the day.

When they recalled the general the next morning, they once again turned to the question of fraud and mismanagement in the Indian Bureau, querying him as to the extent he believed it contributed to the Indian wars. Crook replied simply, "If you will investigate all these Indian troubles, you will find that there is something wrong of this nature at the bottom of all of them."[48]

Crook was the last military witness. After he stepped down the committee called for civilian testimony, summoning several Indian agents and chiefs. While the military had been unanimous in its support of the transfer, the agents, predictably, were not taken with the idea. Nor, interestingly, were the commission's Indian witnesses, evidently unenthusiastic over the army's more disciplined approach to their management.

When the committee finally published its report the following January, its recommendations were divided along political lines. Because of its partisan nature and general indecisiveness, the report had little credibility, and Congress subsequently again rejected a bill that would have transferred control to the military, opting for the status quo and leaving it in the hands of the Interior Department.[49]

The commission's departure from Omaha freed Crook to once again turn his attention to the Northern Cheyennes. He found that, as he had predicted and contrary to Sheridan's apocalyptic fears, their flight failed to precipitate an uprising among the Sioux. By mid-October he reported that affairs among the Brulés and Oglalas were "quiet and satisfactory" and that in all likelihood the Cheyennes would bypass the Sioux reservations without incident and head for their homes in the north. Moreover, Red Cloud, the Sioux chief, had assured Crook's officers that "if the Cheyennes come on the Reservation, they [the Sioux] were prepared to give them up to the army."[50] A week later the wily chief revealed his motive for betraying his one-time allies when he requested that he be allowed to keep any horses and guns his people might seize from his former allies.[51] Though Sheridan's forebodings had proven groundless, he remained adamant that, once apprehended, the northerners should be returned to Indian Territory. To Sherman he expressed his continuing worry that "the remaining Cheyennes in the Indian territory will go north if these Indians are allowed to go free."[52]

Unaware of Sheridan's decision, the Northern Cheyennes completed their five-week, five-hundred-mile hegira in steadily worsening weather. Their tattered clothing offered scant protection from the elements, and they had long since run out of supplies and had begun shooting their remaining ponies for food. Exhausted and filled with anxiety as they approached the imagined sanctuary of the now-deserted Red Cloud and Spotted Tail agencies, they divided into two factions. Not far from Camp Robinson, Chief Dull Knife, the conciliator of the tribe, believing that the soldiers would allow them to remain at the Red Cloud agency, convinced many of his people that they ought to give themselves up to their Sioux brothers. Little Wolf and the majority of the young men, distrustful of the army and perhaps fearing punishment for the depredations some of them had committed in Kansas, decided to continue on to their homeland in Montana, avoiding all contact with the military. Thus, the two chiefs and their respective followers parted ways. Little Wolf's band headed north into the Sand Hill country of western Nebraska, where they would winter before proceeding to Montana. Dull Knife, with a few warriors and most of the elders, women, and children, made for the old Red Cloud agency, unaware that their Lakota allies had moved many miles north to the Missouri the year before.[53] At one o'clock on the afternoon of October 23, a patrol from Camp Robinson discovered them struggling through a snowstorm on Chadron Creek, about thirty miles from the post. The soldiers were shocked at their appearance. Numbering 149 souls, the once proud Cheyenne now peered fearfully at the troops from beneath their threadbare robes, shivering in the cold and blowing snow, their faces gaunt with hunger.[54] Though the soldiers demanded the surrender of their ponies and weapons, because of the Indians' skittishness and fearing bloodshed, the officer in charge failed to search the Indians individually. This error in judgment allowed some of the younger braves to conceal a few guns on their persons. These they carried with them to Camp Robinson and hid in the barracks where they were confined pending a decision as to their disposition.[55]

After receiving word of Dull Knife's surrender, Crook wired Sheridan of his intention to travel to Camp Robinson to personally lead the search for Little Wolf.[56] Despite his fifty-one-year-old general's willingness to take to the field in midwinter, Sheridan remained unconvinced of Crook's commitment to the mission. In a letter to Sherman, he voiced his suspicion that "increased discontent has been given these Indians by encouragement from interests in the Department of the Platte [a reference to Crook?] to induce them to come back north." Sheridan's doubts may have been fanned by an article in a Salt Lake paper reprising some of Crook's testimony before the recent congressional hearings in Omaha. The story quoted Crook as remarking in passing that one could not teach an Indian "anything on an empty stomach," an unsubtle reference to the Cheyennes' plight at Darlington.[57] To Sheridan this may have betrayed an undue sympathy for the Northern Cheyennes.

Sheridan's suspicions were, however, unfounded. True, Crook made no secret of his belief that returning the Tsitsistas to Darlington would be a tragic mistake, publicly stating "that there must have been some good grounds for their leaving Indian Territory."[58] Further, he knew and admired the tribe's courage and integrity, having seen their fighting skills at the Rosebud and witnessed their ability and loyalty when

they served as scouts later in the war. Nevertheless, he was a professional soldier and an ambitious one, all too aware of the premium
his commander put on loyalty in carrying out his orders. So despite
his sympathy for the Cheyennes' plight, he conscientiously executed
Sheridan's directives, exhorting his officers in their pursuit of Little
Wolf and laying the groundwork for the return of Dull Knife's faction
to Indian Territory.[59]

But that did not preclude him from trying to change Sheridan's
mind. To that end, he made sure that his commander was fully
apprised of the despair and desperation that overwhelmed the Camp
Robinson prisoners at the thought of their return to Darlington. On
November 1, he forwarded a telegram that he received from the post
commander informing him that "if these prisoners were to be taken
south, it would 'be necessary to tie and haul them.'" In an accompanying memorandum, Crook warned that rather than accept removal, the
Indians might well resort to mass suicide, pointing out that Red Cloud,
fearing just such an eventuality, had pleaded with the army to confiscate any knives possessed by the Cheyennes lest they use them to harm
themselves.[60] He also made sure that Sheridan knew that the prisoners,
mainly women and children, were not involved in the Kansas depredations, again invoking Red Cloud, who was convinced that the young
warriors who now rode with Little Wolf had carried out the raids.[61]

But Crook's arguments only reinforced Sheridan's suspicion that
Crook was encouraging the Northern Cheyennes in their refusal to
return to Indian Territory. In a letter to the adjutant general of the
army, he coldly noted: "It looks to me as if there was an unnecessary
amount of sympathy in the Department of the Platte for these Indians. . . . The condition of these Indians is pitiable, but it is my opinion
that unless they are sent back to where they came from, the whole reservation system will receive a shock which will endanger its stability."
For that reason he remained wedded to his decision to send them back
to Indian Territory and to jail the ringleaders in Florida.[62] His only
response to the reported threat of mass suicide was to instruct Crook
to increase the guard at Fort Robinson.

The Interior Department, ultimately responsible for the management of the Tsitsistas, wholeheartedly supported Sheridan's position.
Interior Secretary Schurz was far less concerned about the wellbeing
of the tribe than about the depredations the young warriors had com-

mitted against the settlers and ranchers in Kansas and the potential effect of the breakout on the reservation system as a whole. As to the warriors who had participated in the raids, he thought that they should be turned over to the civilian authorities for punishment, which at the time meant hanging, and that "the remainder of said Indians [should] be returned to their Agency in the Indian Country."[63]

By mid-December Dull Knife's people had begun to lose all hope. Though army rations kept starvation at bay, the prisoners were still clad in the rags they had worn at the time of surrender. Housed in drafty barracks heated only by a single, inefficient woodstove, they endured subzero temperatures. To ease their suffering Crook asked that the Indian Bureau issue them clothing from supplies available at the Sioux reservation.[64] Then, before the matter of clothing could be resolved, Sheridan abruptly ordered the prisoners shipped immediately to Kansas, where, per Schurz's recommendation, those identified as involved in the depredations would be turned over to the civil authorities and the remainder sent back to Indian Territory. Because of continuing threat of suicide, the order was kept secret until the last minute.[65]

Crook made one final effort to delay the move. He wired Sheridan's Chicago headquarters that the "mercury in vicinity of Camp Robinson has not been as high as zero for a number of days and it will be inhuman to move these Indians as ordered. Attention invited to my dispatch of the 20th inst. regarding clothing for them." And then, stalling for time, he wrote, "It will take some time to get transportation for their removal."[66] Sheridan neatly sidestepped responsibility. His headquarters replied that "the Lieutenant General wishes the Indians moved *as soon as it is right and proper to do so* [emphasis added], and that such measures as may be necessary to accomplish this be adopted." The matter of clothing, it was curtly noted, had been referred to Washington.[67]

Throughout late December and much of January, Crook had been confined to his residence with a severe cold that soon led to a bout of malaria. Consequently, even if the weather had permitted him to do so, he would have been unable to travel to Fort Robinson to assess the situation firsthand. On December 28 he acceded to Sheridan's pressure. From his Omaha headquarters he wired Captain Henry Wessells, the post commander at Fort Robinson, to prepare for the "safe removal of the Indians." Arrangements, he wrote, had been made for transportation and a military escort, and if the Interior Department failed to furnish clothing in time, as he believed they would, the captain was to issue the needed apparel himself, presumably from military stocks. Finally, though he hoped that the removal would be "effected without difficulty," his promise to Wessells to furnish any "handcuff required" indicated that he had his doubts. In hindsight, it is tragic that he offered no guidance to the captain, a well-meaning but not particularly sensitive officer, as to how or when to break the news to the Northern Cheyennes of their impending move.[68]

On January 3 Wessells assembled Dull Knife and the other chiefs and bluntly informed them that Washington had decided to send them south immediately. They reacted by angrily rejecting his request that they cooperate in the move.[69] Frightened by the prisoners' avowed determination not to yield meekly to his directive, the captain resorted to draconian measures. He cut off all food (and later, water and fuel) to the prisoners, hoping to force them to submit. Informing Crook of his decision, he noted that he tried to ameliorate the severity of his measures by offering to feed the young children, a gesture that the beleaguered prisoners rejected out of hand.[70] Crook supported Wessells's actions and blamed the government for the need to implement such harsh measures. "If the removal had been made two months ago, the great suffering which must ensue and much opposition to going would have been obviated," he wrote in a letter to the adjutant general. In a vain attempt to shift responsibility to the Interior Department, he asked that they superintend the move under military escort.[71] Interior, having no wish to become involved, met that suggestion with silence. Nor, despite Crook's frantic reminders, did they provide the clothing he had requested. In desperation, Crook asked that the quartermaster's department issue the badly needed apparel.[72]

As late as January 7 Wessells remained optimistic that he would be able to peaceably remove the Indians.[73] But events were rapidly slipping beyond the control of anyone in government. The Northern Cheyennes held out for two more days, subsisting on scraps of tallow and beef and a few handfuls of cornmeal that the women had secreted against an emergency. When Wessells cut off their water and fuel, they assuaged their thirst with melted snow from the window ledges and then frost scraped from the panes.[74] Without wood to feed the fire, the temperature inside the barracks plummeted, and the atmosphere became fetid with the stench of unwashed bodies and accumulating excrement and urine.

Seeing that his harsh tactics had failed to produce results, Wessells somehow convinced himself that Chief Wild Hog, one of the principal headmen of the band, was preventing his people from surrendering. If he could be removed, the captain reasoned, all resistance would collapse. On January 9 he arrested the chief and one other, holding them as hostages in a last-ditch attempt to secure the band's agreement to removal. But he badly misread the situation. Instead of destroying their will to resist, the arrest of their chiefs galvanized the prisoners, now convinced that the army was preparing to use deadly force to remove them.[75]

A full moon rose early on the evening of January 9. Its pale light reflected off the snowy fields that surrounded the post, casting the compound into stark relief. While Washington squabbled over who would furnish clothing to the Cheyennes, Fort Robinson girded for trouble. The Indians had denied entrance to the barracks to anyone for some days, and on the morning of the ninth had hung blankets over the windows to conceal their movements. From outside, the soldiers heard sounds that indicated that the Indians were preparing for something. Captain Wessells posted additional sentinels, but at sundown he withdrew them, thinking that the moment of danger has passed.[76]

It had not. The Indians possessed firearms—twelve long guns and three pistols, by one count—that had been secreted under the barracks floorboards for such a moment.[77] Minutes after ten o'clock, the stillness of the night was rent by an explosion of gunshots and shattering glass as the young men, firing through the barracks windows, shot down several of the sentries. Under the covering fire, the rest of the band, including women and children, hurled themselves through the jagged glass of the windows on to the porch and made for the wooded banks of the White River and the steep bluffs west of the post. Cheyenne Dog Soldiers, whose duty it was to protect the band, conducted a fearless rearguard action, sacrificing their lives to aid the elders, women, and children in their escape. But weakened from lack of food and water and hampered by the snow, the escapees were easy prey for pursuing troopers, and many were shot down as they scrambled across the open fields that surrounded the barracks.[78]

The following morning, in a dispatch devoid of details, Wessells reported the breakout to Crook, noting that thirty-five had been recaptured at the outset and thirty killed, including, he erroneously reported, Dull Knife. The rest had fled, but, Wessells predicted, "We will have many more before dark."[79] Crook's immediate response reflected his frustration at the lack of information and his surprise and shock at the number of casualties among the Indians. "Report at once full particulars of the outbreak," he wrote. "Did those Cheyennes have any arms, if so where did they get them, and what necessity was there for killing them?"[80]

Further word from the captain was slow in coming, and Crook was forced to rely on newspaper accounts for any additional information. On January 11, two days after the breakout, the *New York Herald* carried the story beneath a screaming headline: "Massacre of Cheyennes." Under lurid subheadings, "Outbreak of Prisoners and Its Fearful Consequences" and "Shot by Dozens in the Snow," the reporter graphically described the carnage. Among the dead brought in for burial, the article said, were eight "squaws" and two children. Preparatory to writing the article, its author had interviewed Crook. The embarrassed general was forced to confess to his ignorance of the facts and to admit that the information he had received to date had been sketchy. Perhaps seeking to avoid responsibility for the horror, he again insisted that had the Indians been returned south immediately after their capture, the whole situation could have been avoided. Staying so long in the north, he told the reporter, they had become convinced they would be allowed to remain, and their resistance to removal had hardened, resulting in the death not only of several Indians but of a number of soldiers as well.[81] Such an explanation for the tragedy is hardly credible. He and others in the government were well aware that at the time of their surrender in October, the Cheyennes had made it clear that they would rather die than accept return to Darlington.[82]

The day after speaking to the reporter, Crook, upset by allegations of indiscriminate killings by the soldiers and embarrassed at his apparent ignorance of the facts, fired off another telegram to Wessells. News stories, he wrote, were conveying the impression that the escaping Cheyennes had been killed "whenever caught." "The mere fact that they resisted their pursuers is not sufficient excuse for killing them unless the resistance they offered tended to imperil the lives of your soldiers." He now demanded a more complete and detailed accounting of the breakout and the reasons for it.[83]

The beleaguered captain responded with a lengthy report of the history of the affair from his perspective and described his futile attempts to avoid bloodshed in the face of the Cheyennes' adamant resistance. Detailing the precautions he had taken to prevent their escape, he was less precise in his handling of the pursuit, perhaps because he did not witness much of it firsthand. Choosing to overlook the mayhem that had attended it, instead he emphasized his own humanitarian efforts to evacuate two wounded "squaws" and a two-year-old child whom he had found in the snow to "a comfortable place." There was no mention of other women or children. He referred to the other dead and wounded as "bucks," if they were male; the remainder he simply called "Indians."[84]

Only later did Wessells attempt to respond to Crook's concerns about the indiscriminate killings, saying that his soldiers had trouble distinguishing between men and women in the dark and confusion. That difficulty and the fact that some women fought alongside the men, he said, may have accounted for the presence of women and children among the dead and wounded.[85] This explanation seems disingenuous. Though the deaths of some noncombatants might have been expected under the circumstances, the nature and extent of the wounds suffered by some of the twenty-three Cheyenne survivors attest to levels of ferocity, anger, and indiscriminate violence on the part of Wessells' soldiers that belie his attempt to excuse the killings as either accidental or defensive. This impression is strengthened when one considers that witnesses later testified that in the aftermath, civilians from the surrounding settlements were permitted to mutilate and loot the dead, observed but unhindered by the troops.[86]

Sheridan received his first news of the breakout by telegram from Crook on January 10.[87] Ironically, Crook's wire arrived the same day as the Interior Department announced its approval of the purchase of clothing for the Cheyennes, limited "to an amount not exceeding five hundred dollars."[88] The next day the *Herald's* story detailing the casualties among the women and children circulated at the lieutenant general's Chicago headquarters. Like Crook, Sheridan was concerned. Never unduly worried about the death of Indians, he did care about the army's image. Knowing the sensitivity of the eastern establishment

to allegations of mistreatment of the Indians, he had no wish to confront another firestorm of controversy like those that had followed
the attacks on the sleeping villages on the Washita and Sand Creek.
Accordingly, he cautioned Crook that Wessells's hunt for the prisoners still at large "should, and I know will, be governed by the highest
regard for humanity."[89]

Several days later Sherman weighed in. The commanding general
had initially reacted to news reports of the "the massacre" of the Cheyennes by telling reporters that the Indians, whom he characterized as
"insubordinate, cunning, [and] treacherous," "were treated just as they
deserved to be." But after learning that President Hayes was disturbed
by reports of "unnecessary cruelty by Army officers," he was suddenly
struck by the need for a thorough investigation of the affair.[90]

For the time being Crook could only supply his superiors with
information gleaned from Wessells's reports. Based on what he knew,
he reassured Sheridan that "great care was taken not to hurt either
women or children from the commencement to the end of the whole
affair."[91] But evidently lacking confidence in his own assertions and
frustrated by the fact that the papers seemed to know more about the
situation than he did, he dispatched his aide, Lieutenant Schuyler, to
Fort Robinson to act as his eyes and ears on the ground.[92]

Meanwhile, operations at Fort Robinson were not going well. By
January 15, the sixth day following the breakout, a substantial number
of the prisoners were still unaccounted for. As yet unaware of President
Hayes's concern in the matter, any anxiety Sheridan felt about humane
treatment of the prisoners had taken a backseat to his irritation that so
many of them were still at large. He expressed his ire to Crook, wiring
him that he found Wessells's assertions that he was "sparing no efforts
to recapture the escaped Cheyennes not creditable. . . . How fifteen or
twenty savages with twenty five or thirty squaws and children should
get away from five companies of cavalry, or even two companies of
cavalry, seems strange."[93]

Faced with Sheridan's skepticism and undoubtedly harboring his
own doubts, Crook, too, focused the blame on Wessells. Under a *Herald* headline reading, "Responsibility of the Blunder at Fort Robinson
as Placed by Crook," it was reported that the general believed Wessells
ought to have recaptured the escapees at the outset, adding that, as
senior officer of the garrison, the captain was responsible for execut-

ing Sheridan's (and Crook's) orders.[94] To Wessells, Crook wrote, "I am very much disappointed that the Cheyennes made their escape. Follow them with all your available force and don't leave their trail until they are recaptured as much depends on this."[95]

On January 16, goaded by Sheridan's criticisms, Crook concluded that Wessells needed reinforcements and ordered Major Andrew W. Evans, a veteran Indian fighter and commanding officer at Fort Laramie, to "send out all available troops from your post to take up [the Cheyennes'] trail and not abandon it until the Indians are recaptured."[96] As Evans outranked Wessells, he assumed command of the pursuit. Days later, after the chase had ended, he would become the senior member of the board of officers that, together with Schuyler and Captain John M. Hamilton of the Fifth Cavalry, would carry out Sherman's mandate to formally investigate and report on the entire affair.[97]

But Evans would not arrive on the scene until January 19, and in the meantime Sheridan's attention turned to a related matter. His earlier concerns that the Sioux might join the Northern Cheyennes in open rebellion were reignited by the Fort Robinson breakout and a report from Dr. James Irwin, the Indian agent at Pine Ridge, that "the Sioux are much excited over the Cheyenne troubles."[98] It appears that some Oglalas had relatives through intermarriage incarcerated at the fort. They had visited them in their barracks prison and were appalled by their condition. When word reached Pine Ridge of the escape attempt and the deaths of several women and children, their anxiety climbed to a new level. Red Cloud, always politically attentive to the mood of his people, asked that children of mixed Cheyenne and Sioux parentage who had survived the breakout be allowed to join the Lakotas on the reservation. Crook thought this an excellent idea and advised Sheridan that if pursued, "the effect will be good."[99] Sheridan concurred, hoping that the move would placate both the Sioux and the public at large.[100]

While Washington mulled over Red Cloud's proposal, however, the *Herald* published a story that threatened to unravel any good that might have resulted from the chief's plan. The paper reported that Red Cloud had been asked to allow Oglala scouts from Pine Ridge to aid the army in their search for the escapees still at large. This idea may have originated with Wessells, who was by now desperate to bring the pursuit of the Cheyennes to a rapid and successful conclusion. But it was

Lieutenant Schuyler, Crook's aide, who brought the idea, which might even have originated with his boss, to Red Cloud for his consideration. Predictably, the chief was unhappy with the idea, and his Indian agent, Irwin, joined him in opposing it. But according to the *Herald* reporter, Lieutenant Schuyler's diplomatic skills prevailed. Red Cloud reluctantly consented, and Crook authorized the scouts' recruitment.[101] Sheridan and Sherman disliked the proposal, fearing that the army's use of Oglala scouts to the hunt down Cheyennes might stir further unrest in the Lakota community. To minimize that risk, Sherman suggested that the scouts' role should be strictly limited "more with the object of securing the surrender of the escaped Cheyennes than for the purpose of fighting them."[102] This advice, though well intended, would prove difficult to implement as, in the end, the escapees were determined to fight rather than surrender.

The affair reached its brutal conclusion on January 22 near Hat Creek, just forty-five miles from Fort Robinson. Seventeen men and fifteen women and children, the last remnants of the band, were finally run to ground by a contingent of 147 officers and men of the Third Cavalry. Huddled in a narrow declivity carved into the bank of a dry creek bed, the only available shelter on the windblown, wintry prairie, the Cheyennes defiantly refused to surrender. The troops then surrounded the pit and fired more than two hundred rounds at point-blank range into the compact mass of Indians. The Cheyennes resisted "with extraordinary courage and fierceness," in the words of one officer, and though low on ammunition and exposed to murderous return fire, managed to inflict several casualties on the troopers. Three troopers died the fight and five others, including Captain Wessells and a Lakota scout, were wounded.[103] All of the Cheyenne men were killed, the last three armed only with knives and empty pistols, in a suicidal charge against the massed troopers. Only eight women and children emerged from the pit alive, two of whom died the following day.[104] Most had multiple wounds, though the warriors had covered them with their bodies in an attempt to shield them from the blue coats' bullets. The survivors would join the seventy others captured earlier and held at Fort Robinson to await their fate.[105]

In the last analysis, the tragic and entirely avoidable affair had cost the lives of sixty-four Northern Cheyenne men, women, and children. Seventy-eight were recaptured, many of them wounded. Seven were unaccounted for and presumed dead by the military. The list of presumed dead included Dull Knife, his wife, and surviving children, who had in fact escaped. Eleven soldiers died, while Captain Wessells, nine enlisted men, and one scout were wounded, substantial casualties for an Indian war engagement.[106]

Upon learning the details, Crook nevertheless warmly praised the troops, acknowledging not only their courage in the face of the Indians' fierce resistance, but their conduct "in trying to save women and children" and the privations they suffered during the pursuit in sub-zero temperatures.[107] Despite the horrific casualties, his words probably accurately reflected the conduct of a substantial majority of the soldiers. Most seemed to have behaved with commendable restraint as one might expect of men who, after all, had come to know their prisoners as individuals over a greater than two-month period of captivity.

The issue yet to be resolved was the disposition of the survivors, most of them women and children who were now widows and orphans. The day following their recapture, Crook raised the matter with Sheridan's headquarters in a wire that might have seemed to contain a hint of irony. "Shall the Cheyenne Indian prisoners now at Robinson, except those who are too severely wounded to travel, be now sent to Railroad for transportation to Fort Leavenworth?"[108] Sheridan's adjutant general initially responded stiffly that the execution of the original order returning the prisoners to Darlington had only been delayed, not modified.[109] But this was not the final word.

Crook's inquiry had prompted a reappraisal of the situation at what seemed an opportune time. There had been a substantial public outcry over the army's handling of the breakout, as well as considerable unrest in the Sioux community. Both the War Department and Interior were aware that how they dealt with the surviving prisoners might well affect the popular mood as well as peace on the reservation. The government had yet to rule on whether to grant Red Cloud's request to be allowed to accept the widows and orphans of mixed Sioux and Cheyenne blood on the Sioux Reservation. Crook, in line with his general opposition to the return of the prisoners to Indian Territory, strongly favored Red Cloud's proposal as the better and more humane alternative. To Sheridan he wrote, "It is important that these Indians [the Lakota] should not be disappointed. . . . Besides, these women and children have no relations living now outside the Sioux."[110] His arguments carried the day. On January 28 he received orders to deliver those of Lakota blood to their relatives at Pine Ridge. Three days later thirty-three women and twenty-two children, "covered with wounds and gaunt with hunger," boarded wagons from Fort Robinson for the five-day journey to the Oglala reservation, "in deference," as Crook phrased it, "to Red Cloud's request."[111]

The surviving adult male prisoners and the remaining women and children, lacking relatives among the Sioux, were not so fortunate. Governor George T. Anthony of Kansas, purporting to speak for his outraged citizens, demanded that the Cheyenne men who had not died in the escape—Wild Hog, Old Crow, and five others—be turned over to civilian authorities to stand trial for the atrocities they were alleged to have committed as they passed through the northwest corner of the state. These included, by Anthony's estimation, the slaying of over forty settlers and drovers and "many women ravished and worse than murdered."[112] Ignoring Crook's opposition, the federal government acceded to Governor Anthony's demands, and the seven Cheyennes were sent to Leavenworth where they were turned over to the Kansas authorities. The women and children were to be returned to Darlington.

Though the Kansans' desire for revenge was understandable, most historians have agreed with Crook, who argued that trying Wild Hog and Old Crow for the depredations made little sense. These chiefs were not involved in the killings, which, as now seems clear, were committed by the young men of the band acting independently and against Little Wolf's orders. Most of those involved had gone north with Little Wolf's group or, if they had remained with Dull Knife, had died in the breakout. In the end the court in Dodge City, where the seven were taken for trial, sensibly dismissed all charges against the old chiefs in the absence of any evidence linking them personally to the killings.

Understandably, Little Wolf later distanced himself from the depredations. The young men, he said, "killed some citizens, but I think not many. They did not tell me much of what they did because they knew I would not like it." By most accounts, he was probably telling the truth.[113]

Dull Knife was not with the group sent to Kansas. He and members of his family had successfully eluded the soldiers during the breakout and, after much suffering, reached the new Red Cloud agency in dreadful shape. As Guy Dull Knife Jr., the chief's great-grandson, would later recount, some of the Lakota "began to cry when they saw them. They looked like dead people. They were nothing but skin and bone. Their faces were hollow and they were half-naked, wearing next to nothing. Some were barefoot and their hands and feet had frozen."[114] Their wretched condition so moved Red Cloud that he concealed their presence from the army until things calmed down and later convinced the government that the chief and his family should be allowed to remain on the reservation.

As Sherman had ordered an inquiry into the entire affair, Crook immediately appointed a three-officer board to review it. Their report was delivered on January 25, 1879, just three days after the last survivors were recaptured. In their most telling statement, the officers opined that the Tsitsistas' dread of being sent back to Darlington was so great that "the return of these Indians to the South could only have been accomplished by bloodshed." That being the case, the board asked, "Did the dignity of the government require the forcible removal of these people back to the Indian Territory, at any rate prior to a full investigation into the merit of their complaints?" Since the War and Interior Departments had already decided that it did, the authorities at Fort Robinson had no alternative but to try to minimize the slaughter. While criticizing Wessells's decision to starve the Indians into submission and his lack of precautions against a breakout, the board ultimately decided that no blame could attach to the officers involved in view of the inevitable nature of the events set in motion by the government's decision. General Crook endorsed these findings, which he found "very complete." General Sherman wisely had nothing to add.

Dull Knife's band no longer presented a threat, but Little Wolf's people remained at large. After splitting from Dull Knife and wintering in the Sand Hills, they headed north, eventually surrendering to General Miles at Fort Keogh, Montana. While in Montana many of the young warriors volunteered to scout for Miles against Sioux holdouts still roaming that part of the country. Because of their service and the fact that popular sentiment now favored the Northern Cheyennes, the government made no move to return them to Darlington.

As for Crook, he defended his role in the affair in his September 1879 annual report to the secretary of war.[115] Backed by his board's finding, he loyally supported the conduct of Wessells and the troops in his department during the breakout. Like the board, he maintained that in the face of the northerners' adamant refusal to accept return to Indian Territory and Washington's equally stubborn insistence on their removal, neither he nor Wessells had any alternative but to use force to execute the order. Nevertheless, he considered the decision to return the Northern Cheyennes to Darlington manifestly unjust in view of their prior contributions to the government. Among these Cheyennes, he said, were "some of the bravest and most efficient of the auxiliaries who acted under General Mackenzie and myself in the campaign against the hostile Sioux in 1876 and 1877," a distinguished service that "the government seems to have forgotten." As to their refusal to return to Indian Territory, he declared that "during twenty-seven years of my experience with the Indian question, I have never known a band of Indians to make peace with our government and then break it or leave their reservation, without some ground of complaint; but until their complaints are examined and adjusted, they will constantly give annoyance and trouble." Finally, he addressed the matter of Little Wolf's band still in limbo in Montana. He thought it "a very unnecessary exercise of power" for the government to send some members of the tribe back to Darlington while allowing others to remain in the north. Clearly, his implication was that all should have been allowed to remain in their home country.[116]

The Indian Bureau, under the leadership of Commissioner of Indian Affairs Ezra Hayt, continued to insist that the Cheyennes should be returned to Indian Territory. Hayt characterized Dull Knife's people as "the evilest and most dangerous element of their tribe" and declared their decision to break out of Darlington completely unwarranted.[117] But support for his position had eroded substantially, particularly after a select committee of Congress that investigated the affair contradicted Hayt's position in every respect. The committee concluded that the government had violated its treaty agreements with the tribe and that shortages of supplies had created disastrous conditions at Darlington that impelled the Indians to flee north. They agreed with Crook that "unless [the Cheyennes] were living in a place they could look upon as home, it was unlikely that they would ever gain the independence of

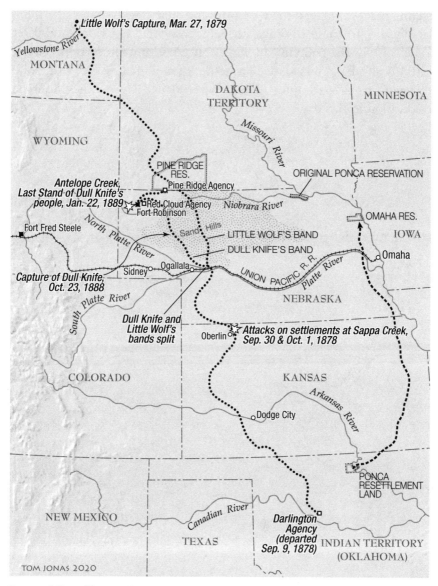

Routes followed by Northern Cheyennes and Poncas on their respective returns to their homelands in 1879. Map by Tom Jonas.

feeling that would lead them to work for their own living."[118] In 1883, largely due to these findings, the government backed down and set aside land for the tribe in Montana near the Crow reservation. There, Little Wolf's band was allowed to settle, soon joined by the Dull Knife survivors from Darlington. Their descendants live on the Montana reservation to this day.

CHAPTER THREE

I Am a Man

No doubt the knock on the front door of his offices at the Omaha *Daily Herald* in the early hours of a Sunday in late March 1879 surprised Thomas Henry Tibbles, the paper's thirty-nine-year-old assistant editor. Tibbles often worked late preparing the next day's edition, but he did not commonly entertain visitors at that hour. When he opened the door, in the light of the open doorway he saw two men and a woman standing on his threshold. He immediately recognized all three. The tall, erect gentleman in comfortable civilian attire was General Crook, commanding general of the department, whom Tibbles had come to know over the past couple of years. Beside him were a round-faced, swarthy man of middle age whom Tibbles identified as Iron Eye, a distinguished chief of the Omaha tribe, and a young woman Tibbles knew as the chief's daughter. The chief was clad in white man's clothing but wore his thinning hair long in the Indian manner. The young woman was of lighter complexion, her face betraying Caucasian features. Her black hair, tied back in a severe bun, and her ankle-length dress gave her the appearance of a Presbyterian schoolmarm, which, indeed, she was.[1] Though the tall, well-built newsman towered over the diminutive young lady, the warmth of his greeting must have quickly set her at ease. He ushered the three callers into his office, thus initiating a series of events that would ultimately have a lasting impact on how the law would deal with the American Indian.[2]

The editor and the general had previously established a rapport, which explains Crook's presence on Tibbles's doorstep that Sunday evening. Though quite different in personality—Crook, private and reticent, Tibbles, extroverted and voluble—by the spring of 1879 the two men had developed an affinity for one another that, in part, reflected their common backgrounds and shared interests. Both had spent their boyhoods on the Ohio frontier. Both loved hunting, the West, and the opportunities it presented for adventure. And both shared a familiarity with and respect for the Indians and a desire to see them treated fairly and with justice. Their interactions with the tribes had led to both being inducted into the Soldier Lodge, a secret society of the Omaha people—a singular honor rarely accorded to whites.[3]

Crook's reliance on Tibbles's public-relations savvy dated back to 1877, when he had turned to the editor for assistance in helping Brulé chief Spotted Tail fight the removal of his band to a site on the Missouri.[4] A year later the general had used Tibbles's newspaper, the *Omaha Herald*, as a platform to publicize his frustration with the government's policies toward the Bannocks.[5] During the Cheyenne breakout, the *Herald* published articles descrying the treatment of the Northern Cheyennes, using information that would probably not have been available to the editor without the connivance of the increasingly disillusioned general. In one issue an editorial undoubtedly drafted by Tibbles demanded that the government "order General Crook to Washington, make him show all the papers, telegrams and endorsements of his office that bear upon this subject. If he be the guilty one punish him, but if not, and we are willing to wager heavily that he is not, then let the one who is delinquent be sacrificed."[6] Given their mutual history, Crook's arrival at Tibbles's door on that late Sunday evening was obviously not happenstance but a logical next step in a growing clandestine collaboration between the two men to ameliorate the injustices inherent in the government's Indian policies.

Described as a man who could easily pass for "a country parson or a tub-thumping politician," Tibbles was an imposing figure. With an unruly thatch of black hair, soon to turn gray, crowning his leonine head, he conveyed an overall impression of forceful tenacity, buttressed by a prominent jaw, partially concealed at the time under a goatee, and penetrating gray eyes that peered out at the world from beneath bushy

Thomas Henry Tibbles. Courtesy of Nebraska Historical Society.

eyebrows. He appeared to be, and was, a man driven by ideals and a fearless resolve to act on them.[7]

The newsman's character had been shaped by early privations and adventure. Born in 1840 near Crook's home in southwestern Ohio, he was only ten when his father died, leaving an aging wife with three youngsters to care for and few resources. As the eldest child, Thomas assumed responsibility for the family's care. Not long after he had begun farming a patch of frontier land to support them, the local authorities stepped in and broke up the family, binding Thomas out to work for another farmer. The work was hard and the farmer indifferent to the young boy's needs. Within a year, with his mother's blessings, Thomas fled west to Kansas, where he embarked on a rolling series of adventures that included a brief tour as a fighting abolitionist in the border warfare that raged across the territory; a year with a nomadic Indian tribe that earned him membership in the Soldier Lodge secret society of the Omahas; and the infiltration of a gang of horse thieves who poisoned him upon learning his identity. After a period of convalescence during which he attended a local college in Ohio, he enlisted as a Union scout during the Civil War. After the war he headed west once again, working his way as a hunting guide and later a preacher until he found his niche as a crusading newspaperman. With such a history, he could justifiably claim that he had never shied away from trouble for a good cause. And on that day in March 1879, if he read his friend's expression correctly, trouble seemed to be in the offing.[8]

Now in his fiftieth year, Crook showed his age. His features, partially concealed under a bushy beard that naturally forked beneath his chin, were deeply furrowed, weathered by decades of service in the field and scored by the stress of unremitting campaigning. The unhappy consequences of the policies he was forced to carry out, most recently with respect to the Bannocks and Northern Cheyennes, seemed to weigh heavily on him. Only two weeks before he appeared on Tibbles's doorstep, he had received word that Little Wolf's band had surrendered at Fort Keogh, bringing an end to the Northern Cheyennes' tragic struggle to regain their homeland.[9]

Now, with scarcely a respite, a new—and by now all too familiar—tale of government injustice threatened to envelope him, one that caused him to seek the aid of the *Herald* editor. But it was the Omaha chief, Iron Eye, who described the plight of a small band of Ponca Indians who had recently sought sanctuary on his reservation. Crook had been aware of the presence of the group and their chief, Standing Bear, since March 7, after Secretary of the Interior Carl Schurz had notified the War Department that thirty Poncas had left their agency in Indian Territory in violation of federal law and were currently on the Omaha reservation. He had requested the army "have the nearest military commander detail a sufficient guard to return [them] to the agency where they belong."[10] Notified by the War Department, Crook had dispatched a detachment of Ninth Infantry troops under the command of Lieutenant William L. Carpenter to apprehend the small band and bring them to Fort Omaha pending their return to Indian Territory.[11]

On March 27 Fort Omaha's commander, Colonel John H. King, notified Crook of the Poncas' arrival, twenty-six in all, "eight men, seven women, and eleven children." Noting that "several of the Indians are sick with chills and fever," King said that that they would have to remain at the fort for several days to recover before making the journey back to Indian Territory.[12] In the interim he housed them in tents on the grounds of the fort. Like the Cheyennes before them, the Poncas had made it known that they would rather die than return to Indian Territory.[13]

There appears to be no official record of Crook's meeting Chief Iron Eye and his daughter prior to his arrival with them at Tibbles's door. This may have been deliberate, in order to obscure the general's role in what would become, in effect, a conspiracy to undermine official government policy. The emotional involvement that Crook exhibited during his meeting in Tibbles's office certainly indicates that he had spent some time earlier that Sunday afternoon in discussions with the two Omahas regarding the Poncas' unfortunate history.[14]

Crook had known Iron Eye for some time. He was principal chief of his tribe and a familiar figure to the white community under his American name, Joseph La Fleshe. Of mixed French Canadian and Omaha parentage, the chief took pride in his dual heritage, giving his children both Omaha and French names. His daughter, whom he had brought with him on this occasion as a translator (though he was fluent in French, the chief's English was rudimentary), was known both as Susette and by her Omaha name, which in her language meant Bright Eyes. Overcoming painful shyness, she had received a finishing-school education in the East and was now principal of the government school on the Omaha reservation.[15] Lieutenant Bourke later described her as "an Indian lady of excellent attainments and bright intellect."[16]

Iron Eye described the Poncas as a peaceful folk who had originally occupied the prairies of the lower Missouri River basin near present-day Omaha. The tribe had always coexisted with whites, regarding them both as valuable allies against their powerful and aggressive Lakota neighbors and as a source of trade goods they could obtain in exchange for pelts.

Despite their friendly relations with the whites, as the tide of westward immigration swelled, the Poncas, like other western tribes, were
gradually squeezed onto smaller and smaller reservations. Altogether,
the government concluded four treaties with the tiny tribe. The first,
in 1858, allotted the Poncas a small reservation in their traditional
homeland on the north bank of the Niobrara River near the border of
present-day Nebraska and South Dakota. The land was fertile and the
Poncas quietly accepted the move, abandoning their nomadic lifestyle
and turning successfully to farming. Many even opted for two primary
indicia of nineteenth-century Euro-American civilization: Christian-
ity and literacy. Ignoring their faultless adjustment, in 1865 the government moved them east along the Niobrara, supposedly to protect
them from their traditional enemies, the Sioux. Though they lost the
improvements they had made on their previous farmsteads, the Poncas
again complied without protest.

Three years later, due to careless drafting, the government erroneously ceded the entire Ponca Reservation to the Sioux under the Fort
Laramie Treaty. Though the error was soon acknowledged, nothing
was done to correct it, and their lands were given to the Brulés. The
Interior Department then ordered the Poncas resettled in Indian Territory, claiming they would be safer there than living near their old enemies. While the Brulés resisted the move to the Missouri River lands,
to the Poncas, it was home. As Standing Bear, one of their principal
chiefs would declare: "This land is ours, we have never sold it. We have
our houses and our homes here. Our fathers and some of our children
are buried here. Here we wish to live and die."[17] But their protestations
were ignored. In 1877 a delegation of Ponca chiefs was escorted south
to select land for their new home in Indian Territory with assurances
that if they did not find an acceptable site, they would be free to remain
on their home reservation.

Later, Standing Bear would testify that "the land they showed us
was stony, and I did not believe we could make a living on it. I was
afraid my people would get sick and die. We could not come here."[18]
Accordingly, he and his fellow chiefs insisted that, as promised, they
be returned to Nebraska immediately. Their escort, Edward Kemble,
a former newsman now acting as a roving inspector for the Indian
Bureau, was incensed by their refusal to consider other locations and
refused to pay their way back to Nebraska. He simply abandoned them

in Indian Territory.[19] Penniless and without a word of English, the seven chiefs made the five-hundred-mile journey back to the Missouri on foot in midwinter, surviving on the occasional kindness and charity of tribespeople and white settlers whose lands they crossed on their way.[20] Unfortunately for the Poncas, Kemble had reached the Niobrara before them with orders to remove the tribe's seven hundred men, women, and children, to Indian Territory—forcibly, if necessary. A portion of the tribe, mostly those of mixed race, accepted the move. But the rest, against their will, were ousted from the reservation by the army in an action so hasty that they were forced to leave behind most of their possessions and livestock, accumulated over years of labor.[21] The government's promise to deliver these possessions to them at a later date was conveniently forgotten.

As a cost-saving measure, rather than transport the Poncas by rail to what is today Oklahoma, Kemble decided to march them to their destination. On May 19, 1877, the tribe set out on a nightmarish journey. Beset by summer heat, insects, and severe storms and weakened by insufficient food, many of the people sickened. Nine died along the way, among them Standing Bear's own daughter.[22] In July, after a forced march of fifty days, the survivors reached Indian Territory. There they were settled on the Quapaw Reservation without the consent of its current occupants. The soil was infertile and poorly watered, and the area swarmed with malarial mosquitoes. Because the Poncas had arrived too late in the season to sow crops, the Indian Bureau had agreed to provide them with rations to sustain them over the winter. But it failed to do so, forcing them to share in the Quapaws' meager allotment, which was barely sufficient to provide one meal a day for each member of the tribe.[23]

As with the Cheyennes and other northern tribes who had preceded them to Indian Territory, the Poncas were soon devastated by disease brought on by malnutrition, poor sanitation, insect infestation, and the unaccustomed climate. According to the Interior Department's annual report for 1877, during the first year "the Poncas . . . have already lost 36 by death, which, by ordinary computation, would be the death rate for the entire tribe for a period of four years." Nevertheless, the department blandly expressed willingness to accept such losses as the normal and predictable consequence of its removal and consolidation policies.[24] Yet by the following summer (1878), their death rate was so high that Standing Bear was permitted to journey to Washington to plead his case for return to their homeland to the Great Father, President Hayes.

Hayes seemed genuinely surprised by the chief's tale, having supposed that the tribe had been happily settled on their new reservation. But rather than set a precedent, he refused to return the Poncas to the north, instead assuring them that their people would acclimate to the country and that soon their death rate would decline. He did, however, permit the Poncas to select an alternate site on which to settle, one supposedly more suitable for crops.[25]

Standing Bear followed Hayes's instructions and chose new land for his people. But he would later relate: "The sickness was worse than ever. Families . . . were scattered around. The whole family would be sick and no one would know it. In some of these families, persons would die and others would not be able to bury them. They would drag them with a pony out on the prairie and leave them there. Men would take sick while at work and die in less than a day."[26] Soon, one third of the tribe was gone, 158 souls, including Standing Bear's sister and a beloved teenage son, Bear Shield. On his deathbed the young man, fearing to enter the spirit world alone, had told his father, "I would like you to take my bones back and bury them there where I was born." Deeply moved, the chief vowed to do so.[27]

As fall passed into winter and sickness continued to afflict the tribe, Standing Bear resolved to save a few of the remaining souls. "If I failed," he said, "it could be no worse than to stay there."[28] He gathered a small group of twenty-seven people, fourteen men and boys and the remainder women and young children, who he thought were sufficiently healthy to survive the journey. He hoped to resettle them on their homeland and then send for the rest of the tribe. On January 2, 1879, they loaded the sick, the very old, the very young, and the bones of Standing Bear's son in four wagons and stole off into the night. They had only a few scraps of food saved from their rations and twenty dollars in cash money to sustain them along the way.

Word of the Poncas' departure immediately filled the local papers, triggering memories of the Cheyennes' recent flight and subsequent depredations. The army pursued them, but the Poncas evaded detection, keeping to thinly settled country and changing direction frequently. Their food and money lasted for twenty days, and from then on they subsisted on the charity of the occasional homesteader who, moved by the Indians' emaciated condition, shared their meager resources with them. They, in turn, remained true to their peaceful nature. As John Bourke would later write, "Not a shot was fired at anyone; not so much as a dog was stolen."[29]

In this fashion the Poncas arrived in northeastern Nebraska at the end of February. The Omahas, who had learned of their flight and anticipated their arrival, welcomed them with open arms. Chief Iron Eye was particularly effusive. The Poncas could stay with them on the reservation for as long as they needed. The Omahas would share their land, tools, and seed with them. And, if they wished, in the coming summer they would help the Poncas return to their traditional lands, ensuring Standing Bear's son's burial in the ground of his ancestors.

The Omahas could only conceal the Poncas' presence from their Indian agent, Jacob Vore, for a short time. On March 4 he learned of it, placed them under arrest—though he had no place to confine them—and informed Secretary Schurz of their presence, setting the wheels in motion for their forced return to Indian Territory.[30]

Lieutenant Carpenter's detachment arrived on the reservation on March 23 to escort the Poncas to Fort Omaha as the first step on their return to exile. Though obviously moved by the piteous condition of the Indians, the young officer could do little but listen to their sad story before marching them to his post. But he did give the people some hope, telling Standing Bear that on arrival at the fort he would have a chance to talk to General Crook. The chief had heard from Iron Eye that Crook was a good man who could be trusted. Perhaps he could help them.[31]

Bright Eyes (Susette La Flesche), Iron Eye's daughter, like almost everyone who met the Poncas, had been deeply moved by their plight and impressed with the dignified manner in which they handled themselves. She and her father discussed ways in which they could help and finally decided to visit the fort to personally request General Crook's assistance. On Friday, March 28, after completing her teaching duties for the week, she and her father undertook the hundred-mile journey to Fort Omaha. If Tibbles's account is accepted as fact, their efforts motivated Crook's midnight visit to the *Herald*'s offices.

"I could see by his face that something had gone very wrong," Tibbles later observed. And Crook wasted no time unburdening himself.

While the Victorian prose Tibbles put in the general's mouth was undoubtedly shaped by the editor's penchant for drama, there can be little doubt that the journalist captured the frustration and outrage that colored Crook's account.

> During twenty-five or thirty years that I've been on the plains in government service, . . . I've been forced many times by orders from Washington to do most inhumane things in dealing with the Indians, but now I'm ordered to do a more cruel thing than ever before. I would resign my commission, if that would prevent the order from being executed—but it would not. Another officer would merely be assigned to fill my place. I've come to ask if you will not take up the matter. It's no use for me to protest. Washington always orders the very opposite of what I recommend.[32]

It was probably Iron Eye and his daughter who narrated the Poncas' sad saga to the editor. But it was undoubtedly Crook who sought to enlist Tibbles's energies and resources to do battle with the "Indian Ring," the shadowy cabal that the general blamed for many of the wrong-headed Indian policies he had witnessed over the course of his career. "You have a great daily newspaper here which you can use. . . . You're perfectly acquainted with all the crimes of the Indian Ring at Washington. I ask you to go into this fight against those who are robbing these helpless people. You can win; I'm sure of it. The American people, if they knew half the truth would send every member of the Indian Ring to prison."[33]

In Tibbles's narrative Crook concluded with an eloquent appeal to the editor's well-known idealism. "No matter what we do, all any of us can get out of this world is what we eat, drink, and wear, and a place to shelter us. If we can do something for which good men will remember us when we're gone, that's the best legacy we can leave. I promise you that if you take up this work, I'll stand by you."[34] Readers familiar with Crook's pedestrian prose might have difficulty believing that the general delivered himself of such heroic oratory. More likely, Tibbles embellished the general's words in the interests of a good story. Yet Crook's statement must have been persuasive, as Tibbles promptly agreed to join the fray.

Washington had failed to put a timetable on the return of the Poncas to Indian Territory, leaving Crook free to defer action until he received a direct order. That created a window of opportunity Tibbles could exploit to marshal public opinion to pressure the government into reversing its course. Crook had arranged to meet with the Ponca chiefs at ten o'clock on Monday to hear their case against returning to Indian Territory. He had invited Tibbles to attend. But the editor was too energized to wait until Monday to hear more of the details. He awoke at dawn on Sunday after only a brief nap, bolted a hurried breakfast, and walked the four miles to Fort Omaha to seek out the Poncas. On reaching the post he called on Standing Bear at his tent on the fort's parade ground. At first the chief was hesitant to speak to the journalist before meeting with General Crook, but his reluctance disappeared when Tibbles revealed his membership in the Omaha Soldier Society. Calling together his chiefs, Standing Bear instructed them to relate their story, which they delivered with such emotion and sincerity that any doubts Tibbles might have had about the justness of their cause evaporated.[35]

Monday morning found the indefatigable editor in Crook's office for the scheduled meeting. John Bourke was present and recorded the proceedings verbatim in his diary. The diarist intended, he said, "to show the cruel and senseless way in which [the] Government of the United States deals with the Indian tribes who confide in its justice or trust themselves to its mercy," undoubtedly a reflection of his commander's own disillusionment with federal Indian policy.[36]

Standing Bear was a handsome and imposing man. His craggy face, square jaw, high brow, and intelligent visage might remind readers of a certain vintage of Nelson Rockefeller in his middle years. He had dressed for the occasion in the clothing he wore in contemporary photographs. He presented, in Bourke's words, a "tall and commanding presence, dignified in manner and very elegantly dressed in the costume of his tribe." He wore a blue flannel shirt ornamented with brass buttons, leggings of the same fabric, deerskin moccasins, and had draped a red-and-blue blanket over his shoulder. His hair, parted in the middle, fell to his shoulders in two braids, and, as Bourke admiringly noted, he wore a necklace of grizzly claws. His appearance was all the more striking for its contrast with the garb of his fellow chiefs, who wore Anglo clothing beneath plain green blankets.[37]

Standing Bear, Ponca Chief. Courtesy of the Nebraska Historical Society.

The Poncas, who bore with them the small trunk holding the bones of Standing Bear's son, crowded into Crook's spartan office. Together with Tibbles, several officers, and an interpreter, they filled the small room to capacity. In the confined space, the atmosphere was electric with emotion. Standing Bear spoke first through an Omaha interpreter, relating a history of government perfidy in heart-rending detail. Though everyone present had heard the tragic tale in one form or another, Standing Bear's eloquence was profoundly affecting. Yet Crook responded in the only way a soldier could under the circumstances—he was bound by his orders. In Bourke's account, the general, who had been down this road before, added, "If we intercede for them, it will do more harm than good."[38] The most he could publicly offer was to allow the exhausted Poncas to "stay here a few days to feed and rest their stock and then move on down slowly, taking all their stock with them."[39] When Standing Bear meekly requested "a little money to put in my pocket so I can spend a little once in a while" to help his sick and weak family, Crook replied through the interpreter, "It is not our place to give them money; they must get that from Washington. We will give them plenty to eat while they are here."[40] As by this time his sympathies lay wholeheartedly with the Poncas, dealing so coldly with them must have been painful, but it was, perhaps, a strategic maneuver. The very severity of the general's pronouncements, recorded by a member of the press, would be sure to reach and likely inflame the public and build sympathy for the tribe. And, as anticipated, Tibbles filled the next day's *Daily Herald* with a detailed account of the harsh, unyielding treatment accorded Standing Bear's people and then telegraphed the story to New York, Chicago, and other cities throughout the nation.[41]

The resultant surge of support for the Poncas left Secretary Schurz unmoved. Despite his reputation as a liberal idealist and ardent reformer, the secretary's interest in Indians affairs focused narrowly on eliminating corruption and mismanagement in the Indian Bureau and cutting costs, basic tenets of President Hayes's administration. Furthermore, he was firmly committed to maintaining a disciplined reservation system as the most effective means of assimilating the Indians into American society. He worried that compromising with the Poncas would show a lack of firmness that would undermine the system.[42] Nevertheless, to put a humanitarian face on his policy, he claimed that if he failed to return the Poncas to Oklahoma, the tribe would wander about the country, becoming vagrants who would be "killed off in detail."[43]

It did not take long for Tibbles to realize that the power of the press alone would be insufficient to change the interior secretary's policies. In his third-party narrative of the affair, he wrote that when casting about for a solution, he turned to the law. Guided by his abolitionist background, he "found the key" to his dilemma in the recently adopted Fourteenth Amendment to the Constitution. Although originally passed to extend equal rights to the newly freed slaves, it broadly "defined the right of any *person* [the italics were Tibbles's] in the United States to his life, liberty, and property unless they were removed by due processes of law." At the time the law did not consider Indians to be "persons," as the term was used in the amendment, and therefore they were not entitled to due process. To Tibbles, this made no sense. Were not Poncas "persons" within the meaning of the provision? Only the courts could decide that question.[44]

Tibbles, not a lawyer, was unable to determine with certainty whether his theory had merit. But he knew a prominent Omaha attorney, John L. Webster, who might.[45] The editor sought him out and described the plight of the Poncas and his theory that the Fourteenth Amendment might be applicable, suggesting to the perhaps bemused attorney that he, Tibbles, believed "that a writ of *Habeas Corpus* could be used to bring the case to the court's attention."[46] Webster, moved by Tibbles's tale, pondered the matter overnight and decided that the editor had "raised a constitutional question of vast importance." In fact, he was so inspired by the issue that he offered to take the case without fee. But given "the magnitude of the questions involved," he decided he needed the assistance of another well-known attorney, Andrew J. Poppleton.[47]

Poppleton, chief counsel to the Union Pacific Railroad and a revered figure in early Nebraska history, was equally animated by the Poncas' story and the opportunity to take on such a landmark case.[48] He joined Webster's legal team, and it was he who later credited Crook, not Tibbles, with the suggestion that a writ of habeas corpus might be used to appeal to the courts for protection.[49] Notwithstanding his West Point education, nothing in Crook's history remotely indicates an interest in the law or any practical experience from which such an theory might have sprung. But if Poppleton was correct, perhaps the idea originated with one of his urbane aides: either Schuyler or Bourke comes to mind.

Regardless of the origin of the proposal, both Webster and Poppleton agreed that a writ of habeas corpus (Latin for "you may have the body") was in fact an appropriate way to bring the case before a federal court.[50] An ancient legal form inherited from the British and subsequently enshrined in American law, the writ compels a government official responsible for an arrest to produce the individual before a court of law for a determination of the legality of the detention. If the arrest is found illegal, the individual must be released immediately. In this case, as the army had detained the Poncas, the writ would be served on General Crook as the responsible officer, ordering him to produce the tribesmen in federal court for the requisite determination.

To rule on the legality of the Poncas' arrest, the court would first have to find that Standing Bear and his people were entitled to invoke the writ: in legal parlance, that they had standing to sue. Prevailing case law held that they did not. An Indian, like a minor, was deemed unqualified to come before the courts and hence did not have the right to the protection offered by the writ. So only if a judge was willing to overturn that precedent would the Poncas have standing to sue.

The government's obvious response would be to invoke current precedent and, in the unlikely event that failed, to defend the legality of the arrest, which in the Poncas' case was based on a law making it a crime for an Indian to enter or leave a reservation without proper authorization. The court would then have to rule on the applicability of that law to the Poncas or on its constitutionality.

As the arresting official was a federal officer, the writ would have to be brought in federal court—in this instance, the U.S. district court in Lincoln, Nebraska. The presiding judge, the independent and well-respected lawyer Elmer Dundy, was the first judge appointed to serve on the Nebraska court after its establishment in 1868. Like both Crook and Tibbles, he was a transplanted Ohioan. Stern, often intimidating, he was nevertheless widely regarded as fair and open-minded. He also had some familiarity with the question of the status of Indians under the law, having recently ruled that federal courts had no jurisdiction over crimes committed on Indian reservations.[51] Crook and Tibbles knew the judge as an avid woodsman and had hunted with him on several occasions.[52]

Indeed, the judge's love of hunting presented an immediate problem for the Poncas' legal team. At the time they sought the writ, he was deep in the wilds on a bear hunt. This was a source of considerable worry to the Poncas' lawyers. They needed to institute the proceedings immediately, before the Interior Department delivered its final order to Crook to remove the Poncas south, an action expected imminently. Only the issuance of the writ could forestall such a move. Tibbles later wrote that while the search for the judge continued, "General Crook, constantly dreading interference from Washington, was the most anxious person I ever saw to have a writ served on him."[53]

Much to Crook's relief, on April 4 the judge was located, and Webster and Poppleton filed their petition. Entitled *United States ex rel. Machu-nah-zha (Standing Bear) v. George Crook, a Brigadier General of the Army of the United States and Commander of the Department of the Platte*, it was presented in behalf of twenty-six Ponca tribesmen, who, the petitioners alleged, had separated themselves from the Ponca tribe in order to return to their homeland. When arrested and detained they had been peacefully residing on the Omaha Reservation with the consent of that tribe. The petitioners now requested that they be "restored to their liberty."[54]

The Poncas and their supporters waited breathlessly for four days before Judge Dundy accepted the writ and served it on Crook. Under oath the general filed the required response, stating that he had detained the Indians on orders from the secretary of the interior and requesting that the complainants be returned to him so that he could discharge his duty and return them to Indian Territory. With the formalities completed, the judge scheduled a hearing on the issues for April 30, and Crook duly notified General Sheridan to that effect.[55]

News of the case traveled rapidly up the chain of command to the secretary of the interior. As the coconspirators had intended, the Interior Department was now barred from taking any action with respect to the Poncas pending a determination whether they were being held under proper authority. In the days before the trial, the parties engaged in a battle for public opinion. Ezra Hayt, Schurz's commissioner of Indian affairs and a firm believer in the sanctity of reservation policy, wrote a letter that, though addressed to the secretary of the interior, was obviously intended for public consumption.

The letter was shockingly callous and slanted. Hayt dismissed the fact that the tribe "had lost a large number by death" as "inevitable in all cases of removal of Northern Indians to a Southern latitude," and he declared that on a recent visit to the agency, he found the people's condition "very much improved, both as to their outward circumstances and their feelings." Among the Ponca chiefs, "only Standing Bear was dissatisfied," showing "bad spirit." Hayt claimed that he was "constantly grumbling . . . and seemed full of discontent, which he took no pains to conceal." Having dismissed the Poncas' claims and undermined their chief's credibility, the commissioner moved on to what he and the Interior Department considered the real issue in the case, its potential to destroy the reservation system. While admitting that "the removal of Northern Indians to the Indian Territory was probably not good policy," he blamed that decision on the previous administration. But what was done could not now be undone, as there was no legal basis for allowing a tribe to return to their old reservation or any other place. Nor, in the commissioner's opinion, ought there be one.

> If the reservation system is to be maintained, discontented and restless or mischievous Indians cannot be permitted to leave their reservation at will and go where they please. If this were permitted the most necessary discipline of the reservations would soon be entirely broken up, . . . and in a short time the Western country would swarm with roving and lawless bands of Indians, spreading a spirit of uneasiness and restlessness even among those Indians who are now at work and doing well.[56]

Hayt's letter stirred up a hornet's nest. Speaking through Tibbles and the press, Standing Bear angrily questioned the right of the government to give the Ponca lands on the Niobrara to the Sioux and refuted Hayt's claim that there was no longer sickness in Indian Territory. He also produced numerous testimonials to rebut the commissioner's slurs on the chief's attitude and conduct while in Oklahoma.[57] The Omahas quickly joined the fray, submitting a petition of their own endorsing the Poncas' claims and affirming the tribe's right to remain peacefully on the Omaha Reservation. This, too, received wide publicity.[58]

While the parties warred in the press, the government assigned a young, ambitious U.S. attorney, Genio Madison Lambertson, to represent it in court. Lambertson, lantern-jawed, self-confident, and ambitious, was twenty-nine years old and had been in the job for only five months. This was by far his most high-profile trial, and he was confident of victory, believing that the case would be thrown out of court as soon as he raised the issue of standing. He undoubtedly said as much when he met with General Crook at the latter's Fort Omaha office to discuss the case. Given Crook's reputation for impenetrability, one suspects that Lambertson left his office with no idea of the general's true motives.[59]

Spring flooding delayed Judge Dundy's departure from Lincoln, causing the case, scheduled for hearing in Omaha on April 30, to be put over until the following morning, a hot and muggy day that turned the packed courtroom into a veritable sauna.[60] General Crook had abandoned his usual civilian attire for the occasion and was clad instead in the stiff, full dress uniform of a brigadier general, complete with epaulets and sword. Captain Bourke and Major Horace B. Burnham, a representative of the judge advocate general, accompanied him. They, too, wore formal military attire and were probably equally uncomfortable. For their part, the Poncas were dressed in ragged, cast-off white man's clothing except for Standing Bear, who appeared in full traditional regalia.[61] Anyone familiar with courtroom theatrics would rightly assume that the petitioners' lawyers had deliberately costumed the parties so as to contrast the might of the U.S. government with the powerlessness of its Indian victims.

The trial opened with each side laying out their theory of the case. In order to establish the Poncas' right to invoke habeas corpus, attorney Poppleton explored the basis for denying them standing: the prevailing legal fiction that Indians were neither citizens of the United States nor members of a foreign nation. As they owed allegiance to their tribes rather than any government, Indians were regarded as people without a country and hence outside the protection of American jurisprudence. Poppleton argued that passage of the Fourteenth Amendment changed this situation by guaranteeing equal protection to "citizens born or naturalized in the United States, and subject to the jurisdiction thereof." The latter phase was originally included in the clause to exclude Native Americans who belonged to tribes that were not subject to court jurisdiction. Poppleton argued that the language in an 1870 Senate Judiciary Committee report on the drafting of the amendment demonstrated that Congress intended to make an exception for Indians who had dissolved their relationship with their tribe and followed the "white man's road." By adopting "civilized" values and forsaking their tribal allegiance, they voluntarily submitted themselves to the jurisdiction of the United States and, as native-born Americans, qualified as citizens entitled to full protection of the law under the Fourteenth Amendment. This argument required not only that the court accept this theory but that the Poncas had, indeed, become detribalized Indians.[62]

Lambertson rose to challenge Poppleton's argument, but the railroad lawyer objected on technical grounds, arguing that the government had no right to speak to the issue, having failed to address it in its initial filings. Judge Dundy concurred but allowed the U.S. attorney time to amend his response to correct the error.[63] Webster followed, presenting testimony designed to prove that the Poncas intended to shed their tribal identity and adopt the white man's civilization. Lambertson refuted this contention on cross-examination. The trial continued in this vein until the judge declared a break for lunch.[64]

When the court reconvened that afternoon, Webster called Standing Bear to the stand and was immediately rewarded with his first hint of Judge Dundy's inclinations in the case. Lambertson attempted to block the chief's testimony by questioning his right as an Indian to appear in a United States' court. At that, Dundy intervened, declaring that as to witnesses, "the Law makes no distinction on account of race, color, or previous condition."[65] The term "previous condition" normally referred to slavery. But Dundy used it to refer to tribal membership, signaling his acceptance of Poppleton's theory of the detribalized Indian.[66] Of equal significance, his ruling gave Standing Bear the opportunity to deliver a moving description of his peoples' travails and to testify to his desire to become a self-supporting citizen of the United States.[67] On cross-examination, U.S. Attorney Lambertson failed to shake the chief's renunciation of his tribal affiliation.

Standing Bear was the petitioner's last witness. As the government had no one to call, his testimony ended the evidentiary portion of the trial and cleared the way for the lawyers to deliver their summations. Webster took the lead. But before he could approach the bench,

Lambertson asked to read into the record his amended response to the writ. Prepared during the lunch break, it addressed the issue he had failed to include in his initial filing: whether the Poncas had, in fact, severed themselves from the tribe.

Crook had willingly signed the government's original response because it was limited to the undeniable assertion that he had arrested the Poncas on orders from above. Now he was sleepily ensconced in the stuffy courtroom, digesting his lunch and steeling himself for the hours of arcane legal arguments that stretched before him. Suddenly he was jolted from his torpor by Lambertson's voice reading a document proclaiming that the petitioners had not dissolved their relations with the Ponca tribe, that they continued to pay allegiance to its chief, and that they had not adopted or pursued the habits of "civilized life."[68] Crook was shocked. He regarded these statements as patently untrue. Lambertson had barely concluded his recitation before the general leapt to his feet and startled the courtroom by vehemently objecting to the inclusion of such language in a document that he was required to sign under oath. When Dundy cautioned him that he could not at this point address the court, the irate general refused to be put off. Turning to Major Burnham, he instructed him to register his objection. After Burnham had done so, the judge tried to calm the still angry Crook, explaining that he would not be signing the document as an individual but as a representative of the government. Unimpressed with the technicality, Crook, through Burnham, hotly denied the truth of the allegation to which he was being asked to attest. To his knowledge, he said, the chief and his people had, in fact, severed their relations with the tribe and made every effort to follow the white man's road, and he would not sign a statement to the contrary. Again Dundy attempted to explain that signing the document was a mere formality, but he could see that his words made no impression. With the agreement of the lawyers on both sides, he simply ordered the clerk of the court to include the amended response in the return.[69]

Crook's outburst sent a ripple of excitement through the crowded courtroom. Here was a general in the U.S. Army, the named respondent in the writ, openly defying his superiors by expressing his opposition to a key issue in the government's case. But Dundy, apparently unfazed by the interruption and eager to conclude the trial, ordered Webster to begin his summation. However, the hour was late, and

Webster was so exhausted that he asked for an adjournment, which the judge grudgingly granted.[70]

The following morning the attorney, restored by a night's rest, delivered his summation. He spoke from ten until noon and then again for an hour after lunch, expounding on the law and the facts. He traced the history of the relations between the Omahas, the Poncas, and the federal government, arguing that both native peoples had sought to emulate the whites and till the soil, abandoning the nomadic lifestyle that previously characterized their lives on the plains. He then expounded on legal precedents pertaining to Indians who had severed their tribal relations.

After Webster's presentation, Lambertson stood. For five hours he argued that the law did not regard an Indian as a citizen or a person—hence he was not entitled to the protection of the writ.[71] When he finished, Poppleton rose to rebut him, speaking in excess of two hours. Leaving aside the rhetoric, his argument boiled down to a single proposition. Since the law makes the writ of habeas corpus available to "any person or party," the court only had to consider whether Standing Bear was a person. To respond in the negative, he said, was to deny the Indian his humanity.

Poppleton completed his argument well after ten in the evening. As the hearing appeared to have been concluded, the marshal, on instructions from the judge, murmured in a low voice that the court was adjourned. General Crook and his fellow attendees, likely dazed by nine hours of testimony in the close courtroom, did not hear him. This was exactly as Dundy intended. What the courtroom heard was the judge telling Standing Bear that he might now address the court.[72]

The evening before, the chief had approached Tibbles. He had become increasingly restive as words he could not understand ricocheted about the courtroom. He told the newsman he wanted to address the court in his own words, to present his case in terms that meant sense to *him*. Tibbles agreed to bring the matter to Dundy's attention, and the judge, after facetiously asking whether Standing Bear had been admitted to the bar, consented to the unusual procedure.[73] To avoid a challenge to the irregularity of his ruling, he resorted to a sleight of hand, adjourning the case prior to the chief's address so that it did not become part of the trial record.

The speech was high drama. Bright Eyes acted as Standing Bear's interpreter. Her command of English—and perhaps more importantly, of the chief's confidence that she would accurately and eloquently translate his words—amply qualified her for the role.[74] She stood at his side as he silently turned to fix his eyes on the hushed courtroom. After a long moment, he turned toward the judge and began to speak, pausing at the end of each sentence to allow Bright Eyes to interpret his words, an artifice that greatly enhanced the impact of his delivery.[75] The speech was not long—he had been instructed by his lawyers to keep his remarks brief. After repeating an abbreviated, but still heart-rending, description of the tribulations his people had endured, he addressed what he saw as the core of the matter: Poppleton's question. Was he a person in the eyes of the law and hence entitled to its protections? Tibbles recorded his simple and straightforward words in the next day's paper and later repeated them in his books. They are so reminiscent of Shylock's speech in Shakespeare's *Merchant of Venice* that one wonders again whether the editor might have reshaped them to satisfy his penchant for melodrama.[76]

In Tibbles's account, the chief addressed his rapt audience, his hand dramatically extended. "That hand is not the color of yours. But if I pierce it, I shall feel pain. The blood that will flow from mine will be of the same color as yours. I am a man. The same God made us both." Turning back to the judge, he described the rocky path that faced his people in pursuit of their destiny. Then, with bowed head, he declared that only one man would decide which way that path would lead and, raising his troubled eyes to Judge Dundy, he quietly ended: "You are that man."[77]

Standing Bear's words had a profound impact on the courtroom. According to Tibbles, "No one who reads the speech can possibly imagine its effect on people who knew of the Poncas' sufferings when they heard it spoken by the sad old chief in his brilliant robes." As the journalist rendered the moment, the deep silence that followed the chief's concluding words was broken only by sobs from the audience. Tears clouded the judge's eyes, while General Crook leaned forward in his seat, covering his eyes with his hand. Then the marshal broke the stillness with the traditional "All rise," and the courtroom erupted in a great shout of acclamation. Surging forward, they crowded around the chief and pumped his hand, Crook in the lead.[78]

While the Poncas waited in suspense at Fort Omaha under Crook's benevolent but watchful eye, Judge Dundy pondered. Then, on May 12, ten days after the trial, the parties were summoned to hear his decision. Crook, as respondent in the case, was among the throng that gathered in the stuffy courtroom to listen to the judge's carefully crafted opinion.

From the outset it was apparent that Dundy's sympathies lay with the Poncas and that he recognized that General Crook, whom he described as a "brave and distinguished officer," had "no sort of sympathy in the business in which he is forced by his position to bear a part so conspicuous." Like the general, the judge, too, had to put personal feelings aside and deal with the matter before him in accordance with his professional responsibilities. This was a case, he said, that "must be examined and decided on principles of law."

After laying out the facts of the case, Dundy methodically rendered his opinion, issue by issue, beginning with the threshold question of the Poncas' standing to sue: that is, whether they were persons in the eyes of the law. Relying on Noah Webster's dictionary, the judge defined a person as "a living soul; a self conscious being; a moral agent; especially a living human being." Recalling Standing Bear's "I am a man" speech, the judge ironically concluded Mr. Webster's definition was sufficiently comprehensive to include "even an Indian." Dismissing the lack of precedent as irrelevant, he famously declared that Indians "are *persons*, such as are described by and included within the laws before quoted," cutting at a stroke the Gordian knot that had denied an entire race the protections afforded by the American legal system.[79]

Having made this benchmark ruling, the judge quickly disposed of the issue regarding the legality of the Poncas' arrest and detention, finding that though Crook acted properly in following his superiors' orders, the orders themselves were deficient. By law the army could legally go on the Omaha Reservation to apprehend persons (the Poncas) not authorized to be there. However, the statute conveying that power required that once arrested, those prisoners must be turned over to civil authorities "to be proceeded against in due course of law."[80] Crook's orders did not specify such a transfer. As he had kept the Poncas in military custody, he had violated the requirements of the statute and must, therefore, release them from custody immediately. Signaling the completion of his reading with a brisk rap of his gavel, the judge touched off an eruption in the courtroom and "great joy" among the Poncas.[81]

The country's reaction was substantially less enthusiastic. The decision sparked controversy from coast to coast, implying as it did a first step on what some viewed as the slippery path to Indian equality. In the West, particularly, there was fear that should the opinion become the law of the land, Indians would quickly be granted citizenship and reservations would become a thing of the past. "Savages" would once more freely roam the countryside, engaging in a riot of rapine and plunder or, reduced to pauperism, become a plague of beggars upon the land. Easterners, having long ago eliminated their own "Indian problem" by pushing their tribes west of the Mississippi, were less fearful and hence more sympathetic. To them, despite the laudable efforts of Standing Bear and his followers to assimilate into white culture, that culture had wronged and oppressed them.[82]

The government's reaction ranged from outrage to cautious support. The Interior Department quickly denounced the judge's decision. In a public letter Commissioner Hayt described the ruling as "a heavy blow to the present Indian system, that, if sustained, will prove extremely dangerous alike to whites and Indians."[83] On the other hand, Secretary of War George W. McCrary ignored an Interior Department announcement of plans to proceed with an appeal. On May 19, only a week after Judge Dundy's decision, he ordered the immediate release of Standing Bear and his people and their relocation elsewhere on government land.[84] Though required by the judge's decision, the promptness with which the order was issued and the decision to resettle the Indians on government land strongly suggests that the secretary's sympathies, like those of Crook, lay with the Indians.

But the army was not unanimous in this regard. Its commanding general, Sherman, and many of his subordinates vigorously endorsed the Interior Department's opposition to the ruling. Only months before Sherman and Sheridan had participated in a vituperative exchange with the department on the latter's fitness to manage Indian policy. They had described the department as "nearly always too late to prevent trouble or even understand the cause."[85] Yet now Sherman joined Hayt in voicing his displeasure at Dundy's ruling and Secretary McCrary's response. In a letter to the latter, he repeated the specious argument that these decisions would turn Standing Bear's people into "paupers turned loose on the community." That being the case, he sarcastically opined, Dundy ought now to assume the expense of their care.[86] Two days later Sheridan wired Sherman asking whether, in view of the Standing Bear case, he should order the arrest of several Poncas who had remained in Indian Territory who had also left their reservation without permission. In an interpretation obviously intended to restrict the scope of Dundy's ruling, Sherman ordered Sheridan to proceed with the arrest, remarking, "The release under *Habeas Corpus* of the Poncas in Nebraska does not apply to any other than that specific case."[87] Sherman's disapproval and the prevalence of like opinions among many officers must have given Crook pause. He had taken a great risk in defending the Poncas' cause and could only hope that his relationship with President Hayes would spare him the consequences.

Several days after Dundy rendered his decision, Lambertson filed an appeal on behalf of the government. Tibbles and other supporters of Indian rights, including, one supposes, General Crook, had looked forward to such an appeal, as a Supreme Court review of the case, if it affirmed Dundy's decision, would make it the law of the land, forever settling the legal status of Indians. But their expectations were dashed. When Lambertson submitted his application for an immediate hearing to Supreme Court Justice Samuel Miller on June 5, the justice initially refused to consider the petition as the Poncas were not at the time before him.[88] Before they could be rounded up, Secretary Schurz abruptly instructed the prosecutor to drop the suit. After reading the U.S. attorney's brief, he could not, he explained in a letter to Indian rights advocate Helen Hunt Jackson, "approve the principles upon which [Lambertson's] argument is based."[89] As he later remarked in a second letter to Jackson, lest there be a misunderstanding of his motives, no purpose would be served in "testing a question which has been tested more than once, and has been decided by the Supreme Court so clearly and comprehensively."[90] In other words, why waste time pursuing the appeal of a decision so obviously inconsistent with past precedent? More likely Schurz feared that the court would rule in favor of the Poncas, enshrining Indian equality in constitutional law, an outcome that would be difficult, if not impossible, to reconcile with government policy of the time.

While Dundy's decision produced momentary exultation among Standing Bear's supporters, in practice it a created dilemma. As detribalized Indians, the Poncas were no longer wards of the government and therefore could not legally remain on an Indian reservation. Their new status almost caused them to fall into a trap set for them by government attorneys. The officials had arrived unexpectedly at the Ponca camp before the tribe's official release date, telling the people they could now return "perfectly safely to their old home on the Niobrara."[91] Chief Standing Bear naively assumed that his visitors were acting in his interest and, eager to return to his homeland, immediately set off with his people toward the Niobrara. Tibbles knew better, aware that by entering on Indian lands, the Poncas would be breaking the law and could then be arrested for trespassing. Fortunately, he intercepted Standing Bear before he reached his destination and convinced him to return to Fort Omaha to await the date set for their release by the secretary of war.[92]

With only days to go before the government set the band free, Crook faced the problem of where to relocate them. Secretary McCrary had stipulated that it would have to be on government land but not on an Indian reservation. Scanning maps of the area, the general hit upon the idea of settling the Poncas on one of several small islands carved out by the channels formed by the Niobrara as it flowed into the Missouri. Located about two miles from the town of Niobrara, it was government property and lay outside the boundaries of the Sioux Reservation.[93] This would be only a temporary solution, as the Poncas would have no legal title to the land and would thus be subject to removal at any time at the government's discretion, which in the past had been exercised with little regard of the tribe's welfare.

For Crook, Tibbles, the Indian rights community, and the Indians themselves, the real goal remained the Poncas' return to their traditional lands, now unoccupied but reserved by treaty to Spotted Tail's Brulé. The issue assumed new urgency when, in June, a second group of Poncas fled Indian Territory in an emulation of Standing Bear's heroic effort and headed north for their Niobrara home. Destitute, they finally made their way to the Santee agency, where they awaited permission to complete their journey. For the time being the government made no effort to interfere with them, but obviously their future remained as uncertain as Standing Bear's.[94]

To offer financial support to the Poncas and press for their return to their homeland, Webster, Tibbles, and other Nebraskans formed the Omaha Ponca Relief Committee, which would soon widen its scope to include the advocacy of Indian rights throughout the United States.[95] Though precluded from membership because of his official position, Crook worked diligently with the group. In mid-June he met "long and often" with Tibbles and attorney Webster to discuss strategy. In Tibbles's words: "We could see a hard struggle stretching out ahead, but we firmly believed that by winning it we should free every Indian in the country from ever again dreading that the whims of everyone in Washington could willfully control his person or his belongings or could hinder his liberty to live his own life reasonably. And we cared not a rap whether our campaign would land heavily on the toes of the red-tape Washington men."[96] The group's fervent approach to this crusade would demand a level of public and personal commitment from Crook at which his prior efforts in the arena of Indian reform had only hinted.

A campaign on the scale contemplated by the Omaha Ponca Relief Committee would require extensive funding and influence beyond its members' resources. Though moved by idealism, these men were pragmatists who realized that the real political and financial power needed to effect change in government Indian policy lay in the East. To elicit support in the region, they decided that Tibbles, with his proven skill as a speaker and publicist, should conduct a speaking tour of eastern cities, contacting like-minded religious and lay groups to enlist them in their crusade. To lend credibility to his cause, he would carry with him documentation of the injustices inflicted on the Poncas, including a transcript of Standing Bear's trial, the endorsements of prominent members of the Omaha clergy, and a lengthy letter from Crook setting forth his views of current Indian policies.[97]

The letter is an important document. By 1879 the general had acquired a national reputation for expertise in Indian matters, not only as a soldier who had subjugated some of the fiercest tribes in the West but also as an administrator who thoroughly understood the needs and desires of the Indians. The Ponca Relief Committee anticipated that his word would carry great weight. Thus, his endorsement was an invaluable asset in Tibbles's campaign for Indian rights. But the letter was more—a manifesto setting out the beliefs that animated Crook's actions throughout the remainder of his career. Writing such a letter knowing that it would be widely disseminated was a daring move, one that he might have been emboldened to make because of his relationship with the president.[98]

To those not already aware of Crook's bona fides, the letter opened with a summary of his qualifications to address Indian policy: "My experiences with the red men embraces much more than a quarter of a century, during which time I have been thrown in contact with them, both in peace and war . . . and have had under my control reservations whereon were congregated Indians in numbers varying from several hundreds well up to thousands." Referring to those he had fought against, he noted that his career had afforded him "excellent opportunities for studying the character of Indians who roam, or lately did roam," over much of the West, adding that he had known many "as friends and allies in war."[99]

The George Crook who penned this letter was not the same man who, as a young officer serving on the California coast, had depicted Indians as "filthy, odiferous, treacherous, ungrateful, pitiless, cruel and lazy."[100] Over time his open and inquiring mind—and the influence of his enlightened aide and amateur ethnologist, John Bourke—had led him to conclude that Indians were, after all, not that different from whites. Distinctions that obviously did exist he attributed to the radically different environmental influences to which the two races had been exposed. Yet, as he now said in his letter, notwithstanding these differences, Indians "act under precisely the same impulses and are guided by identically the same train of reasoning as would white men under like circumstances."

In some instances in recent memory, he wrote, they had even responded in a superior manner. As an example, by 1879 all of the tribes had made their peace with the whites "either of their own seeking or under compulsion." Overall, the Indians had "adhered more closely to the spirit of treaty stipulations than the white man or the white man's government has ever done." Admittedly, some had resumed hostilities. Sometimes, he allowed, it was because of "want of suitable employment" or "the craving of eminence among their fellows," but most often they had taken to the warpath due to, as he diplomatically phrased it, "the general lack of tone of our system of dealing with them." Indian leadership understood that their only hope of survival lay in "adopting the white man's ways," but regrettably "to a great degree [they] have lost confidence in our people and their promises."

Likely recalling the lot of the Bannocks, Northern Cheyennes, and most recently, the Poncas, he continued: "Let a tribe remain at peace, [and] we starve them. Let them go to war and spring suddenly upon our scattered settlements, [and] we make every promise, yield every concession. Thus the Indian learns that by being 'bad' he is all the more certain to be the recipient of kind treatment."[101]

A "new and greater danger" now loomed, more fundamental than broken promises, starvation, and corrupt management:

> The Indians have absolutely no status for claiming protection under our laws. . . . It seems to me an odd feature of our judicial system that the only people in this country who have no rights under the law are the original owners of the soil. An Irishman, German, Chinaman, Turk, or Tartar will be protected in life and property, but the Indian commands respect for his rights only so long as he inspires terror for his rifle. . . .
>
> The red man is in danger of annihilation, of starving to death in the center of a country which is feeding the world with its exuberant harvests, or of being killed for trying to defend rights which the negro and Mongolian are allowed to enjoy. The true, the only policy to pursue with the Indian is to treat him just as one should a white man; if he makes war . . . punish him, but after he has been reduced to submission, protect him in life and property. Keep the white thieves from plundering him; let him see that peace means progress; that he has a market for every pound of beef and every hide, and every sack of grain, and, take my word for it, he will make rapid advances. Self interest will impel him to imitate us, to send his children to school, to adopt clothing, perhaps our language, and to devote his attention to raising cattle and horses and eventually to qualify himself of citizenship.[102]

Crook's opinions, while expressed in the ethnocentric language of his day, were a bold departure from the views of most of his fellow white Americans. From a modern perspective, he, like other like-minded progressives of his day, unfortunately failed to see merit in the customs, beliefs, and practices of societies other than his own. Such bigotry, alive even today, was, in Crook's era, rooted in the ingrained belief in the superiority of European civilization. Within that framework Crook and his contemporaries defined progress as movement toward integration in the dominant (Euro-American) society. To nineteenth-century reformers the solution to the "Indian problem" therefore lay in transforming the Indians into a mirror image of their white neighbors. Tribalism, or the communal nature of Indian society, was widely considered a major impediment to achieving such assimilation. If the primacy that Indian culture placed on societal rather than individual needs could be eradicated, the Indian would become an individualist and consequently a capitalist and, *ipso facto,* a productive member of the American body politic. In a statement that makes today's progressive cringe, Crook noted without a hint of irony, the Indian "will frequently, at feasts and dances, give away the bulk of his possessions to needy friends and relatives. We must endeavor to correct this defect in the Indian character."[103]

For all their shortcomings, Crook's progressive views led him unflinchingly to a conclusion not widely shared at the time, one that formed the underlying premise of Judge Dundy's decision. Once set on the road to assimilation, the Indian should naturally be entitled to all the benefits and privileges that pertained, including citizenship and the full panoply of constitutional privileges and protections. And that was the objective that Crook articulated in his letter to Tibbles.

CHAPTER FOUR

The Ponca Commission

Crook's involvement with the Poncas was temporarily suspended by Tibbles's departure for the East. In the interim, before he was drawn back into the fray, he had the opportunity to indulge his love of the wilderness West through a visit to the newly created Yellowstone National Park, the nation's first. The visit would also afford him the chance to become better acquainted with Carl Schurz, the secretary of the interior whose orders had initially propelled him into the Standing Bear litigation.

The secretary chose to travel to Yellowstone during the summer of 1880 as part of an inspection tour of the West. This would not be an official visit. From its establishment in 1872 until the National Park Service was created in 1916, the park would be under the jurisdiction and control of the War Department, though civilians would manage it.[1] Consequently, Schurz's visit was a personal affair, motivated by his desire to see Yellowstone's wonders. Nevertheless, as secretary of the interior he was afforded all of the courtesies given a visiting dignitary on official business. Though the chance of an encounter with hostile Indians was remote, this included a military escort under the command of General Crook, commander of the military department that encompassed the park.

Prior to joining Schurz in Yellowstone, the general had been reconnoitering the Ute Reservation in Utah to find an appropriate location for a military post to oversee the Colorado Utes who were soon to be settled there.[2] The reservation lay in the Uintah Mountains in the southernmost limits of his department, and, like the Yellowstone trip, the visit gave him the chance to explore relatively wild and unknown territory. With perhaps a hint of irony, he informed his superiors that he "was agreeably surprised to find the Reservation to be such a fine region."[3] John Bourke and the newest addition to his staff, Captain Cyrus Swan Roberts, accompanied him. Roberts had served as Crook's aide during the Civil War and, following Appomattox, had rejoined the general's staff in North Carolina during Reconstruction as a newly commissioned second lieutenant in the regular army. He went on to serve in the Seventeenth Infantry and now, as a captain, rejoined Crook's staff where he would serve intermittently until the general's death.[4]

Bourke, the inveterate diarist, kept a detailed record of both the Uintah reconnaissance and the Yellowstone expedition. Significantly, while in the Uintahs Bourke made several entries that referred to mining operations the party encountered in its travels. His mention of the potential for huge profits to be made in such ventures may indicate that this trip was the origin of Crook's burgeoning interest in investing in mining stock, an interest that would unfortunately soon ensnare him.[5] The diary, while describing Crook's trek through the scenic and game-filled mountain country, also provided a rare snapshot of the general in his wilderness habitat.

> Genl. Crook takes his tin cup of coffee, soaks in a hand-full of hardtack, sits down and gets through his meal in silence. He is remarkably abstemious, rarely drinks coffee or tea except on a trip in the Mountains, can scarcely ever be prevailed upon to touch whiskey and then never more than a spoonful. . . . We have no books with us this time, but to him, *The Great Book of Nature* [emphasis in original] always lies open. He knows the rivers and the trend of the mountains, as if by instinct, and can find his way through dark and tangled forests with the certainty of an aborigine.[6]

After completing their reconnaissance, Crook and his aides joined Secretary Schurz's rather large entourage. En route to the park, Crook's own party had also grown. The president's son, Webb Hayes, the general's frequent hunting companion and surrogate son, and Major Thaddeus H. Stanton, a fellow officer and old friend, had joined him.[7]

While he undoubtedly welcomed the opportunity to tour Yellowstone, Crook must have approached his meeting with Schurz warily. The two men had, after all, been on opposite sides in the Ponca controversy, and the general was an outspoken advocate of the transfer of control over Indian affairs from Schurz's Interior Department to the military. Leaving these differences aside, how these opposites, the German-born intellectual and the plainspoken Ohio farmer's son, would get along was an open question. It turned out, however, that—in the woods at least—the two men had much in common. Crook, of course, never recorded his thoughts on the secretary. But Bourke, who often reflected the general's opinions, experienced a remarkable change of heart. Only months before he had dismissed Schurz as a "spindled shanked Mephistopheles," further alluding to him as "an unprincipled German adventurer, unmindful of God or man, caring for nothing but self."[8] Now, on closer inspection, he found him to be "a very genial companion, puts on no airs whatever and exerts himself to make everything run along smoothly." And even more significantly, at least for General Crook, Schurz was "a very good shot and by his skill has done much for our table. He rides well, is very wiry and can stand almost any amount of fatigue." As icing on the cake, the secretary enjoyed a good story around the campfire.[9] And so, by all accounts, the two men got along famously.

In this atmosphere of harmony, the group journeyed through the park, attended by Tom Moore, Crook's peerless packer, and guided by Mr. Philatus Norris, the park's superintendent.[10] Accompanied by an assortment of troops and cooks to see to their every need, they rode through the magnificent mountain valleys, admiring the scenery, gawking at the geysers, and observing the wildlife, much like any tourist in our own time. But, unlike park visitors today, they carried guns and made liberal use of them to kill as much game as time and opportunity allowed.

The pleasure of their jaunt was only slightly marred by hordes of mosquitos that infested the well-watered region and an encounter with a bear that apparently chased Webb Hayes and General Crook some distance into camp, fortunately damaging only their egos. Of Indians, there was no sign. Interestingly, Crook, the vaunted expert on all things Indian, reported erroneously to his superiors that the tribes rarely penetrated the interior of the park because of the severe winter climate and "perhaps . . . the superstitious dread of the geysers and other phenomena."[11] He was likely repeating a bit of misinformation supplied by Norris, who had previously incorporated it in his annual report to the secretary of the interior in 1878.

In fact, there were other reasons for the absence of Indians. Several tribes, including the Blackfeet, Shoshones, and Crows, had histori- cally frequented the park to hunt. Though respectful of the geysers as inhabited by spirits, Indians often bathed in the hot springs, prizing their medicinal qualities. One tribe, the Sheepeaters, actually made its home in Yellowstone's high mountain valleys for much of the nine- teenth century. They had risen against the whites in 1879 in sympathy with the Bannocks and had consequently been removed by the army to one or the other of the Shoshone reservations. The other tribes who formerly hunted in the region were then summarily notified that they were no longer welcome to wander freely within the confines of the new park. Thus, at the time of Schurz's visit, only a scattering of desti- tute Sheepeaters remained within Yellowstone's boundaries.[12]

The group continued to tour, viewing the park's many attractions and shooting its game until August 18, when the secretary and his peo- ple left Yellowstone and headed north to visit the Crow agency. Crook and his contingent spent several more days hunting before hurrying back to Omaha to greet President Hayes as he passed through the city on a visit to the West.[13]

As the year 1880 passed into history, Crook found himself once again involved with the Poncas. Following the tribe's temporary resettlement on the island in the middle of the Niobrara River, the future of Stand- ing Bear's people remained uncertain. Neither the Interior Depart- ment nor Congress had made an effort to find a permanent home for them. In his annual report for 1879, Schurz had acknowledged the obvious: that the removal of the Poncas to Indian Territory had "griev- ously wronged" them. However, he and his subordinates in the Indian Bureau soon concluded that the portion of the tribe that had remained in Oklahoma had adjusted to life in the south and "would soon be more prosperous than [they had] ever been before." Having reached that conclusion, the department seemed in no hurry to propose any measures to Congress to alleviate the plight of those who had gone north with Standing Bear.[14] In May 1880 a Senate committee investigating the removal pompously agreed that "a great wrong has been done to the Ponca Indians." But like the Interior Department, Congress preferred to take no action other than recommending generous remuneration for the Poncas for which no funds were appropriated.[15]

On December 18, 1880, almost exactly a year and a half after Dundy had rendered his decision, President Hayes finally bestirred himself, appointing a commission to once again "ascertain the facts in regard to [the Poncas'] removal and present condition." Of more practical importance, he mandated that it "determine the question as to what justice and humanity require should be done by the Government of the United States" and report to him their conclusions and recommendations.[16] Such a commission, coming on the heels of the Senate's vacuous report, might uncharitably be viewed as kicking the can down the road. But more consistent with his character, it may well have been that Hayes intended to clear the impasse created by Congress and the Interior Department and finally do something to help the Poncas.[17]

Hayes had good reason to do so. He was a lame duck president, having declared at the time of his election in 1876 that he did not intend to run for a second term. James A. Garfield, who had won election in 1880, would be succeeding him in March 1881. Under such circumstances, the mind of a president frequently turns to his legacy. Other than expressing his sympathies for their condition, Hayes had done little for the Poncas. Now he had the opportunity to leave a positive historical record without incurring political harm. In fact, by extending a helping hand to the tribe, he would be able to ride a growing groundswell of public opinion that, as a result of Tibbles's campaign, was sympathetic to the Ponca cause.

He was perhaps encouraged by members of Congress, especially from his own party, who demanded that he take some action on behalf of the tribe. Leading this movement was Republican Senator George Frisbie Hoar of Massachusetts, a well-known crusader against government corruption and a notable champion of Indian rights. As a member of the Congressional Election Commission in 1876, Hoar had played a key role in settling the disputed Tilden-Hayes election that resulted in Hayes winning the presidency. Aside from having great respect for the senator, Hayes undoubtedly considered himself in Hoar's debt.[18]

A new urgency was lent to resolving the issue after Secretary Schurz received a letter in October from a coalition of chiefs purporting to represent the 521 Poncas who had remained in Oklahoma. The chiefs claimed that they and their people had adjusted to life in Oklahoma and accordingly wished to remain in Indian Territory. They offered to relinquish their claim to their ancestral lands on the Niobrara if Congress provided them with $140,000 in full compensation for all losses suffered by the tribe as the result of their removal.[19]

Though the proposed settlement would wipe out all other claims, including any made the northern Poncas, the Oklahoma chiefs tendered their offer without consulting Standing Bear or his people, who were known to be adamantly opposed to renouncing their rights to the Niobrara land. Indian rights reformers believed that Secretary Schurz had engineered the chiefs' letter to undermine Standing Bear's claims. An investigation seemed required to determine whether the Oklahoma chiefs had acted in their own interests or were being coerced. If the offer was genuine, the government would have to decide how to resolve the competing claims of the two Ponca groups. A commission seemed the perfect body to make these determinations and propose a settlement acceptable to both groups.

Hayes moved quickly to fill the commission's ranks and directed it to complete its work before his term ended and Congress adjourned.[20] Crook was summoned to the White House to meet with General Sherman and the president on December 12.[21] After the meeting he lunched privately with Hayes. The two old friends then strolled over to view the as yet uncompleted Washington Monument. During the walk Hayes described his expectations for the commission and asked Crook to chair it. The subject may have again come up that evening at a state dinner held to honor former president Grant.[22]

Things proceeded rapidly from that point. On December 16 Hayes wrote to Senator Hoar regarding his plan to appoint members to a Ponca commission and suggested that one of those would be General Crook. He expected the others, two or three in number, to be selected by Indian rights advocates from among private-sector members of their community.[23] The next day Crook met with Hoar and other interested senators—including Henry L. Dawes, another prominent Indian rights activist—to confer on the commission's composition.[24] On December 18 Hayes announced the formation of the commission and formally named Crook to chair it. The general and Colonel Nelson Miles would represent the government, while William Stickney of Washington, D.C., and Walter Allen of Massachusetts represented the private sector.

Crook cannot have welcomed the idea of Nelson Miles's appointment. Nor would Miles have been pleased to serve under Crook. However, the colonel was regarded as experienced in Indian affairs. Furthermore, as General Sherman's nephew by marriage, it may have been thought that his participation would earn the general's favor, critical in gaining support for the commission's recommendations. Any concerns Hayes might have had about Miles's rocky relationship with Crook may have been assuaged by knowing that Miles certainly knew of the president's friendship with Crook and, as a very political and ambitious officer, would accordingly behave in a collegial manner.[25] It is also possible that Hayes hoped that Crook's serving on the commission with Miles might help the officers resolve their longstanding differences.[26]

If that, indeed, was his purpose, the effort apparently came to naught. Bourke, undoubtedly mirroring Crook's own bias, described Miles as "brave, energetic, and ambitious, selfish, conceited, and inordinately vain." As to Miles's work on the commission, the lieutenant dismissed it, allowing that he had "done hard work against the Indians on the North West border . . . and has done it well, but his contributions on the Ponca matter were not up to the same standard. As a member of the Commission, he has been anxious to thrust himself forward as the most experienced of the list, but I err greatly if he has not been the least of value of any."[27]

On the private-sector side, Stickney was a member of the Board of Indian Commissioners, established in the 1870s by President Grant to oversee Indian affairs. Bourke dismissed him as "a well-meaning, psalm-singing Christian—of that class whose religion has given them the heart-burn." He was a bit more generous in his description of the fourth member, Mr. Allen, a reporter for the *Boston Advertiser*. He found him to be "a gentleman of great mental cultivation, a little bit too inclined to the humanitarian side of the Indian question," too prone to find dishonesty in Secretary Schurz's "every act," yet for all that, "an intelligent, clear-headed, hardworking and valuable member of the Commission."[28]

The Indian rights movement seemed to share Bourke's lack of enthusiasm for the appointments, with the notable exception of General Crook. Helen Hunt Jackson, an ardent and outspoken activist, wrote Senator Dawes, "For God's sake, . . . don't let that committee go as it stands. . . . Not a man in it can be absolutely trusted not to be either hoodwinked or influenced [by Schurz] except Gen. Crook."[29] It would transpire that her pessimistic assessment proved unwarranted.

The job of recording the commission's proceedings fell to Crook's aides, Bourke and Roberts. They diligently recorded lengthy verbatim accounts of the testimony, some of which appeared in the commission report. Much more of it, together with Bourke's insightful asides and descriptions of the conditions under which the commission worked, found its way into the pages of Bourke's diary.[30]

To determine the truth of allegations that Secretary Schurz had coerced the Oklahoma Poncas into relinquishing their claim to their northern homeland, the commission summoned their chiefs to Washington on Christmas Eve for interrogation. Meeting in the offices of the Indian Bureau, located in the ornate halls of the Patent Office, the Poncas recounted the conditions under which they had been removed to Oklahoma, until Crook pointedly interrupted to ask their spokesman, White Eagle, why they had decided to remain in Oklahoma. To that point, he asked whether "any threats or promises [had been] made to induce them to change their minds."[31] Though White Eagle assured the commissioners that the decision had been entirely voluntary, Crook, still skeptical, continued to probe, inquiring whether White Eagle spoke for all of his people. The chief answered in the affirmative. With this troubling issue temporarily addressed, Crook adjourned the proceedings, announcing that they would resume in Indian Territory following the holidays.

On January 5 the commission reconvened at the Ponca Agency.[32] Representatives of the Interior Department were excluded from the proceedings to allow the Indians to speak freely.[33] Crook and Allen, not yet entirely satisfied by the chiefs' Washington testimony, posed a series of questions to clarify why the Oklahoma Poncas wished to remain in Indian Territory after all they had suffered. White Eagle, again speaking for his people, insisted that they wanted to remain where they were and cultivate the land "so as not to be moving about."[34] Moments later, Allen inquired whether they would prefer to return to the north if the

Great Father wished it. White Eagle's depressing response indicated the tribe, now thoroughly disillusioned, had come to believe that the government never intended to provide a permanent home for the Poncas in the north. "If the Great Father should want to make that for me, I should think he'd have me wandering around and for that reason, I should be unwilling to go and should want to remain here."[35] The cynicism implicit in this remark could hardly have escaped the commissioners' notice.

Under further questioning White Eagle added that unless Standing Bear's faction rejoined the tribe in Oklahoma, he believed they should not have any part in the cash settlement requested by the Oklahoma Poncas. To Crook's query whether White Eagle thought that he and the other chiefs could convince Standing Bear to return to Oklahoma, the chief replied that he thought he could. But when asked whether he would go north to talk personally with Standing Bear, he begged off, pleading fatigue and proposing that the tribe write a letter instead. Crook, unhappy with that response, urged that one of the chiefs go north to negotiate with the Standing Bear faction.[36] Reluctantly, they agreed.

Following these discussions, the commission, accompanied by several representatives of the southern branch of the tribe, journeyed north to Dakota, where, in temperatures that hovered around twenty-eight degrees below zero, Standing Bear awaited them.[37] The two Ponca factions seemed genuinely happy to see one another, but the warmth between them chilled perceptibly when Crook, speaking for the commission, explained the reasons for the visit and had the southerners' letter to Secretary Schurz read aloud.[38]

An aroused Standing Bear rose to address the issue. He blamed Schurz, whom he contemptuously called "the Dutchman with the eyeglasses," for misleading the Oklahoma faction in order to convince them sell the Poncas' homeland. It belonged to the tribe. Spotted Tail, the Brulé chief, had confirmed this when his people had been mistakenly granted the land by the government. He had told his fellow Brulés that they "must not retain this land, but must give it back to the Poncas who wanted to live upon it." Now, Standing Bear declared, "Tho' he [the Great Father] were to give me a million dollars I would not give him the land. I wish to take back my people from Indian Territory. I wish them to live."[39] To calm the chief the commissioners explained

that no decision had yet been made; only at the end of their deliberations would they make a recommendation about the disposition of the
land. Under the circumstances it would be best if the Poncas could
decide among themselves what they wanted to do. After three days
of hearings, it was evident that there was little room for compromise.
Each group was equally adamant in its desire to remain in place. On
this note, the commission adjourned.

The four-day return journey to Washington was plagued by cold
and snow, and the delegation was thoroughly exhausted by the time
they that arrived in the capital on January 18.[40] While the commissioners recuperated, Bourke and Roberts labored to produce a fifty-
page report containing the commission's recommendations, which
they managed to place on President Hayes' desk on January 26.[41] The
commissioners' near unanimity regarding both the findings and recommendations allowed three of the four members to sign the report
without reservations. Mr. Allen, the lone holdout, submitted his own
report. Though he agreed with the majority's conclusions, he felt that
it lacked a detailed account of the supporting facts, which he supplied
in his own addendum.[42]

Like all before them who had examined the issue, the commissioners
found that the original removal of the Poncas to Oklahoma had been
"injudicious and without sufficient cause"; consequently, the tribe had a
rightful claim to recompense. They also concluded that the Oklahoma
faction's offer to renounce their claim to their northern lands was made
in good faith and without coercion. They had simply "finally despaired
of regaining their rights [to their homeland], under the belief that the
government would not regard their title to the land in Dakota as valid,
and they could obtain stronger title to the land in Indian Territory, as
well as other prominent considerations." As to the Indians who had
come north, the members opined that they "have the strongest possible
attachment to their lands and a resolute purpose to retain them."[43]

The commission's commitment to allowing the Poncas to determine their own futures and a recognition of the need to accommodate
the disparate desires of the two factions gave their proposed solution
the strong imprint of Judge Dundy's decision and General Crook's own
philosophy of Indian management. Rather than provide reservations
to either or both factions, the commissioners recommended that the
land be allotted in severalty, allowing tribal members the opportu-

nity to determine their own destiny. They would have six months to make the decision whether their holdings, one hundred and sixty acres allotted to each man, woman, and child in the tribe, would be on the current reservation in Indian Territory or upon the original Ponca reservation in Dakota. In addition to land, the tribe would receive the amount of $53,000 per year in damages for a period of five years to be distributed to the people on a *pro rata* basis. They would also immediately receive $25,000 for the purchase of agricultural implements, stock, and seed, of which $5,000 would be exclusively for the benefit of Standing Bear's people and the remainder divided among the entire tribe. A further $10,000 was recommended for the construction of dwellings and schoolhouses at both locations. This settlement would extinguish all future claims by the Poncas. Finally, the commissioners endorsed Judge Dundy's determination that Indians should be allowed recourse to the courts for vindication of their personal and property rights. How otherwise, the commissioners asked, could Indians be expected to understand their duties in civilized society unless "relieved from the uncertainties and oppression frequently attending subjection to arbitrary and personal authority"?

Hayes was pleased. Regarding the report as "practical, judicious, wise, and based upon common sense," he committed himself to see that its recommendations were implemented. Then, in the words of Lieutenant Bourke, "the Ponca Commission withdrew & dissolved."[44]

Unhappily, the commission's work failed to resolve the matter. In the latter part of December, as the commission commenced its work, a senate select committee chaired by Senator Dawes had also held hearings on the Ponca issue. On January 29, three days after the commission's report had been delivered to the president, Dawes reconvened his committee and summoned the commissioners to appear before it. Crook did not appear, but the two civilian members and Colonel Miles were closely questioned regarding their recommendations and, once again, on whether the Oklahoma Poncas had been coerced by the interior secretary into giving up their claim to their northern homeland. The senators seemed more interested in discrediting Schurz than in eliciting the truth. Despite the commission's finding that the chiefs had acted voluntarily, the senators seized upon the Poncas' having lost hope of ever regaining title to their Dakota homeland to cast dispersions on the secretary.[45]

Press coverage of the commission's recommendations and the congressional hearings generated renewed public insistence on a rapid and fair resolution of the Poncas' plight.[46] Dawes responded by introducing a bill on the floor of the Senate that was intended to implement the report's proposals. The Interior Department prepared its own bill, in some ways intended to subvert the Dawes bill, and submitted it to the Committee on Indian Affairs rather than Dawes's select committee. Both bills languished in Congress during the waning days of the Hayes administration.

In the end the controversy was resolved in a very modern way—by amendment to appropriations legislation passed in early March, days before Garfield took his oath of office.[47] That amendment appropriated $165,000 for the use of individuals of the tribe "to secure to them lands in severalty on either the old or new reservations."[48] Dawes and the commissioners had sought to give every Ponca six months during which to freely elect whether to remain in place or select lands in the territory occupied by the other faction. Congress removed this option, electing to freeze everyone in place, Standing Bear's people in the north and the Oklahoma faction in Indian Territory. Thus, the Poncas were denied even this small voice in choosing their own destiny. Adding insult to injury, only months later did the northern faction received the cash promised to alleviate their impoverished condition. They would not receive their allotted acreage until 1890, and only then incidental to the division of the Great Sioux Reservation under the Dawes Act of 1889. Eventually, through their own industry, both northern and southern factions adapted to and thrived on the allotments provided to them, but their road, like that of most Native Americans, would not be an easy one.[49]

The Ponca affair and its aftermath were pivotal in confirming Crook's public stance on Indian rights. Heretofore, he had confined his fight against injustice to the tribes to military channels, though he became increasingly outspoken in his dealings with the press. Now, through his growing friendship with Thomas Tibbles and his involvement with the Poncas, he had earned a reputation in Indian reform community and established the basis of an alliance that would shape his remaining years.

CHAPTER FIVE

Crook House

When Crook first assumed his position as commander of the Department of the Platte in April 1875, like his predecessors he had located his headquarters and residence in the city of Omaha rather than at the closest military installation, Omaha Barracks. The latter had been constructed in 1868 on orders from General Sherman after Omaha was chosen as departmental headquarters because it was served by two major railroads. The general intended to use the railroads as a means to move troops around on the frontier. With ready access to both the Union Pacific and Northern Pacific and to the newly built telegraph system, the city, already a significant rail depot, was an ideal site to furnish administrative and logistical support to forts springing up to its west and to provide troops to protect crews constructing the rail lines. Originally named Sherman Barracks, it was rechristened Omaha Barracks after Sherman allegedly complained about attaching his name to a post so insignificant as to be classified a "barracks" rather than a camp or fort. (The "barracks" designation was used to describe a post with cheap, temporary housing that did not require special legislative funding.)[1]

And that was exactly how Crook found the post when he arrived in the spring of 1875. The garrison was housed in "one-story frame buildings lined with brick, plain batten finish and painted a dull yellow." The structures were heated by wood-burning stoves and lit by coal oil lamps, and all plumbing was outdoors. The camp's sewage drained into a small stream that flowed into the Missouri, a mile away.[2] These shabby barracks framed a rectangular parade ground situated on eighty-two acres of open, treeless prairie, half of which had been purchased by the government and the other half donated by prominent citizens of Omaha after Sherman determined that the original forty-acre acquisition was inadequate.[3] The rudimentary layout of the post was hardly suitable to house the headquarters for the Department of the Platte or its commander, and at the time of Crook's arrival, it never had.

By contrast, the city of Omaha had many appropriate facilities that made the decision to lease property in town to house the department's commander and his staff a natural one. Staff officers assigned to the department had always regarded the choice as highly felicitous. Town life offered many more benefits than the more countrified and run-down military installation. Omaha had restaurants, a theater, and other amenities not readily available elsewhere on the frontier. According to John Bourke, who reflected the elitist attitudes of the officer class, it hosted among its "better classes of inhabitants" persons "noted for their intelligence, refinement and hospitality."[4] Moreover, while Omaha Barracks was located three miles north of the city and its rail depot, offices in the city were no more than a short walk from the Union Pacific station, a great convenience to military officers who traveled often and frequently hosted arriving visitors on army business.

However much the officers stationed in Omaha appreciated the arrangement, paying rent for civilian quarters when free accommodations were available at a nearby military post did not sit well with the cost-cutting Congress. In the spring of 1878 it enacted legislation requiring all military departmental headquarters, with few exceptions, to be relocated onto military reservations.[5] Consequently, while Crook was preoccupied with the trial of Standing Bear, his staff was unhappily packing and moving from their comfortable offices on Fifteenth Street in downtown Omaha to a temporary wooden building on the Omaha Barracks parade ground prepared for their use. They would remain there until the post's soldiers finished constructing the brick buildings that would become permanent departmental headquarters. Crook had originally resided in rental housing in downtown Omaha, first at Nineteenth and Davenport and then at Fifteenth and Harney. Now, he too moved temporarily into a wood structure on the post, while the troops worked on a permanent brick building that was to be his official residence.[6]

Crook House, Omaha, as it appears today. Author's photo.

Work on his new home, begun the summer before, was just being completed in the spring of 1879, around the time Standing Bear's case was argued in court. The house was built from plans drawn by George W. Field, a Civil War veteran and experienced civil engineer hired by the Military Department of the Platte to work on the design and construction of many of the buildings on the new headquarters site.[7] It was of solid brick construction with thick interior and exterior walls, built to withstand the climatic extremes that prevail on the Great Plains.[8]

A two-story, five-thousand-square-foot structure of Italianate design popular in America during the period, the building was intended to be both stylish and spacious enough for a general officer's family. Modified somewhat to reduce its ornateness, perhaps in deference to General Crook's taste and character, it had hipped roofs and two open porches supported by Doric columns and adorned with a cornice of galvanized iron.[9] The house was situated on a knoll, commanding a fine view of the grounds of the post and beyond that, in the distance, the Missouri River.

Despite many other issues that vied for his attention, Crook appeared to have taken an active interest in the construction of the residence, primarily, it seems, in an effort to reduce its cost. The use of soldiers to carry out construction projects on military posts was common in Crook's day, hailed by Congress as a cost-saving measure and a way to keep the troops busy in an era when training seems to have been regarded as largely irrelevant. Thus, soldiers participated in building the home and, according to one source, so did the Poncas, while they were confined to the fort pending the outcome of their case.[10]

Frugality in construction seems to have been a matter of pride to Crook. Though $10,000 was appropriated for the job, he seemed determined to do it for less. One strategy he employed was to use alternative (cheaper) materials for the more decorative aspects of the house. The flooring on the first story was of alternating walnut and oak boards, but on the second floor savings were incurred by substituting pine painted to look like mahogany or grained to resemble oak for the woodwork. Further economies were realized when, at Crook's insistence, plaster of paris painted to give the appearance of walnut was substituted for wood in the crown moldings and arches on the ground floor. Oak-grained plaster of paris was used for these features in the second-floor rooms, while imitation maple sufficed for the servants' quarters. At the general's insistence, further savings were achieved by eliminating the closets in the original plan, except for those in his own bedroom and in a large room that would become the Presidential Bedroom. A marker placed in front of the home by the Nebraska State Historical Society and the Douglas County Historical Society—the latter cares for the residence today—documents the success of his efforts. It boasts that the cost of construction was reduced by employment of troop labor and the clever use of substitute materials to an enviable $7,716.[11]

The house was heated by a coal furnace in the basement, which supplied hot air to the rooms above through vents and registers in the floor. Additional heat, if required, was provided by coal-burning fireplaces built into nearly every room, perhaps in an effort to keep Mrs. Crook, a Maryland native, from fleeing east each year to escape Nebraska's notably severe winters. The building was also piped for gas lighting, a very modern innovation in 1879. Running water, another modern convenience, flowed by gravity from a cistern on a hill behind the house, supplying the kitchen and the home's only bathroom, located above the kitchen in the servants' sleeping area. The decision to place the bathroom in the servant's quarters was not a democratic gesture but a practical choice, it being the best-situated location for the pipes to take advantage of the slope used to direct water into the house.

The downstairs, perhaps dark and gloomy by today's standards, in Crook's time represented the height of late Victorian fashion. From photos taken in the 1890s, we know that in accordance with the style of the day, the walls and ceilings of most of the rooms on the first floor were wallpapered. But to further reduce cost, Crook chose relatively inexpensive, local, machine-made wallpaper. To the modern eye the deep, rich colors and busy patterns seem lavishly ornate, but they were plain by Victorian standards, chosen not, as one might suspect, to accord with Crook's simple tastes but rather to accommodate to the differing preferences of the frequently changing occupants assigned to the post.[12]

When it came to outfitting the knobs and hinges of the doors throughout the house, Crook spared no expense. All are of solid brass, and the knobs on the front doors are embossed with the U.S. Treasury seal. Entering the house through these doors required a steep climb up stairs from the street level, but an alternate access was provided via a carriage mount on the north-facing side of the building, which allowed visitors to dismount from carriages and enter the house directly. Passing into its interior through the front door, visitors find themselves in a main hall that opens into a reception room, dining room, and parlor where Crook entertained visitors. By all accounts, these were important and often-used rooms as, during this period, Fort Omaha provided the venue for many of the city's social activities.[13] Also on the first floor is a modest study where the general could retire to work on his collections of birds' nests, eggs, and butterflies. The kitchen and pantry are located in the rear of the house.

The second floor is reached by a stairway off the main hall. No substitutes here, as the stairs leading to the second floor were meant to impress. Walnut was used for the risers and bannisters, while the treads were oak. Facing east toward the front of the house, on the right of an upstairs hallway, is the master bedroom suite. Mary had her own sleeping chamber at the front of the house, where it was warmer in the winter and cooler in the summer. Next to it was the "morning room," a place to dress and perform the management duties for the general's household. George's bedchamber, slightly smaller than Mary's, adjoined her room and connected to it by a door. Its simpler décor and modest size again appropriately mirror Crook's self-deprecating personality and dislike of ostentation. Separate sleeping areas allowed the general's aides to have access to him during the night should circumstances warrant, while maintaining Mary's privacy.

Across the hall from the master bedroom suite are two additional bedrooms, one for ordinary guests and a second, designated the Presidential Bedroom, for more important visitors. President Grant would sleep in this room while visiting Omaha during Crook's tenure. A room for servants, a bath, and a storage room make up the remainder of the floor. Several steps descended to this section of the house, symbolic of the lower level of society servants occupied in the Victorian era relative to their employers.[14]

Completed in September 1879, the new home was among the first buildings in Omaha to receive a telephone. Frank Burkley, telephone and telegraph operator for the headquarters staff at that time, recalled that the phone "was the object of considerable interest not only on the part of the Fort Omaha residents, but also by the people of Omaha, many of whom were curious to talk over a wire five miles long and to get me to play the mouth organ so that they and their friends could hear music by wire this great distance away." Aside from calling attention to the great novelty represented by the telephone in that era, Burkley's recollections reflect the close relationship that existed between Omaha's citizenry and the nearby military post.[15]

Though Crook's house was ready for occupancy when former president Grant and his wife arrived for a three-day visit in November, the family had not yet received the shipment of furniture ordered for their new home. Rising to the occasion, the citizens of Omaha and officers on the post loaned furnishings from their homes to the family so that the couple could be properly entertained. During the Grants' stay, Mary Crook hosted a large, informal reception for them in the first-floor parlor, which proved large enough to accommodate not only the numerous guests but also the Ninth Infantry orchestra that entertained them.[16] By all accounts, it was Mary who worked out the arrangements for this and other entertainments held at the home, as the general had little interest in such affairs and was in fact said to dislike them. He may not have been overly upset when, by happenstance or prior arrangement, he was called away to Chicago on the day of the Grant reception, missing the event entirely.[17]

It has been written that President Hayes also stayed at the Crook House. However, there is little evidence that that was the case. A review of contemporary sources reveals that though Hayes visited Omaha on at least two occasions, one was well before the house was built. A second visit does not appear to have involved a sleepover. The Nebraska historical marker in front of the home describes a more limited connection: "From here, President Rutherford Hayes reviewed the Fort's troops on September 3, 1880." In the fall of that year, Hayes had embarked on a seventy-one-day tour of the West. Accompanied by his family, General Sherman, and various other notables, he began his trip by attending a reunion of Civil War veterans in Canton, Ohio. There, Crook, who had been his commanding officer during the war, joined him and addressed his former troops.[18] A special train then took the president and his party westward, making a stop in Omaha en route to Ogden, Utah.

The train pulled into the city's Tenth Street Depot at 8:30 a.m. on September 3. The president's party descended to the platform in a downpour, clambered aboard a series of carriages and army ambulances, and, huddled beneath umbrellas, hurried off to Fort Omaha. While the local paper described the president's arrival at the post as "a scene of beauty and gayety that was pleasant to look upon," it was probably considerably drearier. The troops stood wetly at attention in front of the Crook residence, while the post's artillery fired a twenty-one-gun salute and a sodden military band played tunes for the president. At 10:30 a.m. the band completed its renditions, and Hayes and his party set off for a rainy tour of Omaha.[19]

Some years before the president, a temperance man, had purchased land in Omaha, and a scandal had developed after it was learned that a saloon had been constructed on the site. One of the places he asked to see during his tour of the town was the building that had caused all the trouble. As they drove by it, the president turned to his famously abstemious spouse, known popularly as Lemonade Lucy, and said, "Lucy, there's your saloon."[20] Following his tour of the town, Hayes and his family continued on to the depot and boarded the presidential train that departed at one p.m. for Ogden.

It is probable that General Crook was not in Omaha on this august occasion. While he was present at the Canton, Ohio, reunion, there is no mention of him aboard the train for Omaha or of his presence at the Fort Omaha festivities.[21] As one of the most prominent citizens of the city, if he had been in Omaha, his presence certainly would have been noted. It is more likely that, having traveled east as far as Ohio to attend the reunion, he then continued on to visit family in nearby Dayton or perhaps traveled to his wife's home in western Maryland. In either case, he missed the opportunity of formally hosting his friend, the president, at his new residence, a circumstance that he probably did not find too troubling.

Having a comfortable and relatively permanent residence must have been a joy for Mary. She had endured the nomadic existence of an army officer's wife for many years and would have been delighted to finally have a home to care for. But sadly for her, at least, the couple's residence at Crook House was short-lived. They only occupied the house for a year before the general was reassigned to Arizona.

Despite the army's decision to build him a lavish residence, Crook, like his officers, had not been happy with idea of relocating to Fort Omaha. In March 1880, only a few months after moving into his new quarters, he wrote to General Sherman, pointing out the fort's short-comings. Not only did the military have an uncertain leasehold interest in over half the acreage that encompassed the post, in Crook's opinion the location was impractical, unhealthy, and uneconomical. The land itself was "barely sufficient to contain the necessary improvements." Further, "Even the higher ground where the officers' quarters are situated is now rapidly becoming poisoned by drainage from privies and stables." These situations, he predicted, would soon force the government to purchase additional land if it expected to maintain the post permanently. Finally, the site was too far from the railroad depot in Omaha, involving "too great an expense for the transportation of supplies." Though he did not come out and say it, he was probably equally disturbed by the lengthy commute he was required to make when he embarked on his frequent travels about the West. For once, Washington listened to his complaints. In 1881 his headquarters were returned to downtown Omaha, and he and Mary once again moved into rented quarters in the downtown area. Upon his return to the Platte in 1887, he would continue to reside in rented quarters in Omaha, for a time on Chicago Avenue and then at the city's Paxton Hotel.[22]

CHAPTER SIX

Cowboys and Indians

Crook was widely renowned throughout his career for his consummate management of Indian affairs. However, in his dealings with civil authorities, fortunately rare, he sometimes demonstrated an inability to grasp underlying political or social implications lurking beneath the more obvious aspects of an issue. In the spring of 1879, as Judge Dundy prepared to hear the Ponca case, the general became entangled in a civilian controversy that demonstrated his shortcomings in that regard.

Following the conclusion of the Sioux War, relative peace with the Indians and the advent of the railroads brought new conflicts to the West. A surge of homesteaders, predominantly small farmers and immigrants fleeing poverty abroad, flooded the rich grasslands that typified the Great Plains. They staked out patches of land, usually at or near water sources, and fenced them to keep out cattle that roamed freely on the prairie, clashing with the ranchers who owned the livestock. The ranchers, many of whom were wealthy entrepreneurs from the East or Europe, had arrived a few years earlier, freely grazing their cattle on the land recently emptied of buffalo and Indians. Convinced that these grasslands were theirs by right of occupancy, they felt threatened by the homesteaders, whose fences prevented access to free water and grass and who occasionally preyed on their herds. Isolated incidents blossomed into bloody range wars between the two groups. Local law enforcement, already overburdened by general lawlessness,

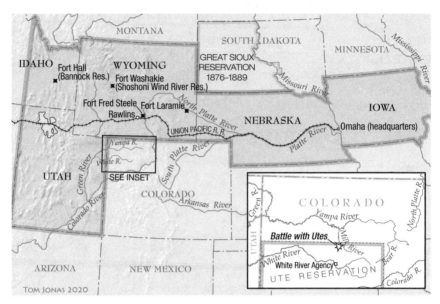

Department of the Platte showing locations and events related to Bannock and Ute conflicts, 1878–79. Map by Tom Jonas.

did not have the resources to handle the situation and looked to the military for assistance.

Since the early days of the republic, the government has recognized the need in certain situations for the army to intervene in matters touching on civilian law enforcement. A series of congressional enactments, relying on the ancient English common-law theory of posse comitatus, permitted such intervention on authority of the president in extreme situations where violence threatened civil order. But Americans have always been hostile to the idea. Following the Civil War, federal troops were employed to maintain peace in the South during Reconstruction and to deal with labor unrest in the East. Such deployments aroused deep antipathy toward the army in the South and in the urban North, spurring a coalition of politicians from these areas to pass legislation to restrict what they regarded as abuses of posse comitatus authority. In 1878 statutory language for that purpose was included in the annual military appropriation bill. Soon known as the Posse Comitatus Act, the law, still in effect today, forbade the use of the army (and now the Air Force) to execute civil laws except where expressly authorized by the Constitution or an act of Congress. Under the Constitution the president has the power to use the military to preserve order, but the act placed under close scrutiny the instances where local or federal officials could request military intervention, making it the exception rather than the rule and requiring express presidential approval in each instance of military intrusion in civilian affairs.[1]

In the spring of 1879, only months after the new law came into effect, Crook became entangled in its complexities after the governor of Nebraska asked him to intervene in the trial of a rancher, Isom Prentice "Print" Olive, who had been arrested for the murder of two homesteaders. A Confederate veteran and former Texas cattleman, Olive was a notorious and polarizing figure in frontier Nebraska, and his trial became emblematic of the conflicts over land that roiled the Great Plains during this period.[2] In 1877 Print and his brother established a ranch in central Nebraska near the town of Plum Creek. The ranch prospered, but rustlers plagued their herd, despite the brothers' warnings that they would shoot anyone found with one of their cows. The Olives suspected homesteaders. In the summer of 1878, true to his word, Print intercepted a sheriff's wagon transporting two farmers accused of rustling and shot and hanged the hapless prisoners. That probably would not have caused much comment, but there was general outrage upon the discovery of the charred remains of the two men by the side of the road.[3]

Print, now referred to by Nebraskans as "Man-burner," and one of his employees were arrested and scheduled for trial. Because popular feelings ran high in Plum Creek, the authorities moved the case to Hastings, a hundred miles away. But when Hastings began to fill up with armed cattlemen, the prosecutor, fearing that they intended to shoot up the town and free Print in the event of his conviction, asked the local sheriff to wire the Nebraskan governor, Albinus Nance, to request military intervention. The sheriff complied with a telegram that conveyed a sense of desperation: "The crucial time has arrived. Do not feel safe with such guards as I can get. Send troops from other points than this city for reason you know. Have them here by special train at noon tomorrow (Friday)." He dramatically concluded his plea, "For God's sake, don't fail."[4]

Rather than call on state militia to handle the matter, Governor Nance deemed it politically advisable to pass on the sheriff's request to the federal government, distancing himself from the decision-making process. He directed his communiqué to General Crook, the commander of the Military Department of the Platte, and, perhaps to enhance its effect, he timed its dispatch to ensure delivery in the early morning hours. Awakened by a cry for help in the dawn hours, Crook took the message seriously. It read: "Sheriff Martin of Adams County, Nebraska has called on the governor of Nebraska for military assistance to aid him in guarding the Olive gang from outlaws who, from official authority received at these headquarters will attempt the rescue of the prisoners in the sheriff's custody. Can you furnish the State with a company of U.S. troops for duty at Hastings, Nebraska? Have them report there this morning by special train that will be furnished at Omaha. Please answer immediately."[5] Note that the governor's message converted the cowboys' suspected intentions into a fact and transformed them into outlaws, while Olive and his ranch hands had become the "Olive gang."

Crook had apparently learned little from a previous unfortunate intervention in civilian affairs during Reconstruction. Then, too, he had been manipulated by local authorities who urged him to use military force to prevent an alleged uprising by freedmen in Wilmington, North Carolina. Without investigating the circumstances further, he had ordered that the freedmen be disarmed. He would later learn to his chagrin that the claims of a black insurrection were entirely spurious and that he had been duped into using his soldiers to render newly freed slaves helpless so that they could be subjugated by the white power structure.[6]

On this occasion, perhaps moved by empathy for the homesteaders and townspeople of Hastings, it seems that Crook reacted viscerally, without properly ascertaining the facts or considering the consequences. Within hours of receiving the governor's request, he dispatched an infantry company from Fort Omaha by rail to the town to save it from what he assumed was an impending attack by a criminal gang of desperate outlaws. Although aware that the new posse comitatus legislation required presidential approval before ordering troops to intervene in a civil matter, so convinced was Crook by the governor's urgent plea that he believed that any delay to obtain the president's approval would be fatal. Confident of his judgment, he undoubtedly also believed that his friend President Hayes would back his play.

Three days later, Crook sent a dispatch to General Sheridan that demonstrated the depth of his concern. "Knowing the desperate character of the Olive gang," he wrote, "and of their friends, the outlaws referred to, and that if not prevented in their designs, there was great danger of their injuring many persons and perhaps of their burning the town, I ordered a company of Infantry to proceed from this post to Hastings." He had ignored the requirement for presidential approval, he informed his bemused superior, because "the desperate character of the individuals referred to, being well known to me, I felt confident they could carry out their determination to rescue Olive at any cost and that they would do so if not prevented before the consent of the President could be obtained." In any event, he informed Sheridan, he had "telegraphed the Governor of the State that he [the governor] must obtain by telegraph from the President of the U.S. the requisite authority as required by the Constitution and laws for the use of the troops in the suppression of domestic violence." Unfortunately, as the embarrassed general later admitted, "as the President has declined to grant the permission, the troops have been ordered to return to their station."[7]

Did Crook overreact? The president obviously thought so, as did General Sheridan and Secretary of War McCrary. The latter, responding in Hayes's behalf, cautioned Crook that the law forbade the use of troops before a demonstrated need existed. Regulars could be dispatched under defined circumstances, but only "*after* a regular call for aid from the President" (author's italics).[8] Sheridan was even more emphatic. He agreed, he said, with President Hayes that the evidence presented by the governor had *not* warranted intervention. In fact, he lectured, Crook's hasty intervention had precluded a calm assessment of the true nature of the situation.

John Thurston, the judge who acted as special prosecutor in the Olive trial, expressed a quite different view. He maintained that the troops, regulars under the command of Captain Andrew S. Burt, one of Crook's most trusted officers, had saved the day. As Thurston dramatically described the situation, at about 11:15 on the morning of the troops' arrival, he had been arguing the case, stalling for time with an ear cocked for their appearance. Suddenly, he had heard the thin notes of a bugle sounding through the open courtroom window.

Jurors, lawyers, and observers alike rushed into the street to watch as a company (Thurston thought two companies) of infantry, armed with carbines and a Gatling gun, deployed diagonally across from the courthouse, where they remained for the duration of the trial. "I never saw so surprised and so quiet a crowd of men in all my life as those cowboys were. They would cheerfully have attacked five hundred untrained militiamen, but ninety-two regular soldiers with a Gatling gun and the flag, and Little Andy Burt in command, put the fear of God in them in two seconds. Trouble was all over. We went back into court and the trial was resumed."[9] Olive was convicted of murder and sentenced to prison for life. Who knows but that the presence of troops may have stiffened the jury's backbone and allowed it to make that determination.[10]

Crook suffered no further censure for his handling of the Print Olive affair, but his reprimand was said to have had a chilling effect thereafter on the willingness of commanding officers throughout the army to authorize military intervention in cases involving civil law-enforcement issues. Historians Clayton Laurie and Ronald Cole, authors of an extensive treatise on the role of military forces in controlling domestic disorder, attribute the prolonged lawlessness that continued to infect Arizona and Utah well into the 1880s to this phenomenon.[11]

During the summer and early fall of 1879, as the furor over the Olive affair faded from the news, the papers in nearby Colorado were filled with tales of unrest among the Utes, the predominant tribe in the region. Lurid accounts spoke of homesteaders' cabins and acres of forests burned by "the unruly savages," depredations against peaceful miners and farmers, and Indians wandering the countryside wantonly slaughtering game and threatening settlers. The stories had little to do with reality, yet headlines in the Colorado papers blared "The Utes Must Go," and local politicians quickly took up the cry.[12] Though the new state of Colorado lay beyond General Crook's immediate jurisdiction (it was in the adjacent Military Department of Missouri, commanded by Brigadier General John Pope), he would soon find himself involved, with tragic consequences.

The anti-Ute sentiment that pervaded the white population of Colorado had its origins in the tribe's traditional control, confirmed by treaty, of over twelve million acres, about a third of the state, encompassing some of the region's richest farmland and mineral wealth.[13] For hundreds—perhaps thousands—of years the Utes ranged over the land they called the Shining Mountains, a mountainous region extending west from the front range of the Rockies across the Continental Divide, and some 450 miles south into Utah. Divided into seven bands, three in the south and four in the north, they prospered in their mountain fastness, pursuing a nomadic lifestyle and hunting in some of the most game-rich country in North America.

During the first half of the nineteenth century, the inaccessibility of their rugged territory spared them from the ruination caused by immigration routes and railway lines elsewhere in the West, and the tribe had maintained friendly relations with whites entering the region.[14] In America's wars against the Utes' traditional enemies—the Sioux, the Arapahos, the Cheyennes, and Apaches—the tribe's warriors served the army as fighters and scouts. One, Nicaagat (Ute John), an influential chief with the White River Utes, had accompanied Crook in the recent Sioux War.[15] According to Bourke the chief had attached himself to the general, and his irreverence for Crook's august rank provided the troops with "a considerable share of amusement."[16] Ute cooperation with the whites and the negotiating skills of their chief, Ouray, won them the right to remain on a major portion of their land after other tribes had been exiled to remote and barren locations.[17]

The discovery of gold and silver in the Front Range in the 1860s and subsequent statehood in 1876 brought a tide of immigration into Colorado and an increased demand for land. Hegemony over almost twelve million acres of valuable land by a tribe that numbered between only four and six thousand members was anathema to white Coloradans, and they vied with each other for excuses to remove the Utes from the state. The new governor, Fredrick Pitkin, who had a substantial interest in local mining, led the charge. "The presence of Indians in the State still constitutes an obstacle to the advancement of Colorado," he declared. "Even those who do not fear the Utes, dislike them and would be glad to see them banished to some more appropriate retreat than the garden of our ever-growing state."[18] The Interior Department supported Pitkin's efforts. In his report for the year 1877, Indian Commissioner Hayt recommended that all of the Indians in Colorado (together with those in Arizona) be removed to Indian Territory. Making no effort to disguise his motives, he wrote, "There is no hope of civilizing these Indians while they reside in Colorado, as all the arable land in the State is required for its white settlers."[19] But bills submitted in 1878 to Congress to achieve this purpose had, at least for the time being, failed to pass after intense lobbying by the Indian reform movement.[20]

If the Utes could not be removed, Colorado's whites demanded that at least they ought to be confined to their reservation. The Bureau of Indian Affairs obliged, establishing several agencies on Indian land to control their nomadic habits and making them liable to arrest if found outside the reservation without permission.[21] Restricting the Utes' ability to hunt would make them wholly dependent on government rations. Then, it was thought, they would be forced to abandon their nomadic habits and become "civilized" farmers.

The Utes at White River agency proved especially resistant to this plan. The agency was located in the remote, inaccessible northwest of the reservation where an abundance of game might allow the tribe to indefinitely postpone "the time when they should be compelled to adopt civilized habits and means of subsistence."[22] In 1878, to counteract such an eventuality, the Indian Bureau appointed Nathan Meeker, a religious zealot with a messianic belief in the benefits of agriculture, as agent to the tribe.[23]

Meeker, a remarkably insensitive individual, assumed that the tribe would welcome his efforts. But, like most Western tribes, the Utes remained deeply committed to their nomadic culture and disdained agriculture. Recently forced to cede nearly four million acres to the government after gold was discovered, they had also become increasingly resentful of white America's obvious hunger for their lands.[24] But Meeker appears to have been oblivious to these concerns and to the anger engendered by his efforts.[25]

Predictably, Meeker's relationship with the Indians deteriorated rapidly. During the summer of 1879, just at the beginning of planting season, the tribe left the reservation on an annual hunt, as was their custom. The agent, incensed by what he considered their willful disregard of his efforts, wished to make them return. Under existing law the army provided military assistance to the Interior Department if the department requested it to quell Indian unrest. As Fort Steele, in the Department of the Platte but on the Colorado-Wyoming border, was the nearest post to White River, Meeker wrote its commander, Major Thomas T. Thornburgh, complaining of Indian depredations and asking that troops be sent immediately to compel the Utes' return to the agency.[26]

Thornburgh, a West Point graduate and classmate of Bourke's, was well known to Crook, who thought him a fine officer, an exceptional hunter and woodsman, and a man of good judgment and sensibility.[27] Though the general placed great trust in the major, as soon as Thornburgh informed him of Meeker's request, he recognized the sensitivity of the issue and its potential for causing a violent confrontation. Leaving nothing to chance, he traveled personally to Fort Steele in July to assess the situation but returned immediately to Omaha after learning that Thornburgh intended to thoroughly investigate the agent's allegations before taking any action.

As Crook had suspected, Thornburgh found that the Indians had indeed left the reservation on their customary annual hunt, but he found no evidence to support Meeker's allegations of misconduct. Interviews with "nearly every ranchman residing within 100 miles of the post" failed to confirm any depredations.[28] Under the circumstances, the major ignored the agent's request for troops.[29]

As Thornburgh had Crook's complete confidence and as the major's findings seemed to confirm his own conclusions, any concerns the general might have felt about Ute unrest were now allayed, and he so informed Sheridan. In his dispatch to his division commander, Crook also took the opportunity to point out that if depredations should occur, which to date had not seemed to be the case, Thornburgh's troops could not respond in a timely manner because of the distance and remoteness of the White River agency. He suggested that only a military post constructed on the reservation itself would deter impending trouble. Crook clearly considered that any problem between the Utes and their agent was outside his jurisdiction.[30] Not long after writing to Sheridan, confident that the issue did not require his further attention, Crook departed on leave to his wife's family home in Oakland, Maryland. He would not return to Omaha until September 22, almost two months later.[31]

Had Crook visited the White River agency, he might not have been so sanguine. The tribe was probably aware that Meeker had requested military intervention. They certainly knew he had been the source of stories of depredations that appeared in the papers, and they feared that his largely fictional complaints would spark retaliation.[32] In addition, they were heartily sick of his high-handed and dismissive attitude. In this climate of distrust and resentment, Meeker, insensitive to the unrest he had stirred, decided to relocate his agency buildings to land prized by the tribe for grazing and racing their ponies and to plow up a portion for crops. Coincidentally, he decided to do this at a time when a delay in the arrival of their yearly annuity had already darkened the tribe's mood.[33] In that tense atmosphere it was not surprising that when Meeker sent a plowman to begin tilling the ground, the Indians drove him off with gunfire.

On September 8 Meeker sent a lengthy complaint to the commissioner of Indian affairs, declaring, "This is a bad lot of Indians. They have had free rations so long and have been flattered and petted so much, that they think themselves the lords of all."[34] On September 10, before his dispatch reached Washington, he wired hysterically that he had just been assaulted by a "leading chief," "forced out of my house and injured badly, but was rescued by employees."[35] Apparently, the tribe's medicine man, who grazed his horses on the land being plowed, had angrily confronted the agent at his home. The assault occurred when Meeker told the shaman that he should rid himself of the horses. The angry tribesman responded by shoving Meeker out the front door.[36] Without bothering to investigate further, the Interior Department asked the army to send troops from the nearest post "to arrest such Indian chiefs as are insubordinate and enforce obedience to the requirements of the agent."[37]

While still on leave in Maryland, Crook received word of these events from his adjutant, Lieutenant Colonel Robert Williams. Pursuant to ground rules established by the War and Interior Departments for the management of Indian affairs, the general had no choice but to advise Williams, "Should the Interior Department make the proper application, order the troops to give them (the agency employees) necessary protection." Immediately thereafter, he set out for Omaha.[38]

Passing through Chicago en route, Crook learned that in response to Interior's request, General Pope, the Department of the Missouri's commander, had dispatched a regiment of Buffalo Soldiers to the Ute Agency to investigate. After discussions with Sheridan, it was decided to recall Pope and his troops and send Thornburgh, closer to the scene, in their stead.[39]

Upon receiving his orders Thornburgh, now believing that "the Utes mean mischief," asked for reinforcements to handle the mission.[40] Crook approved and ordered two additional companies of cavalry from Fort Russell to join Thornburgh's command.[41] With a column now numbering two hundred men, the major embarked for the White River agency on September 21.

Slowed down by cumbersome army supply wagons, Thornburgh took a full seven days to reach the Milk River, the boundary to the Ute Reservation. In the interim Crook became increasingly uneasy about the column's safety. No one in the military, least of all Crook, had forgotten the Custer debacle, and he knew the Utes to be formidable warriors. On the September 23 he wired Thornburgh through Williams, urging him to "proceed with utmost prudence and if you have cause to believe you have not sufficient force, communicate at once . . . stating the number you require. In the absence of reliable information, Department Commander leaves matters entirely to your discretion and good judgment."[42]

Meanwhile, Thornburgh had opened communications with Agent Meeker, who informed him that the Utes were watching Thornburgh's progress toward the Milk River with growing nervousness. If the troops crossed the river, the tribe indicated that they would view the advance "as a declaration of real war." With a rare flash of insight, the agent suggested that, to allay their concerns, the major should camp on the north bank of the Milk and come into the agency with only five soldiers to talk with the Indians.[43] Thornburgh decided to adopt Meeker's suggestion and proceed with only a few men to the agency for talks. He informed headquarters that he did not anticipate trouble.[44]

But after another two days on the trail, Thornburgh reconsidered, fearing that leaving his troops outside the reservation would be a violation of his orders to bring his column onto the agency. Also, if his men remained on the far side of the river, his force would be divided, making him vulnerable if things went wrong. On September 29 he crossed the Milk onto the reservation with his full command, intending that once across, he would proceed with a few men to the agency.[45] This was a fateful and tragic decision. To the Indians, Thornburgh crossing the Milk with his full command was a breach of his promise to come to the agency alone, and they interpreted the troop movement as an act of war.[46] As the vanguard of the major's force crossed the shallow stream, they were met by three hundred Ute warriors. Though Thornburgh tried opening negotiations, it was too late. As soon as he moved additional troops across the river to reinforce his forward guard, firing broke out and the battle was on.

As he attempted to disengage and retreat back across the river, the major, who wanted nothing more than to resolve the conflict peacefully, was struck by a bullet and killed. His second in command, Captain John S. Payne, though wounded, assumed command and completed the retreat across the river. There, they hastily constructed a redoubt, using wagons, bags of feed, and the bodies of horses and mules killed by Indian sharpshooters. Besieged, they fought through the remainder of the day, suffering twelve killed and forty-three wounded, including all but one of the remaining officers. Further, all of the column's livestock was slaughtered, making escape impossible.[47]

When fighting broke out at the river, the Utes had sent messengers back to their fellow tribesmen at the agency reporting what they deemed an attack on the reservation. The news touched off an emotional explosion in the highly charged atmosphere of the agency; a party of young warriors unleashed their anger and frustration, brutally attacking the agency's white employees. All eight were killed, including Nathan Meeker, who was later found with a logging chain wrapped around his neck and a barrel stave hammered through his mouth into his skull, presumably intended to stop his lies. Meeker's wife and grown daughter and an employee's wife and two children were taken captive.[48]

Trapped in the redoubt, Captain Payne dispatched a courier with word of the command's precarious situation and a request for reinforcements. At Fort Omaha, Lieutenant Colonel Williams, still in command of the post in Crook's absence, had awakened to news of the attack at 3:30 a.m. on October 1 and promptly relayed the information to Crook and Sheridan in Chicago. Crook reacted with shock and rage at what he assumed was an unprovoked attack on his men and at the news of Major Thornburgh's death. He ordered the various posts throughout the department to assemble troops at the town of Rawlins, near Fort Steele, and march under Colonel Wesley Merritt to the relief of Payne and his beleaguered command. That force would total some five hundred troops.

Bourke, who on Crook's orders had been preparing to join Thornburgh's column as an observer, woke that night to the same terrible news.[49] He, too, was shocked. Reacting emotionally to his friend's death, he filled his diary with rumors regarding Ute depredations. Echoing the army's then-prevailing opinion that Meeker's efforts to promote farming had provoked the Utes, he wrote that because it "resembled work for the Indians, . . . they kicked."[50] On the train to Rawlins, en route to join Merritt's expedition, he was exposed, perhaps for the first time, to a different perspective. Some of his fellow passengers, many of whom lived in the area bounding the reservation, said that they hoped that Meeker, whose fate was as yet unknown, had been killed, blaming "his inefficiency or rascality" for bringing about the revolt. One man opined that Meeker, though honest, was "utterly impractical and visionary and without any ability to manage Indians or whites."[51]

Bourke caught up with Merritt's fast-moving command on October 4, and the next day he accompanied the relief force to the site of the siege. He described the battlefield as reminiscent of the devastation outside of Petersburg after the mine explosion that precipitated the Battle of the Crater. The Utes had departed, having killed every animal in the command. The bloated and rotting corpses gave off a stench that caused Merritt to evacuate the site immediately, pausing only to bury the dead soldiers and recover Thornburgh's sun-blackened corpse, which had lain outside the redoubt for the entire week of the siege.[52] The body was returned to Omaha, where, on October 22, despite a chill north wind, "nearly all the prominent citizens of Omaha," including Crook and his staff, grimly turned out for the funeral, "the largest ever seen" in the city.[53] From the battle site Merritt's troops hastened to the agency, where they found the bodies of the agent and his employees but saw no sign of the women and children. The Utes had disappeared into the surrounding mountains.

Though anger ran deep in the military community, cooler heads prevailed, and it was decided not to pursue a campaign of revenge against the Utes. Instead, General Charles Adams, an officer in the Colorado militia and a former White River agent well respected by the Utes, was appointed as a special representative of the Interior Department to deal with the aftermath.[54] With Chief Ouray's assistance he secured the release of the captive women and children, unharmed, and then participated in the investigation that followed.

A commission was appointed to investigate the causes of the out-break and determine what to do with the tribesmen who participated. Chief Ouray acted as a sort of defense counsel for the White River band, while Adams took the lead for the government. As a result of their efforts and the impartiality of the commission, the Milk River fight was correctly assessed as the result of a series of misunderstand-ings. The commissioners found that the Indians had acted largely in the mistaken belief they were under attack. As a result, the ambush of Thornburgh's force was treated as an act of war rather than a murder-ous rampage warranting criminal punishment, though one warrior, identified as having molested the women, was sent to prison.[55] Though with this one exception, the band escaped criminal penalties, the Utes' fate was sealed. Within two years the treaty under which the tribe held sway over their mountain homeland was abrogated, and Utes were forced to consent to expulsion from Colorado and removal to a reser-vation in Utah where the remainder of the tribe resided.

Though the government had once more broken its word to the Indi-ans, and though the removal worked a distinct hardship on the tribe, Crook never raised his voice in their defense. Despite the commission's findings and moved by anger at the death of Thornburgh and his men and the army's apparently lenient response, he advocated a strong hand in dealing with "our worst disposed and fiercest tribes." He pointed out that while retribution had been meted out for the slaying and moles-tation of the civilians, the killing of the soldiers at the Milk River—which he characterized as cold-blooded, treacherous, and unprovoked murder—had gone unpunished. This lack of response, he thought, was both "unjust and unwise" and created a dangerous precedent, devalu-ing the life of soldiers killed by unwarranted Indian depredations. As a measure of recompense, he recommended that Congress at least autho-rize the award of brevets for bravery to soldiers serving in the Indian wars, an honor not available to them at the time. Finally, he recom-mended that military posts be built near any Indian agencies where uprisings were likely to occur.[56]

Crook's outrage over Thornburgh's death and the attack on his troops, and perhaps his own guilt at misjudging the gravity of the growing unrest among the Utes, does not entirely account for the gen-eral's apparent indifference to the injustice later inflicted on the tribe. There may have been yet another factor at play. Though Crook usually framed his advocacy of Indian rights in pragmatic terms, being human, he often seemed influenced by his personal feeling for the tribe involved. His actions on behalf of Apache scouts or the Bannocks who had served him in battle appear to have been largely motivated by feelings of gratitude and admiration. His personal interactions with Standing Bear probably provided a substantial incentive for his intervention in the Poncas' behalf and could well have influenced his conduct with respect to Spotted Tail, the Brulé leader as well. On the other hand, such connections did not exist with respect to Eskiminzin, an Apache chief whom he disliked, and the Oglala leaders, Red Cloud and Crazy Horse, with whom he had been unable to establish rapport. With respect to these men, Crook had not acted as diligently in their behalf, though their causes seemed equally deserving.

There had been little to bond him to the Utes. He had never visited their reservation and had no personal relationship with any of their leaders, other than Nicaagat, and consequently, had far less personal interest in helping them. With respect to Nicaagat, while his irreverent style may have amused Crook, the chief had disgusted a good many observers at Slim Buttes, possibly including the general, when he had scalped a number of women slain in the battle.[57] The absence of any personal connection with the tribe or its leaders may have prevented Crook from seeing past his anger at the deaths of his men, and insulated him from the outrage that so often moved him to come to the aid of other mistreated bands. It was perhaps an understandably human, though not particularly admirable, response.

CHAPTER SEVEN

Investing in the Future

In the fall of 1879 Crook celebrated his fifty-first birthday, a moment when many pause to take stock of their lives, contemplate their mortality, and look toward the future security of their family. For an officer in the nineteenth-century frontier West, the prospect of sudden death or crippling injury, an ever-present aspect of their profession, furnished an incentive to provide for their loved ones not common to many other professions. This was particularly true in the nineteenth-century army, where retirement compensation, a recent innovation, was far from generous and ceased altogether upon the officer's demise.[1]

Although blessed with extraordinary good luck—during years of exposure to danger, he had remained virtually unscathed—Crook had attended the funerals of many of his fellow officers and seen others retire with debilitating illnesses or injuries. Though he did not have children, he was naturally concerned about how his wife, Mary, would be cared for upon his death. During his thirty-year career as a soldier, he had amassed little personal wealth. As a junior officer he had been able to save little, as his pay barely sufficed to cover the high cost of living in the West. As a brigadier general he earned a far more substantial salary: $5,500 per annum, an amount equal to about $122,000 in today's dollars. It was an amount adequate to meet his current needs and responsibilities as a department commander, but it left little in the way of savings to provide for the future. On retirement his pension would be reduced to $4,125 (about $91,500 today), still a handsome sum, but it would cease altogether at his death.[2]

To augment his pay and accumulate the extra income necessary to leave behind an inheritance, Crook, like other officers, often sought outside opportunities for financial gain.[3] To make ends meet as a young lieutenant in California during the Gold Rush, he had tried his hand at farming and commercial hunting with limited success.[4] But in the rigid cast structure of the Victorian era, such work did not accord with his present status as a senior military officer. Nor would such enterprises be expected to generate the amount of additional income to which he aspired.

As the Department of the Platte was in the midst of a sustained period of relative tranquility, Crook had ample time to explore investment as a means to augment his income.[5] And he was well placed to do so. In the American West of the 1880s, financial opportunity seemed to lurk around every corner, though in some cases it could prove ephemeral, whisked away at the last minute by unforeseen (at least by the investor) disaster. Many of Crook's civilian friends and hunting companions, and several of his fellow officers, had accumulated wealth by speculating in the region's booming economic environment. Opportunities to invest capital in ranching operations, real estate, and the newly discovered mineral bounty of the region frequently presented themselves, especially to well-connected figures like Crook. Mining held a particular attraction. The papers spoke constantly of spectacular gold, silver, and copper strikes throughout the West. On a single train ride in the fall of 1879, Captain Bourke reported rubbing shoulders with passengers who had mining interests in Colorado, California, Nevada, and the Black Hills of Dakota. These men were full of enthusiasm and rosy predictions. He had learned, he wrote, that Colorado that year had added $17 million to the national fund of gold and silver and would be producing wealth at a rate of $200 million per annum within five years.[6]

Crook began his brief foray into mining speculation in early 1879 with the purchase of shares in the Murchie mine. The mine, discovered in the 1850s, was located near Nevada City in California's Grass Valley, the second-largest gold-mining district in California. Murchie was a hard rock mine; that is, the gold was found in veins of quartz usually running far beneath the surface. The mine soon showed itself less productive than originally anticipated, yielding between $5 and $17 a ton, a meager return compared to a similar mining operation in New Mexico which assayed at $160 a ton. Efforts to increase the value of production by sinking deeper shafts proved unsuccessful, and its operators could only keep the mine open using profits from a crushing mill that extracted gold from surrounding quartz. Thus, it appears that Murchie's history had been a frustrating saga of digging ever-deeper shafts in the failed hope of increasing the value of its yield, a sad history that raises a question: Why did Crook and his fellow investors ever considered buying shares in the mine in the first place? The answer probably is that the shares were relatively cheap.[7]

Much of what is known about Crook's participation in the enterprise comes from correspondence with his aid, Walter Schuyler, whose role in the operation is outlined below, and from interviews conducted by Martin Schmitt, editor of Crook's autobiography, with the general's nephew, Oliver Crook. Oliver was about seventeen years old at the time of the purchase. His uncle George sought to involve him in the project hoping that he would acquire the practical experience to pursue a career in mining.[8] Details such as who brought the investment to Crook's attention, when he actually bought his shares, or the exact extent of his investment remain unknown. Nor do we know the precise extent of his involvement in the mine's management, though he seems to have taken a leading role as liaison between Schuyler and the investors.

Crook acquired his shares as a member of a consortium that included, among others, General Sheridan and Brigadier General Delos Sackett, the inspector general of Sheridan's Division of the Missouri. The president of the consortium was Andrew Snider, a successful businessman whom Crook had known and hunted with since the entrepreneur had served as post sutler at Fort Terwaw in northern California in the 1850s.[9] The consortium also drew in a number of small investors from among the junior officer corps, including Crook's aide Lieutenant Bourke and Captain Charles King, an officer who had known and admired Crook since serving in the Fifth Cavalry during the Sioux War.[10] King had been forced to retire due to an old wound. With a family to support on a disability pension of $2,000 a year, he, like the others, had been attracted by tales of the rich of gold deposits in that area of California and by Crook's enthusiasm about the mine's prospects. Any misgiv-

Lieutenant Walter Scribner Schuyler, circa 1880. Courtesy of Mark Kasal.

ing they might have had were swept away by their high regard for the general's integrity and, perhaps, by a misguided belief in his business acumen.

Reference to Crook's connection with the mine first appeared in Bourke's diary in July 1879. According to Bourke, before departing for Oakland and while still investigating rumors of Ute unrest, Crook dispatched his aide, Lieutenant Schuyler, to California to inspect the mine and "see what could be done to make it produce."[11] Though Schuyler, a West Point graduate, had no discernable mining experience, Crook

placed great reliance on his good judgment. He must have felt vindicated because, as the year drew to a close, he secured an extended leave
of absence for Schuyler, allowing him to go to California to manage the
mine's operations on behalf of the consortium, this despite his lack of
familiarity with the business. One can only imagine Schuyler's uneasiness at his commanding officer's jaunty assurances that he and the other
stockholders had great confidence that the young officer would "bring
it through all right."[12]

The lieutenant's early correspondence was hopeful, conveying a high
expectation of success.[13] But after three months the mine had yet to
show a profit. While Schuyler continued to express optimism, Crook
grew increasingly nervous, especially when Schuyler suggested that
continued operations might require an additional infusion of cash from
the investors. Apparently under increasing pressure from his partners,
particularly Generals Sheridan and Sackett, Crook tartly informed his
aide that a call for additional funds from the investors at this juncture
would be perceived as "ruinous to people here and must be avoided."
It seems that Crook and some of his partners were concerned that such
a demand, coming on the heels of a previous assessment of funds from
the stockholders, would push many to sell their stock rather than contribute more money to the project. That in turn would put too many
shares on the market, depressing the share price.[14] This worry caused
the consortium to contemplate ways of bailing out of the investment
altogether. To that end, Crook instructed Schuyler to "endeavor to
give a good impression to outsiders as to the value of the property
and in the meantime get all the statistics of the mine and those of the
neighborhood . . . anything that will go to show that our property is
in the best localities in the country. This may all be useful in trying to
sell our property in the future."[15]

Within a week of writing this letter, Crook received news that
rekindled his optimism. General Sackett, a moving force in the consortium, had learned about a refining process developed by Professor
George W. Maynard, a well-known mining engineer in New York,
that was said to increase the amount of gold yielded by raw ore. Sackett
asked Crook to forward a description of the process to Schuyler. If the
lieutenant could crush a "couple of hundred pounds" of Murchie ore
and forward it to him, he (Sackett) would then send it to the professor
to determine whether the process would enhance the mine's output.

Sackett was so bullish about the potential of Maynard's process that he inquired into the possibility of buying or leasing other mines in the area with similar problems.[16]

Schuyler did not share Sackett's optimism. In a follow-up letter to Crook (evidently no longer extant), he apparently again broached the idea of an additional assessment on the investors to cover mounting operational costs. At the same time, desperate for relief from the burden of managing a failing mine for a group of anxious investors that included so many of his superiors, he raised the possibility of being reassigned back to Arizona. That suggestion touched a raw nerve. Crook quickly informed Schuyler that when he had mentioned the lieutenant's Arizona proposal to Sheridan, the latter "got up in arms at once and said it would never do and gave his reasons." He added, pointedly, that he (Crook) fully appreciated Sheridan's concern. As an alternative he passed on the lieutenant general's generous offer to extend Schuyler's leave "as long as you wanted it," a prospect that must have had very limited appeal to the disheartened lieutenant. Nor was Sheridan thrilled with Schuyler's idea of increasing the investors' contributions. That "would not do" either, Crook cautioned. Instead, at Sheridan's urging, he proposed securing a short-term loan to cover the mine's operations. He further recommended that in the meantime Schuyler "shut down" until additional funding could be secured. Evidently Sheridan did not like that idea either, as Crook soon withdrew it.[17]

As the mine continued to lose money, Schuyler struggled to escape from the enterprise, even proposing an assignment to China. Crook scotched that suggestion with a mix of flattery and a thinly veiled threat. "The Murchie investors have great confidence in your integrity and judgment and none more so than General Sheridan," he said. "We all believe you have done your best and want you to remain there. You have not suffered a particle in reputation by your connection with the mine, but," he warned, "should you leave it now, it would leave room for hard things to be said about you."[18]

Then, suddenly, the whole complexion of the situation changed. Professor Maynard's process seemed to work, and samples from the mine now assayed at $30.74 a ton.[19] This news was sufficient to seduce the investors into putting more money into the operation. In June, Crook reported to Schuyler "the assessment boom has already started and I think that it can be levied as soon as you want." But, he cautioned,

"I do hope that this . . . will be sufficient as many here will not stand another [assessment]."[20]

For the next several months the enterprise continued to limp along. Professor Maynard's process soon proved less beneficial than originally anticipated. Other "processes" were explored and discarded. Crook, who evidently had staked not only a considerable amount of his savings in the venture but also his reputation, became increasingly gloomy about the prospects of success. Things looked up briefly in December 1880. While Crook was occupied with chairmanship of the Ponca commission, Schuyler deepened the mineshaft, striking a richer vein at the four-hundred-foot level.[21] But though the discovery evoked a temporary euphoria among the backers, their enthusiasm quickly faded when, in March, the lieutenant, once more running short of funds, proposed yet another assessment. As Crook had predicted, the investors balked and Schuyler was reduced to running the mine at a minimal level, producing only sufficient profit by the end of 1881 to pay its debts.[22]

The consortium had had enough. Almost two full years after Crook first sent Schuyler to California, the partners decided to close the operation. To his discredit, the general made his diligent aide a scapegoat for the mine's failure and removed him from his staff. In a letter dated December 31, 1881, he wrote, "I think it better all things considered, that you resign from your position as ADC. I write you this now in order that you may assign your own reasons for this step."[23] The following year Crook traveled to California and personally closed down the mine, sending his nephew, Oliver, to Sonora to close other operations the consortium had evidently purchased there. In Martin Schmitt's words, "The dreams of the miners were over."[24]

Moved by ambition for advancement as well as by the same desire for financial security that had propelled him into his mining venture, during this time Crook had mounted a campaign for promotion to major general. At the outset of the Civil War, Crook had resigned his commission as a captain in the regular army to accept an appointment as a colonel in an Ohio regiment in the volunteer service.[25] Thereafter he had advanced rapidly to major general and corps commander at a time when vacancies and promotions were far more common in the greatly expanded military machine. After Appomattox he had been forced to accept a reduction in grade to lieutenant colonel in the reconstituted and greatly downsized postwar army. Then, in 1874, to facilitate his appointment as commander of the Department of Arizona, he had been advanced to brigadier general, a controversial two-grade promotion that leapfrogged him over more than forty colonels of the line.[26] As a brigadier, opportunities for further advancement were rare. In the absence of a mandatory retirement age, promotion beyond brigadier depended on the death or voluntary retirement of one of the major generals currently occupying the few allocated positions. Thus, when rumors began circulating during the last months of 1881 that Major General Irvin McDowell planned to retire at some time in the near future, interest among brigadiers, including Crook, quickened.

The selection of an officer to fill a vacancy among the army's higher ranks was a process that, while guided primarily by seniority, was not immune to political influence; Crook, viewed by many western politicians as a hero of the Indian wars and a champion of a strong military presence in their region, thought himself well positioned in that regard. In fact, the territorial delegates from Arizona, Dakota, Idaho, Montana, New Mexico, and Wyoming expressed their support for his candidacy for the next vacancy in a petition to the president in February 1882. Senator Sanders of Nebraska made a similar request.[27] Additionally, the general counted on support from an even more august figure, former president Rutherford Hayes.

Crook's preoccupation with the promotion process manifested itself in a series of letters that he wrote to Hayes's son, Webb, in late December 1881, hoping to enlist him to his cause. In his initial missive, he announced his intentions and his desire for Webb's assistance. He ended the letter on an urgent note: "What is done should be done at once, as delay may be fatal."[28] In his next letter, responding to an apparently encouraging reply from Webb, Crook outlined the details of his campaign for the position, employing what was for him the familiar terminology of a battlefield report. He aimed, he said, to marshal the "humanitarians who take such an interest in Indians," together with General Grant and Jay Gould, to act in support of his candidacy; and to "[concentrate] all my forces and get McKinley to command them during my absence." William McKinley, in 1881 a congressman from Ohio and a rising star in the Republican Party, had served on Crook's staff as a young officer during the war and remained a loyal friend to his former commander.[29]

A bill mandating the retirement of military officers at sixty-four was then before Congress. Crook's certainty that it would pass bolstered his feelings of confidence. "Consequently," the general excitedly wrote Webb, "McDowell & all others eligible will have to go."[30] As he had foreseen, the bill was enacted into law six months later. Under its terms, McDowell, who would turn sixty-four in October 1882, would necessarily retire that fall.[31]

Three days after penning his letter on the retirement legislation, Crook followed up with another, cautiously advancing the hope that Sheridan, and through him Secretary of War Robert Lincoln, might also support his candidacy.[32] Stopping at Chicago en route to New York on leave, Crook called on Sheridan, his former West Point roommate, to explore the possibility. But his expectations were disappointed when the lieutenant general coolly informed him that he would endorse no one for McDowell's position. Though Crook may not have known it, Sheridan was a weak reed for him to rely on. Little Phil had indicated in communications with Sherman during the Sioux War that he had revised his opinion downward regarding his old friend's qualities as a soldier based on his perceptions of Crook's performance during that conflict.[33] But Crook, a keen student of the Indian mind, could be obtuse in reading his fellow officers. He optimistically described his Chicago meeting to former president Hayes, quoting Sheridan as telling him "he would rather see me have the place than any of the rest." But this may have been merely Sheridan's way of avoiding confrontation with his prickly subordinate, since, according to Crook, he also said that "the person who had performed the greatest amount of service ought to have the place."[34] Crook may have thought these words referred to him, but Sheridan, who probably had no wish to antagonize any of the factions among his fellow generals, ultimately chose to follow tradition, recommending the promotion be awarded based on seniority. In his last letter to Webb Hayes on the subject, Crook, grasping at straws, suggested without supporting evidence that John Hay, President Lincoln's former secretary and a prominent Ohio Republican, might endorse him.[35]

Though his campaign seemed to be flagging, it must have still appeared promising in some quarters as several of his fellow officers were now galvanized to oppose it. On March 29, 1882, a group signing itself only as "EIGHTY SIX OFFICERS OF THE ARMY"

Lieutenant General Philip H. Sheridan. Courtesy of Mark Kasal.

submitted a petition to President Chester Arthur, who had succeeded to the presidency following Garfield's assassination. The document was remarkable in its intemperate language and its vagueness, the reason, perhaps, why its authors delivered it under a cloak of anonymity. Their precautions were of little use, however, as the identities of some among them were soon revealed by their stated reasons for opposing the promotion. One of two accusations they leveled at Crook was that "this officer was advanced to his present rank from the grade of *Lt. Col.* to the prejudice of every Colonel of the line." In approving the promotion, the petitioners allowed, the president (Grant) had demonstrated his "*credulity* [emphasis in original]" in accepting the "puffs" in the newspapers, planted, they surmised, by a member of Crook's staff (i.e., Bourke, whom some regarded as little more than the general's press agent). Crawling a bit farther out on the limb they had constructed, the officers then described former president Grant as profoundly ignorant for believing such untruths that were "contrary to the opinion and knowledge of every officer of the Army." Who but an officer like Nelson Appleton Miles, then vying with Crook for the promotion, would have the overweening ambition and arrogance to mount such an attack on President Grant, still widely esteemed as a national hero?[36]

Another group whose hand may be detected in the language of the petition was likely comprised of the officers of the Third Cavalry regiment who had served under Crook at Powder River and the Rosebud. These men, led by Colonel William B. Royall, had been infuriated by Crook's decision to court-martial their regimental commander, Colonel Joseph J. Reynolds, for incompetence at Powder River. They had been further alienated by Crook's handling of the regiment at the Rosebud.[37] For these reasons they, too, had motive to join in this effort to block Crook's chances for promotion. They left their fingerprints on the petition when they declared, "Had Genl. Merritt preferred charges against Genl. Crook (as he should have done) in 1876, for the imbecility he exhibited during his campaign against Sitting Bull, he would not now figure as an aspirant in promotion. . . . It is a disgrace," they concluded, "that he should belong in the Army at all! But it would be insulting, should his imbecility and dishonesty be rewarded by promotion."[38]

It is doubtful that such a document carried much, if any, influence in the promotion process. However, Crook did not receive the appointment. In the end it was awarded strictly on the basis of seniority. When McDowell retired on October 15, 1882, "by operation of law," General John Pope, whose promotion to brigadier antedated Crook's by several years, was named to fill his slot.[39] There is no extant record of Crook's reaction to Pope's appointment. By then the general was far too deeply embroiled in events in Arizona to have much time to ruminate on his failed hopes.

CHAPTER EIGHT

Return to Apacheria

September 1882. The troops at Arizona's remote Fort Apache had anticipated Crook's return to the territory since early July.[1] Private Will C. Barnes, a signalman, may have been the first to spot the arrival of Nantan Lupan, as the Apaches referred to Crook. Riding near the post, the young man observed a plume of dust rising from a trail to the west, and emerging from beneath it, a file of horsemen headed in his direction. By pushing his mount hard, he managed to intercept the small column and quickly identified its leader: a man with a "full grizzled beard" who sat astride a large gray mule. To the young man, filled with tales of this storied figure, the rider presented a disappointingly unmilitary appearance. Clad in a "yellow canvas coat and a pair of blue soldier trousers, much the worse for wear," he sported equally eccentric headgear, "one of those white East Indian pyramidal hats, built on the lines of a present-day 'tin hat.'" Instead of an officer's pistol, he was armed with a double-barreled shotgun casually slung across the pommel of his saddle. Despite the man's odd appearance, Barnes admitted to being thrilled "at his first sight of this famous soldier, who had subdued the Apaches and brought peace to Arizona in 1873."[2]

George Crook was at the top of his game. Ordered back to Arizona to restore the peace among the Apaches that he had secured before his departure in 1875, he was no longer the indecisive, self-doubting figure he had become in the immediate aftermath of the battle of the Rosebud. By now he had resumed the personae of the bold, confident

Crook, mounted on his mule Apache, accompanied by his White Mountain Scout Alchesay. Courtesy of Arizona Historical Society.

officer who had tamed the Indians of the Great Basin and the fearsome tribes of Arizona. At a send-off dinner in Omaha that September, as he prepared to depart on his new assignment, he had been toasted by the city's mayor, among others, who remarked, "I know of no one whose leaving Omaha will cause such genuine and general regret as General Crook." The mayor then described Crook's transfer to Arizona as an honor and a recognition of merit "before which all promotion along the beaten paths of military life grows pale."[3]

While the general might not have shared the mayor's enthusiasm for his transfer, he approached his new assignment with the confidence of a man returning to familiar territory and the scene of past success. He was convinced that he knew the Apaches, understood the attitudes of the white Arizonans, and grasped the topography of the country. In his thinking it only remained for him to learn why Arizona had lapsed into turmoil since his departure and what he must do to restore it to its former tranquility.

The Arizona to which Crook returned in the fall of 1882 was not the same sparsely settled frontier territory it had been on his departure seven years before. When he departed for the Platte in 1875, he had left behind a country at peace for the first time since its acquisition from Mexico. The Apaches and other warlike tribes had been subdued and settled on reservations and, as far as he could predict, were progressing toward a self-sustaining agrarian lifestyle. Their subjugation and the coming of the railroad had opened up a vast region to exploitation, particularly in the southern part of the territory By 1880 Arizona had forty thousand non-Indians living within its borders, and that number was growing at a rate of over ten thousand newcomers each year.[4]

But now this progress appeared threatened. The Apaches were once again in a state of unrest and, in some cases, open hostility. There had been an apparent mutiny by formerly loyal Apache scouts at Cibicue Creek on the White Mountain Reservation and a breakout by the Chiricahuas, who were now ravaging the Mexican countryside. The current commander, Colonel (Brevet Major General) Orlando O. Willcox, had achieved some military success but had failed to completely restore peace. Instead, much to General Sherman's annoyance, he had become embroiled in controversy with other commanders in the field. Willcox, though a highly regarded officer with an excellent record of service, had displayed little insight or ability in his dealings with Indians, especially the Apaches. Sherman had chosen to replace him, though he took pains not to blame him for his effort, believing that Willcox had done his best in an extremely difficult situation. The officer whom Sherman selected to replace Willcox was George Crook. He reasoned that "these Apaches know Gen. Crook and fear him. Therefore his assignment to the command of the Department is wise and right."[5]

Replacing Willcox with Crook was certainly wise. But Sherman's stated rationale for choosing him reflected a misreading of the current situation in Arizona and an incomplete understanding of the basis for Crook's success in dealing with the Apaches. True, Crook had succeeded in defeating the Apaches on the battlefield, largely because he was able to instill fear in them through relentless campaigning and his employment of their kinsmen to hunt them down in their mountain lairs. But thereafter his success in settling them peacefully on the reservation had been the result of an entirely different set of circumstances. This, General Sherman, who shared with his friend Sheridan a dislike and distrust of Indians, had failed to grasp.

As soon as the tribes had agreed to lay down their arms and settle on the reservations set aside for them, Crook had substituted fairness, honesty, and trust for fear, forging a bond with the Apaches based on honoring promises and respectful treatment. His appreciation of the Apaches was sincere. Having absorbed the tales of their depredations prior to his initial arrival in Arizona, he had been skeptical of their nature. However, as he came to know them, he became convinced of their humanity and their unique character among the other tribes in Arizona. Writing to Herbert Welsh of the Indian Rights Association in the summer of 1884, he remarked, "Speaking for myself, . . . I do not hesitate to put the Apache at the very head for natural intelligence and discernment. . . . Were he a Greek or a Roman, we should read with pride and enthusiasm of his determination to die rather than suffer wrong." As to his faults, they are "identical with those of which we ourselves should be guilty under similar provocation."[6]

The Apaches responded to his sincerity by placing their confidence in him, as documented in the remarkable work of oral historian Eve Ball. During the 1950s and 1960s Ball, a former English teacher, conducted extensive interviews with the sons and daughters of some of the great Apache leaders of Crook's time, recording their recollections of their parents' memories and attitudes. While doing so she became "the only white person [in that period] in whom they had complete trust," a trust that allowed her to elicit their unvarnished opinions concerning the whites whose lives intersected with those of their parents' generation.[7] About Crook, she reported, "Every one of the older Apaches interviewed told me that, though Crook was their enemy, he was an honorable enemy and they respected him."[8] He had earned their respect just as she had, on the basis of trust. Eugene Chihuahua, son of one of the most revered Chiricahua warriors, told Ms. Ball, "The one bit of hope was our faith in the promise made by General Crook. For though he was our enemy, he was an honest enemy."[9]

Now, entering upon his second tour of duty in the Department of Arizona, Crook intended to build on the Apaches' belief in his integrity. As John Bourke later recounted, upon arriving in the territory in 1882, the general had been overwhelmed with tales "of gross outrages perpetrated upon the men and women who were trying faithfully to abide in peace with the whites. . . . No one had ever heard the Apaches' story, and no one seemed to care whether they had a story or not."[10]

General Crook intended to hear their voices. Seeking out the leadership of the Western Apaches, men whom he had known from his earlier tour in Arizona, as well as former scouts who were now labeled as mutineers, he would elicit their views of the events that had transpired since his departure in 1875. Only then would he determine what was needed to repair the bond broken in the intervening years and restore peace to Arizona.

Crook arrived at Whipple Barracks, site of his former headquarters, on September 4. Anxious to get to the real work of reconciliation, he remained only long enough to assess the readiness of his command for combat should that prove necessary. After that, he proposed to set off immediately for Fort Apache, the epicenter of the present unrest. At Whipple he rapidly concluded that if further fighting was required, and the depredations committed by the Chiricahuas in Mexico seemed to indicate that it would be, his cadre of Apache scouts was too small and his pack trains in too poor a condition to mount an effective campaign.

The department's scouting contingent at that time consisted of only five companies of twenty-five Indians each, spread thinly over five forts in eastern Arizona. The posts closest to the San Carlos Reservation, Forts Apache and McDowell, had only one company each.[11] This scouting force was, in Crook's opinion, insufficient to meet the potential threats of an incursion from Mexico or further breakouts from the reservation. Consequently, he fired off a memorandum to the Division of the Pacific requesting authorization to recruit 125 additional scouts because, as he put it, "catching Indians if done at all must be mainly thro' their own people." At the same time, to strengthen his pack trains he asked for the immediate reassignment to his department of one hundred mules currently in Cheyenne, Wyoming, together with his old pack master, Tom Moore.[12] Then, exactly a week after his arrival, he mounted his own mule, Apache, and headed for Fort Apache to begin his inquiries.[13]

Situated high above the hot desert floor among the pines on the White Mountain Reservation in northeastern Arizona, Fort Apache was well known to Crook. He had first visited the post in July 1871, shortly after beginning his assignment in the department. Then, too, he had been seeking a way to bring peace to the territory, albeit through military means. At that time, as was his habit before embarking on an offensive, he wanted first to reconnoiter the area and familiarize himself with the local tribes. Impressed with stories he had heard of the White Mountain people, he had called at their reservation to assess their suitability to serve as scouts in future campaigns. If they proved adequate and amenable, he planned to recruit them. On his arrival, Chief Pedro, his son, Alchesay, and Chief One-Eyed Miguel had greeted him.[14] Impressed by their demeanor and professions of friendship, he had enlisted a number of the White Mountain warriors on the spot. And they had served him well.

Miguel had died in the interim, a victim of intratribal warfare, but Crook hoped to counsel with old Pedro, though he was now lame and hard of hearing, as well as Alchesay, now a prominent tribal leader in his own right, and other tribesmen who had remained aloof from the current unrest.[15] To that end he pitched his tent about a mile away from the post on the banks of the White River, where he thought the Indians could speak freely without the intimidating presence of his troops.[16] After completing these discussions he planned to travel into the mountains to meet face-to-face with those who had participated directly in the recent fighting and who had gone into hiding to avoid retribution.

Crook did not ride alone, though his entourage was so small that it is doubtful it could have withstood a determined attack. To ensure accurate communications with the Apaches, whose difficult tongue few white men ever mastered, and because he had previously experienced misunderstandings due to inept translation, he brought with him two extremely reliable and competent linguists. The first, Corydon Cooley, was a white frontiersman and rancher who had married into the White Mountain tribe, wedding two of Chief Pedro's daughters.[17] Fluent in their language and well respected by his father-in-law's people, he also had a long association with the general, both as a leader of scouts and interpreter for his adopted people. The other interpreter was Severiano, a Mexican captured in childhood by the Apaches who had risen in the tribe and married Chief Miguel's daughter.[18] With these two translating, Crook believed that he would receive an accurate rendering of the concerns of the White Mountain community.

Other than the interpreters, his detail included half-dozen cavalry troopers, army surgeon John O. Skinner, and Captain John Bourke. Bourke was familiar with Fort Apache and the White Mountain tribe from his first tour in Arizona. Additionally, only the year before, while en route to do anthropological fieldwork among the Pueblo tribes of the southwest, he had called at Fort Apache, arriving just as its commander, Colonel Eugene Carr, was about to depart for Cibicue Creek on what would turn out to be a near-fatal mission.[19]

Carr had been ordered to arrest a medicine man and subchief of the Cibicue band of Western Apaches who was rumored to be stirring up his followers with talk of driving the whites from the country. The medicine man's cult, for such it seemed to have become, had thrived in the atmosphere of dissatisfaction and restlessness that now infected the Western Apaches, who only a few years before had been a contented people. During his stay at Fort Apache, Bourke had listened with apprehension to Carr's ominous prediction that the arrest of the shaman might result in violence.[20] Like Sherman, Carr attributed Crook's power over the Indians to their fear of him. Hoping to intimidate the shaman's followers before his departure for Cibicue, the colonel asked Bourke to visit Chief Pedro and "give [him] a good dose of Crook, they haven't forgotten him and the licking he gave them. He is the only bulge we have on them now."[21]

Bourke visited Pedro's camp, finding it in turmoil. The chief's warriors were drunk, heavily armed, and galloping wildly about on their war ponies. Though they warmly welcomed Bourke, he worried about their questions about his recent visit to the Navajos. Their curiosity seemed to confirm rumors he had heard that the Navajos planned to join their Apache relatives in rising against the whites. With growing concern, he later commented that "the Apaches were acting in a more bold and saucy manner than I have ever known them to do and I have been among them eight years."[22] In retrospect, there was good reason for his alarm. A few days after Bourke departed Fort Apache, the shaman's followers attacked Carr's patrol following the colonel's arrest of the medicine man at his camp on Cibicue Creek. The incident triggered the unrest that now had brought Crook to Arizona, accompanied by Bourke, the latter reassigned to Crook's staff at the general's request. It seemed that the two men had now come full circle.[23]

Crook soon learned that the incident at Cibicue was the culmination of a chain of circumstances that had unfolded following his departure from Arizona. In 1875 he had left his successor and former West Point classmate, August Kautz, with a military department that for the first time in generations appeared free of hostilities. Pursuant to President Grant's peace policy and Crook's campaigns against the Western Apaches and Yavapais, the various Indian bands in the territory had been settled, each within the boundaries of its own reservation.

Crook had never been at ease with the government's policy of confining Indians to reservations. On the Pacific coast he had observed firsthand the disease, idleness, and dislocation that prevailed after its adoption. But in the intervening years he had come to view it as unavoidable because it protected the tribes from white violence, among other reasons. Though he saw the merits of their removal to areas at a safe distance from the travel routes and settlements of whites, he fought to settle the tribes on, or as near as possible to, their traditional homelands—or at least on land that was conducive to good health and self-sufficiency. Unfortunately, his efforts in that regard often met with failure because whites coveted such land and, as he somewhat defensively pointed out, the Interior Department, not the military, was responsible for "the selection of reservations or the designation of reserves to which particular bands should be assigned."[24] Nevertheless, once reservations had been established and when they were under army control, those under Crook's management were administered with humanity and with the objective of preparing the Indians for their eventual assimilation into white society. However, in his view, after oversight was transferred to the Interior Department, misguided policies, poor management, and corrupt agents undermined the progress he had made. Events in Arizona certainly seemed to bear out his opinion.

Yet even under military control, Crook would have admitted, the adaptation of many Apaches to reservation life had not been smooth. Their nomadic habits and warrior culture made their adjustment to the regimentation and confinement of the reservation precarious. The harsh environment prevalent in some areas of the reservation made it all the more difficult. Unaccustomed food, climatic differences, and a host of diseases to which they had little immunity caused their death rates to soar, especially among the young. Added to these troubles, the Apaches chaffed under the strict discipline of military control and the enforced idleness of reservation life. To counter their restlessness, Crook believed that the Apaches needed to be "kept at work." As a stopgap measure, they could gather forage and firewood for the army, but a more permanent solution lay in farming and raising stock. In 1874

Crook believed that, with the provision of seeds, equipment, breeding animals, and a modicum of education, "there will be no further trouble with [the Apaches] and they will gradually become self supporting."[25] By the following year he had become even more sanguine. Just prior to his departure from the territory, he reported that the tribes under his jurisdiction (which would exclude the Chiricahuas, who had been exempt from his control) had abandoned raiding as a form of economic endeavor and were well on their way to agricultural self-sufficiency.[26] Or so it had seemed to him at the time. Now, as he rode toward Fort Apache, he hoped to learn how and why his rosy projections had gone awry.

As he prepared to confer with the friendly bands around Fort Apache, the general dispatched messengers to the Indians involved in the Cibicue incident the year before, who were now hidden in the nearby mountains. His couriers, who included Alchesay, were instructed to inform these holdouts that the Gray Fox planned to come to them to hear what they had to say. They bore the message that "if no killing of white people occurred in the meantime, not a shot should be fired by the troops."[27] No one had any idea how the warriors would react. Cooley, who knew them well and feared the worst, prepared for the mission by making out his will, fully expecting that he might not return alive.[28]

While his couriers reached out to the dissidents, Crook conferred with Pedro and some forty others of the White Mountain band who lived near the post and had taken shelter at Cooley's ranch during the fighting. The general opened by saying that he intended to set down everything he heard, "because what goes down on paper never lies." They should speak freely, telling the truth about what happened in his absence "without fear, and . . . in as few words as possible, so that everybody can read it without trouble." Bourke recorded these conversations and later summarized them in his book, *On the Border with Crook.*[29]

Reading Bourke's narrative, it is apparent that Crook's assurances encouraged the tribesmen to speak frankly and that both the captain and the general were deeply moved by what they heard. The Apaches spoke passionately of corrupt and tyrannical Indian agents who diverted reservation supplies to traders in surrounding white settlements and, without any reason the Indians could discern, destroyed the crops that the Apaches relied on for their sustenance. They told of the arrest of the shaman for causes they claimed were beyond their comprehension, and afterwards, the incarceration for months at a time, without proof or trial, of Indians suspected of participating in the Cibicue fight. And they angrily denounced the steady encroachment on reservation lands by surrounding whites: Mormon settlers to the north and east and prospectors and miners to the west and south.[30]

Mose, the only scout who had not mutinied at Cibicue, gave Crook his version of the events that occurred. His words painted a picture wholly at odds with the government's perception that the incident had been planned in advance, and he characterized the fighting as a spontaneous response by the scouts to shots fired at them by Colonel Carr's cook, without, at least to Mose's perception, any apparent provocation.[31]

Though Crook would ultimately need to know the immediate reason for the mutiny, at the outset of his inquiry he was focused on determining the root causes of the unrest that had precipitated it and finding a means to address them. He had come to Arizona firmly believing that the ferment that followed his earlier departure was related to the policies and practices of the Interior Department in its management of the Apache Reservation. Nothing he was hearing now disabused him of this notion.

Crook had long opposed the hegemony over Indian policy given by Congress to the Indian Bureau. In the years before he had attended West Point, the army had held sway over Indian affairs because relations between Indians and whites was commonly marked by hostility. However, from the 1840s, after the Indians were removed from the East and many were placed on reservations, responsibility for their supervision and care had been transferred to the Interior Department unless armed conflict demanded military intervention. Many in the army opposed the change, believing it resulted in a significant worsening in the government's relations with the tribes, and they never ceased to try and reverse it.

Historians generally attribute the Indian turmoil that plagued Arizona Territory following Crook's earlier departure to the Interior Department's unswerving decision to consolidate the Indians on increasingly fewer and smaller reservations for reasons of efficiency and economy. Crook certainly ascribed to this view. The policy was politically and economically popular with a parsimonious Congress and even more so among whites in the West. There the economic benefits of consolidation were so pronounced that Crook and others believed that the mysterious "Indian Ring," a shadowy cabal of politicians and entrepreneurs, was behind it. Concentrating the Indians in areas near towns made the reservations a more accessible and profitable market. And if the tribes were settled on lands poorly suited for agriculture, well, this only increased their dependence on the often-adulterated and overpriced rations supplied by local merchants. Perhaps the greatest attraction of consolidation was that it opened up thousands of acres of fertile and mineral-rich Indian land for exploitation. Ranchers, farmers, miners, and land speculators who expropriated the land justified their actions by saying that Indians occupied far too much territory given their small numbers and their lack of interest in tilling land.[32] The Interior Department's policy even found supporters among Indian reformers, who declared that radically reducing the size of reservations would make the Indians more amenable to control. Also, denying them access to their traditional hunting and gathering grounds facilitated their conversion to farmers and their ultimate assimilation into white society.[33]

But consolidation was a disaster for the native peoples. It created overcrowding and drove some tribes into proximity with historic enemies, sparking violent clashes. By making it easier for corrupt Indian agents and contractors to siphon off already-inadequate rations and supplies and provide inferior substitutes, consolidation also caused widespread hunger among the tribes that ultimately led to unrest. To soldiers who believed as Crook did, a change in this system of management was essential to preserve peace.

While to its Anglo population Arizona Territory was the perfect place to practice consolidation, for the Apaches, it was the worst. The relocation site chosen was the San Carlos agency. Situated on the White Mountain Reservation, midway between Tucson and Fort Apache, it was within easy reach of merchants of Arizona's southern towns. Agency headquarters was located on a bleak stretch of infertile land in disease-ridden lowland country on the Gila River.[34] The area was aptly described by one Apache informant as "the worst place in all the great territory stolen from the Apaches. If anybody had ever lived there permanently, no Apache knew of it. Where there is no grass, there is no game. Nearly all of the vegetation was cacti. . . . The heat was terrible. The insects were terrible. The water was terrible. What there was in the sluggish river was brackish and warm." Stagnant river water served as a breeding ground for swarms of malarial mosquitos, which caused such widespread illness that Camp Goodwin, built at the site in 1868, had been abandoned in 1877 after a quarter of the soldiers stationed there died from the disease.[35] And the place teemed with rattlesnakes, tarantulas, Gila monsters and centipedes.[36] Crook had been quick to point out that the hot, arid location made little sense, if for no other reason than it was most unsuitable for any type of agricultural endeavor. Nevertheless, it was here that the Indian Bureau sought to crowd together hundreds of Apaches for conversion from nomadic raiders to sedentary farmers and pastoralists.

Consolidation at San Carlos began in February 1875 while Crook was still in command of the department. Notwithstanding the general's firmly stated opposition, fourteen hundred Yavapais and Tonto Apaches were moved from the Verde Reservation and resettled there. The move ignored the excellent adjustment the two tribes had made at Verde, and even more egregiously, it overlooked the long-standing enmity between the two groups. The latter—an oversight that would plague many removals, particularly in Arizona—stemmed from the government's seeming inability to grasp that animosities could exist even between tribes that shared similarities of language and culture. And among the Apaches these hostilities were exacerbated at San Carlos, where the bands were packed too close to one another, often causing violent flare-ups.[37]

Only three months after their arrival, the mutually antagonistic Tontos and Yavapais were joined by the White Mountain and Cibicue Apaches. These tribesmen had been plucked from their traditional mountain homes near Fort Apache as the result of an ongoing struggle between Interior Department officials and the military commander at Fort Apache over control of the White Mountain Reservation. The commissioner of Indian affairs thought to resolve the conflict by exiling the Indians to San Carlos, out of the reach of the military.[38] No one, least of all the commissioner, considered the consequences of moving a mountain people into a lowland desert environment. And again, the department failed to attend to existing feuds between the two bands or to the fact that many among the White Mountain band had served as scouts in Crook's campaign against both the Yavapais and

Tontos, who now awaited them at San Carlos. The uneasiness of the White Mountain Apaches at moving into the vicinity of those they had helped subjugate was palpable.[39]

Before the Indians from Fort Apache had properly adapted to San Carlos, the fractious Chokonen, Nedni, and Bedonkohe bands of the Chiricahuas, the most aggressive and martial of Arizona's Apaches, arrived. The Chiricahuas, under their chief, Cochise, had formerly occupied a reservation in their traditional homeland in the Dragoon and Chiricahua Mountains in southern Arizona under a treaty negotiated with General Oliver O. Howard. Unfortunately, the reservation boundary had been drawn so that its southern edge lay on the Mexican border, giving the tribe unfettered access to Sonora and Chihuahua in northern Mexico, their favorite raiding grounds since the days of the Spanish conquest.[40] While Cochise had agreed to cease raiding on the Arizona side of the line, he had made no such commitment with respect to Mexico, where his young men, particularly members of the Nedni and Bedonkohe bands, continued their raiding. These were bloody affairs that drew bitter complaints from the Mexican government. Pursuant to Howard's agreement, Crook's troops were barred from the reservation, placing the Chiricahuas outside the ambit of his authority.[41] When Crook proposed to intervene to end the depredations in the mid-1870s, he was rebuffed by the War Department, which had no wish to renew hostilities with the Chiricahuas so long as Cochise kept the peace in Arizona. Not surprisingly, prior to his departure from Arizona in 1875, Crook found the situation extremely frustrating and the open door to Mexico a constant thorn in his side.

After Cochise died in 1874, his sons, Naiche and Taza, inherited his mantle. While they continued to respect the agreement not to raid into Arizona, depredations in Mexico continued unabated. The Chiricahuas' troublesome history and the value of their land to the surrounding white community made their removal from their border homeland an inevitability, awaiting only an excuse. In the spring of 1876, well after Crook's departure for the Platte, several Chokonens, drunk on whiskey, killed two stage-line employees and a nearby rancher. The Interior Department seized on the incident as the pretext to move the entire tribe to San Carlos.[42] A June 24, 1876, editorial in the *Arizona Weekly Citizen* may have inadvertently spelled out the real reason for the move. "The [former] home of the Chiricahua Apaches . . . is a rich domain of mountain and valley embracing some of the best mineral and agricultural features of the Territory. . . . Some of the valleys are said to be the best watered, and the stock ranges the finest in southern Arizona. The region will probably soon be thrown open to settlers."[43]

At San Carlos the Chiricahuas were placed on a desert tract on a bend in the Gila River, not far from the former site of malarial Camp Goodwin. Despite its evident drawbacks, most of the Chokonens accepted their new home and attempted to adjust to the new reality. Others, primarily from the militant Bedonkohe and Nedni bands, fled to Sonora, and a few joined the Chihennes, a related branch of the Chiricahuas, on their reservation in New Mexico.[44]

Also known as the Mimbres or Warm Springs Apaches, the Chihennes had been exempted from the original move to San Carlos because they resided in New Mexico, where they enjoyed a relatively peaceful existence in their beloved traditional homeland under their chief, Victorio. However, some young warriors, stirred by the influx of their Bedonkohe and Nedni relations, became restless; in May 1877 the Interior Department, worried that they now presented a danger, resettled them alongside the rest of the Chiricahuas on the Gila.[45] Finding removal from their homeland intolerable, the Chihennes attempted to return to their reservation in New Mexico. When the Indian Bureau refused to allow them to do so, they joined forces with dissident Bedonkohes and Nednis and embarked on a two-year-long war against the residents of New Mexico and Sonora. In January 1880 the Bedonkohes and Nednis, tired of the fighting, voluntarily surrendered, but the Chihennes fought on until Victorio and many of his followers were killed by Mexican troops at the battle of Tres Castillos in the Chihuahua desert. The survivors were then returned to San Carlos.[46]

The agents chosen by the Indian Bureau to manage the increasingly discontented Apache bands that now crowded the San Carlos agency aggravated rather than ameliorated the situation. John Clum, the bureau's first appointee, was honest and energetic. At first he seemed an excellent choice. He actually liked and got along with the Apaches. But at twenty-three, his youth belied a self-confidence that bordered on arrogance. Ambitious and self-promoting, he became a convinced proponent of consolidation as a means of strengthening his own power and authority, welcoming every opportunity to bring new bands under his wing.

To Clum the army represented competition in his quest for control of the Indians, and his consequent resistance to the military set the pattern for the agents that followed. His efforts brought him into constant conflict with officers at nearby posts, often with the support of his Interior Department superiors in Washington.[47] The infighting made management of the reservation even more difficult, since the Apaches were quick to sense discord among their overlords and take advantage of it.

Clum resigned in July 1877.[48] The agents who came after continued to oppose military intervention in reservation affairs but added corruption to the mix. Clum's first two successors were both dismissed for dishonesty and self-dealing. The Indian Bureau, despairing in the short term of finding an honest civilian, turned to the army to provide them with a man of integrity to manage the agency while they searched for a civilian replacement. The officer selected, Captain Adna R. Chaffee, made an honest attempt to reform his predecessors' corrupt practices, but his tenure was all too brief. After a little more than a year, in June 1880, Joseph C. Tiffany, a civilian, replaced him.[49] Tiffany's management would contribute substantially to the conditions that led to the events at Cibicue.

By 1881, according to Pedro and others who spoke to Crook, life at the now overcrowded San Carlos agency had become close to unendurable. As the Gray Fox listened attentively, they told of the starvation and disease that afflicted its inhabitants. Watching their children die from hunger and illness ratcheted up the level of tension, already high under conditions of confinement, idleness, boredom, and intratribal hostilities. In this suffocating atmosphere, many were driven to seek relief in *tiswin*, their potent, corn-based homebrew.

As Crook well knew, even under normal conditions, among the Apaches the capacity for violence lay just below the surface, only awaiting the accelerant provided by alcohol. Motive was always present, as revenge and the cycle of vengeance killing were deeply embedded in their culture. Blood feuds between bands, clans, and even individual families were commonplace and long-lived.[50] Among the Western Apaches, trapped in the claustrophobic confines of San Carlos, relations between the Cibicue and the White Mountain bands, never warm, dissolved in a maelstrom of murder. Several prominent leaders of both bands were killed or maimed, leaving their people fragmented and directionless.[51] Deprived of authority figures to guide them, severed from their homelands and tribal traditions, alienated from one another, and plagued by the circumstances of their confinement, the Western Apaches had become a lost people. In this condition they were highly receptive to the prophesies and teachings of a diminutive, charismatic White Mountain chief and medicine man, Noch-ay-del-klinne, who now came to prominence among them.[52]

The slight, light-skinned shaman had been known to the white world since 1871, when, still in his mid-twenties, he had probably served with the original White Mountain contingent enlisted by Crook to fight the Tontos.[53] He later became a shaman and prophet among his people, incorporating Christian dogma learned at mission school into his teachings.[54] His prophecies involved the restoration of Indian land, the resurrection of fallen leaders, and the return of the buffalo, all to be brought about by the disappearance of the white man and a return to the old ways. His teachings paralleled those of other shamans dating back to Tecumseh, and they reappeared in the Ghost Dance movement that preceded Wounded Knee, a predictable response to the white man's seizure of Indian lands and destruction of native culture.[55] Foreshadowing the Ghost Dancers, Noch-ay-del-klinne preached that his prophesies could be hastened to fruition through dances that he first introduced in June 1881 and that continued throughout that summer. They attracted increasingly large crowds, often including bands formerly regarded as hostile to one another, inspiring dread in the white population, who were certain that they were the prelude to an insurrection.[56]

Of special concern to the army was the participation of their Indian scouts, Western Apaches whose loyalty had formerly gone unquestioned but who now returned from the dances surly and insubordinate, apparently under the spell of the medicine man.[57] In August 1881 Colonel Carr, who commanded the Sixth Cavalry at Fort Lowell, attended one of the events and promptly concluded that a general uprising seemed likely.[58] Carr shared his concerns with General Willcox, Kautz's successor as department commander. Carr reported that the medicine man attributed his failure to resurrect any of the dead chiefs to date to "the presence of the white people; that when the white people left, the dead would return," and that "the whites would be out of the country when the corn was ripe."[59] It was late summer and the corn was already ripening on the stalk. To Carr and many others, this portended that the insurrection was imminent. Responding to these rumors, Carr had sent Bourke to visit Pedro's camp after Willcox had directed the colonel to consult with Agent Tiffany at San Carlos and arrest the shaman, if deemed necessary "to prevent trouble."[60]

Tiffany had been Indian agent a little over a year before Noch-ay-del-klinne began his dances. A political appointee, he completely lacked experience in the West or with Indians. The Apaches had related to Crook "that [their civilian agents] ran from bad to worse, being dishonest, indifferent, tyrannical, and generally incompetent." Tiffany, whom they named "Big Belly," they regarded as tyrannical, perhaps because of his tough disciplinary attitude and his great reliance on his Indian police to keep order. Presumably, they also questioned his honesty. Though he was never convicted of any wrongdoing, more than a whiff of corruption lingered over him during his entire career, including his time at San Carlos.[61] Despite never meeting the man, Crook had acquired a particular distaste for him, probably based on his reputation.[62]

It was Tiffany who lit the fuse that ignited the outbreak at Cibicue. During the spring and early summer of 1881, he, too, had become alarmed by stories about Noch-ay-del-klinne's activities, including rumored references to the disappearance of the whites before the corn was harvested. When the shaman moved his camp to Cibicue Creek, some forty-five miles from his agency and out of view, the agent found it particularly troubling. His concern turned to fear when Noch-ay-del-klinne declined the agent's request that he conduct future meetings with his followers under Tiffany's view and refused the agent's summons to come to the agency for talks.[63] Tiffany then ordered his Indian police to arrest him. When they returned two or three days later, downcast, without either their weapons or the medicine man, Tiffany became convinced that an uprising was imminent and wired Carr, pleading for guns and a contingent of scouts to protect the agency. "I want [the shaman] arrested or killed or both and think it had better be before dance next Saturday night," he demanded.[64]

On the morning of August 29, though aware that his action might precipitate a general uprising, Carr led a column of troopers, packers, and twenty-three White Mountain scouts to Cibicue Creek to arrest

Noch-ay-del-klinne and return him to Fort Apache. Carr took the medicine man into custody without incident, but that evening, as he was making camp, the shaman's adherents surrounded his campsite. When fighting broke out, almost the entire Apache scout contingent joined in on the side of the shaman. What actually precipitated the incident or whether it was premeditated was not known at the time. Whatever the immediate cause, seven soldiers were killed, including an officer, while among the Apaches, the medicine man and his wife and son, together with some eighteen others, including six scouts, lost their lives.[65]

At nightfall, after the shooting died away, Carr's outnumbered troops withdrew and made their way safely back to Fort Apache, where they were greeted with relief by the garrison, who thought them wiped out.[66] Excited by rumors of the fighting, Apaches in the vicinity of the post had attacked nearby settlers and the next day staged an abortive attack on the fort, which Carr repulsed. Two days later Apache raiders attacked ranches in the adjacent Pleasant Valley, killing two more whites and stealing stock.

That seemed to end the affair, but the white community, panicked by initial reports that greatly exaggerated the extent of the fighting, feared that it was the precursor to a major uprising. The reports from the field prompted an equally intense reaction from the army. The first sketchy news of the attack led General Willcox to send his immediate superior in San Francisco, Major General McDowell, a wire extravagantly describing the affair and warning that it was a possible harbinger of a widespread outbreak. McDowell passed the news to General Sherman in Washington, stoking the fire by adding word of a rumored attack on Fort Bowie the same night, a tale that in fact had no foundation in reality.[67]

Sherman, envisioning a reprise of the recent war with the Sioux, fired off a series of telegrams of escalating stridency over the next week.[68] They culminated with a directive to Colonel Ranald Mackenzie, district commander in New Mexico and one of the army's most celebrated Indian fighters, to lead a contingent of cavalry to Arizona to reinforce Willcox's already substantial forces.[69] Mackenzie's presence complicated the ensuing hunt for the scouts, now labeled mutineers. Through a series of miscommunications and misunderstandings, over the next few weeks Mackenzie and Willcox engaged in a struggle for command that generated bad feelings and confusion up and down the chain of command.[70]

It soon became evident to anyone with a modicum of objectivity that reports of a general uprising had been greatly overblown. Ironically, Agent Tiffany was one of those who helped calm the situation by providing a surprisingly accurate analysis of the extent of the outbreak. He reported that only about four hundred of the reservation's five thousand Indians seemed to have been involved, primarily members of the Coyotero and Cibicue bands. The other tribes had either remained friendly or had at least held themselves aloof from the fray. His estimate of those involved was later revised downward to about 220 men.[71]

But Tiffany's numbers did little to calm Willcox.[72] Spurred on by Sherman's belligerent telegrams and the belief that he confronted a war that could drag on into the foreseeable future, he ordered most of his 1,300 troops to Fort Apache and authorized the sale of 250 arms and 50,000 rounds of ammunition to the whites in the area for self-protection.[73] Soon the troops, their numbers swollen by Mackenzie's force and additional soldiers from neighboring departments, flooded the reservation, searching for the warriors who had participated at Cibicue.

The Indians at San Carlos had not seen uniformed troops on the reservation since 1876 and found their presence unsettling. Though the Western Apaches, most notably the Cibicues and Coyoteros, were the army's primary target, the Chiricahuas were the Indians most unnerved. While they had not participated in any of the attacks, the reservation was rife with rumors that the soldiers had come to deport the tribe to Indian Territory or possibly kill them.[74] The Nednis and Bedonkohes were particularly skittish. Having only recently returned to the reservation after hiding out and raiding with Victorio in Mexico, they suspected that they were the true objective of the increased military activity. Their leaders, Juh and Geronimo, who had previously seen the inside of white prisons, were especially nervous. So when a cavalry troop entered their camp searching for the scouts, tensions reached a fever pitch.[75] On the night of September 30, 375 Chiricahuas, including 74 of the most renowned fighting men in the tribe, broke from the reservation under Juh and Geronimo, and struck out for Mexico.[76]

Meanwhile, an announcement by Agent Tiffany that any Apache who failed to surrender by September 21 would be treated as hostile and hunted down induced many of those involved to surrender themselves. By Tiffany's deadline over sixty of the mutineers had given themselves up.[77] Only a few of the participants now remained at large.[78]

The capture of the remaining holdouts proved difficult, most likely because of the treatment accorded those who had already surrendered. Sherman, eager to make an example of the mutineers and deter other Indians from going on the warpath, had pressed not only for prompt and vigorous prosecution of the hunt for the holdouts but also for harsh punishment of those already in custody. In November, in obedience to his orders, an army court-martial found four of the imprisoned scouts guilty of mutiny, desertion, and murder. One received a life term at Alcatraz, an army prison at the time, and the other three, known to whites as Dandy Jim, Deadshot, and Skippy, were sentenced to hang. On March 3, 1883, President Arthur confirmed their sentences, and the three men were executed, still protesting their innocence from the gallows platform.[79] A witness at their trial, Second Lieutenant Thomas Cruse, would later reflect that he "always regretted the fate of Deadshot and Skippy. The former was the sage of the Indian company, the latter our clown and wag. I doubted at the time if they had an intentional part in the firing upon us. It seemed to me that they were swept into the fight by excitement and the force of evil circumstances." Their deaths devastated the tribe. Though suicide was almost unknown among the Apaches, Deadshot's wife hanged herself on the day of her husband's execution.[80]

Predictably, the executions hardened the determination of those Western Apaches still at large, as well as the Chiricahuas in Mexico, not to surrender. To reinforce his band and ensure their survival in Mexico, Geronimo returned secretly to San Carlos in the spring of 1882 and coerced Chief Loco and his Warm Springs Apaches into joining him. With these additional warriors, the Chiricahuas now raided with virtual impunity throughout Sonora and Chihuahua.

Meanwhile, the Western Apache holdouts resupplied themselves in a series of attacks of their own throughout northwestern Arizona. But their success was short-lived. Willcox's troops caught up with and decisively defeated them at Big Dry Wash in July. This victory, however, came too late to salvage the department commander's reputation. After the battle, though Willcox boasted that only eleven mutinous scouts remained free, the continuation of Chiricahua raids in Mexico gave his words a hollow ring.[81] In August, Sherman relieved him of command and replaced him with the Apaches' erstwhile nemesis, General Crook. It was now Crook's responsibility to finish the job.

CHAPTER NINE

There Is Not Now a Hostile Apache in Arizona

Skeptical of the official version of Cibicue and its aftermath, Crook wanted to hear from the actual participants in the affair. Having counseled with Chief Pedro and others of his tribe, he now summoned the officers of Carr's command who had been present at the fight. Among the first to appear was Lieutenant Thomas Cruse, commander of the mutinous scout company. Cruse later recalled that he and his comrades had faced the general's inquiry with considerable trepidation. Suspecting that the Indians had already provided a completely different story than he had to tell, he worried that if Crook accepted their version of events, he was "due for difficulties." His fears were not allayed when he entered the general's tent and stood before the Gray Fox himself. The latter viewed him with a "fixed stare, seeming to bore through me." Then Captain Bourke proceeded to cross-examine him as would a "prosecuting attorney," while Crook "sat there like a graven image . . . running his fingers through that long beard," giving no hint of his reaction to the lieutenant's testimony. To Cruse's relief, he later learned that Crook had no intention of making him a scapegoat. In fact, to the lieutenant's evident surprise, he discovered that the general's only interest was "in getting the whole situation clear in his mind—the legitimate grievances of the Apaches, the real character of their leaders, the best method of returning all Apaches to their reservation."[1]

Having learned all he could at the White River, Crook set out to meet with the eleven scouts who, with their Cibicue allies, remained sequestered deep in the nearby mountains. The emissaries that the general sent from Fort Apache had, it seemed, been successful in convincing the suspicious tribesmen of his peaceful intentions, as they agreed to meet with him on their own turf. But having been labeled mutineers and hunted by the troops for a year, no one was sure how they would receive Crook and his entourage. Now accompanied by a number of curious Indians from Fort Apache, the general approached the fugitives' campsite with some anxiety. Their wickiups were scattered along the banks of the Black River, some fifteen miles from the White, in a canyon that seemed an ideal site for an ambush. The only approach was by a narrow, rock-strewn trail that threaded through a dark ravine "walled in by towering precipices of basalt and lava" topped by stands of juniper and pine. The path followed the swift and roiling river, which, Crook noted with interest, played host to numerous trout amid the many rocks that broke its passage. As the tense and exhausted men neared the camp, it must have been with considerable relief that they heard the tinkle of laughter from Apache women and children.[2]

The good humor of their dependents contrasted sharply with the mood of the warriors, at first, "sullen and distrustful." But after Crook "shamed" them for not having faith in one "who had always been straightforward with them," they opened up to him.[3] They were soon reciting all-too-familiar complaints of corrupt agents, stolen lands, and inadequate rations.[4] But it was their description of the events at Cibicue that drew the general's attention. The future of these men would depend in large measure on his determination whether the fight had been a premeditated mutiny, as the military now insisted.

What he heard closely paralleled the tale Mose had told. For some time prior to joining Carr's mission to arrest the medicine man Noch-ay-del-klinne, the scouts were assailed by rumors that the troops planned to disarm them and either kill them or send them into exile. So when they set out from Fort Apache, they were confused and anxious, believing that the march might portend their arrest or worse. If the soldiers fired on them, they resolved that it would be "better [to] die fighting like men than be crushed underfoot or driven out."[5] Some of the scouts professed not to know what had triggered the melee. Others confirmed Mose's version of events, saying that Carr's cook was the first to fire, and the rest of the soldiers followed his lead. Crook believed the uniformity of most of their accounts lent them credibility.

If true, they clearly indicated an absence of premeditation, contrary to the army's belief.

It was not unusual for individuals who shared information with the general to come away with no idea of how he had received it. On this occasion, however, he recognized that the scouts' futures hung on his conclusions, so he was quick to share them:

> I have heard all that you have said and I think I understand you. It is believed by the white people that these Indian soldiers turned against the white soldiers at the Cibicue; when white soldiers do such a thing as that we always kill them. The whole matter seems to be wrapped up in a good deal of mystery and confusion. Each side has a different story. The promptness with which you have come in here makes me think you are telling the truth as you know it.[6]

Following his meetings at Black River, Crook held additional interviews with other scouts camped nearby and then proceeded to San Carlos. There he convened yet a different element: Indians who had remained on the reservation during the breakout. Once more he listened to an identical litany of wrongs they had suffered at the hands of agents, the soldiers, and the surrounding white population.[7]

After completing his interviews, Crook drafted a report to General McDowell, division commander, outlining the causes he believed had led to the unrest and the measures he intended to implement to restore peace.[8] He began by reciting the Indians' take on the events that had transpired, giving great credence to their views and concluding that only by understanding their perspective could one expect to address their concerns fairly and effectively.[9] Even today such a modus operandi is rarely followed in formulating policies effecting the powerless and disenfranchised. In Crook's era, when the Indian perspective was viewed as largely irrelevant, it was even less likely to happen. Yet as the general wisely pointed out, failure to take their views into account so often invited a recurrence of the problems that had precipitated unrest in the first place.

Based on the Apaches' testimony and surrounding circumstances, Crook told his superior that he believed that the scouts had acted in self-defense rather than with premeditation. Had it been otherwise, "not one of our soldiers could have gotten away from there alive."[10] Furthermore, General Sherman's punitive measures had convinced the "mutineers" that they had nothing to lose by continuing their depredations. Emboldened by this attitude, they became an ongoing danger to the surrounding white population and a nucleus of discontent for the Apaches on the reservation. As the tribesmen believed they had acted in self-defense against a premeditated attack by the soldiers, Crook asserted that any attempt to punish them "would bring on war."[11] Instead he planned to offer a general amnesty to the holdouts, hopefully inducing them to return peacefully to the reservation. If this worked, and he was confident that it would, he intended to take measures needed to redress the grievances that had led to the outbreak. He would then turn his attention to the Chiricahuas presently wreaking havoc in the countryside of northern Mexico.[12]

During the weeks that followed, Crook implemented the policies set out in his report. On October 5 he issued a general order to his officers that was obviously also intended for Indian ears. He had found among the Indians, he wrote, "a general feeling of distrust and want of confidence in the whites, especially the soldiery; and also that much dissatisfaction, dangerous to the peace of the country exists among them." To win their trust, they were to extend the principles of justice equally to Indians and whites alike, and they were to exercise extreme caution in their use of force, lest through inexperience or haste, they "allow the troops under them to become the instruments of oppression."[13]

He then moved to win over the former "mutineers" by demonstrating his personal commitment to justice. That fall he had an opportunity to do so when eleven Apache prisoners were brought up before a grand jury in Tucson in connection with their role in the Cibicue affair. Crook wrote to the territorial prosecutor, repeating that, contrary to popular opinion among white Arizonans, the Cibicue incident had not been premeditated, that the Indians thought they had been acting in self-defense, and that consequently, any attempt to punish them "will bring about a war which will be destructive to the growing interests of this Territory and New Mexico." His administration would be "very seriously embarrassed," he said, "unless the Apaches can be made to feel that they are to be tried upon a basis of exact and even-handed justice . . . and not punished without sufficient cause."[14] The letter arrived after the grand jury had already discharged the prisoners, but Crook's words helped persuade the Apaches of his sincere desire to secure fair treatment for those who returned peacefully to the reservation. Seeing that there were no reprisals taken against them and that military patrols no longer hunted them, the remaining dissidents accepted Crook's word and shortly thereafter began returning to San Carlos to reunite with their families.[15]

In the months that followed, Crook recruited many of these men as scouts for the ensuing campaign against the Chiricahuas. Their assistance would prove critical, and he would reciprocate. In 1884, as a gesture of gratitude and an acknowledgment of their role, the general asked his superiors to release the two remaining Cibicue prisoners still confined at Alcatraz. The secretary of war agreed to his request, and they were freed to return to the reservation.[16] The legacy of trust that Crook created during this period had a lasting effect. Western Apaches would continue to join scouting units in the Southwest well into the twentieth century, creating an exemplary record of service up to 1947 when the Indian scout companies were finally disbanded.[17]

While laboring to bring about the return of the "mutineers," Crook also sought to rectify the wrongs that had precipitated the outbreak in the first place, a task he viewed as essential to maintaining permanent peace on the reservation. Unlike many government agents, the general did not view the reservation system as method of incarceration intended to prevent the Indians from marauding. To him, reservations would serve as safe harbors where Indians could be furnished the skills and acculturation required to make them self-sustaining and capable of adjusting to white society. And all reservations under his control were managed to that end.

To Crook, the Interior Department's consolidation policy figured prominently as among the chief causes of Apache unrest. Crowding five thousand southwestern Indians from disparate bands into the hot, unhealthy, barren flats at the confluence of the San Carlos and Gila Rivers had made life a misery and farming an impossible dream. But San Carlos itself was only a small section of the Apache Reservation, which Crook considered "abundantly large enough for all the Indians belonging to it," containing "every variety of soil and climate suited to their different requirements."[18] Why not disperse the Indians over this wide area, a change in policy that would facilitate their conversion to farming and reduce friction between the bands?[19] With respect to the

White Mountains and Cibicues, he saw no reason why they should not be returned to their homes in the mountains surrounding Fort Apache. There they would be within the reservation's boundaries but still subject to military oversight. As to the other tribes, there was "no necessity for concentrating all the bands at one point." They could be distributed according to their varied needs and preferences to any of the lowland areas up or down the Gila and San Carlos Rivers, well away from the barren, malarial area where they were now congregated.[20]

Crook anticipated that his recommendation would meet unyielding opposition from the Indian Bureau and the Interior Department. He would need a measure of authority over the reservation to circumvent their resistance. Thus he argued that, with the Chiricahuas and a number of Western Apaches still at large off the reservation, military necessity justified the temporary transfer of reservation control to the army.

Such a transfer of authority from one cabinet department to another would normally be accomplished through an interdepartmental agreement, a time-consuming and tedious process. But Crook, impatient of bureaucratic niceties and confident he could get away with it, simply assumed immediate control over the reservation.[21] In his annual report for 1883, he would frankly, and arrogantly, declare that he considered the memorandum of agreement ultimately concluded between the two departments in July 1883 as "merely a reiteration of directions which I had found it necessary to issue the previous autumn." His rationale for putting the cart before the horse was simple and straightforward: he knew best. As he put it, "A thorough examination of the status of the Indians on the White Mountain Reservation convinced me that the safety of the Territory and the welfare of the Indians required that I should assume the police control of the reservation and which I virtually did."[22] There was nothing virtual about it. Though Crook tried to disguise his usurpation as a limited exercise of police power, in truth it was far more. By November 1882 he had taken over the entire administration of the reservation, save only the issuance of rations and annuities to the Indians. These functions, funded with Interior Department appropriations, he graciously left to the Indian Bureau.[23]

Such a blatant power-grab would probably have met serious opposition from an activist Indian agent like John Clum. Fortunately for General Crook, his task was greatly facilitated, at least at the outset, by the active—even enthusiastic—cooperation of the reigning agent at San Carlos, Philip P. Wilcox, Agent Tiffany's replacement after the latter resigned in June 1882. Assuming his position on September 1, only days before Crook's arrival in the territory, Wilcox was a political appointee with few qualifications other than his friendship with Secretary of the Interior Henry M. Teller.[24] He had little knowledge of or interest in the Apaches and was perhaps more than a little intimidated by them.[25] In truth, he had accepted the job only after learning of the unavailability of more lucrative opportunities in government. His primary interest seems to have been in the pecuniary advancement of both himself and his son-in-law, John A. Showalter, whom he hoped to appoint as post trader on the reservation. Considering Arizona "a hole not fit for a dog," he planned to return to his home in Colorado as soon as possible, leaving his day-to-day duties in the hands of his clerk, Samuel B. Beaumont. One source asserted that Wilcox would only return once or twice to San Carlos during the next three years, probably an exaggeration, but not much of one.[26] Given Beaumont's genial personality, as described by a lieutenant who worked with him, Wilcox's absence, at least in the beginning, probably promoted good relations between civilians and the military. The lieutenant described Beaumont, who answered to the honorific of "colonel," as "a fine old gentleman, an ex-officer of the Civil War, and an immediate buddy of ours."[27]

Given his lack of interest in the job and his attitude toward Arizona and the Apaches, Wilcox seemed perfectly satisfied to have Crook assume control. On one of his frequent visits back to Colorado, he was asked by a reporter for the *Denver Tribune* why there had been no clash between himself and General Crook. He replied enthusiastically, "General Crook has been fair and wise in all his propositions and I heartily concur with his policy. He is doing splendid work and I will aid him all I can. We do not disagree on any subject. When one makes a suggestion, the other acquiesces in it and acts upon it." As to the spirit of cooperation that now prevailed, this, he crowed, "was the first time in the history of Indian affairs that such a thing has occurred."[28]

The cozy relationship between the two men would soon dissolve, but in the interim it greatly facilitated Crook's efforts at reform, beginning with his "suggestion" that the Apaches at the San Carlos agency be allowed "to choose lands for themselves in different parts of the reservation." When Wilcox ventured that such a policy violated Indian

Bureau rules that "required him to keep the Indians at the agency," Crook simply ignored the objection. Thereafter, he later recalled, the agent readily assented, stipulating only that the military "assumed the responsibility of allotting lands within the Reservation limits . . . and be held responsible for [the Indians'] behavior."[29]

By reversing a major component of the Interior Department's concentration policy, Crook could fulfill a promise he had made to the Western Apache bands that they would be able to return to their mountain homes. And they did so without delay. Most of the other bands dispersed to lowland areas at some distance from the agency along the Gila and San Carlos Rivers where the soil and the climate was more conducive to agriculture. These movements, Crook believed, eased tribal tensions that had previously contributed to unrest at San Carlos and greatly assisted the various tribes in achieving self-sufficiency.[30] And, because dispersing the Indians made a daily headcount difficult, Crook eliminated the much-disliked requirement, at least temporarily.

Neither the absence of a headcount nor the dispersal of the bands implied that Crook intended to slacken military control over his charges. His primary objective would always be the maintenance of stability and peace on the reservation. For that reason, and in light of continuing depredations by the Chiricahuas, he soon reinstituted the headcount, requiring passes for all Indians wishing to travel outside the bounds of the reservation. These policies, though unpopular with the Apaches, enabled the army to keep track of the agency Indians, and knowing their whereabouts helped officers counter false accusations that their charges had participated in the violence that sometimes afflicted the surrounding settlements. To ensure that the headcounts were accurate, Crook conducted a census of the reservation tribes and then enrolled all members of the various bands and issued each man old enough to bear arms a brass identification tag. These were coded to identify the band to which the Indian belonged and bore a number assigned to him upon enrollment. The tribesmen were required to carry these tags at all times.[31]

In Crook's view, the disciplined and honest administration he required lay beyond the capabilities of the Indian Bureau's civilian employees, so he appointed officers from his command to manage the reservation, a task that might seem familiar to the "nation builders" in today's army. It was not his style to micromanage his subordinates. Rather, he gave

road directions and then stood aside to allow his officers to implement them as required by exigencies on the ground. He expected the
men who filled these positions to be highly motivated, honest, and
innovative, capable of functioning independently and exercising good
judgment. Having previously commanded many of the troops currently stationed in Arizona, he was fortunately well positioned to make
appropriate choices. The officers he selected were among the very best
in the territory. Dedicated, intelligent, and sympathetic to the Indians,
they shared Crook's own enlightened views and, as he had, would soon
earn the trust and respect of the Apaches under their supervision.

To oversee the San Carlos agency, he selected Captain Emmet
Crawford, and to assist him as his chief of scouts, Britton Davis, a
young lieutenant fresh from West Point. He designated a third officer, one already widely respected by the Apaches, Second Lieutenant
Charles B. Gatewood, to supervise the White Mountain and Cibicue
bands at Fort Apache.

Crawford had begun his military career as an enlisted man in a
volunteer Pennsylvania regiment during the Civil War. Wounded at
the second battle of Fredericksburg, following his recovery he was
selected to command colored troops, an assignment that many officers sought to avoid. But he continued to serve with black units for
the remainder of the war and into Reconstruction, an indication that
he liked the work and was good at it. He had been assigned to Fort
Verde in Arizona during Crook's first tour, and he fought with the
Third Cavalry alongside the general in the Sioux War before returning to Arizona with his regiment. Britton Davis, who worshiped
Crawford, considered him "mentally, morally, and physically . . . an
ideal knight of King Arthur's Court." The wife of the post surgeon at
Camp Sheridan was similarly struck by Crawford's knightly virtues,
finding him "gentle, kind, and chivalrous and ever ready to undertake any perilous duty for which he might be detailed."[32] Over six
feet tall and lean, with deep-set gray eyes, a goatee, and drooping
mustache, he presented a serious, even melancholy, face to the world.
Davis thought that perhaps he had suffered some sadness in his early
life, for although Crawford had a keen sense of humor, Davis never
heard him laugh aloud. Modest and self-effacing, "he delighted in
assigning to his subordinates opportunities and credit he might well
have taken to himself."[33]

Captain Emmet Crawford. Courtesy of Mark Kasal.

Not much can be said about Lieutenant Davis's prior experience, since he arrived in Arizona newly graduated from West Point. But the wisdom of Crook's selection soon became obvious. His assignment was a boon to future historians, as he was to record the fascinating events that subsequently unfolded in a memoir entitled *The Truth about Geronimo,* a work later described by Robert Utley, the dean of Western

Britton Davis as a West Point cadet. Courtesy of the Arizona Historical Society.

historians, as "one of the best books, both as a source and as literature, to come from the frontier."[34]

For the post at Fort Apache, Charles Gatewood was an equally fine choice. Just under six feet tall, he had a lanky build and a thin, handsome face browned by the sun and dominated by a prominent nose and sad-looking gray eyes. The nose earned him the nickname Scipio Africanus at West Point because of a fancied resemblance in profile to the Roman general. The less classically inclined Apaches called him Nantan Bay chen daysen, Big Nose Boss.[35] His fellow officers, at least the ones who left written records of their experiences, uniformly lauded

Lieutenant Charles Gatewood, circa 1880. Courtesy of the Arizona Historical Society.

his integrity, courage, professionalism, and ability to manage the Apache scouts under his command.[36] But their descriptions included none of the warm, humorous anecdotes that colored their narratives of other officers. He was not a man given to easy familiarity. Stubbornly moral, serious and reserved in demeanor, he was a loner who preferred his own company and thoughts to the fellowship of the officers' mess. During Crook's initial Arizona tour, Gatewood had established a reputation for getting along with the Apaches, though, according to some sources, he neither liked nor trusted them.[37] Apparently he overcame or hid this predilection well, because after observing his leadership of a company of Apache scouts, Crook thought enough of him to appoint him to administer the White Mountain Reservation at Fort Apache. Gatewood suffered from recurring inflammatory rheumatism, malaria, and the various intestinal ailments that frequently accompanied duty in the Arizona Territory. Yet he invariably demonstrated both endurance and courage in the field. Because of his unflinching bravery, his willingness to consult with and listen to his scouts, and his even-handed treatment of the Apaches on the reservation, he won their admiration, respect, and confidence They, in turn, taught him something of their culture and language.

In his annual report to the secretary of war for 1883, Crook noted that on November 2 he introduced a gathering of chiefs at San Carlos to the officers who would be overseeing them. His opening remarks soon demonstrated his intention to usurp the Indian Bureau's authority on the reservation. Initially, he maintained the fiction that Wilcox was in charge, crediting him with the decision to disperse the Indians about the reservation while describing him to the chiefs as the authority "who gives you all you are entitled to." If they should need advice, he told them, the agent would supply it. But as he outlined his new policies, the agent's authority faded into the background, replaced by references to the army and military control.[38]

Taking as his theme greater freedom and greater responsibility, he began by emphasizing the latter. With the bands scattered about the reservation in areas remote from the agency, Crook declared that the chiefs would be accountable for the behavior of their people, assisted by the scouts and Indian police. Only in the event that the chiefs were unable to maintain the peace would the white soldiers intervene.

Noting that wife beating and the cutting of noses of adulterous women would no longer be tolerated, Crook was especially emphatic and uncompromising on the subject of alcohol. Though raised a Methodist and a teetotaler, he had tolerated drinking in his various commands unless it interfered with his troops' ability to carry out their duties. But with respect to the Apaches, he was not prepared to be so indulgent, demanding rigorous adherence to the Indian Bureau's frequently flouted ban on the making and consumption of tiswin, the tribes' beloved homebrew. Drunkenness in Apache society was a plague, leading to confrontations that often ended in violence and caused blood feuds that carved deep divisions within and between tribes. As Crook put it to the assembled chiefs, drinking causes you to "let all your brains run down in your stomachs." In the future they would be responsible for strictly enforcing the tiswin ban. This rule would soon loom large in the military's relations with the Apaches.[39]

On a more positive note, within their tribal areas the chiefs would now have greater autonomy in choosing the locations where their people could live, grow their crops, and raise livestock. As they would be expected to reduce their dependence on the government's largesse, rationing would continue only until the Indians could raise sufficient food to sustain themselves. The grumbling that followed this announcement was somewhat muted when the general declared that he would no longer require headcounts. Nor would they be required to obtain passes to travel off the reservation "so long as there is no disturbance." But the enrollment of Indians would continue, and all adult males would receive identity tags that they were expected to carry at all times, a policy that would later facilitate the reintroduction of the hated policy.[40]

Knowing that at some time in the future he might need to enlist their warriors in a campaign against the Chiricahuas, Crook warned the chiefs that "so long as the Chiricahuas are out, you cannot expect to have a secure peace; and I may have to call upon you to settle that matter." His words met with a tepid response, since some among the Western Apache leadership had relatives among the Chiricahuas. But over the next several years their reluctance would dissipate as friction between the two bands increased, and the White Mountain warriors would become indispensable in tracking and fighting the Chiricahuas.

As a final gesture toward Indian Bureau authority, as Wilcox was absent, Crook concluded by introducing Sam Beaumont, the agent's clerk, to the chiefs. Beaumont made a few brief remarks, touching on rations and annuity goods, the only areas of responsibility remaining within his purview. As a Civil War veteran, he seemed to have no problems accepting military presence on the reservation and assured the attentive Indians that "[Wilcox] will work in perfect harmony with General Crook," words that he might soon recall with embarrassment.[41]

Though he made no mention of it to the chiefs, one of Crook's priorities was to protect the tribe from white intrusions on their lands. Past Indian agents had winked at or, on occasion, abetted such incursions, but under the army's administration that would no longer be the case. Miners and squatters invited onto the reservation by past Indian agents were expelled, and the general and his officers resolutely opposed any future efforts to curtail the reservation's boundaries; nor did they countenance threats to remove the Apaches to Indian Territory in order to take their lands.[42] A survey of the reservation then underway and scheduled to be completed by spring would clearly define the boundaries of the Apaches' territory and assist in fending off white encroachment.

Under the management of Captain Crawford and Crook's other appointees, the lives of the reservation Apaches began to show immediate improvement, no doubt aided by the fact that, at least for the time being, relations between Indian Bureau employees and army officers justified Beaumont's rosy assurances of "perfect harmony." During Wilcox's frequent absences, Beaumont cooperated fully with the officers as they began the work of rooting out corruption on the reservation.[43]

While under Indian Bureau supervision, the issuance of rations to the Indians had frequently been the object of many of the abuses afflicting the reservation system. Adulteration and shortages were a constant irritant. Looking into the procedures followed when issuing rations, Beaumont reported that the agency scales used to weigh beef rations had never been tested. When Crawford asked him to check them, he found they had been rigged so that the beef contractor "was getting paid every week for about 1,500 pounds of beef that he did not deliver." The animals themselves, all skin and bones, were so weak that Davis suggested that they must have been transported to the agency on ponies, an accusation the beef contractor hotly denied. Davis and Beaumont also learned that before driving the cattle to the reservation on ration day, the contractor would deprive them of water for a period of time. Then, just before delivery, he would herd them into the river where they would drink their fill and arrive at the scales "looking like miniature Zeppelins."[44] The guilty supplier's contract was terminated and a new agreement entered into with a nearby rancher who was thought to possess greater probity.

The trader's store on the reservation provided another opportunity to cheat the Indians. The post trader who operated the store had a monopoly on trade on the reservation, allowing him to provide goods on a "take it or leave it" basis and thus reap huge profits by offering substandard goods at high cost. It was this coveted position that Agent Wilcox had successfully obtained for his son-in-law, John Showalter. In response to a number of complaints from the Indians, Crawford visited the store and found that Showalter had, indeed, been charging extortionate prices for his goods. As Davis put it, "After the captain had a talk with him, prices were cut practically in half."[45] While salutary for the Indians, this reduction in his son-in-law's profit margin surely riled Wilcox, probably inspiring some of the animosity that would soon roil his relationship with Crawford.

Crawford also moved to address the troubling the issue of idleness and boredom among his charges. The Apaches, no longer able to raid or hunt and loathe to perform the "woman's work" of farming, had little to occupy their time. To fill the hours they turned to drink, which bred violence. Knowing this, and not wishing to see the Indians reduced to a state of dependency, General Crook had advocated their gainful employment, both as a cure for boredom and a means to "earn at least a portion of their keep." The cavalry and pack trains under Crawford's command created a constant demand for wood and hay, both available locally. With the captain's encouragement the Apaches began a flourishing business cutting hay and wood for the garrison. The work not only alleviated boredom but also put some cash in their pockets, allowing them to augment their rations and purchase goods at the trader's store.[46]

These reforms lifted the mood of the Indians on the reservation. When Davis and Crawford had first arrived at San Carlos agency, they felt "the sullen, stolid, hopeless suspicious faces of the older Indians challenging [them]."[47] But before long, Davis observed that "with just rationing, fair prices at the trader's store, and a little money to buy the simple things they craved, the rancor of the Indians quickly faded away. . . . We were gaining their confidence, of all things the most necessary to our control of them."[48]

For his part, Crook labored at maintaining good relations with Agent Wilcox. In February, in a letter to the agent's boss, Secretary of the Interior Teller, he leapt to Wilcox's defense when local business-men, eager to take over mineral-rich reservation lands, attacked him in the press. In that missive the general went out of his way to laud the agent's cooperative attitude.[49]

CHAPTER TEN

Preparations for a Campaign

With trusted officers and humane policies in place, Crook grew confident that the unrest that had previously plagued the San Carlos Reservation was a thing of the past. Having established firm control over Indian affairs in Arizona, he was no longer the uncertain and frustrated Rosebud George. His rapid and bloodless restoration of peace among the Western Apaches seemed to have rehabilitated his reputation in the eyes of his superiors and the citizens of Arizona. Once again, he was regarded as the consummate authority on Indian affairs, well positioned to address the problem of the Chiricahuas, the only remaining threat to security in his department, Accordingly, with his customary self-assurance he began preparations for a campaign to return the illusive bands now terrorizing the Mexican countryside to San Carlos.

Upon his initial arrival at Whipple Barracks in September, anticipating that such a campaign would be needed and convinced that his current force of Apache scouts and the condition of his pack trains were inadequate to ensure success, Crook requested, and duly received, permission to recruit up to five companies of scouts and a shipment of mules.[1]

As he envisioned it, two columns of Apache scouts would form the backbone of his Mexican expedition, one commanded by Captain Crawford and the other by Lieutenant Gatewood. Al Sieber, a German-born frontiersman and veteran of Crook's Tonto campaign, would supervise the Apaches day-to-day. He would hold the title of superintendent of pack trains, a fiction that enabled Crook to pay him from his generous transportation budget.[2] Archie McIntosh, who had served as a lead scout for Crook since his days in the Great Basin, and Sam Bowman, of black and Choctaw ancestry and formerly Carr's chief of scouts, would assist Sieber.[3]

To communicate with his scouts and, if need be, with the dissident Chiricahuas, Crook chose Mickey Free as interpreter for the units. Free, fluent in Spanish and several Apache dialects, was a colorful and somewhat mysterious figure deeply interwoven into the fabric of Arizona history. He was an odd-looking man, described by Tom Horn, a scout who knew Free well, as the "wildest dare-devil in the world at the time. He had long, fiery red hair and one blue eye."[4] A frontier official who apparently despised him as a "half-breed" described him in less flattering terms: "He was of small stature, slim with long, tawny hair, straight, ragged and unkempt. . . . His appearance with a defective eye, his ugly features and sneering countenance, gave him a decidedly repulsive appearance."[5]

Born in Mexico of Sonoran parents, Free, then named Felix Telles, was taken by his mother to live in Arizona, where she moved in with John Ward, an Irish American rancher. Young Felix's stay on Ward's ranch was brief. In 1861 Aravaipa Apaches raided the ranch and captured the then thirteen-year-old boy. His kidnapping became the focus of a rescue effort that precipitated a decade-long war between Cochise and his Chiricahuas and the army that failed in its objective to free Felix. The boy would be traded by the Aravaipas to the White Mountain people. Raised by them, he was eventually accepted as a full member of the band. Like many captives, he fully adapted to Indian life and to his new family.[6] In 1872 John Bourke recruited the young man to serve as a scout in Crook's Tonto campaign, beginning Felix's long career in the army, where his linguistic skills secured him steady employment. Consequently, when Crook enlisted Felix in his Mexican campaign a decade later, the general would have been familiar with his qualifications, though he now knew him as Micky Free, so named by soldiers who, unable to pronounce his Apache name, gave him the nickname because of a fancied resemblance to a character in an Irish romantic novel. And Micky Free he would remain, both to his contemporaries and to history.[7]

Mickey Free, scout and interpreter. Courtesy of Arizona Historical Society.

Crook's scouts were enlisted for six-month terms and formed into two companies, each with twenty-six Apaches of the rank of private and four Apache noncommissioned officers, a first and second sergeant and two corporals, who were selected from among the chiefs and prominent members of their own bands. The scouts' assigned duty was to track down their dissident brethren and, where possible, talk them into surrender. But more often than not, they would take the lead in combat because they were usually the first troops on the scene.[8] When not on campaign, they performed a less commonly noted secondary function: gauging the mood and temperament of the reservation Indians and reporting back to their officers on the happenings in the now-dispersed camps about the reservation. Crook became so reliant on their intelligence that he supplemented it with an additional cadre of "secret scouts," including several women. This network, established at San Carlos by Captain Crawford, was charged with ferreting out any "indication of discontent or hostility" in the population. To enhance the network's effectiveness and protect its members from reprisal, their identity was kept closely guarded, even from one another, and they delivered their reports clandestinely at night, directly to the white officers who supervised them.[9]

A fundamental element in Crook's management style was his belief in self-governance on the reservation, which he held to be preparation for the Indians' future assimilation into white society. In line with this philosophy and to maintain order on the reservation, he continued the Indian agents' practice of establishing an Indian police force separate from the scouts, its membership selected from "among the best of their several tribes."[10] In addition to their normal police functions, they, too, were expected to report any signs of unrest among the reservation's population. Together with the scouts and secret scouts, they formed a well-developed and extensive intelligence-gathering network that greatly facilitated Crook's ability "to think like an Indian." Without the services provided by his Apache spies, the lives of his officers and men would have been at greater risk, and his effectiveness both in the field and on the reservation would have been severely curtailed.

One of the reasons Crook deployed such an elaborate intelligence network was his distrust of the Chiricahuas. Though he expressed empathy and admiration for most Apache peoples, from his early days in Arizona he characterized the Chiricahuas as "the worse band of Indians in America."[11] His negative attitude dated back to September 1871 when he led his troops into the Arizona desert seeking Cochise's band, which was then on the warpath. He hoped to establish a reputation for invincibility among the tribesmen by defeating the Chiricahuas, which in turn might hasten the surrender of all. But Cochise's people eluded his grasp, and his future efforts to bring them to heel were thwarted by the peace policies of the Grant administration and then by a separate peace negotiated with the chief by General Howard.[12] Frustrated and angry, Crook had denounced the tribe's depredations and the Howard agreement in his annual reports and in his correspondence with his superiors, and he later heaped scorn on Grant's peace emissary, Vincent Colyer, for allowing the Chiricahuas to be "subsisted and protected" (his words), alleging that they used their reservation as a base for their depredations.[13] In one of his dispatches he contemptuously (and inaccurately) described Cochise's followers as a "band of Indians [who] were originally made up of outlaws and the disaffected of the different adjacent tribes, confederated together for the purpose of murdering and robbing."[14] In reports during 1873 and 1874, he continued to complain bitterly of the freedom that the tribe enjoyed under Howard's agreement, devoting an entire paragraph of his annual report for 1873 to the subject. Not only had the Chiricahuas' frequent raids into Sonora and Chihuahua caused constant complications with the Mexican government, he declared, but they also fomented unrest among the Apache bands at San Carlos.[15] He found it especially galling, he said, that the Indians on the "Chiricahua," as he referred to the reservation, were not enrolled or counted, preventing the authorities from holding them accountable for their murderous conduct.[16]

Now, almost a decade later, events in 1882–83 seemed to confirm the Gray Fox's concerns. Once more on the warpath, based in their reputedly impregnable redoubt in the Sierra Madre Mountains of Mexico, they threatened Crook's hard-won peace in Arizona. When the Mexican consul in Tucson complained to the American government that Western Apaches were leaving San Carlos and raiding into Sonora, the general firmly corrected him. The Chiricahuas, he declared, and not the Indians on the reservation had committed these depredations, pointing to the head counts and tagging requirements he had instituted at San Carlos as conclusive proof that the reservation's residents had not been involved. And he could not resist the opportunity to mention to his superiors that he had a decade earlier "ventured . . . to predict what has since come true, that our people would have cause to rue the failure to put the Chiricahuas under strict yolk [sic]."[17]

Notwithstanding his abiding resentment and distrust of the Chiricahuas, Crook was committed to exploring a peaceful means to return the tribe to the reservation. In this he was undoubtedly influenced by the potential cost in human suffering of a military campaign into Mexico.

Such an operation would be a cruel and pitiless affair that might drag on for months, and the Chiricahuas, who had a great many women and children with them, would undoubtedly incur terrible casualties, as would his own troops. Yet Crook's primary motivation was practical rather than humanitarian. An experienced Indian fighter, he realized that there were major drawbacks that made a purely military solution a daunting and perhaps impossible objective.

A major obstacle was the Mexican government's historic unwillingness to permit American troops to operate south of the border. In July 1882 the United States had entered into an agreement with Mexico motivated by the two nations' mutual desire to eliminate the Apache threat. It sanctioned cross-border troop movements. But Mexico's suspicions of American intentions hedged the agreement with preconditions that, if literally interpreted, would hamstring the type of operation that Crook envisioned as essential. The agreement allowed troops to cross the border only when in hot pursuit of an enemy and only in unpopulated areas at least two leagues from any town or encampment on either side of the line. Further, if at all possible, prior notice to the nearest Mexican military command or civil authority was required before crossing the border, and certainly at the time of such transit. Worst of all in Crook's view, the agreement required that "the pursuing force shall retire to its own territory as soon as it shall have fought the band of which it is in pursuit or have lost its trail. In no case shall the forces of the two countries, respectively, establish themselves or remain in the foreign territory for any time longer than necessary to make the pursuit of the band whose trail they follow."[18] The general's own experience told him that such a narrow window was woefully inadequate. The terrain of northern Mexico and the Apaches' ability to maneuver in it precluded such a quick in-and-out operation. Only a dogged and prolonged pursuit, during which trails would be lost, regained, and lost again, would win the day. And such a campaign could only be carried out in the context of a carefully planned and executed operation over an extended period, an eventuality ruled out by the "hot-pursuit" doctrine.[19]

Even if the Mexicans were to permit a more extended operation by U.S. forces, locating and defeating the enemy in his mountain redoubt would be a fearsome task, requiring precise intelligence and a force

capable of fighting in incredibly challenging terrain. The Chiricahuas'
traditional refuge was located deep in the Sierra Madre, a range that
originates just south of the U.S. border at the New Mexico and Arizona line and extends about six hundred miles into central Mexico.
While the Indians were on intimate terms with every wrinkle and
dip of the range, for Crook and his troops, as historian Dan Thrapp
suggests, it would have been "a labyrinth of uncharted, unexplored,
and even unknown canyons, forests, defiles, gorges, and retreats, into
which no white man was ever reported to have penetrated." Thrapp
vividly describes the geology of the region:

> It is as though a huge wrinkle developed on the earth's surface,
> bending sheets of rock upward into a giant fold. Over eons of
> time, the arch of the wrinkle was worn away by water, wind,
> and time, and the packed formations tilted upright were eaten
> away to varying degrees, depending upon the resistance of the
> types of rock which composed them. The result is an interior
> fearfully rough and varied, a mass of ridges, gorges, bald rock,
> timbered recesses, and barren knobs, like the bared skeletons
> of dead animals.[20]

For troops to find the Indians in this maze, let alone fight them,
represented a huge and unknown challenge. Nor was terrain the only
issue. In assessing the prospects of a military campaign, Crook realized
he would be forced to deal with a skillful and ferocious foe whom he
described in one letter as "nothing but Malays running amok."[21] A less
colorful but perhaps more helpful description of the fighting qualities
of the Apaches comes to us from Frank Lockwood, a noted student
of their history. "They were," he writes, "endowed with great acute-
ness of perception; marked ingenuity in overcoming the asperities of
climate, soil, and topography; shrewdness in forecasting the actions
of their enemies and in coordinating their plans, though operating in
widely scattered bands over a vast region of the country."[22] Add to this
their superb physical conditioning, skill in the art of concealment and
ambush, and an astounding mobility that allowed them to travel from
seventy-five to one hundred miles in a twenty-four-hour period. Then
arm them with repeating rifles and you have the makings of a truly

formidable foe. In Crook's view, fighting such warriors, their instincts sharpened by desperation, would be a long and costly affair, both in men and material.[23]

Given such obstacles, the general believed that a negotiated peace was vastly preferable to risking his soldiers and reputation on a military campaign. Thus, at the end of September, probably on or close to his fifty-fourth birthday, he rode south from San Carlos to the Mexican border on a mission that combined a peace initiative with intelligence gathering. He was accompanied by a small contingent of Western Apache scouts and several Chiricahuas, friends and relatives of those tribesmen who had remained behind when Juh and Geronimo had led their followers off the reservation a year before. Their tales of a growing desire among some of their kin to return to San Carlos had aroused Crook's expectations, and at his urging they had agreed to try and contact the dissidents.[24] His objective, as he described it to his superiors, was to "locate [the tribe's] whereabouts and ascertain if they would be willing to come back and remain at peace upon the reservation." If they were not, he wrote, displaying a confidence that masked the grim reality of the situation, he would "enlist a sufficient no. of scouts to go over the line and clean them out."[25]

In this instance his initiative fizzled. The Chiricahuas he sent into Mexico returned quickly because, as Crook sardonically reported, "the Mexicans were having a revolution that week," and there were too many of their troops about. Fearing the Mexican army's habit of shooting Apaches on sight, the emissaries had deemed it prudent to beat a hasty retreat over the line. The mission did produce some intelligence. While on the border Crook's scouts intercepted two Chiricahua women returning to San Carlos who confirmed that the tribe was, as Crook suspected, camped deep in the recesses of the Sierra Madre, a safe distance from the border.[26]

In October and again in November, Crook sent additional Apaches into Mexico, hoping to learn more about the location of the tribe and, if possible, induce them to return peacefully to the reservation. These missions also failed to produce results, as his messengers were met with threats from the Chiricahuas whom they encountered, forcing them to retire precipitously back across the border.[27]

It was now clear to Crook that he would have to use military force, at least at the outset, to attain his objective. Although realistic about the difficulties involved, he yet remained optimistic about the possibility of success. Strangely, the remoteness and inaccessibility of the Chiricahuas' redoubt in the Sierra Madres offered him hope. Based on his long experience in Indian warfare, he knew that while Indians remained extremely vigilant when in actual contact with a foe, their wariness would often be dispelled when they believed their enemy to be at a safe distance. Thus, deep in the Sierra Madre, hidden in mountainous terrain never penetrated by the troops that had hunted them for generations, they might be vulnerable to the element of surprise. His use of scouts, Indians to fight Indians, gave him confidence that he would be able to make maximum use of this tactic.[28]

Though realistically planning for war, Crook had not given up his search for a peaceful resolution. In the latter part of October, he ordered Crawford and three scout companies to the border town of Cloverdale, Arizona, just north of the line dividing Sonora and Chihuahua. They were to patrol the boundary, watching for Apache raiders who might venture into Arizona. At the same time, the captain was to send spies south in a final attempt to locate and open communications with Juh's and Geronimo's bands. Three scouts rode sixty miles into Mexico but failed to make contact with the dissidents.[29]

While scouts vainly probed Sonora and Chihuahua in search of them, Juh and Geronimo raided throughout the Mexican countryside, acquiring food, horses, and supplies, and from time to time engaging in pitched battles with pursuing Mexicans. The savage fighting had taken its toll on the band. During the ten months following their breakout, they had lost an estimated 150 women and children killed or captured.[30]

The two leaders and their followers remained together until early winter 1882 but then split into separate parties. Juh, feeling the need to move deeper into the mountains for safety, led his people, more than half the tribe, to a site about fifty miles south of Geronimo's camp. There he was confident he would be secure from the Mexican authorities who rarely ventured into the high mountains in the wintertime.[31] He misjudged his enemy. At dawn on January 29, 1883, a volunteer force of Tarahumara Indians led by Mexican officers fell upon Juh's unsuspecting camp. Greatly feared by the Chiricahuas because of their persistence and cruel ferocity, the Tarahumaras fought mercilessly against their ancient enemies, inflicting heavy losses.[32] As was usual in such frays, few warriors were killed, but several prominent leaders whose families had been with Juh—among them Chatto, Geronimo, and Naiche—suffered devastating losses. Juh himself lost his wife, and his only daughter was wounded. The attack dealt his prestige a terrible blow from which he never recovered. He sank into melancholy, began drinking heavily, and abandoned his role as a determining voice in tribal affairs, leaving Geronimo as the supreme authority in the tribe.[33] The disastrous defeat also strengthened the desire for peace among some of the less-militant Chiricahuas, particularly Loco's Warm Springs people, many of whom had only reluctantly left San Carlos because of Geronimo's threats.

Crook learned of Juh's defeat and the ensuing losses from relatives of the dissidents who had remained on the reservation. The information strengthened his resolve to go into Mexico, as he suspected that the attack had further weakened the band's resolve to fight on.[34] While Geronimo and a hardcore group of his followers might continue to resist, the majority could well be persuaded to peacefully return to San Carlos.

But several preconditions remained to be fulfilled before Crook could launch his expedition. The hot-pursuit agreement with the Mexicans required a trigger, an incident that would allow American troops to cross the border. Further, since he had no intention of limiting his operations to the narrow confines stipulated in the diplomatic agreement, Crook needed an understanding with the Mexican authorities that they would not interfere if and when his campaign exceeded the terms of the hot-pursuit doctrine. Of equal importance, he required authority from his superiors to undertake such a diplomatically risky venture. And, finally—and critical to the success of the enterprise—he had to determine the whereabouts of his quarry.[35]

At this juncture events unfolded that would resolve most of these issues. In late winter of 1882–83, Geronimo's band camped in Sonora near the town of Fronteras, not far from the U.S. border, awaiting spring's arrival so they could replenish their stocks of food and ammunition. In early March, as the desert began to bloom, Geronimo unleashed his warriors in a two-pronged offensive for that purpose. He and Chihuahua, a noted Chokonen subchief, led the bulk of his men south on a raid along the Sonora River. He directed Chatto (Broken Nose), a stocky, brash young warrior, to lead a simultaneous lightning

Geronimo (*mounted left*), Bedonkohe shaman who became leader of the dissident Chiricahuas; and Naiche (*mounted right*), son of Cochise and chief of the Chiricahuas. Photo taken by C. S. Fly, Tombstone photographer, circa 1886. Courtesy of Mark Kasal.

strike into Arizona to seize livestock, arms, and ammunition and to gather the latest news from San Carlos. Chatto's second in command was Benito (Bonito), a White Mountain Apache who had participated in the Cibicue fight and then, fearing retribution from the army, joined Geronimo in Mexico. Among the best of Geronimo's men, these two led a formidable group of twenty-four other prominent young warriors that included Naiche and Mangas, the sons of Cochise and Mangas Coloradas.[36]

Heading north toward the border, Chatto's raiders killed several Mexicans and expatriate American ranchers before passing swiftly and unobserved through the Huachuca Mountains into Arizona on March 20. Over the next six days they pursued a four-hundred-mile rampage through Arizona and New Mexico, murdering eleven whites and gathering horses, weapons, and ammunition to resupply the band. They then slipped back across the border into Mexico, taking with them a six-year-old captive, Charlie McComas, the son of a prominent New Mexico judge and his wife whom they had slain in their final attack on U.S. soil. In the process the raiders lost only one warrior, Beneactiney,

Chatto, Chiricahua warrior who later became one of the foremost of Crook's scouts.
Courtesy of the Arizona Historical Society.

Chihuahua, Chokonen subchief and Apache war leader. Courtesy of Mark Kasal.

Chihuahua's son-in-law. The death of this single man would have unanticipated but momentous consequences for the Chiricahuas.[37]

Chatto's raid, and in particular the murder of the McComas couple and the kidnapping of their young son, aroused the Anglo population in the Southwest and, indeed, the entire nation, contributing to a swelling chorus of criticism directed at Crook and the army and renewing cries for the extermination of the Apaches. Tucson's *Arizona Star* demanded that "these bloodthirsty savages," by which the paper meant not only the raiders but also all Apaches in Arizona, "be annihilated or removed." The *Phoenix Herald* warned, "If the military cannot suppress them . . . it is the proper thing for the citizens to take the matter in their own hands." The *Tombstone Epitaph,* long a critic of the army in general and Crook in particular, blamed the raid squarely on the general, claiming he and his soldiers had been sequestered safely at Fort Whipple and other posts throughout the territory while the Indians plundered and murdered the citizens. Like the *Herald,* the *Epitaph* advocated citizen intervention.[38]

The papers reported that some of the raiders had worn red headbands like those of Crook's scouts, who had begun wearing such headbands at the request of Mexican officials, to allow their troops to distinguish the Indians from hostile Apaches.[39] Since the Cibicue affair attitudes toward the enlistment of Apaches in the army had soured, few recalling their contribution to the success of Crook's campaign against the Tontos. Arizonans now pointed to the headwear as evidence that the scouts had participated in the raid and called for their expulsion along with all the other Apaches in the territory. The remote hint, no matter how farfetched, that the McComas tragedy had involved Crook's scouts fed the popular rage.[40]

Virulent personal attacks in the press and slurs directed against his troops were troubling to Crook, and insinuations against the scouts were especially galling since they threatened a vital resource in his campaign against the Chiricahuas. Yet he exercised diplomatic restraint in countering them. While he took care to refute the more dangerous canards, he diplomatically expressed his understanding of the fear and anger that gripped the population, even agreeing that, as the press insisted, the Chiricahuas were incorrigible.[41]

Perhaps one reason why the thin-skinned general weathered these attacks with such equanimity was that he secretly welcomed them.

Public outrage provided the *casus belli* he required to justify his planned foray into Mexico, meeting a necessary precondition for his campaign against the Chiricahuas. But he was politically savvy enough to take measures that would meet Arizonans' demand for domestic action to alleviate their anxiety. He issued a flurry of orders dispatching troops from throughout the department to the border in a declared attempt to interdict the raiders as they attempted to cross back into Mexico. Such deployments, tried many times in the past, rarely met with success. The Apaches were known to cross and recross the mountainous border like wisps of smoke, so it is likely that the troop movements were mostly for show.[42] In the end, as one journalist informed his readers, "Easily as the swallow darts through between the poles of a telegraph line, the elusive raiders slipped through the necessarily coarse meshes Crook had spread for them."[43]

Chatto's raid was a reminder of the ease with which the Chiricahuas could penetrate the international border and extend their depredations deep into New Mexico as well as Arizona, a threat that prompted Crook to coordinate defensive strategies with Colonel Ranald Mackenzie, New Mexico's military commander. On March 27, even before it was certain that Chatto's warriors had returned to Mexico, Crook hastened to Albuquerque to confer with Mackenzie.

Before departing Crook wired his superiors in Washington, making it clear that he intended to respond to Chatto's raid with a campaign into Mexico and asking for authorization to do so. The response came while he was still in Albuquerque. Framed in General Sherman's peremptory style but delivered through General John Schofield, the wire seemed to give Crook the broad discretionary authority he sought. Sherman directed that he was "to destroy hostile Apaches, to pursue them regardless of department or national lines, and to proceed to such points as you deem advisable," adding that Mackenzie "will cooperate to the fullest extent."[44] Read literally, the telegram authorized Crook to pursue the Indians wherever their trail led, and if it led outside the boundaries of his department, including into Mexico, so be it. Perhaps that is how Sherman intended it at the time.

Having completed his discussions with Mackenzie and with Schofield's wire in hand, Crook boarded a night train for the return trip to Arizona, disembarking in Willcox, the railhead near the border where he intended to mass his troops and launch his expedition into Mexico.[45]

It was there that he received a telegram from Britton Davis containing information vital to the coming campaign. There had been a defection in the ranks of the raiders.

As Davis would later recount, on the night of March 28 he received word at his camp at San Carlos of the murder of Judge McComas and his wife. The killing had taken place near Silver City, New Mexico, not far from the Arizona border. As the raiders were reported to be riding west from there, they were thought to be headed for San Carlos to induce some of the more dissatisfied Indians to join them, and they would arrive within a day or so. Based on these reports Davis considered that "the massacre of all the whites at the agency was not at all improbable." As a result, for the next two nights he "slept with one eye and half the other open." About midnight on the second evening, he awoke to the sound of someone stealthily entering his room. Leveling his revolver at the shadowy figure, he was prepared to fire when the man identified himself as one of his secret spies. Breathlessly, the man whispered, "Chiricahua come!"[46]

Unsure of how many Chiricahuas were coming, Davis rounded up his scouts and went to investigate. To his relief, it turned out that he was dealing with a single warrior, a White Mountain Apache named Tzoe, who was married to a Chiricahua. Tzoe, known to the soldiers at San Carlos and to history as Peaches because of his light, smooth complexion, was a member of Chatto's raiding party.[47] After his best friend, Beneactiney, had been slain, Peaches claimed to have lost his desire to fight. Lonely and bereft, he felt that he could no longer remain with the Chiricahuas and so had returned to the reservation to be with his family.[48]

As Peaches expressed willingness to share his extensive knowledge about the raiders with the military, Davis immediately contacted Crook at Willcox and then brought the defector there to meet him. The young warrior proved a fount of intelligence about the Apaches' life in Mexico: their strength, their weaponry, and the current mood in their camps.[49] Crook found the information about the state of Apache morale of particular interest. It confirmed earlier rumors that some of the Chiricahuas, tiring of the fugitive life, were prepared to quit the warpath and return to the reservation. Peaches told the general that while in Arizona, Chatto had sent two members of his party to contact Merejildo Grijalva, a former Apache captive and army scout, to sound out reservation attitudes toward the dissidents.[50] So it appeared that even the most hardened warriors were reaching out to learn what kind of reception they could expect should they return to San Carlos. Perhaps the most important information that Peaches conveyed was his readiness to guide the general to Geronimo's camp in the recesses of the Sierra Madre and his confidence that it could be taken by surprise.

Davis had taken the precaution of transporting the Apache to Willcox in irons. But the general was so impressed by both the detailed manner and the sincerity of the man's presentation that he enthusiastically offered to strike off the prisoner's bonds immediately and enlist him as a scout. The warrior demurred, saying that "he would prefer to wear shackles until his conduct should prove his sincerity." But Crook would not be denied. He had the irons removed on the spot. And in that moment, Peaches "was installed in the responsible office of guide of the contemplated expedition."[51]

With a casus belli, his superiors' authorization to go forward, and a guide to Geronimo's camp in hand, Crook lacked but one element to launch his campaign: the consent of the Mexican government to exceed the limits of the agreement with the Americans. A formal relaxation of the convention's stringent requirements for hot pursuit would require a legislative enactment by Mexico's congress, a remote possibility given the suspicion with which that government regarded its northern neighbor. To circumvent such a time-consuming and likely fruitless process, Crook hit upon the idea of meeting with his local Mexican counterparts in Chihuahua and Sonora to obtain their informal agreement to achieve the same result on the local level. As both states had long suffered from the depredations of the Chiricahuas without appreciable help from their central government, he suspected that local military officials would be receptive to his overtures. Such meeting would have the added purpose of apprising local authorities of his planned campaign, allowing them to keep their troops out of his way and avoid clashing with his scouts.[52]

On April 8, without informing his superiors in Washington, who undoubtedly would have found it difficult to approve, Crook boarded a train south to Guaymas, the railway's Sonoran terminus. There, he conferred with Major General Bonafacio Topete, the Sonoran officer in charge of the state's operations against the Apaches, and his superior, Major General Guillermo Carbo, the overall commander of the

Sonoran military zone.[53] Accompanying Crook were aides Bourke and Roberts and Lieutenant Gustav J. Fiebeger, the engineering officer who would map out Crook's route through the unexplored regions of the Sierra Madre. Bourke, as usual, faithfully recorded the substance of the meetings between Crook and the two Mexican officers as well as additional discussions with officials in Chihuahua.

In both states Crook solicited the cooperation of the local American consul, whom he later credited with rendering him "valuable assistance." The nature of that assistance must have been purely logistical since there was little of substance for the consul to contribute. From the outset it appears that the general knew exactly what he expected to accomplish, and for their part the Mexicans seemed to have been in full accord with his objectives. All present, Mexican and American, had experienced the horrors of Apache warfare, and as Crook had anticipated, local Mexican officials were more than willing to look the other way while the Americans attacked the problem. Perhaps Crook mentioned the consuls in his report to mollify the State Department, the government entity that would normally take the lead in such diplomatic initiatives.[54]

General Carbo was a sophisticated officer. He recognized that elimination of the Apache threat required noninterference from his own troops and meant giving the American general considerable latitude to operate on Mexican soil. He knew that the current agreement was far too restrictive to give Crook that latitude. But though he sympathized with his American counterpart's dilemma, he also had to contend with his own lack of authority to unilaterally alter those terms. He resolved his conundrum with carefully phrased wordplay: "He would impose no objection [to Crook's operations in Mexico], provided his superiors made none." He went on to suggest that the two governments should reopen negotiations to correct "the imperfections of the present agreement." In the meantime, "should General Crook find it necessary to cross the Border before these changes had been perfected," he asked that the general's Indian allies "wear a distinctive badge" to distinguish them from the hostile Apaches—the red headbands referred to in the Arizona press. In addition, he asked that Crook keep his subordinate, Major General Topete, fully apprised of his operations.[55]

Having achieved the hoped-for results, Crook journeyed to the Sonoran port of Hermosillo to meet with Don Felizardo Torres, the governor of the state. The American general was warmly received and feted at an elaborate state dinner and ball. The next morning he and Torres reached an understanding that the governor, too, would refrain from interfering with the American's operation in the state. Having gotten what he came for, Crook wasted no time in returning to Arizona before the Sonorans changed their minds.

On April 13 the general headed south once again, this time to Chihuahua, where he again met with local army officials as well as the mayor of the Chihuahua city, from whom he received assurances similar to those he had been given in Sonora.[56] Only after returning from this second visit to Mexico on April 18 did Crook inform Sherman of his foray into international diplomacy. All parties had agreed, he informed the presumably startled general, that "a literal construction of the terms of the present agreement will bring about failure in the settlement of pending Indian hostilities." Hence, Crook stated, it was "all important that we on the ground be permitted to vary these stipulations to the extent required by the best interest of the two Governments." Should his advice not be heeded, he warned, "troops on both sides" would be powerless to prevent "another blood curdling raid." Looking to ensure a prompt reply from Sherman, he added that he would be beyond reach of telegraph within ten days. Crook was clearly emboldened by his diplomatic successes in Mexico, convinced of the correctness of his position, and confident of success. He now had the bit firmly between his teeth.[57]

Why Sherman waited a full ten days to respond is not known. But his dispatch reached Crook at the Slaughter Ranch at San Bernardino Springs on the Mexican border on April 28, two days before his planned departure into Mexico. In tone and content the commanding general expressed strong dissatisfaction with his subordinate's high-handed manner and his plan to mount a campaign in Mexico that defied the international agreement between the United States and Mexico. Sarcastically referring to the fact that he had been forced to learn of Crook's proposed expedition from the newspapers, Sherman tartly informed him that "the Secretary of War deems it proper to instruct you that *no* military movements must be made into, or within the Territory of Mexico, which is not authorized by the agreement [Sherman's emphasis]. . . . Negotiations for modifying [the agreement] now going on with Mexican Government but it cannot be inferred that Gov't will assent to any modification."[58] In a series of articles later published in *Outing Magazine* in 1885 and ultimately reprinted as *An Apache Campaign in the Sierra Madre,* Bourke would write that Sherman's message ordering Crook to conform his operations to the terms of the agreement "left him [Crook] as much in the dark as before." As Sherman's wire appeared entirely unambiguous, one can surmise that the good captain was simply trying to protect his general's rear.[59]

Crook's replied to Sherman in a wire dramatically datelined "in the field, San Bernardino Springs." He knew that the campaign he contemplated, an operation whose details he had not shared with the commanding general, rendered meaningless the concept of hot pursuit embodied in the agreement. Nevertheless, in his telegram to Sherman he disingenuously declared that his mission to Mexico had not been intended to circumvent the understandings between the two governments: "My object was to arrange for cooperation and in case my troops followed hostiles into Mexico, *to see if I could not secure a literal* [perhaps he meant liberal] *interpretation of the terms of the agreement in regard to the time I could be allowed to remain*" (author's emphasis).[60]

Crook willingness to ignore Sherman's clear orders to adhere to the agreement stemmed from his confidence in the ultimate success of the enterprise. If he succeeded, he was gambling that his violation of the agreement would go unmentioned by either government. Yet he knew that if he failed, the army would disavow his actions and most probably terminate his career. At that moment, as historian Dan Thrapp writes, "Crook was a man on a limb, sawing furiously and hoping to get back successfully before the limb fell."[61] On April 30 Crook sent Sherman his final message: "It is my intent to start tomorrow morning in pursuit of the savages in accordance with the treaty."[62] For a career military officer approaching fifty-five, an age when many professionals are already contemplating retirement, Crook's decision to undertake such an expedition marked him as an officer of both great courage and enormous self-confidence.

CHAPTER ELEVEN

Into the Sierra Madre

Adhering to the schedule that he had shared with Mexican officials in Sonora and Chihuahua, Crook intended May 1 as the jump-off date for his departure into Mexico.[1] On April 23, in what Bourke described as a "disagreeable sandstorm," the general had set out on a five-day march south from the Southern Pacific Railway to his base camp at a ranch on the border at San Bernardino Springs. With him were his scouts, a small contingent of troopers, and, of course, his pack trains carrying the supplies needed for the expedition. Captain Crawford joined him there with a hundred additional scouts and another mule train. The number of Apache scouts under Crook's command now totaled 193.[2] It was at San Bernardino Springs that he received Sherman's wire, and on April 30 he dispatched his final reply to him and wired the government of Mexico to announce his imminent departure.[3]

Later that day he called his scouts and their leaders together for a talk. The scouts were recruited primarily from the White Mountain, San Carlos, and Tonto Apache bands, together with a sprinkling of Yavapais. As they would serve as the bulk of his force and the backbone of the campaign, Crook wanted to ensure they clearly understood what was expected of them.[4] Standing in ranks in the open air, the scout companies presented a deceptively ragtag appearance, having substituted field garb for the uniforms they normally wore in garrison. They were now clad in loose-fitting calico shirts of various colors and baggy cotton pants that reached down to their moccasins. Many had been

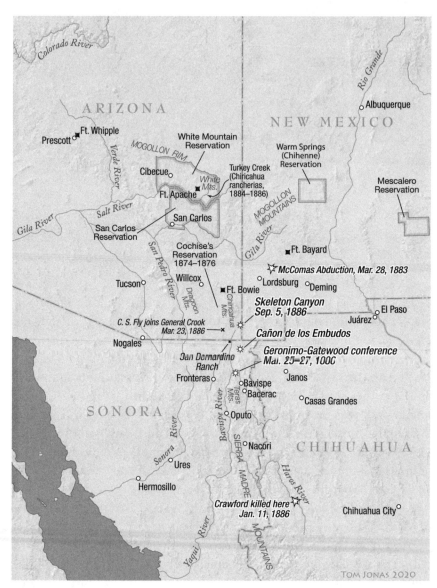

Arizona, New Mexico, and Old Mexico showing locations and events, Geronimo campaigns, 1883–1886. Map by Tom Jonas.

on the march for some time, and their clothing showed hard wear—
except for their moccasins. These they had resoled for the expedition.
Experienced desert campaigners, the Indians regarded their footwear
as the most critical item of apparel. Though they used horses on raids
when rapid mobility was desirable, more typically, because of the difficult desert and mountain terrain, they preferred traveling on foot. Hot
deserts and stony mountain trails made walking barefoot an unpalat-
able option, even for these hardened warriors, making moccasins a
necessity. These they had adapted over the centuries to suit their environment. To protect from spikes and spines of the desert flora, they
were fashioned with buckskin leggings reaching to mid-thigh. When
the men were on the march, the leggings were tied off below the knee
and folded over, so that they hung loose about the leg for freedom of
movement. The sole also differed from an ordinary moccasin, cut so
that it extended beyond the big toe and turned upward, protecting the
wearer's toes from thorns and sharp stones.[5]

Each scout was armed with a Springfield breech-loading rifle and a
knife described by contemporaries as a butcher knife. Around his waist,
he wore a cartridge belt, which, in addition to holding forty rounds,
also held the warrior's shirt and pants in place. For this expedition
the scouts had been issued lengths of red flannel that they fashioned
into headbands to distinguish them from their Chiricahua quarry. This
innovation would prove so useful that it became a standard part of their
uniform. Apaches on the warpath carried little on their persons other
than their weapons: the only exceptions were the small buckskin medicine bags tied to their waists. These contained amulets and fetishes to
protect the wearers from various evils and a small quantity of Hoddentin, a sacred pollen that symbolized life and renewal and was used
in most Apache rituals.[6]

For the meeting Crook and his officers seated themselves beneath a
large canvas that provided shade from the burning sun. Arrayed before
them were the scout companies' first sergeants, backed by their second
sergeants. Behind them stood the ranks of each company.[7] The scouts'
dark eyes focused intently on the Gray Fox, their expressions betraying nothing of their thoughts as they listened to his words, translated
by Mickey Free from English into his ungrammatical Spanish and
then repeated by Severiano in the Apache tongue.[8] Crook leaned forward and asked, "Do you think we will find [the Chiricahuas]?" One

sergeant boldly answered in the negative. The Chiricahuas were like coyotes and could smell danger a long way off, he said. Crook waited patiently for the translation and then, unperturbed, replied:

> I think we are going to catch these Chiricahuas, all of them, and we are going to keep after them till we catch them all. We have orders from Washington where the President lives to catch these Chiricahuas. We are all wearing the President's clothes now and eating his grub, and I want you to help him. . . . I am the man in charge of all this outfit and now I am going to sign my name on this paper so that even if I get killed, the President will still know what we all did and the record won't be lost. Thus, no matter if I die or live, the government will know that it must reward you.[9]

The scouts greeted Crook's words with approval. Though remuneration was important to them, many among them had additional, more traditional, motives for volunteering to serve against the Chiricahuas.[10] Particularly among the San Carlos and White Mountain bands, there were many who bore grudges against Geronimo and his followers for slaying friends and relatives as well as a widely regarded White Mountain police chief the year before. They regarded Crook's campaign as a means to avenge their losses, a matter of great importance in Apache culture. More than a simple emotional response to an injury or loss, revenge had a religious connotation. Raids undertaken for that purpose were preceded by ritual and ceremony, including a war dance held the night before a raiding party departed. The dance dramatized the warfare to follow and provided an opportunity for each warrior to pledge his courageous participation. Al Sieber, attuned to the doings of his scouts, knew of his scouts' desire for revenge and relayed the information to Crook. The latter, fully aware of its importance, used the custom to his advantage.[11] To allow the scouts to honor their tradition, Crook ended his meeting with the scouts by ordering them to hold a dance that evening, which they did.[12]

At sunrise on May 1 Lieutenant Gatewood gave the command: "Ugashe." The scouts "started as if shot from a gun," fanning out rapidly in a broad skirmish line, moving in "a rough shambling walk," a deceptively leisurely pace that in reality easily covered four miles an hour.[13] They were followed in short order by General Crook astride his mule, Apache, leading the small force of army regulars he had chosen to accompany the expedition: forty-two troopers from the Sixth Cavalry commanded by Captain Adna Chaffee and two subordinates, Lieutenants Frank West and William W. Forsyth. Five separate pack trains driven by Crook's experienced packers brought up the rear. A force under Major James Biddle remained behind at the border base camp in reserve. They were to guard Crook's flanks and rear and, in coordination with the troops garrisoning posts in the interior, form a cordon at the border to protect the settlements should the Apaches attempt to circle back around the expedition and go on the offensive.[14]

The column's destination lay approximately two hundred miles south of the border, deep in the Sierra Madre, the rugged mountain range that formed the north-south border between Chihuahua and Sonora. Crook anticipated that it would take about sixty days to travel to the Chiricahua camp, accomplish the mission, and return. Like the scouts, the officers and regular soldiers traveled light, as was Crook's custom. Rations were meager: salt pork, beans, bread, and coffee, supplemented by whatever game the men could shoot along the way. The scouts would carry and cook their own rations, while the officers and men messed with the packers. The packers' cook, a former teamster, was less than an accomplished chef, but complaints were muted after he threatened to "kick a lung" out of any man who grumbled about his fare.[15]

Fiebeger and Bourke were allotted a mule between them to carry their "bedding, etc." Bedding was one blanket, and the "etc." was sixty days' ration of hard bread, coffee, and bacon, one hundred and forty rounds of ammunition per man, and a single change of flannel shirt and underwear. Notwithstanding these severe limitations, the column required seventy-six packers and 266 mules to meet its needs, the bulk of their loads being fodder and grain for the livestock. The train was divided so that each company had its own mules, identifiable by the unique cut of their manes and tails.[16]

As the column disappeared into the dust and heat haze of northern Mexico, to the world outside his command Crook seemed to have dropped off the ends of the earth. He would not be heard from again for another forty-one days, leaving behind him a citizenry that was far from confident that he would survive.[17] Though the general's use of Apache scouts was widely recognized as the basis for his success during his earlier campaigns, the so-called Cibicue mutiny had cast a thick cloud of suspicion and fear over their service. Many who heard of Crook's plan to lead a force into Mexico that included over three times as many Apaches as white troops regarded it as a foolhardy exercise and predicted the direst consequences. It was not long after the column's departure that the newspapers carried word from "a reliable citizen" in Tombstone that the scouts had mutinied and massacred nearly the entire command. Sheridan, who had heard such tales before, was said to have promptly advised a reporter following up on the story that he placed little credence in it—less, in fact, than he would to a report that the "column had met defeat at the hands of the hostiles." Generals Grant, Schofield, and Howard, all familiar with Crook's style of campaigning, also scoffed at such "news."[18]

Crook never doubted his scouts' loyalty and cast the doubters as disgruntled Anglos who had not been selected to scout for the column. In newspaper interviews granted before his departure, he had tried to allay concerns about the scouts and reassure the public by conveying his own sense of confidence, which was firmly rooted in long experience. His present force contained many of the same Western Apaches and San Carlos warriors he had recruited for his 1873 campaign against the Tontos and Hualapais, their loyalty now reinforced by their desire for vengeance against the Chiricahuas.[19] Praising the scouts' qualities, he told a journalist, "Our people cannot teach them anything about the kind of war we have in this country. . . . They are as full of fidelity to a man in whom they have confidence, and I would trust myself with them as readily as I would with regular soldiers; much more readily in such work as I now have on hand."[20] After the campaign had concluded, he felt free to add another factor that ensured their loyalty. As he told a reporter for the *New York Herald,* the scouts all had families camped around San Carlos or Fort Apache who were, in effect, hostage to their good behavior. Perhaps embarrassed by the unseemly nature of this assertion, he hastily added, "I have often been out with Indian scouts when I really had no hold upon them except the confidence which they had in me."[21]

For the first three days the column followed the narrow confines of the San Bernardino River valley, traveling south through country long depopulated by Apache raids stretching back to the days of the

Spaniards. The men marched under a blazing sun past abandoned villages, farm fields and pastures overgrown with mesquite, and riverbanks choked by thick stands of cane and matted sacaton. This coarse grass, native to alkaline soil, formed an impenetrable barrier that forced the column away from the flat riverbed and onto the surrounding steep slopes. On this higher ground the troops' progress was impeded by numerous ravines filled with spiked and thorny vegetation, their menace concealed by gorgeous spring plumage. Footprints of an occasional Apache moccasin were the only signs of human life, though the countryside was home to small game and an unpleasant number of large rattlesnakes.[22]

For three more days they labored south along the San Bernardino to its confluence with the Bavispe River, where they found their first signs of human habitation: the squalid and ancient hamlets of Bavispe and Basaraca. With the scouts in the lead, the column entered Bavispe under the fearful gaze of the residents, who brightened perceptibly at the sight of uniformed soldiers.[23] Crook chose not to halt but continued south a few more miles to Basaraca, where the town's impoverished inhabitants, clad in ragged and dingy clothing, lined the rooftops and streets to welcome them. Long the prey of Apache raiders who had reduced them to a miserable state of fear and want, they viewed Crook as their rescuer. They reported recent depredations in the neighborhood and pledged their cooperation, offering to provide local guides if needed. The general politely declined, saying he lacked the resources to feed them; he later confessed that he was also skeptical of their usefulness. He did not believe "that any guides could be equal to those which we had been following.[24]

That evening the residents of Basaraca held a *baile,* or dance, to entertain the column. Judging from the descriptions of the event provided by the attendees, the villagers' dire poverty did not allow for lavish entertaining. But mescal, a liquor brewed by the villagers from the maguey cactus, was plentiful, and Bourke enlivened the affair by teaching the village orchestra to play the old Mexican standby "La Paloma."[25] Marching out of Basaraca the next morning, the captain recorded that there were "many swelled heads among the packers," a testament to the potency of the mescal.[26]

Despite their hangovers the column made eighteen to twenty miles the next day before camping at a ranch called Tesorabibi, abandoned years before as the result of Apache depredations. This would be their last camp before entering the foothills of the Sierra Madre. During the sunlight hours of the following day, May 7, they rested in preparation for the arduous journey that lay ahead, waiting for nightfall to cloak their advance into the mountains. As they rested they were visited by Mexican officers who informed the bemused Americans that they planned a scout into the Sierra Madre in the next week with a force of some four hundred men.[27] Crook never mentioned this encounter in his official report, perhaps because he discounted the value of the officers' information.

As darkness fell, the column set out on the final and most difficult stage of its journey, the scouts in the lead. Upon entering the Sierra Madre foothills, the expedition encountered a succession of rough, oak-clad slopes crisscrossed by numerous ravines. It was called to an abrupt halt when several of the scouts ran to Crook's side, declaring their unwillingness to proceed. A photographer and journalist accompanying the expedition, A. Franklin Randall, had captured a young owl, which he now displayed on the pommel of his saddle. Unversed in Apache lore, he had unwittingly precipitated a crisis. Regarded as the material incarnation of ghostly spirits, the owl was greatly feared by the tribesmen.[28] The bird's presence on Randall's saddle horn would bring extreme bad luck down upon the expedition. Crook wisely ordered the bird released and the march resumed.[29] Three days later five pack mules plunged off a mountain trail and were killed. One of them carried Mr. Randall's photographic equipment, which was "smashed to smithereens." If any among the chroniclers of the expedition saw this as somehow connected to the owl, they failed to record it.[30]

The column now moved forward into the secluded and forbidding range that comprised the Chiricahuas' traditional refuge. To avoid detection and the possibility of ambush, caution became the watchword. In addition to traveling in darkness, Crook forbade the making of fires for the next several days unless absolutely necessary.[31] Only after they had entered a region of looming peaks and deep canyons that concealed their movements did they feel secure enough to travel during the daylight hours. With Peaches' guidance, they followed a narrow trail frequently used by the Chiricahuas to drive stolen livestock into the mountains. The steep path was littered with the carcasses and skeletons of cattle and horses slaughtered along the way, either for food or because they could no longer go on. The trail ran along the mountain-side with no barrier to break a fall, and each day mules lost their footing and slipped off the edge, tumbling end over end down precipitous slopes. Some could be recovered, but many others were lost, together with their irreplaceable loads.

"Climb! Climb! Climb!" Bourke scribbled in his diary on his second day in the mountains. The march was an ordeal for the white troopers. "Up the summit of one crest, only to learn that above it towered another, the country fearfully corrugated into a perplexing alternation of ridges and chasms." Two days later, he wrote:

> Up! Up! Up! Perspiration running from every brow, the trail zigzagging up the vertical, or almost vertical, slope of a ridge, very nearly a thousand feet above the water. "Look out!" comes the warning cry from those in the lead, and then those in the rear dodge nervously from the trajectory of some piece of rock which, dislodged by the feet of horses or men, has shot downward, gathering momentum each second as if shot from a catapult. To look at this country is grand; to travel in it is hell.[32]

Yet all around the white soldiers, the Indian scouts ran effortlessly up and down ridges, ferreting out the signs of the Chiricahua bands who had occupied this country only days before. Reminders of the enemy's presence appeared with unnerving frequency: the burnt embers of cooking fires, places where they slept or held a dance, a flat stone on which the women had pounded acorns into flour, a rawhide rope, the occasional live pony—and everywhere the scattered horns and bones of cattle and horses. Most affecting were the grisly remnants of a recent battle between Mexican and Apache forces in which the Mexicans seemed to have received a severe drubbing.[33]

On the afternoon of May 10 signs indicated that the Chiricahuas were not far ahead, and in this terrain an ambush or an accidental blunder into the enemy's camp seemed likely. To prevent these eventualities and knowing that the scouts could travel far more rapidly and silently than his troopers, Crook ordered Crawford and Gatewood to accompany one hundred and fifty scouts forward to "scour the country in front and on our flanks." He planned to follow at a slower pace with the remainder of the column.[34]

As the scouts prepared to depart, Crook delivered a brief lecture to them, laying out the rules of engagement. Knowing they thirsted for revenge, he cautioned that only if the Chiricahuas refused to submit should they slay them. The scouts argued that they should put the leaders, miscreants like Geronimo, to death even if the rest surrendered. Crook replied that if the Chiricahuas fought, the scouts could not kill enough to suit him, but he cautioned that they should spare the women and children and grant mercy to all who asked for it, adding, "We should take prisoners back to San Carlos and there teach them how to behave themselves."[35]

At dawn the next day the advanced party set out, rationed for four days. The rest of the expedition—the troopers, a small contingent of scouts, and the pack trains—remained in place. Crook established strong picket posts on the surrounding hills and then, characteristically, he eased his inner tensions by striding off into the bush to shoot birds. Perhaps his men wondered at this, given the extraordinary measures they had taken to conceal their presence from the enemy, but no one appears to have raised the point. That evening a message arrived from Crawford that he had encamped after a march of twelve miles.[36]

The general started out early the next morning, amid ever-freshening signs of a strong Chiricahua presence. Rounding a bend in the trail, the column met Gatewood returning from the advance party leading several ponies they had captured along the way, a further indication of the foe's proximity. As they continued forward, Peaches pointed out a natural amphitheater, a stronghold that Geronimo had only recently abandoned. A glance satisfied Crook that it would have cost him a hundred men to take it had the enemy not left of their own accord. He decided to camp on the spot, taking advantage of the protection it afforded, and remain there with the pack trains and troopers while Crawford's scouts continued ahead to search out the enemy's rancheria.

On the afternoon of May 14, while still in the amphitheater, Crook received a message from the captain. He had discovered a rancheria showing signs of recent occupation. Peaches had inspected the ground and, based observation and knowledge of the band's habits, concluded that the main body of Indians was now marching toward a mountain retreat about three days beyond Crawford's present position. The captain asked that Crook bring his troops to the rancheria that evening, while he (Crawford) scouted the country ahead in preparation for the column's arrival. He believed that the Chiricahuas remained unaware of the column's presence.[37]

At first light the next morning, Crook moved his force out on Crawford's trail. They had marched for ten miles through sooty, scorched terrain when they encountered two packers bearing another message from Crawford. He had come upon the Chiricahuas' rancheria. But before he could surround it, the Indians had been alerted to his presence when one of the scouts prematurely discharged his weapon, and they had scattered into the mountains with the scouts in pursuit. As Crook absorbed this information, the sound of distant gunfire told him that the scouts had now engaged the enemy, and he promptly ordered the regulars to ride to their assistance.

Their presence proved unnecessary. Crawford and his scouts scored a decisive victory on their own. In a fight that lasted for several hours, nine of Geronimo's warriors were killed without the loss of a single member of Crawford's force. John Rope recalled that almost all of the Chiricahua dead were males, though a vengeful scout had cut down an old woman in cold blood, despite the vehement objections of his White Mountain comrades. In addition to the casualties inflicted, the scouts recovered a great deal of booty and captured four children and a young woman later identified as Bonito's daughter.[38]

The old woman turned out to be an aunt of the band's subchief, Chihuahua. Her death would have tragic consequences, as it resulted directly in the murder of young Charlie McComas, whose rescue had been one of the campaign's chief objectives. A search of the Chiricahuas' camp and its environs after the fight had failed to disclose any clue to the child's whereabouts, though several of the captured Chiricahuas admitted that he had been with the band up until then. His fate remained a source of speculation for over seventy years, until the last surviving member of the band, Betzinez, wrote a memoir in 1959 that revealed the truth. The son of the murdered woman, enraged by his mother's senseless death, had dashed the little boy's brains out with a rock immediately following the attack. The body, hidden among the rocks, was never found.[39]

Though most of the band escaped during the fighting, the scouts took justifiable pride in the fact that they, themselves, had suffered no casualties. As Bourke recorded in his diary, "This is the first time that the Chiricahuas have suffered so great a loss without inflicting any punishment whatever upon their assailants." Perhaps of even greater significance, the scouts' surprise attack had demonstrated that the tribe's Sierra Madre retreat was not the impregnable refuge they had thought. That their fellow Apaches had carried it out—and that one of their own had led the force to their lair—only added to the Chiricahuas' insecurity.[40] Crook had often said that when Indians realized that their own people would ally with an enemy against them, it would have a profoundly demoralizing effect. Ensuing events would show that, in this instance, his insight proved well grounded.

Crook questioned Bonito's daughter, the oldest of the captured children, regarding the bands' current state of mind. She, like Peaches, believed that her people were eager to make peace and return to San Carlos. She also informed him that at the time Crawford attacked the rancheria, most of the warriors had been raiding with Geronimo in Chihuahua, a circumstance that probably contributed substantially to the scouts' one-sided victory. To facilitate a peaceful resolution, she offered to arrange for a delegation of those who been in the rancheria to come in and talk to him.

Impressed with the young woman's sincerity, Crook believed her assertion that the band wanted to return in peace to the reservation.[41] In reality, because the Chiricahuas were now aware of his presence, peace talks with them remained one of his only available options. As he later described his predicament, "We could never hope to catch [the Indians] in the rugged peaks and the effort would surely cost the lives of many men, each rock being a fortress from behind which the Chiricahuas could fight to the death with their breech-loading guns."[42] Under the circumstances he could either attempt to convince the Indians to return peacefully to San Carlos or retreat to the border and try to surprise the band at a later date. Since he considered it unlikely that the Mexican government would permit a second U.S. expedition into their territory, the latter did not seem a realistic alternative.

Given these circumstances, Crook chose to negotiate, a difficult course at best that required the surrender of the most warlike and suspicious Indians in North America. The entire band would have to agree to the terms proposed. If only a few warriors chose to remain on the warpath, it was likely that his entire mission would be viewed as a failure. Even if all yielded and returned peacefully to San Carlos, he would still have to face a hostile populace that demanded the extermination of the Apaches or, at minimum, their expulsion from the territory.[43]

The day following the battle, May 16, Crook took up the challenge. Summoning Bonito's daughter to his tent, he instructed her to convey to the band's current ranking subchief the army's desire to return the Chiricahuas peacefully to San Carlos. To signal his respect for this as yet unidentified leader, he asked the young woman to present him with a fine horse captured from the band and an offering of tobacco.[44] A thin curl of smoke rising from the brow of a hill near the rancheria later that day signaled that the gift had been received. The next day, a little past noon, Severiano, the interpreter, reported the approach of two women carrying a white flag. One of them was the sister of a scout. She reported that the band had taken heavy casualties in the fight and that they had a young American captive whose description resembled that of little Charlie McComas. The women pointed to a white horse with a Mexican saddle that one of the scouts had captured during the fight. If Crook wanted Chihuahua, now identified as the leading subchief, to be his "friend," he should give them the horse. Crook promptly complied and she disappeared into the hills with it.[45]

Over the next two days a trickle of women and children came in to break bread with the scouts, who worked hard to put them at ease. On May 18 Chihuahua made his presence known. As John Rope recalled the scene years later, the proud warrior, who had served as Geronimo's second in command on a recent raid into Sonora, rode swiftly into the soldiers' camp astride a white horse, undoubtedly the one Crook had given to the woman two days before. The mount was adorned with strips of red cloth that fluttered from its tail and bridle, and its rider, emphasizing his readiness to make war, brandished a lance in one hand and carried two pistols ostentatiously thrust into his belt. Guiding the horse swiftly on a direct path to Crook's tent, he forced his way through a group of scouts seated beneath the branches of a large oak, scattering them and the troopers gathered in the vicinity. Reining the horse in front of the tent, he dismounted as the general emerged through the tent flap. The two men shook hands. At this point the description of events related by Bourke and Crook, the white officers, and John Rope, the Apache scout, diverged. According to the scout Chihuahua appeared angry. Without further preliminaries he demanded to know why Crook had killed his aunt, the old woman slain by the San Carlos scouts. "If I was trying to make friends with someone, I would not go and raid their camp and shoot their relatives," he declared. Crook's response, not included in Rope's reminiscence, must have partially mollified the chief, who then accepted an offer of food and tobacco from the officers before riding off as abruptly as he had come.[46]

Bourke and Crook painted a far more pacific, and less credible, portrait of the exchange. Describing Chihuahua as brave and intelligent, they credited him with expressing an earnest desire for peace. As Bourke recorded the event, "Chihuahua had a very pleasant talk with the commanding general, after which he was given permission to go out and hunt up the remnant of his band, promising he would have them back by tomorrow."[47] Crook and Bourke both stated that while Chihuahua complained bitterly about the Mexicans, he assured the officers that his people would be glad to make peace with the Americans, though, of course, he could not speak for Geronimo or his warriors. Crook added that Chihuahua said that the captive boy, Charlie McComas, was alive and well.[48] John Rope's description seems the more plausible. It may be that Crook found it expedient to exaggerate the subchief's willingness to make peace and to play down his arrogance in order to calm a jittery Anglo Arizona. More on that later.

Throughout the next day women, children, and elders continued to arrive in Crook's camp, but neither Chihuahua nor any of his warriors made an appearance. On Sunday, May 20, a "perfect avalanche" of women and children poured into the camp, their presence creating a pleasant and peaceful scene. However, men of fighting age remained conspicuously absent.[49] Their failure to appear and an over-arching concern about how Geronimo would react to Crook's peace initiative cast a long shadow. The infamous war leader was expected momentarily; in fact, many in the camp suspected that he had already arrived, causing widespread fear that he and his warriors would open fire on the troops before realizing that Crook had come in peace. To guard against that happening, Chiricahua women tore up flour sacks to make white flags that they posted throughout the camp as a sign of the soldiers' peaceful intent. But the wary scouts, leaving nothing to chance, built barricades of rocks and pine logs as cover in case of an attack.[50]

Before dawn on Sunday morning, several of the band's older women, convinced that Geronimo's warriors now lay concealed on the opposite slopes, climbed up on the ridges around the campsite and called out to them that Crook's men had come in friendship and should not be fired on.[51] Then, according to Bourke, at about eight o'clock in the morning "a fearful hubbub was heard" on the surrounding cliff tops. Armed Indians suddenly appeared against the skyline, "running about from crag to crag, evidently much perplexed and uncertain of what to do."[52] Fight, flight, or peace—all depended on Geronimo.

CHAPTER TWELVE

Geronimo—Hunter and Prey

Though neither a chief nor a subchief, Geronimo had become the undisputed leader of the Chiricahuas who had fled San Carlos the previous year, owing to both happenstance and his uncompromising and charismatic personality. Respected and feared for his courage and ruthlessness as a warrior and for his reputed supernatural endowments, he had been overshadowed by a cohort of Apache leaders of almost mythic stature throughout much of his life. This unusually brilliant constellation of personalities—Cochise, Victorio, Mangas Coloradas, and Juh—dominated the political and military affairs of the Chiricahuas during the middle decades of the nineteenth century. While closely allied with them, Geronimo remained very much a secondary character in the Apache story until the mid 1870s. Once these chiefs, with the exception of Juh, had passed away, they left behind a less-impressive generation of leaders. By then Geronimo's star had risen, bolstered by his military astuteness, his prowess in battle, his stubborn refusal to submit to the laws and strictures imposed by whites, and, perhaps most of all, his "power." The latter consisted of a mystical ability to see into the future and sometimes well beyond the immediate range of his senses. In addition, he was reputed to have several ancillary talents, including rainmaking and the ability to adjust time so that the night would last longer.[1] For a military leader, these talents were of incalculable value.

Throughout much of his career, the shaman had allied himself with Juh, a Nedni chief of great military prowess who was married to one of Geronimo's cousins.[2] A cocaptain with Juh during the 1882 breakout from San Carlos, Geronimo had finally assumed full command after Juh's stunning defeat and demoralization at the hands of the Tarahumaras.[3]

At the time of his encounter with Crook, the shaman looked younger than his sixty years. His muscular physique made him appear stocky, though in reality he was somewhat taller and heavier than the average Apache warrior, standing about five feet nine, a bit shorter than Crook, and weighing about 170 pounds. Contemporary whites often portrayed him in terms that mirrored his popular reputation in their world. Hence, in the year following the Sierra Madre campaign, a white Arizonan, on encountering the Apache leader, described him only as "vicious." Another saw his eyes as "keen and cruel" and found the lines in his face indicated a "superior degree of craftiness, and giving forth the idea of his cold, sneering character."[4] Greater objectivity seemed to prevail during his captivity, when he was regarded as more of a curiosity than a threat. Then, an officer found that he had "a good head, strong Apache features, a certain dignity and bearing, indicating a man of authority and self-respect."[5] There are many photos of the shaman, allowing modern readers to form their own mental image. But it requires no great imagination to see in his grim visage a life marked by great violence and equally compelling tragedy, the life of a man and a people who survived as both hunter and prey.

Much of the story of Geronimo's early life is found in his autobiography, recounted to S. M. Barrett, a white school superintendent in Lawton, Oklahoma, when the old Apache was in his eighties.[6] According to two of the most authoritative of the shaman's recent biographers, Robert Utley and Angie Debo, Barrett's book should be read with care, particularly those sections dealing with Geronimo's later years when he was at war with the United States. And parts of his tale seem obscure due to difficulties in translation, an Apache's different sense of chronology, and likely deliberate obfuscation. Yet the narrative of his youth, his life among his people before the whites came to Apacheria, and his early struggles with the Mexicans contains much that historians find accurate and illuminating.[7]

Geronimo, named Goyakla (He Who Yawns) in his youth, was most likely born in 1823 on the upper reaches of the Gila River into the Bedonkohe band, the smallest of the Chiricahua subtribes, one closely affiliated with the Chihennes or Warm Springs Apaches.[8] The Bedonkohes had been so reduced in number by the time of Goyakla's childhood that they merged with the Chihennes for protection. Thus, Goyakla grew to manhood under the chieftainship of Mangas Colora-das, a Bedonkohe who had married into the Chihennes and succeeded to leadership of both bands. Mangas was an extraordinary individual, both in his physical person and character. Well over six feet tall, pos-sessed of a matching physique and great intelligence, he was an aggres-sive warrior and a wise diplomat.

Under Mangas's leadership, Goyakla's boyhood years were spent in relative tranquility.[9] Nevertheless, he was trained from childhood to be a fighter, as were all young men in the tribe, and he participated in raids into Mexico. Following his father's death, which happened when he was probably still in his early teens, Goyakla assumed responsibil-ity for the care of his mother and siblings and married and started his own family.[10]

In 1850, while on a trading expedition in Mexico, the warriors, including Goyakla, left their women and children in camp and went into a nearby town to trade.[11] On returning to the rancheria, they discovered that Mexican troops had attacked and burned the camp, killing or capturing many of its occupants. Among the ashes of the wickiups Goyakla found the burnt corpses of his mother, his wife, and their three small children, scalped by the soldiers in order to claim the bounties offered by their government for dead Apaches.[12] The loss of his entire family devastated Goyakla and converted the historical enmity against the Mexicans that he shared with his people into a personal vendetta that spurred him to remorseless acts of violence against them throughout the rest of his fighting life.[13] Sometime after this tragic event, Goyakla, consumed with the desire to annihilate his enemies, is said to have acquired the name Geronimo, but its significance remains uncertain.

Though they vigorously continued their revenge raids against the Mexicans prior to the Civil War, Geronimo and his fellow Chirica-huas maintained an uneasy peace with the Anglos north of the bor-der. But this changed in 1863 when Geronimo's old mentor and ally,

Mangas Coloradas, was falsely accused of stealing livestock belonging to a group of Arizona miners who seized and brutally flogged him. Outraged and humiliated, Mangas declared war on the Americans and in alliance with Cochise terrorized the Southwest in the 1860s. After a decade of savage warfare, the aging chief, now in his seventies and tired of the incessant violence, attempted to negotiate a peace with the army. Instead he was taken prisoner and, on orders from the general who had taken him, treacherously murdered by soldiers "while trying to escape," and his corpse mutilated.[14] Mangas had been one of most important and beloved figures in Geronimo's life, and the shameful circumstances of the chief's death marked him indelibly.[15] He would later say that it was "perhaps the greatest wrong ever done to the Indians."[16]

Although Geronimo fought the Americans following the death of Mangas Coloradas, he did not receive his great notoriety north of the border until the mid 1870s, after the removal of the Chiricahuas to San Carlos. Not long after the move, instead of submitting to reservation life, he, Juh, and their followers fled the reservation and joined Victorio's band in their war against the whites. He was then officially labeled a renegade by the government and became infamous throughout the Southwest.[17] In the spring of 1877 he was captured through trickery by the Indian agent at San Carlos and spent four months in the agency guardhouse.[18] His sojourn in prison, like so many other incidents in the shaman's life, further honed his already guarded and suspicious nature. Fear of a second imprisonment has been cited as contributing to his decision to flee the reservation in 1882 in the aftermath of Cibicue.[19]

Geronimo's reputed mystical powers in no small part contributed to his rapid rise in leadership. Crook, who knew little about him before his flight into Mexico, may have been aware of the supernatural tales that surrounded him but likely regarded them with the skepticism that most whites reserved for the beliefs of Indian peoples. Perhaps he would have had second thoughts after learning why Geronimo's men had so abruptly broken off the raid in Chihuahua and returned to their Sierra Madre rancheria. That story comes to us from Jason Betzinez's memoir of his days as a member of the shaman's band. It is widely regarded as reliable. Its author was educated in both Apache and Anglo traditions. Betzinez, Geronimo's nephew, was still a young man at the time of the surrender of the Chiricahuas. Thereafter he attended Carlisle Indian School and embarked on a life of assimilation into white society. He married a white missionary, worked for a time in a steel mill in Pennsylvania, and later farmed in Oklahoma. His book, published in 1959 when the author was almost a hundred years old, bears every indication that advanced age had not dimmed his intelligence or memory, leading historian Robert Utley to describe him as "the most authoritative voice on the Chiricahua past."[20]

Betzinez's description of Geronimo's powers at the time of his meeting with Crook explains a great deal about the shaman's charismatic hold over his followers. As the old Indian remembered it, the raiders were deep in Chihuahua and had just captured several Mexican women, whom they intended to use as hostages to exchange for members of their families captured during the attack on Juh's camp months before. They had gathered around a fire and were dining on stolen Mexican beef, Betzinez seated next to Geronimo. The shaman suddenly dropped his knife, exclaiming, "Men, our people whom we left at our base camp are now in the hands of U.S. Troops! What shall we do?" There was no explanation of how he knew this. The camp was, after all, about 120 miles away. But his followers expressed not the slightest doubt as to the truth of his statement, and all agreed to return immediately to the rancheria. As they started out, Geronimo announced that the next day they would see a man standing on a hill to their left, and he would howl to tell them that the troops had captured their base camp. The next afternoon a man appeared just as Geronimo had described it, let out a howl, and then, descending the hill from the left, informed them that Crook's men had taken their rancheria. Hurrying on, they reached the rim of a canyon overlooking their supposedly impregnable campsite and confirmed that, indeed, soldiers now occupied it. Moreover, to their dismay and confusion, they could see their people mingling with their captors down below.[21]

As he awaited the arrival of Geronimo and his men on that Sunday morning, Crook recognized that as the band's leader and the most wary and suspicious of the Chiricahuas, the shaman was the key to the peaceful resolution of his mission. Though nothing was certain in dealing with these unpredictable and highly individualistic people, if Geronimo could be convinced to return peacefully to San Carlos, the others would likely follow.[22] Yet Crook had never personally met Geronimo and had little history with the Chiricahuas. He would essentially be flying blind in his dealings with the man, relying only on his general knowledge of the Apaches with whom he had worked and fought during his years in Arizona and ever mindful of the Chiricahuas' fearsome reputation. He knew that he would have to treat them with extreme caution. They lived their lives poised on the knife-edge of flight or fight. At any instant they could erupt in a frenzy of lethal violence, or, depending on the circumstances, they could take flight like a flock of startled birds, disappearing into their mountain fastness without a trace detectable to white eyes.

In the past Crook's history with the tribe had led him to denounce them repeatedly. But these diatribes hardly disguised his growing respect and admiration for their skill and ability as warriors and his emerging empathy for their courage in their fierce struggle for survival. Bourke undoubtedly reflected his commander's admiration when, upon observing Geronimo's warriors as they descended into camp on that Sunday, he confided to his diary that they were "certainly as fine-looking a lot of pirates as ever cut a throat or scuttled a ship; not one among them who was not able to travel forty to fifty miles a day over these gloomy precipices and along these gloomy canyons. In muscular development, lung and heart power, they were, without exception, the finest body of human beings I had ever looked upon."[23] At the same time, Bourke, like Crook, was all too aware of "the fear of treachery and ambuscade ever present in their minds."[24] It would be no easy task to win the trust of these hardened, wary warriors and convince them to submit to the general's authority.

Though their imminent arrival had been widely anticipated, the sudden materialization of Geronimo and his warriors on the canyon rim above the camp surprised and stunned the troops below. Bourke noted that even the scouts were not immune. They "grasped their guns, took to the trees and set up a fearful yelling." Geronimo's men were equally disconcerted, a thousand questions coursing through their minds. How had these troops unearthed their lair? What was their intention? Who had betrayed them? And how had the Apache scouts, men that they had counted among their friends and relatives, come to be in this place? Overwhelmed by uncertainty and fear, at a loss as to what to do next, in Bourke's words, they hovered "like hawks or vultures to the protecting shadows of inaccessible pinnacles one thousand feet above over our position."[25]

Geronimo, for all his courage and mystical power, shared in the confusion. Unsure of how to proceed, he sent two old men to investigate. If they did not return, he would attack.[26] But they did return, climbing to the canyon rim to report that the Gray Fox appeared indifferent whether the warriors came in or not. That was up to them. He would react in accordance with their decision. As Bourke put it, "If they wished to see [Crook], they could come in without fear of molestation; that he did not intend to hurt them *for the present* and would refrain from active work for a day or two to allow such as were so inclined a chance of surrender" (emphasis added).[27] The consequences if they chose not to speak with him were unstated, but there could be no mistaking Crook's intentions.

The scouts made independent efforts to open up communications. Among them were men related to Geronimo's people, including the shaman's father-in-law. These men began a shouted dialogue with their counterparts on the canyon's rim. As the sun rose in the sky, their words took effect, and individual warriors began picking their way through the rocks, descending the slope to meet the warm embrace of family and old friends. Though some may have seen him as a Judas, Peaches thrust himself into the forefront of this effort[28] But at no time did the Chiricahuas drop their guard. As Crook later reported, they were so wary that "in surrendering they would not trust themselves in our hands all at once, but came dropping in from all sides in small fragments. . . . Had I seized upon the first who came in, no others would have followed."[29]

Notwithstanding the welcome his men received, Geronimo and his leading men remained aloof, perched on the canyon heights. They had experienced too many betrayals during their lives to completely entrust themselves to these unknown soldiers. The fate of Mangas Coloradas years before likely weighed heavily on Geronimo's mind. Clearly, as one steeped in the culture of revenge, he also would have considered the prospect of retribution for the numerous victims of his depredations should he return to Arizona. And finally, at this stage, as Lieutenant Fiebeger pointed out, Geronimo "had never seen Crook before and was not certain of his protection."[30] Thus it was no surprise that the Chiricahua leadership continued to hang back.

Yet as Crook later described it, at around sundown "the Chiricahuas came in rapidly from all points of the compass—men, women, and children. All the chiefs surrendered, gave themselves up."[31] What tipped the balance has never been conclusively resolved. Contemporary accounts provided by Crook and other white men who were there are vague. The general never publicly provided a reason, and his aides, perhaps acting on their commander's instructions, were no more forthcoming. Bourke simply recorded that Geronimo and his followers came into the soldiers' camp "while we were eating supper." Crook "received them coldly," and the initial conference "did not last many minutes, and amounted to but little, but was followed by another and longer one as the night advanced."[32]

Lieutenant Fiebeger observed the initial encounter between the shaman and the general but was out of earshot and so could record only the visual aspects of the conversation. Crook was "sitting at the middle of a log apparently taking little interest in the proceedings when Geronimo came up behind him and seated himself at the end of the log, facing in the opposite direction." The general ignored his presence, leaving it to the Apache to begin the conversation. As soon as Geronimo spoke, Crook sent for his interpreter. Regarding the ensuing discussion, Fiebeger speculated that the shaman inquired as to why Crook was there, and Crook presumably replied that he was there to "show the Chiricahuas that they were no longer safe in their stronghold and it was up to them to decide whether they would return to the reservation or fight it out.[33]

Geronimo later provided Barrett, his biographer, with his own version of the event. "When I arrived, General Crook asked me 'Why did you leave the reservation?'" He said he replied, "You told your soldiers to put me in prison, and if I resisted to kill me." According to Geronimo, Crook denied that he had given any such orders. (In fact, he was not in Arizona at the time.) Then, skipping over two days of prolonged negotiations, Geronimo concluded, "I agreed to go back with him to San Carlos."[34]

None of this explains what allowed the Apache leadership to overcome their fears and enter Crook's camp. For that, we turn to John Rope, the Western Apache scout, for a plausible rationale. Rope's recollections, recorded by anthropologist Grenville Goodwin half a century after the fact, lack precise details, as one might expect. But they paint a picture that, though uncorroborated and general in nature, may provide the reason why the Apache leadership came to place their confidence in the Gray Fox.

According to Rope, while Geronimo's foot soldiers were filtering into Crook's camp, the general "was off on one side . . . hunting birds with a shotgun by himself. When he was there, all Chiricahua chiefs came to him. They grabbed his gun away and took the birds he had shot. They said he had been shooting toward them. Mickey Free went over there. They all sat on the ground and talked. After about two hours, the general came back with all the Chiricahua chiefs to camp."[35] Clearly, if Rope's account is accurate, and most prominent historians regard him as a reliable and significant source, something that occurred during this meeting convinced the Chiricahua leaders that it was safe to enter into discussions with the Gray Fox.[36]

Though Rope's tale did not appear until 1932, published versions of the story of Crook's "capture" began to dog the general shortly after his return to Arizona. The earliest known mention, a distorted and embellished version of Rope's account, can be found in an October 1883 clipping from the *Chicago Times* that found its way into Bourke's diary. The story was attributed to a St. Louis man who was vacationing in Arizona during the period immediately after the campaign. He, in turn, claimed to have heard the tale from certain unnamed officials. Replete with dialogue that could have been lifted from a Victorian drama, this third- or fourth-hand account has Crook awakening early on that Sunday morning and finding his camp surrounded by Chiricahua warriors, their rifles pointed down at him from the heights. To Captain Crawford, he declares, "We are surrounded and possibly shall all be massacred, and we might as well go to our fate bravely." With that, he grasped his shotgun and told his officers, "I will go up on the side of the hill and pretend not to see them." Naturally, he was spotted and taken prisoner by the Chiricahua leadership. The chiefs held him hostage until noon, forcing him to accede to their demands in order to save his own life and those of his men. What these demands entailed was not mentioned. But reputedly, when Crook first proposed that the Chiricahuas should return with him to San Carlos, they laughed at him.[37] In time this story would be used to discredit the general by creating the appearance that his decision to grant the Apaches amnesty and return them to San Carlos was made under duress.

Based on Rope's narrative and the *Chicago Times* story, Dan Thrapp's account of the Sierra Madre campaign offers an alternate—and to this writer, entirely reasonable—theory of the "capture." He contends that

Crook had deliberately arranged his "apprehension." In support of this admittedly controversial premise, the historian points out that while the general was indeed an avid hunter, even known to have indulged in the sport while deep in Indian country, it is hardly credible that he would have chosen such a precarious moment in his campaign to go off by himself to shoot birds. Further, it seems inconceivable that this veteran of so many Indian conflicts would be so careless as to allow himself to be captured under such circumstances unless he intended it. That being the case, Thrapp contends that Crook staged the event in order to provide an opportunity for face-to-face discussions with the headmen of the band under circumstances that would put them at their ease.[38]

Prior to Geronimo's arrival on the canyon rim, Crook had already concluded that the Chiricahuas, weary of life on the run and seeing their redoubt breached by soldiers, would, if permitted to do so, return peacefully to the reservation. Only interference by Geronimo and his hardcore warriors, fearful of retribution, might prevent them from doing so. Crook's challenge was to convince the shaman and his militant followers that he was able and willing to protect them. Since he was virtually unknown to them, this would be a difficult task. According to Thrapp, by allowing himself to be "captured" and hence putting himself in the chiefs' complete control, Crook was be able to foster an atmosphere conducive to gaining their trust.

The plan was a dangerous one, given the Chiricahuas' unpredictability and propensity for violence. Some would have justifiably regarded it as foolhardy. But to Crook it seemed a gamble worth taking. He may have been influenced by his knowledge that the Apaches placed a great premium on courage. What better way to demonstrate his bravery than by putting himself at the mercy of these noted warriors? But it seems unlikely that he would have taken such a risk had he not had unshakeable confidence, demonstrated time and again over the years, in his ability to read the Indian mind. Beyond that, he had an ace in the hole. Many of the Chiricahuas—warriors, women, and children—were now in the soldiers' camp. In effect, they had become hostages to their leaders' good behavior. If Rope's account is to be believed, the ploy worked. The Gray Fox met with his "captors" and within two hours was back in camp, the leadership in tow.

We can never know with certainty what finally induced the chiefs to lay down their arms and return to the reservation. Dan Thrapp speculates that while a "captive," the general probably made them a preliminary offer of terms, but what they were we will likely never know. As Thrapp points out, since Crook never promised more than he could deliver, it is doubtful that he would have promised them full amnesty—such a commitment was not his to make. But he must have offered them some measure of protection, and it seems clear that Crook's power sufficiently impressed the chiefs to put their lives in his hands. He had, after all, unearthed their hidden lair in the Sierra Madre and turned their own relatives and friends against them. Could not such a man protect them from the wrath of Anglo Arizona?[39]

Going out on a limb for the Chiricahuas would not have been easy for Crook. He had little reason to trust them and knew that there would be much opposition to any gesture of leniency from his superiors and from Arizonans generally. However, he had few, if any, other options. As the historian Hubert Bancroft recognized not long thereafter, whatever inducements Crook offered, a negotiated surrender was his only feasible alternative. "Successful prosecution of the campaign at this time and in this country [Mexico] was impossible, because to withdraw and await a more convenient opportunity . . . would involve renewed disaster to the scattered settlers, and because the Chiricahua outbreak had been caused to a considerable extent by unfair treatment."[40]

But if Crook's strategy was well thought out and constituted his only option, why did he and his aides not mention it in their accounts, especially since it proved successful? A possible answer lies in the general's need to gain popular support for his plan to allow the Chiricahuas to remain in Arizona. Fear of their return ran strong and deep in territory, not only within the Anglo and Mexican population but even among other Indians. The popularly preferred solution was summed up by Tucson's *Arizona Weekly Citizen,* which declared that "the leaders should be tried and hung and the balance sent to the Indian Territory as was the case with the Modocs."[41] A mass meeting in Tombstone similarly resolved that the government ought to "look upon the mutilated bodies and desolate homes of our people and . . . remove the Apache Indians from the territory."[42] Powerful elements in the government, particularly within the Interior Department, agreed. In such a poisonous atmosphere, if stories of Crook's "capture" were widely circulated, Crook's opponents would argue, as they ultimately did, that the unrepentant Chiricahuas had forced their will on him

and that they remained unbowed and a continuing threat to peace
in the Southwest. In order to prevent this, Crook needed to portray
the Chiricahuas not as proud and unbroken warriors but as a beaten
and submissive foe, eager only to be allowed to live in quiet harmony
with their neighbors—as indeed it seemed most of the tribe's members
were. Incidents such as Chihuahua's bold ride into the enemy camp or
Crook's "capture" while bird hunting conflicted with that image, and
it seems logical that Crook and his officers would not mention them
in their reports. It would be neither the first nor the last time a public
figure shaded the facts to attain a desired objective.

Whatever the truth of the matter, late on that Sunday afternoon, the
Chiricahua leadership voluntarily abandoned the safety of the canyon
rim and entered Crook's camp to begin (or continue) discussions with
the general that ultimately led to their surrender. The talks took place
over a period of several days. If Crook had previously striven to win the
trust of the chiefs, now, he reported, he took a substantially hard line,
his customary approach on such occasions.[43]

> [The chiefs] wanted to make peace and return to the San Car-
> los reservation. I replied that they had been committing atroci-
> ties and depredations upon our people and the Mexicans and
> that we had become tired of such a condition of affairs, and
> intended to wipe them out; that I had not taken all this trouble
> for the purpose of making them prisoners; that they had been
> bad Indians, and that I was unwilling to return without pun-
> ishing them as they deserved; that if they wanted a fight, they
> could have one any time they pleased. I told them that the
> Mexican troops were moving in from both sides, and it was
> only a matter of a few days until the last of them should be
> under the ground.[44]

The packer Tom Horn claimed to have witnessed these conversations, alleging that he interpreted for Crook during this time. This was
probably not true. Nevertheless, his account likely reflects information
he gleaned from the man who actually interpreted for Crook, Mickey
Free. It is certainly representative of the prevailing atmosphere. Horn
claimed that Crook threatened the Chiricahuas, telling them that if
they rejected his peace offer now, he would return to Mexico with

a large war party "able to operate all over the mountains at once," a reminder of his Tonto campaign of 1873. "Then will the Chiricahuas be doomed." Horn quoted him as saying he wanted no misunderstandings and so spoke frankly, telling them that he would not hesitate to make war on them, but he would first give them a chance for peace. He then gave Geronimo and the others a day to think over his ultimatum. The packer described Crook's harsh words as creating such tension among the Chiricahuas that, when he offered them the choice of peace or war, Sieber, sitting nearby, anticipated an immediate and violent reaction and slipped his hand under his shirt and gripped the butt of his pistol. Whether fact or fiction, this colorful and oft-quoted passage from Horn's memoir certainly conveys an accurate picture of the risk that Crook faced in confronting the volatile, heavily armed Chiricahuas deep in their mountain fastness.[45]

Most of Crook's tough talk was bluff veiling the actual fragility of his negotiating position.[46] Though there was always the chance that the Apaches might suddenly erupt into murderous violence, it was not a pitched battle that Crook most feared. From the time he had planned the expedition, he had been firmly convinced that he had sufficient military strength to overwhelm the outnumbered tribesmen in open battle; in any case, he now believed them to be "almost destitute of ammunition."[47] His real concern was that, having lost the element of surprise, any attempt to subdue the Apaches by force would doom his mission. The Indians could simply scatter, fading into the rough mountain terrain. His troops, even with the help of the scouts, would never find them, leaving it unlikely that he would ever have another opportunity to decisively end the conflict, certainly not on Mexican soil. Thus, he relied on psychology to convince the chiefs that their best hope lay in accompanying him peacefully to San Carlos, and it was far from certain that he would succeed.

Later, some observers, including Horn, would insist that only an offer of amnesty would have persuaded the chiefs to return to the reservation. That Crook made such an offer is doubtful. As mentioned previously, making it would have been out of character. Furthermore, he had to know that any such guarantee could be withdrawn by his superiors, destroying both his career and his credibility with the tribes and leaving the Indians vulnerable to the questionable mercy of Arizona's civil authorities.

Yet Crook seems to have presented his terms to the chiefs in sufficiently vague language that must have sounded very much like an
offer of amnesty. He reported that he informed them: "I could not
close my eyes to the atrocities of which they had been guilty; many
of the Americans wanted their band rooted out. If I took them to San
Carlos, no doubt a cry would be raised for their blood. . . . They could
not expect me to fight their battles or palliate their villainous conduct."[48] However, according to Bourke, when he presented his terms
to Geronimo, he told him, "If [he] was willing to lay down his arms
and go to work farming, General Crook would allow him to go back
[to San Carlos]; otherwise the best thing he could do would be to
remain just where he was and fight it out."[49]

At this juncture, in the eyes of the Chiricahua, Crook appeared
cloaked by an aura of omnipotence. Shocked by his ability to locate
and capture their camp and to bend their fellow Apaches to his will,
the tribespeople regarded him as having almost supernatural powers. Their awe was documented by most of the whites present. These
observers shared a widespread agreement that, at least outwardly, upon
entering Crook's camp, the Chiricahua leadership displayed a deferen-
tial, even submissive, attitude toward the general.[50] Geronimo himself
later admitted that he had been astonished to find the general in his
rancheria. In accordance with the Apache belief system, the shaman
assumed that only magic could have allowed Crook to accomplish such
an unimaginable feat. Perhaps Geronimo was gilding the lily when
he told Captain Crawford a year later that he thought that the general
"was so powerful that he could command the sun, the moon, and
everything," but he seems at the time to have sincerely believed that
the general's abilities were not entirely of this world.[51] And if Geronimo had such respect for Crook, the other leaders did as well. Their
attitude was likely: What choice do we have? Perhaps such a man really
can protect us from the government's wrath.

But underlying the Chiricahua leadership's respect and deference
was an uneasiness at submitting to Crook's control, accompanied by a
deep resentment and thirst for revenge directed at the scouts for their
part in this affair. The reminiscences and diaries of the expedition's
officers did not reflect any awareness of these undercurrents. They
were either oblivious or chose not to report them. But the scouts and
their white chief, Al Sieber, were clearly sensitive to the emotional

turmoil that pervaded the tribe. Horn's account is full of ominous indications of their restiveness.[52] Anthropologist Grenville Goodwin later
interviewed former scouts who confirmed the uneasiness. Curley, a
Western Apache, told Goodwin that despite their professed eagerness
to return in peace to San Carlos, Geronimo and his warriors were nervous about submitting to the will of the white general.[53]

In fact, the Chiricahuas seem to have been more than nervous. They
were actively devising a plot that, if carried out, would have entirely
destroyed Crook's initiative. The scout John Rope described the plan
to Goodwin.[54] The chiefs decided to hold a dance on the evening
of May 22 and invite the scouts. While the latter danced with the
women, the Chiricahuas intended to fall upon them and kill them
all. According to Rope, Geronimo's father-in-law, Dji-li-kine, (Pine
Pitch House), much esteemed by the band for his wisdom and courage,
vehemently opposed the idea, having many friends and relatives among
the scouts. His opposition was ignored, but somehow Al Sieber became
aware of the plot and foiled it. Knowing that Apaches were reluctant
to hold a celebration when a death occurred, he asked that the dance
be cancelled as a scout had died that day. Out of respect for Sieber,
Geronimo and his chiefs agreed, thus ending the threat.[55]There is an
indication that the officers may have had some inkling of the Chiricahuas' plans. Bourke notes in his recollections that a dance was planned
"for the purpose of stealing cartridges from our scouts; but in this the
Chiricahuas were disappointed."[56] If Bourke had some knowledge of
the incident, surely Crook did also. Perhaps, consistent with the theory
that he wished to avoid arousing the fears of the Arizona public, he
omitted mention of it from his official report.

Sieber's intervention appears to have ended any contemplation of
armed resistance among the Chiricahuas. Despite their hidden resentments and uneasiness, their peace faction won out. But to keep the
pressure on, Crook "kept them waiting for several days, and each day
they became more and more importunate. Jeronimo [sic] and all the
chiefs at last fairly begged me to be taken back to San Carlos." They
told him, "We give ourselves up; do with us as you please."[57]

To further gain the confidence of the Chiricahuas, Crook took a
carefully calculated risk. He informed Geronimo that he would not
require his people to surrender their arms. This concession seems to
have greatly impressed the Apaches, and the shaman in particular,

though the general would be much criticized for it later on.[58] Speaking to a reporter from the *New York Herald* upon his return from the Sierra Madre, Crook explained the logic of his decision. He said that he never disarmed Indians under such circumstances, because if the white soldier keeps his arms and disarms the Indian, it sends a clear signal that the soldier is afraid of him. Besides, he added, when Indians are asked to surrender their arms, they invariably hide their good weapons and only surrender those to which they do not attach much value.[59] Later he would raise another consideration, one that illustrates that his decision was both strategic and evidence of his empathy for the Chiricahuas. "It is unfair to deprive [the Apache] of the means of protecting his home and property against the white scoundrels who, armed to the teeth, infest the border, and would consider nothing so worthy of their prowess as the plunder of ponies and other property of unarmed Indians."[60]

Although Geronimo and his chiefs were clearly impressed by Nantan Lupan, fear of the Mexicans may have tipped the balance, finally convincing the band to submit to the general's authority. As part of his bluff, Crook had told chiefs that the Mexican army was fast approaching "from both sides, and it was only a matter of a few days until the last of [the Chiricahua warriors] should be under the ground."[61] Most Apaches were contemptuous of the Mexican soldiers' fighting abilities, but they feared their treachery. Concerned for the safety of their families and low on ammunition and food, the prospect of an attack by a coalition of Mexican and American forces that included their own Apache brethren would have been a daunting proposition.

Nevertheless, speaking for the chiefs, Geronimo asked Crook to delay his departure for the border. Many members of his band remained scattered in the mountains, and he claimed that he wanted to return to the reservation with his entire people and needed a few more days to collect them. Playing on Crook's strong desire to recover little Charlie McComas, the child taken by Chatto's raiders, he also suggested that additional time would facilitate search for the boy, whom Crook still believed to be alive.[62]

Crook agreed to Geronimo's request, though he suspected that it was simply a cover to permit the Chiricahuas to augment their herd at the expense of Mexican ranchers before their return to San Carlos. But he had his own reasons for delaying his departure. A continuous trickle of Chiricahuas had come into his camp over the past several days, but they did not include several key chieftains, including Juh, regarded by the Americans as the most important and dangerous of the Chiricahua chiefs; Chatto, the leader of the raid that had precipitated Crook's expedition into Mexico; or Chihuahua, who not been seen since his initial meeting with Crook on May 18. Including these men among the returnees would greatly enhance public perception of the success of Crook's mission, and the longer he waited, the greater the chance they would come in.

Somewhere around May 23—the date is uncertain—Crook's patience began to bear fruit. Chief Loco was the first to arrive.[63] The general greeted the Chihenne chief warmly. Loco had always been a reluctant rebel. The year before Geronimo had used duress to force his band to join the irreconcilables in the Sierra Madre, and now Crook had every reason to regard his desire for peace as genuine.[64] Loco was followed by Nana, an old and weathered chief of the Nedni band, who came in with fifteen of his warriors. The elderly warrior was something of a phenomenon, even among the Apaches. Bourke described Nana, then probably in his seventies, as having "a strong face, marked with intelligence, courage, and good nature, but with an under stratum of cruelty and vindictiveness." Though reported killed "no less than a dozen times during the past three years," he appeared in camp very much alive and in good health. Well-respected as a leader despite his advanced age, his agreement to return to San Carlos with Crook's column added great credibility to the general's efforts.[65]

Then Chatto arrived.[66] For Crook, his appearance was particularly auspicious because of his fame throughout Arizona due to his recent raid. Over a breakfast of hard tack and coffee with the general, Chatto asked for an additional delay of four days to enable him and his fellow chiefs to round up their remaining tribespeople.

This time Crook refused. He was anxious to move on. Logistical issues were pressing: the expedition had been camped at this site for over a week, and the lengthy occupation had rendered the place unhealthy and depleted its supply of wood and grass. In addition, the expedition was running short of rations. Its basic supply of food and forage, intended for the column alone, now fed an additional four hundred Chiricahua men, women, and children as well as the Apaches' livestock.[67] In any event, it was time to make for the border. There was always the chance that the mercurial Apaches would change their minds about returning to San Carlos. And, of course, there was the real possibility that Mexican soldiers might arrive on the scene at any moment. Their presence would certainly complicate the situation and likely cause the Apaches to scatter. In his official report, almost as an afterthought, Crook would add one more reason. If he tarried any longer in the Sierra Madre, he wrote, he would be in violation of his agreement with the Mexican government, which forbade his remaining in the country once he had broken off engagement with the enemy.[68] This obviously disingenuous statement may have been a last-minute effort to smooth a few ruffled feathers in the diplomatic community.

On May 24 Crook began his journey north to the border. Among the tribe the very young, the very old, and the feeble were mounted on mules, donkeys, and ponies, while the rest moved out on foot in a long, single-file column, garlanded with "cotton-wood foliage to screen them from the sun."[69] He initially led his motley crew only a few miles north to the banks of the Bavispe River.[70] There they spent several idyllic days resting on the river's banks, where the soldiers sprawled on the flat rocks lining the stream, watched the children frolicking in the water, and took occasional cooling dips in the river's silvery pools. The Apaches, at least the men, also found the respite relaxing. The scouts gambled with the Chiricahua warriors, fleecing them of some of the loot they had acquired on their raids, while the women jerked meat and roasted mescal for the journey to the border.[71]

Crook soon decided it was time to move on. Unable to delay the column any longer, Geronimo suggested that Crook move slowly toward the border while he and his fellow warriors scoured the hills, gathering up the rest of the band. If they failed to overtake Crook at the border, they would make their way alone back to the reservation.[72] In fact, Bourke overheard the shaman comment that he needed additional mules and horses to transport his people back to San Carlos, more likely the real reason for his suggestion.

Crook obviously understood Geronimo's intentions, aware that the shaman and Juh had gone on a similar livestock raid before they had come back to the reservation three years earlier.[73] In this instance, in his haste to return to the camp, Geronimo had been forced to abandon his captured livestock to the Mexican army. Sieber had warned the general that he planned to make up for these losses before crossing the border.

Under the circumstances, Crook was not eager to accept Geronimo's proposal. He could only imagine the outcry when he showed up at the border without the shaman and his warriors, and it was learned that he had unleashed them on the Mexican countryside to steal livestock. But he had little choice. Refusing Geronimo's request would likely result in his taking his band back into the mountains, leaving the general empty-handed. So he reluctantly acceded, though he refused a brazen request for safe conduct passes that would allow the warriors to proceed unmolested to San Carlos.[74]

Bourke was disappointed by Crook's decision. In his diary he confided that Geronimo's proposal was "a plan to work off all surplus women and children and decrepit men upon this command, leaving the Apache incorrigibles free to continue depredations upon Mexico."[75] But the captain may have been too hasty in his judgment. While only force could have prevented the warriors' departure, the premium Apaches placed on family all but guaranteed that if Crook returned the tribe's women and children to San Carlos, the men would follow, perhaps not immediately, but soon enough. It was a gamble, but one that he was almost certain he would win. At least one Tucson paper, albeit one that usually favored the general's policies, agreed. In the bigoted parlance of the day, the paper commented that "the captives can be used to good effect in bringing in or inducing the surrender of the warriors. However savage and heartless they may be, they have a love for their squaws and papooses, and they will make concessions to secure them or be with them."[76] Nonetheless, it was a decision that could have grave consequences for Crook's future. In making it he demonstrated yet again his confidant reliance on his ability to read the Indian mind. Shortly thereafter, as if to confirm the wisdom of his judgment, the shaman and chiefs Chatto, Chihuahua, and Ka-ya-ten-nae, delivered 116 more of their followers to the column, bringing the total of Chiricahuas in the camp to 384.[77]

On May 30 Crook broke camp and, minus many warriors and most of their leaders, escorted the rest of the tribe to the border. The column, guided by Tuzzone, a member of Chatto's band, wound its way out of the mountains on a trail different from the one the expedition had followed south. Crook had selected a path leading northwest across the eight-thousand-foot Sierra Madre divide and then down the less precipitous Chihuahua slope of the range.[78] This route circumvented settled areas and minimized any chance encounter with Mexican troops or civilians, thereby avoiding complications that were likely to ensue.[79]

Contrary to Crook's expectations, Juh, among the foremost of Apache leaders, had not joined the others in the soldiers' camp. Preferring to remain in Mexico, the country of his birth, the great warrior chief would never return to Arizona. He had begun drinking heavily after the attack by the Tumanoros and was probably intoxicated when, that autumn, while riding on a bluff overlooking the Casas Grandes River in Chihuahua, he fell from his horse and tumbled down the steep slope into the river. He was either killed on impact or drowned as he lay unconscious in the water, a tragic and meaningless ending to the life of one of the most able Chiricahua chiefs.[80]

The column encountered no one on the trail to the border and only briefly interrupted its progress to inspect a grisly battlefield where, the year before, the Mexican army had ambushed and inflicted heavy losses on the Apaches. The ground was still littered with the bones of slain Indians, picked clean by scavenging animals, that lay scattered among the graves of the Mexicans who had died in the fight.[81] The only mishap occurred when the expedition almost incinerated itself after "a careless Chiricahua squaw" started a prairie fire, fortuitously extinguished by the soldiers and scouts.[82] On June 1 Geronimo visited Crook's camp for the last time, held a lengthy discussion with him, and then departed the next day. Their conversation went unrecorded, but it seems that it did not diminish Crook's confidence that the shaman would show up at San Carlos as promised.[83]

Nine days later the expedition reached the border just to the south of San Bernardino Springs and camped on the spot they had left a month before. To mark the occasion, Crook called his officers into his tent and offered them the contents of "the only bottle of liquor left in camp," a "very good brandy" that the abstemious general had long secreted in his saddlebags for a special occasion.[84] The next morning, June 10, the command crossed the border and at ten o'clock arrived at Camp Supply on Silver Creek, a base established to await his return and guard the border. Only 325 Chiricahuas—52 warriors, including the chiefs Nana, Loco, and Bonito, and 273 women and children—now remained with the column, a count that indicates that 83 members of the tribe must have slipped away during the march.[85]

Major James Biddle, the officer Crook had left in command of Camp Supply, had little forewarning of his superior's appearance. Because Crook had not considered it necessary to send couriers ahead with expedition news, false and misleading reports about his activities in Mexico cropped up in the newspapers right up to the time he suddenly materialized at the border. Major Biddle only learned of Crook's impending arrival two hours before it occurred, when a lieutenant, whom the general had thoughtfully dispatched at the last minute, rode into camp to announce his commander's approach. Characteristically, Crook downplayed the occasion. Obviously savoring the moment, he casually greeted Biddle in perhaps conscious imitation of Stanley's nonchalant salutation to Livingstone. "Nice morning, Colonel," Crook was widely reported to have commented before heading for a nearby washbasin, rolling up his sleeves, and thoroughly scrubbing the trail dust from his face and hands.[86] Only after he had completed his toilette did he turn to Biddle, who by this time was undoubtedly afire with curiosity. Drawing up a campstool, Crook sat back and spoke "about his campaign in an offhand way, as if hunting the fiercest and most cruel foe on the continent, in the wildest and most inaccessible country to be found, was a matter of everyday occurrence."[87]

The general remained at Silver Creek for several days, drafting a report on the expedition for his immediate superior, Major General Schofield. Delivered by courier to Tombstone on the evening of June 11 and wired from there to San Francisco, it became the first official word of the campaign's results to reach the public.[88] Headlines in papers across the country trumpeted the news that Crook's scouts had fought and won a signal victory over the Chiricahuas without incurring a single fatality and that the column had rescued five Mexican women held captive by the tribe and had returned with considerable Apache plunder. The number of Chiricahua "prisoners" figured prominently in the accounts, as did the disquieting information that Geronimo and most of his warriors were still at large in Mexico.

Americans from areas remote from the site of recent Apache depredations seemed ready to overlook the news about Geronimo and to applaud Crook's achievements. The eastern press, the farthest away, was the most enthusiastic. The *New York Daily Tribune* editorialized that "the whole campaign has been admirably managed and adds fresh laurels to [Crook's] fame as an Indian fighter." While commenting that

Crook "apparently stretched the treaty provisions to their limit if he did not actually violate them," the press opined that since "his expedition has proved highly successful, the Mexican authorities may now be too grateful to make trouble even if, upon reflection, they think they have cause to complain."[89] Equally effusive, the New York Times wrote, "No other officer than Crook would have had the hardihood to venture on foreign soil with no reserve resources but his own, with only a handful of soldiers and 200 savage Indians to subdue hostiles but little more treacherous than his own scouts."[90]

The western papers, closer to the reality of Apache warfare, were somewhat less fervent in their praise. For instance, while lauding Crook's success, the San Francisco Tribune voiced skepticism about his plans to resettle the Chiricahuas in Arizona. Foreshadowing a chorus of demands for the removal of the "renegades to Indian Territory," the paper favored Secretary Teller's call for the punishment of the Apache leaders, a demand that would soon drown out the applause.[91]

In Arizona the papers were divided about the magnitude of Crook's success. None exhibited more vitriol than the Tombstone Epitaph and Globe's Arizona Silver Belt, long-time critics of the general. The Silver Belt claimed that the expedition had been pretty much a farce. Crook, the paper editorialized, went into Mexico knowing that he ran no risk from the Chiricahuas, who had been more than willing to return to San Carlos, and in any event had no ammunition with which to fight. To prove their point, the paper cited the fact that the column had suffered no casualties and had only killed "helpless women." The article concluded, "Where is the sense in growing jubilant over a man who conquers women and children and brings them to feed upon the brothers of the men they have murdered, upon the government whose laws they've outraged while their husbands are still killing in Mexico?"[92] Local papers spewing such venom circulated in Crook's camp at Silver Creek, and word of their content soon reached the ears of the Chiricahuas, making them restless. Bourke blamed these accounts for Geronimo's subsequent delay in returning to San Carlos.[93]

Nevertheless, at least for the time being, the tone of most news stories and the welcome accorded Crook in Tucson and elsewhere in the territory indicated that the naysayers were in the minority. The public in general seemed hopeful that the Sierra Madre campaign had ended the Apache menace in the Southwest. Crook was not so sure.

Memories of past difficulties in persuading the government to accept his recommendations left him far from certain about the tribe's ultimate fate. Though confident that the Indians would keep their part of the bargain, when asked whether his campaign would put an end to further outbreaks, a journalist reported that "he answered with a grim smile, 'You know a great many people made money out of the Indian troubles. These same people [still] exercise considerable influences in the control of the Indians.'"[94]

CHAPTER THIRTEEN

Fire in My Rear

While still in Mexico Crook had received word that a small band of Loco's followers, including the chief's wife, son, and son-in-law, had attempted to surrender themselves at San Carlos on May 31. To his surprise and dismay, he learned that Agent Wilcox had turned these Warm Springs Apaches over to the military, recommending that they be held for trial for participating in Geronimo's raids.[1] For Crook this was a completely unexpected and disturbing turn of events.

Prior to his departure for Mexico, Crook had what he regarded as a collaborative relationship with Wilcox. Accordingly, before he left he had met with the agent and tribal leaders at San Carlos to discuss the resettlement on the reservation of the Chiricahua band should he succeed in bringing them back from the Sierra Madres. As long as they remained on the warpath, he explained, their depredations would likely endanger the reservation Apaches, who would be blamed for them. A promise to return the band to Arizona might facilitate their surrender. Realizing the truth in Crook's words, the tribal leadership had agreed to accept them. At the time Wilcox, too, appeared amenable. The agent apparently changed his mind in the interim, and Loco's people, from the outset reluctant participants in the outbreak, now bore the brunt of his perfidy.

What had altered Wilcox's attitude? In retrospect, it appears that while Crook was in Mexico, the agent had successfully weathered several crises at San Carlos and as a result seems to have grown confident of the peaceful intentions of the Western Apaches and his own ability to control them. This reduced his dependence on the army at a time when he had become intensely frustrated by the growing domination of reservation affairs by Crook and his officers. Not only did the military infringe on matters he now regarded as his prerogative as Indian agent, but in some cases officers had, as we have seen, directly interfered with the ability of he and members of his family to enrich themselves at the expense of the Indians. With Crook and Crawford in Mexico, Wilcox decided that the time had come to rid himself of their unwarranted intrusion into Indian affairs and reassert civilian (Interior Department) control over the reservation.[2] The appearance of Loco's destitute and harmless relatives at the San Carlos agency seems to have presented him with the opportunity. In what one historian described as an act calculated to "undermine Crook and sabotage his plans," Wilcox refused to allow the Indians on to the reservation; instead, with the blessings of the interior secretary, he turned them over to the military for prosecution. In doing so, he had to be aware that his action would receive widespread approval throughout the Southwest and, more importantly, embarrass Crook, because when it became known to the Chiricahuas, they would flee back to Mexico.[3] Fortunately, the officer in charge of the department in Crook's absence, departmental adjutant James P. Martin, was sensitive to the potential consequences of taking any action against Loco and his people and so ordered them held in loose confinement at Fort Thomas pending Crook's return from Mexico.[4]

Crook, undeterred by Wilcox's machinations, did not waiver in his plan to return the Chiricahuas in his custody to San Carlos.[5] As soon as he reached the border, he wired Wilcox stating that he had several hundred Apaches in tow and expected them to be rationed and settled on the reservation. The agent, again with Interior Department support, informed Crook that these Indians, like Loco's band, would also be denied entry to San Carlos. As justification, he claimed that the rest of the Apaches on the reservation feared that if the Chiricahuas were allowed to return, they would disrupt the peace and destroy all the gains they had made through the agent 's efforts.[6] Interior Secretary Teller fired off a harsh letter to Secretary of War Robert Lincoln in support of his agent, writing:

I do not think these Indians should be allowed to return to the agency. . . . There can be no permanent peace if these Indians are allowed to murder the people, steal their stock, and then surrender themselves and return to the agency to be supported by the Government. I think the criminals should be held as prisoners and punished for their crimes. The children should be taken from their parents and put in school.[7]

Not to be outdone, Teller's assistant secretary, Merritt L. Jossyln, told the press that "if the head men caught by General Crook could be taken out and hung, the effect upon the remainder would be wholesome."[8] Lincoln wisely delayed action on Teller's request until he had an opportunity to discuss it with Crook, instructing the general to keep the band apart from the other Apaches pending resolution of the burgeoning dispute about their fate.[9]

Crook did not intend to back down, but in obedience to Lincoln's order, he instructed Crawford to escort the Chiricahuas from Camp Supply to San Carlos, and once there to keep them separate from the reservation Indians under the watchful eyes of the scouts.[10] Undoubtedly suspicious of Wilcox's allegation that the reservation Indians opposed the Chiricahuas' return, subsequent events indicate that he probably also instructed the captain to determine whether the agent had accurately represented the mood on the reservation. In the interim he planned to return Fort Whipple, where he could remain in close communication with his superiors.

Before departing Camp Supply, Crook assembled the scouts, their officers, and the Chiricahuas who had guided them, offering his formal congratulations on the success of the expedition. With unabashed pride, he told them, "You thought you would never catch the Chiricahuas, but now you see we have got them all." He concluded by enjoining them to keep watch over the Chiricahuas at the reservation. He then headed to the nearest railhead to board a train for Tucson, the first stop on his triumphal return journey to his headquarters.[11]

On the train Crook drafted a telegram to General Schofield laying out his rationale for returning the Chiricahuas to Arizona. Describing Wilcox's attempts to sabotage his efforts as "this fire in my rear," he asserted boldly that any attempt to hold these Indians "responsible for their acts before their surrender will drive them back to the cliffs and gorges of the mountains, and we shall the have to fight them till the last one dies." Instead, the government ought to treat the Apaches as a defeated nation, because "in their code all the depredations committed on ourselves and the Mexicans while at war were legitimate," a novel argument that must have raised eyebrows. He reflected that the Chiricahuas "are no worse than the 6000 Apaches I put on the reservation 10 years ago," adding that, with respect to those Indians, he had only a few soldiers and scouts to discipline and control them. Now he had "the valuable assistance of all the other Indians who would watch with jealous eyes the slightest movement the Chiricahuas might make." He warned that "if I am not sustained now, they will not surrender to us again." In case Schofield missed the point, he concluded, with a thinly veiled threat to resign if Secretary Teller's recommendations were accepted: "I shall be only too glad to get rid of the hard work and responsibility [the Chiricahua's] management will entail."[12] His threat proved entirely superfluous. General Schofield had already communicated his support for Crook to Washington.[13]

On the evening of June 19, a reporter observed General Crook disembarking from the train at the Tucson depot, describing him as "a medium sized man with bushy whiskers dressed in a gray suit with a Japanese summer hat, without any military trappings or style whatsoever." Such was the general's grand entrance into the town. But the city's elite, swept up in the nation's euphoric mood at his miraculous return from the Sierra Madres, was not about to allow their conquering hero to pass so simply through their municipality. They feted him in grand frontier style, escorting him to the theater one night and on the next throwing a lavish banquet in his honor.[14]

While the general rested in his hotel room between festivities, a reporter from the *Arizona Weekly Citizen* called on him to request an interview. He readily agreed, eager to explain to the citizens of the territory his rationale for returning the Chiricahuas to Arizona. But the reporter's first question indicated that his interest lay elsewhere. Had Crook promised the Indians anything to induce them to return to San Carlos? He had not, Crook replied. He had told them that "as far as I was individually concerned the past would all be wiped out, but that they had committed so many outrages upon my people that they would be liable to be shot wherever found." How then did he induce them to surrender? Crook's answer demonstrated both his great self-confidence (some might say ego) and, more likely, his insight into the minds of the Chiricahua leadership. "Well, it was this way," he said. "They have an abiding faith that I am all-powerful and that I can succeed in anything I undertake and that it is bad medicine to fight against me. So when they asked me to be allowed to return to San Carlos, and I told them I would not be responsible for any harm that befell them, they refused to believe me. . . . They surrendered on their implicit faith in my power to shield them from danger should they surrender."[15]

Did he get all the chiefs? Not Juh, Crook admitted, but Nana and Loco had come in with his column. As for the rest, he employed Geronimo's subterfuge, telling the reporter, "I sent the others [Geronimo, Natches (Naitche) and Chatto] out into the mountains to look up the squaws and children who had scattered [following the attack by Crawford's scouts]." When asked how many were still out, Crook estimated their number at about one hundred.[16] As to whether there was any likelihood that those still out would *not* come in, Crook confidently replied, "None, whatever, as we hold all their important families, *unless their faith with me is broken,* then it will be good-bye John to all the Chiricahuas" (emphasis added).[17]

The reporter next inquired whether the general had heard from Secretary Lincoln, a reference to the dispute about returning the Chiricahuas to the reservation. Crook elected not to answer this question directly. Instead he used the opening to attack the Interior Department's recent recommendations regarding the treatment of the Chiricahuas, repeating the arguments he had made to Schofield. If Secretary Teller's suggestions were followed, he cautioned, the tribe would flee into the mountains and it would be useless to attempt to go after them. Comparing the Apache nation in defeat to the South after the Civil War (Reconstruction had ended less than a decade before), he advocated treating them with similar leniency. He peremptorily brushed aside Wilcox's claim that the other Indians did not want the Chiricahuas on the reservation, declaring it "all bosh." He was confident, he said, that if allowed to return to the reservation, the tribe could easily be controlled by the military. The reporter concluded his interview with a question about little Charlie McComas, whom Crook optimistically declared would be recovered shortly. In this, of course, he was sadly mistaken.[18]

On June 22, the day before publication of Crook's interview in the *Weekly Citizen* and with the Chiricahuas now only a day away from their destination, Secretary Lincoln approved their temporary resettlement at San Carlos. At the same time, he ordered the general to report to Washington for a meeting to decide the tribe's final disposition.[19]

As Washington mulled over the fate of the Chiricahuas, Crawford had shepherded them through the dust and heat of an Arizona summer toward San Carlos. Progress was slow in parched country broken only by infrequent waterholes, called tanks in that part of the country. As the column passed through Fort Thomas, Loco's people joined their fellow Chiricahuas.[20] Crawford was alerted to the possibility of trouble on June 22, when local civilians along the route told him that at San Carlos he might find the agency Indians opposed to the Chiricahuas' return. Like Crook, he had not anticipated such resistance and approached the reservation the following day with some trepidation.

As the column neared the Gila River, the reservation's boundary, the scouts spotted flashes of sunlight reflected off dozens of looking glasses, signaling the presence of a large crowd of Indians awaiting them at the agency. Crawford halted, reordered the column into parade formation, and waded across the shallow stream onto the flat bottomland formed by the confluence of the San Carlos and the Gila. Accompanied by Sieber, he marched the column between rows of Indians lining both sides of the trail to the weather-beaten schoolhouse near the agency where they were to camp.

There, Crawford learned that Wilcox was absent, whether in Denver or Washington was unclear. Had the agent really believed there would be open hostilities between the Chiricahuas and agency Indians, his absence would have been notable. But contrary to the warnings Crawford had received, on the surface, at least, all was peaceful. Yet beneath the surface, there must have been tension. Betzinez would later recall that the other bands did not welcome the Chiricahuas' return, probably because of lingering anger at Geronimo's murder of their highly regarded chief of the Indian police the year before.[21]

An experienced officer, intimately familiar with these Indians, Crawford was undoubtedly aware of these undercurrents, but had other business to take care of. He now faced the challenge of replacing his scout companies whose enlistments were expiring. Most now returned to their homes. Prior to their departure several cowboys arrived driving a number of fine horses that they offered for sale to the scouts. John Rope believed that the horses were delivered at the request of General Crook, who had encouraged the scouts to take up stock raising as an appropriate and sustainable means to support their families.[22]

The War Department's decision to allow the Chiricahuas onto the reservation did nothing to dampen Wilcox's campaign to sabotage their resettlement. As part of his effort, he now loudly complained that Crook had "forced the Chiricahua on the reservation," pointing to the fact that they had arrived under guard. When the War Department's adjutant general, Richard C. Drum, asked Crook to respond to this latest sally, Crook fired back that the agent was mistaken. The tribe, he said, had chosen to return to San Carlos. The presence of the guards had been ordered by the secretary of war to keep the prisoners separate from the other Indians on the reservation, so that, Crook sarcastically remarked, "the Indians at San Carlos are in no danger of being contaminated by contact with the Chiricahuas."[23]

Once the Chiricahuas were settled into their camps, Crawford called the prominent chiefs together to look into Wilcox's allegations regarding the agency Indian's hostility toward the returnees and to assess the potential for future trouble. On June 26 he telegraphed his conclusions to Crook. The agent, he wrote, had greatly exaggerated the situation. When the bands had learned of the impending return of the tribe, they had initially acquiesced. The consensus seemed to be that they did not like the Chiricahuas, "for some of them are bad people, but if the General says he wants them here we will let them come." Several days later, however, white men circulated among the Indians, spreading word that the Chiricahuas would cause another outbreak and provoke the Arizona Rangers to attack the reservation. The Rangers, purported to be a mob recruited from the saloons of Tombstone, had previously attempted to attack the agency. The possibility that they might return alarmed the Indians, causing them to reverse position and oppose the Chiricahuas' return. More recently, according to Crawford, their fears had been calmed by the presence of his troops. After talking to representatives of the various bands, he now concluded that only the non-Apache Yumas and Mohaves (traditional enemies of the Chiricahuas) continued to oppose the return of the tribe. The Apaches, he said, "are indifferent except for the White Mountains who have friends and relatives among the hostiles and want their return, but will not say so."[24]

Fortified by Crawford's findings, Crook and Captain Bourke arrived in Washington on the evening of July 5. The next morning they attended a meeting with the secretaries of war and the interior convened by Lincoln to resolve the differences between the two departments regarding the Chiricahuas' fate. Teller continued to oppose Crook's resettlement plan, claiming the tribe's presence on the reservation would be disruptive and endanger the safety of the agent and other agency employees. He also objected to allowing the Indians to escape punishment for their depredations, maintaining that they were thieves and murderers and should be tried and hanged. Secretary Lincoln, apparently persuaded that following Teller's course would in fact result in further protracted hostilities, decided in Crook's favor, ruling that the Chiricahuas should be recognized as prisoners of war and treated accordingly.[25]

There remained the issues of where to put the tribe and who would manage them, the latest iteration in the ongoing quarrel between the Interior and War Departments over control of the tribes. Aware that this broader issue could not be conclusively resolved in the context of the matter before him, Lincoln wisely focused only on the Chiricahuas. Again, not surprisingly, he came down on Crook's side. He proposed that the Chiricahuas be allowed to settle at San Carlos under the aegis of the army, which, he suggested, would also exercise police powers over the entire reservation to ensure peace was maintained.

When two cabinet secretaries disagree on a course of conduct, the president ultimately makes the final decision. In this instance the press speculated (probably correctly) that Secretary Teller did not find Secretary Lincoln's proposal very much to his liking, but he likely knew that he was outgunned. Rather than accede to Lincoln's position and reach final resolution that day, as a face-saving measure and to allow tempers to cool, Teller agreed to adjourn until the following day without announcing any final decision.[26]

After the meeting Lincoln and Crook proceeded to the White House, evidently to secure President Chester A. Arthur's support. Arthur, who ascended to the presidency after the assassination of President Garfield in 1881, had originally endorsed the decision to send Crook to Arizona following the Cibicue imbroglio, so he knew something about the general. A New Yorker with little knowledge of Indian affairs, he was undoubtedly impressed by Crook's reputation as an Indian fighter and the results of his recent campaign in the Sierra Madres. He was also said to subscribe to Crook's views on how best to assimilate the Indians into American society. Most importantly, in the final analysis, Arthur, a particularly political animal, was undoubtedly reluctant to undercut a general who was currently being lionized in the Eastern press for his brilliant work in Mexico. And, of course, he did not want to risk another Indian war on his watch. It is probably safe to say that he warmly received his secretary of war and his grizzled general and endorsed Lincoln's proposed resolution of the controversy.

Consequently, the next day, as expected, Secretaries Lincoln and Teller jointly announced the conclusion of a memorandum of agreement permitting the Chiricahuas to resettle at San Carlos. The agreement covered those Indians who had returned from Mexico with General Crook as well as those who were expected to come in thereafter. All were placed under the complete control of the military, a ratification of the de facto authority that Crook had exercised on the reservation during the past year. In addition, the agreement entrusted the army with complete "*police control of all of the Indians* [emphasis added]" at San Carlos; that is, responsibility for keeping peace on the reservation. To calm any concerns Wilcox might have had for his personal safety, the agreement provided that the tribe could not be settled near the agency headquarters without the agent's consent, and Crook's troops were specifically charged with protecting the agent's person in the discharge of his duties.[27]

The conclusion of this agreement was a signal victory for General Crook. He had kept his word to the Indians and demonstrated his power to control events on their behalf. He believed that he could look forward to the return of the remaining chiefs and warriors to the reservation and, with the military in charge of the reservation, the end of warfare with the Apache tribes.

Exhausted by the pressures of the campaign and its politically charged aftermath, he now planned a few days of well-deserved leave with Mary at her family home in Oakland, Maryland, and a brief visit to Omaha on personal business before returning to Arizona. Prior to leaving the capital the weary general still found time to give yet another newspaper interview, this time to the *New York Herald*. Expressing great satisfaction with the agreement, he assured the reporter that within a short time all the Indians currently outside the reservation "will be glad to join their comrades," putting an end to the Apache threat in Arizona. Anxious to repair his battered relationship with Wilcox, he then effusively praised the agent's ability and "fidelity." Wilcox's efforts, he expected, would promote "the intentions of the government in making this Agency an exception to the regulations governing other Indian reservations." Then, taking advantage of this public forum, he pronounced on an issue that had been of great concern to the family-oriented Chiricahuas. He flatly declared that his management plan for the reservation did *not* include removing Apache children from their parents to attend school, as Secretary Teller had previously proposed. While that might be a determination for future consideration (as indeed it was), to do so now, he said, would only arouse the Indians' suspicion and distrust. Finally, he emphasized that the agreement had provided him with absolute authority at San Carlos, so that "the Indians may know that their confidence [in his word] will not be betrayed."[28]

Crook's departure for Oakland marked the beginning of a six-month period during which he would be without his long-time aide-de-camp, John Bourke. The strain of the Sierra Madre campaign had taken a toll on the health of both men. But the captain, despite his younger age, had much the worst of it. He appears to have suffered from what he identified as nervous prostration: extreme mental and physical fatigue brought on by the strain of the campaign, what today might be labeled post-traumatic stress disorder. His symptoms—anxiety, depression, and sleeplessness—were sufficiently acute that, upon examining him on his return to Arizona, an army surgeon pronounced him unfit for duty and ordered him to take a convalescent leave for six months. This seems to have fit neatly into the captain's life plan. Prior to his transfer to Arizona, he had engaged in a secretive courtship with Miss Mary Horbach, the daughter of an Omaha businessman. The need for rest and recuperation created a forced hiatus in his career that provided an ideal opportunity for marriage followed by a lengthy honeymoon in Europe, Bourke's first real vacation since his graduation from West Point in 1869.[29]

It is not known whether Crook was aware of Bourke's courtship and intention to marry before the general departed for Maryland. But two weeks before the nuptials were scheduled to take place, the general wrote his aide from the Glades Hotel in Oakland, an inn owned by Mary's father where the couple stayed while in the town. The letter chiefly concerned a sum of money that Crook had borrowed from the captain and had forgotten to repay. It made no mention of his aide's impending marriage. Yet the general concluded by wishing Bourke "all kinds of good luck and happiness on your journey," a clear reference to the honeymoon and possibly to the captain's future life in matrimony.

After a small, private ceremony at the bride's family home in Omaha, the couple departed on a six-month honeymoon in Europe. Married life and a six-month European vacation seem to have cured the captain of his malady. When he returned to duty in January 1884, Crook happily found him "so much better, he seems to have gotten over his nervousness and irritability, and take a broader view of things."[30]

Settling Down the Chiricahuas

Crook wasted no time in implementing the July 7 interagency agreement. In many respects it was, after all, merely a formal ratification of the measures he had instituted the previous year before crossing into Mexico. On July 24 he issued General Order No. 13, reassigning Crawford to San Carlos, this time making him overall military commander of the reservation pursuant to the terms of the agreement. His duties now included not only the exercise of police power for the entire reservation, but, with respect to the Chiricahuas, complete control over their activities, including the issuance of rations.[1] Under the order Crawford was responsible for carrying out Crook's primary objective: integrating the fractious tribe back into reservation life in the hope of bringing to an end Apache depredations in Arizona. A troop from the Third Cavalry was transferred from Fort Thomas to assist him.

Crawford established his headquarters at San Carlos on a stony bench at the confluence of the San Carlos and Gila Rivers, not far from the site where past Indian agents had located their agency. On this arid, insect-infested stretch of desert—christened by Britton Davis as "Hell's Forty Acres"—the Interior Department had tightly packed over four thousand Apaches of various bands and seven hundred Yavapais (so-called Apache Mohaves and Apache Yumas).[2] For his use and habitation, Crawford took over a series of sturdy adobe school buildings that had been constructed during Tiffany's tenure. They served as storerooms and officers' quarters for himself and his assistants—a quartermaster, an adjutant, a provost officer, and a surgeon. The Third Cavalry troopers were housed in tents around the agency.[3]

With Crawford in overall command, Crook appointed Lieutenant Gatewood to serve as commander of Fort Apache in the mountains to the north of San Carlos to keep watch over the nearby White Mountain and Cibicue bands with whom he had had a long association. Lieutenant Britton Davis was assigned to supervise the Chiricahuas, initially at San Carlos and later in the White Mountain country where they would be resettled.

When the Chiricahuas first arrived, Crawford situated them below the bench on the flats next to the river where he could keep a sharp eye on them. Yavapai and San Carlos bands were camped nearby, but these Indians, who regarded the recent returnees with dislike and suspicion, remained aloof from them. According to Davis, the Chiricahuas, scorned by their fellow Indians, turned to the society of the young lieutenant and his troops for consolation. Under the pressure of circumstances, their initially stiff and formal interactions soon blossomed into companionship as the once mortal enemies discovered their common humanity.[4]

By appointing officers in whom he placed implicit trust, Crook believed that he now had the situation on the reservation firmly under control. Yet the continued absence of Geronimo and his followers remained a source of concern. In Mexico the shaman had committed to meeting the general's column at the border or, failing that, he would lead his people directly to San Carlos. Britton Davis recorded that he had promised that this would occur within two moons.[5] At the time, as mentioned, Crook believed he had little choice but to accept him at his word. But the weeks passed and reports of Apache depredations in Sonora and Chihuahua continued to come out of Mexico. The shaman's assurances became increasingly suspect, placing Crook in an awkward position, jeopardizing his policies, and subjecting him to a barrage of embarrassing press criticism.

Crook had recognized from the outset, of course, that the shaman's purpose had really been to acquire livestock and booty rather than, as he had told the general, to gather his people. But he had assumed that, as skilled raiders and stock thieves, the Apaches would have accomplished their mission and returned to San Carlos well within the time Geronimo had stipulated. The delay was becoming increasingly

difficult to explain. Moreover, how could Arizonans be asked to tolerate the return of the Chiricahuas to the territory and forgive their
past depredations when a goodly portion of the tribe continued to
engage in mayhem south of the border in violation of their commitment to Crook?

Seizing on the situation, the Arizona press embarked on a campaign
of vicious personal attacks against the general. Tucson's *Arizona Weekly
Citizen* declared that Crook "thinks more of a dirty Apache than he
does of our white citizens" and that there "never was a commander as
over-rated, [nor] an officer less competent to command . . . than this
same General Crook. . . . The longer he remains in Arizona the more
transparent will his unfitness appear to the people of Arizona and the
country at large."[6] The *Arizona Silver Belt,* the strident voice of the
small mining town of Globe, was even less restrained. Harking back
to Chatto's raid, its editor wrote, "After [Chatto] came, [Crook] could
not leave Whipple post till he received his new invoice of night shirts
and tooth powders, and so, for nearly two weeks, the murderous devils
destroyed property and took lives . . . before Gen. de–Wellington-
Boots-Crook got his lordly shape near where blood had been spilled."[7]
Such attacks fueled a growing uneasiness throughout the territory,
exacerbating anxieties already kindled by detailed, lurid accounts of
Apache raiding that spilled over the border from Mexico. Would these
Indians ever honor their commitment to return to San Carlos? Or
would they continue their bloody raiding in Sonora and Chihuahua
and perhaps even expand their depredations into Arizona, as Chatto
had done only months before?

Initially, Crook's only defense was to publicly dismiss these concerns. On July 23 he wrote, "The fact that the Indians left behind
have not come in is a matter of no significance. Indians have no idea of
the value of time." After all, he pointed out, it had taken Loco's family 66 days to come into to San Carlos from Mexico.[8] But the horror
stories emanating from Mexico undermined his confident assertions.
On July 20 the *New York Times,* generally sympathetic to Crook and
to the Indians, complained that "the Indian fugitives have not come
in to any great extent and advices from Mexico show that, relieved of
their non-combatants, they have again taken to their favorite pursuit
of robbery, rapine, and murder." A Mexican force sent against them,
reported the *Times,* had been "repulsed with considerable loss, and the

people of the region are berating Gen. Crook, who has only left the most warlike of the Chiricahuas to pursue their plans."[9] On September 15 Tucson's *Weekly Citizen* reported that, according to the Mexican Consul in that city, "No less than twenty Mexican citizens have been murdered by the Apaches in Moctezuma and Sahuaripa districts since General Crook visited that locality last June." The consul added the theft of "a large amount of stock" and the destruction of property to his catalog of depredations.[10]

Crook next tried to blame the delay on an abundance of caution on the part of the Apaches. By this time, he said, they were keenly aware of the heightened feelings against them in Arizona and were hesitant to come in. Bourke loyally endorsed his general's explanation, writing that the headmen of the band "hid back in the mountains until they could learn exactly what was to be their fate"[11] In support of this explanation, Crook reported that he had learned that several Chiricahua warriors had appeared at the border in July and August, intending to go to San Carlos. But they had "mysteriously" turned about and disappeared back into Mexico after talking to white ranchers in the area.[12] In a report a week later, he repeated the story, this time specifically asserting that the local press stirred up prejudice against the tribe, hindering "for some months the return of the Chiricahuas who surrendered to me in the mountains."[13]

Tales of the presence of Chiricahuas on the border during that summer turned out to be questionable. In separate interviews, two prominent Apache chiefs who had been in Mexico would later deny that any of their people had tried to cross into Arizona during the period in question. Historian Edwin Sweeney implied that Crook had made up the story to explain the Chiricahuas' failure to appear at San Carlos. Since the general actually dispatched troops to the border in reaction to the tales, it is more likely that he honestly accepted rumors of an Apache presence as true. Furthermore, as Sweeney admits, Crook ordered chiefs on the reservation interrogated to establish the veracity of the claims. Had he fabricated the story, it seems improbable that he would have ordered an investigation that would likely expose him as a liar.[14] In any event, anyone reading the virulent articles that regularly appeared in several Arizona papers, notably Tucson's *Arizona Weekly Citizen* and Globe's *Silver Belt,* would recognize that Crook's explanation had some truth in it. It was highly probable that press reports did cause Geronimo's warriors trepidation regarding the reception they could expect to receive upon their return to the territory.

With the benefit of hindsight, we now know that there was an additional reason for the Chiricahuas to delay in Mexico: their desire to recover members of their families who had been captured during the attack on Juh's village. Toward the end of July one of Geronimo's wives, captured during the attack, had escaped from her Mexican captors. After a remarkable forty-four-day journey during which she survived on roots and berries, she found her way to her husband's redoubt, bringing the band word that thirty-five of its members had survived and were being held in Chihuahua City.[15] Among them were Chatto's wife and children and two other wives of Geronimo. Chatto—and undoubtedly Geronimo—immediately resolved to negotiate their return. To that end, they entered into truce talks with the authorities in Chihuahua and Sonora. The Mexicans suspected that this was but a traditional device often used by the Apaches to buy time to rest and rearm. So, following their own traditions, Mexican officials pretended to be receptive, hoping to lull the Apaches into complacency, lure them into town, ply them with alcohol, and then wipe them out, a rather shopworn ploy that had been surprisingly successful in the past. During the summer and fall of 1883, these two mortal enemies engaged in this ritualistic dance. And while doing so, the Chiricahuas continued their depredations and the Mexican army continued to hunt them.[16]

Meanwhile, their fellow tribespeople on the reservation, all too aware of the ongoing hate campaign in the press and the growing hostility in Arizona, became increasingly uneasy about the delay, causing Crook to worry that they would take flight and join Geronimo in Mexico.[17] Of equal concern to him was the possibility that settlers along the border, aroused by news stories of Apache atrocities in Mexico, might attack Geronimo's warriors when and if they did return to Arizona.[18] Either eventuality would destroy Crook's chances of bringing his hopes to fruition.

The Apaches' promise that they would return to Arizona in "two moons" would have put them at the border in late July.[19] But July ended and the first weeks of August slipped by without any sign of them. Thus, when Crawford wired Crook on August 17 to suggest that he be allowed to send a few of the subchiefs into Mexico "to hunt up their people," the general leaped at the offer. A week later, Bonito, a White Mountain Apache married to a woman in Geronimo's band and a friend to Chatto, departed San Carlos for the Sierra Madre with two Chiricahua comrades.[20]

While awaiting the results of this mission, Crook was beset by angry Mexican government officials. Outraged by Geronimo's resumption of raiding, they demanded that the U.S. government prosecute the Chiricahuas on the reservation for the depredations. Crook fended them off. Punishing those now at San Carlos, he asserted, "would be an act of perfidy and bad faith and would unquestionably prevent the return to the agency of the Chiricahuas left in the Sierra Madres, [and] would precipitate an Indian war." The officials reluctantly backed off, at least for the time being.[21]

No sooner had that matter been put to rest than the general found himself responding to a claim by the Mexican chargé d'affaires in Washington for the return of Mexican property captured from the Indians during the Sierra Madre campaign. Crook dismissed this request, too, saying that he considered the property in question, mostly livestock, the legitimate spoils of war and had distributed it to his scouts as compensation for their services. He added that the return of such stock would only precipitate a flood of claims from Mexico, many of them fraudulent, which could never be sorted out.[22]

While the Mexicans pursued their demands, closer to home the McComas family continued to press for the recovery of Judge McComas's missing son, Charlie. In the aftermath of Chatto's raid, many had believed the boy was alive and was still being held by the Apaches in Mexico. His return had been a primary raison d'être for the Sierra Madre campaign, especially for Crook, who was fully sensible to the widespread outrage and shock caused by the murder of the boy's parents and the grief the surviving family members felt at little Charlie's loss. Though many of his subordinates thought the boy had not survived, the general clung to the hope that he lived, and his failure to find the boy was as frustrating to him as Geronimo's continued sojourn in Mexico. In June he had written to his superiors that he remained anxious "to get in the last of this band, so as to leave nothing undone for the recovery of the captive boy," an indication that the missing child and the return of the Chiricahuas were inextricably linked in the general's mind.[23]

At the end of August Charlie's uncle, Eugene Ware, a former cavalry officer who was now a Kansas state senator, complained to the secretary of state about the army's supposed lack of diligence in searching for the boy. He touched a raw nerve. Though Ware expressed admiration for Crook's efforts, his bitter disappointment at the military's failure to rescue young Charlie caused him to lash out at the institution. "It may be true," he wrote, "that our officers are too busy playing poker and the men drinking whiskey, and having amateur theatricals at their barracks to render much assistance."[24] When the senator's letter reached his desk, Crook responded with restraint, though the legislator's remarks surely angered him. He coolly replied that he had no news about the boy but was hoping to hear something from Bonito's mission.

But when he received a similar complaint from Judge John M. Wright, the former law partner and friend of the slain Judge McComas, Crook snapped. Without Bourke to help him formulate a tactful response, Crook's reply rivaled Ware's in its offensiveness, although perhaps unintentionally. With scant regard for the family's feelings, he abruptly informed the judge that the family's campaign to win Charlie's release had only damaged his own efforts by allowing the Indians to see how badly the Americans wanted the boy returned. For his part, he said, he had tried to gain Charlie's return by convincing the Indians "that we cared very little for the boy."[25] Obviously, he did not mean this literally, but then clarity in composition had never been Crook's forte. The letter unfortunately received wide circulation in the press, particularly in the Southwest, and the public, not to mention the grieving friends and relatives, was left with the impression that general was indifferent to the child's plight.[26]

In Arizona that fall, whites and Apaches alike coexisted in an atmosphere of mutual apprehension and mistrust. Given their level of anxiety, the Chiricahuas at San Carlos must have communicated to their relatives in Mexico their fervent wish that they return quickly to the reservation. In any event, in late September their chiefs reported to Crawford that they had received word that the warriors—except for Geronimo and Juh (the latter had died by that time)—would be coming in within sixty days. Crawford relayed this information to Crook. The general then ordered Captain William A. Rafferty, commander at Fort Bowie, to lead a troop of cavalry to San Bernardino Springs to meet the returnees when they crossed the border and escort them to

San Carlos, protecting them from possible attacks by angry ranchers along the route. The general also ordered Britton Davis and a detachment of scouts to lend their support to Rafferty. Among the scouts were Chiricahua warriors whose presence, it was hoped, would reassure Geronimo's followers and prevent them from bolting. An anxious Crook had Davis send three of his scouts, two of whom were relatives of the subchief Chihuahua, into Mexico to keep an eye out for the band and hurry them along. However, these men, fearing an encounter with Mexican troops, turned back after riding only a short distance across the border.[27]

Finally, in late October, after several weeks "of weary waiting," the first returnees, seventy-nine in number, appeared in company with Bonito, the messenger dispatched in late summer to make contact with Geronimo. Several days previously, unaware of Rafferty's presence at San Bernardino Springs, Geronimo had sent a member of Bonito's delegation ahead to alert the garrison at Fort Bowie of his impending arrival. Low on food, he had requested rations be delivered to them at Silver Creek, about ten miles north of their crossing point. Consequently, a troop of cavalry from Bowie had already arrived at Silver Creek with the requested rations by the time the warriors crossed into Arizona. Rafferty, Davis, and the scouts met with the returnees on October 26, and two days later the captain sent a dispatch detailing the arrivals to Crook. Besides Bonito, the group included two prominent chiefs: Naiche, son of Cochise, and Chihuahua. With them were about a dozen warriors and "twice that number of women and children." Rafferty reported that he anticipated the subsequent arrival of Chief Ka-ya-ten-nae with "nine bucks and one squaw" and of Chatto and Geronimo with eight additional warriors within eight days by another route.[28] Ka-ya-ten-nae, who likely succeeded Victorio as the chief of the Chihenne Chiricahuas, was a prominent and respected figure among the Chiricahuas, important enough for Rafferty to delay his departure for San Carlos until the chief arrived.[29]

While waiting for Ka-ya-ten-nae, Rafferty questioned the returning warriors about the reasons for their delayed appearance. They responded by detailing their attempts to negotiate the release of their relatives held captive by the Mexican government, stating that in the end they had belatedly realized that the negotiations were simply a pretext by the Mexicans to entrap and exterminate them. Too low on ammunition to fight and despairing of ever seeing their families again, they had escaped to their mountain hideout. There they found Bonito, who by chance had just arrived. He convinced them that they would be well received in Arizona, so they decided to accompany him to the border.[30]

The Chiricahuas also gave Rafferty a complete accounting of the whereabouts of those members of the band still in Mexico. Of the 146 tribespeople who had remained there following Crook's departure, four men had died, including Juh. Ten men and two women were currently on their way to San Carlos by an alternative route. Ten boys and twenty women and younger children had remained in Mexico but would be coming in as soon as they had gathered the remainder of their stock.[31]

On November 3 Ka-ya-ten-nae duly appeared at Silver Creek with his followers and a sizeable herd of horses and mules, recently captured in raids along the Sonora River.[32] The day after the chief's arrival, Rafferty, who was fast running out of rations to feed the Indians, insisted that the group set out immediately for San Carlos. As they moved north Ka-ya-ten-nae, who claimed to have never been on a reservation before, displayed increasing nervousness, either because he suspected treachery or simply at the prospect of confinement at San Carlos.[33] A portent of his future rocky adjustment to reservation life, his uneasiness communicated itself to the others, and only Bonito's constant reassurances prevented the band from bolting.[34]

While en route the Indians camped apart, refusing the soldiers entry to their rancheria, probably to conceal the number of horses and mules they had acquired during their raids and, more significantly, to hide the presence of three white children. But Mickey Free discovered the children's presence after insinuating himself into the camp. He erroneously concluded that one of them was Charlie McComas. His report raised hopes that were dashed after the group arrived at San Carlos on November 21, and Bonito, who had captured Charlie during the Chatto raid, emphatically informed Crawford that the boy was not among the captives. The white children he identified as captives taken during recent raids in Mexico.[35] Crook regretfully reported this to Judge Wright, the family's representative, who after personally inspecting the children was forced to agree. Despite this disappointment, Crook continued to hold out hope that Charlie remained alive and might come in with Chatto.[36]

The protracted failure of Chatto and Geronimo to appear at the border soon became a source of much embarrassment to the general.[37] Not only were these two considered by Arizonans as the most culpable of the Apache leaders, but the general feared that until they returned, there was always a possibility that the rest of the band might bolt once again for Mexico. He warned his superiors that although a total of 423 Chiricahua men, women, and children had now returned to the reservation, this was no time to relax vigilance. The Indians were extremely wary. Many had hardly recovered from the trap laid for them by the Mexicans at Casas Grandes and "required very careful and delicate handling." While Arizonans might consider such a policy as too lenient and accommodating for their taste, for Crook "the security of life and property both in this country and in Mexico" depended on it.[38]

After delivering Ka-ya-ten-nae and his band to the reservation, Rafferty and Davis returned to the border to await the arrival of Geronimo and Chatto. Displaying his usual abundance of caution, Geronimo had sent word that before returning he wished to consult with his son, Chapo, for information about the kind of the welcome he could expect at San Carlos. Crook willingly accommodated the shaman's concerns, dispatching Chapo, Chihuahua, and a small delegation into Mexico.[39] In the meantime warriors continued to trickle across the border.

On February 7 Chatto himself appeared with nineteen followers. Of course, Charlie McComas was not with him.[40] Davis accompanied the Indians to San Carlos and then returned once more to the border to await Geronimo. On February 26 Crook's patience was at last rewarded when the shaman and his band crossed into New Mexico near Skull Canyon, a border point that later assumed considerable significance. When his scouts reported Geronimo's approach, Davis rode his mule down to the line to meet him. Anxiously scanning the arid Sonoran countryside for signs of the Apaches, he finally discerned a line of tiny figures in the distance, winding their way toward him. He observed a great cloud of dust rising to their rear and feared it might be Mexican troops in pursuit. But as the group drew near, he could see that, though cautious, the Apaches did not appear rushed or excited. Geronimo, mounted on a white pony, rode at the head of a column that Davis estimated to include "fifteen or sixteen of his men and some seventy women and children."[41] To allay any concerns they might have about the officer awaiting them, Davis sent two scouts ahead to reassure them. Geronimo and the scouts conversed briefly. Then the shaman defiantly edged his pony toward the young lieutenant, making no move to check his progress until his mount bumped the shoulder of Davis's mule. Reining in his pony, he demanded to know why his people needed an escort to San Carlos. Davis responded that they were there to protect the Chiricahuas from harm at the hands of whites along the route. In turn he asked the shaman to explain the dust cloud that continued to hover behind the Indians. Snapping out a single word—"*ganado*," Spanish for cattle—Geronimo pointed to the herd of 350 Mexican cattle, horses, and mules his warriors had stolen on their march to the border.

Knowing of Crook's urgent need to know of Geronimo's arrival, Davis promptly wired him with the news, including a short message dictated by the shaman. "Tell General Crook," the Apache leader had said, "we have left the mountains and are going to San Carlos as we told him we would when we surrendered to him last summer. Some of us have never been on this reservation, but now we are all going there and all that we want is to live in peace. We have had enough of fighting."[42]

Though Geronimo's herd substantially slowed the column's progress, with patience, cunning, and considerable luck, Davis successfully guided the obdurate and rebellious shaman and his nervous companions and stolen livestock across 175 miles of Arizona territory and safely to the reservation. In the process they eluded angry whites lusting for revenge and a U.S. Marshal from the Southern District of Arizona with a warrant to arrest the notorious Apache for his depredations.[43] At San Carlos the shaman was irate to learn that Crook planned to sell his stolen cattle at auction and return the proceeds to the Mexican government to compensate their owners. This appropriation of his herd became another in a long list of Geronimo's grievances against the white man. When years later he dictated his autobiography, he said that the general told him that if he tried to recover the stock, he [Crook] had given orders that he be arrested. If he resisted, he would be killed. This, Geronimo claimed, was one of the reasons why he absconded from the reservation a year later, an explanation that is suspect at best given the circumstances that attended that breakout.[44]

Somewhat mollified by Crook's decision to allow his people to keep their stolen horses and mules, the shaman seemed to outside observers to adjust relatively well to reservation life. He settled with Chatto and Ka-ya-ten-nae in a place apart from the rest of the Chiricahuas and seemed content to accept Crawford's efforts to put the band to work raising crops. To questions about Charlie McComas, he replied that he knew nothing of the boy's whereabouts, leaving the boy's family with only the mournful hope that he might be with a small band of stragglers even now on the final leg of their journey to San Carlos.[45] This hope, too, soon faded when the rearguard arrived in April without the child. Though it brought no comfort to the McComas family, the return of this last remnant of the band from Mexico was significant. As Crawford proclaimed on Crook's behalf, "For the first time since the establishment of the reservation, all tribes of the [Arizona] Apache nation in their entirety were upon it."[46]

CHAPTER FIFTEEN

Move to Turkey Creek

Crook greeted Geronimo's arrival at San Carlos with relief. At last all but a handful of the Chiricahuas were out of Mexico and gathered under the army's watchful eye. He could finally turn away from the bloody and frustrating work of fighting the Apaches and focus his full attention on setting them on a path that he believed would lead to permanent peace and, ultimately, to their assimilation into American society.

The general was keenly aware that an environment that accommodated the Apaches' basic need for security and sustenance was essential to his objective of transforming these wary nomadic warrior tribesmen into peaceful farmers and ranchers. Achieving these conditions was both his most urgent priority and his greatest challenge. Well aware of the tribe's turbulent history as both hunter and prey, Crook knew that they were apt to bolt at any perceived threat to their safety, shattering the hard-won peace. Consequently, he devoted considerable energy over the next two years to diffusing situations that might portend such an eventuality. He would encounter obstacles at every turn: opposition from the citizens of Arizona who feared and hated the Apaches; interference from the economic and political interests who profited from unrest; resistance from elements within the government itself who disagreed with his policies; and significant challenges from the Indians themselves.

At first things seemed to go well. In the fall of 1883 Crook conducted a monthlong inspection tour to observe how dispersal of the various bands across the reservation had affected their wellbeing. He observed great improvements in both their mood and material condition. He found the White Mountain bands around Fort Apache entirely self-supporting. Residing in an area cooler and more fertile than San Carlos, they raised corn, vegetables, and melons and sold hay to the post. To continue this progress, Crook recommended that the tribe be provided with farm implements, seed, and a gristmill to grind their own flour, presumably through the Interior Department. In justification he pointed out in his murderous grammar that the "distribution to the value of the amount saved [by] the gov't in the item of beef issues alone in the last six months would place them in a condition to make their future beyond question."[1] As to the bands he had dispersed in the San Carlos area, he claimed that "the Indians have planted more extensively than ever before, and their condition is consequently much improved as contrasted with former years."[2]

While Geronimo had been occupied with depredations in Mexico, the Chiricahuas who had already returned to the reservation had been settled near the San Carlos agency under Crawford's watchful eye. The location proved unsuitable as they chafed under the scrutiny of the military and grumbled about the unaccustomed heat and aridity and the hostility of the neighboring tribes.[3] Sympathetic to their complaints, Crook planned to resettle them with the White Mountain band in the mountains near Fort Apache. There they would enjoy a climate more akin to what they were used to, would have access to fertile lands, and would be distanced from hostile neighbors. But Crook would not authorize the move until Geronimo had rejoined the tribe on the reservation, believing that they required continuing oversight to prevent them from bolting across the border. He was also concerned about the hostility displayed toward the Apaches by whites in towns and on ranches surrounding the reservation. "Incendiary articles" appearing in the local papers stirred up the citizenry to the point that, on one occasion, Arizonans had actually attacked a peaceful Indian camp. "Careful and judicious management," Crook wrote, "can hardly be expected to keep these Indians quiet, if such unprovoked and malicious acts are repeated."[4] For the time being he kept the tribe close to the San Carlos agency under careful observation.

But how to keep these nomadic warriors occupied? Crook had long considered idleness to be among the greatest evils of the reservation system. The Chiricahuas at San Carlos graphically illustrated the problem. The Apaches' already restless nature was exacerbated by idleness and consequent boredom. To ameliorate its effects, the general decided to put the tribesmen to work while they awaited Geronimo's return and their move to a more permanent location. Eager to get them started as farmers, as he had done for the White Mountain tribespeople, he asked the army, now responsible for the Chiricahuas, to supply them with seed and farm implements. As this was not a normal budget item for the War Department, he rationalized his request by pointing out that while the Interior Department would probably not provide such resources, the army could justify the expenditure as a "military necessity." Without these supplies, he argued, "it would be extremely difficult to keep [the Chiricahuas] quiet."[5]

In the meantime Lieutenant Britton Davis found gainful employment for the Chiricahuas in his charge gathering fodder for the livestock and chopping wood, which they then sold to the military. The lieutenant reported a marked improvement in their mood as money from their labor began to flow into their hands.[6] While the Chiricahuas' adaptation to life on the reservation showed signs of progress, Crawford reported that they remained wary and uneasy, stirred not only by the rhetoric in the newspapers but also by the disruptive influence of the Chihenne chief, Ka-ya-ten-nae. Crawford described him as "very suspicious & . . . a bad man among them," whose restlessness caused sympathetic ripples among other members of the tribe.[7] In an attempt to assuage Ka-ya-ten-nae's discontent, Crawford appointed him to a position of responsibility in the scouts. In the short run, this course seemed successful.

While Crook worked with Crawford to curb the Apaches' restlessness, yet another potentially disruptive influence appeared on the horizon. The reservation had been subject to repeated invasions by the surrounding white population, covetous of its rich agricultural and mining potential. Its mineral wealth made it particularly vulnerable. To the east and in the area where the town of Globe now is located, land rich in copper had been stripped away from the reservation. Acres of good grazing and productive cropland tempted the settler population, and Mormon farmers had recently established homesteads on such land in the northern sector of the reservation. A little research educated Crook to the fact that these usurpations of reservation lands had been accomplished without thought of compensation to the Indians, a circumstance that had not escaped their notice.[8]

In 1881 prospectors had discovered a coal bed on Deer Creek on the reservation's southern border and petitioned to lease the land on which it was located. Though the Indian agent at the time, Joseph Tiffany, supported their request, Secretary of the Interior Teller's predecessor had, to his credit, refused to approve it. So the miners went to Congress to obtain legislation to "segregate," or carve away from the reservation, the coal-producing land. Several bills were introduced for this purpose, but none so far had been enacted into law. Despite this, the prospectors who discovered the coal had begun extracting it. In 1883, after the military assumed control of reservation affairs, Crook, with the support of Secretary Teller, ordered the eviction of the miners as well as the Mormons. The Mormons left, but the miners persisted. In March of the following year, they promoted the introduction of yet another bill in Congress to allow them access to the coal.[9]

Crook responded to this latest initiative with a lengthy letter to the army's adjutant general, explaining that he could tolerate the mining of the coal but not the absence of compensation to the Indians for its extraction. He then traced the history of past curtailments of reservation lands without compensation and described the Apaches' awareness of and growing anger at this violation of their treaty rights. He concluded with a warning that should the Deer Creek lands "be taken from them without arranging for a satisfactory royalty or other compensation, it will be a grave and just source of grievance and may lead to serious results." His efforts were successful in blocking the mining operation for the remainder of his tenure, but only so long as he remained in Arizona.[10]

In the spring of 1884, about the time of the Deer Creek affair and Geronimo's return to San Carlos, agricultural implements ordered for the Chiricahuas finally arrived on the reservation. At the same time, Crawford purchased seeds for the tribe in Tucson. He soon reported positive indications of the tribe's adaptation to reservation life, resulting, it appears, from the availability of agricultural supplies and Geronimo's return. May was planting time in Arizona, and Crawford, calling attention to the Chiricahuas' longstanding desire to settle in the mountains, urged that they be relocated there before the season passed.[11] The captain's assurances and Geronimo's reappearance convinced Crook that it was now safe to allow the tribe to resettle at a distance from the agency.

The Chiricahua leadership favored the move to the White Mountain's country. It was at a higher elevation and hence cooler than San Carlos, and they were more comfortable surrounded by White Mountain tribespeople instead of the Western Apache and Yavapais who lived around the San Carlos agency.[12] To facilitate the tribe's participation in deciding where to relocate, Crook authorized Crawford to permit Ka-ya-ten-nae, now seemingly adjusted to reservation life, to travel with Mangas and Loco to Turkey Creek, about fifteen miles south of Fort Apache, to view the site as a possible home for the tribe. The chiefs were favorably impressed. It was a good place: mountainous, like the Chiricahuas' former home, well watered, and rich with game.[13] Pleased with their chiefs' reports, the band asked for permission to move and Crook agreed.

In late March 1884 the Chiricahuas gathered their livestock and the agricultural equipment and seeds recently received and moved under military escort to Turkey Creek. Arriving at the site, Betzinez recorded that the tribe happily found their "beloved General Crook," whom they had not seen since he delivered them to Arizona a year before. Assembling them in conference, the Gray Fox gave them what the old Indian later recalled as "some good fatherly advice, mainly to settle down and go to work"—a standard Crook lecture.[14] Then the tribe settled in to their new home, erecting their wickiups on pine-covered slopes and upland meadows teeming with deer and wild turkeys, the latter not eaten by the Apaches, and traversed by clear streams full of trout, which were also not part of the Apache diet.

But though the Chiricahuas welcomed Crook's homily and trusted in his protection, they were not entirely satisfied with their new lives. Before they departed for Turkey Creek, Crawford, on Crook's orders, had informed the tribes that they would be subject to the same rules as had applied to them at San Carlos, many of which they deeply resented. Designed to facilitate military control as well as to protect them from the surrounding hostile white population, Crawford's commitment to enforcing these measures had significantly contributed to Crook's willingness to permit the band's relocation under the supervision of only a single officer, Britton Davis.

MOVE TO TURKEY CREEK   247

For Crook, among the most important of these measures was the issuance of brass identity tags to every male Indian fourteen years or older. He had introduced this requirement during his first tour in Arizona, and he continued to regard it as particularly important. Quite naturally the Apaches disliked it then and disliked it still.[15] But with the tribes dispersed throughout the vastness of the reservation in widely separated and remote small camps, Crook saw the system as more necessary than ever to keep track of their whereabouts.

In preparation for issuing the tags, Captain Crawford conducted a census, identifying every man and boy on the reservation deemed capable of bearing arms and the camp and tribe to which he belonged. Tags of different shapes were then issued, each representing a different tribal affiliation: a letter identified the bearer's band or subdivision of a tribe, and a number was assigned to him personally. The tag holders' names, tribal affiliations, and numbers were then recorded in books kept for that purpose. Every tag-holder had to wear it at all times and to present it when drawing rations. Rigorous enforcement and frequent roll calls made it relatively easy to identify and place every individual on the reservation at any given time. On occasion the tags operated to the benefit of the Indians, as they could be used to verify that a warrior accused of depredations against settlers or ranchers had been on the reservation at the time.[16]

Even more unwelcome than the tags was Crook's prohibition of certain practices dear to the heart of any Apache warrior. Most unpopular was a ban on the making and consumption of tiswin. The "tiswin-drunk" was a widely practiced and cherished custom of the Apaches. The abuse of alcohol is a problem in every society, and the Apache leaders could not understand why drinking tiswin was any more reprehensible than the consumption of whiskey so liberally indulged in by their military guardians. The military and civilian administrators on the reservation, however, saw the practice among Apaches as particularly iniquitous. Under the influence of the fermented corn drink, they seemed capable of committing the most appalling and senseless acts of violence. And in a society that prized revenge, tiswin-fueled incidents often led to an escalating cycle of mayhem. So Crook had no hesitation banning the practice despite its popularity. He also forbade wife-beating and the custom of cutting off the noses of unfaithful wives, prohibitions that Apache menfolk viewed as infringing on their absolute authority over their households. Indian police were charged with preventing these practices and apprehending those who violated the prohibitions. Transgressors could land in the guardhouse for a stay of ten days to two weeks. Violence resulting in death could lead to forfeiture of the miscreant's life.[17]

The Apache scouts, no longer needed to track down their rebellious fellow Indians, formed the Indian police force. They not only enforced the new measures and kept order on the reservation but also served as informants, keeping Lieutenant Davis aware of the mood of the people and breaches of agency rules. A guardhouse was maintained at San Carlos under the control of a white officer who served as provost and scouts who served as guards. Cases were tried before the provost or the commanding officer himself and were judged by Indian juries, a system that later drew objections from Wilcox, the Indian agent.[18]

Notwithstanding their resentment of the army's strict discipline, in the beginning most of the tribe settled quietly into their new homes. Each family group was assigned a plot of arable land near Turkey Creek. Using the stream's water for irrigation, they began to grow crops— corn and potatoes that first year. Typical of most warrior nomad societies, enthusiasm for agriculture seems to have been confined to the women. According to Davis, "None of the [male] Indians were making anything more than a bluff at farming." Most, he recalled, were happy to loaf and gamble and, when they wanted something, to trade a pony for it.[19]

The salubrious surroundings disguised the undercurrents that continued to roil the community. Particularly affected were the tribespeople recently returned from Mexico. Among them were individuals who had never experienced outside constraints on their behavior. Ka-ya-ten-nae, only temporarily mollified by his position in the scouts, allied with other disaffected leaders, including Geronimo, Chihuahua, and Naitche, all proud men who remained openly aloof and wary of military authority.[20] They complained bitterly to Davis about the prohibitions on making and drinking tiswin and against wife beating, claiming that these restrictions had not been included in the agreement they had negotiated with Crook in Mexico.

Davis soon learned from his spies that Ka-ya-ten-nae was openly advocating resistance to Crook's rules. In mid-June the lieutenant assembled the chiefs to discuss the matter, but neither side would give ground and the meeting ended on a sour note. Several days later Davis was informed by one of his spies that Ka-ya-ten-nae was not only counseling resistance but had participated in a tiswin-drunk that had culminated in a plot to kill the young officer. According to his informant, while Ka-ya-ten-nae and his cohorts surreptitiously sipped illegal tiswin in the bush, they had heard Davis approaching. Though the lieutenant was actually hunting turkeys, the warriors thought he had come to arrest them, so they hastily devised a plan to kill him from ambush and then flee to Mexico. Davis inadvertently foiled their plot, turning away from the path leading to the designated ambush site after hearing a turkey call from another direction. With only his spy's words as proof of the incident, Davis could not arrest the chief without exposing his source, so he took no action. But several days later, at a dance on June 21, Ka-ya-ten-nae was heard to brag of previous victories in his fights with the whites and "hinted of future engagements in which they [the Apaches] might hope to be equally fortunate."[21] This was enough for Davis, who now decided to arrest the chief.

Anticipating trouble because of Ka-ya-ten-nae's prominence in the community, the lieutenant sent a message to Fort Apache explaining the situation and asking for four troops of cavalry to help in the arrest. At sunrise on June 22, with troopers on hand, he assembled the tribal leadership, including Ka-ya-ten-nae, at his tent. Though obviously aware of the reason for the meeting, the Chihenne chief angrily demanded to know why Davis had summoned him. The lieutenant, feigning a calm he certainly did not feel, replied that Ka-ya-ten-nae was under arrest and would be sent to San Carlos for trial. With only two scouts by his side, Davis now found himself in a tense standoff. He was hemmed in between fifty or so armed chiefs and an apoplectic Ka-ya-ten-nae, and facing them, a line of troopers from Fort Apache, their guns drawn and cocked. He feared that at the very least he would be mowed down in the crossfire. Acting with a boldness he certainly did not feel, Davis reached out and relieved Ka-ya-ten-nae of his pistol and cartridge belt. To the amazement of all, the chief, apparently stunned by the young officer's boldness, seemed "suddenly to wilt, his bravado falling from him like a discarded cloak," in Davis's words. Having allowed himself to be disarmed, the chief had no choice but to meekly submit to his arrest.[22]

Crawford, who awaited Ka-ya-ten-nae at San Carlos, had already decided to make an example out of the chief. He appointed an Indian jury of Western Apache headmen eager to do his will and drew up charges alleging that the chief had fomented unrest among the Chiricahuas and plotted Davis's murder. Though Ka-ya-ten-nae vigorously denied the accusations, the die was cast. Crawford, determined to back Davis, had already decided on a conviction, and the jury voted accordingly, recommending that the chief be punished severely for his misdeeds.[23] The captain then imposed a harsh sentence of three years confinement and recommended to Crook that it be served at Alcatraz federal prison in San Francisco. There, the chief would be kept in irons, forced to wear white man's clothing, and required to perform manual labor.[24]

Crook seemed unconvinced that the evidence warranted the harshness of Crawford's proposed sentence, particularly the recommendation that it be served at Alcatraz.[25] At the time, the infamous prison was likely very much on his mind. Not long before Ka-ya-ten-nae's trial, he had asked his superiors to commute the sentences of several Apaches imprisoned there for their participation in the Cibicue fight, citing conflicting evidence at their trials and the salubrious impact their release would have on their fellow Apaches.[26] Ka-ya-ten-nae's case presented similar, if not identical, considerations. More importantly, the Gray Fox viewed the chief as an influential and respected leader and potentially an invaluable ally in Crook's effort to control the skittish bands. Yet respecting Crawford's judgment and agreeing that Ka-ya-ten-nae had been a disruptive force within the tribe, on balance, he reluctantly endorsed the captain's recommendation. However, he proposed a modified plan that would both turn the chief's incarceration to his advantage and ameliorate the severity of the sentence.

On August 2 Crook wrote to the Division of the Pacific's assistant adjutant general in San Francisco advising that Ka-ya-ten-nae be kept at hard labor in shackles for one month and then allowed to go about the island and the nearby city of San Francisco under guard. His exposure to white civilization, Crook reasoned, might impress the chief with the benefits of following the white man's road and thereafter make him a positive influence on his people upon his return to the reservation. The general's alternative was accepted, and, whether the chief was impressed or cowed by his exposure to the white world, it seemed to work. In March 1886 the general had Ka-ya-ten-nae released from Alcatraz. Other reservation leaders opposed his return, fearing he would stir unrest. But to their gratified amazement, in John Bourke's words the chief became an "Apostle of Peace" and, as Crook had hoped, played a key role in his peoples' adjustment to life on the reservation.[27]

Crook again demonstrated concern for the Chiricahuas' peace of mind in the case of the Chokonen scout My-klitz-so (Yellow Coyote), known to whites as Dutchy because soldiers thought his broad countenance lent him a Germanic appearance.[28] Dutchy was a complex character. He was as lethal as any of Geronimo's warriors, an equal-opportunity killer who slew both whites and Indians with apparent impartiality and lack of conscience. In July 1881, while breaking out of San Carlos to join Geronimo, he shot down a teamster in cold blood; and while with the shaman in Mexico, he had participated in Chatto's cross-border foray, evidently committing some of the murders that gave the raid its notoriety.[29] Yet in his earlier life on the reservation, he had scouted for the army. While doing so, he had demonstrated his loyalty in a somewhat perverse manner. At the request of the Indian agent, he had hunted down his own father, accused of killing a white man, and delivered the old Indian's head to the agent "with a smile of great satisfaction."[30] Later, again enlisted as a scout, he gained the support of Britton Davis, who was undoubtedly influenced by his conduct at the time of Ka-ya-ten-nae's arrest. It had been Dutchy who staunchly stood beside the young lieutenant as they faced the guns of both the army and his own people. Davis admired his loyalty and, for reasons not quite so obvious, found him extremely likeable, with "a keen sense of humor."[31]

In November 1883 the scout's propensity for violence caught up with him. Captain Crawford reported to Crook that the civil authorities in Graham County, Arizona, issued a warrant for Dutchy's arrest for the 1881 murder of the teamster. The captain asked the general whether he should cooperate.[32] A letter from U. S. Marshal Zan L. Tidball arrived on Crook's desk on the heels of Crawford's request, asking for the army's help in arresting Dutchy to avoid a serious incident.[33] Because a federal marshal was involved, Crook found it politic to refer the matter to the War Department. But he warned that since Geronimo and his followers remained at large in Mexico, if Dutchy were arrested, they would believe that they, too, could be apprehended and tried for similar wrongdoings and would refuse to return. It was also possible that those presently on the reservation would flee to Mexico, fearing a similar fate. Not to put too fine a point on it, he concluded, "I regard the decision asked for as of first importance as it will really decide whether or not we will have a continuance of warfare heretofore waged in this territory and Mexico."[34]

Though Crook had addressed the matter to the secretary of war, the latter passed the buck to Secretary Teller, who referred it back to Crook with a brief note: "Whether [Dutchy] ought to be surrendered to the civil authorities on process is for you to determine."[35] Crook, who may have expected such a response, refused to give up the scout.

Marshal Tidball did not give up. He made a second attempt to arrest Dutchy after Geronimo returned to the reservation. But Crook held fast to his original recommendation, informing the marshal's Justice Department superiors that the Chiricahuas "understand that their past offences will be overlooked provided they behave themselves in the future," Dutchy's arrest would be considered a breach of faith. Even an acquittal would leave them "with feelings of insecurity and a want of trust in the intentions of the Government." And though it might not cause a breakout, the arrest would occasion difficulties in managing the tribe.[36] The secretary of war agreed and ordered the marshal to stand down.

In November the persistent Tidball made a final attempt after a federal grand jury returned an indictment against Dutchy for the murder.[37] Crook remained adamant. Citing "grave results" that might ensue, he urged his superiors to make a "decisive" end to the matter.[38] Though local Arizona authorities did not abandon their efforts to arrest the scout, Washington continued to support Crook's decision. Dutchy remained in the army, serving ably and loyally. But all did not end well for him. In 1893 his homicidal nature and a life-long love of strong drink caught up with him, and he died in a drunken brawl with a soldier at Mount Vernon Barracks in Alabama.[39]

During the summer of 1884, while Geronimo's presence stirred new undercurrents of unrest at Turkey Creek, Crook contended with yet another factor that preyed on the Chiricahuas' mood. The small band, historically beleaguered by outsiders, had always focused on the preservation of their families. The prolonged captivity of several kinsmen, among them relatives of Chatto and Mangas, cast a heavy pall. In July Crook attempted to ameliorate the situation by asking the army to help repatriate two groups identified by the tribe. One group, Loco's followers, was held at Fort Union in New Mexico. The other, women and children captured and enslaved by the Mexicans during the recent fighting, was in Chihuahua.[40] In April 1885, after almost a year of foot-dragging, General Sheridan and the commissioner of Indian affairs finally agreed to transfer the Fort Union prisoners to Fort Apache, where they were reunited with their families.[41]

The case of the captives in Mexico proved more complex. Mexican authorities at first denied they held them. To refute this obvious falsehood and learn the extent of the problem, the Department of State intervened, asking Crook to compile a list of all tribal members the Chiricahuas believed to be captives.[42] Crook supplied ninety-five names furnished by their families. Confronted with this evidence, the Mexicans eventually agreed to return the children, but declared the adults ought to be given a choice whether to rejoin their people. In response Crook warned that unless the Mexicans released everyone, the Chiricahuas might use their continued captivity as an excuse to resume raiding in Chihuahua.[43] The governor of Chihuahua ultimately released thirteen of the captive women, setting them adrift to make their way home alone on foot. They finally reached Turkey Creek after an arduous journey of several months, rejoining their euphoric relatives.[44] Crook persisted in his effort to repatriate the remaining captives. In his 1884 annual report to the secretary of war, he reiterated that the failure to release them remained an irritant and a motivation for the tribe's young men to engage in reprisal raids into Mexico.[45]

Not all Crook's problems during this period related to the Chiricahuas. He had long emphasized that corruption was a major contributing factor to instability on the reservation, attributing it to employees and contractors of the Interior Department and using it as an important argument for army control over Indian affairs. So he was embarrassed and dismayed in the spring of 1884 to receive a report from Crawford that Archie McIntosh, one of Crook's most trusted scouts, had allegedly misappropriated supplies from the Indians and sold them to whites off the reservation.

McIntosh had first scouted for Crook in Idaho and Oregon and had accompanied the general to Arizona in 1871.[46] Despite his initial reluctance to make the move, the scout remained in the territory following Crook's departure for the Platte. Moving in and out of government service in various capacities, he married an Apache woman and bought a ranch near Globe. Upon Crook's return he joined the Sierra Madre campaign and was responsible for provisioning the Chiricahua scouts after their surrender, apparently without a hint of scandal.[47] He had even unearthed corruption in the rationing system at San Carlos, and his disclosures had been a crucial piece of evidence used to support Crook's takeover of management of the reservation. Crawford's report of McIntosh's malfeasance caught the general off guard.

Despite the scout's long and loyal service, Crook could not now afford to overlook the situation, particularly one involving the agency supply system. He ordered Crawford to investigate the allegations and discharge the scout if they proved true.[48] The charges proved well founded, and, with Crook's concurrence, Crawford fired McIntosh but granted the scout's request for a final appeal to the general. McIntosh used the reprieve to convince several Chiricahua leaders, whom he may have bribed with purloined supplies, to sign a petition to Crook asking that he be kept on. Discovering the scout's machinations, Crawford angrily expelled him from the reservation and berated the chiefs for allowing themselves to be used.[49] Crook approved his captain's handling of the situation. So Archie McIntosh, who served the Gray Fox faithfully for over twenty years and even saved his life on one occasion, rode into forced retirement, perched on a mule-drawn wagon loaded with the meager household effects acquired during a lifetime in government service.

CHAPTER SIXTEEN

More Fire from the Rear

As Crook worked to put the Chiricahuas on the road to assimilation, a most persistent obstacle to his progress was not the settler population, Tucson's "Indian Ring," or even forces within the tribe. It was the unwillingness of the Department of the Interior and its Indian Bureau to accept Crook's assumption of authority at San Carlos. The general was no longer a young man. In addition to the normal deterioration that accompanies aging, thirty years of military service, most of it spent campaigning under severe conditions, had exacted its toll on his body and health. Recurring bouts of malaria and other ailments sapped his energy, and, to Crook, the Indian Bureau's seemingly endless provocations added unnecessary stress to his usual burdens of command.

In the months following Crook's return from the Sierra Madre, San Carlos agent Wilcox and his boss, Secretary Teller, had eagerly sought opportunities to derail the July 1883 interagency agreement, which they regarded as usurping their legitimate authority over the reservation. The general, profoundly committed to military control, realized that there was some legal justification for the Interior Department's perspective and thought he was being as accommodating as possible to minimize bureaucratic squabbling. He labored to create an atmosphere of collegiality with the agent and at least initially believed himself successful.

Peacetime management of Indian affairs was an aspect of military service many cheerfully avoided. But Crook welcomed the duty. He sympathized with the Indians, admired them in many respects, and wanted to ensure their survival in the culture that was rapidly enveloping their homelands and threatening their extinction. Believing that assimilation was the only solution, he sought to retain management of the reservations to that end. In Arizona he now had the authority and rank he thought would, at last, allow him to prevail.

To mollify Anglo Arizonans, many of whom thought his policies coddled the Indians, he presented his position in terms of the territory's self-interest. His aim, he said at every opportunity, was peace and security at the lowest possible cost. Every instance of unrest among Indians could be attributed to broken promises and mistreatment, and the accompanying loss of life and property and the military expenditures surrounding Indian unrest retarded the economic progress that was the great promise of westward expansion. The simple solution was for whites to never lie to the Indians, to treat them fairly, and to furnish them with what they had been promised: a secure interest in land that could sustain them, education for their children, the means to attain self-sufficiency, and adequate food supplies until they could become self supporting. Under such a regimen, Crook predicted, the Indians would quickly acquire a stake in American society and become part of it. It was "better to have [the Indians] raise corn than scalps."[1]

Dealing with frontier society was, at least, fairly straightforward. Relations with the Interior Department were more complex and controversial. As outlined in chapter 8, Crook returned to Arizona in 1882 convinced that Indian Bureau policies and corrupt agents were responsible for the so-called mutiny at Cibicue. His subsequent investigations reinforced this conviction and led him to conclude that assuming control over the San Carlos Reservation and assigning his own officers to run it was the solution. Ignoring historical precedent, Crook convinced himself that the Interior Department would accept this plan.

At first, as we have seen, things went smoothly. Crook made decisions and Agent Wilcox supported him, a pattern that from his perspective seemed to make perfect sense, given the agent's inexperience, apparent indifference to his charges, and ignorance of their ways. In return for Wilcox's cooperation, the general worked to portray him in a positive light.

As long as Wilcox remained uncertain of his competency or his ability to control the Apaches, the relationship ran smoothly. He was so completely dependent on Crook's expertise and the trust and confidence that the Apaches reposed in the Nantan and his officers that he passively accepted the military's authority.[2] He freely admitted to Crook that he knew nothing of the Apaches and had so little confidence in his ability to deal with them that "he would not remain at their Agency if [Crook] were to leave the Department." Further, Wilcox assured the general, he "would do all in his power to assist him in controlling them."[3] For his part, Crook did his best to promote this collegiality. As mentioned in chapter 9, just prior to his departure for Mexico in February 1883, Crook had written Secretary Teller to defend the agent against charges of incompetence and corruption that had appeared in a local paper. In the letter he had frankly acknowledged the pitfalls of joint departmental control, warning that "the functions of the War and Interior Departments in a place like the San Carlos Agency touch so closely at the edges, and even overlap so frequently, that unless the respective officials be men of peculiar fitness for their duties, constant wrangling must result with the most disastrous consequences to the best interests of government." Nevertheless, with Wilcox at the helm Crook allowed that he did not anticipate such a problem. In fact, he could "unhesitatingly say that if you do not support him fully you will most certainly regret it."[4] Wilcox gratefully responded that "I shall never forget your kindness and hope, at sometime, to have an opportunity of demonstrating the extent of my appreciation."[5] Such expressions of mutual gratitude and admiration permitted Crook to depart for Mexico confident that he was leaving behind an Indian agent who would do his bidding. Sadly, he was soon disabused of that notion.

As most of the soldiers stationed at San Carlos had joined Crook's campaign in Mexico, Wilcox found himself with few troops for protection, and he was saddled with almost exclusive administrative responsibility over the reservation. Of necessity, he developed some facility in dealing with the tribespeople and experienced a newfound confidence in his abilities as an agent. With this emergent self-assurance came a diminished sense of his dependence on the army's protective presence and a desire to assert prerogatives that he had formerly ceded eagerly to the military.[6] Though he still considered Crook a partner in Indian management, he began to fancy that he was the more senior.

Wilcox demonstrated his new assertiveness in a letter to Crook in May 1883, delivered while the general was deep in the Sierra Madre. The subject was Captain William E. Dougherty, one of Crook's officers at San Carlos, who, the agent complained, had trampled on Wilcox's authority and impugned his reputation. The origin of the agent's outrage was a news story recounting his refusal to honor the captain's request for seeds for the Western Apaches at Fort Apache in furtherance of Crook's policy of promoting self-sustainable agriculture on the reservation. Rebuffed by the agent, the captain had purchased the seeds on the commercial market, and he told the Apaches to ask Wilcox for rations to sustain them during the period between planting and harvest. The article reported that the agent denied this request also, leaving the Indians destitute. In his letter to Crook Wilcox freely admitted to refusing these requests because "supplying the Indians of this reservation is my prerogative." The agent saw the captain's actions, taken "without so much as saying 'by your leave sir,'" as a clear usurpation of his authority. Not only that, he believed that Dougherty had planted the story in the press to embarrass him.[7]

Wilcox had a point. By involving himself in Western Apache agricultural affairs, Captain Dougherty had clearly infringed on the agent's turf. Under the agreement Crook had reached with Secretary Teller, aside from the Chiricahuas, the army's authority on San Carlos Reservation was limited to maintaining the peace, and then only at the request of the Indian agent. Agricultural activities were off limits. Nor did the army have any authority with respect to rations. Even though Dougherty had overstepped his authority, Wilcox's response demonstrated a marked lack of concern for the welfare of his charges and a preference for bureaucratic nicety over practical and humanitarian considerations. To Crook the agent's complaint must have seemed not only petty but also suggestive of a previously unimagined aggressiveness that boded ill for his future relations with the military.

Upon his return from the Sierra Madre, the general had anticipated resistance from the local population to resettling the Chiricahuas at San Carlos, but probably not the persistent opposition now mounted by Wilcox and his Interior Department superiors in Washington. The imposition of military control on the reservation had never been acceptable to the Interior Department, and Secretary Teller made every effort to subvert it. He received support from a powerful combination of Ari-

zona economic and political interests and local newspapers, all working in concert to perpetuate fear of Apache depredations. Removal
of the tribe from the territory would open fertile and mineral-rich
reservation lands for white exploitation. Stirring anxiety in the white
population also ensured a continuing flow of government dollars into
the territory in support of the military presence, a financial bonanza to
the Arizona business community of over $2 million annually. So there
were sound economic reasons to oppose Crook's efforts to bring peace
to the territory.[8]

To discredit the general, stories began to appear in newspapers in
widely scattered locations shortly after his return from Mexico. They
alleged that the Chiricahuas had captured Crook in the Sierra Madre
and that the terms of their surrender had been extorted from him in
exchange for the lives of his command.[9] The stories were so similar
that the general later surmised that "their common origin was apparent." He suspected that Teller or his minions had planted them and
added that they were "evidence that the Interior Department was not
in sympathy with my views."[10]

In public Crook brushed aside the allegations, asserting that the secretary of war had already denied their validity. But in private they
stung him deeply. In a letter to Secretary Lincoln, he complained bitterly of this "systematically prepared falsehood." While claiming to
"overlook the design and intent to injure and misrepresent me," he
could not ignore the damage such allegations would cause to his ability
to solve "this intricate Indian problem." His calls for an inquiry into
the problem were ignored.[11]

Despite Crook's repeated denials, the tale took on a life of its own.
A former Texas state senator named Barnett Gibbs, a hardliner on the
Apache question (and possibly motivated by business interests in Arizona), widely circulated the story, embroidering it to suit his needs.
Claiming a source in the military, he put forward the image of powerful and unrepentant savages forcing their will upon Crook and the
army. The general and his command, he announced, had been captured by the Apaches and then "promenaded . . . in triumph back to
civilization." Some of the more thoughtful papers considered the story
vastly overblown. The *New York Times* found "some improbabilities
about Gibbs's story, but it was sufficiently out of the ordinary to serve
in hot weather and the result was its wide circulation."[12]

When a journalist queried Secretary Teller about the accuracy of the tale, he equivocated: "I do not know. [Crook] is an honorable man and I suppose what he said was true." Secretary Lincoln far more emphatic, dismissing Gibbs's tale as "utterly without foundation."[13] Captain Bourke also leaped to Crook's defense. Interviewed by a reporter while on a visit to Philadelphia, he declared that Crook "was not defeated. I say this positively, without regard to the assertions of so-called state senators or of military dudes in Washington."[14] The "military dudes" Bourke referred to may have been "certain frontier officers" who, the captain speculated, might have repeated the canard out of jealousy.[15] A week later Bourke, by then in Nebraska for his wedding, took time out from his nuptials to again publicly "deny to our Omaha friends the lies about Crook which have been manufactured by military dudes in Washington."[16] Though generally discredited today, the tale would persist for years to come.[17]

While forces opposed to Crook worked to undermine him in the press, Agent Wilcox launched his own campaign to subvert the general's authority on the reservation. His previous attempt to scuttle Crook's plan to settle the Chiricahuas at San Carlos was an opening salvo, designed to embarrass the general by forcing him to renege on his commitment to keep the tribe in Arizona and trigger a stampede back into Mexico. By thwarting that plot and securing the interdepartmental agreement that installed him on the reservation, Crook made it obvious to Wilcox and Teller that a frontal assault on the general would not succeed. The secretary, wary of a confrontation with President Arthur, cautioned Wilcox to try and get along with Crook, at least for the time being.

But the agent was no longer the pliant neophyte he had once been. Only two months after the agreement went into effect, he wrote to the secretary to advocate for the agreement's repeal. Portraying joint management of San Carlos as a temporary expedient only needed to protect the Chiricahuas during the immediate period following their return from Mexico, he recommended it be phased out. Continuing it, he wrote, would in effect simply engender conflict and hinder progress in turning the Apaches toward agrarian pursuits.[18] When his suggestion was ignored, he launched a yearlong, rolling barrage of complaints against Captain Crawford, Crook's alter ego at San Carlos. Lower in rank than the general, the captain seemed more vulnerable, someone who could be ousted if the agent could demonstrate his unfitness to manage Indian affairs. With Crawford deposed, Wilcox might then be able to convince the government to remove the army from the reservation altogether.[19]

Crawford's personality and the manner in which he performed his duties made him an inviting target. When Crook first assigned him to San Carlos in the months preceding the Sierra Madre campaign, the captain's proactive management style reflected that of his commander, and it worked in the cooperative atmosphere that then existed between Crook and Wilcox. But following Crawford's return from Mexico, the situation changed.

Though the interdepartmental agreement limited the military's jurisdiction to the exercise of police powers for all tribes but the Chiricahuas, Crook and his subordinates, especially Crawford, shared a far more expansive view of their authority. Activists by temperament, they were firmly convinced of their superior expertise in Indian affairs and equally skeptical of the competence and perhaps the honesty of the Indian Bureau's staff.[20] Operating under such preconceptions, they were wont to intervene often in areas beyond their purview. As Crawford admitted, "The Indians are continually coming to me asking advice in regard to farming and to settle difficulties over the location of their lands. I always give them what little information I possess and settle their difficulties for them."[21] By "Indians" he meant all of the bands on the reservation, not just the Chiricahuas. Since his detailed reports to Crook did not evoke censure, his commander obviously approved of his overreaching.

Crawford's encroachments outraged Wilcox and gave the agent ammunition for his campaign. His anger was fueled by personal animosity that apparently originated when, upon his return from Mexico, Crawford had met with tribal leaders to assess their attitude toward the return of the Chiricahuas. These gatherings had exposed the agent's attempts to stir up opposition to the tribe, embarrassing him and ultimately undermining his efforts to sow dissent. His growing resentment was further exacerbated by what he perceived as Crawford's "gruff, dictatorial, and self-important" manner.[22] Motivated by animus and by what he believed to be a just cause, Wilcox now focused on Crawford's multiple invasions of the agent's "prerogatives."

Crawford had his own grievances against Wilcox. He found it particularly galling that the agent persistently claimed credit for improvements on the reservation that he himself had initiated. Crook, while sympathetic, was anxious to avoid unnecessary complications with the Interior Department bureaucracy that might impede his own work. So he attempted to calm the waters, cautioning the captain to swallow his pride and get on with business.[23] Though Crawford agreed to try, it is evident that he was not terribly motivated, and any willingness he had dissipated in the face of Wilcox's virulent attacks.

The agent began his campaign in the early months of 1884, raising an issue related to sending Apache children to the Carlisle Indian School in Pennsylvania. Though the idea of doing so originated with Crawford, Wilcox, as Indian agent, was responsible for recruiting pupils for the school. The agent wrote to his superiors, saying that the captain had "greatly embarrassed the agent in his efforts" by recruiting the children himself. The accusation came to nothing after Crawford revealed that Wilcox had, in fact, asked for the captain's help when his own attempts had failed. The captain's error, it seems, was to make the agent appear inept.[24] This fracas was the first of many instances in which Wilcox disregarded or distorted facts in bungled attempts to demonstrate that Crawford exceeded his authority and ought, therefore, to be relieved.

Not long after the school fiasco, the agent brought a new charge against Crawford, this time objecting to the captain's allowing a horse trader to come on the reservation to sell his mounts to the Apaches. In a letter to Commissioner of Indian Affairs Hiram Price, Wilcox charged that Crawford had usurped the agent's exclusive legal authority to authorize traders to come on the reservation.[25] Trade with the Indians was a particularly sensitive area to Indian agents as it touched on the pecuniary benefits available to them to augment their salaries. But again, Wilcox omitted pertinent facts in framing his allegations. It soon developed that Crawford had indeed allowed the trader to sell his horses on the reservation, but only to Apache scouts enrolled in the military. As such, Crawford's action had been an appropriate procurement by the commanding officer of the scout detachment, and once more the agent's charge dissolved when confronted by the facts.[26]

While the horse trader dispute was still winding its way up the chain of command, Crawford unwisely stoked Wilcox's outrage by intruding in an area in which the agent did have unquestioned authority: the reservation rationing system. From the beginning of his tenure at San

Carlos, the captain had taken a keen interest in the quality and quantity of the food supplies provided by the government to the Indians. From Crook's perspective, Crawford's focus was not only warranted but laudable. Corruption and mismanagement in the rationing system was often a source of unrest at San Carlos and other reservations throughout the West. On this occasion, Crawford inspected cattle being delivered to the reservation under a procurement contract between the agent and a local rancher. He found that some of the animals intended as breeding stock were "a miserable lot of scrawny cows, several of them very old and barren." Believing that both the government and the Indians were being cheated, Crawford suggested to Crook that an officer be detailed to inspect all cattle before they were issued to the Indians.[27] His observations drew howls of outrage from the contractor and, of course, the agent.[28]

Crawford's meddling in the beef contract gave Teller what he considered clear justification to request the captain's removal, and Wilcox, of course, enthusiastically agreed and penned a lengthy letter to the commissioner of Indian affairs enumerating the captain's "misdeeds." Careful to avoid criticizing General Crook directly, Wilcox had no such inhibitions when it came to Crawford, whom he now accused of implementing the interdepartmental agreement so as to "deprive the agent of all voice in the management of Indian affairs on the reservation." His interference was so pervasive, the agent claimed, that the Indians had come to believe that he (Wilcox) had no function other than to issue weekly rations. The captain's conduct, the agent concluded, rendered the agreement "only productive of unprofitable results to the Indians."[29]

In support of his contention, the agent provided a litany of every grievance, real or imagined, he had endured at Crawford's hands. Commencing with the captain's "use of influences amounting almost to coercion" to force the reservation Indians to accept the Chiricahuas back at San Carlos, Wilcox charged the captain with abuses that ran the gamut from intervention in Apache agricultural practices to harboring a murderer (Dutchy).

Saving what he considered the best for last, Wilcox ended his screed with the tale of Crawford's involvement in the trial of a scout named Charley, accused of murdering his adulterous wife. Not only had Crawford allowed the miscreant to be tried by an Indian jury, but upon his conviction the captain had surrendered the murderer to the relatives of the victim for punishment. Subsequently, the agent indignantly declared, the prisoner's mangled remains had been found near the agency and had been buried by a detachment of prisoners under guard of Crawford's scouts. Wilcox believed that this sequence of events proved beyond a doubt the captain's "unfitness . . . to remain among the Indians upon whom the Interior Department desires to impress the benign usefulness of Christian civilization."[30]

Crawford regarded Wilcox's allegations, if left unchallenged, as potentially damaging to his career. He therefore demanded a military court of inquiry to investigate and clear him of the charges. Crook saw the inquiry as an opportunity to defend his own ideas on Indian management. He laid out his position in a dispatch to Major General Pope, commander of the Division of the Pacific, intended for inclusion in the court's record. Its tone belied Crook's annoyance at the agent's ill-considered attacks, and unsurprisingly, its content defended Crawford's conduct in every respect—and by extension, Crook's own policies.[31]

Reviewing Wilcox's past history at San Carlos, the general argued that the agent had willingly ceded his authority to the military, not only over reservation policing but over agricultural activities as well. His acquiescence led Crawford, at Crook's direction, to assume "police-control [evidently broadly defined] of the entire reservation, Agent Wilcox being of assistance only so far as he dealt honestly with the Indians." Under these circumstances, Crook claimed "astonishment and perplexity" when upon his return from Mexico he was inexplicably confronted by Wilcox's "complete change of front." Crook asserted that the agreement of July 1883, so vehemently condemned by Wilcox, simply ratified the status quo that had existed prior to his departure into Mexico. If anything, it reinforced the army's authority over the Indians. "The only difference being," Crook caustically noted, "that the Agent no longer received the credit for managing the Apaches, with whose management he had really so little to do."[32]

Of all the charges made by Wilcox, Crook seemed most disturbed by those that pertained to the trial and punishment of the scout Charley. The agent's criticisms struck at the heart of what Crook regarded as a core concept of reservation management. Introducing Indians to the Euro-American judicial process was an essential step in moving them toward acceptance of the white man's concept of civic responsibility.

In the instant case, it involved the right to dispense justice in matters internal to the tribe, an idea that Crook had sought to put into practice in Arizona as early as 1874.[33]

As to the severity of the punishment meted out, he had this to say:

> The Apaches are a fierce, treacherous people, in dealing with whom only the most stringent methods are of the least efficacy. It is impossible to make them abandon their life-long traditions of blood and cruelty unless by the severest punishment their unruly and turbulent spirits can be impressed with a cause of their responsibility to the law. . . . Whether or not the severity of the punishment, in the present case, may be deprecated, it is their view of what is just and proper under the circumstances.

He expressed hope that as the Apaches became more assimilated into American culture, a direction in which he believed they were at present headed, the prevailing system of blood atonement would give way to our "milder and humane methods of dealing with criminals." The reader is free to consider the irony implicit in this latter conclusion.[34]

The Crawford inquiry became an arena in which the War and Interior Departments laid out their respective claims for control over Indian affairs, but in this instance the military judged the merits. Unsurprisingly, after a review of the record, the court of inquiry ruled that not only had Wilcox's allegations "failed of proof, but almost every allegation contained in [his letter] has been disproved." The court further found that Crawford's actions had been "wise and for the best interests of the Indians." General Crook predictably approved the court's findings.[35] The army lined up solidly behind the general and his broad assumption of control over all the tribes at San Carlos and absolved the captain of responsibility for overstepping the bounds of his authority. General Pope, Crook's division commander, exemplified the military's position. He officially endorsed the court's conclusions in every respect, finding them "entirely conclusive in regard to the charges made against [Crawford]." He also offered his unsolicited opinion that joint jurisdiction over the San Carlos agency had been a bad idea from the outset, though it may have been the only solution to the situation at the time. The continuation of disputes between the agent and the captain, he opined, had, as Crook had predicted, caused "serious injury to the public interests, danger to the peaceful status of the Indians, and in all respects, bad administration." To remedy the situation, he suggested that the management of San Carlos should be given exclusively to one or the other department. Since the present arrangement had been Crook's idea in the first place and since the War Department had endorsed it, Pope thought the general ought now to have exclusive control of the reservation.[36] Pope's outburst fell on deaf ears. Control on the reservation remained divided and, as neither Wilcox nor the Interior Department agreed with the court's findings, the quarrel between the agent and Crawford continued unabated. Unfortunately, but typically, it was the Indians who bore the brunt.

While the Apaches and Yavapais were making some progress in raising their own food, it was insufficient to sustain them. The government made no move to make up for the shortfall. During the summer of 1884 the situation became so dire that Crawford worried that an outbreak might result unless additional rations were forthcoming from the Indian Bureau. According to the department records, from June 28 to July 25, the Indians received only half the amount due them. From July 25 to August 8, no beef was received at all. And from August 8 to the 21st, only half the issue was provided. During this time no sugar, coffee, or salt arrived on the reservation, and the flour issued was unfit for consumption.[37] Conditions reached such a pass that the Indians requested Crook's permission to kill their breeding cattle for food. The general refused, believing that the destruction of their breeding stock would retard the tribes' progress toward self-sufficiency. Instead he telegraphed his superiors in the Division of the Pacific pleading that the Department of the Interior institute a regular system of adequate rations to ameliorate the situation, which now threatened to become a crisis. The Indian Commissioner denied Crook's request, spitefully citing Crawford's testimony at his court of inquiry that the Indians under military control at San Carlos were now "entirely self-supporting." In the absence of evidence to the contrary, the commissioner, apparently bent on using hunger to provoke unrest and thus demonstrate the ineffectiveness of military management, ruled that there was no need for additional rations.[38]

Despairing of receiving rations from the department, Crawford issued passes to two groups of Apaches, numbering about six hundred Indians, to allow them to forage from traditional sources off the reservation. The passes were narrowly drawn, limiting the Indians' access to sparsely occupied areas to the south and north of the reservation. There, it was hoped, they could find the game, mescal, and the fruit of the saguaro cactus to supplement their dwindling food supplies, leaving local settlers undisturbed. Nevertheless, the local populace was aroused. To ranchers and farmers in the region, the effect of sightings of large numbers of reportedly well-armed Apaches riding over the landscape was immediate and electric. Though no incidents were reported, local Anglos put together a petition expressing their outrage and submitted it to the Indian agent through his clerk. Without properly investigating the complaint, Wilcox promptly forwarded it to the Indian commissioner, spitefully adding a gratuitous canard—that Crawford had allowed the Indians off the reservation "to gratify his hatred of white citizens." The commissioner happily sent the petition on to the War Department, obviously hoping that this might at last result in the captain's removal. After receiving Crawford's full report, General Sheridan, who had succeeded to the post of commanding general following Sherman's retirement, dismissed the matter out of hand, as not a single incident of an untoward nature had actually occurred. The foraging parties had, in fact, presented no threat. They had been composed primarily of women and children and had each been accompanied by an escort of scouts under an officer and Chief of Scouts Al Sieber.[39]

Wilcox and Crawford's feud culminated with something less than a bang. Crawford apparently provoked the final disagreement, which involved an employee named Gilson who had been hired to advise the Indians on agricultural matters. With permission from Wilcox, Gilson had built a farmhouse, corral, and well on the reservation beside the road leading to Globe. The well was primarily a convenience for whites using the road—it was the only water source between San Carlos and the town—but Gilson also allowed Indians to use it. Aside from attending to travelers on the road, Gilson also grazed his cattle on nearby reservation land and watered them at the well, again with the agent's permission. Like Crook, Crawford took a dim view of non-Indians trespassing on reservation land and requested that the man be removed from the reservation. He justified his action as an exercise of his police powers as such encroachments were a source of discontent among the Indians.

Once again, the controversy boiled down to the old issue of civil versus military authority. The War Department at first sided with their man. However, when Secretary Teller and his commissioner of Indian affairs pressed their support of the agent, Secretary Lincoln ordered Crawford to withdraw his objections. In September, despite having won that battle, Wilcox, never too enamored of either Arizona or Apaches, had had enough. He resigned, remaining on the job only long enough for his replacement, Charles D. Ford, to arrive.[40]

Ford, too, was a political appointee and like his predecessor had no prior familiarity with the Apaches. Possibly for that reason, on arrival he followed Wilcox's example and initially cooperated willingly with the army, in this case with Crawford. Unlike Wilcox, however, Ford brought to his work a commitment to carry out his duties to the best of his ability. Along with this seriousness of purpose, he possessed a relaxed and pleasing personality.[41] Nevertheless, Crawford, frustrated and jaded by his prolonged feud with Wilcox, rejected the opportunity for a fresh start. Instead he treated the new agent coldly and exhibited little interest in his gestures of cooperation. Less than a month passed before the two men became embroiled in confrontation.

The dispute arose in December when the Interior Department's annual issue of clothing and other annuity goods arrived at the agency. By law the annual distribution was given into the custody of the agent to be distributed under his aegis. With custody came fiduciary responsibility, rendering the agent personally liable if any of the goods were lost or stolen. A portion of the goods was designated for distribution to the White Mountain people and to the Chiricahuas around Fort Apache, who were in dire need of the allotment's blankets and clothing to tide them through the winter. Without bothering to inform Ford or involve him in the distribution, Crawford ordered Davis and Gatewood, the officers respectively in charge of the two tribes, to send a pack train to transport the annuities north to their post. When informed of Crawford's orders, Ford reluctantly agreed to allow the military to ship the goods, but he insisted on accompanying them to the post in fulfillment of his legal responsibilities. Crawford stubbornly rejected the agent's condition, unfairly suggesting that it was part of an Interior Department plot to withhold the goods from the Indians in order to "cause an outbreak if possible." Rather than allow Ford to accompany the pack train, he sent the mules back to Fort Apache without the allotted supplies.[42]

Of course, it was the Indians who suffered, deprived of their annuities and forced to endure a mountain winter without the warm clothing and blankets they had been promised. According to Davis they quite naturally manifested "considerable dissatisfaction" at this state of affairs. Some went so far as to blame the problem on Crook. And to an extent they were justified in doing so. Despite the suffering and possible unrest that resulted from Crawford's action, the general did not intercede to have the goods released. Confronted with a situation that pitted the Interior Department against the military and wishing to support an officer who had served him so well, he opted to do nothing, despite the suffering his captain's wrong-headed action inflicted on the Indians.[43] The incident demonstrates that, on occasion, Crook's humanitarian concerns for the Indians were not immutable. When faced with a choice between the welfare of the tribes and the prerogatives of the military, he could ignore Indian interests in favor of the army to which he owed his career.

In January, with the annuity issue at a stalemate, Crawford overreached yet again, arresting and ordering the removal of two agency employees whom he accused of hostility to the army and interfering in military functions. An exasperated Crook countermanded the order.[44] His commander's failure to sustain him was a severe blow to Crawford. Yet he continued to meddle in areas beyond his purview.

Matters with Agent Ford finally came to a head over an irrigation ditch being dug by Yuma tribesmen under the supervision of one of Crawford's lieutenants. When the agent's request that the Indians desist was ignored, he confiscated their tools and reported to the commissioner of Indian affairs that "the right to direct the farming operations of my Indians has been assumed and is now being exercised by Capt. Crawford."[45] The quarrel soon escalated to Crook's level. Perhaps feeling the need to atone for not backing his captain in his previous squabble, the general attempted to defend the captain's behavior, arguing in a dispatch to General Pope that agricultural matters should fall under military authority because food issues often caused unrest on the reservation. To this stale argument he added, somewhat dubiously, that the Chiricahuas were so widely dispersed on the reservation that the army could not assist them without also helping the other tribes who farmed alongside them. To emphasize his support for Crawford, he ended his letter with the now-familiar threat to resign should the War Department not sustain him in this matter. General Pope, Crook's immediate superior, endorsed the dispatch, ominously predicting that should his general's authority "be curtailed or modified in any way there are certain to follow very serious results, if not a renewal of Indian wars and depredations in Arizona."[46]

Crook's threat must have rung hollow, even to himself. The Apaches had been quiet for the entire year while under his management, probably for the first time since before the Mexican War in 1848. No one in government wanted to upset that apple cart, so there would be little support for replacing him.[47] Secretary Lincoln had no intention of relieving Crook, yet he had no wish to see the feud between the agent and the captain continue. As that would be the likely result of sustaining the captain, he disregarded Crook's arguments and threats and ordered Crawford to stop interfering in agricultural affairs at San Carlos. Humiliated and exhausted by the struggle, Crawford requested reassignment to his former regimental company, now stationed in Texas.[48] While warmly commending Crawford for his service, Crook reluctantly granted his request, tacitly acknowledging that the officer's usefulness at San Carlos had now come to an end.

Crawford's replacement was Captain Francis E. Pierce, First Infantry, a Civil War veteran and experienced professional.[49] Immediately prior to his San Carlos assignment, he had served with the Hualapais, a tribe not affiliated with the Apaches. Consequently, while he had some knowledge of territorial affairs, he had none of the deep familiarity with the Apaches that had characterized Crawford's relations with the tribe. For that reason, he lacked the trust and confidence they had placed in his predecessor. Despite this, Pierce proved an excellent choice and was regarded by at least one of his fellow officers as "one of the best 'Indian men' that we ever had."[50] Unburdened by the past differences that had afflicted Ford's relationship with Crawford, he moved swiftly to resolve any disagreements with the agent. The two men soon developed a collaborative relationship and began working in tandem to improve the lot of the reservation's Apaches.[51]

The personnel shifts at San Carlos coincided with a change of administration in Washington. In 1885 Grover Cleveland became the first

Democrat to enter the White House since the short, unhappy reign of Andrew Johnson. The new president regarded himself as a reformer on the Indian question, and, like Crook, he believed in assimilation. Perhaps the similarity in their views on the Indian question persuaded the president to consider broadening Crook's mandate in the management of San Carlos. Not long after his inauguration, Cleveland's newly appointed secretary of war, William C. Endicott, wrote to his equally new counterpart at Interior, Lucius Q. C. Lamar, suggesting that General Crook be given charge of the entire reservation.[52] Lamar was a Southerner, so valued for his intelligence and integrity that within two years he would be elevated to the Supreme Court. He, too, saw himself as a reformer committed to fair treatment for the Indians and to the removal of corrupt and incompetent employees from the ranks of the Indian Bureau, including its agents on the reservations. He would also become an ardent subscriber to the concept of private ownership of tribal lands as the key to assimilation, a major tenet of General Crook's Indian philosophy.[53] With this background and an apparent familiarity with Crook's administrative record, Lamar was favorably disposed to Endicott's suggestion. He ordered an inspection of the agency and asked that Agent Ford express his opinion on the proposal. Quite naturally Ford opposed ceding control to the army over all aspects of reservation management, but he was open to surrendering jurisdiction over Fort Apache and its environs—in other words, over the Chiricahua and White Mountain bands.[54]

Whether Ford's recommendation would have carried the day will never be known, since it was superseded by other events in the spring of 1885. In the meantime, during the fall and winter of 1884 Crook could view the situation at San Carlos and throughout his department with considerable satisfaction. The Chiricahuas had apparently integrated themselves into reservation life, and there was growing comity between the Indian agent and military officers that heralded a period of tranquility on the reservation. As no crisis demanded his urgent attention, Crook was able to contemplate a brief break from the bureaucratic obligations that bound him to his desk at Fort Whipple. Never enamored of paperwork, he much preferred indulging his interests in the natural world: hunting, fishing, and exploring the still-unsettled western backcountry. Hence, when in November 1884 the opportunity arose for such an outing, he seized it.

According to Bourke, who would accompany him and who perhaps first suggested the expedition, its impetus came from a visit by a delegation of the tiny Havasupai tribe to Fort Whipple a year earlier. In June 1882, by executive order, President Hayes had awarded the Supai, as they were sometimes called, their own reservation on the floor of Cataract Canyon, a narrow, half-mile-deep declivity carved out by the rushing waters of Cataract Creek, one of the tributaries that had formed the Grand Canyon. The reservation, twelve miles long and five miles wide and accessible only by means of a single, narrow trail, stretched along the banks of the creek. It was as remote a site as one would hope to find in Arizona.[55]

The Supais had come to Whipple to report the presence among their people of an Apache Mohave, or Yavapai, from San Carlos who was wanted for the year-old murder of an Apache scout. While generals do not normally travel long distances to apprehend fugitives, even murderers, Crook evidently saw this bit of stale news as an excuse for adventure and learning. He had taken such a trip once before in Arizona, in 1875, just prior to his reassignment to the Platte, during a similar period of low activity. He and Bourke, a keen student of Indian culture, had paid a visit to the Moquis using a similarly tenuous excuse.[56] Now known as the Hopis, the Moquis were, coincidently, closely related to the Supais, both geographically and culturally. Piqued by his own curiosity, and probably with a little prodding from Bourke, Crook now decided to call on the Supais not far from the area he had visited a decade before. While there he would, of course, apprehend the fugitive and return him to San Carlos for trial.

On November 6 Crook, accompanied by Bourke and a California artist named Alexander Harmer, traveled by rail from Fort Whipple north to the small village of Ash Fork. There they were joined by another Crook aide, Captain Cyrus Roberts; Cowarrow, a Hualapais chief; and Charlie Spencer, a former scout married to a Hualapai woman. Cowarrow and Spencer would serve as guides and interpreters. From Ash Fork the men and their small pack train set out, Crook astride his favorite mule, Apache, for the trailhead into the canyon some sixty miles away.

Despite his fifty-six years and his occasional bouts with illness, Crook considered himself to be in good condition and evinced no apparent qualms about embarking on what all anticipated would be a strenuous journey. Proud of his fitness, he was always on the lookout for opportunities to demonstrate it to his colleagues. So this would be another of his Spartan exercises. As no troop escort accompanied the group, each officer would be responsible for the care of his own horse or mule. Further, his guides had advised him that since they were headed into a land of few watering places and sparse forage, it would be unwise to encumber the expedition with a large pack train of thirsty animals. Consequently, Crook restricted his companions' baggage to a minimum. Though they could expect cold weather at these elevations—two inches of ice formed in their water buckets the first night—the travelers would take no tents and only "the most necessary bedding and clothing."

After ascending for three days into the high Grand Canyon country, they caught their first sight of the Supais' home. Described by Bourke as "a tremendous gash in the bosom of Nature," it presented an awesome spectacle, a gaping abyss framed by "hideous escarpments and on each hand other walls equally grim and deadly." Snaking its way along the sides of this formidable fissure, they could see "the narrow trail, rocky, steep and perilous . . . passing over a chasm which seemed to fairly yawn for victims" before disappearing into the canyon's shadowy depths.

Bourke's fearsome description soon proved no exaggeration. After a tortuous, hour-long descent on foot, leading their mules, Crook and his officers reached the canyon floor, exhausted but elated at their survival, a euphoria that quickly turned to horror. Looking back to view the mules picking their way cautiously down the trail, they watched aghast as one of the animals lost its footing and rolled and tumbled three or four hundred feet, shot over a vertical wall "like a projectile from a catapult, hurled through the air a thousand feet until it struck with the deafening report of a cannon upon a towering mass of sandstone, [and] burst into two pieces." When the mule's remains rolled to a stop several hundred feet away from the appalled officers, little was left of the beast save an unrecognizable mass of flesh, bone, entrails, and the shattered and misshapen contents of its load, the expedition's entire mess outfit.

Gathering the mangled remnants of their eating utensils, cups, and plates, the party continued down the canyon floor along the dry bed of Cataract Creek until fatigue forced them to camp amid the cacti and other spiny flora that crowded most of the available space on the stream's banks. A restless night among the thorns was followed by a sparse breakfast served on their few still useable mess tins and a lengthy, exhausting trek through fine, deep sand down the winding course of the canyon. Crook led the march and got so far ahead of his comrades that by the time they reached their next camp, he had already built fires to welcome them.

Bourke's diary entry describing the evening's entertainment provides a rare glimpse of a more whimsical aspect of the general's personality. At dinner the captain sought to impress his audience with a description of the unearthly cries of a mountain lion that had followed them at a distance along the trail. "The attempt made by General Crook," he defiantly recorded, "to bribe Cowarrow into saying that we had been unnerved by the braying of a Supai donkey or the hooting of an owl failed miserably."

They had camped very close to the Supai village and probably could have spent the night there instead of camping out among the cacti. But rather than impose on the villagers by arriving unheralded in the night, Crook tactfully waited for morning to send Cowarrow into the village to announce their presence, a bit of frontier courtesy that Bourke did not find sufficiently unusual to comment on. After the morning meal Cowarrow returned with a small delegation of their Supai hosts to the campsite. At its head was the village chief, a well-built Indian wearing a hat adorned with the feathers of a golden eagle. The chief, Navajo by name, warmly greeted the general and invited him and his companions to visit the village. In return, Crook, adhering to Supai protocol, politely invited the chief to first partake of a meal of coffee, bread, meat, and tobacco. Navajo accepted and while eating noticed the lack of fodder for the animals around the campsite. He generously offered to allow Crook to graze his stock in his own harvested fields. Then, after a modest breakfast and a companionable smoke, the Supai led the party into the village.

Bourke immediately noticed that despite the aridity of the canyon, the tribe seemed amply provided with food. Irrigated fields of maize, peach orchards, and a variety of other crops common to the Southwest surrounded the village. Strolling among the houses, which were "of comfortable construction," the visitors saw women hard at work on household chores to a background chorus of noisy dogs whose howling echoed off the canyon walls and filled the air. As with the Moquis, the visitors observed all manner of artfully crafted items for which they eagerly traded. Not to be outdone by his villagers, the chief presented Crook with a beautiful blanket of Navajo design.

In the village and while hiking further upstream to the cataracts that gave the creek its name, Bourke, ever the anthropologist, observed and later recorded in his diary both the natural beauty of his surroundings and various manifestations of the Supai culture. Finally, after the party had exhausted its curiosity about the tribe and its customs, Crook brought up the official reason for his visit, the accused murderer. In due course the chief surrendered the fugitive, who was plainly shaken, believing that he was to be killed outright. The gift of some tobacco reassured him, and, whatever his ultimate fate, he seemed resigned to it, as he returned meekly with the party to San Carlos.

The next morning, November 11, the party worked with the Supais to repair an alternate trail by which they could more safely and rapidly exit the canyon, avoiding the need to retrace their steps up the steep and dangerous path by which they had entered it. The next day, with prisoner in tow, the party set out for the canyon rim. Though superior to the former route, this trail, too, was steep and often narrow. Yet rather than ascend on foot, Crook insisted on riding his mule, Apache, the entire way, a decision that Bourke quickly characterized as "very reckless." Safely reaching the rim, the travelers divided, most returning south to the rail line to catch the train back to Whipple, while Crook, Bourke, and some of the others turned west for a quick glimpse of the Grand Canyon before returning to what they undoubted anticipated would be the routine issues of the Department of Arizona.

CHAPTER SEVENTEEN

Breakout

As the winter of 1884–85 drew to a close, to most observers the Chiricahuas seemed to be adjusting well to reservation life. In a letter to his
superiors, Crook cheerily predicted that their progress in agricultural
production was likely "to lead them from a life of vagabonds to one
of peace and self-maintenance."[1] Some support for the general's optimism could be found in the reservation's overall production figures as
reported by Captain Pierce in 1885. Pierce described "eleven hundred
acres under cultivation" and an annual harvest of over 800,000 pounds
of barley. The White Mountain Apaches had delivered 700,000 pounds
of hay to the post quartermaster at Fort Apache, and the yield in corn
was predicted to be an impressive 3.5 million pounds. The corn yield
would soon become a most significant statistic, though for reasons not
found in Captain Pierce's report.[2]

Yet the Chiricahuas, while credited with some production, did not
quite fit into this rosy picture. A few of the former warriors, such
as Jason Betzinez, viewed their time at Turkey Creek as "an opportunity to learn farming with a real worthwhile future." Many more
were considerably less enthusiastic about agrarian pursuits, and not
without reason. Most of the good agricultural lands in the environs of Fort Apache had been allocated to the White Mountain and
Cibicue bands, who had settled there first. Plots left to the Chiricahuas
required irrigation, a labor-intensive practice that did not always pay
off in an area afflicted by flash flooding and long dry spells. Leaving

aside these constraints, these were not a people accustomed to a quiet pastoral existence. Throughout their history the Chiricahuas had successfully pursued a migratory cycle that provided them with a usually adequate supply of nature's bounty, joyously supplemented by raiding their more sedentary neighbors. The men of the tribe regarded themselves as warriors, first and foremost. Farming, if it was done at all, was women's work.[3]

Geronimo's approach to agriculture was perhaps typical. After planting barley that spring, the shaman proudly exhibited a small blister on one of his palms as evidence of his labors. But when Lieutenant Davis visited the old warrior's fields, he found him "sitting on a rail in the shade of a tree with one of his wives fanning him. The other two were hoeing a quarter-acre patch of partially cleared ground, in which a few sickly-looking sprouts of corn were struggling for life."[4] Davis found other signs that farming had not found its place among the aspirations of these nomadic warriors. Tools were missing, sold or gambled off to the White Mountain people. Wagons were in a state of disrepair, their wheels and underpinnings smashed in wild rides over the mountains. Pierce confirmed Davis's findings. After inspecting the Chiricahua fields adjacent to those of the White Mountains', he found them neither as well cultivated nor as well fenced as those of their neighbors. While impressed with the tribe's natural abilities, he opined that they would make far better progress if they spent less time drinking and gambling. Agent Ford, who accompanied Pierce to observe the distribution of the annuity goods, reported similar shortcomings.[5]

While Pierce, only an occasional visitor, had noted the tribe's lack of enthusiasm for farming, he failed to detect the growing restlessness that lurked just beneath the surface. The power struggles at San Carlos that pitted Crawford against Wilcox and then Ford had not gone unnoticed by the Apaches, especially the tribes' chronically suspicious and restless leadership. Britton Davis, living in isolation with his charges, had a better grasp of its impact. He wisely observed that "the seed of divided authority sprouts and bears its natural fruit—defiance of all authority." In his daily interactions with the tribe, he thought he saw evidence of this defiance in the brutal treatment of the women of the tribe and an increase in tiswin consumption.[6] A modern observer might have attributed these conditions to the hopelessness and despair engendered by the economic and cultural dislocation the tribe suffered in consequence of its confinement on the reservation. But there can be little doubt that the feuding between the authority figures upon whom the Apaches were totally dependent for their safety and sustenance caused them considerable angst.

And their uneasiness grew as the result of personnel changes that they observed over the winter of 1884–85. The sudden disappearance of Crawford, a familiar and reliable officer with whom Geronimo, in particular, had established some rapport, was especially troubling. Captain Pierce was an unknown quantity to the Chiricahua leadership, particularly to the distrustful shaman. Further, Geronimo seemed to believe that if Crawford had left the reservation, Crook, too, must have passed from the scene. The Chiricahuas chafed at Crook's interference with their freedoms, and Geronimo himself nursed a personal grudge against the general for confiscating the cattle the shaman stole in Mexico. Nevertheless, to the Chiricahuas the Gray Fox was a comforting presence whom they relied on to protect them from vengeful and covetous elements in the white community.

Lieutenant Gatewood, who knew the Chiricahuas intimately, attributed the Chiricahuas' uneasiness, at least in part, to changes in the legal system as it affected the Indians. After settling the Apaches at San Carlos, Crook had mandated that crimes Indians committed on the reservation were subject to the jurisdiction of the Indian courts that he established. Presided over by the officer in charge, the courts tried cases and imposed sentences in accordance with the decisions of Indian juries. But in March 1885 Congress passed legislation that transferred jurisdiction over some classes of offenses from reservation to civil courts. The military communicated these changes to their charges on the reservation a month later, and, according to Gatewood, the news that they would have to submit to the judgment of hostile civilian authorities deeply disturbed them.[7]

Yet in mid-May, when Pierce visited the Chiricahuas to distribute their supplies, he seemed unaware of these undercurrents. Upon his return to San Carlos he would maintain that despite the Chiricahua's indifferent attitude toward farming and fondness for drink and gambling, "they were no worse today than many other Indians on the reservation."[8] His failure to recognize the extent of the unrest then sweeping through the tribe would have consequences that, in the words of Britton Davis, would "cast the shadow of unmerited censure over the closing days of the brilliant career of a general of the army, bestowing honor where honor was not due; and whose only highlight in the dull horror of massacre and fruitless pursuit was one example of personal courage as fine as any the army can boast."[9]

While there may have been any number of reasons underlying the restlessness of the Chiricahuas in late spring 1885, an objective evaluation of the events that occurred in the days following Pierce's departure from Turkey Creek would identify tiswin—or "gray water," the Apaches' beloved homebrew—as the primary accelerant.[10] When the captain proudly reported that corn topped the list of the tribe's agricultural outputs, he failed to appreciate the fact that this crop was the principal ingredient in tiswin. More corn meant more tiswin.

Crook's strict prohibition of the making and consumption of tiswin infringed on one of the Apaches' most cherished traditions and, of equal importance, had serious economic consequences for their womenfolk, whose prerogative it was to brew and sell the drink.[11] Foremost among the brewers was Huera, the wife of Mangas, son of Mangas Coloradas and a prominent chief in his own right. Huera's product was of such merit that few could resist its charms.[12] A particularly strong-willed woman, she apparently prodded the usually good-natured and compliant Mangas to confront Davis about Nantan Lupan's prohibition policy.[13]

Davis, concerned about the steady increase in the consumption of tiswin among the Chiricahuas and an accompanying surge in spousal abuse, arrested several tribesmen for these infractions, further inflaming the tribe's leadership.[14] In protest, Mangas and Chihuahua, a sub-chief known for his militant attachment to Apache tradition, planned a tiswin-drunk involving about three quarters of the men of the tribe. With that many men involved, they reasoned that the lieutenant would be unable to make any arrests and therefore would be forced into embarrassing inaction. Thus, they would have made their point, suffered no consequences, and set a precedent for future celebrations. They scheduled the event for May 14.[15]

Geronimo joined the protesters, apparently believing that he could use the occasion to encourage a breakout from the reservation. He must have been contemplating the action for some time. His outward adjustment to life at Turkey Creek apparently masked his seething resentment at the restriction of his freedom and his unslaked desire for revenge against all Mexicans and Americans. Other factors, too, were at work, including a fear that plans were afoot to punish him for his past depredations, an anxiety fed by demands in the Arizona papers for his arrest and trial and by the recent Congressional action transferring criminal jurisdiction from the Indian courts to civil authorities. In addition, Davis had been unable to disabuse the shaman of the notion that Crawford's disappearance meant that Crook, too, had abandoned him, leaving him and his people vulnerable to white retribution. Finally, months later, trying to justify his role in the events that transpired, he told Crook that he broke out because over the course of that spring, he had come to believe that Chatto, together with Mickey Free and Lieutenant Davis, were plotting to have him arrested and hanged. It was a tale seemingly without foundation, but one carefully nurtured by Huera to draw Geronimo into her tiswin plot. Though Crook would dismiss these claims as excuses invented after the fact, the shaman's suspicious nature makes his belief in them credible.[16] Certainly, concern for his personal safety played a part in his decision, and joining Chihuahua and Mangas in staging the tiswin-drunk fit neatly into his scheme.

On the morning of May 15, the day following the tiswin-drunk, Davis emerged from his tent at sunrise to find the chiefs and other tribal leaders, about thirty warriors in all, arrayed before him. Though they carried no weapons other than their knives and an occasional pistol, the lieutenant found the absence of any women or children in the crowd ominous. His scouts had also gathered in small groups about the tent, among them Chatto. They were fully armed, but their presence did little to allay his trepidation as he ushered the chiefs into the tent for a parlay.[17]

Once inside, it was Chihuahua, clearly inebriated and quite angry, who spoke. Though drunk, he addressed himself quite cogently to Crook's policies, arguing that his people were not children and did not need to be told whether they could drink or how to treat their wives. Davis tried to explain Crook's rationale, at which point Nana stood to leave, muttering angrily in Apache. At Davis's insistence, Mickey Free reluctantly translated his words: "The stout chief [as the Apaches called Davis because his stocky build contrasted with the lean Crawford and Gatewood] can't tell me how to treat my women. He is only a boy. I killed *men* before he was born." Davis took this as "a solar plexus blow to my dignity," particularly as the assemblage met it with approving murmurs.[18]

Following this interruption Chihuahua challenged Davis, declaring that the Apaches had all drunk tiswin the night before. What was the lieutenant going to do about it? He had no jail big enough to hold them all. The lieutenant, in a tight corner, bought time by replying that the issue was too big for him to decide, and he would need to consult with Nantan Lupan as to how he should handle it.[19]

Military protocol required any communication sent by Davis to Crook at Fort Whipple to be routed through Davis's commanding officer, Captain Pierce at San Carlos. Only after the latter had read and approved it could it be forwarded to the general. Knowing it would take some time before he received a reply, Davis hurriedly drafted a telegram for Pierce's review. Because telegraphers often leaked such messages to the press, he would have to be circumspect. Yet he fully expected Crook to quickly grasp the gravity of the situation. His wire gave a sketchy summary of the incident and outlined his proposal for dealing with it. The guardhouse would not hold all of those involved, and besides, he anticipated trouble if he attempted to arrest the chiefs. So he proposed to arrest only the women who made the tiswin and one scout involved in the drunk. He concluded by telling Crook that he had informed the Indians that he "would lay the matter before the General." To the lieutenant, this last meant that he would take no action until he received instructions from Crook.[20]

Upon receiving Davis's wire, Pierce, new to San Carlos and uncertain what to do, hastened to consult with Al Sieber, his resident expert. Awakened from a deep sleep after a night of drinking and gambling, Sieber was not at his best. After reading Davis's message, he failed to assess its importance. He groggily dismissed the incident as "nothing but a tiswin drunk" and airily advised the captain not to pay attention to it as "Davis will handle it." He then returned to his bed. Pierce, perhaps lulled into a false sense of security by his recent visit to the tribe, took Sieber at his word. Thinking it not worth General Crook's time, he did not forward the message. Nor did he respond to Davis. The general thus remained unaware of the problem, and Davis was left awaiting instructions that would never arrive.[21]

At Turkey Creek, after their meeting with Davis, Geronimo and the Chiricahua leadership, except for Chatto, retired to the shaman's camp to await the Gray Fox's response. When no reply came, they were troubled by what this might mean, though it seems that neither Chihuahua nor Mangas were as yet prepared to flee the reservation.

But Huera, inspired by her hatred of whites and fear that she would be punished for her role in the tiswin-drunk, gave a fiery speech, prodding the warriors to take up arms. Geronimo was undoubtedly delighted. By now he had concluded that Davis's delay in responding to the chiefs was evidence that he and Crook were hatching a plan to arrest or, more likely, kill the prominent chiefs and exile their people to some remote location. For Geronimo there was but one option: flight.[22]

But first the shaman needed to whip up support among his fellow tribesmen. This would not be easy. While not enamored by conditions at Turkey Creek, most Chiricahuas preferred the reservation to life on the run. So Geronimo needed to convince the leadership to join him. Mangas seemed the most malleable because of Huera's influence. But though he was the son of Mangas Coloradas and a prominent figure in the tribe, he lacked the prestige to convince many others to accompany him. To assemble a reasonable following, Geronimo needed to gain the support of the more influential leaders: Naiche, son of Cochise, and the respected Chihuahua. To convert them to his cause, Geronimo told them that, on his orders, two of the scouts had been sent to murder Lieutenant Davis and Chatto. In fact, the two warriors lost their nerve and failed to carry out the plan. Nevertheless, Geronimo lied, telling the chiefs that the plot had been successful in order to convince them that there was no turning back. On the strength of his representations, Chihuahua and Naiche, and eventually Mangas, believed they now had no alternative and joined him in the breakout.[23]

On Sunday afternoon, May 17, Davis was umpiring a baseball game at Fort Apache when Mickey Free and Chatto hurried onto the post parade ground with the news that an unknown number of Chiricahuas had fled the reservation and were headed for Mexico. Davis's prompt attempt to notify Crook was foiled when the Indians cut the line.[24]

As any hope of catching the Apaches required speedy action, the lieutenant mounted an immediate pursuit with a contingent of White Mountain scouts under Gatewood and a detachment of Fourth Cavalry troopers led by Captain Allen Smith, commander of Fort Apache. They chased the Indians through the night, riding east into the rugged Mogollon Mountains. The following morning, as the exhausted column crested a ridge overlooking a broad valley, they saw in the distance the dust of the Indians' ponies ascending the opposite slope. To Davis they appeared to be heading into the mountains of New Mexico, a secure avenue south to the border. As he watched them disappear into the hills, the lieutenant was acutely aware "that further pursuit by troops was useless and that we were in for a long campaign in Mexico." For the sake of appearances, Davis ordered Smith and Gatewood to continue the chase, while he returned to Fort Apache to draft a report on the debacle to General Crook. For their part, the Apaches demonstrated their incredible mobility, traveling 135 miles in two days through some of the most impassable country in North America, leaving Smith and Gatewood to do little more than mark the direction of their flight.[25]

Because of a delay in repairing the downed telegraph lines, Crook did not learn of the breakout until the day after it occurred. Having never received Davis's initial telegram, he had no inkling of the disaster that was about to befall him.[26] The news could not have been more devastating. For some months he had been working to negotiate the release of Chiricahua captives in Mexico, the final impediment, he believed, to gaining the tribe's acquiescence to reservation life and consequent assimilation into American society. At the same time, he had labored to improve their lot on the reservation and concurrently to secure title to lands previously promised them by President Hayes that lay adjacent to San Carlos. In this context, to General Crook, Geronimo's unanticipated departure must have appeared as a betrayal of trust.

The Apache uprising, for that is how most Arizonans viewed it, sent a wave of fear and anger rolling across the territory and was marked by an almost daily outpouring of scorn and condemnation in the Arizona press.[27] News accounts of atrocities committed by the fleeing Chiricahuas abounded, prompting cries for revenge against all Apaches and allegations of Crook's supposed incompetence. Arizona's *Clifton Clarion* was typical, holding the general responsible "for the death of every citizen . . . since the late Indian breakout." Further, " His temporizing policies," the paper claimed, "have encouraged the savages to renew and repeat the diabolical acts characteristic of the bloodthirsty Apaches."[28] Meanwhile, Tucson's *Arizona Weekly Citizen,* representing

the editorial policy of many of the southern Arizona papers, described
Crook's efforts to apprehend the renegades as a campaign of "brilliant
stupidity" intended to "protect Indians and afford them an opportunity
for daily plunder and to escape safely to Mexico with their booty."[29]
Equally troubling to Crook was the public outcry for the removal of all
the San Carlos Apaches to Indian Territory, exactly the sort of "solution" that he had striven to avoid.[30]

The general responded by publicly placing the blame for the breakout on the Department of the Interior. In an official dispatch he identified the department's chronic mismanagement of Indian affairs and
its agents' constant interference in Crawford's efforts to carry out his
duties on the reservation, together with dual control of the reservation
as the primary, if not immediate, cause of the breakout. Reminding
his superiors of his earlier request to be relieved of his responsibilities
unless his authority was strengthened, he stressed that now, more than
ever, he needed complete control over the reservation if he was to
remain in charge of the Chiricahuas.[31] His reasoning had the advantage
of absolving both the Chiricahuas and the military of responsibility.
Rather than removing the tribe from Arizona, the government had
only to remove the Interior Department from the reservation.

Months later he would again hammer on this theme in his 1885
annual report to the secretary of war. He opined that the decision to
curb the military's authority over agricultural activities on the reservation and Crawford's subsequent transfer had had a profound impact
on the Apaches. In the management of Indians, he wrote, "a power
once exercised can never be withdrawn from the person in charge
without loss of respect and influence." Warrior tribes like the Chiricahuas must believe that "the person in charge of them has *absolute
power* [Crook's emphasis] and this belief cannot be weakened without
danger." The Apaches were keen observers, and in the present situation
they were fully aware that the military's power had been undermined
and with it, Crook's authority. Since they looked to him personally as
their benefactor and protector, they viewed any diminishment of his
powers with anxiety.[32]

Ultimately, the government deferred to Crook's concerns and terminated the system of dual control that he had initially fostered but now
found so troubling. The end came in the dog days of that summer of
1885. Indian Agent Ford, who, like Wilcox, had become increasingly

militant in opposing the army's usurpation of his prerogatives, intervened to prevent a military officer from arresting an agency policeman. His cause may have been just, but his timing was bad. The officer appealed to Crook. Crook, in turn, called on his division commander, Pope, a reliable ally in such situations. Faced with the usual arguments for military supremacy, this time Interior Secretary Lamar did not back his agent. Instead, he ordered Ford to accede to the officer's authority and in a surprising turnabout recommended that Secretary of War Endicott name an officer to take temporary charge of the San Carlos agency. On August 6 President Cleveland suspended Ford, and three weeks later Captain Pierce assumed control, beginning a sixteen-year reign of exclusive military hegemony over the reservation.[33]

Though Crook publicly held the Interior Department responsible for the outbreak, he certainly realized that other factors had played a par, including his misplaced confidence in the Apaches' adjustment to reservation life.[34] Months after the breakout Crook grudgingly admitted that his belief that the Chiricahuas had adapted well to life on the reservation had "probably" resulted in "a little over confidence" and "possibly" a relaxation of vigilance among his officers. They, in turn, had not sensed the darkening mood that prevailed among the tribe's leadership. In his annual report he even suggested that had someone of his experience in Indian matters been present at Turkey Creek, he would have seen the signs of impending trouble and moved to stop it.[35] One could also reasonably suppose that had the general read Davis's reports more closely and spent more time personally observing the Chiricahuas, he might have taken a more skeptical view of his officers' optimistic assessments. But his insights gave little indication that he accepted any responsibility for the breakout. With the benefit of hindsight, historians might criticize him for neglecting to take measures to minimize the threat, perhaps by stationing troops with Davis at Turkey Creek as he had done at the San Carlos agency. The presence of soldiers might have deterred Geronimo and the others from defying young Davis's authority.

Despite Crook's well-known sensitivity to public criticism, he did not allow the waves of vituperation that now broke over him to stampede him into overreaction. He never lost his sense of perspective in that regard. Though acknowledging the need for military force to resolve the crisis, he remained committed to preventing the punishment of the entire tribe for the deeds of a few. He recognized, if others in Arizona chose not to, that the situation, while serious, involved only a small percentage of the Apaches on the reservation and that a significant portion of the Chiricahuas had not been involved. Even among the actual participants, there were several who did not support Geronimo. While he knew that he would have to pursue and perhaps kill the ringleaders, Crook retained the hope that, as he had done in the Sierra Madre, he could greatly shorten and minimize the brutality of the campaign and pursue a negotiated surrender rather than a war of annihilation. His strategy from the outset was to use the scouts and other willing Chiricahuas "to get in among the refugees and work upon the dissatisfied ones especially Natchez [Naiche] . . . and thus . . . induce a return of those who are least guilty and destruction of the ring-leaders if possible."[36]

The lack of unity among the Apaches who fled the reservation favored his plan. As Crook had gleaned from Davis, far from being a cohesive unit, in reality they were an uneasy coalition of several bands, each with different objectives and often at odds because of the hostility of their leaders toward one another.[37] Chihuahua and Naiche, reluctant participants from the beginning, had become even more disaffected when, shortly after leaving the reservation, they discovered that Geronimo had lied when he told them that Chatto and Davis had been murdered. Chihuahua was so incensed that he went looking for the shaman, intending to kill him. The two men and their followers would pursue separate paths for the rest of the time they remained at large and never truly reconciled thereafter. Naiche generally remained with Chihuahua. And Mangas, who had his own disagreements with Geronimo, made his own way, seeking sanctuary for his people deep in Mexico and remaining there until his surrender the following year.[38]

A schism also opened between those who participated in the breakout and the majority of the tribe who had remained on the reservation. Initially, Crook had received word that the number of escapees was small, only about fifty.[39] A later headcount made by Davis expanded the total to include the followers of Naiche and Chihuahua. In the final analysis, Crook reported that among the Chiricahuas at Turkey Creek, including the Mimbre or Warm Springs band, "thirty-five men, eight tagged boys, (those old enough to bear arms), and 101 women and children were missing." Their leaders included Chihuahua, Geronimo and

Naiche, Mangas and Nana. Almost double the number of warriors, seventy-six men and boys of fighting age, and their families, including such prominent men as Loco, Chatto, and Ka-ya-ten-nae, remained at Turkey Creek.[40]

Most who refused to join Geronimo did so because they had no desire to return to a fugitive existence. But some who stayed, especially among the Warm Springs band, despised Geronimo, blaming him for much of the strife and bloodshed that had afflicted them over the past several years. Crook, who often relied on intratribal friction as a means of controlling Indians, surmised that these disaffected tribesmen would willingly participate in the campaign against the shaman. He was correct. By the close of the campaign, of the seventy-six warriors who remained on the reservation, at least fifty-seven volunteered to serve as scouts. Further, among those Chiricahuas serving as scouts at the time of the breakout, only two, those assigned by Geronimo to assassinate Davis and Chatto, would desert and join the shaman. In light of later events, it is worth noting that five hundred additional San Carlos Apaches from many different bands would also join Crook in the subsequent search for the fugitives.[41]

Apart from exploiting divisions within the tribe, Crook hoped to play on the pervasive longing among the Chiricahuas for the return of their relatives held captive in Mexico, whose freedom he had been laboring to achieve before the breakout. Most members of the tribe recognized that Geronimo's actions jeopardized these efforts, as it was unlikely the Mexican government would release the prisoners as long as Apaches continued raiding in Sonora and Chihuahua. Of the prominent tribesmen who remained on the reservation, Chatto probably had the most at stake. His wife and children were among the Mexican captives, and, as Davis informed Crook, the chief was "very bitter," knowing that Geronimo's actions, unless checked, might destroy any chance he might have of ever seeing them again.[42] This consideration and his long-standing rivalry with the shaman for primacy in the tribe provided him with strong motivation to end the breakout. Already a leader in the scouts and an intelligent and charismatic warrior, he was to become an invaluable and steadfast ally to Crook in the pursuit of both diplomatic and military initiatives in the coming campaign. Uniquely aware of the strategies that the bronco leadership would pursue on the warpath, he also proved a priceless asset in tracking their movements and an extremely persuasive advocate for peace to those in Geronimo's band with captive kin.

Crook saw the tribe's desire for the return of the captives as such a powerful motivating factor that he told Davis to employ not only scouts formally enlisted in the army but also "Indians outside the scouts as desire to go in pursuit." Emphasizing the relationship between the return of the escapees and the release of their relatives, he instructed Davis to pass the word to the chiefs that success with regard to the latter would depend on the outcome of the former.[43]

While he hoped for a peaceful solution in the long-term, Crook was all too familiar with the personalities involved and the warlike nature of the tribe to believe that peaceful persuasion alone would win over Geronimo's followers. While some might be convinced to return by more pacific means, only force would suffice with respect to the more militant members of the band, the shaman and his loyalists in particular. Further, he knew that a prompt and vigorous military response would reassure the frightened citizens of the territory and curb a backlash that would damage the reputation of the military and destroy his chances of keeping the Apaches in Arizona. Consequently, as soon as news of the outbreak reached him, Crook implemented measures to safeguard the far-flung and isolated settlements, ranches, and mines that would likely be the first targets of opportunity for the fleeing Chiricahuas.

In addition to protecting the populace, Crook had to at least attempt to interdict the Apaches before they reached Mexico. On its surface such a strategy would seem a priority. Once the band crossed into Chihuahua and Sonora, efforts by the army to dislodge them would be a long, drawn-out affair, mired in a morass of diplomatic and logistical complexities, grim hardship, and danger. Crook knew from bitter experience that interdiction would almost surely be unsuccessful, given the Apaches' extraordinary mobility and their intimate familiarity with the many passes that existed in the wild and mountainous country between the reservation and the border. But regardless of these realities and mindful of the storm of outrage that inaction would inevitably provoke, he ordered the commanders at posts in southern Arizona and New Mexico to dispatch a host of troopers to scour the region where the Chiricahuas were thought to be. Additional troops, accompanied by Apache scouts, were assigned to guard all the passes and water holes between the Southern Pacific Railroad and the Mexican border on the off chance that they might stop Geronimo from crossing into Sonora and Chihuahua.[44]

As it appeared that the Apaches were headed east toward New Mexico, which lay in a separate military department, Crook's superiors, hoping to facilitate his efforts, granted him temporary military control over that territory. On May 31, cloaked with this additional authority and feeling the need to be nearer to the action, he moved his headquarters from Fort Whipple to Fort Bayard in New Mexico, close to the Mexican border. Colonel Luther Bradley, the military commander in New Mexico, also traveled to Bayard to supervise his own troops participating in the chase, creating the potential for conflict between the two commanders. To avoid unnecessary turf squabbles and in a gesture more generous in appearance than in reality, Crook placed Arizona troops operating in New Mexico under Bradley's immediate command. But he retained direct control over those columns that included detachments of Apache scouts, knowing full well these were the only ones likely to make contact with Geronimo.[45]

As he knew they would, Crook's interdiction efforts came to naught. On June 2 he ruefully admitted that the nine columns of troopers and scouts that he had dispatched into the countryside had failed to "catch the raiding parties or afford citizens so scattered among the mountains protection from such parties." Nor had they prevented any of the bands from reaching Mexico. He soon learned from his trackers that after leaving the reservation the "refugees had split into four groups," reflecting the divisions between the bands.[46] Geronimo had fled across the border to escape Chihuahua's wrath. The latter initially sought shelter in Arizona's Mogollon country, hoping to return to the reservation now that he knew that Davis and Chatto had not been killed. But after spotting Davis's troops on his trail, he had discarded that hope and begun raiding in earnest. Leaving a trail of at least seventeen dead civilians and the corpses of about 150 mounts strewn in their wake, he and his followers ultimately attacked a cavalry patrol guarding Guadeloupe Canyon, one of the entry points into Mexico, and fled across the border. Naiche had also planned to return quietly to San Carlos and dispatched his family back toward the reservation for that purpose. But they, too, saw Davis's troops and turned about and fled across the border, reuniting with Chihuahua's followers in Sonora.[47] Mangas and his people reached Mexican territory at about the same time, having engaged in depredations against isolated ranches and lone travelers along their route, all reported in grisly detail in local newspapers. Public outrage at the reported atrocities greatly diminished Crook's hope of a quick and peaceful resolution to the breakout.[48]

Reluctantly, the general now began preparations for what he realized would be a prolonged and difficult campaign in Mexico. Employing tactics used in the Tonto Basin and perfected in the Sierra Madre, he planned to deploy multiple columns operating independently of each other. They would pursue the Chiricahuas relentlessly into their deepest sanctuaries, giving them no rest until they surrendered or were killed. As he had in the Sierra Madre, he would place his scouts in the forefront of the action, using his regulars only in a supporting role. Though the strategy had previously subjected Crook to withering criticism, it had proven its worth.

The breakout had not diminished Nantan Lupan's faith in either the loyalty or the fighting abilities of his scouts. He believed that only an Apache had the knowledge of the terrain and the tracking skills, stamina, and fighting abilities to hunt down other Apaches. And among the Apache bands, he considered the Chiricahuas without peer. Moreover, he believed that only the Chiricahuas had the shared values and familial relations needed to persuade their fellow tribesmen to return peacefully to San Carlos. Consequently, his columns, though commanded by experienced officers, would be composed almost entirely of Apache scouts, Chiricahuas whenever possible. In the words of Britton Davis, the regular troops would only serve as "a rallying point for the scouts, increasing their morale and protecting the pack trains."[49] To implement his strategy, Crook asked General Sheridan for authority to recruit additional Indians for the service, though fully aware that the lieutenant general and many others in the Southwest and in Mexico would be discomfited by his plans.[50] Shrugging off their opposition, he remained supremely confident that, as in the past, he would be vindicated by the outcome.[51]

With the outlines of his military strategy in place, Crook turned to the international complications created by the Chiricahuas' flight into Mexico. His earlier success in the Sierra Madre had done little to abate the Mexican government's suspicion and resentment at the thought of U.S. troops on its territory. The treaty between the two countries, renewed in 1883, was about to expire again. It still stipulated that the armies of either country could not enter the territory of the other unless in hot pursuit of the enemy and could remain only so long as that pursuit continued.[52] These provisos were obviously as inconsistent with Crook's present strategy as they had been during the 1883 campaign. Further, the Mexican authorities and the country's citizens could hardly be expected to greet the appearance of large numbers of armed and mounted Apache scouts on their soil with enthusiasm, though accompanied by army regulars. Rather than rescind the restrictions, Crook believed that the government in Mexico City would more likely construe the treaty narrowly, making the chance of an armed clash between Mexican and American forces eminently foreseeable. So he wired Sheridan on June 5, asking for assurances that the Mexicans would not interfere with his columns and that his troops would be "freed from present vexatious treaty stipulations." He reiterated this plea on June 9, pointing out that his plan would fail if subject to the letter of the current agreement. This second message carried a note of urgency since, at that moment, he was poised to dispatch his first columns across the border. In fact, without waiting for a reply, he ordered the lead column into Mexico two days later.[53]

Unlike the Sierra Madre campaign, Crook had decided not to personally command the operation in the field. Tactical and political considerations required that he remain in Arizona where he could oversee and coordinate the entire operation and where communications facilities existed to meet any contingency, including the possibility that the Apaches might cross back into the United States. He also desired to be on hand to fulfill his superiors' constant demands for information and to be available if and when the opportunity arose to negotiate a peaceful end to the conflict. Because he chose not to lead his troops in the field, he would have to rely on trustworthy officers to carry out the task. His first choice was Emmet Crawford, whom he recalled from his duty station in Texas. Of all his officers, Crawford was the most familiar with the Apache leadership as well as the area of operations in Mexico and Arizona. He and his scouts represented Crook's greatest hope to find the dissidents and either defeat them or negotiate their peaceful return to Arizona.

But Crawford would not be alone. His command would operate in conjunction with a second column under Captain Wirt Davis of the Fourth Cavalry, later described by one historian as "the unsung officer of the Geronimo War."[54] Like many of his compatriots, Davis was a Civil War veteran. Enlisting as a private, he received a field commission upon demonstrating his leadership abilities. He was ultimately awarded two brevets for outstanding service and commissioned first lieutenant after the war ended. Over the ensuing years he earned an enviable reputation as an Indian fighter, both on the northern plains and in the Southwest. At forty-six, his hair had already turned gray, and his weathered face, dominated by a huge walrus mustache that softened his pugnacious jawline, had the benign appearance of "a gentle-hearted grandfather," an impression further fostered by his quiet and common-sense demeanor. But outward appearances belied the tough and dedi-cated soldier within—he was an expert shot with a pistol and a hard drinker, though one who abstained while in the field.[55]

While Davis and Crawford pursued the fleeing Apaches in Mexico, Crook guarded against the potentially devastating possibility that the Apaches might cross back into the States. He stationed troops at every water hole along the border and assigned regulars and scouts to patrol between these outposts. As backup he deployed a second line of troops along the Southern Pacific Railway, and in case that line was breached, he had cavalry transferred from Texas and stationed north of the rail-way, poised to pursue any Apaches who managed to get through. By the beginning of June, as Crawford readied his column to cross into Mexico, Crook had no fewer than twenty troops of cavalry and two hundred scouts patrolling throughout southern Arizona and New Mexico, an outlay of manpower that would soon be put to the test.[56]

CHAPTER EIGHTEEN

Pursuit into Mexico

On June 6, 1885, five days before launching Crawford's column into Mexico, Crook warmly greeted the captain as he stepped off the train at Deming, New Mexico, the depot nearest Crook's Fort Bayard headquarters. He and the captain were deep in discussion when a wire arrived from Sheridan with the welcome news that Crook's request for two hundred additional scouts and more mules and packers had been approved, the latter now en route from Wyoming. At the same time, knowing his general's minimalist approach to communications with higher authority, Sheridan urged that he move his headquarters from New Mexico to a point of his own choosing in Arizona on the Southern Pacific line, where he would have rapid and easy communications by the telegraph and enhanced mobility by rail.

Sheridan's suggestion undoubtedly accorded with Crook's own preference. Conducting operations in New Mexico, another general's bailiwick, was inherently awkward. So after completing his talks with Crawford, Crook relocated to Fort Bowie, hard by Apache Pass. Closer than Bayard to the Southern Pacific line, Bowie had the advantage of being the southern terminus of the telegraph system that connected the department's military posts and was, of course, in his own department.[1]

Among the general's first tasks at Fort Bowie was to oversee the formation of Wirt Davis's column. Like Crawford's force, scouts formed the backbone of the outfit—one hundred White Mountain Apaches led by Lieutenant Gatewood. Troopers from the Fourth Cavalry, Captain Davis's own regiment, and two pack trains comprised of mules and packers fresh from Wyoming would support the scouts. Like Crawford, Wirt Davis was expected to seek out his quarry among the canyons and slopes of the Sierra Madre, pursuing them without respite until they had been brought to bay. But his departure was delayed to await Gatewood's scouts, who had received last-minute instructions from Crook to reconnoiter the Mogollon and Black ranges to ensure that no Apaches remained in U.S. territory. The tribesmen were long gone but searching for them consumed the better part of a month, so Captain Davis did not leave for Mexico until July 13, almost a month after Crawford.[2]

Having deployed his troops, Crook now found himself at loose ends. Far removed from the action and uncomfortably aware of his inability to affect the unfolding events of the campaign, he had time on his hands and little to do beyond awaiting reports from the field. It was during this hiatus that his thoughts apparently turned to a personal undertaking that had been germinating in the back of his mind for some time—authoring his memoirs. He never explained his reasons for undertaking the project or for its timing. He was not a vain man, but he may have seen it as a means of securing recognition long denied him for his achievements during the war. There is some evidence that he was also moved by the possibility that a memoir might reap some financial rewards and leave a small legacy for Mary upon his death.[3] Or it may simply have been a distraction during this stressful period. In any event, he took pencil in hand and, on the backs of order forms and other papers that lay about his office, began recording recollections of his military career. Characteristically, he produced a barebones narrative, providing scant insights into his motivations or emotional reactions to events.[4]

At the same time as he began work on his memoir, Crook started a diary. Though he possibly kept journals earlier in his career, the two slim volumes that he filled, beginning that summer and continuing up to the time of his death, appear to be all that have survived, now all but forgotten in the archives of the U.S. Army Heritage and Education Center in Carlisle, Pennsylvania. As with his autobiography, he did not explain why he began the journal. Perhaps knowing that the next few months would be of momentous importance to his career, he intended it as an *aide memoire* related to his projected autobiography. Or not.

There is a more interesting explanation. With the caveat that historians are sometimes tempted to make too much of such things, it is possible that confiding his thoughts to the diary served a therapeutic purpose, either consciously or unconsciously, as a stress reliever. Journals, especially those of public figures, often serve as an outlet for the expression of private thoughts and opinions that the writer is unable or unwilling to confide to others. It is logical to speculate that this might have been a course that a man with Crook's reclusive temperament would pursue. But that seems not to have been the case. Despite the fact that the entries were often written during dramatic and emotion-filled periods, Crook's diary, like his memoir, is marked by the absence of introspection or personal feeling. Instead—at least during the first years he kept it and with few notable exceptions thereafter—it is a dry and banal record of his day-to-day doings, giving no hint of the turmoil that surrounded him during this time. In some cases it even omits reference to important events that must have stirred him deeply. This very absence of emotion and confinement to the ordinary suggests the diary's therapeutic value. Cataloging the commonplace in its pages may have been Crook's way of creating an alternative reality that banished from his thoughts stressful events and relieved the grief, anger, and frustration that they brought into his life. Imagine him, each night, hunched over his desk, pencil in hand, scribbling the two or three lines in his spikey handwriting recording the sanitized recollections of the day's events that he would carry into sleep that night.

His first entry, dated August 13, 1885, is typical and sets the tone for what followed. It reads: "Major Roberts returned from Whipple Barracks today. Showering today but little rain at the post. Heavy showers in San Simon Valley."[5] From that day forward, his entries almost always began with a brief mention of the day's weather before moving briskly to a snippet of trivia from his daily life—a game of whist or billiards, a walk, a picnic, or a dinner with a fellow officer—usually including no more than the names of those present and the location of the event. It is especially frustrating that he rarely refers to his professional responsibilities, though they surely occupied much of his time and thoughts. Work-related entries are usually limited to arrivals and departures of official visitors, followed occasionally by a brief notation that meetings or conversations took place but rarely their content. In the neutral universe of his diary, the barbs of newsmen and politicians or the petty jealousies and machinations of fellow officers have no place; nor, for the most part, do violence, grief, disappointment, loss, recrimination, and self-doubt.

Only when Crook traveled—on hunts, official trips, and sightseeing expeditions—were his entries more detailed and lively. In the case of his hunts, they include meticulous lists of the species and number of animals bagged by himself and his fellow hunters. The diary also reveals that the frequency of his hunts increased markedly during periods of stress, particularly during his time at Fort Bowie. Overall, his journal provides a fascinating, though frequently dimly lit, window into the mind of an otherwise inaccessible personality.[6]

While Crook took his first tentative steps into the world of letters, at Separ, a dusty hamlet in the New Mexico boot heel, Emmet Crawford assembled his column for its departure into Mexico. The command included thirty-two scouts under Al Sieber, one troop of the Sixth Cavalry, and a pack train managed by veteran packer Henry Daly. In early June Crawford led his column south to Skeleton Canyon, just north of the border, where he rendezvoused with Britton Davis and sixty additional Chiricahua and White Mountain scouts under Chatto, a separate pack train, and Mickey Free, his interpreter. Crawford was impressed by Chatto and quickly made him his principal advisor on Apache matters.[7]

On June 11, in 120-degree heat, Crawford's small force crossed the border and wound its way south into Sonora, following the route Crook had used two years before.[8] Eight days later, as the column neared the town of Oputo on the Bavispe River, three scouts in the vanguard of the column were fired on; one was killed and another wounded. When word of the ambush reached the column, Davis recorded that "hell or at least the threat of it, broke loose in the scout camp." Assuming Mexicans were responsible, several scouts, mostly White Mountains, for it was one of their number who had died in the ambush, stripped for war and prepared to wreak havoc on the nearby town. The officers, with the help of the more clear-headed scout leadership, calmed the warriors, and the column resumed its march south. Although the villagers were spared White Mountain wrath, a herd of Mexican cattle spied along the trail later that day was not. The scouts slaughtered the entire herd in an orgy of revenge. During the 1883 expedition only Crook's presence and the iron discipline he imposed had prevented such occurrences.[9] Without his restraining authority, the historic, deep-seated hatred that characterized relations between Mexicans and Apaches would prove a recurring problem.

Two days later all thoughts of vengeance were forgotten upon discovery of fresh tracks belonging to one of the bands they had been seeking. Crawford halted the column and, fearing that Lieutenant Gatewood and Sieber would slow the scouts and perhaps alert their quarry, had the two white men remain in camp while detailing thirty of the Apaches to take up the trail. The scouts, with Chatto in the lead, tracked the band for two days in pouring rain to a small rancheria later identified as Chihuahua's. Chatto later related that as his men were attempting to surround the camp, they were spotted and forced to attack prematurely. Consequently, their quarry—fifteen warriors and some of the women and children—escaped. But an equal number of women and children were captured, among them Chihuahua's wife and children and the family of Chihuahua's brother, Ulzana, whose young son was mortally wounded during the fighting. It was widely thought that the capture of the families of the two prominent Chiricahuas would encourage their surrender. But the opposite occurred—the loss of his family members and the death of his nephew hardened Chihuahua's resolve to fight on, spurred his hatred of Chatto, and instilled in him a burning desire for revenge.[10]

After sending the captives and the two scouts wounded in the encounter back to Fort Bowie, bringing Crook his first word of the fight, Crawford continued south to the small Sonoran town of Nacori. He then turned east onto the steep slopes of the Sierra Madre.[11] Appalling conditions marked the column's progress. In addition to the heat, the men contended with insufficient water one day and torrential rains the next, rancid and moldy rations, and a profusion of unpleasant insects and rattlesnakes. The pursuit was unequal and frustrating. The column was slowed by the weight of their rations, forage, and supplies, while their foes had "nothing to carry but themselves." Crawford's men rode increasingly worn-out stock while their quarry acquired fresh horses along the way, killing them when the mounts tired and surviving on their flesh and wild fruits.[12] Adding to its frustrations, the column had to contend with attacks by hostile Mexicans, who believed the troopers, their uniforms by now reduced to rags, to be civilians—"Texans and bronchos [sic]"—invading their territory.[13]

Their arrival at the crest of the Sierra Madre yielded magnificent views of its eastern slopes but no sign of either the Indians or of Wirt Davis's column. The trek had exhausted Crawford's rations, leaving him ill-equipped to continue into the arid Chihuahua desert. So he doubled back to the valley of the Bavispe River where forage was more plentiful and from there sent the pack trains back to the border for fresh supplies. On August 2, after their return, convinced that Chihuahua's band was to his east in the Sierra Madre, Crawford broke camp and led his men once more up the daunting slopes of the range.[14]

A week later Britton Davis, riding in advance of the column, encountered two white men and some thirty armed Apaches in a clearing. The whites were "scarecrows," dirty and unshaven, clad in tattered clothing, their feet wrapped in bloody strips of flannel. They revealed themselves to be Lieutenant Mathias W. Day and Charlie Roberts, a civilian chief of scouts. They and the Apaches with them were from Wirt Davis's command.[15] They had been trailing Geronimo's band for three days. Before catching up to them, they had exhausted their food, and their moccasins had dissolved in the wet weather, leaving them barefoot on the thorny, rock-filled terrain. Though the Apaches spotted his men before they had completely surrounded their camp, Day's scouts killed a woman and a teenage boy and captured fifteen women and children. The rest of the band, including the shaman and his warriors, had escaped, scattering in different directions. Among the prisoners were eight members of Geronimo's family.

An account of the engagement was forwarded to Crook at Fort Bowie, who passed it on to his superiors with evident satisfaction.[16] Unfortunately, the report was garbled. While correctly listing the number and identities of the captives, the information about those killed was erroneous. One woman and a teenage boy somehow became four warriors and a woman. Two of the supposed dead were unaccountably identified as Nana, the old Mimbre chief, and Geronimo's twelve-year-old son, Chapo.[17] It also listed Geronimo as having been wounded. In fact, Nana, whose demise had been reported several times in the past, had escaped death yet again because he was not in the camp.[18] Chapo, too, had survived the fight. Geronimo himself escaped unscathed, though one of his warriors was shot in the leg. The shaman later recollected that only "one boy was killed and nearly all of our women and children were captured."[19] The source of the report's confusion remains a mystery. Though not attributable to General Crook, he must have found it embarrassing.

Perhaps to dampen unrealistic expectations fostered by his original dispatch, the next day Crook followed up with a second, more sobering appraisal of the affair, emphasizing the difficulties inherent in campaigning against the Apaches, though he expressed optimism that the harrowing ordeal his men endured would ultimately be rewarded. He predicted that the fragmented band would come together, probably in November, and "this will perhaps lessen the difficulties . . . to be overcome." But, he warned, "in no event can anything except the most severe arduous and persistent work or unlooked for accidental good fortune accomplish any important good results." The campaign would prove every bit as arduous as Crook predicted, and "accidental good fortune" continued to be in short supply.[20]

After skirmishing with Lieutenant Day, Geronimo and his remaining followers fled across the Sierra Madre toward the state of Chihuahua with Crawford's column on their trail. Aware that the plodding pace of his pack animals and weary mounts could never match that of the swiftly moving band, Crawford once again deployed his scouts in advance of the column. But this time he ordered Britton Davis and Sieber to accompany them in order to impose the discipline that he felt was absent when the scouts took to the trail on their own. Lightly rationed and carrying the minimum of clothing and equipment, the detachment set off, anticipating that they would rejoin the column after a few days. But that was not to be. In fact, the march became an ordeal lasting the better part of a month. Unable to catch up with their more mobile foe, Davis would pursue their trail across the mountains and into Chihuahua, contending with incessant rain, dwindling rations, and, most dangerous of all, encounters with hostile Mexican regulars and local militias.

These armed and angry men, in many cases little more than bandits, roamed the countryside in bands searching for Apaches. The scouts and their American officers—whose uniforms were tattered and filthy after months on the trail—were hardly distinguishable from their quarry. Running out of rations, the column, like Geronimo, began supplementing their diet with Mexican cattle, the butchered remains of which they left strewn along the trail.[21] Though Crawford had authorized Lieutenant Davis to issue receipts in payment for the slaughtered stock, these bits of paper had little meaning to Mexican peasants and did little to alleviate a growing anger directed by the local population against the intruders.

On August 25 smoldering resentment and misunderstandings threatened to turn into tragedy. Lieutenant Charles P. Elliot, en route from Crawford's column to Britton Davis's detachment with supplies, was fired on by Mexican irregulars who had found the carcasses of several cows slain by Davis's scouts on the trail and assumed Elliot's men were responsible. With difficulty, the lieutenant restrained his Indians from returning fire, and he identified himself as an American officer. Unimpressed, the Mexicans appeared ready to kill him. Fortunately, a company of Mexican regulars rode up at that moment and took custody of Elliot's men, turning them over to Britton Davis, who by then had also arrived on the scene. Though the incident ended without bloodshed, it signaled an ominous escalation of tension between local and American forces and reinforced Lieutenant Elliot's already low regard for Mexico and its people.[22]

Crook, unable to influence the course of action from his distant vantage in Arizona but fully aware of the dangers posed by such incidents, did what he could to reduce friction. The most recent treaty with Mexico was scheduled to expire at the end of October and had as yet not been renewed.[23] So the general fell back on his own resources. Perhaps spurred by word of Elliot's encounter, in early September Crook met with the governor of Sonora, Luis Torres, in Benson, Arizona. Torres, who appreciated the Americans' efforts, assured Crook that he was amenable to reciprocal border crossings by military units and would not interfere with American troops hunting Apaches in his state. He followed up by issuing orders to his prefect commanders to render the U.S. military all possible aid in apprehending the Chiricahuas. Unfortunately, Mexican anger at the butchery of their cattle by hungry scouts and the continuing Apache depredations on Mexican civilians guaranteed future incidents that Crook's understanding with Torres would be powerless to avert.[24]

Meanwhile, Britton Davis and his scouts continued on Geronimo's trail, which now turned north toward the border. This change of route led Davis to believe that the shaman planned a raid on the Mescalero reservation in New Mexico to recruit additional warriors.[25] Though the lieutenant had little chance of catching up with the band, he pressed his pursuit, hoping at least to prevent them from laying waste to the countryside along the way. But he was again intercepted by hostile Mexican troops, and this time he was ordered out of the country. As he was plainly in violation of the hot-pursuit doctrine, he had no alternative but to comply, abandoning the chase and returning to the States.

Crossing the border at El Paso in early September, Davis made his way to Fort Bliss, where he wired Crook to report of his belief that Geronimo was headed for Mescalero. Thinking he was probably correct, Crook ordered Colonel Bradley to mount a force "to clean out this party." In the interim, Davis, while recuperating in Texas, encountered an American with a large cattle operation in Chihuahua who offered him a job managing his holdings. The lieutenant, weary of Indian warfare, accepted the offer, resigned his commission, and then traveled to Fort Bowie to inform Crook of his decision. The news must have shocked and dismayed the general, but characteristically, his diary entry that evening read simply, "Lt. Davis wishes to resign to accept business proposition." And so, with only this passing reference, Crook closed the book on a promising young officer whom he had looked upon fondly and in whom he had reposed great trust and responsibility.[26]

While Britton Davis's detail had been harassed by Mexican troops in Chihuahua, Crook had learned from Crawford's dispatches that he too had experienced similar difficulties and was peremptorily ordered out of the country. Though angered and humiliated by the confrontation, Crawford, like Davis, was forced to obey. The treaty sanctioning his presence in Mexico had by now expired, leaving his column in limbo. After considering the fruitlessness of Crawford's recent efforts, the worn-out condition of his men and livestock after three months in the field, and the approaching expiration of his scouts' enlistments, Crook ordered him to withdraw to Fort Bowie. On October 10 the captain presented himself at Crook's headquarters, tired but prepared to refit his troops and recruit fresh scouts and renew his hunt for the dissidents.[27]

Davis and Crook misread Geronimo's intentions. Though the shaman did, indeed, return to U.S. territory, he was not headed for

Mescalero. From the outset his objective had always been to rescue family members captured by Lieutenant Day, whom he believed were still at Fort Apache. While Crook dispatched troops to apprehend him at Mescalero, the shaman, in company with five warriors and four or five women, easily evaded soldiers stationed along the border and slipped into New Mexico. The small band then headed northwest toward the safety of the Mogollon Mountains, within striking distance of his objective 150 miles further east.[28] Along the way, they killed several whites—men, women, and children—and kidnapped the eleven-year-old son of a rancher named McKinn, who would remain with the band through the coming months and later provide a firsthand account of the raiders' depredations.[29]

On September 23, headed for Fort Apache, Geronimo learned that his family, with the exception of one of his wives, She-gha, had been transferred to Fort Bowie. That evening an embarrassed Crook received word that the shaman had slipped by soldiers guarding the Indian encampment near Fort Apache and carried off She-gha, her daughter, and another woman, along with several horses belonging to the White Mountain tribe. He had then fled back into the Mogollons with angry White Mountain warriors in pursuit.[30]

The same day Geronimo struck the Chiricahua rancheria at Fort Apache, Wirt Davis's column, now operating alone in Mexico, encountered Chihuahua's band in the Teras Mountains. The ensuing fight proved insignificant, but as the shooting died away, one of Davis's scouts who was related to Chihuahua shouted to him that the army was willing to accept the band's peaceful surrender. Before Chihuahua could respond to this offer, Davis, fearing treachery, abruptly broke off the discussion, thus missing what might have been an opportunity to secure the surrender of more than half the dissident Chiricahuas.[31]

When Captain Davis reported this skirmish to Crook, he warned that these Indians, too, seemed headed north on a path that would bring them back into Arizona.[32] Chihuahua did not disappoint. Out-distancing Davis, he crossed the border on September 28, linking up with Naiche's band in New Mexico. The two chiefs easily eluded the network of troopers guarding the area and disappeared into the mountainous New Mexican countryside on a trail that indicated that, like Geronimo, they were probably headed into the Mogollons and perhaps then to Fort Apache.

Faced with the return of two marauding bands to his jurisdiction, Crook issued a warning to the citizens in the area that the Indians would be passing through, probably on the lookout for livestock.[33] And to prevent the shaman from raiding Turkey Creek for relatives and additional warriors, he accepted Crawford's suggestion and transferred the Chiricahuas still there to San Carlos, where troops were available to guard them. As the transfer was for their own protection, he cautioned Captain Pierce to treat them as guests rather than prisoners.[34]

Crook was now under great pressure, embarrassed and angered by the seeming ease with which the dissidents had been able to elude his troops and raid throughout the territory almost at will. The harassed general wrongly blamed the White Mountain scouts for his troubles, claiming they had shown insufficient ardor in their pursuit of the shaman following the raid on Fort Apache. In fact, he had no reason to question the loyalty or the dedication of the tribe. They had suffered much at the hands of the Chiricahuas and had given good service to the army. Ignoring such evidence, he decided to spur them to greater efforts by authorizing a bounty of one hundred dollars on the head of any "hostile Chiricahua buck brought in by a scout or volunteer," a crude but effective device he had employed during his 1873 campaign against the Tontos and Yavapais.[35] On September 30 he had Roberts send a dispatch to Gatewood at Fort Apache informing him of the new policy. Its tone unmistakably conveyed his annoyance with the tribe. "Tell the White Mountain Indians," it directed, "that the general . . . is getting tired of doing all of their work for them and that he will ask to go away from here and they will probably then get another big-bellied agent who will move them all [back] to San Carlos."[36] Crook's previous threats to resign had been directed to his superiors. Perhaps now he thought it would work with the Indians. Whether it had any effect in this case is unknown. But his decision to offer a bounty for Chiricahua heads certainly produced results, and they were tragic for the White Mountain people.

In addition to placing a bounty on the raiders' heads, Crook ordered Crawford and Wirt Davis, now back in Arizona, to join in the pursuit of the raiders. With such formidable enemies on their trail, the Chiricahuas wisely turned back toward the border. Hotly pressed, Chihuahua's band was almost caught by pursuing cavalry. But just as the Apaches' mounts began to fail and the troopers drew near, the Indians were saved by the negligence of local ranchers. Ignoring Crook's warnings of the Apache threat, cattlemen had gathered for a fall roundup squarely in the path of the Indians' flight. They failed to post guards before retiring for the night and, predictably, awoke the next morning to find their horse herd gone. These fresh mounts, which Crook bitterly described as "about thirty of the best horses in Arizona," allowed Chihuahua to easily beat the pursuing troopers to the border.[37] More galling still, in the confusion caused by Chihuahua's escape, Geronimo, too, crossed easily back into Mexico.[38]

Perhaps emboldened by the ease with which they had evaded Crook's forces and still desirous of liberating their families from their enemy's clutches, Chihuahua put aside his anger at Geronimo long enough to formulate a plan for a joint operation. At Casa Grandes in late October, they decided that while the shaman and Nana remained in Mexico plundering the countryside, Chihuahua would return to Arizona in a raid again aimed at freeing their captured relatives and, if possible, at recruiting additional tribesmen to their cause. The raid would also serve to provide Chihuahua and his brother, Ulzana, an opportunity to exact revenge on Chatto for leading the earlier attack on their band in the Sierra Madre. Once across the border the raiders intended to separate into two bands. Chihuahua, with a small party of eight warriors and two women, would make diversionary attacks in southern New Mexico to draw the attention of the army. Meanwhile, Ulzana and his own band of twelve, unaware that their relatives had already been transferred to San Carlos, would make for Fort Apache to recover them.[39]

In mid-November, to Crook's consternation, the Apaches appeared in New Mexico. Chihuahua's diversion worked perfectly. Though soldiers picked up his trail, efforts to apprehend him failed, and the band disappeared into the New Mexican countryside, leaving several civilians and scouts dead in their wake.[40] For the remainder of the month, he continued to hold the army's attention, hitting ranches and settlements in southern New Mexico, killing a reported forty whites, looting stock, and drawing multiple troops of cavalry into fruitless pursuit. In December he disappeared back into Mexico.[41]

While Chihuahua diverted the army's attention in New Mexico, Ulzana's band unexpectedly appeared near Fort Apache on the White River on November 23. For Ulzana, avenging himself on Chatto was of more immediate interest than liberating the captive families. The chief scout had a farm in the area, and Ulzana's warriors found him and his wife working their fields. Somehow intuiting impending danger, Chatto managed to get himself and his wife safely to the fort. But Ulzana, though he now knew that his relatives were no longer at Fort Apache, so longed for revenge that he remained in the area for the remainder of the day, hoping for a second chance at the scout. While awaiting an opportunity to strike, he and his warriors killed two white stockmen and the cattle they had been guarding and ran off a horse herd belonging to Bonito, payback for his refusal to join in the breakout. Later that afternoon, the raiders paused for a meal, posting a young man as sentry on the ridge above their camp. As they ate, a local chief crept up and killed the young man, severed his head, and delivered it to Fort Apache in the hopes of collecting Crook's bounty.[42]

The Apaches had long been hunted for bounties placed on them by both the Americans and the Mexicans, and the tribe carried memories of many instances of treachery used to collect the blood money. So the emotional impact of this killing on Ulzana's band far exceeded their reaction to the slaying of a single warrior. Infuriated by the death and mutilation, they turned on the White Mountains and in a frenzy murdered twenty-one of their people, including eleven women and six children, and kidnapped an additional three women. These acts, in turn, enraged the White Mountain warriors, who immediately set out in pursuit of the band. But Ulzana was too quick for them. Slipping into the Mogollons, he raided into New Mexico throughout December, defying all attempts by troops to apprehend him, and then, at the end of the month, rejoined his brother in Mexico.[43]

Ulzana's raid was particularly galling to Crook. Despite the presence of hundreds of troops combing Southwest in search of them, Ulzana's warriors achieved spectacular results. When sufficient time had elapsed for him to view the event with something like objectivity, the general was able to accurately describe its achievements. The war party, he wrote, had "travelled probably not less than one thousand two hundred miles, killed thirty-eight people, captured and wore out probably two hundred and fifty head of stock, and though twice dismounted, succeeded in crossing back into Mexico with the loss of but one, who was killed by friendly Indians."[44]

The havoc caused by Ulzana's raid and the army's failure to bring the raiders to bay gave new life to a storm of criticism directed at both

Crook's generalship and his plan to keep the Chiricahuas in Arizona. But despite the outcry, the general did not curtail his efforts to prevent the tribe's permanent removal or diminish his belief that force alone would never resolve the crisis. The apparent ease with which this small band of Chiricahuas had eluded the military's attempts to capture them only hardened that conviction. He was now more than ever wedded to the idea of a negotiated surrender and to policies that supported that end.

After Geronimo fled the reservation, Crook had initially decided that when he eventually apprehended him and the other chiefs, he would turn them over to the civil authorities for trial and punishment. But now he realized that such a course would make a voluntary termination of hostilities impossible. As long as the Indians believed they would be tried in a civilian court—where loss of freedom or, more likely, death by hanging would result—they would never willingly give up their arms. Further, Crook had consulted with lawyers and learned that turning the Indians over to a civilian court would be a useless gesture: their conviction would be highly unlikely. Discarding the notion of involving the civil authorities, he now argued that a negotiated surrender would be feasible only "if [the leaders] are assured their lives will not be forfeited and they would simply be transported [exiled from Arizona]."[45]

In the Southwest, at least, Crook's recommendations were greeted with derision and a renewed outburst of criticism. But in September, before Ulzana's raid, the idea of a negotiated surrender had received support from an unlikely source: General Sheridan. In the early days following the breakout, the lieutenant general had lavished praise on Crook and his handling of the crisis, absolving him of any responsibility for it. In his annual report to the secretary of war that fall, Sheridan had expressed "the greatest confidence" in General Crook's ability to capture or kill the shaman. Moreover, to counter the popular notion that Crook cared more for the Indians than the good white people of Arizona and New Mexico, Sheridan had publicly reassured the uneasy Anglo population that their lives, property, and business interests were uppermost in the general's mind. Finally, in words that he must now have looked upon with bitter regret, he announced that "General Crook is the best man we have to deal with these hostile

Indians and will accomplish more in the end than perhaps any man in the Army."[46]

While praising Crook, Sheridan initially took a punitive attitude toward the "hostile Chiricahuas," declaring that they "have forfeited their lives by their outbreak and savage acts of butchery and deserve no consideration whatever." He had briefly considered and rejected a suggestion by Brigadier General Nelson A. Miles, commander of the Department of the Missouri, that the entire Chiricahua tribe, both participants and nonparticipants, be removed from San Carlos to Fort Leavenworth and placed under Miles's control. Sheridan came to believe that such action would only further inflame Apache resistance. Instead, perhaps influenced by Crook, he had concluded that to end this "weary struggle" his old West Point roommate should have the authority to treat the fugitives as prisoners of war, "to be transported to some distant point . . . [and] never be allowed to return to Arizona and New Mexico." The secretary of war supported this plan after he had been assured that it was meant to apply to all of the dissident Chiricahuas, not just their leadership. The secretary's endorsement identified for the first time the location of Sheridan's "distant point"—Fort Marion, Florida. For better or for worse, the government thought that it had now fixed the terms under which it would accept surrender.[47]

Sheridan had made his recommendation prior to Ulzana's raid, an event that greatly embarrassed him. Not two months later Ulzana had suddenly materialized in Arizona, hundreds of miles from the border, as if deliberately seeking to make fools of the army and General Crook. Under the circumstances, Sheridan's initial reaction appeared relatively mild. On November 19 Crook noted in his diary that the lieutenant general had wired that the president "was much annoyed at the frequent complaints of depredations in Arizona and New Mexico" and had inquired whether "there is any likelihood of the war terminating soon" and whether he [Sheridan] could assist Crook.[48] Hoping to avoid a visit from his commander, Crook immediately responded: "All has been done that in my judgment can be done for the suppression of these Indian troubles. . . . I know of nothing that would be of assistance to me more than I now have."[49] Four days later Ulzana surfaced in the White Mountains. Six days after that, Sheridan, obviously unimpressed by Crook's response, arrived on his general's doorstep.

Little Phil was no longer in a liberal frame of mind. Ulzana's presence had reinforced his conclusion that Crook's plan to allow the loyal Chiricahuas to remain in Arizona was not feasible. In his opinion the entire tribe had conclusively demonstrated their incurably predatory nature. Only their immediate removal to a distant place from which they would never return would afford the people of Arizona complete protection from their depredations. Secretary of War Endicott agreed. But with commendable caution, he directed that before making a final decision, Sheridan discuss the matter with Crook. Accordingly, the lieutenant general eased his now corpulent five-foot-five frame on to the padded seat of a railcar bound for the Southwest. Stopping briefly in New Mexico to pick up Colonel Bradley, with the colonel in tow, he hurried on to Crook's Fort Bowie headquarters, arriving on November 29.[50]

Eight days previously, Wirt Davis had departed Fort Bowie on his second campaign into Mexico with a hundred newly recruited scouts to replace his original, and now weary, White Mountain Apaches. The new scouts were a mix of men from the Yuma, Tonto, Mojave, and San Carlos bands, with a scattering of White Mountain tribesmen.[51] Captain Crawford, with one hundred Chiricahua and White Mountain scouts, was scheduled to follow him into Mexico. Fortuitously, he was still at the post at the time Sheridan arrived.[52]

Crook took full advantage of Crawford's presence. Acutely aware of his own shortcomings as a persuasive speaker, he was not above looking to a more articulate subordinate to argue his case—in this case the eloquent and experienced Captain Crawford.[53] Crook's greatest concern at this point was the impact on the Chiricahuas should they learn of Sheridan's current plan to exile their entire tribe from their homeland. It would be disastrous if it caused those who had volunteered as scouts to withdraw from the coming campaign, as they formed the backbone of the command. They were to compose its entire fighting force with the exception of a few officers, and their presence was considered vital to any effort to persuade their fellow Chiricahuas to surrender. So Crook desperately needed to change Sheridan's mind about the removal, and he believed that Crawford was the best person to do it. Not only was he experienced and well spoken, but his very life might depend on the outcome, a circumstance that would undoubtedly make him all the more persuasive.[54]

As Crook had foreseen, Crawford's presentation and Sheridan's opportunity to observe the scouts firsthand won the day. Despite long-standing reservations regarding Indian scouts, Sheridan was greatly impressed by Crawford's professionalism and by the appearance and evident discipline of his men. And he seemed convinced by the captain's logic. The Chiricahuas could hardly be expected to endure the dangers and emotional turmoil involved in fighting their own people knowing that their reward was to be exile for themselves and their families. Crawford's presentation did not change Sheridan's opinion about the reliability of Indian scouts or alter his longstanding concern that Congress might cut military appropriations if it believed that scouts could be used as a temporary substitute for troops in moments of crisis. Yet he was sufficiently impressed by the captain's arguments not to undercut him on the eve of his departure on such a dangerous and difficult campaign. So he temporarily ignored his reservations and agreed to support the deployment of Crawford's scouts for the remainder of the campaign. More importantly, he shelved his proposal to remove the Chiricahuas from Arizona until a later date.[55] At the same time, to Crook's delight, he extended the latter's authority to deal with Apache depredations by widening his jurisdiction to include the Military District of New Mexico.[56]

Sheridan's decision to give Crook command in New Mexico did not sit well with Crook's fellow brigadier, General Miles. Miles, like his late friend George Armstrong Custer, was an officer of undeniable ability and courage. His immense ego, voracious ambition for advancement, and relentless self-promotion also invite comparison to Custer. But unlike his ill-fated fellow officer, Miles was well connected, having married the daughter of John Sherman. A prominent U.S. senator and a formidable power in the Senate, his father-in-law was also a former cabinet secretary and, not incidentally, the brother of the commanding general of the postwar army, William Tecumseh Sherman, a relationship that did not always work to Miles's advantage.

Miles had been openly scornful of George Crook's reputation as an Indian fighter dating back to Crook's elevation to brigadier in 1873. At the time of Crook's promotion, Miles had been a full colonel, one of several that President Grant had passed over to appoint Crook, a lieutenant colonel, general and commander of the Department of Arizona. Miles considered Crook inferior to him in ability and military achievements. Moreover, while he would later dismiss the importance of seniority when the issue was inconvenient to his own campaign for a general's star, he seems never to have gotten over the fact that Crook had won the appointment despite Miles's own seniority. Their joint service on the Yellowstone during the Sioux War had heightened the competition between them and did not enhance Miles's opinion of Crook's abilities as an Indian fighter. He kept a keen eye out for weaknesses in Crook's performance to exploit in the likely event that the two officers would again find themselves in competition for promotion.[57]

In 1880 Miles vied for brigadier rank, using the influence of his powerful father-in-law and other influential friends. He won the promotion, replacing retiring Brigadier General Ord, despite the circumstance that six other colonels out-ranked him in length of service and in the face of opposition from General Sherman, who truly believed in the principal of seniority.[58] In 1885, as a brigadier, Miles convinced General Sheridan, Sherman's successor and the best man at Miles's wedding, to assign him to the Department of the Missouri. His new command included New Mexico Territory, a happenstance that put him squarely in Crook's path, opening a new chapter in their rivalry.

During that summer of 1885, newly installed at his headquarters at Fort Leavenworth, Kansas, Miles first turned his gaze toward the Southwest, where, to his delight, Crook appeared to be floundering following Geronimo's breakout. Coincidently, the impending retirement of General Pope, commander of the Division of the Pacific, in March 1886 had created a rare opportunity for advancement to major general. In this context Miles viewed the conflict with the Chiricahuas as both a chance to discredit Crook and an opportunity to garner enough glory to earn the additional star that he so craved. Consequently, he unhesitatingly injected himself into the situation, expressing loudly and publicly his dissatisfaction with Crook's Apache policies and even, as we have seen, advancing solutions of his own.

Ulzana's depredations in New Mexico and Crook's inability to prevent them provided Miles with fresh ammunition. Against the background of public criticism of Crook's response to the raids and despite his own lack of experience with the Apaches, Miles advocated removing Crook and consolidating New Mexico and Arizona under his own command. He even recommended General Eugene Carr, who

Major General Nelson A. Miles in full dress uniform. Courtesy of Mark Kasal.

had crossed swords with Crook in past assignments, as his subordinate to take charge of the field operations against the Apaches. But neither General Sheridan nor General Schofield, Miles's immediate commander, thought that removing a commanding officer in the middle of a campaign was a good idea. Both agreed that Crook should remain in charge, at least for the time being. But to Miles's likely chagrin,

Sheridan chose to adopt the brigadier's concept of consolidating the two jurisdictions and, as we have seen, selected Crook rather than Miles to command them.[59]

Despite this setback, Miles did not give up his campaign for the Pope vacancy. Four brigadiers were in line for it—Generals Howard, Terry, Crook, and Miles. While Howard and Terry had seniority, both Crook and Miles had reputations as experienced and competent Indian fighters. Miles evidently dismissed the qualifications of the two longer-serving generals, conveniently ignoring their seniority. He saw Crook as his only real competition and continued to look to the latter's Apache problems as fodder for his campaign, which he launched in the fall of 1885 with the aid of well-positioned surrogates.

Part of Miles's strategy was to undermine Crook's reputation as an Indian fighter, a celebrity he regarded as entirely undeserved. As he wrote to a former aide and loyal ally: "[Crook] has never succeeded to my knowledge in sending away Indian trouble."[60] He recognized that Crook's use of Indians as scouts made him vulnerable in an administration skeptical of native auxiliaries and made him enemies among those within the military angered by the fancied insult implied by Crook's preferred use of Apaches on his expeditions into Mexico. Seeking to play upon these prejudices and ignoring his own lack of experience in Apache warfare, Miles offered Sherman his unsolicited opinion that "if called upon, I believe those Apaches can be destroyed by U.S. troops." In an interview in the *New York Times* in September 1885, he expressed doubt that Indians scouts, especially those of the same tribe as those hunted, could be expected to help the military against their own people. While publicly denigrating the value of using Apache scouts, Miles also urged the removal of all Chiricahuas from Arizona, a recommendation sure to please his superiors and garner him political support in the Southwest. He made no secret of these views, though he must have also known that they might undermine the morale and effectiveness of Chiricahua scouts currently risking their lives in Mexico.[61]

As the military did not look kindly upon self-promotion or on officers criticizing one another, surrogates often waged campaigns for promotion. Captain Bourke, obviously a Crook partisan, alleged that Miles or others working on his behalf orchestrated a newspaper campaign to undermine the Gray Fox. In support of his contention, Bourke's diary included several editorials published in big-city papers in early January

1886 as the campaign was heating up. All assailed Crook's efforts to capture Geronimo and advocated his replacement by Miles. Bourke suspected that the almost simultaneous appearance of these articles calling for Miles to replace Crook "smacks of the Literary Bureau style of pre-arrangement."[62] The *New York Times,* demonstrating that not all the newspapers were in Miles's camp, endorsed Bourke's views. The paper opined that the proliferation of such articles was part of a concerted plot to win Miles the promotion to major general, a charge that drew denials from General Sheridan and the War Department.[63]

Crook's supporters, too, seemed to have few qualms about using papers favorable to their man to promote his cause. An article friendly to Crook appeared in the *San Franciscan,* a California paper, naming Arizona's Indian Ring as part of the plot to replace Crook with Miles These "mining sharks and cattle swindlers" either benefitted from continuing Apache unrest or coveted Apache lands on the reservation. Consequently, the *San Franciscan* alleged, they wished to see Crook removed from command and replaced with a less experienced officer. Of General Miles, the paper wrote, it was unfortunate that at this time "military jealousy, backed by family and petticoat influences at Washington [a reference to Miles's wife's family connections] should lend itself to the scheme for 'downing' a brother officer."[64]

A number of other partisans joined the fray on both sides. Edmond Ross, the territorial governor of New Mexico, viewed the Apaches as a roadblock to settler immigration and favored any policy, no matter how ruthless, that removed them from the scene. Skeptical of Crook's use of scouts and impatient with his apparent lack of progress in killing off the marauders, he saw General Miles as the preferable officer to manage the Geronimo campaign. Warmly supporting Miles's efforts, he took a leading role in New Mexico in campaigning for Crook's removal, adding his signature to a letter to the president from federal officials in New Mexico calling for the removal and even pressing the governor of Arizona to do the same.

An active Crook partisan, William H. H. Llewellyn, the Indian agent at the Mescalero Reservation and a prominent New Mexican Republican, vigorously opposed Ross's lobbying efforts. He wrote to Crook impugning the governor's motives for favoring Miles's candidacy, claiming that in turn for his support, Miles had promised Ross to move the military departmental headquarters from Santa Fe to

Albuquerque, a move that would allegedly benefit the governor's business interests. In addition to spreading rumors about the governor's corruptibility, Llewellyn also reported that Ross was working hard to undermine Crook's support within the Nebraska congressional delegation, but he had met only limited success due to Llewellyn's own activities to thwart the effort.[65]

Another Miles partisan was Francis Barlow, a former general, great friend, and long-time supporter. Retired from the service, he was not constrained by the army's reluctance to attack its own. In a letter-writing campaign in support of Miles's candidacy, Barlow wrote a friend that "General Crook was made a Brigadier General by Grant in 1873, over all the colonels in the Regular Army, and since then he does not appear to have done anything to warrant his new position."[66]

During the Sioux War Miles had tried to induce several Sioux chiefs to surrender to him rather than Crook in order to garner credit for ending the conflict.[67] He had failed then, but now, Captain Bourke alleged, he sought to use a similar strategy in his campaign for the coveted promotion. According to Bourke, Miles sent an aide to the Mescalero Reservation in New Mexico to enlist the Mescalero Apaches in an effort to persuade Geronimo to surrender to Miles rather than Crook. Bourke credited Agent Llewellyn with foiling the plot by using his influence to dissuade the Mescaleros from helping Miles. The indefatigable agent had then written to President Cleveland describing the general's trickery. There is no record of what, if anything the president might have made of this tale.[68]

Crook was anything but oblivious of Miles's machinations and their potential impact on his career. In a letter to the division headquarters in San Francisco, he complained bitterly, if ungrammatically, that "General Miles occupies the position that by moving troops to certain points he can satisfy public opinion and by catering to individual interests can make capital at my expense, without any corresponding benefit being accomplished. I shall still be responsible for all the outrages while he can thro[w] responsibility on my shoulders on the ground that he is unable to use his own troops." Crook was so annoyed by Miles's efforts that he suggested that he, Crook, ought either to be given responsibility for command of all troops in New Mexico or be relieved of responsibilities in that district.[69] His resignation offer was, of course, ignored by superiors now used to Crook's histrionics. But, as we have seen, in the end he achieved his goal when Sheridan gave him the New Mexican command. Miles's reaction was predictable. He regarded Sheridan's action as a personal affront and shortly thereafter, when Sheridan praised Crook in his report to the secretary of war, Miles called the plaudits "unwarranted."[70]

The president appears to have been unimpressed by the antics of the two generals and their supporters. The rivalry intensified for a short time when a second vacancy in the ranks of major generals opened up upon the unexpected death of General Hancock. In the end, however, all the sound and fury came to nothing. In March 1886 the president, adhering strictly to the principle of seniority, named Generals Howard and Terry to fill the two openings. Crook remained a brigadier, and with Geronimo still at large, his future as commander of the Department of Arizona appeared far from certain.

CHAPTER NINETEEN

A Tragic Loss

The closing weeks of 1885 and the dawning of the New Year were a time of growing uneasiness for General Crook, a situation for which Miles was only partially responsible. Having failed to intercept Ulzana's band in the Dragoon Mountains, Crawford, on Crook's orders, had disappeared into Mexico to join Captain Wirt Davis in scouring the volcanic maze of slopes and canyons in the Sierra Madre in search of the elusive dissident Chiricahuas. Crook's hopes reposed with the two captains, yet he remained completely in the dark regarding their whereabouts or the day-to-day operations of their columns.

Even today, the U.S.-Mexico border is too long, too rugged, and too porous to prevent anyone with sufficient knowledge, ability, and determination from breaching it. And as Ulzana's raid had demonstrated, the Chiricahuas certainly possessed these qualities in abundance. The raid, together with Crawford's failure to find Ulzana in the Dragoon Mountains, had underscored the army's inability, even with legions of troops at its disposal, to locate the Indians or afford protection to the widely scattered settlers and miners who resided in the territory. It had become painfully clear that so long as the dissident Apaches remained at large in Mexico, they were a sword of Damocles hanging over the entire Southwest. The only solution was, as Crook phrased it, to "break up their main nest down in old Mexico."[1]

On December 3 Crook laid out his strategy for Frederick Tritle, Arizona's governor, and Colonel Bradley, New Mexico's military commander. Bradley had argued that rather than send Crawford into Mexico, Crook ought to deploy his forces in Arizona's Mogollon and Black ranges where he thought the Indians were hiding. Crook, now Bradley's superior officer, dismissed this suggestion out of hand. While it might be useful to deploy additional troops between the border and the railway, he told Bradley, "when the Indians get into the rough country north of the railroad, it is practically impossible to do anything with them. . . . The country is so indescribably rough that any pursuit is almost a farce."[2] He shared the same reasoning with Sheridan on Christmas Eve, writing that "troops cannot catch [the Apaches] in this country except by accident."[3] Rather, he would stay with his Mexican strategy, relying on the competence of Crawford and Davis—and especially on their Apache scouts—to locate the Chiricahuas, despite the officers' dismal track record to date. He was optimistic that their luck would improve during the winter season when cold weather would make it more likely that the bands would congregate and remain longer in their campsites, making it easier to find and engage them.[4]

But his public optimism masked a host of doubts. The reality was that too many uncertainties were involved for him to have the confidence he outwardly displayed. While he heard nothing from Mexico, he was besieged daily with reports of Ulzana's continuing depredations in his own backyard and his troops' failure to counter them. Ignorant of the activities and whereabouts of his two Mexican columns, surrounded by critics and second-guessers, he was a man under siege. Beset by tension, he confided in no one. His natural reticence inhibited him from seeking the advice and support of his aides, and while many married officers confided in their wives, there is no evidence that the general ever adopted the practice, despite the closeness of their relationship. At any rate, she was in Maryland visiting her family.

To pass the time and likely to relieve his stress, the beleaguered general fell back on his favorite form of relaxation, hunting. He whiled away many a morning or afternoon shooting and trapping birds and small game. His almost daily hunts in the desert scrub surrounding Fort Bowie, a seemingly benign way to manage his stress, worried his aides. There was always the potential that unfriendly Apaches might appear at any time in the neighborhood. This was a realistic concern. In early December, when Crook had extended his hunting into the

Chiricahua Mountains, only a day or so after he left the area Ulzana's band passed through on its way back into Mexico.[5]

The general's diary records a litany of short hunts juxtaposed with troubling occurrences. On December 7 Indians stole two horses; three days earlier they had burned a ranch. That day Crook went hunting, trapping one fox and slaying a dozen quail. The following day he trapped another fox and killed six quail after receiving word of the slaughter by Apaches of two men near Alma, New Mexico. On December 14 he received news that a week before, Lieutenant Fountain of the Eighth Cavalry had battled the Indians in the Mogollons. Though he had captured their stock and supplies, his men failed to kill or capture any members of the band. The next day, fox traps empty, Crook compensated by shooting one quail and two cottontails.[6]

As Christmas approached and Crook moved on to deer and turkeys, President Cleveland nervously called his department commander's attention to news reports of public furor in the Southwest over Ulzana's raid and the army's seemingly ineffectual response. Crook's pessimistic response and Sheridan's continual carping about the failure of the general's efforts did little to allay the president's concerns. At the end of December, Crook recorded glumly in his diary that Sheridan had wired him to inform him that the president wanted "to know if I could not give him some good news." Later in the day Crook shot five quail and two doves before drafting a discouraging reply indicating that he had none to share. Instead, he described a large force—four troops of cavalry and forty Navajo scouts—that in the days following the Fountain fight had unsuccessfully pursued Ulzana and his ten fellow warriors after they killed an army doctor and four soldiers. The Indians escaped without suffering a single casualty. Crook blamed the fiasco on the Navajos; frightened of the Chiricahuas, they had refused to follow the raiders' trail despite their superior numbers.

The Navajos' perfidy (according to Crook) clearly demonstrated why he preferred Chiricahua scouts for such work. For Sheridan, the report likely confirmed his low opinion of Indian scouts in general, a sentiment only reinforced by news of yet another debacle. A Mojave scout had shot and killed two black troopers. A subsequent investigation determined the first shooting was accidental and the second was the result of a misunderstanding due to language differences, a finding that did nothing to alleviate Sheridan's concerns.[7]

Crook closed out his communications for the year 1885 in a black mood, reporting that while Crawford and Wirt Davis had been in Mexico for almost three weeks, he had yet to hear from them. "News from these commands may be expected at any time," he wrote, in a half-hearted attempt to cast a little sunshine on the report. The next day he bagged five quail and two doves.[8]

Almost another month passed before Crook finally received word about Crawford's command. It arrived with the sudden and explosive force of a thunderclap. Crawford was dead—murdered, it appeared, during an attack by Mexican forces on his column south of Nacori in Sonora. These sketchy facts were outlined in a brief dispatch from First Lieutenant Marion Maus, Crawford's second in command, and delivered to Crook at Fort Bowie on January 27. The poignancy of the tragedy was compounded by the additional news that, just prior to the calamity, Geronimo had agreed to meet with the general and discuss terms for ending the hostilities. The captain would never realize the fruits of his hard campaigning. Several more weeks of silence followed before Crook would learn anything further.[9]

After abandoning his fruitless search for Ulzana's trail in the Dragoons, on December 11 Crawford had crossed into Mexico. Accompanying him were four companies of Apache scouts, three officers, and a contract surgeon to care for the wounded.[10] His second in command, First Lieutenant Maus, was a levelheaded, thirty-five-year-old West Point graduate and veteran of the Sioux War and Nez Perce campaign. He commanded two of the scout companies. The other two officers were Second Lieutenants William E. Shipp and Samson L. Faison, both also West Pointers and both new to the West and Indian warfare. The former would command the remaining scouts, while the latter served quartermaster and commissary. The army contract surgeon, Dr. Thomas Davis, brother of Union general Jefferson C. Davis, had served alongside Crawford at San Carlos and thus was probably on familiar terms with many of the scouts.[11] Al Sieber initially joined the column as chief of scouts but turned back short of the border when Crook decided his presence was needed to calm unrest at San Carlos caused by Geronimo's breakout.[12] Tom Horn replaced him. A packer on the first Sierra Madre expedition and a Sieber protégé, Horn spoke Spanish and some Apache and was also well known to the scouts. Three pack trains, each with its own pack master, carried supplies for the column. Henry Daly was one of the pack masters. He, like several other whites on the expedition, would write an account of it.[13]

The core of Crawford's force was the cadre of one hundred Apache scouts recruited from the White Mountain, Cibicue, and Chiricahua bands. They were divided into four twenty-five-man companies split into two commands under Lieutenants Shipp and Maus. The lead scout, given the rank of sergeant major, was Noche, a Chokonen Chiricahua who was, by all accounts, a highly competent and reliable leader. He replaced Chatto, who had refused to reenlist for this mission, having been worn out by the exigencies of Crawford's first expedition. Chatto's nephew had signed on in his stead, together with Dutchy (Britton Davis's loyal but, from all accounts, murderous scout). During a previous campaign, Dutchy had refused to fight against his people and had subsequently been charged with mutiny, but Crawford regarded him as too valuable to leave behind on this occasion. To demonstrate his faith in him, the captain appointed him as what Lieutenant Shipp termed his "body servant." By most accounts Dutchy would reward Crawford's trust.[14]

Crawford hoped to coordinate his operations with Wirt Davis's column, which had been fruitlessly scouring the eastern (Chihuahua) slopes of the range for the past several weeks. Though this would be his third journey into the Sierra Madre, there is evidence that the forty-one-year-old Crawford was uneasy about this mission. Weeks before, while visiting a fellow officer and friend at Fort Grant, he had expressed pleasure at receiving General Crook's assignment to this command but confided that he had a premonition that "when I go into Mexico, I will not return."[15]

Immediately after crossing the border into Sonora, Crawford had reported his presence to the Mexican authorities at Fronteras, twenty miles to the south of the line, ensuring that the government was well aware of his presence and purpose.[16] From the border region he planned to go deep into the Sierra Madre and then hook northward, hoping to come at the Indians from an unexpected direction. To that end, he proceeded south, following the now-familiar route from Fronteras to the small Sonoran town of Nacori Chico. There he divided the column into separate detachments to search the surrounding slopes of the Sierra Madre for signs of any of the dissident bands. No trace of them was found, but several reports indicated that they had been seen farther to the south.

On December 31, while Crawford was camped in the valley of the Bavispe River, a deputy marshal from Tombstone arrived with an arrest warrant for Dutchy for the teamster's murder he had allegedly committed three years before. Crawford successfully put off the lawman by telling him that arresting Dutchy would create what he euphemistically termed "dissatisfaction" among his fellow scouts. The impact of the incident on Dutchy was unclear, but the scouts could now concentrate on the search for Geronimo without distraction.[17]

Four days later, while camped near Nacori Chico, the captain received word that Geronimo was close by. Filled with anticipation, he set off immediately with his officers, Tom Horn, and the scouts, leaving his slower pack animals to catch up when they could. Unimpeded by the mules the column moved swiftly, and four days into the chase, Horn, leading an advance party, struck Geronimo's trail. From the tracks his scouts concluded that Naiche and his people were with the shaman.

Like hound dogs on a scent, the column relentlessly tracked the dissidents into raw, mountainous country aptly named Espina del Diablo, the Devil's Backbone. They moved on foot over extremely rough ground broken by steep canyons. It was a perilous and arduous exercise since they were forced to travel at night to avoid detection. Marching in total darkness, the men stumbled blindly over the stony ground, falling into unseen crevices and suffering stabbing pain as jagged rocks pierced the thin soles of the moccasins they had donned to muffle their footfalls. Their path led upward over steep ridges marked by sharp drop-offs, and as they ascended into higher altitudes, the air grew chill. Each man carried only a single blanket, and the biting cold made sleep difficult on the brief occasions when they stopped to rest. As they drew closer to their quarry, they found their route strewn with the gory remains of hastily slaughtered cattle. Each of the beeves had only a few pounds of meat cut from it, evidently eaten raw as the fleeing Apaches had little time to stop and cook their meals.[18]

At dusk on January 9 the forward scouts reported that they had found Geronimo's rancheria a night's march to their front. The column halted in preparation for the trek that would bring them to the camp at first light. Crawford, exhausted by the pace, now suffered severely from the ill effects of his years of hard campaigning compounded by enduring travel in such harsh country. Still, he did not falter. Taking Lieutenants Maus and Shipp and about eighty scouts, about half of them Chiricahuas, he set off into a moonless night, using his rifle as a crutch to support himself over the rough ground.[19]

Reaching Geronimo's camp just before sunrise, he deployed his force, hoping to surround the sleeping warriors. But as had happened so frequently, before they could get into position, the Apaches discovered their presence, this time alerted by the braying of their burros. Led by Geronimo and Naiche, the rancheria's eighty inhabitants (twenty or so warriors and sixty women and children) escaped in the confusion and uncertain dawn light without suffering a single casualty. But in their haste they abandoned their scant food supply, equipment, and nearly all of their livestock.

The fugitives were now in deep trouble. They had no provisions, clothing, equipment, or livestock and were adrift in piercing, mid-winter mountain cold. Even more demoralizing was their grim aware-ness that fellow tribesmen who knew their every hideout had brought them to this pass. Under these disheartening conditions, Naiche, never wholly committed to this enterprise, dispatched a woman to Craw-ford's camp to ask for a parley. The captain received her cordially and after hearing her tale knew that the moment had at last arrived when the Apaches might be induced to surrender. But his interpreter was with the pack train, still several hours to his rear, so he thought it wise to delay negotiations until his arrival. To signal his good intentions, the captain sent the woman back to Naiche with some food and word that he would meet with the chief the next morning at a place about a mile from the camp. He then sent a runner to hasten his column's arrival.[20] Confident that they now had nothing to fear from the shaman's band, Crawford's exhausted force built huge fires to warm themselves and settled down for a much-needed rest. Secure in the knowledge that Geronimo would not attack him in the night, Crawford posted no guards that evening, perhaps a fatal error, since doing so might have averted the tragedy that would soon unfold and alter the course of future events.[21]

The column awoke at dawn on January 11 in a heavy fog. Many were still in their blankets when a shouted warning rang through the camp. Mexican soldiers were approaching. Tom Horn and Lieutenants

Maus and Shipp, all too aware of the potential combustibility inherent in any contact between their scouts and Mexican troops, leapt to their feet and rushed toward the oncoming intruders, hoping to avert a misunderstanding that might erupt into hostilities. Shouting in Spanish as they ran (both Maus and Horn spoke the language), they identified themselves as an American military unit. The advancing Mexicans either ignored or did not hear their shouts and began shooting into the camp, wounding several scouts and forcing the rest to take cover in the rocks. The scouts immediately returned fire, and the two forces exchanged shots for perhaps fifteen minutes while the three Americans continued their frantic efforts to identify themselves.

Stiffened by the cold and slower than the younger men, Crawford arrived on the scene some moments after the firing had begun. Taking command, he and Maus moved forward toward the approaching Mexicans, shouting that they were Americans. As Maus later described the moment, "Several of them approached and Captain Crawford and I went out about fifty yards from our position in the open and talked to them. . . . Captain Crawford then ordered me to go back and ensure no more firing. I started back when again a volley was fired. . . . When I turned again, I saw the Captain lying on the rocks with a wound in his head, and some of his brains upon the rocks."[22] According to Lieutenant Shipp, who actually witnessed the shooting, the captain had climbed atop a boulder in order to be seen more clearly and was waving a white handkerchief in token of his peaceful intent. Suddenly, a single shot rang out that knocked him senseless. A glancing blow to his forehead had cracked his skull.[23] He would live for several days thereafter, but the wound to his brain was mortal.

Whether Crawford's death was the result of a misunderstanding or a deliberate act remains in dispute. The commander of the attacking Mexicans would later assert that the shooting occurred because his men misidentified the scouts as raiders whom they had been tracking. The Mexican government blamed the American government for Crawford's death, arguing that the U.S. Army had brought Indian scouts into Mexico in violation of its treaty with Mexico. Moreover, they challenged the veracity of Maus's report, calling it a fabrication and claiming that Crawford had been killed by his own troops.[24]

Based on the accounts of his officers, Crook had no doubts that the Mexicans were aware that they were attacking U.S. soldiers at the time Crawford was killed.[25] In his own report he wrote that the shot that ultimately killed Crawford "seemed to be the agreed upon signal, as at once the firing became general." He mocked the claim of mistaken identity, pointing out that the Mexican soldier who shot Crawford was standing only twenty or thirty yards from him at the time, that the captain was in uniform, and that he had identified himself to the advancing force as an American officer. In a later interview with Charles Lummis, a Los Angeles reporter, the general bluntly claimed that the men who attacked Crawford were "simply banditti, after scalp money and plunder. It was no mistake. They knew who he was. . . . The only mistake they made was in our numbers. They didn't know how strong our force was, and thought they could get away with it."[26] Crook's characterization of the attacking force seems to have been correct. It was later identified as a unit in the Seguridad Pública, civilian irregulars described by packer Daly as "similar to the state rangers of Texas." (Possibly he meant the Arizona Rangers.) More accurately, they seem to have been similar to American militia units that patrolled the frontier during the Indian wars. For the most part they were an unpaid, undisciplined rabble, rewarded for service with whatever they could loot. In this case they included Tarahumara Indians, blood enemies of the Apaches who were much feared for their pitiless brutality and dogged tracking ability.[27]

There may have been a third explanation for the shooting. Absent from Lieutenant Maus's official report, but included in an account he provided General Miles, was a description of the scene just before Crawford was shot. "Looking to the rocks, we could see the heads of many of our Indian scouts with their rifles ready, and could hear the sharp snap of the breechblocks as cartridges were inserted. I can well recall the expression on the faces of these Mexicans, for they thought our scouts were going to fire; indeed I thought so myself."[28] Maus's description led historian Jerome Greene to surmise that the Mexicans fired on Crawford by mistake. While discounting the Mexican government's claim of American responsibility and its allegations that Maus had fabricated his report, he postulated that the click of the scouts' breechblocks startled the Mexican troops, causing one to fire when Crawford showed himself in an effort to effect a ceasefire.[29]

Crawford's shooting did not end the affair. The firing continued for about a half hour, until the Mexicans, having incurred a number of casualties and now aware of their opponent's strength, asked for a parley. Though they apologized for the confrontation, they presumptuously asked the Americans to provide them with rations and horses to transport their wounded and for Doctor Davis to tend to them. Maus's position was precarious. His captain was alive but comatose, and his men, both scouts and officers, were exhausted and short of rations and ammunition. The Mexicans remained threatening, and the intentions of Geronimo and his people, who had delightedly observed the fighting from a nearby ridge, were uncertain. Would they attack, flee, or adhere to their previous agreement to return peacefully to San Carlos? Given these considerations, the lieutenant felt that he had little choice but to comply with the Mexicans' requests. The next day the Mexicans repaid his generosity by taking him hostage until he agreed to replace Indian ponies that he had given them with more tractable mules.[30] Only then did the Mexicans, apparently satisfied, withdraw.[31]

The next day Maus began the sad and difficult journey north to the border. The first evening the column received a visit from two women, emissaries from Geronimo with an offer to parley. The lieutenant eagerly accepted and the next day conferred with Naiche and Geronimo. The Apaches wanted to meet face-to-face with General Crook "near the line in one month," after they had time to round up the rest of their people and their livestock. As a token of good faith, they agreed to leave nine members of the band with Maus as hostages. Among the nine were old Nana and members of both Geronimo's and Naiche's families.[32]

After his talks with the shaman and fearing a renewed assault by the Mexicans if he tarried, Maus resumed his march north. His progress was slow because of his need to care for the wounded, including Crawford, who awakened only once briefly before lapsing into a coma. There was little they could do for him but arrange him as comfortably as possible on a litter outfitted with a makeshift canvas shade to protect him from the sun.[33] The trail was steep and uneven, and two packers were required to attend the litter, easing it over rough spots and around sharp bends in the trail. Finally, on January 17 one of the men lifted the canvas to check on the captain and found that he had died sometime that day. At the small town of Nacori, they temporarily interred the captain's body, wrapped in a blanket and placed in a rude coffin constructed from boards salvaged in the town, just outside a small cemetery on the outskirts of the village.[34] That evening Maus dispatched a message to General Crook relating the facts surrounding Crawford's demise and Geronimo's proposed parley with the general. As to the latter, he noted that he was impressed by the sincerity of the dissident chiefs and believed that they "mean to do as they say."[35] What Crook made of Maus's assurances—and whether Geronimo would live up to his word—remained to be seen.

CHAPTER TWENTY

Cañon de los Embudos

As communications from Mexico were problematic, Crook did not receive the news of Crawford's death until January 27. Maus's dispatch bearing word of the killing had first traveled by courier and wire to Fort Bowie. From there it had to be relayed by Crook's aide, Roberts, to Albuquerque, where the general was conferring with General Williams, his adjutant general. Two weeks earlier, on the morning Crawford was shot, the general had recorded in his diary that he had experienced dizziness upon awakening, likely a symptom of his recurring bouts with malaria rather than a portent of impending tragedy.[1] Ignoring the momentary weakness and unaware of the events that were now unfolding in Espina del Diablo, he diligently attended to routine matters. Ironically, these included drafting a response to a complaint from Luis Torres, Governor of Sonora, regarding recent depredations in the Sierra Madre that the governor attributed to Crawford's scouts. Assuring Torres that he was forwarding his concerns to the captain for investigation, Crook promised that if his allegations were found to have substance, severe punishment would be meted out to the guilty parties. These words must have come back to haunt him when he learned that at the time he wrote them, Crawford lay mortally wounded, killed by members of the Mexican armed forces.[2]

The sudden and unexpected news of Crawford's brutal slaying and the uncertainty surrounding Geronimo's proposed peace talks brought Crook's spirits to a low he had not experienced since the aftermath of the Rosebud fight and the Custer debacle almost a decade before. Then, too, he had confronted loss while facing a future filled with uncertainty, his career and even his life dependent on circumstances beyond his control. Though he might have drawn some comfort from Geronimo's offer to talk, Crook knew better than to place too much reliance on the words and deeds of the impulsive and mercurial shaman and his followers. The outcome of any such discussions was far from certain.

Geronimo, always wary of treachery, had stipulated that he did not want any soldiers to accompany the general to the meeting site. Though probably not Crook's primary concern, there is evidence that the physical threat implicit in the coming talks, should they even occur, certainly was on his mind. On several occasions during this period, he made written reference to the murder of General Edward Canby by the Modoc chief Captain Jack in 1873 under similar circumstances. The Modocs were fierce warriors, much like the Apaches, and fighting them had proved frustrating and difficult, making the prospect of a negotiated peace attractive. Canby, eager to end the conflict, had agreed to the chief's offer to meet him unarmed and unprotected by troops. Captain Jack, bowing to pressure from his lieutenants, had then shot and killed Canby and another of the negotiators, afterwards escaping to continue the war. The talks that Crook now contemplated with Geronimo held the prospect of a similar outcome. The danger in this case was exacerbated by the shaman's insistence on holding the meeting south of the border, where an approach by Mexican troops might ignite a violent response from the volatile Chiricahuas.[3] Aside from such worries, Crook seriously doubted that the Indians would surrender unconditionally and accept the prospect of removal to Florida. Should the talks fail, the Gray Fox would face the embarrassing and potentially career-ending eventuality of returning empty-handed from Mexico, leaving the Chiricahuas free to continue their depredations indefinitely.

In Albuquerque, when he received news of Crawford's death, Crook had been enjoying a rare respite from the serial crises that characterized the Geronimo campaign. The holiday aspect of the trip must have been enhanced when Mary joined him, having arrived by rail on January 25 on her return from the East.[4] The sudden, unanticipated news of the fate of his highly regarded and beloved longtime subordinate was undoubtedly a heavy blow to absorb. Yet his habitual reticence and self-control did not desert him. He left no clues of his reaction to the tragedy, not even confiding his emotions to his diary. Whatever feelings he had can only be inferred from external sources.

Perhaps one indication of the extent of his inner turmoil was that after officially relaying word of Crawford's murder to his superiors on January 27, he made no mention of it in his diary, either that day or for many days thereafter.[5] The omission seems intentional. The entry for January 27, the date he received the news, is distinguished only by the utter banality of its contents: a description of being fitted for a coat and vest, an unsatisfactory conversation he had with a Colonel Head, whom he grumpily characterized as "a big humbug," and a visit by Mrs. Crook to the rail office to check her bags. The entry for the following day noted his arrival in Deming, where he stopped en route back to Bowie. It described an encounter with several officers at the depot, where "no special news" was exchanged. How extraordinary, given that Arizonans had only learned of Crawford's death the day before. Another officer in Arizona, traveling by rail at the time, recalled that "the talk on the train was all about Crawford." A week later Crook, now at Fort Bowie, wrote that Wirt Davis had arrived from Mexico "badly used up. Gives no news of importance." Again, one wonders. Was Crawford's death not discussed? If it was, was the conversation really so insignificant?[6] While speculation as to the thoughts and motives of one long dead is inherently suspect, it may be that Crook's omission of the mention of Crawford's death in his diary was one means of avoiding the pain it caused him. By refusing to acknowledge the loss, he managed to cloak it in a cloud of mundane details that deadened its impact.

Aside from his studied failure to mention Crawford's demise, Crook's diary provides another clue as to his state of mind. In the days following his receipt of Roberts's telegram, the general's entries document almost daily shooting expeditions. Despite inclement weather and a potentially dangerous mishap—a cartridge prematurely exploded in his hand, burning an ugly hole through his beard and singeing his eyebrows—he spent nine of the fourteen days following the news of Crawford's death shooting quail. Was this almost daily slaughter intended to assuage his grief, perhaps even feelings of guilt? It had been Crook, after all, who had recalled Crawford from a safe berth in Texas to the dangerous assignment that led to his death.[7]

Though Crook may have been able to keep Crawford's death at arm's length on a personal level, he could not avoid dealing with it professionally. First, there was the distressing matter of the disposition of the captain's remains. On February 8 he received word that Crawford's brother had asked that the body be returned to the family home in Kearney, Nebraska, for burial. A week later the general met with the Santa Fe undertaker who had volunteered to travel to Nacori to recover and then transport the captain's body to Nebraska. That meeting provided the first occasion on which he made reference to Crawford's death, albeit briefly, in his diary: "Undertaker from Santa Fe came to see about Capt. Crawford's body." The next day he wired Washington for authority to spend the funds necessary to cover the expense of recovering and reinterring the remains.[8] And on the February 17 he penned a formal letter of appreciation to the secretary of state of Sonora, thanking him for facilitating the body's return to the United States.[9]

The arrival of letters sent by Crawford to his family in Nebraska must have been particularly painful. Crawford's brother had forwarded the letters to verify that the captain wished to have his remains sent home for burial. Crook, obviously deeply affected by their contents, reassured the family that there was no question but that the body would be returned to the family. Even now, he added, it was on its way from Mexico, housed in a casket not unlike the one used for the remains of President Garfield. His communications with the family go unmentioned in the diary, and when Lieutenant Maus's report arrived on the 28th with the heartrending details of Crawford's death, it, too, received only a passing reference.[10]

Events concerning the Apaches unfolded swiftly now, leaving Crook little time to dwell on the tragedy of Crawford's death. On February 1 Sheridan wired Crook that the president had been made aware of the shaman's desire to meet with the Gray Fox. Rather than congratulate Crook, he appended a warning instead. Make "no promises at all to the hostiles *unless* it is necessary to secure their surrender" (emphasis added). The "unless" seemed to imply, possibly inadvertently, that Crook had some latitude in his negotiations.[11] That same day Crook was encouraged to learn that, at least for now, the administration agreed that turning the Indians over to the territorial authorities for trial would impede peace negotiations with Geronimo. Accordingly, the president instructed the federal district attorney in Arizona to prevent the civilian authorities from interfering with "any Indians that Crook might have as prisoners until further word is received from the Department of War as to their disposition."[12]

Ten days later a dispatch from Maus, now on the Mexican border, brought additional welcome news. The dissidents remained of a mind to surrender and would soon name the place where they wished to meet. At the same time, scouts returning to Fort Bowie confirmed Maus's belief that Geronimo was sincere in wanting peace, adding that some of his people, spotted near the border, had ignored fire from overeager troopers and indicated by signs their friendly intentions.[13] A week later other returning scouts carried more hopeful news. Though the Apaches were still scattered throughout the mountains, for the first time they had committed to setting an approximate date for their meeting with Crook—the middle of the next month (March). Nevertheless, as he cautioned his superiors, the scouts also warned that the Indians were extremely wary "and may not be willing to surrender unconditionally. . . . Any attempt to coerce or exact too rigorous terms with any part of them will stampede the whole."[14] Washington cannot have welcomed the flexible approach that Crook's words implied.

For the next two weeks Crook tensely awaited final confirmation of the meeting with Geronimo, even as he prepared for it. Though occupied with the emotionally fraught issues related to Crawford's final interment, he marshaled the energy to fight off initiatives that he believed would weaken his hand in negotiations. One such undertaking, an attempt to remove troops from Arizona in anticipation of peace with the Indians, he opposed as premature, believing it might encourage Geronimo to take a hard line in negotiations. On the other hand, he scotched a renewed effort by U.S. Marshals to arrest Dutchy on the old murder charge. What would Geronimo think if he saw the general surrendering one of his own scouts to the civil courts? Meanwhile, he fended off Sheridan's nervous inquiries as to why the Indians continued to delay their appearance at the border.[15]

On March 16 word finally arrived from Lieutenant Maus that he had at last reached agreement with the "hostiles," as he referred to them, on the terms for the coming meeting with the general. All but Mangas's band had now congregated within twenty-five miles of the lieutenant's camp in northeast Sonora. Four emissaries had come to him, announcing Geronimo's terms. The meeting must be held in Mexico, but close to the border and at no great distance from where Maus was then camped. Furthermore, to allay Geronimo's fear of treachery, Crook must travel to and attend the meeting without escort, a demand that surely revived memories of the Modocs. Maus concluded his dispatch by urging Crook to make haste, lest the skittish Apaches take flight at the approach of Mexican troops or some other perceived danger.[16]

Crook would not be rushed. He had always begun negotiations with the tribes on his own terms, and his dealings with the Chiricahuas would be no different. He had no intention of allowing himself to be stampeded and thus betray his eagerness to bargain. Rather than rush to join Maus, as the nervous lieutenant had urged, he moved forward with deliberation. To convince Geronimo of his authority, he wanted Ka-ya-ten-nae, the respected Chihenne leader he had ordered imprisoned at Alcatraz, at his side during the negotiations. So he arranged for the chief's release. As Crook had predicted, incarceration in the island penitentiary had worked a wondrous conversion on the Apache leader, and he had become, in Bourke's words, "a white man" and "an apostle of peace."[17] Several days would elapse before the chief arrived at Bowie from San Francisco, and the general delayed his departure for Mexico to await him.[18] On his arrival on March 22, Crook immediately dispatched him to the border under the watchful eye of Alchesay, the White Mountain scout who had loyally served Crook for many years, and Tom Moore, the general's longtime pack master, who now appeared with his mule train from Wyoming.[19]

That same day, as Ka-ya-ten-nae began his journey south, Geronimo and Naiche announced their choice of location for the parley: the Cañon de los Embudos (Funnel Canyon), poetically referred to by the Apaches as the place of "Green Water Running." Described by one of Crook's packers as "a pretty little canyon, some 345 feet deep, filled with cottonwood and Sycamore trees," it lay eighteen miles south of the Arizona border. The canyon floor, about two hundred feet in width, was watered by a small, tree-shaded stream. With good water, plentiful grass, and high country to the south and east that afforded the security that Geronimo craved, it was a good campsite and an ideal place to hold the talks.[20]

Maus arrived at the site first, making his camp on a low mesa at the base of the canyon by the creek. The next morning Geronimo appeared with most of his people. Maus's scouts, many of whom had lost families to these fighters, watched with narrowed eyes as the dissidents, mounted on stolen livestock, swept around the base of the mesa "like a whirlwind, dashing by as if in review." They had obviously already scouted the location and carefully chosen where they wanted to set up their rancheria. Disappearing into some nearby timber, they could be heard making their camp on a conical hill above the canyon, situated about five hundred yards distant from Maus and hidden from view behind rough outcroppings of lava rock and steep ravines that lay between the two forces.[21]

And this is where Crook found them when he finally showed up on March 25. Two days before, accompanied by aides Bourke and Roberts and Roberts's twelve-year-old son, Charlie, for whom Crook seems to have developed a special fondness, the general had departed Fort Bowie in a buckboard. As agreed, he traveled without military escort, but with him were thirteen armed packers, ostensibly to attend to his mules and supplies.[22] Charlie kept a daily account of the expedition, an important historical record that demonstrated the boy's unusual powers of observation and precociousness.

Their first day on the road had been a ten-hour ordeal. The track was so rough in places that the party was forced to switch at intervals from their wagons to mules to negotiate it. That evening they made camp at a water hole with the unappetizing name of Mud Springs, still in Arizona but near the border. Here Tom Moore, Ka-ya-ten-nae, and the rest of the advance party awaited them. Here, too, the general received word that Maus had camped near the Apaches at the designated meeting site about a day's ride to the south.

According to most accounts, it was at Mud Springs that several others joined Crook's party, including Mayor Charles Strauss of Tucson and, of greater interest from a historical perspective, a mustachioed, flamboyant character named Camillus Sydney Fly. The latter ran a successful business in Tombstone photographing the town's notables.[23] His appearance at Crook's camp was probably no coincidence. Prior to departing for the canyon, Crook had received an inquiry from another Tucson photographer named Willis P. Haynes asking for information about the Geronimo campaign. Crook, by then heartily sick of the wildly inaccurate reporting that characterized so many stories in the local and national press, was anxious to set the record straight. He told Haynes that there was not a word of truth to recent articles about the shaman's surrender and other events in the campaign. Lieutenant Maus, he said, was in camp south of San Bernardino Springs, and he himself was departing for the site the next day to "have a talk with the hostiles." The specificity with which Crook discussed his plans hinted at an open invitation to join him. Haynes did not bite but must have passed along the information to Fly, a fellow photographer. And the latter, known to be a daring character, lunged at the opportunity. Having given fairly precise information about when and where he would be carrying out his mission, Crook was probably not surprised, or for that matter disappointed, when Fly showed up. He consented to bring the man along, and the pictures that he took over the next several days provided a priceless photographic record of the historic event.[24]

The next morning the travelers journeyed by wagon to San Bernardino Ranch, briefly visiting en route one of the border outposts established to interdict the Apaches. The party then crossed into Sonora, camping for the night at Contraband Springs—as the name implies, a known haven for smugglers.[25] They were now only eighteen miles from Maus's camp.

On the 25th Crook had the party on the trail by seven a.m., as was his habit. As they rode down the San Bernardino valley, a herd of wild pigs foolishly darted across their path. The scouts took off after them, and Ka-ya-ten-nae shot one through the head while riding at full gallop, demonstrating that his sojourn in Alcatraz had not diminished his warrior skills.[26] They arrived in Maus's camp around lunchtime, and, as lead packer Henry Daly noted with pride and amusement, Crook went straight to the packers' camp, "expecting to get a good meal with us."[27] While they were eating, Daly—who claimed great insight into the Indians' state of mind—warned the general that the Apaches were in "an ugly mood," irritated by Crook's late arrival and hung over after a night spent guzzling cheap whiskey and mescal. The liquor, Crook learned to his displeasure, had been furnished by a Swiss-born army beef contractor and general no-account named Tribolet, who had set up shop about three miles from the camp and was selling booze to all comers.[28] Given the Indians' mood, Daly advised Crook to temper his usual harsh approach to avoid antagonizing them. As soon became apparent, the general, though well aware of the threat presented by the presence of alcohol at such a gathering, ignored this advice.

Naiche's opening gambit seemed to underscore Daly's warning. Upon learning of Crook's arrival, the chief galloped his pony through the packers' camp in search of Crook, scattering their carefully prepared luncheon in all directions. His sudden appearance startled the scouts, who leapt to their feet and ran for their rifles. According to one of the packers, "Crook turned pale at this sign of impudence but was perfectly calm." Ordering the men not to shoot, he advised the muleskinners to take their dinner and get to the top of the hill, fortifying their position as best they could. "No telling what these Indians intend doing," he said. He remained seated by the fire and finished his meal. While the packers scurried up the hillside and barricaded themselves behind their packsaddles, the general leisurely assisted the cook in packing up his outfit.[29]

Naiche's dramatic entrance may have been a prearranged signal. Dismounted warriors now began to move warily in and out of the campsite, never more than five to eight at any given time. Bourke, always the keen observer, noted that they were in prime condition, most fully armed with Springfield breech-loading carbines or Winchester repeaters and wearing full belts of ammunition ostentatiously draped across their chests. That, and the fact that they were dressed in new shirts and blankets, led the captain to surmise that they had completely refitted themselves since their encounter with Crawford's scouts two months before. Bourke thought them "apprehensive of treachery and ready to meet it." Crook would describe them "as fierce as so many tigers."[30]

Realizing that the packers' campfire was not a place where the Apaches would be comfortable, Crook moved to a more neutral site in a nearby grove. In this bucolic spot, shaded by slender sycamores and enormous old cottonwoods, he met with the leaders, Geronimo and Naiche, while their warriors hovered in the background.

It was not Crook's way to seek to overawe the Indians with military formality, a common ploy on such occasions. On the contrary, by carefully arranging his party of unarmed soldiers and civilians, including two youngsters (in addition to Charlie Roberts, a small boy who had

Surrender talks at Cañon de los Embudos, Mexico. Photo taken by C. S. Fly. On lower left is Captain Roberts. Geronimo, wearing a headcloth, sits to his left. On the right, opposite Geronimo, is Crook wearing his Japanese campaign hat. On his right sits Captain Bourke and on his left young Charlie Roberts (*partially cut off*). Courtesy of Mark Kasal.

followed the party from San Bernardino Ranch was also in attendance), before the fully armed Apaches, the general effectively projected an impressive image of complete self-confidence to the watchful Chiricahuas.[31] Avoiding any display of military pomp, he entered the grove dressed in the modest civilian garb he wore on the trail: a frayed brown canvas coat and pants, buckskin gloves, moccasins on his feet, and his familiar cork hat perched squarely on his head. Seating himself on a flat rock outcropping with young Charlie Roberts at one elbow, Bourke at the other, and the remainder of his party clustered about him, Crook opened the parley. He began by asking Geronimo, who sat across from him, to explain his reasons for leaving the reservation.

The shaman, too, wore his everyday dress: shirt, vest, breechclout, and high Apache moccasins, a bandana tied about his head. Through an interpreter, he responded to Crook's request with great emotion and eloquence, delivering a litany of wrongs meant to justify his breakout and subsequent depredations. Though articulate and compelling, Crook viewed it as being short on truth, weaving paranoid fantasies and fabrications into a tale of mistreatment and treachery. While the shaman spoke, the general sat before him, his eyes fixed on the ground, his face a mask of indifference, saying nothing. His posture infuriated

Geronimo. Beads of sweat began coursing down the shaman's face. Clutching a "buckskin thong" tightly in his hand, he demanded to know why Crook would not look at him, speak to him, or smile at him: "Quivering with fury, he fairly hissed, with all the venom of his wild nature, 'I want no more of this!'"[32] Crook, seemingly unfazed, calmly waited for Geronimo to finish speaking. Then he addressed him.

From Charlie Robert's gleeful summary, we know that the Nantan did not heed Daly's advice to go softly. Instead, maintaining a pose of uncompromising indifference, a tactic he had found useful on many occasions in the past, he told Geronimo that he was a liar, and in obedience to Sheridan's orders, demanded the Apaches' unconditional surrender. Bourke's verbatim transcript added some detail to Charlie's account, but the gist was the same. Refuting many of Geronimo's accusations, Crook concluded: "Everything that you did on the reservation is known; there is no use for you to try to talk nonsense. I am no child. You must make up your minds whether you will stay out on the warpath or surrender unconditionally. If you stay out, I'll keep after you and kill the last one if it takes fifty years." He then abruptly dismissed the shaman with the words, "I have said all that I have to say; you had better think it over tonight and let me know in the morning."[33]

In the midst of this tense dialogue, someone cried out that the Mexicans were coming. This caused a stir amongst all present, but it soon became apparent that in reality the "Mexicans" were Chihuahua's band, coming to join Geronimo for the talks. With him rode Ulzana and those who had participated in the raid that had resulted in the deaths of so many White Mountain tribespeople. Masking any insecurity they might have felt entering a camp populated by kinsmen of those they had so recently murdered, the band rode arrogantly into the glade. Equally disciplined, the White Mountain scouts held their anger in check. Chihuahua, who had up to now been in a state of towering rage at the thought of his family in captivity, came forward and politely shook Crook's hand. This simple act seemed somehow to purge him of anger, enabling him to peacefully attend the talks.[34]

While high drama and tension filled the canyon with palpable electricity, photographer Fly diligently went about his work, taking pictures of the participants "with a 'nerve,'" as Bourke put it, "that would have reflected undying glory on a Chicago drummer." As if he were photographing a Tombstone belle in his studio, he moved among some of the most fearsome warriors in the West, asking them "to change position, and turn their heads or faces, to improve the negative." None seemed to mind except Chihuahua, "who kept dodging behind a tree, but was at last caught by the dropping of the slide."[35] Among the pictures taken that day is the now-famous photograph of Geronimo, Crook, and the other attendees, seated in the canyon grove, while Apache warriors hover like shades among the trees, rifles at the ready. A version of that iconic photo, cast in bronze, would one day grace one side of the monument that marks Crook's grave at Arlington National Cemetery.

After the Apaches departed for their camp, Crook returned to his own campsite to contemplate the day's events. During the talks he had followed Sheridan's instructions, offering the Indians an opportunity to surrender unconditionally. But he had grave doubts whether they would accept. That night he sent a dispatch to the lieutenant general, telling him that he feared "it would be impossible to get a hold on them except on conditions that they be allowed to return to the reservation on their old status," terms he was well aware were unacceptable to his superiors and the people of the Southwest.[36]

To gain further insight into the Apaches' reaction to the day's talks, Crook sent Ka-ya-ten-nae and Alchesay, well respected among the broncos, into their camp. They reported back that the Indians were in such an excitable state that the two emissaries feared even mentioning the possibility of surrender: "Geronimo told his people to keep their guns in their hands and to be ready to shoot at a moment's notice."[37]

Despite the tension, the following day the talks proceeded in a calmer and more positive atmosphere. During private conversations with Geronimo, Naiche, and Chihuahua, Crook softened his approach, raising the possibility of a temporary exile in the East where they would remain for enough time to allow the anger against them in Arizona to cool. Exactly how long this would be was apparently not discussed, but the proposal clearly implied an amnesty for their crimes, for otherwise they could never return safely to their homeland. Though clearly not the unconditional surrender envisioned by President Cleveland and General Sheridan, after assessing the mood of the Chiricahuas, Crook apparently felt that his offer was consistent with Sheridan's instruction to make no promises to the Indians "*unless necessary to secure their surrender*" (emphasis added).[38]

After their lengthy discussions with Crook, the chiefs retired once again to discuss his proposal with their warriors. Alchesay and Ka-ya-ten-nae accompanied them, under instructions to keep the Indians off-balance by "dividing their councils, exciting their hope, and enhancing their fears." For his part, Crook wired Sheridan that notwithstanding his doubts of the night before, he now believed that "things look more favorable."[39]

On the morning of March 27, the third day of the parley, Chihuahua sent "a secret message" to Crook expressing his belief that the entire band intended to surrender. But whatever the rest decided, he would surrender his own people and come into the soldiers' camp.[40] In some measure this change of heart may have been the result of interventions by the two scouts who had, on Crook's orders, concentrated their efforts on the more pliable Chihuahua and Naiche. Crook had reasoned that if they accepted the proposal, Geronimo and his lieutenants would have no choice but to also agree. At noon a relieved Crook welcomed all of the chiefs, including Geronimo, to a council in a grove of sycamores not far from the original meeting site. He seated himself beneath one of the large trees, and the Indians squatted in front of him at a distance of several paces. Then Chihuahua rose to speak.

The chief's speech was sincere and moving. For whatever reason, like Chatto and Ka-ya-ten-nae he seemed to have experienced a total conversion from bitter enemy to loyal friend of the whites. Such spontaneous reversals, and they do not seem limited to the Apaches, were documented on several occasions in the history of the frontier. Perhaps, as in this case, they can be attributed to events or circumstances that drove home with shocking suddenness and force the stark realization of the inevitability of Euro-American domination of the Indian tribes and the futility of further resistance. Some chiefs, like Chatto, seemed to have been susceptible to such fatalism, while others—such as Geronimo, Victorio, Mangas Coloradas, and the great Cochise—seemed more resistant. Though previously one of the most prideful and militant of the Apache resisters, Chihuahua evidently was not among those unmoved by circumstances. Standing before the general whom he had berated two years before, he now delivered a speech remarkable for its submissiveness. He now surrendered to Crook, he said, "because I believe in you and you do not deceive us. You must be our God; I am satisfied with all that you do." With startling humility, the once-proud chief concluded, "Whenever a man raises anything, even a dog, he thinks well of it, and tries to raise it up, and treats it well. So I want you to feel towards me, and be good to me, don't let people say bad things about me."[41]

Naiche followed, declaring, "I think it is now best for me to surrender and not remain out in the mountains like fools, as we have been doing. . . . I surrender to you and hope that you will be kind to us, as you have always been a good friend to the Indians and tried to do what was right for them. I have changed all my thoughts. I surrender to you." Geronimo was the last to speak. With unaccustomed brevity, he delivered a brief and sad affirmation of his intentions. Taking General Crook's hand, he, too, seemed humbled: "I give myself up to you. Do with me what you please. I surrender. Once I moved about like the wind; now I surrender to you and that is all."[42]

Though the terms that Crook offered were far more generous than either the president or General Sheridan had contemplated, they appeared required by circumstance. There is every indication that the general's instincts were correct. Had he adhered to his original position of unconditional surrender or a fight to the death, the Apaches would likely have scattered into the mountains, and there would have been little Crook and his small force could have done to stop them.

According Bourke and Crook, the terms of surrender were the result of a compromise that emerged during the talks. The Indians, Crook reported, had initially insisted upon returning to the reservation immediately "on their old status." As this option was plainly unacceptable, they were left with the choice of either returning to the warpath or, if Crook were to strictly follow his instructions from the president, banishment from their homeland forever. Neither alternative was palatable to the Chiricahuas. To break the stalemate Crook had offered temporary exile in the East. The duration of the exile had not been defined but seems to have evolved from discussion between the parties. Ultimately, as Crook wired Sheridan on the 29th, it was agreed that the Chiricahuas "should be sent back east for not exceeding two years, taking with them such of their families as so desired, leaving at [Fort] Apache, Nana who is 70 years old and superannuated."[43]

Mangas and his thirteen followers were absent from the talks. But as they had not been involved in any depredations on American soil, Crook saw no reason not to include them in the understanding with the other dissidents. Believing that when Mangas heard of the agreement, he would surrender his own people, Crook ordered that all efforts to apprehend the chief be halted.[44]

By accepting the Chiricahuas' surrender under the terms offered, Crook knew that he had gone out on a very long and extremely shaky limb. It would require a great deal of salesmanship to win the approval of the president and the people of Arizona to an agreement that permitted the tribe's return to Arizona after only two years in the East. Yet if the compromise truly brought an end to Apache depredations in the territories, Crook would win plaudits and perhaps elevation to major general, a capstone to his career of almost forty years. Of equal moment, it would secure his long-term policy objective, the eventual permanent return of the Chiricahuas to their homeland. To him, it must have seemed worth the risk.

But government endorsement of his terms required his presence to argue on the Indians' behalf, and Crook felt it critical that he return to Fort Bowie immediately in order, as he put it, "to be within telegraphic communication with the War Department."[45] Accordingly, he decided to depart with Roberts and Bourke early the next day, leaving Lieutenant Maus and his scouts with the ticklish task of escorting the Indians back to Arizona.[46]

On leaving the meeting, Charlie Roberts had written in his journal, "We all think this will be the end of the Indian troubles at least for a good long time." Others did not share young Charlie's optimism. Henry Daly was one. After the participants had drifted out of the grove on the last day of the talks, the packer, who had been watching Geronimo carefully, later claimed that he had an intuition that the shaman had no intention of participating in the surrender. Circulating among the Chiricahuas, he said he learned that Geronimo and his band deeply resented Chihuahua's role in the talks and blamed him for undermining their original position: that they be allowed to return to the reservation immediately and without consequences. The shaman and Naiche were also angry because Chihuahua, who was only a subchief, had taken center stage at the conference, diverting attention from the two principal leaders. To this flammable mix of anger and resentment, the whiskey peddler Tribolet added the dangerous accelerant of alcohol, a known incitement to violence among the Apaches. His activities would have dire—and perhaps intentional—consequences.[47]

CHAPTER TWENTY-ONE

Too Wedded to My Views

The evening before Crook departed Cañon de los Embudos, "pande-monium again reigned in the camp of the Chiricahuas." Apache cries echoed throughout the ravine and bullets fired from the camp whistled around the tents of the scouts and soldiers. According to Daly, after Lieutenant Maus expressed concern to his commander about the situation, Crook summoned the veteran packer to his tent to garner his opinion on the likelihood that the Indians would adhere to the agreement. When Daly said he doubted that the Indians would go to Fort Bowie, Crook curtly replied that the chiefs had promised to go and that he had never known an Indian to break his word to him.[1] That seemed to end the discussion.

The following morning Chihuahua assured Crook that despite their drunkenness, the Chiricahuas intended to keep their word and would depart with Lieutenant Maus for the border. Perhaps because of his urgent desire to return to Fort Bowie, the general was too eager to be convinced by Chihuahua's assessment. In any event he ignored an array of red flags that, had he heeded them, signaled a developing situation that might have caused him to remain with Maus and escort the Indians to the border. For example, though Crook never mentioned it, Naiche, in a drunken stupor, had shot and wounded his wife in the chaos of the night before. In fact, at the time of the general's departure the chief was still too drunk to stand upright. Nor did the general report that on their way out of camp, he and his aides encountered Geronimo and four of his warriors "riding on two mules, drunk as lords." Disregarding these portents, he and his aides, with young Charlie in tow, rode north and left Maus and his scouts to deal with the dangerously drunk and fractious tribesmen now scattered about the countryside.[2]

Following Crook's departure, Chihuahua remained true to his word. As promised, he gathered his band and joined Maus as he started his march to the border. Geronimo and Naiche joined the procession, though, drunk and hung over, they lagged behind. But later that day the situation began to deteriorate. While still in Mexico, Geronimo insisted that the party make camp. The following morning, having advanced only a few more miles, Geronimo again refused to cross into Arizona, an unmistakably dangerous sign. Though the line was only a short distance away, he settled down not far from Tribolet's ranch. To counter the threat posed by the trader's proximity, Maus sent Shipp and a detachment of troops to destroy his liquor supply. But it was too little, too late. Soon the Apaches were again roaring drunk.[3] Sometime during that night, Tribolet, evidently not content with simply supplying the Apaches with whiskey, also filled Geronimo's head with the dire fate that awaited him in Arizona, undoubtedly ending with the shaman's death at the end of a rope.[4] Spurred on by liquor and paranoia, later that night Geronimo, Naiche, and twenty of their warriors, with thirteen women and children in tow, stole silently past the sleeping lieutenant and his scouts into the darkness.[5] Chihuahua kept his word. He, together with his brother, Ulzana, Nana, and ten other warriors—whom Maus later described as the "most daring renegade Indians to prey upon civilization"—remained behind, along with most of the women and children, leaving a total of eighty persons in the camp.[6] Needing to make at least a show of pursuit, Maus ordered his second in command to escort Chihuahua's people to Bowie and set off with a contingent of scouts after Geronimo. As expected, his efforts proved futile. The tiny band simply disappeared into the surrounding mountains.

Crook received the grim news late in the evening of March 30 and communicated it at once to Sheridan. Though undoubtedly anticipating an angry reprimand, Sheridan's response took him aback: "Your dispatch of yesterday received. It has occasioned great disappointment. It seems strange that Geronimo and party could have escaped without the knowledge of the scouts."[7] The general was profoundly affected by

Sheridan's insinuation of collusion between Geronimo and the scouts, regarding it not only as an uncalled for attack on his men's loyalty and integrity but also as an indictment of a fundamental cornerstone of his strategy as an Indian fighter. He and his former West Point roommate and friend had endured many rough patches in their relationship as commander and subordinate, particularly during the Sioux War.[8] But he had usually found that he could rely on Sheridan's support. Now it seemed Little Phil had abandoned him. Crook's reaction was immediate and firm. "There can be no question," he wrote, "that the scouts were thoroughly loyal and would have prevented the hostiles leaving had it been possible." Geronimo was too wily and his actions too unforeseeable to have been forestalled.[9]

No sooner had Crook dispatched this telegram than he received another, equally unsettling message. Dated March 30, it had evidently been sent just before Sheridan had received word of Geronimo's escape. It contained President Cleveland's blunt rejection of any concessions allowing the Chiricahuas to return to the reservation after two years in the East. Instead, Cleveland ordered Crook "to enter again into negotiations on the terms of their unconditional surrender, only sparing their lives."[10] Such a change in conditions undercut any hope of a negotiated settlement with Geronimo. If unconditional surrender had been unacceptable to the shaman before he had absconded, it certainly would not be any more appealing now. The only option left was a long costly war of extermination.

Sheridan's wire also raised another, more personal, concern. Throughout his career Crook had carefully nurtured a reputation among the Indians as one who told the truth and kept his promises. These core principles were a matter of personal pride and honor and an acknowledged reason for his success in dealing with tribes throughout the West. Chihuahua had agreed to surrender based on the conditions Crook had offered and had remained steadfast because of his faith that the Gray Fox would keep his word. Obedience to the president's current directive required that Crook renege on his agreement with the chief, likely damaging, if not destroying, his credibility and staining his honor. This was anathema to him.

His first course was to try to change the president's mind by appealing to reason. To that end, he wired Sheridan that Chihuahua's people were coming in peacefully. The shaman and his followers were long gone. Changing the surrender terms now would simply cause those who had kept faith to scatter into the mountains, Crook wrote, "and I can't at present see any way to prevent it."[11]

Whether Sheridan even relayed these words to the president is doubtful. Without bothering to respond to Crook's contention, he pointedly suggested that his general concentrate his efforts on protecting the people of Arizona and New Mexico from the depredations that he was sure would now follow. Noting sarcastically that the forty-six companies of infantry and forty troops of cavalry currently on hand should be sufficient for the job, Sheridan asked Crook for an outline "of what you contemplate for the future."[12]

On April 1 Crook replied. Tiredly, he explained, as he had so many times in the past, that regular troops, regardless of their number or deployment, would be unable to provide protection against such a mobile force in such a large and mountainous region. And once again he ended his communiqué with an offer to resign. But this time his words conveyed a sincerity that had been notably absent on prior occasions: "I believe that the plan upon which I have conducted operations [using scouts to hunt down the Apaches in Mexico] is the one most likely to prove successful in the end. It may be, however, that I am too much wedded to my own views in this matter, and as I have spent nearly eight years of the hardest work of my life in this Department, I respectfully request that I may be now relieved from its command."[13] Perhaps on reading these words, Sheridan understood Crook's fatigue and disappointment and sought to do him a favor. More likely, he saw an opportunity he had been awaiting and perhaps had engineered.

At about noon on the day after Crook had offered to resign, Lieutenant Faison appeared on the ridgeline south of Fort Bowie, Chihuahua's band in tow. The straggling column of Indians followed the lieutenant into the swale that contained the post's scattered buildings. Crook stood on the porch of his headquarters and briefly greeted them as they road by on their way to their designated campsite, adjacent to the scouts' encampment about a half mile west of the post.[14]

Duty, as well as common politeness, required Crook to have a formal parley with Chihuahua later that afternoon. But how much could or should he tell the chief about the president's decision regarding the surrender terms? He had already made up his mind. As he had informed Sheridan in his telegram of March 31, if word of Cleveland's terms reached Geronimo's ears, he would never voluntarily surrender. The same would probably be true if the shaman learned that Chihuahua's band was imprisoned for any length of time in Arizona. For these reasons Crook recommended that if the prisoners were to be sent away as the president wished, it should be done without delay. To further reduce the risk of Geronimo's discovering the change in terms, he also asked approval to withhold from Chihuahua the change in surrender terms until after his arrival in Florida. If that course were followed, Crook argued disingenuously, it would be easier to obtain his people's consent to remaining indefinitely, "if they can be shown that their future will be better by remaining than to return."[15] What he did not say, but knew to be true, was that once in Florida the Apaches would be prisoners, a continent away from Arizona and powerless to escape or resist.

While the impact of the president's decision on "those still out" was a critical consideration for Crook, preserving his reputation for honesty among the western tribes seemed to be equally imperative. Indians, invested in a belief in the general's omnipotence, would hardly credit that Crook had been over-ruled by higher authority. They would believe he had lied to them. Concealing the change in terms from Chihuahua until he was well away from the Southwest might, he may have reasoned, prevent other Indians in the West from learning of the Nantan's apparent perfidy.[16] Thus, pending word from Sheridan, Crook remained guarded with Chihuahua. When the chief expressed hope that the general's punishment would not be too hard, Crook made no reply.[17]

Not surprisingly, on April 5 Sheridan assented to both of Crook's recommendations. Rationalizing the change in surrender terms as a product of Geronimo's breach of faith, he ignored the fact that Chihuahua had punctiliously adhered to his agreement with Crook. As a result of *Geronimo's* actions, Sheridan wrote, "the Indians now in custody [Chihuahua's people] are to be held as prisoners and sent to Fort Marion without reference to previous communications and without in anyway consulting their wishes in the matter."[18] In compliance with Sheridan's order, Crook now directed that Chihuahua and his followers board the train to Florida. They would do so in ignorance of their destination and the fact that they were never to return to their homeland.

Chihuahua had arrived at Fort Bowie on April 2, the same day that Captain Bourke was scheduled to depart as escort for Emmet Crawford's remains on its rail journey to Kearney, Nebraska, for burial. The transfer of Crawford's coffin from the post to the railway station at Bowie was a somber event. Accompanied by four companies of infantry and a company of scouts, it was performed with great ceremony in a blinding sandstorm. Bourke recalled that "in the glare of the locomotive headlight, the scene was solemn, sad, and strangely impressive" and made no mention whether Crook had been present.[19]

Whether he was in attendance at the station, the occasion would have been an emotional one for Crook. Not only was it a stark reminder of Crawford's untimely death, but it forced him to confront the reality that Bourke, his loyal and longtime aide, would be absent from his side for the foreseeable future. After attending the funeral, the captain would journey to Washington, D.C., where he had been reassigned to the Smithsonian to complete for publication the write-up of the anthropological field notes that he had compiled during his time in the Southwest. Since first becoming a member of Crook's staff in 1872, Bourke had received several other assignments. In fact, he had only recently been recalled from duty in Texas to assist the general in managing the Geronimo crisis. Whether he would be returning to Crook's staff from this latest assignment was far from certain. While the general had always supported Bourke's anthropological work, including the present task, he must have found his aide's departure at this crucial moment deeply affecting. None of this emotional turmoil is reflected in Crook's diary. Turning to the page for that date, one finds simply a notation that Bourke "with Capt. Crawford's remains left for Kearney, Nebraska."[20]

This entry is followed by shocking news, rendered in equally unemotional terms. "Received orders relieving me from the command of this Dept." The apparently unconcerned manner in which he recorded this momentous information is, of course, vintage Crook. Yet it also reflects the manner in which he wished his dismissal to be viewed: as a welcome relief from an unpleasant assignment. He expressed this view some days later. When a journalist voiced his regret that the general would soon be leaving Arizona, Crook replied "promptly and earnestly: 'Well, *I'm* not. I have had to worry along with these fellows for eight years, and have got enough of them. Now, let some of the others try their hands.'"[21]

Perhaps to underscore his calm acceptance of the events of that date, Crook chose to complete his entry on an upbeat note. The sheriff of Cochise County had appeared at the post on April 2 to serve a warrant for the arrest of Chihuahua and his followers. The previous day Crook had rejected a similar request from Arizona's governor, Conrad M. Zulick, and a U.S. Marshal. Confident that he had the administration's backing, at least on this point, Crook had told the governor that he had been instructed by the War Department to hold the Indians as prisoners of war, and thus he could not, for that reason, give them up. Now he recorded with obvious relish that he had responded to the sheriff in the same manner. At least he had spared Chihuahua's band the indignity of civil prosecution and trial.[22]

Though Geronimo's escape had cast a dark shadow over Crook's reputation and perhaps what remained of his future in the army, many who had known him over the years, inspired by his leadership, integrity, and wisdom, continued to stand by him. They included members of the military and the political establishment as well as an assortment of journalists who had covered him in the field. Among the latter were reporters who had initially been drawn to him as "good copy" but who had eventually become his friends. Generally, they were men who wrote their stories from firsthand observations in the field instead of relying on tales garnered in the saloons that lined the streets of most frontier towns. A recent member of this elite cadre was an ardent and energetic twenty-seven-year-old novice reporter named Charles Fletcher Lummis.

Like Crook, Lummis is often defined in the popular mind by his eccentricities. A bright but obstreperous son of a New England Methodist minister, he had gone to Harvard, paying his way by writing poetry, which he printed on birch bark and sold to visitors to the White Mountains resort where he worked during his summers. But school proved too tame for the adventurous youth. Liberated by his newfound ability to support himself by writing, he quit college and found work as a journalist for a small but venerable weekly in Chillicothe, Ohio, before moving on to a new and feisty paper called the *Los Angeles Daily Times* that had just opened its doors in California. The publisher, Colonel Harrison Gray Otis, who also possessed an independent streak, had been impressed with Lummis's energy and writing and had hired the young man sight-unseen after a brief correspondence.[23]

In an exploit characteristic of his energy and boldness, rather than take the train Lummis had walked from Ohio to California to assume the duties of his new job.[24] Wearing a "white flannel shirt tied at the neck with a blue ribbon, knickerbockers, red knee-high stockings, a wide-brimmed felt hat, and low cut street shoes," all topped off with a large canvas duck coat, he set off from Chillicothe in September 1884.[25] He completed the 3,500-mile journey in 143 days and along the way fell deeply in love with the Southwest and its peoples. On arriving in Southern California, he sent word to Otis, asking him to meet him in San Gabriel, a Los Angeles suburb ten miles outside the city. Together the two journalists hiked the last leg of Charlie's trek into town, where they celebrated with dinner at a fashionable downtown restaurant, Lummis, still clad in a variant of the outfit he had worn throughout his journey. As Otis later recalled, "His garb was not reassuring to the timid."[26]

Lummis's first year at the *Times* was, by all accounts, a success. The paper nearly doubled its circulation, largely due to his lively coverage of the fast-growing city. Yet he yearned to make his mark beyond Los Angeles. Whether he or Otis came up with the idea of a trip to Arizona to cover the last days of the Geronimo campaign is unclear. Otis had served in General Crook's Army of West Virginia during the Civil War. Familiar with the general's character and military skills, he had been supportive of his management of the campaign against Geronimo. It is possible he reckoned that Lummis's reporting would be favorable to the general and help bolster his battered reputation. But as the *Times'* publisher, a boost in circulation was likely his primary concern.

Lummis arrived in Tucson on March 30 in a gloomy frame of mind. Just as he departed Los Angeles, he received word that the war he had planned to write about appeared over. The Apache leaders had surrendered to General Crook. Since all the arrangements had been made for the trip, Otis agreed not to cancel it, allowing his reporter to "detail the many points of interest which a man of his industry and love of adventure can gather."[27] By the time he descended from the train at Bowie Station on March 31, he learned that there was still a story. Geronimo had absconded and Crook was in deep trouble with his superiors.

Crook met the young journalist almost as soon as he arrived at the post from the train station. What the general made of the eager reporter is unknown. Having just submitted his request to be relieved of his command and preoccupied with the handling of the Apache prisoners, Lummis's arrival did not merit mention in his diary. But Lummis had a lot to say about his first interview with the Gray Fox. From the outset he liked the "grim old General," finding in him "that . . . which makes one want to take off one's hat." He is "as kindly as he is reticent." The young journalist was, as Otis had undoubtedly anticipated, sympathetic toward his beleaguered subject. No commander since the war, he wrote, "has been more persistently, more savagely, more cruelly hounded by jealousy, opposition, and many other masked influences, than has Crook. . . . He has been cursed, and alleged acts of his made up out of whole cloth. . . . But let the lying go on as it will, . . . he is here to fight, not to justify himself."[28]

Lummis quickly established himself as a keen observer with the ability to paint portraits of his subjects in vivid and revealing language. He described the fifty-eight-year-old Crook as

> a tall well-knit man, without an ounce of superfluous flesh. He is straight, but does not convey that impression, for his well-turned head has that peculiar droop of the habitual hard-thinker. It is as though the weight of care and thought behind the seamed forehead dragged it forward from its poise. The deep, clean lines that mark his face are further tokens of the hard brain-work he has put into this campaign. He is an indefatigable worker, and keeps at the knotty problems all day and well into the night. . . . His forehead is high and broad; his eyes clear and penetrating; his nose large and very strongly hooped aquiline. He wears nothing to denote his rank or even his profession, but paces thoughtfully up and down the porch in a plain, but neatly kept civilian suit, topped by a big, buff slouch hat.[29]

Crook seems to have taken to Lummis, at least enough to invite him to attend the general's initial meeting with Chihuahua after the chief's arrival at Bowie. Over the next two weeks he allowed the journalist frequent access, not only to himself but to others on his staff, thus enabling Lummis to give *Times* readers a steady stream of dispatches that provided an accurate, firsthand snapshot of events as they unfolded. His stories provided an immediacy and detail unavailable elsewhere, not only to *Times* readers but to future historians.

On April 2 the paper carried the reporter's dispatch describing Crook's replacement as department commander by General Miles, and the next day it noted the arrival of Lieutenant Maus with the grim news that Geronimo continued to elude capture.[30] On April 6, only three days after Crook himself had received word from General Sheridan, the reporter broke the news to his readers in Los Angeles that Chihuahua's people, seventy-six in all, would be transferred as prisoners of war to Fort Marion in St. Augustine, Florida. The site was chosen by President Cleveland as it had been previously used as a prison for Indians in the aftermath of the Red River War.[31] Lummis remarked that the Chiricahuas had philosophically absorbed the news of their exile, but his story made plain that they were as yet unaware of their destination. Loomis reported that the chief told Crook that he "hoped he would not suffer imprisonment too long, because he would lose a wagon he had at the reservation."[32] To which the general had tersely replied, "Oh, I'll tell your relatives to take care of that."[33]

The evening before their departure, the prisoners hosted a dance to bid farewell to the scouts. The next day, April 7, Chihuahua's band loaded their meager possessions on a variety of mounts and formed a ragged procession that wound its way down Apache Pass fifteen miles to Bowie Station. On their flanks rode a company of soldiers from the Eighth Infantry, led by General Crook riding in a buckboard with Captain Roberts, and his son, Charlie.[34] At the station the warriors surrendered their weapons, an exercise that, as Crook acknowledged in his diary, caused "considerable nervousness amongst the men." Whether he referred to his soldiers or the warriors remains unclear.[35] Then, in what must have been a painful moment for both Crook and the Apaches, the Nantan stood aside and watched as the Indians and their escort boarded their assigned rail cars. As the train departed a dispirited Crook remounted his buckboard and made his way back up the pass to Fort Bowie to await the arrival of General Miles.

The trip to Florida would prove arduous for the Apaches, who had never been away from their home country or ridden in a train. The soldiers guarding them were there not so much to prevent their escape as to protect them from hostile whites along the route. As Lummis pointed out to his readers, "There are plenty of alleged white men who would jump at the chance to signalize their bravery by shooting a captive squaw through a car window, if they received sufficient notice to brace themselves with brag and whisky." Crook, fully alert to the danger, had cautioned the reporter not to give his paper the date of Chihuahua's departure.[36] To further safeguard the prisoners, the windows on the train were nailed shut, and the Apaches were forbidden to leave the cars at any time during the seven-day trip to St. Augustine, not even to wash or relieve themselves. The condition of the cars upon arrival can only be imagined, but white reporters who viewed the Apaches as they detrained in Florida described them as a "dirty, ragged, half-clad" rabble with "unkempt locks of coarse black hair flying loose about their heads."[37] Their ordeal, which would last well into the next century, had just begun.

CHAPTER TWENTY-TWO

Changing of the Guard

Consistent with his protestations that he was relieved to have the burden of the Arizona command lifted from his shoulders, Crook wound up his affairs at Fort Bowie without fanfare or sentiment. As he had voluntarily resigned his departmental command, as senior brigadier in the army, he retained the right to request his next assignment. He chose to return to his old post as commander of the Department of the Platte, replacing General Oliver Otis Howard, who was being transferred to command of the Division of the Pacific following his promotion to major general. General Miles would replace Crook in Arizona, a fact that Crook undoubtedly found galling.

But his demeanor revealed none of this. As he awaited his successor, he went about saying his goodbyes. The day before the prisoners had been put aboard the train for Florida, he had met with his scouts and told them of his imminent departure. He thanked them for their good works and imparted advice like a concerned father seeing his children off to school, counseling them on the evils of tiswin, the advantages of stock raising, and the like. To Lummis—who now enjoyed the general's trust, which permitted him to attend such meetings—Crook appeared "tired and preoccupied." Lest readers misinterpret the general's intentions, the journalist, by now very much a Crook man, assured them that "it is worse than foolish to construe his application for relief into an admission of failure," as some of the Arizona papers had done.[1]

But though Crook continued to have faith in his methods, which, after all, had resulted in the pacification of all but a small handful of Apaches, he had no illusions as to how the public would view his abrupt transfer. His resignation, accepted with alacrity by General Sheridan, was a repudiation of the policies that had made him famous as one of military's premiere experts on Indian affairs. Indian scouts had been a cornerstone of his strategy in both war and peace. This had been particularly true in Arizona. In several of his campaigns, especially during the early days of the Sioux War when he had been unable to secure Indians as scouts, he had employed white or mixed-race men instead, often with considerable success. However, the Southwest presented its own unique difficulties. The martial qualities of the Apaches—their unparalleled knowledge of and adaptation to the unforgiving terrain and climate, their physical prowess, and their consequent mobility— had convinced the general of the overwhelming superiority of these bands (especially the Chiricahuas and perhaps the White Mountain Apaches) in finding and fighting their fellow tribespeople. To that end, he had built and nurtured a scouting force that matched the capabilities of their unreconstructed brethren. Now these same Indian scouts on whom his successes had been built were about to be tossed aside, along with his own reputation as an authority and leader in the formulation of Indian policy.

Added to Crook's worries about his own career was his grave concern about how his notably unsympathetic successor would treat his scouts and the rest of the Apaches, especially the Chiricahuas. Miles had publicly expressed his skepticism regarding the usefulness and loyalty of the scouts, in many respects echoing the low opinions expressed by the white and Mexican citizenry of the Southwest.[2] He also was an early and persistent champion of the banishment of all Chiricahuas from the Southwest.

For the time being Crook kept his concerns private. It was in his nature to do so, and he knew that the military took a dim view of any officer who publicly criticized a fellow officer. So when he bid farewell to his scouts and they asked him whether Miles was "a good man, or will he lie to us the same way other people have lied to us," Crook responded diplomatically. He allowed that his successor was "a good and honest man." And when they asked whether Crook would write a letter on their behalf telling Miles that "we have done right, and to do right with us," Crook assured them that he would make such a recommendation, though he must have realized it would be of little use.[3]

On April 11, in the suffocating heat of a parched Arizona afternoon, General Miles arrived by train at Bowie Station amid a cloud of flies. Alone and without aides, outwardly he appeared undaunted by climate, insects, or the enormity of the task before him. His inner doubts were another matter. He would later claim that he "never had any desire to go to this section of the country or to engage in a campaign of that character," a declaration that most would have considered perfectly reasonable.[4] Miles had risked little in criticizing Crook's performance in Arizona from a safe distance, but to personally wade into that swamp appeared a needless gamble. Much smarter to stand back and leave Crook to complete his own self-immolation. But Miles's persistent criticisms of Crook's performance had fallen on receptive ears, convincing the secretary of war and General Sheridan that Miles would be able to resolve the Apache troubles. Now he owned the problem.[5]

During the dust-choked ambulance ride from the depot and his subsequent meeting with General Crook at his Fort Bowie headquarters, Miles maintained his pose of equanimity. A bemused Lummis watched as the new arrival "undemonstratively" greeted the man whom he was about to replace while a six-pounder boomed in the background. Then the two generals walked to the post commander's quarters for what must have been an awkward luncheon before retiring to the privacy of Crook's office for a late-afternoon conversation.[6] With no one else present, what the two men talked about went unrecorded. Yet Miles's public criticism of Crook's management of the Geronimo campaign and his vocal opinions regarding the use of Apache scouts, though probably not on the agenda, must have hovered like a dark cloud over their meeting. Before retiring for the evening, the two men wrote out complementary general orders, Crook relinquishing command and commending his men for their zeal, courage, and energy, Miles simply noting his assumption of command over the Department of Arizona.[7]

That night, in the privacy of his quarters, Miles reflected on the reality of his assignment. In a letter to his wife, Mary, he unburdened himself of the concerns that had begun to undermine the breezy self-confidence and braggadocio he had previously displayed in picking apart Crook's performance from afar. Describing his meeting with the Nantan, he refrained from gloating over his assumption of command, noting only that Crook "appears to feel very much disappointed but does not say much." As for his own feelings, he wrote candidly that "in many respects, this is the most difficult task I have ever undertaken, on account of the extensive country, the natural difficulties and the fact that the hostiles are so few in number and so active. Still I can only make the best effort possible."[8] He certainly did not share these thoughts with General Crook or anyone else.

The next morning the two men again met to complete Miles's briefing. While they were doing so, the scouts, whose enlistments had expired, came to bid Nantan Lupan farewell. Several of their leaders, including Alchesay, who had served Crook for over a decade, threw their arms around the general, patting him affectionately on the back while he smiled in embarrassment and awkwardly "told them to be good Indians."[9] At one o'clock that afternoon, dressed in an old linen duster, Crook bid his farewells to his staff, including Captain Roberts, who was also moving on to a new assignment. He then mounted a buckboard for Bowie Station.[10] To General Miles, Crook seemed "very much worried and disappointed" and his troops "somewhat disheartened, as they had all hoped to go home."[11] A less self-absorbed officer might perhaps have acknowledged that the troops' unhappiness perhaps lay in the loss of a respected commanding officer.

At Bowie Station, Crook boarded the train to Prescott and nearby Fort Whipple. There he joined Mary in packing their belongings, consigning what they no longer needed to a local auction house. Several days later, accompanied by Mary; her sister, Mrs. Reid; Peison, his long-serving striker; and his Chinese cook, Lee, Crook departed Arizona for Omaha to resume his old command.[12]

His departure from Arizona did not go unremarked. A substantial number of the territory's residents acknowledged and appreciated his contribution to their welfare. The previous December the Arizona General Assembly had drafted a joint resolution thanking the general "for his distinguished service in our behalf," the second such resolution passed by that body in twelve months. The Society of Arizona Pioneers had also publicly lauded his efforts.[13] To mark his departure, his supporters organized a reception in his honor in Tucson with hundreds in attendance.[14]

Others did not mourn Crook's leaving. The *Tombstone Epitaph*, never a friend to the general, captured their mood in a single sentence.

"Crook was telling the truth when he said that he was glad to get out of the country, and he might have added that the people were glad to see him go and would have parted with him without a pang of regret if he had gone several months ago."[15]

In view of General Miles's oft-repeated criticism of Crook's management of the Geronimo campaign, it might seem ironic that the new commander's strategy would ultimately converge with that of his predecessor. But initially Miles was determined to chart his own course, described by Britton Davis as "a policy midway between Crook's and that demanded of Crook by Sheridan."[16] It would soon become apparent that Sheridan's exhortations, like Miles's carping prior to his assignment to Apacheria, had been dictated by considerations that had little to do with the realities of Apache warfare.

From the outset Miles confronted the same issues that had plagued Crook: the challenge of finding and defeating an elusive guerrilla force on unfriendly foreign soil while simultaneously defending a thinly populated but vast and rugged terrain. Meanwhile, he must meet Washington's demand for a swift conclusion to the conflict through either unconditional surrender or annihilation of the enemy. Lurking in the background as Miles struggled with these problems was the embarrassing question as to why with five thousand troops at his disposal—at that time roughly one quarter of the U.S. Army—it was so difficult to bring to book a ragtag band of thirty-six fugitives.[17]

Crook had long realized that a war of annihilation would be too protracted to satisfy either his impatient superiors or the restive population of the Southwest. Instead he had hoped to bring the matter to a more rapid conclusion by employing the unique capabilities of his Apache scouts to secure a negotiated settlement, as he had in the Sierra Madre two years before. He had stubbornly adhered to this plan despite growing evidence that the entire Cleveland administration and his military superiors viewed it with undisguised skepticism and pressed for unconditional surrender.

Following Geronimo's stampede after the negotiations at Cañon de los Embudos, doubt had turned to disaffection. Blaming the scouts for the debacle, Crook's superiors had replaced him with Miles, accepting the latter's boast that regular troops, if given the opportunity, could accomplish the victory that native scouts were unable or unwilling to achieve. To ensure that Miles got the point, Sheridan instructed his aide to tell the general to conduct "the most vigorous operations looking to the destruction or capture of the hostiles." Further, though "he [Sheridan] does not wish to embarrass you by undertaking at this distance to give specific instructions, . . . it is deemed advisable to suggest the necessity of making active and permanent use of the regular troops of your command."[18]

At first Miles had no quarrel with Sheridan's policy, fully aware that it had been a major reason for his appointment. As he planned to rely on his regulars to bear the brunt of the fighting, he allowed the enlistments of the Apache scouts to expire and replaced them with a small number of Indians from the Yuma and Pima tribes who would function in a far more limited capacity.[19]

As Crook had done, Miles deployed his troops to guard the border and Arizona and New Mexico's civilian population, assigning a few scouts to accompany them as trackers and messengers. Infantry would guard the waterholes, passes, and supply depots along the border, while cavalry patrolled the international boundary and the plains between the border and the mountains of the two territories. Domestically, his only tactical innovation, one in which he took special pride, was to use the heliograph, a system that employed sunlight and mirrors to flash coded messages, to ensure rapid communications between units.[20] The heliographs, intended as a counter to Apache mobility, might have been more useful had Geronimo's warriors spent more time raiding into the American Southwest. But the system never played a significant role in the campaign that followed as, except for two brief, but embarrassing, cross-border forays, Geronimo confined the bulk of his depredations to Mexican territory.

Miles also adopted Crook's strategy of deploying a column into Mexico to seek out the fugitives. But in obedience to Sheridan's directive, he assigned regular troops rather than scouts to "capture or destroy any band of hostile Apache Indians" and follow every trail.[21] He limited his cross-border deployment of scouts to about a dozen Indians drawn from tribes other than the Chiricahuas to act as trackers. To lead this force, Miles chose Captain Henry Lawton of the Fourth Cavalry. Lawton, a tough, hard-drinking, self-confident officer, had impressed Miles with his outspoken insistence that "the Apaches could be outmaneuvered, worn down, and subjugated by white soldiers."[22]

His sterling Civil War record, brawny 250-pound physique, and great physical strength and stamina also convinced Miles that the captain would prove more than a match for the Chiricahuas. A young and exuberant army surgeon named Leonard Wood would serve as the column's medical officer and second-in-command. While his "keen intelligence, physical endurance, and resoluteness of spirit" certainly qualified him for the position, his assertion that "white men were more than a match for savages" undoubtedly added to his appeal to his superiors.[23]

Before Miles could complete his domestic deployments, the Apaches struck. Driving north from Sonora under the joint command of both Naiche and Geronimo, they crossed the border into Arizona on April 26 and raided into the Santa Cruz Valley. Though they lost horses and equipment in skirmishes with the white troops and were forced southward after only three days, they suffered no casualties and eluded every attempt to bring them to bay. Replacing their lost equipment and stock and inflicting heavy casualties on the local population, they overlooked Miles's cavalry and returned safely to Sonora.[24]

In late May, Naiche crossed the border again with a party of eight men and nineteen women, apparently heading for Fort Apache. It has been said that, tiring of life on the run, he had a vague intention of surrendering to Crook, unaware that the Nantan was no longer in command. But if he wanted peace, he made little effort to demonstrate it. He and his band remained in Arizona for eighteen days, during which they slaughtered thirteen Americans. While suffering no casualties, the band did lose one warrior, who, with his fellow raiders' apparent acquiescence, left the group to rejoin his family on the reservation, laying down his rifle for the hoe.[25]

In early May, Lawton took his column into Mexico. Like Crawford and Davis before him, his efforts proved in vain. He spent four fruitless months combing the Sonoran Mountains but failed to come to grips with Geronimo's band. Forced by the terrain and heat to abandon their mounts within days of entering the mountains, Lawton's cavalry soon joined the infantry, campaigning afoot. High temperatures, torrential rain, and unforgiving terrain caused intense suffering and fatigue among the troops, notwithstanding the fact that they had been chosen for their superior strength and endurance. Hindered by their Yuma scouts, who were not as good at tracking as the Chiricahuas and did not know the country as well, the regulars had little hope of success. They had difficulty locating the enemy, and, when they did pick up a trail, they lacked the stamina to catch up with them.[26]

In July, Lawton received replacements for his exhausted troops, but only when he briefly adopted Crawford's tactics did he come close to success. On July 14 he sent some of his scouts forward alone. Without the white soldiers to slow them down, the Indians located and attacked a small party from Geronimo's band, seizing their ponies and camp equipment. But by the time Lawton and his regulars arrived on the scene, the Apaches were long gone and soon made good their losses at the expense of the local population. This was Lawton's only contact with his elusive foe. The campaign seemed to have stalled.[27]

Unable to prevent the Apaches from raiding into Arizona and New Mexico or to engage them in Mexico, Miles awakened to the fact that the war to the knife that Sheridan demanded now appeared threatened with humiliating failure. So protracted and barren of results was the campaign that Miles began to fear that it would damage not only his reputation as an Indian fighter but also his future career. In early July, as Lawton's heroic efforts continued to produce no tangible gains, Miles turned reluctantly to his predecessor's idea of a negotiated end to the conflict.

To assess the feasibility of such an endgame, he interrogated the lone defector from Geronimo's group, now quietly farming near Fort Apache. The warrior offered the hopeful opinion that the pressures of constant warfare and life on the run were eroding the band's morale to the point that many might now be anxious to surrender.[28] His words encouraged Miles. But how to reach out to Geronimo? He did not have Crook's reputation for trustworthiness among the Indians. To convince Geronimo that he could be trusted, Miles would need Apache support.

This was not an easy decision for Miles. He was deeply suspicious of the Apaches, and he had repeatedly censured Crook for using them as scouts in his campaigns. But in May, with Naiche cutting a swathe of destruction deep into Arizona, he decided that he had few other options. As yet unwilling to deal with the Chiricahuas, he wrote to Captain Pierce, now in command at San Carlos, asking him to seek out any non-Chiricahua Apaches at the agency who might be induced to carry a peace initiative to Geronimo. But the other bands feared and distrusted the shaman, and Pierce replied that there was "no one here who will venture into the hostile camp." An offer of a $2,000 reward for Geronimo, dead or alive, to these same Apaches elicited no better results.[29] In desperation Miles turned to Lieutenant Colonel James Wade, commander at Fort Apache, and queried whether any of the Turkey Creek Chiricahuas would be willing to undertake a peace mission. The results were the same. Divisions within the band had become so pronounced that no reservation Indian would venture into Geronimo's camp.[30]

At a loss, Miles consulted Noche, the Chiricahua warrior who had led the scouts during Crawford's second Sierra Madre expedition. This time he hit pay dirt. Noche offered to introduce the general to former scouts Kayitah and Martine. Both men had relatives with Geronimo and knew him well. They had received confirmation from their kinfolk of the band's low morale and desire for peace. Martine's son, George Martine, would later relate that Miles asked both men to approach the shaman's followers and offer them land on Turkey Creek and a $70,000 reward if they "came back alive and Geronimo surrendered." According to George, the offer of land convinced them to take the risk.[31]

In light of Miles's opinion of the Chiricahuas, it was no surprise that he did not trust the two Apaches to handle this delicate mission alone. Nor would he allow such negotiations to proceed without the oversight of at least one white officer to claim credit for the army. So he chose as the mission's leader Lieutenant Gatewood, possibly the only officer remaining in the command that the tribe still had confidence in and respected.[32] Gatewood accepted the challenge with extreme reluctance. His health was poor, and though he believed that the Apaches trusted him, he did not reciprocate the feeling. Besides, he considered the mission "a fool's errand," according to one biographer. His instructions were to demand Geronimo's unconditional surrender with the understanding that the shaman and his people would be removed to Florida or elsewhere in the East, with the final decision as to their disposition left to the president. He was further told that he should not approach the hostiles camp with an escort of fewer than twenty-five soldiers.[33] In Gatewood's estimation, even if he managed to get to Geronimo—which, with an escort of so many soldiers, he deemed impossible—the shaman would reject the terms outright.

Accompanied by reservation interpreter George Wratten, the reluctant Gatewood and the two scouts entered Mexico on July 19. Plagued by continuing illness and the hot, humid summer weather, Gatewood finally caught up with Lawton's column on August 3. He was not warmly received. The captain was outraged when he learned the details of Gatewood's mission. He had come to Mexico on orders from the president to kill or capture Geronimo and not to negotiate his surrender. Only after an extensive parley did Lawton reluctantly agree to allow the mission to go forward. But he did not want any part of it. "If Gatewood wants to treat with [Geronimo], he can do so on his own hook," he declared dismissively.[34]

Rumors of Geronimo's whereabouts finally led Gatewood to Fronteras, where he learned that the shaman was camped on a steep slope outside the town. On August 24 the two scouts made the dangerous climb to the camp under the watchful eyes of the shaman's lookouts. Recognizing Kayitah and Martine and urged on by his warriors, Geronimo reluctantly agreed to talk to them and then to meet with Lieutenant Gatewood the next day.[35]

The tense negotiations that ensued have been recounted on multiple occasions in books and on film.[36] It is sufficient to note that the turning point came when Geronimo declared to Gatewood that he would surrender, but only if he was allowed to return to the White Mountain reservation to rejoin his family. Gatewood's response stunned him. The Chiricahuas were no longer at the White Mountain agency. They had been rounded up by General Miles and sent to Florida. If Geronimo were to return to the agency, he would find himself alone among the White Mountain people, now his enemies. Though he continued to bluster, it was plain that he was shaken by this unexpected news. When he asked Gatewood, "What would you advise? Should we surrender, or should we fight it out?" it became plain that the tide had turned. Gatewood responded, "I would trust General Miles and take him at his word," a phrase that he might later have regretted. But Geronimo apparently accepted it at face value. The two men then agreed the shaman would meet with General Miles near the border, at a point to be determined. The die was cast for the surrender of the only group of Indians still at war with the United States.[37]

Geronimo's shock was understandable on learning that not only had Chihuahua and *his* followers been exiled to Florida but the rest of the tribe as well. Chihuahua's people had, after all, joined the shaman on the warpath. But the remainder of the tribe had remained peacefully on the reservation following the May 1885 breakout. Why had General Miles sent them into exile? With little evidence to substantiate it, the general had incorrectly assumed that the tribe would join the shaman or, at minimum, supply his people with enough ammunition to allow them to continue raiding indefinitely.[38] In fact, the Chiricahuas had to all appearances adjusted well to life on the reservation and had given every indication that they were well on the road to assimilation. Less than one third of the tribe had accompanied the shaman into Mexico, and, contrary to Miles's expectations, during the fifteen months that followed, not one of the warriors remaining at Fort Apache had joined Geronimo or provided any form of support to his band. On the contrary, many had enlisted as scouts to fight *against* him.[39] After Miles replaced Crook, the Chiricahuas, though no longer allowed to serve as scouts, continued to remain aloof, offering no aid or comfort to their tribespeople in Mexico and even, on occasion, providing General Miles with information about Geronimo's activities. Perhaps the best indicator of the reservation Chiricahuas' peaceful intentions was the decision of the two former Chiricahua scouts to volunteer, at considerable risk to their lives, to assist in surrender negotiations with the shaman.

Given these circumstances, Miles's decision to send the entire band into exile in Florida seems simply a reflection of his unshakable belief that the entire Chiricahua tribe was incorrigible and that they were a menace to peace in the Southwest. If they were allowed to remain in the territory, he predicted, "every few years a new generation of their boys and young men [would grow] to manhood and become full fledged warriors and their only hope of achieving distinction according to the tradition, practice and influence of their fathers, was in committing acts of cruelty and devastation."[40] Miles's continuing distrust of the Chiricahuas would continue to fuel his feud with General Crook.

Some historians have speculated that Miles might also have had political motives for removing the Chiricahuas from their White Mountain reservation. While the land at San Carlos, arid and pestilent, was undesirable to white settlers, the Chiricahuas' new home at Turkey Creek was in a fertile, well-watered, and timbered area coveted by Anglo Arizonans. Removing the Chiricahuas from Arizona would free up that land, perhaps increasing the general's popularity among westerners, an important constituency in the event that, as widely speculated, he should ever decide to run for president.[41] Leaving aside possible presidential ambitions, removing the Chiricahuas was such a popular notion in the territory that, as John Bourke confided to his diary, Miles's identification with it might help insulate him from criticism sure to arise should his campaign against Geronimo prove unsuccessful.[42]

Exiling the reservation Chiricahuas was not universally well regarded. General Sheridan, for one, opposed it. As he advised the secretary of war, "The whole history of the Indian wars in this country shows that they are generally traceable to the action of the Government in removing tribes from the locality where they had become established."[43] Sheridan aside, removal was guaranteed to arouse Crook's supporters, a not inconsequential political force. Nevertheless, Miles decided to proceed with the removal of the more than 80 warriors and 350 women and children currently who had peacefully resided at Turkey Creek. Among those banished were friends and relatives of the two scouts who were now risking their lives for him, which seems to have troubled him not at all. Nor was he apparently concerned about the potential impact of his action on the Chiricahuas whose surrender he now sought to negotiate.

In June, Miles visited the tribe's camp at Fort Apache in an effort to persuade its leader to voluntarily accede to removal. The visit was not a success. The Indians did not welcome removal, and the general found much else that displeased him. The camp "was a perfect pandemonium." The Indians were brewing tiswin and engaged in "drunken orgies every night." Furthermore, "the young men were insolent, violent, and restless, and anxious to go on the warpath."[44] How much of this was exaggeration designed to justify their removal is difficult to know. But he often used the experience to bolster his argument that allowing the band to remain in Arizona would be a serious mistake.

Florida was not Miles's destination of choice for the tribe. To his credit, he realized that sending these mountain people to a hot and humid lowland locale boded ill for their future. His preferred option was Indian Territory, the nation's current home for tribes removed from their homelands. Unexpectedly, he ran into strong opposition from Washington. Secretary of War Endicott, Secretary of the Interior Lamar, General Sheridan, and, most importantly, President Cleveland all objected to Miles's idea. Even Congress opposed it, having already enacted a law prohibiting any of the Apache tribes from being sent to Indian Territory—a statute, Miles now suggested, that ought to be repealed. In the end the president's insistence that the Chiricahuas be relocated to Fort Marion in St. Augustine carried the day.[45]

In mid-July, hoping the Chiricahua leadership would be convinced by the Great Father to accept the fate he planned for them, Miles sent a delegation of thirteen prominent warriors, including Chatto and Ka-ya-ten-nae, to Washington to meet with the secretaries Endicott and Lamar and ultimately the president. They were escorted by one of Miles' aides, Captain Joseph H. Dorst.[46] Much to Miles's annoyance, John Bourke joined the delegation upon its arrival in the capital. Though deeply engaged in his ethnological work at the Smithsonian, Bourke had been drawn back into Apache affairs at the request of Secretary of War Endicott and Herbert Welsh of the Indian Rights Association, whom the captain, with Crook's encouragement, had been advising regarding the Apaches' future. Fiercely opposed to Miles's intentions, Bourke argued vigorously against removal, relying heavily on the tribe's uneventful three-year history of residency on the reservation. Chatto, too, spoke out against the move, stating that for himself, he wished only to remain on his farm at Fort Apache.[47] Secretary Lamar presented the chief with a large silver medal left over from the Arthur administration, but he ignored the Indians' protestations. The next day Chatto met briefly with President Cleveland, who also appeared deaf to his entreaties.[48]

On July 31 the president reconvened his officials. Bourke and Dorst were allowed to attend, but not the Indians. It was immediately apparent that Cleveland had already made up his mind, as he promptly announced his decision to send the tribe to Florida. In a last-ditch effort to change his mind, Bourke recalled General Crook's promise that the Chiricahuas could remain in their homeland. The decision to exile them, he warned, might provoke the tribe into breaking out and joining Geronimo. The president, determined to implement the move without further delay, brushed aside his protestations.[49] Further, apparently convinced that the scouts had contributed little to the campaign and could not be trusted, he ruled that they would accompany their brethren into exile. Bourke came away from the meeting with a profound contempt for the president. In his diary he wrote, "[Cleveland] impressed me as being self-opinionated, stubborn, and not too tenacious of the truth; a man of great sinuosity of morals, narrow in his views, fond of flattery."[50]

As if determined to demonstrate his "sinuosity of morals," the president resorted to subterfuge in his handling of Chatto and his delegation. Fearing that if allowed to return to Arizona they might warn the rest of the tribe of their impending exile and precipitate a breakout, he ordered them temporarily detained in the East on a pretext and then sent them directly to Florida. To lull any suspicions, the chiefs were hustled off for a brief visit to the Indian school in Carlisle, Pennsylvania, where some of their children were enrolled. From there they boarded a train heading west, assuming that they were returning to their White Mountain homeland. Instead, they were detained at Fort Leavenworth until their families were dispatched to Florida.[51] At Leavenworth, on instructions from Miles, they were told that if returned to the Southwest, they would be tried for past crimes. Alternatively, they could rejoin their people at Fort Marion and receive land, farm equipment, and a monthly cash stipend in return for ensuring their peoples' submission. Confined at Fort Leavenworth, they had no alternative but to accept exile in Florida.[52] Several years later, in a letter to Crook, Chatto bitterly asked the Nantan, "Why did they give [the medal] to me? To wear in the guardhouse? I thought something good would have come to me when they gave me that, but I have been in confinement ever since I have had it."[53]

The removal of the Chiricahuas at Fort Apache was conducted under similarly discreditable circumstances. On August 29, with Miles supervising by telegraph, Colonel Wade's command at Fort Apache rounded up the 382 tribespeople at Turkey Creek, including those who had served as scouts in the Geronimo campaigns. General Miles later recorded the scene as relayed to him by the fort's telegrapher. When the Indians assembled for their customary Sunday head count, they suddenly found themselves surrounded by a large body of troops, who disarmed them and confined them in the quartermaster's building on the post while arrangements were finalized for their transport by rail to Florida. On September 7 the closely guarded band left Fort Apache on an eight-day march on foot over the hundred miles to Holbrook, Arizona, where they boarded the train that would carry them into exile.[54] The glaring injustice of the president's decision, particularly with reference to the scouts, would have consequences that, in the future, gave him more than a little cause to regret his actions.

While Miles busied himself with the removal of the Chiricahuas at Turkey Creek, events continued to unfold in Mexico. Geronimo had insisted that he would only surrender if he could do so personally to General Miles. After some discussion the Apaches chose the location—Skeleton Canyon, in the Peloncillo Mountains on the Arizona side of the border, about sixty miles south of Fort Bowie.[55] It fell to Captain Lawton's command to escort the shaman and his band to the spot.

When Geronimo met with Lawton, he insisted that he and his followers ought to be allowed to return to Turkey Creek. Lawton correctly believed that this demand was pure bluster. At this point there was nothing for the holdouts on the reservation. The entire tribe had already been shipped to Florida. As the captain knew, the band, exhausted by months on the run, was well aware that they had little option but to accept unconditional surrender and exile or face continued warfare, misery, and, ultimately, death.[56]

Despite the near certainty that the band would surrender, Miles remained reluctant to risk a meeting without a firm guarantee of success, fearing that, like Crook, he would suffer an embarrassing denouement should the mercurial Apaches decide once more to decamp. At one point this concern became so acute that there was talk of assassinating the shaman should the opportunity arise.[57] The general continued to procrastinate until he was finally propelled into action after Lawton reported that the Apaches were becoming increasingly restless and might become violent if Miles did not arrive soon. Yet still he delayed his departure at the last moment, deciding to attend a banquet in his honor in Tucson. In the end, he did not arrive at Skeleton Canyon until September 3.

When Miles and Geronimo at last found themselves face-to-face, they talked for two days. Accounts varied as to the terms they agreed upon, but there is general agreement that Miles told the Apaches that if they surrendered, they would be treated as prisoners of war and, as such, not turned over to civilian authorities for prosecution. They would be sent to Florida where they would be reunited with their families and Chihuahua's band, then en route to Fort Marion from

Turkey Creek. It was primarily the desire to rejoin their families that impelled the shaman and Naiche to accept these terms.

On September 5 the two Apache leaders and four of their warriors boarded an ambulance with Miles and drove rapidly to Fort Bowie. Lawton and his command followed close behind with the rest of the band. Geronimo's warriors, like Chihuahua's men, refused to give up their arms until their arrival at Fort Bowie, fearing an attack by angry whites once they crossed the border into United States territory.[58]

The situations faced by Crook and Miles in negotiating the surrender of Geronimo and his followers were not exactly comparable. Crook had orders to "secure the surrender of the Chiricahuas in Mexico upon terms of their being held as prisoners of war."[59] He had been given some flexibility in negotiating terms, since Sheridan had told him that he could grant additional concessions if absolutely necessary to induce surrender. The Nantan took full advantage of that latitude, but to his chagrin, President Cleveland had repudiated the agreement as too lenient after Geronimo had fled the scene.

Miles's orders were more restrictive. His instructions precluded him from accepting any terms other than unconditional surrender. The term "prisoners of war" was not used. Nor was incarceration in Florida specified. Eventually, like Crook, Miles had decided that though the president had stipulated that he would accept nothing less than unconditional surrender, the wary Chiricahuas would not agree to such terms without knowing what they implied. So Miles sought to frame an explanation that, while harsh, at least held out some hope of a positive outcome. As he had been informed that the president planned to send the prisoners to Fort Marion, he instructed Gatewood to tell Geronimo that he and his people would be sent to Florida as prisoners of war and reunited with their families. Once in Florida they would "await the President's decision as to their final disposition." This formulation provided some specificity but left open the vague possibility of the tribe's eventual return to Arizona.[60] This hope, added to the promise of reunification with his family, prompted Geronimo to reluctantly agree to accept surrender and accompany Miles back to Fort Bowie. But the situation would begin to unravel once they arrived.

General Howard, now Miles's superior as commander of the Division of the Pacific, contributed to the ensuing confusion when, in his initial report to the president, he described Miles's terms of surrender only as "unconditional." Based on Howard's brief dispatch, and unaware of Miles's pledge to treat the Apaches as prisoners of war and send them to Florida, Cleveland considered himself free to dispose of the prisoners as he saw fit. This immediately complicated the situation, as he now changed his mind about their disposition. General Sheridan had suggested, and the president agreed, that because of the political climate in Arizona, it would be more expedient to turn the Apaches over to the territorial authorities for trial. Given the popular mood among Arizonans, both men envisioned a rapid and final resolution that would win acclaim in the Southwest for the army and the administration—the expedited trial and hanging of Geronimo and his lieutenants and the exile of the rest of the band to Fort Marion, never to return to Arizona.[61]

Unbeknownst to the administration, Miles, concerned that if he reneged on his promise to Geronimo the band would abscond, moved to implement his commitment to send the band to Florida.[62] When Sheridan learned of this, he angrily demanded that Miles hold the prisoners at Fort Bowie until the president decided on their disposition. Fearing he would be held responsible if the band fled to Mexico, Miles wanted them removed from his jurisdiction. So he equivocated, responding that Arizona's posts were unsuitable to secure the prisoners. Could they not be sent on their way and held in Texas or in Florida for safety until their final disposition was determined?[63] Hearing of Miles's response, an angered President Cleveland wired Miles directly, ordering that "Geronimo and the rest of the hostiles immediately be sent to the *nearest* fort or prison where they can be securely confined" (emphasis added).[64]

But Miles forged ahead with his plan to rid himself of the shaman, later claiming that he never received the president's telegram.[65] On the morning of September 8, Lawton and Wood escorted Geronimo, Naiche, and their thirty followers to Bowie Station, where they boarded a train bound, they thought and as Miles intended, for Fort Marion.[66] The two Chiricahua scouts, Martine and Kayitah, who had facilitated the surrender at the risk of their lives, were invited to attend Geronimo's departure. At the last moment the unsuspecting scouts were seized by soldiers and forced aboard the train to accompany the shaman into exile, probably because Miles feared they would undermine his public claims of credit for the surrender.[67]

With the last of members of the troublesome Chiricahua tribe now headed off to Florida, a self-satisfied Miles declared that he had scored "a brilliant ending to a difficult problem."[68] But his elation soon evaporated. Two days later, when Cleveland learned that Miles had disobeyed him and that the Apaches were en route to Florida, he indignantly ordered the train halted at San Antonio and the prisoners removed. They were held there, confined at a quartermaster's depot for six weeks while the administration pondered what to do with them.[69]

As the prisoners languished in Texas, the controversy over their future gained momentum. Pressure from Arizonans to try them for their crimes was countered by an outcry against the dishonorable violation of the terms of surrender. The imbroglio embarrassed the administration and precipitated a scramble to determine what had actually been agreed upon. Finding Miles's vague responses unsatisfactory, Washington asked Brigadier General David S. Stanley, who was supervising the incarcerated Apaches in San Antonio, to interview Naiche and Geronimo to learn their understanding of the surrender terms. Both Indians insisted that Miles had promised to send them to Florida to join their families and to forgive them for their depredations.

After consulting with his political advisors, the president eventually concluded that disregarding these terms might not play well in the country as a whole. Perhaps it also dawned on Cleveland's administration that turning the Chiricahua leadership over to civil authorities in Arizona might ignite yet another Apache uprising. So the prisoners once more boarded a train to complete their journey to Florida.[70] Though saved from the noose, they were denied one of General Miles's key commitments: reunification with their families. At least initially, rather than rejoining their relatives at Fort Marion on the Atlantic coast, they were dispatched to Fort Pickens, a crumbling, poorly maintained stone edifice on an island in the Gulf of Mexico that was three hundred miles from Fort Marion.[71]

Instead of earning the accolades he had anticipated, like Crook, Miles now found himself mired in controversy and censure, perhaps a predictable consequence of his failure to obey a direct order from the president of the United States. Typically, he blamed his predicament on an imaginary cabal in which Crook figured prominently. The plotters, he figured, had distorted his communications with the president to create the impression that he had knowingly disobeyed orders by sending the Apaches east. To counter, or at least obscure, this impression and refurbish his image, he now launched a campaign employing his political connections and talent for self-promotion. The latter included the premature release to the press of his annual report to the secretary of war, a self-congratulatory document that ignored the part played by Gatewood, Martine, and Kayitah in the surrender, ascribing it almost exclusively to his own efforts and those of the troops in Lawton's command.[72]

That scenario required that Miles omit any reference to the role of Lieutenant Gatewood and the two scouts from the public narrative. To prevent the scouts from contradicting his account, he had arranged for the deportation of both men to Florida with Geronimo. As to the lieutenant, Miles appointed him to his personal staff, a move he publicly characterized as a reward for Gatewood's services but one more likely arranged to enable him to monitor and control the lieutenant's utterances.[73] Though largely discredited by future historians, Miles's version of events was widely accepted at the time by a public all too willing to subscribe to a belief of the supremacy of white soldiers over a "savage" foe.

CHAPTER TWENTY-THREE

Campaigning for Indian Rights

The warmth of Crook's welcome in Omaha seemed to take some of the sting out of his departure from Arizona, at least in the short term. The city's notables hosted a lavish banquet for him on the evening after his arrival, featuring such exotic fare as frogs' legs, strawberries, and ice cream molded into the shape of a goose, a tribute to his hunting skills. Speeches lauded the general, and he, in turn, had an opportunity to air his version of the recent campaign. He used it to underscore the difficulties of Indian warfare, especially since the advent of repeating rifles, and the perils he faced when meeting with Geronimo at the Cañon de los Embudos. He also damned the press and armchair warriors in the East for their criticisms of his performance with a bitterness that recalled his earlier reaction to the army's failure to credit his achievements during the Civil War. Perhaps referring to General Miles, he sarcastically declared, "One campaign in Washington is worth a dozen in the field." Ending on a more positive note, he confidently predicted that before long, the few holdouts who had absconded with the shaman would return of their own volition to the reservation.[1]

The press would remain a favorite target for Crook in the months to come. He complained frequently that "nine tenths of all [their] dispatches which have been scattered over the country in regard to my operations against the Apaches have not had one grain of truth in them."[2] Miles's treatment of the Chiricahuas and his criticism of the scouts—and, by extension, Crook's operations against the Apaches—

were also "a constant source of irritation and anger." Such attacks were especially galling, as they not only offended the Nantan's pride and sense of honor but potentially threatened his chances for future promotion.[3]

Crook's prickly mood serves as the context for his overreaction to an interview given with an *Omaha Daily World* reporter by Colonel William B. Royall, who had served with the general during the Sioux War. The colonel was visiting Omaha on sick leave from his regiment, then stationed in Arizona, when he was asked by the journalist what he thought of Miles's progress in tracking down Geronimo. The colonel replied that he considered "Gen. Miles combination to catch the Indians is almost perfect," that his vigorous campaign would soon result in the destruction or surrender of the band, and that Miles's troops had "perfect confidence in him."[4] Crook's aide, Lieutenant Lyman Kennon, recorded Crook's reaction in his diary.

It transpired that Crook hosted a dinner for Royall the evening following the publication of colonel's interview. Several other officers were in attendance, including Major Guy V. Henry, who had served with both men at the Rosebud. After the meal, as Royall prepared to depart, he turned to Major Henry and said, "These are all your friends, I suppose." To which Henry replied, "I am Genl. Crook's friend, but no more than I am your friend, Col. Royall." This seemingly innocent response, overheard by Crook, seemed to trigger long-festering resentments now stoked by the *World* interview. Pulling a clipping from his pocket, he angrily declared,

It had come to my knowledge . . . Col. Royall, that you have been going around the country making remarks and statements of a nature disparaging to me. This does not seem to me to be generous or in good taste. For ten years I have suffered the obloquy of having made a bad fight at the Rosebud, when the fault was in yourself and Nickerson. There was a good chance to make a charge, but it couldn't be done because of the condition of the cavalry. I sent word to you to come in, and waited two hours, nearer three, before you obeyed. I sent Nickerson three times at least. Couriers passed constantly between the points where we were respectively. I had the choice of assuming the responsibility myself for the failure of my plans or of

court-martialing you and Nickerson. The failure of my plan
was due to your conduct.[5]

Royall responded with a dignified defense of his actions in which
Henry concurred. But it hardly mattered. Crook's attack on the colonel's performance in the battle—and on Nickerson, especially—was
as unwarranted as it was unexpected. Yet it seemed more a product
of Crook's festering anger at Miles as of old resentments regarding a
Sioux War engagement a decade past.

This incident was followed in November by the publication of the
secretary of war's annual report for 1886. It included a public endorsement by General Sheridan of Miles's skewed account of the Geronimo
campaign, and the following: "Indian scouts could not be depended
upon to fight and kill their own people. . . . General Crook seemed,
however, wedded to the policy of operating almost exclusively with
Indian scouts, and as his experience was of great weight, his policy
could not well be changed without his removal to another field."[6] To
Crook's dismay, Sheridan's rebuke received the approval of Secretary
of War Endicott.

Sheridan's comments reawakened old insults, real and fancied, dating back to Little Phil's failure to honor Crook for his contributions
to the Shenandoah campaign.[7] Crook now envisioned a conspiracy
between Miles and Sheridan to deny him recognition for his part in the
pacification of the Apaches, and he worried that such public criticism
from his superiors, if unanswered, could very well spell the end of his
military career. By now he was a veteran of many skirmishes among
officers jockeying for promotion and knew that something more effective than a fit of pique was needed to counter such an official criticism
of his policies. While the report containing Sheridan's critique had also
included Crook's rebuttal, his narrative had been printed in a truncated
format, omitting all but one of the appendices containing the reports of
his officers, which confirmed the scouts' pivotal role in the campaign.
His first reaction was to have his own report reprinted separately in its
entirety. But he doubted that this alone would be sufficient to counter
Sheridan's criticisms.[8]

In October, in an initial rebuttal, Crook published a lengthy article
defending his use of scouts as a strategy in Indian warfare in the prestigious *Journal of the Military Service Institution of the United States*. Tracing

the history of combat with the tribes in North America, he worked his way up to the present conflict with the Apaches, asserting that with the advent of the breech-loading rifle, the tribe had been transformed into "a foe of the most dangerous character within human knowledge." Terrain and climate, and the Apaches' adaptation to both, had rendered army regulars helpless in the face of this "tiger of the human species." Only a fellow tribesman, preferably the "wildest [he] could get," possessed the skills, knowledge, and physical endurance to track and engage such an enemy. Aiming squarely at Miles and Sheridan, he declared, "For months the statement has been industriously disseminated by interested parties that the Apache scouts were untrustworthy, that they had mutinied, and everything of that kind. But in none of these reports is there a spark of truth. The Apache scouts, for this class of warfare, are as worthy of trust as any soldier in the world, and in all the experience I have had with them they have proved themselves energetic, reliable, truthful, and honest."[9]

But these arguments were perhaps too generic. Something more specific was needed to expressly counter the sting of Sheridan's characterization of his resignation. Ultimately, Crook decided on an independently published refutation. In its final form it was entitled *Resumé of Operations against the Apache Indians, 1882 to 1886.* Beginning with the Chiricahua scouts' role in Crook's efforts to pacify the Apaches following Cibicue, the document addressed, step-by-step, the events that culminated in his departure from Arizona. Each was documented with the telegraphic exchanges between himself and General Sheridan, dating from the surrender at Cañon de los Embudos to the time of his resignation. With assistance from his aide Captain Roberts, he was able to complete the work for publication in December of that year.

In accordance with military protocol, Crook sent a letter to Washington asking for approval to disseminate his rebuttal. In the hope of securing wide distribution, he requested that the government publish it. The secretary of war denied both requests, citing reasons that Crook must have found infuriating. "To publish the letter," Endicott's assistant adjutant general, John C. Kelton, wrote, "would be merely to lay before the public a matter which there is no military reason whatever for bringing to their knowledge, and would re-awaken a discussion in the public press of a subject which now appears to have passed from their attention." Stung by the reply, Crook protested that as he had been publicly censured for his decisions, he thought it only fair that he be allowed to present "facts which justified my action." His argument must have struck a responsive chord, as the government finally directed the Government Printing Office to publish the work. Crook's reaction to that decision demonstrated a sophisticated grasp of Washington political maneuvering. He wrote Bourke that, ultimately, he regretted receiving permission; had it been refused he could have asked Congress to demand it, which, he believed, would have generated more interest in the document.[10]

As Crook had feared, the original publication hit the ground with a muted thud. Only time and historical perspective garnered interest in the *Resumé of Operations* and elicited the reaction that he had sought. In 1970 the document was reprinted in its entirety with a forward by Barry C. Johnson, author and editor of several works on the Indian wars. Johnson characterized the document as "a lucid and logical exposition of Crook's policy and general philosophy in dealing with the Apache problem. It is difficult," he added, pinpointing the reason Endicott had feared the *Resumé*'s publication, "not to conclude that he had the better of the argument, theoretically, with the Commanding General."[11]

The *Resumé* proved to be the opening shot in a campaign orchestrated by Crook to redeem the Chiricahuas who had not participated in the breakout, most particularly the scouts, from their unjust and undeserved exile and imprisonment. Still furious at the shaman's betrayal following the Cañon de los Embudos surrender, the general regarded Geronimo's fate as fully deserved. So the *Resumé* made no attempt to come to *his* defense. While the general's passion stemmed in great measure from his ire at the treatment of the scouts, concern for his own reputation certainly played a significant part. Above all, he regarded Miles's treatment of the Chiricahuas as a betrayal of his (Crook's) own commitments to them, a betrayal that stained his honor and his reputation. In a letter to Bourke written well before publication of the *Resumé,* he privately confided his belief that not only had Miles used deceit in dealing with the Apaches, but the government had broken its (in reality, Crook's) promise to the Indians.[12]

As a prelude to freeing the imprisoned scouts, an investigation was required to document the conditions under which the Indians were being held to underscore the unfairness of their incarceration and arouse public outrage. The general planned to distance himself from any such investigation lest his participation be misconstrued as simply an effort to discredit General Miles as part of the two officers' now very public feud.[13] Indeed, some newspapers favorably inclined toward Miles did portray it that way.[14] To conceal his hand yet still obtain the information needed to proceed, Crook proposed to Bourke that "perhaps Herbert Welsh could send some one of his people or perhaps go to Florida for the Winter, and let them have an interview with these people [the Chiricahuas] eliciting all these points."[15]

Identifying a member of the eastern establishment's reform movement for this task signaled another step in Crook's evolution as a humanitarian. Throughout most of his career, he had subscribed to a perception of the Indian reform movement common to many on the frontier. He (and not a few of his fellow officers) regarded the urbanized eastern reformers as under the spell of James Fenimore Cooper's vision of the "noble Red Man." This view held that easterners, bemused by Cooper's romanticism, completely failed to comprehend the threat posed by Indians on the frontier and were so far insulated from reality by distance, sentimentality, and ignorance as to be disqualified from meddling in Indian affairs. Crook's adherence to this view had been reinforced by his contact with the reformers appointed to implement President Grant's peace policy in Arizona in the 1870s, especially Vincent Colyer, whom the general sarcastically labeled "Vincent the Good."[16] Colyer's activities in Arizona had thwarted Crook's own strategic objectives in the territory, earning the reformer the general's undying contempt, though Crook agreed with many of the man's ideas concerning the resolution of the so-called "Indian problem."[17]

Crook's attitude toward the movement had altered substantially as a consequence of his involvement with the Ponca case in 1879, so much so that by the time he returned to Arizona in 1882, he had come to see these same reformers as allies in his fight for Indian rights in the Southwest. Consistent with this evolution in his thinking, in the years since the Standing Bear trial he had become accustomed to approaching Indian reform groups for assistance on humanitarian issues affecting the tribes. He also found it convenient to use these groups as an unofficial forum on matters on which he could not speak in his capacity as an army officer. Hence, by October 1886 it was not unusual for him to turn to Herbert Welsh and his organization as a resource. Nor did he entertain any doubt that the reformer would be a willing ally.

Herbert Welsh, founder of the Indian Rights Association, circa 1880. Courtesy of the Pennsylvania Historical Society.

Welsh was a relative newcomer to Indian affairs, having established the Indian Rights Association only three years earlier. Still in his early thirties, he was the youngest member of a prosperous Philadelphia family historically involved in both philanthropy and Indian rights as the result of their religiosity and commitment to the ideal of Christian responsibility. Welsh inherited the family's earnestness and zeal. A photograph of him taken in 1883 shows a solemn young man with boyish features, an intense gaze, and a firm jaw, the latter overshadowed by a dramatic mustache, possibly affected to add maturity to his otherwise youthful appearance.[18]

As a youth Welsh had harbored artistic ambitions, although he quickly abandoned them in 1882 after he and a friend spent a month in the Dakotas on the Great Sioux Reservation. They had undertaken the trip to familiarize themselves with the missionary work of William Hobart Hare, Episcopal Bishop of Niobrara, and so spent most of their time at the religious missions on the reservation's various agencies. Welsh was deeply affected by the Indians he met and by the bishop's dedication and views. He was also impressed by the officers he encountered while visiting Fort Niobrara.[19] At the time of Welsh's visit, Crook was still in command of the Department of the Platte, and though there is no evidence that the two men actually met, the young idealist must have surely have learned something of the general and his humanitarian ideas during the visit.

Welsh's western sojourn made such an impression on him that upon his return to Philadelphia, he published his thoughts in a pamphlet and gave a number of talks to groups in and around the city. The views he expressed on Indian reform paralleled those of many ethnologists and reformers of the time and closely accorded with those of George Crook and John Bourke. While these ideas appear quaint and paternalistic today, in contrast with countervailing opinions of the time—largely based on the premise that the Indian was an inferior being best kept in confinement (or better still, annihilated)—they can be considered enlightened for the day. In common with most of his fellow reformers, Welsh believed that all people had equal potential. Societies, however, did not. Indian culture represented a primitive mode of social structure that prevented its adherents from achieving the full benefits of "civilization." By this reformers meant the ascendant Western culture of Europe and North America, universally regarded by Euro-Americans as the gold standard of political, moral, social, and religious beliefs and practices. To be assimilated into this more advanced society, it was only necessary to introduce the Indian to Christian values and beliefs, capitalism (as embodied in the concept of private ownership of land, or "severalty," as it was referred to), and the rule of law. Adherence to these principles, bolstered by firm guidance from competent and honest agents, would bring the tribes to a level of equality with Euro-Americans and ensure their assimilation into the American body politic. Ancillary to these beliefs was an abhorrence of the ration system, which was regarded as promoting corruption on the reservation and fostering dependence on government largesse.[20]

Not content to simply analyze the situation from afar, in December 1882 Welsh created an organization to promote his ideals, the Indian Rights Association (IRA). Under the unassuming title of corresponding secretary, Welsh became the engine behind its activities for the next thirty years, striving to influence public opinion and promote legislative action in support of policies its members believed would contribute to the betterment of the American Indian.[21]

Though he may not have met Welsh during the latter's 1882 trip to Sioux country, Crook soon became aware of the IRA. Conversant with the wealth and influence wielded by such organizations, Crook turned to it for assistance in the spring of 1883, shortly after the organization's birth, to resolve a crisis on the Hualapai Reservation. The general held the Hualapais in high regard because of their loyal service as scouts during an early campaign in Arizona. This had led him to intervene in their behalf some years earlier in an attempt to forestall their removal to a reservation that he believed inimical to their survival.[22] Now the tribe was facing food shortages that threatened them with starvation. Mrs. Crook apparently shared his interest in the tribe, for she and the general cosigned a letter to the association soliciting funds to address the emergency.[23] A correspondence between Welsh and the Crooks ensued, culminating in a generous contribution from the IRA. This was followed by an invitation from Crook to Welsh to come west to meet the beneficiaries of his organization's largesse.

Welsh accepted and in June 1884 he traveled to Arizona, met the general and his wife at Fort Whipple, and then visited the Navajo, Hopi, and, eventually, the Hualapai reservations. The trip opened the young easterner's eyes to the wide variety of cultures and living conditions of the tribes that his organization had been founded to assist. It also began a mutually beneficial relationship between the reformer and the general.[24] Welsh realized that in Crook he had an invaluable informant on Indian matters. Crook, who had worked previously with a similar group from Boston on the Ponca issue, saw in Welsh an influential ally in his fight to protect the tribes.

In September of that year, Crook visited Philadelphia briefly to call on the reformer and enlist the IRA's aid in procuring agricultural equipment and a gristmill to further farming initiatives then being carried out by the White Mountain Apaches. Welsh was much impressed by the general's sincere interest in the welfare of the Apaches and his confidence in their ability to adapt to white civilization. Crook invited the association to send representatives to the White Mountain Reservation to see proof of this for themselves. Welsh accepted the challenge, sending Robert Frazer, a mining engineer and member of the organization's executive committee, to accompany the general's annual inspection tour of the reservation. As Crook hoped, Frazer was favorably impressed, reporting that the Apache was "prepared by intelligence and inclination to become in time and with the acquirement of the English language, a law-abiding and useful citizen." As a bonus for Crook, an ardent advocate of severalty, Frazer even purported to have the insight that for the tribe, "to own their land individually is their heart's desire."[25]

In January 1885 Crook wrote again to Welsh, ostensibly to thank him for aid that the reformer had provided to Mike Burns, a young Yavapai adopted by a military officer following the deaths of his entire family at the Salt River Cave.[26] But his real reason for writing was to convey his support, which as an army officer he was unable to officially express, for a bill being considered by Congress to extend the ballot to the Indians. The content and tone of the letter, which bore the distinct imprint of John Bourke's elegant writing style, indicated an unspoken wish that his words be published. The legislation had stalled after a House committee had reported it out with the notation that its passage would require repeal of legislation prohibiting the sale of liquor to the Indians. As reported by the *Alta California*, the committee believed that "to give Lo the ballot would do him less good than to keep the bottle away from him."[27] Crook's response, subsequently published by the IRA under the title *Letter from General Crook on Giving the Ballot to the Indians*, shows the influence of the Ponca case on his thinking, and is, for its time, a strikingly enlightened discourse on civil rights in American society as applicable to African Americans of the period as to the Indians.

> The proposition I make on behalf of the Indian is that he is at this moment capable, with very little instruction, of exercising every manly right; he doesn't need [to] have the *guardianship*

[emphasis in original] as many people would have us believe; what he does need is protection under the law; [and] the privilege of suing in the courts. . . . If with the new prerogatives, individual Indians continue to use alcoholic stimulants, we must expect to see him rise or fall socially as do white men under similar circumstances. . . . [The Indian] is fully able to protect himself, if the ballot be given and the courts of law not closed against him. . . . If our aim be to remove the aborigine from a state of servile dependence, we cannot begin in a better or more practical way than by making him think well of himself, to force upon him the knowledge that he is a part and parcel of the nation, clothed with all its political privileges, entitled to share in all its benefits. . . . To sum up, my panacea for the Indian is to make the Indian self-supporting, a condition which can never, in my opinion, be attained so long as the privileges which have made labor honorable, respectable, and able to defend, itself, be withheld from him.[28]

Welsh's strengthening relationship with General Crook paralleled his relationship to John Bourke. Closer in age to Welsh and certainly a less formidable presence than the general, Bourke's personality and eagerness to share his expertise in Indian culture allowed a friendship and a lively correspondence to grow between the two men that Crook undoubtedly encouraged. Having Bourke as an intermediary between himself and Welsh permitted the general to maneuver behind the scenes, using the IRA to further his agenda on behalf of the Indians without leaving his fingerprints on the effort. This, in turn, protected Crook from censure by his superiors, and perhaps in the case of the Chiricahua prisoners, it served to blunt the perception that Crook's interest in their fate was simply a cover for a personal attack on General Miles. Concurrently, it allowed the IRA to mount its own initiatives untainted by the animus that existed in certain quarters against General Crook.

Welsh and Bourke were already deep into a correspondence when Bourke received Crook's letter suggesting that Welsh interview the prisoners at Fort Marion. As already mentioned, Bourke had continued his involvement in Apache affairs following his reassignment to the Smithsonian in April 1886. He had been outraged at the campaign to remove the general from command in Arizona, and, like Crook, he was disgusted by Miles's subsequent treatment of the Chiricahuas. He was particularly disturbed by the imprisonment of the scouts, some of whom had been his informants on Apache lore and had become his friends. So he had been moved to accompany Chatto's delegation to its meetings with the government that past summer to oppose their banishment to Florida.

Knowing of Bourke's involvement, Welsh had written the captain asking for background on the government's treatment of the Apaches. Bourke obliged in a letter brimming with indignation. The whites, he said, "had driven these unfortunate people before us, that they are now like rats in a cage cooped up in the mountains of Arizona and must fight or die." He urged Welsh not to accept the popular view of the Apaches as ruthless murderers, noting, "He is a savage, of course, . . . but he is not a bit more savage than many of the factions which now enter into our political equation."[29] After Chatto's delegation had been shipped off to Florida in September, Bourke again wrote to Welsh, heatedly labeling the government's actions toward the loyal scouts "a contemptible outrage."[30] Bourke's expanding friendship with Welsh, together with Crook's familiarity with the reformer, made him the general's likely choice to enlist in the prisoners' cause.[31]

Welsh's IRA was not the only organization interested in the prisoners. In late February 1887 the Boston Indian Citizenship Committee invited the general to visit their city to raise awareness of Indian rights. The committee, which had come to know of Crook through Henry Tibbles's 1879 tour of the city in behalf of the Poncas, was composed of members from the same social stratum as the IRA's Philadelphia reformers and shared their ideals and zeal. Now, perhaps at Tibbles's urging, they had narrowed their focus to the plight of the Fort Marion prisoners. Eager to become involved, they hoped that the general would educate them as to ways in which they could be of assistance. Crook was more than happy to accommodate them.[32] Aware of Crook's need to avoid a direct connection with the issue, they worded their invitation vaguely, informing him only that they wished for his attendance at several meetings they planned and to enlist his "further aid and cooperation in the line of action they have adopted."[33]

Accompanied by his new aide, First Lieutenant Lyman W. V. Kennon, Crook arrived in Boston on February 23, 1887.[34] The consummate woodsman, able to find his way through fog and snow in uncharted mountains and deserts, found the city's geography daunting. To his diary he confided, "I have heard of the crookedness of the streets of Boston, but they are so much more than I had any idea of that I am certain I would get lost within two blocks of my hotel."[35] But under the gentle guidance of the committee, he soon settled down and enjoyed his stay immensely. The visit, almost two weeks in duration, had been arranged to coincide with the presence of Tibbles and his wife, Bright Eyes, whom the journalist first met and subsequently wooed during the Ponca affair. Their presence reinforced Crook's message of Indian equality and assimilation, a theme that he expounded on during the many speaking engagements arranged by the committee. Interspersed with sightseeing and social events, he addressed large audiences of "Indian loving people," as he referred to those who came to hear him. His speeches reprised his years of experience interacting with the Indians and the lessons he had learned, particularly during the Standing Bear case. In one such speech he echoed the Ponca chief's words, declaring, "The Indian is a human being." That being the case, he asked, "How can we preserve him? My answer is, 'First, take the government of the Indians out of politics; second, let the laws of the Indians be the same as those of the whites; third, give the Indians the ballot.'" His message was well received, at least in Boston.[36]

While Crook spoke publicly of the plight of the Indians, in private, after learning that the Boston Committee was "red hot over the Apache business and seem determined to get the bottom of it," he worked with its members to develop strategies to help the Fort Marion prisoners.[37] The committee agreed with Crook that someone needed to visit the fort to assess the actual conditions of the prisoners. Tibbles was eager to go, but his fellow Bostonians feared that his passionate nature might impede the cause. Crook, too, doubted his old friend's judgment and discretion and had already fixed on Bourke and Welsh instead. The captain was well known to the Apaches, and the general believed that they would readily open up to him. But like Crook's own situation, Bourke's involvement would be risky. The captain could not afford to endanger his position at the Smithsonian by alienating the War Department, a potential villain in any negative report on the condition of the prisoners. To disguise his role, Crook suggested that his former aide participate as an investigator but remain in the background "so as not to compromise your position." Welsh, representing the IRA, would lead the mission and be its public face.[38]

The visit to Fort Marion was not easy to arrange. President Cleveland, General Sheridan, and Secretary Endicott all opposed it. They had no wish to see the prisoner issue reopened or to further expose their perfidy with regard to Geronimo's surrender terms to additional scrutiny. But Welsh, with the clout of the Philadelphia reformers behind him, persisted. Ultimately, Endicott gave in after Welsh offered to fund the trip, including coverage of Bourke's expenses.[39]

Bourke and Welsh arrived at Fort Marion on March 8, 1887, to find that conditions there were appalling—worse, in fact, than they were at Fort Pickens, where the more culpable Geronimo was incarcerated. The fort, built by the Spanish in the 1690s of porous coquina stone, was a crumbling ruin. The year before, 500 Apaches had been confined within its walls in a space that could probably safely accommodate not more than 150 souls with any degree of comfort and health. By the time of Welsh's arrival, only 447 remained, of whom 90 were men. Among those, 30 (Chihuahua's band) had participated in Geronimo's breakout. The rest were innocent of any involvement and had farmed peacefully at Turkey Creek or actually had aided the army in the ensuing campaign. Forty-four children had been removed to the Carlisle Indian School. But, as Welsh was shocked to learn, 23 women and children had died during their confinement, a period of less than a year.[40]

Only leaky army tents protected the Apaches from the elements. In a vain attempt to keep out the damp, the tents were equipped with wooden floors and were crowded together atop the narrow ramparts of the old fort in a manner that afforded little privacy. The disposal of human waste and garbage was inadequate and encouraged a proliferation of rats. Rations, which were similar to those doled out to Indians on the reservation—flour, beef, coffee, and sugar—were insufficient and lacked fresh vegetables or fruit, despite the abundance of the latter in Florida. Unused to the climate, provided with only marginally adequate nutrition, forced to live in overcrowded unsanitary conditions, and exposed to the elements, the prisoners suffered from malaria, tuberculosis, and dysentery, all contributing to the high mortality rate.[41]

Following his visit, Welsh gave a lengthy interview to the *New York Tribune*, which to the Boston committee's dismay was published before they had an opportunity to discuss his findings with them. In line with Crook's own priorities, Welsh focused his discourse on the "injustice with which the good behavior, the fidelity and, in some instances, the distinguished services of these Chiricahua Indians have been rewarded by the government of the United States."[42] The reformers thought it insufficiently forceful. Tibbles, too, was disturbed by it. His critique, thankfully confined to a letter to Bourke, characterized Welsh's commentary as so weak "that it will scarcely make a day's sensation." But his real complaint, just as the reformers had feared, was that the reformer "has no interest in anything but the Indians [so] that the treatment of Gen. Crook will not be made a point of. If I had a hand in the affair I would have the whole thing fully ventilated, and Gen. Miles held to an accountability."[43]

Crook, too, found Welsh's article somewhat disappointing. His concern was that the presentation was so weak that it would take the "keen edge off the whole business." But, unlike Tibbles, he believed that the investigation's findings were useful and undoubtedly appreciated Welsh's tactful avoidance of any mention of the circumstances surrounding the general's departure from Arizona. To the reformer he enthused, "This Apache business would furnish a better subject for a novel than did the outrages of Californians on the Mission Indians." He was also optimistic that the Boston committee would now press the campaign as they had with the Poncas.[44]

During the weeks that followed, Welsh labored on his report, which he planned to publish as a pamphlet. The work detailed the unhealthy conditions at the fort and underscored the injustice of incarcerating the scouts by highlighting the notable contributions to the Geronimo campaign made by prominent individuals like Chatto, Martine, and Noche. With Crook's permission, Welsh quoted extensively from the general's *Resumé of Operations* and used materials provided by Bourke, though at the captain's request he concealed the latter's contribution.[45]

Desiring the report to be as inclusive as possible, Welsh asked Gatewood to provide his personal assessment of the role of the scouts. The lieutenant's harsh reply shocked him. Now on Miles's staff and undoubtedly under considerable pressure from the general, the lieutenant wrote not only to Welsh but to the prestigious *Army and Navy Register* that "Chatto and the other Chiricahua scouts could scarcely be considered faithful. They hindered rather than aided the operations of the troops." Moreover, according to Gatewood, "much of the ammunition issued to them went into the belts of the hostiles." When Welsh shared the letter with Crook and Bourke, they were equally astonished. After reading it Crook drily observed that Gatewood's response was "very different from statements which I understand he made upon his return from securing the surrender of the hostiles, & before he was taken on Miles' staff." Though Welsh included Gatewood's commentary in his final report, he refuted it with quotes from reports of other officers who had been in the field with the Chiricahuas. Their repeated declarations as to the value and loyalty of the scouts starkly contrasted with Gatewood's claims, casting doubt on his credibility and on similar disparaging remarks made by General Miles.[46]

Notwithstanding reformers' concerns about Welsh's effectiveness, his *Tribune* interview and the subsequent publication of his report had a profound impact on popular opinion, elevating him to a leadership role in the struggle to free the Apache prisoners. His revelations were so embarrassing to the Cleveland administration that Sheridan, in an attempt to undermine Welsh's report, ordered Colonel Romeyn B. Ayres, the commander of the St. Augustine post, to conduct a secret investigation that he hoped would reveal participation by the reservation Chiricahuas in the aftermath of the outbreak. Unfortunately for the administration, Ayres produced an honest, straightforward assessment that supported Welsh's findings. He reported that of the 82 male adult Chiricahuas remaining at Fort Apache, 65 had served the government as scouts during the entire Geronimo campaign. Four of those who did not were "too old and feeble to be enlisted as scouts," but they had been instrumental in keeping their people "friendly toward the Government." Clearly, Ayres thought that there was little justification for holding these men as prisoners of war. But mindful of the need for discretion because of Sheridan's position in the matter, he tried to keep his findings confidential.[47] His efforts failed because Bourke and the Boston reformers leaked its contents, reinforcing the increasingly popular perception that the government had created a grave injustice in locking away the loyal Chiricahuas.

The negative publicity exerted tremendous pressure on the administration to find a more humane alternative to Fort Marion.[48] Vociferous opposition in the Southwest rendered it politically unwise to return the tribe to Arizona. An alternative—sending the prisoners to Fort

Pickens to join Geronimo, an option strongly supported by General Howard, now commanding the Department of the Atlantic—drew vehement protests from Bourke, probably acting for Crook, and the reformers. Attention then shifted to Mount Vernon Barracks, a 2,100-acre military reservation about thirty miles north of Mobile, Alabama, that seemed to offend no one. Hoping that Bourke would endorse the selection and thereby win the support of the reformers, Secretary Endicott asked him to visit the post to assess its suitability.

On April 11, 1887, Bourke inspected the camp and reacted favorably. The buildings, he reported, "are in excellent condition and the post is as neat as a pin." Though malaria, yellow fever, and cholera were endemic in the swamps that surrounded the area, the sanitary condition of the site itself, "situated on a 224 foot elevation above sea level," Bourke pronounced "excellent." The air was "pure and sweet," and there was an abundance of fresh water. Moreover, Bourke found the climate, though warm during the day, "cool and pleasant at night."[49] The captain found only one drawback. He, like Crook, believed that "continuous and well-remunerated labor" was essential to the development of the Apaches into peace-loving citizens. In consequence, he was disappointed in the quality of the soil at Mount Vernon Barracks. It was too sandy for either stock raising or agriculture, the vocations then considered most suitable for Indians. However, he thought this difficulty surmountable. Some of the men might continue to serve as scouts, while the surrounding area, covered with pine and cypress, could provide the basis for a timber industry.[50]

President Cleveland was impressed by Bourke's report, all the more so because, for once, it supported a decision he was prepared to make. On April 27, only nine days after Bourke had submitted his assessment, the Chiricahuas remaining at Fort Marion were put on trains to Mount Vernon Barracks. Along the way twenty women and eleven children, families of those warriors incarcerated at Fort Pickens, were dropped off in Pensacola to be reunited with their menfolk. At last Miles's promise to Geronimo that upon surrender he would be reunited with his family had been fulfilled. The remaining 354 prisoners continued on to Mount Vernon Barracks.[51] In May 1888 the Fort Pickens prisoners quietly joined them, fulfilling the second part of Miles's commitment. The surviving remnants of the Chiricahua tribe were now reunited in exile.

Sadly, the reality of life at Mount Vernon Barracks did not measure up to Bourke's expectations. Eugene Chihuahua, son of Chihuahua, summed up his experiences there as a child. "We didn't know what misery was till they dumped us in those swamps." The buildings in which the prisoners were quartered were "tumbledown houses with dirt floors. . . . It rained nearly all the time and the roofs leaked. On top of that the mosquitoes almost ate us alive. Babies died from their bites. It was hot and steamy." The Apaches were accustomed to heat, but humidity was another matter. "It was terrible. Everything molded—food, clothes, moccasins, everything." Malaria, or as the Apaches called it, the shaking sickness, was carried by the mosquitos and infected almost everyone.[52] By the end of their first summer at Mount Vernon, the Chiricahuas, malnourished and weakened by malaria and their unsanitary living conditions, began to die, most from tuberculosis. By December 1889 a worried General Howard reported that whereas the death rate for a normal population of the size quartered at Mount Vernon Barracks would be 2 percent, among the Chiricahuas it was "three times as great." Added to this grim statistic was the tragic news that of the children sent north to be educated at the Carlisle Indian School, fully a quarter had died during the past three and a half years, the majority also from tuberculosis.[53]

As early as January 1888 it had become evident to Welsh and others who closely monitored the situation that the Apaches would have to be moved again. Their very survival was at stake. But the War Department, still smarting from criticisms leveled at them in Welsh's report, now ignored its author's pleas. In May, after several frustrating months of failed attempts to get the administration to act, Welsh turned to Crook, now a major general, for help.

As a major general and the new commander of the Military Division of the Missouri, from his Chicago headquarters Crook oversaw a substantial portion of the military establishment west of the Mississippi. His new rank and assignment gave him a far more prestige than that of a mere departmental commander, allowing him to exert considerable influence within the Cleveland administration. He had only received his promotion a month before. At the end of March, Major General Alfred H. Terry, former commander of the Little Big Horn campaign and occupant of Sheridan's old position as head of the Division of the Missouri, had announced his intention to retire due to declining health. His decision signaled a vacancy that would allow advancement to the coveted rank.

Crook was the senior brigadier in the army, having held his rank since 1872, longer than any other serving general. His only serious competition was General Miles. The latter was eight years his junior in rank. However, he was extremely well connected politically and had a career record that rivaled Crook's. But Miles had incurred the wrath of the Cleveland administration because of his handling of the Geronimo surrender and had alienated many of his fellow officers through his arrogance, ambition, and the shameless use of his wife's relatives—the Shermans and the Camerons—to further his career. Even Sheridan, according to Miles's wife, Mary, opposed his appointment: "[He] hates the whole Sherman family," she wrote her uncle, William Tecumseh Sherman.[54]

Crook, on the other hand, still retained his reputation as a premier Indian fighter and administrator of Indian affairs. He also seems to have successfully disguised his hand in the Indian Rights campaign to resettle the Chiricahuas, thus avoiding the enmity of both President Cleveland and Secretary Endicott. By 1887 even Sheridan, as Mrs. Miles had surmised, preferred Crook. Also of significance were the general's own highly placed supporters, among them Rutherford Hayes, his comrade and ally since their days together in the Civil War.

After Terry announced his intentions and the competition for promotion heated up, the former president mounted a letter-writing campaign on his friend's behalf. "I believe General Crook is the senior Brigadier," he wrote in letters to several of his prominent friends. "His appointment will be especially gratifying to all who take an interest in the just and humane treatment of the Indian. His attitude to Mr. Cleveland's administration is not in his way, and he is the most distinguished soldier named for the place." To Melville Fuller, a prominent Democrat and nominee for the then-vacant position of chief justice of the Supreme Court, he wrote, "We know Crook as the brave and successful Indian fighter of the time, and what is better, as the true, judicious, and reliable friend of the Indian. He is, I believe, the senior brigadier and, although no politician, he is a friend of Mr. Cleveland's Administration." Hayes's repeated references to the Cleveland administration are further evidence of Crook's success in keeping a low profile on the Chiricahua issue.[55]

In the end General Miles's liabilities and the warm support of Hayes and other Crook supporters paid off. President Cleveland forwarded the general's nomination to the Senate, and he was confirmed on April 6, 1888. Crook received word of his promotion while visiting Major Roberts, his former aide, in Cheyenne. Characteristically, he played the stoic. To his diary he confided: "Laura [Major Roberts's spouse] was much surprised and excited to rec. a telegram from Gen. Drum, in the afternoon, congratulating me on my promotion." Yet his elation was shadowed by a sad memory. He confided to Hayes, "This comes as a matter of course, and I enjoy it more than I did my appointment as brigadier general for that came by the death of General Canby, one of the best of men."[56]

On May 1 Crook took the oath of office. Three days later he relinquished his command of the Department of the Platte and boarded a train for Chicago to assume General Terry's former command, the Division of the Missouri.[57]

No longer locked in a competition for rank with Miles, Crook no longer needed to disguise his involvement in the prisoner issue. Moreover, he undoubtedly recognized the enhanced power of his new position and was eager to test it. Hence, he responded warmly when in June, Welsh journeyed to Chicago to confer with him about the plight of the Chiricahuas. During their meeting Crook suggested that in the general's name, the reformer might offer the recommendation that the tribe be resettled at Fort Sill on land granted to them in severalty, on which they could raise crops or stock, according to their preference. Welsh liked the idea and presented it to Secretary Endicott. But the secretary, still piqued by the reformer's criticism of the treatment of the Fort Marion prisoners, ignored Welsh's recommendation despite Crook's association with it, leaving the Chiricahuas to languish in Alabama.

The administration's obduracy worried Crook. He was not only concerned about the prisoners' health but also feared that their prolonged idleness at Mount Vernon threatened to turn them into "vagabonds for the remainder of their lives."[58] So during the summer of 1888, he prodded the reformers to press hard for immediate transfer of the Apaches. Impatient at the lack of progress, in August he journeyed to Washington to meet personally with Secretary Endicott and the president. Focusing on the injustice of the scouts' imprisonment, he suggested that recompense was due and repeated his recommendation that they be resettled at Fort Sill. Knowing that the Indian training school at Hampton, Virginia, was being touted as an alternative, he proposed a compromise pursuant to which the Apaches would go first to Hampton to receive agricultural training and then to Fort Sill for resettlement. Leaving Washington, he then rode south to Hampton and, in the stifling heat and humidity of a tidewater summer, inspected a farm proposed as an alternative site. But Cleveland still refused to make a decision. Consequently, when in November the Democrats lost the White House, the Chiricahuas were still confined to Mount Vernon Barracks, while those who sought to aid them were faced with the prospect of dealing with a new administration.[59]

Through Bourke and Kennon, Crook renewed his efforts the following spring with a new cast of characters: a Republican president, Benjamin Harrison; his appointee as secretary of war, Redfield Proctor, a Vermont politician; and the new commanding general, Major General John M. Schofield. Bourke was once more summoned to investigate proposed sites, this time in the Hampton area and then in Cherokee country in the mountains near Asheville, in western North Carolina. Though the Cherokee site appeared promising, by early winter 1889–90 a groundswell of opposition from the Asheville area, and more importantly, from the region's Congressional representatives, stalled the plan. Hoping to rekindle enthusiasm for the North Carolina option, the secretary of war invited General Crook to visit Asheville and inspect the proposed site, thinking his support might calm local fears. On December 28 the general, accompanied by Kennon, visited the area in a chill winter rain. Despite viewing the site in such weather, Crook thought the location similar to the Apaches' home in the Arizona mountains but expressed doubts that it contained sufficient land to settle almost four hundred Chiricahuas.[60]

Crook and Kennon then boarded a train for Mount Vernon Barracks, arriving there in still-falling rain in the early morning hours of January 2, 1890. After breakfast with the post commander and a visit to a small school set up for the Indian children, they were joined by old friends Chihuahua and Ka-ya-ten-nae and guided to the log huts that housed the tribe. There Chatto and numbers of Apaches, streaming in from all points, enthusiastically crowded about the aging general. Crook was of course delighted by their adoration, but when Geronimo, who was teaching a class when the general arrived, attempted to address him, Crook angrily waved him away, denouncing him as a liar. Naiche, Chatto, and other prominent leaders spent the rest of the day at Crook's side, reciting the indignities they had endured. Their words, particularly Chatto's sad tale, left him shaken and renewed his indignation at the unfair and unmerited cruelties visited upon these venerable warriors, many of whom had given him unstinting service.[61]

Crook allowed the intensity of his feelings to show through in an interview that he gave to a *Washington Post* reporter on his return to the capital. His words caused quite a stir. Under a column heading reading "Story of a Great Wrong," he recited a tale of injustice and misery. While singling out Geronimo as an Apache for whom "death is too good," he lauded the vital part the Chiricahua scouts had played in the shaman's surrender, only to be rewarded by imprisonment at Mount Vernon Barracks. There they were to "languish, . . . robbed of employment, cramped in their quarters, breathing the miasmatic exhalations that rise from low and unwholesome land." Asked by the reporter to name those responsible, Crook carefully softened his response so as to absolve his current superiors from blame. But his message was nonetheless clear. "I cannot say," he declared. "It was done during the last Administration. It was one of those hard, those terrible, those dastardly crimes that are committed against people who cannot defend themselves." He wisely avoided getting ahead of the current administration when he refused the reporter's request to name a specific site for the tribe's relocation, allowing only that the prisoners ought to be allotted farms "somewhere" other than the swamp where they currently resided. To calm fears sure to arise in communities that might suddenly awaken to find themselves amongst a people he had once described as "human tigers," the general firmly asserted that "there is no danger that they will return to the warpath." But he warned, "I would not advise the restoration to their homes in the White Mountains of those who *did* go out because, if they ever should make another drunken sortie, as they might, there is no end to the slaughter they might accomplish and the damage they could perform" (emphasis added).[62]

Though he had declined to identify a resettlement site to the *Post* reporter, Crook had no such scruples when submitting his report to Secretary Proctor two days later. Noting that at Mount Vernon the prisoners' "mortality has been much more than normal, and would seem due to homesickness, change of climate and the dreary monotony of empty lives," he suggested North Carolina as an alternative, as it possessed a "climate more like their Arizona homeland than any place else in the East." However, he strongly preferred a site near Fort Sill in Indian Territory (modern-day Oklahoma), which, he felt, more closely mirrored "the country to which they are accustomed." Whether North Carolina or the Indian Territory was ultimately selected, the time had come to right the great wrong that had been done to these "men [who were] not only innocent of offense, but to whom the Government is largely indebted for services of the very greatest value and which they alone could have rendered."[63]

A month later Crook visited Indian Territory to inspect the Fort Sill site, a trip that, for him, confirmed the correctness of his earlier recommendation. Despite chill winter weather, he pronounced it "one of the loveliest country [sic] I ever saw, with good soil in the bargain, a most suitable place for the Indians."[64]

Crook's words, backed by his experience and prestige, galvanized the Harrison administration. Within a week the secretary of war forwarded Crook's Fort Sill recommendation to the president with his own endorsement, although he cautiously left the North Carolina site open as a possibility.[65] With Crook's prestige behind it, Harrison chose the Fort Sill option. But because of the legislation prohibiting resettlement of Apaches in Indian Territory, implementing the administration's decision required congressional action. Under the guidance of Senator Henry Dawes, an activist in the Indian rights cause, a joint resolution supporting the move was quickly passed in the Senate and then referred to the House.

It was in the context of House hearings on the issue that ferocious opposition erupted. To no one's surprise, it emanated from the desert Southwest.[66] Indian Territory, southwesterners declared, was simply a stalking horse for sneaking the Apaches back into Arizona. And if that argument proved too thin, they loudly proclaimed that Fort Sill was close enough to the Chiricahua's homeland to allow these wily savages to make their way back to it, and once there, wreak their terrible revenge on the good people of Arizona.

Many of the territorial papers, longtime and intemperate critics of General Crook, sought to undermine his recommendation by ascribing a variety of underhanded motives to it. One paper characterized it as an effort to honor the agreement "dictated" by that "fiend incarnate," Geronimo, in March 1886 to return the Chiricahuas to Arizona after two years in the East. "Now, 'under the cloak of sympathy [and] determined to undo the military achievements of General Miles,' Crook was attempting to execute the long deferred payoff."[67] Another alleged that "in a fit of jealously over Miles's' success in apprehending Geronimo, Crook merely attempted to undo the accomplishments of his rival."[68] As to Crook's "lugubrious blubber" over the mortality among the Mount Vernon prisoners, the *Tombstone Epitaph* exclaimed, "Why, they did not die fast enough."[69]

Crook, believing he no longer needed surrogates to respond to these canards, dealt with them directly, using the sympathetic *Washington Post* as his forum. Rather than defend his motives, he concentrated on calming fears of the "Apache menace." Characterizing the allegations against him and his scouts as stories circulated with a less-than-honorable intention, he declared that he would definitely not have recommended the relocation of the Mount Vernon prisoners "if there was any probability of their turning like snakes against the Government." Contrary to popular perception, the Apaches "were broken in spirit and humbled to the dust." Geronimo, that once feared menace, was now teaching Sunday school to Indian children and "had lost all hatred of white people." Indian Territory perfectly suited the Chiricahuas, and he would bet any amount that they would behave themselves if allowed to settle there.[70]

Among his enemies Crook's words were met with sarcasm and feigned outrage. Geronimo teaching Sunday school? queried the *New York Herald,* the general's harshest critic during the Sioux War. "Think of that! Geronimo the bloody, teaching Sunday school and pulling the wool over the eyes of a man who has Crook's reputation as an Indian fighter! . . . Wow! General Crook's certificate of good character has stirred the Western heart to unutterable wrath."[71]

General Miles, unable to resist the opportunity to sabotage his old rival's cause, added his voice to the chorus. When called before the House Committee on Indian Affairs to testify on the removal issue, he denounced the Chiricahuas as "the lowest, most brutal and cruel of the Indian savages on this continent." Though he had earlier supported Indian Territory as the place to send the Apaches, he now testified that the Oklahoma climate would be injurious to their health. Moreover, it was no longer safe to send the Chiricahuas, even those who had not committed depredations, to Fort Sill. Disaffected by their treatment in Florida, within six weeks of their arrival in Indian Territory, they would be armed and out again. This novel conclusion, he freely admitted, was based not on firsthand knowledge but on his judgment of the tribe's character observed during his visit to their reservation in July 1886. At that time he had said they were "insolent, violent, and restless." Now, he claimed, he had reliable information that they were planning another outbreak.[72]

As the next witness before the House Committee, Lieutenant Kennon, acting as Crook's spokesman, delivered a skillful rebuttal of Miles's testimony. But logic and fact seemed to play only minor roles in the deliberations. Fear of the Apaches was very palpable and prevalent throughout the Southwest. As unsupported and self-serving as Miles's testimony was, it accurately reflected the mood among whites in the region, their fears stoked by local politicians and by some territorial papers that fanned the flames with rumors of Apache depredations.[73] Unfortunately, not all their stories were fantasy. On March 1 a freighter named George Herbert was murdered, his wagon burned, and his horses stolen by "fiendish Apaches" at Point of Rocks near Phoenix. Though the army tracked down and—to the immense satisfaction of the Arizona public—killed two of the alleged perpetrators, the newspapers used the incident to whip up renewed hostility to "much petted Geronimo and his Apache fiends."[74]

Another circumstance worked against the bill. As the *Prescott Weekly Courier,* a paper firmly in Crook's camp, pointed out, the fate of the Chiricahuas had become thoroughly enmeshed in the feud between Crook and Miles, which had, against reason, survived Crook's promotion. The Miles faction feared that any decision to transfer the Indians to Fort Sill would be perceived as a tacit acknowledgement of the scouts' role in the Geronimo surrender, casting doubt on Miles's claim of exclusive credit for the surrender. That, in turn, could endanger his reputation and his career.[75]

Crook read accounts of the committee hearings with growing concern. In an effort to counter Miles's influence, he wrote a letter to General Howard pointing out that Miles had favored sending the Chiricahuas to Indian Territory following their surrender in 1886. Thus, "it would appear that his opposition [now] is based rather on personal grounds, than a desire that these Indians be treated with humanity and Justice." Pleading with Howard to use his influence with the philanthropic and religious community to correct the injustice to the Chiricahuas, he urged, "Whatever is done, should be done immediately, before the enemies of the bill succeed in poisoning the minds of the Committee. You know it is much easier to defeat, than to insure the success of a measure."[76]

Miles found an ally in the Mexican government, which raised its own objections to the transfer. Their consul in Washington wrote to the administration impugning the integrity of the scouts and claiming that if sent west, the Chiricahuas would return to their old haunts and resume their war against the Mexican people. Crook responded angrily to the consul's fears, dismissing them as "trumped up charges to affect any claim we may ever make for the killing of Capt. Crawford, which they too well knew was a most villainous affair."[77]

Unhappily, any support that Crook's friends in the Indian reform community could bring to bear on the bill was diluted by their lack of unanimity on where to send the prisoners. Herbert Welsh and the IRA had become convinced that North Carolina was the best place for the Chiricahuas. Avoiding entanglement in the Miles–Crook feud, Welsh campaigned vigorously in favor of his choice and against the Oklahoma site.[78]

Still, Crook's support for Fort Sill looked as though it might carry the day. On March 10, 1890, he wrote optimistically to the Boston Indian rights people that he trusted that their influence might be "extended to aid in obtaining for [the Chiricahuas] a location where they too may hope to have permanent homes and become self-respecting and self-supporting," by which he meant Fort Sill.[79] Then, less than two weeks later, Crook died. With his demise and the lack of agreement among those who might have assumed his mantle, interest in the issue in Congress and the administration waned, and the matter gradually faded from sight.

For the remainder of the Harrison administration, the Chiricahuas remained in limbo at Mount Vernon Barracks. Ironically, it was not until the reelection of President Cleveland in 1894 that the issue of their relocation was resurrected, and it was finally decided to move the tribe to Fort Sill as General Crook had recommended. On October 2, 1894, the 259 Warm Springs and Chiricahua Apaches who had survived captivity in Florida and Mount Vernon Barracks were dispatched to Fort Sill. There, the 45 children who had been shipped off to the Indian school in Carlisle, Pennsylvania, would later rejoin their families. Reports of the survivors' condition were dismal: "More than one-half of the men and nearly one-half of the women were unhealthy and crippled."

Technically still prisoners of war, the Chiricahuas remained at Fort Sill until 1913, when they were given the choice of staying in Oklahoma on farms that had been allocated to them in severalty or accepting transfer to the Mescalero Reservation in New Mexico. Seventy-six members of the tribe opted to stay in Oklahoma. The remainder, eager to return to the Southwest, resettled in New Mexico alongside their Mescalero cousins. Never allowed to return to Arizona, their descendants still reside on the Mescalero Reservation.[80]

What of their leadership? Both those who had ridden with Geronimo in 1885 and those who had helped hunt him down—Chihuahua, Naiche, and Chatto among them—worked hard to adapt to their captivity. They farmed or raised livestock, took Anglo-American names, became Christians, and joined the all-Indian army units formed at Mount Vernon Barracks and later at Fort Sill. Chihuahua died at Fort Sill in 1901, never returning to his beloved homeland. Naiche, son of Cochise, led the exodus to Mescalero and lived peacefully there until his death from influenza in 1919. Chatto paid for his loyalty to Crook. Ostracized by many of his fellow tribesmen, he lived apart from them at Mount Vernon. Longing to return to the Southwest, he chose to accompany Naiche to Mescalero, making a life for himself on the reservation until he died in an automobile accident in 1934.[81]

Geronimo, like Chihuahua, never again saw his homeland. Over the years at Mount Vernon and then at Fort Sill, the shaman, once resolutely committed to the Apache way, became, at least outwardly, a tame follower of the white man's road. He wore the white man's clothing, cultivated the soil, and finally, in 1903, agreed to be baptized after all of the other Apache leaders had accepted Christ. At the same time, he relished and even profited from his celebrity, posing at a price for occasional photos and selling handmade bows and arrows to curiosity seekers. In 1905, on the occasion of Theodore Roosevelt's assumption of the presidency, he agreed to ride beside his friend, the Comanche chief Quanah Parker, in the traditional inaugural parade in Washington. In return, he asked Roosevelt to allow him to return to his Arizona homeland. The president refused.[82]

In the end, Geronimo, invulnerable to the white man's guns, fell victim to his whiskey. On February 11, 1909, riding home in the early morning hours following a drinking bout in nearby Lawton, he fell from his horse. He lay unconscious, half-submerged in a pool of freezing water for the remainder of the night. Discovered by his fellow Apaches the following morning, he had contracted a chill that rapidly developed into pneumonia. He lingered for six days, hoping that a son and daughter could come from their distant Indian school to be with him in his final moments. Notified of his illness by letter instead of a telegram, they arrived too late to comfort the dying shaman, but they were able to attend his interment among members of his family in the Apache graveyard in a quiet shady corner of Fort Sill.[83]

CHAPTER TWENTY-FOUR

Omaha Sojourn

Characteristic of Crook's reticence, upon his return to the Platte in 1886 he left no personal records of the angst that he suffered as a result of his quarrels with Miles and Sheridan or the carping journalists, or of his frustrated efforts to help the imprisoned Apaches. Instead, he filled the pages of his diary with accounts of a relaxed lifestyle more typical of a retiree than the commander of a military department on the frontier. After a career marked by thirty-four years of more or less continual warfare, Crook had at last reached a safe harbor where, no longer buffeted by unremitting drama and violence, he enjoyed the company of an admiring and supportive public and had the time to take pleasure in the prerogatives earned after decades of arduous service.

From the date of their arrival in Omaha, General and Mrs. Crook embarked on a bustling social whirl that, if his diary is to be believed, filled almost every evening and many of their daylight hours. He set the tone that first evening, noting in his diary that at the reception held in his honor, there was "just sufficient wine to make all feel good without becoming drunk," an unusual commentary from the normally abstemious general.[1] In stark contrast to his Arizona diary entries, replete with frustrating and horrific references to Apache depredations, his Nebraska entries recount dinners, visits with friends and old comrades, card games, and even the occasional opera, concert, or light musical entertainment, all available in an increasingly urbanized Omaha. In previous postings he might have avoided these latter occasions. But now, usually with Mary at his side when she was not troubled by bouts of ill health or absent visiting family in Oakland, he attended them with evident relish, with only an occasional grumble about a boring evening.[2]

He hobnobbed with the city's elite: businessmen, railroad executives, and bankers, as well as with his fellow officers and their families. Among the many friends and acquaintances recorded meticulously in his diary, the name Jennie McClelland appears so often and in such contexts that readers might be forgiven for suspecting the general of an extramarital interest. But they would be mistaken. Though Jennie is never properly introduced to the reader, multiple entries, such as one describing Mrs. Crook and Jennie at an evening sewing dolls' dresses and another depicting a dance hosted by the general and his wife for Jennie and her friends at their residence, make it clear that Jennie was a youngster.[3] Probably twelve or thirteen years old, she was likely the child of the widow of a fellow officer. No Mr. McClelland was in evidence, and Mrs. McClelland, in the tradition of Victorian widows, kept a boarding house. Jennie joined a small coterie of young people—unnamed nephews and nieces, Charlie Roberts, Webb Hayes, and others—whom George and Mary, childless themselves, took lovingly into their lives.

Though social affairs occupied many of his leisure hours, the amount of space Crook devoted to hunting and fishing in his diary indicates that he was most content when so engaged. His hunts were no longer the near-daily frenetic, stress-relieving campaigns he had waged against the assorted pigeons, foxes, and quail of Arizona. They were more infrequent but lengthier and meticulously planned expeditions, organized and equipped with the same attention to detail Crook employed for his military campaigns, often including the same packers and scouts. Usually accompanied by a select cadre of like-minded sportsmen, he would head off into remote mountain country or to lakes and marshes, often for several days at a time and in all kinds of weather. Transportation was never a problem. Using rail passes freely available to high-ranking military personnel or special cars provided by prominent railroad executives whom he included in his party, he and his fellow sportsmen would travel in comfort to the depot nearest their destination. Then they would continue by wagons or horseback, frequently attended by a small escort of enlisted men, to the remote location where the best fishing and hunting could be found. Once there, the soldiers would set up camp and do the chores, while the notables fished or hunted during the days and wiled away the evening hours telling tall tales or playing cards.

The annual fall hunt had become a treasured tradition for Crook. Commencing in 1878, they continued each year to the end of his life, unless military exigency or ill health intervened. The general and his closest hunting companions went into the mountains of Wyoming or Montana to hunt bear, deer, elk, and mountain lions.

A frequent companion on these adventures was John S. Collins, a prosperous leather merchant from Omaha whose father had partnered with Jesse Grant, President Grant's father, in a tannery business in Galena, Ohio. Sometimes referred to by Crook as "Old Jack Pot," Collins had known the Gray Fox since the early 1870s when Grant had appointed the young man post trader at Fort Laramie. Later, after moving to Omaha, Collins's friendship with Crook had grown, nurtured by social affairs, a shared membership in the Omaha Gun Club, and the memories of numberless hunts and fishing trips throughout the West. Another member of the group was businessman and railroad executive Albert Touzalin. His position as president of the Chicago, Burlington, and Northern Railroad made him a welcome companion, as he could always ensure that the hunters traveled the rails in style and comfort. A third regular was Webb Hayes, the now-grown son of Crook's dear friend, former president Rutherford Hayes. From early childhood Webb had been a surrogate son for the childless Crooks. Each year Crook would plan the details of these annual hunts in bantering correspondence with the younger Hayes that betrayed the general's enormous affection for him and his anticipation at the thought of their spending time together.[4]

Crook's accounts of these hunting and fishing trips always included a tally of the animals taken. The sheer number of kills, the lack of effort to recover wounded animals, and the variety of game slaughtered reveal a profligate attitude toward wildlife that modern readers might find appalling, but such thinking was common at the time. In one day's hunt, Crook recorded that he "killed 11 deer and three elk. I was trying my telescopic sights at 4 & 500 yards at deer. Wounded several, killed one. I poisoned 5 magpies who had been eating my deer. Parties

Fall hunt, taken at Fort Washaki, circa 1886–87. Crook is seated in foreground. Standing (*left to right*) are fellow hunters John Collins, Albert Touzalin, Thaddeus Stanton, and Webb Hayes. Courtesy of Mark Kasal.

who went out after the elk and 4 deer failed to bring them in." The day before, he reported, "John Collins killed a badger and Mr. Hatch a wild cat and I a coyote," animals viewed as varmints suitable only for extermination. Occasionally, concerns about the wantonness of the slaughter would tentatively make an appearance in his diary. On the same day they slew the varmints, the general wrote, "Several antelopes were killed, but we stopped shooting at them as we had all the meat we wanted and the rest would spoil." During a fishing trip in Wisconsin, he wrote that he caught 135 bass. He could have caught many more, he said, but allowed that he "got ashamed."[5] Usually, however, Crook recorded his take with more than a little satisfaction, frequently noting that it exceeded those of his fellow hunters. He obviously had a competitive streak, certainly when it came to bagging fish and game.

In addition to descriptions of hunting adventures, Crook's diary entries during this period reflect an increasing preoccupation with his past, particularly his Civil War service. Perhaps this was a natural consequence of the aging process or maybe a consequence of the work he had begun on his memoirs. Frequently an entry would be triggered by the anniversary of a notable event in his career. On June 10, 1886, for instance, he reminisced about the arrow wound he had received on that date on the Pit River in California twenty-nine years before. Other entries recalled the Rosebud fight, "Custer's destruction," and Civil War conflicts in which he had played a critical role—Antietam, Cloyd's Mountain, and Lewisburg. The diary includes accounts of visits from officers, some long-retired and others in the latter stages of their careers, who shared reminiscences of these battles, making it easy to picture them in his office or around his dinner table chewing over old campaigns.[6]

Especially poignant is his description of the tenth reunion of the Society of the Army of West Virginia and his beloved Thirty-sixth Ohio Volunteer Infantry in Cincinnati in early September 1886. In prior years, preoccupied with the Apaches and perhaps not yet fully in the grip of nostalgia, he had not attended such events. In his absence, speeches delivered on his behalf by Rutherford Hayes are testament to his continued veneration by his former Eighth Corps comrades. In 1884, for example, the former president elicited loud applause from the veterans when he described Crook as an officer "never seeking popularity, but always having it, because he deserved to have it; the men believed in him, and he believed in them."[7]

When the general appeared at the tenth reunion two years later, the aging veterans of the Thirty-sixth, "Crook's Regulars," as they had been known during the war, had gripped his hand in greeting so warmly and so often that by the end of the day, it had become, he wrote, "a little tender." Deeply touched by their regard, he abandoned all attempts at grammar and syntax in a rare display of emotion: "I had never had my feeling stirred up since I have grown up," he wrote in his diary, "as they were at meeting the old gray headed soldiers whom when I had last met them . . . many of them boys not 20 years of age." Among those in attendance were Generals (President) Hayes, Benjamin Kelley, and Sheridan. Putting aside his public spat over the Apache scouts and his longstanding resentment at the lieutenant general's failure to acknowledge his contribution during the Civil War, Crook graciously introduced Sheridan when the latter rose to speak. By his account, the reunion was a huge success and he looked forward to the next one in Wheeling in a year's time. However, the press of other duties intervened, and he was unable to attend. Yet for the remainder of his life, the pull of old battles and former associates continued to draw him into his past.[8]

Crook's active lifestyle—most notably his participation in rigorous outdoor pursuits—bespoke a vigorous man in his prime. But the pages of his diary reflect that, in fact, his health was beginning to decline. By the 1880s both husband and wife had entered what in the nineteenth century would have been considered their senior years. Time and the hardships of a life spent on the frontier had left their mark on both. Mary suffered from rheumatism, neuralgia, and gout, ailments that accounted, at least in part, for her frequent trips to Maryland to enjoy the support of her family and a kinder climate.[9] George was troubled, particularly in warm weather, by debilitating fevers and headaches that signaled bouts of recurrent malaria. From time to time he also suffered from what the doctors termed chronic laryngitis. But of a far more serious nature, toward the end of 1886 he began recording symptoms that indicated the onset of heart disease. On December 12 he complained of "spasmodic pain in the ribs." Early in the new year, he reported that "walking up the hill strained my lungs and had some blood come from my windpipe." A subsequent examination revealed an enlarged heart and the "top of right lung affected." Seemingly undeterred by the diagnosis, Crook continued to maintain an active social and work schedule that included a visit and speaking tour in Boston at the invitation of the Indian reformers in January 1887. Malaria continued to plague him during the spring and summer of 1887. And during the following spring, he recorded awakening with chest pains and spitting blood. The once-vigorous general now had serious health issues.[10]

It may have been that these issues and an accompanying sense of his mortality spurred in him a concern for Mary's future financial well-being, or it may have simply been that he was now surrounded by men of wealth and influence and wanted his share. Whatever the reason, harking back to his Murchie mine venture, Crook became increasingly interested in schemes to augment his income. Prominent among these was a decision to write a memoir like that penned by Ulysses Grant. The latter, published in 1885, had enjoyed tremendous financial success. He also kept on the lookout for investment opportunities.

In April 1888, while still in Omaha basking in the glow of his recent promotion to major general, he accepted a suggestion from his old friend Thaddeus Stanton and bought a thousand shares in the King of the West, a silver mine that had gone into production six years before.[11] Other investments followed in the coming months.

While Crook's diary entries during this period may convey the lifestyle of a retiree, they by no means reflect the entirety of his life. While they contain few references to his official duties, in reality, as his correspondence shows, they continued to occupy a great deal of time and energy.

As Bourke and Roberts, his longtime aides, were no longer at his side, Crook needed a replacement. Among the important qualifications he seems to have considered in filling the position was the ability of the candidate to articulate the general's views in writing, a skill that a lifetime of experience told him he lacked. Fortuitously, a young infantry lieutenant appeared in Omaha who seemed well suited to his needs. Lyman Walter Vere Kennon was an 1881 graduate of West Point recently transferred to Omaha as acting chief engineer after meritorious service in Utah. At twenty-eight years of age, Lieutenant Kennon was a trim, soldierly officer of great initiative, energy, and wide-ranging talent, who possessed a quiet, unassuming manner that must have appealed to Crook. During the five years that had elapsed since his graduation from the academy, he had acquired a remarkably broad range of experience while serving on the Ute reservation in the Department of the Platte, including conducting a census of the tribe, managing a sawmill, building a road, and constructing a stockaded outpost for the protection of troops and supplies. He had also supervised the closure of a deactivated fort. But what surely attracted Crook's notice was the lieutenant's authorship of two works that had garnered intense interest among many in the officer corps. The first was a short pamphlet entitled "Duties of Guards and Sentinels." Despite its uninspiring title, this little handbook was so thorough that the government adopted it as an instruction manual, the first ever to outline the requirements of sentry duty, and distributed it to the troops. His other project, an article published in the prestigious *Journal of the U.S. Military Service Institution of the United States* entitled "Battle Tactics of Infantry," outlined his planned modernization of infantry tactics to conform to recent changes in weaponry. The work had been universally commended by

Lieutenant Lyman W. V. Kennon, Crook's aide, circa 1885. Author's collection.

officers throughout the army and was considered of such moment that it had already been translated into several languages for dissemination abroad. Eventually, it would result in the adoption of the first modernization of infantry tactics since Upton's work in the 1860s. Crook, who advocated similar changes, likely found the effort most interesting. In addition, Kennon had dashed off a study of the Seminole Wars, a strong indication of an interest in military history and Indian warfare in particular.[12] In sum, even a cursory review of the lieutenant's background must have convinced Crook that he had unearthed the perfect replacement for Captain Bourke as his next aide-de-camp. Perhaps, too, he had found someone who could help him to write his memoirs and the several articles he had in mind as a means to earn greater credit for his role in the Civil War. Happily, on July 1, 1886, Crook appointed the young lieutenant his aide-de-camp.[13]

With the addition of Kennon to his staff, Crook now had the capability to manage a military department in need of restructuring. Because of the cessation of Indian hostilities and the confinement of the tribes to reservations, Congress had determined to reduce the military budget and downsize the army. Pursuant to that initiative, Fort Thornburgh had already been dismantled and two additional posts, Fort Fred Steele and Camp Medicine Butte, were also scheduled for closure and their garrisons consolidated into fewer, but larger, forts.

Crook considered these realignments as an opportunity to introduce greater discipline and better training for his troops, but he first had to deal with the problems the changes caused. The sudden concentration of troops at fewer facilities created overcrowding on posts too small and decrepit to serve their garrisons properly. The general had always taken a great interest in the welfare of his command, and he now raised concerns about the inadequacy of the "old, illy-built and unhealthy buildings" that housed his men and officers. The enlisted quarters badly needed renovation. As for the officers, in an era when building supplies could be readily furnished to all posts by rail, he questioned "why an officer's quarters, which while in the service, are his only home, should not have the conveniences that are found in the ordinary houses occupied by civilians."[14]

If post housing was outdated, so were the training and the tactics employed by the frontier army. Training had always been scant for soldiers on the frontier, and, as Kennon had pointed out in his seminal article, tactics had never been modernized to match new and improved weaponry. Crook had always recognized the value of training, having prepared a regiment of undisciplined volunteers to fight during the Civil War.[15] As an outstanding marksman, he found it especially disturbing that any improvement in firepower brought about by the introduction of the newer repeating pistols and rifles had been for years notably diluted by the troops' woeful inability to shoot straight. In large measure, this was due to the army's failure to allow its recruits more than minimal practice using live ammunition. To remedy this situation, target practice was being carried out in his command with "unflagging zeal and enthusiasm" under the tutelage of his old subordinate, Major Guy Henry. Long recovered from the severe wounds he received at the Rosebud, Major Henry now functioned as Crook's inspector of rifle practice. Under his supervision the troops were required to spend more time on the firing range and engage in frequent competitions as an incentive to improved marksmanship.

Improved weapons training not only included marksmanship but also addressed changes in tactics intended to promote more effective use of modern firearms. If soldiers continued to use tactics designed for men fighting with single-shot muskets, Crook opined, "their skill in the use of a rifle is, to a great extent, thrown away." Updated tactics should accompany training in advanced weaponry. To that end, he modeled his training on actual field experience. Simulating campaign conditions, he had his recruits make lengthy marches while "equipped as for field service," after which they would "go into camp, and continue regular target practice for at least six days."[16]

Though Indians no longer roamed freely about the West, they were still popularly perceived as a menace. Thus, though distasteful to him, as departmental commander Crook had to deal with reports of troubles with the tribes, real or imagined. In August 1886, not long after his return to Omaha, it was the Utes, their various bands now consolidated on a single reservation in the southeastern reaches of his department, who drew his attention. Only a few years had passed since the Colorado Utes had been forced off their rich hunting grounds and sent to join their fellow tribespeople in Utah's desert country. Embittered by their exile, they did not get on well with the other bands. Their manifest discontent, the restlessness of their young warriors, and their annual custom of returning to their former range in Colorado for their spring hunt caused uneasiness among whites in that state. To meet these concerns and tighten control over the tribe, General Sheridan ordered Crook to establish a new military post to replace the recently deactivated Fort Thornburgh on the reservation near the Uncompahgre Agency, the new home of the former Colorado Utes.[17]

In search of a suitable site for the post, Crook, accompanied by Kennon and a cavalry escort, traveled to the Ute reservation in the sweltering heat of August. His decision to personally undertake the mission probably had something to do with the fact that the country afforded abundant opportunities for excellent trout fishing. Crook's diary entries reflect this, making the expedition appear to be something of a lark. But though he personally may have enjoyed the trek, the enlisted men who marched with him did not. By their account the expedition was extremely exhausting, requiring a forced march that included a stretch of thirty miles without water, undertaken in conditions that made the column vulnerable to attack. Even Crook admitted that toward the end, heavy rain and bad roads made travel difficult.[18]

On August 20 the departmental commander reached the Uintah River, where he rendezvoused with infantry companies from Fort Bridger. Shortly thereafter the force was confronted by a large party of anxious Indians, armed and in full war paint. They had been told that Crook and his soldiers had come to take away their reservation and put their chiefs in prison. Their anxieties only increased when they learned that two detachments of Ninth Cavalry Buffalo Soldiers were also on their way to the site. These black troops were under the command of Major Frederick Benteen, a survivor of the Little Big Horn. The Utes, somehow imbued with Anglo prejudice against blacks, were outraged at their presence, and it was only after Crook convinced them that they meant no harm and that they were officered by whites that tensions subsided.[19]

Having calmed the Indians, Crook selected a location for the post, which he named Fort Duchesne. Unfortunately for the troops who would build and garrison the fort, the spot chosen, though sited on a river bank, was situated on a flat, dusty plain with only an occasional sagebrush, shad bush, and prickly pear to break the monotony of its burning wastes. The soldiers watched in despair as the general described the task before them, mounted his wagon, and departed for Omaha. For his part, Crook seems to have assumed that he had adequately completed his mission, and he prepared to move on.[20]

But he had not heard the last of Fort Duchesne.

Though the Utes appeared to have been quiescent during this period, Major Benteen, who was responsible for the fort's construction, proved a problem. Four months after his return to Omaha, Crook was embarrassed to learn that the major had failed to complete his assigned task. As summer passed into fall and then winter, the fort, dubbed "Fort Damn Shame" by its forlorn garrison, remained unfinished while the troops huddled in tents on the open plain, buffeted by harsh winds and the pervasive dust storms that swept across its treeless expanse. Sheridan, incensed, demanded to know why the work had not been completed. Crook sent an inspector to investigate.[21]

Subsequent reports verified that the fort remained unfinished. Benteen blamed Crook and the location he had chosen. With justification, he claimed it was devoid of timber needed for construction and remote from a source of wood or any other building supplies. Crook's inspector, who admittedly disliked Benteen, discounted this explanation and instead found the major culpable. Benteen had a serious drinking problem, and in the inspector's opinion his frequent bouts of intoxication and his mismanagement of the project, rather than Crook's site selection, were the problem. After reviewing the matter, Crook court-martialed Benteen for dereliction and for conduct unbecoming, and he was subsequently convicted. Still, the general could hardly escape some blame for the fiasco, since it was he who selected the site and appointed the major to the task. That became painfully clear when late in the summer of the following year, well after the major's departure, a rueful Crook admitted that the post's buildings were "not as good as it was hoped they would be." Rather than accept responsibility, the general pointed to the lateness of the season in which the work began and the lack of appropriated funds.[22]

Nor did Fort Duchesne seem to overawe the Utes as had been intended. In August 1887 Crook was again bedeviled with rumors of unrest. That spring a party of tribesmen, including a band under Chief Colorow, had made their customary annual pilgrimage into the Colorado mountains. They drove before them herds of livestock that they planned to graze on the rich lands that they had formerly occupied, while they hunted to supplement their meager government rations. White Coloradans, especially those now occupying land formerly belonging to the tribe, felt threatened by their presence.

To encourage the Utes' departure, a posse formed to arrest several warriors for violating Colorado game laws, of which they were probably unaware, and for stealing two horses belonging to a local rancher, a misappropriation for which the tribe had already made restitution. When the posse confronted the band, fighting broke out and three Indians were wounded. The whites withdrew but returned within days and attacked and burned a Ute camp. Thoroughly alarmed by the posse's aggressiveness and fearing for the safety of their women and children, the Utes promised to leave the state as soon as they could gather their livestock. The posse refused to accept any delay and continued to harass the Indians. At this point, though the Coloradans now outnumbering the Utes by almost two to one, Governor Alva Adams, worried that they did not have enough firepower to wipe out the miscreants, wired General Crook asking for regular troops to back up his citizens.[23]

Crook was skeptical of the governor's claims of imminent danger. During his time on the frontier, he had heard many settlers and politicians cry wolf. In the present case, he firmly believed that Adams's fears were either the product of an overwrought imagination or, more likely, politically motivated. Not wanting his troops to become pawns in such a game, Crook, having been burned once by the doctrine of posse comitatus for his involvement in the Print Olive case, now invoked the concept to reject the governor's request. The army, he piously declared, could not become involved in a civilian effort to enforce criminal law, even where Indians were involved. Adams then asked Crook to force the Utes to return to their reservation. Again, the general refused, correctly stating that such a request would have to come from the Interior Department.[24] On August 25, while Crook was engaged in standing off the governor, the posse attacked the Indian camp. In a three-hour fight, they lost three men but managed to kill one warrior and three children before the Indians broke off the fight and fled into Utah, abandoning their stock and property.

Fearing that the Utes might return for their stock and to exact revenge on the settlers who had taken the animals, Adams asked the Interior Department to intervene, though the tribesmen were no longer in his state. As Adams was a powerful figure in President Cleveland's own party, Crook was ordered to confer with the governor and resolve the matter.[25] Accordingly, Crook and the Ute Indian agent duly met with Adams on August 31 and again on September 1. At these meetings the governor requested that troops be stationed on the Colorado line to prevent the Utes from reentering the state to reclaim their property.

Over the years Crook had been required many times to execute government Indian policies that plainly conflicted with his concepts of justice and fairness. In many instances, he had been forced to comply, though he knew that doing so would aggravate rather than resolve the situation. In this case he decided not to allow himself to fall into that trap. He doubted that the Utes would attack, and if they did, he knew that his troops would have little chance of preventing them from crossing into Colorado. Blame would then fall on his command, not the governor. So he refused Adam's request and tartly suggested that the proper means to assure that the Utes would not return was to restore to them their missing animals: according to Crook, 300–400 horses and about 2,500 sheep and goats. Until that was done, he declared, the army would not be responsible in any way "for the Utes behaving themselves." On September 2, having said his piece, he returned to Omaha.[26]

Crook's interaction with Governor Adams demonstrated Crook's growing willingness to defy political constraints when they ran counter to common sense and his own sympathy for the Indians. He laid out the case for his superiors: "From the outset the Indians were, with but one slight interruption, pursued incessantly; in every case the whites were the aggressors and fired first. Colorow had no desire whatever to fight, and made use of his weapons in self-defense only for the protection of his women and children and his herds. During the whole time they were pursued . . . five Indians died from effect of wounds received, viz: one 'buck,' one large boy, one small boy and two small girls. Seven others were wounded, one perhaps mortally."[27] He further pointed out that Colorow had resisted his pursuers only because he had been forced to retreat in haste through territory thickly settled by hostile whites, while hindered by the need to protect his women and children as well as his herds. Alluding to allegations that the Indians had committed depredations, he said that they had only been accused of killing cattle. To that charge, he responded, "In a country containing many reckless and unprincipled white men, it is as likely that cattle were killed by them as by Indians." He concluded by reporting that Colorow and his people were now quietly settled on their reservation. If their stock was returned to them, there would be no reason why they would not remain so.

Ultimately, his confidence was justified. Though only a small fraction of the stock taken (125 horses) was ever returned to the Utes, the tribe remained at peace, ending the affair.[28] Though Crook was obviously unaware of it at the time, this would be the last occasion in his long career when he would be called upon to intercede in a conflict between the western tribes and Euro-Americans.

CHAPTER TWENTY-FIVE

Chicago

On April 6, 1888, just two years following his return to Omaha, Crook received word of his promotion to major general and his reassignment to Chicago. The news reached him in Cheyenne, Wyoming, while he was calling at the home of Captain Roberts and en route to Salt Lake to visit old friends. After receiving word of the promotion, he tarried a short time to celebrate the occasion with Roberts and his family. At the time the two officers likely discussed the possible transfer of the captain to the general's staff in Chicago, because not long afterward Roberts joined him in the Windy City, resuming his position as aide-de-camp.[1]

Mary was not with her husband in Cheyenne when he received the welcome news, having returned to Maryland for one of her regular sojourns with family and friends. Though frequent separations were a regular feature of their marriage and Crook made no reference to it in his diary, he must have regretted her absence at this auspicious moment. But he was a soldier and used to disappointments. And after a short stay in Cheyenne, he resumed his journey to Salt Lake.

Arriving in the city on a Saturday evening, he spent the better part of a week visiting his old comrade, Paymaster Thaddeus Stanton, taking in the sights of the capital of Mormonism and luxuriating in the felicitations of friends and admirers. He then returned to Omaha to wind up his affairs and prepare for his reassignment to Chicago. To his delight, waiting on his desk upon his return were "a hat full" of congratulatory letters and telegrams. With ill-disguised pride, he confided to his diary that it took him the better part of several days to reply to them all.[2]

Over the next two weeks, warmed by the congratulatory atmosphere that pervaded the town in reaction to his promotion, the unseasonably cold and rainy weather hardly dampened his spirits. He spent his evenings with admiring friends like Judge Dundy, who had presided in the Ponca case; Colonel Henry, his valued comrade from Sioux War days; John Collins, his old hunting buddy; and, of course, Mrs. McClelland and her daughter, Jenny. Despite the bustle of activities, he made time to attend a reception given by a local national guard unit and looked on with pride as they presented young Lieutenant Kennon with a dress sword in gratitude for his work in training them. Nor, in all the excitement, did he neglect his Indian friends or Lee, his Chinese cook. On April 19 he sent Young Man Afraid of His Horse, a favorite Oglala stalwart, a gift of three turkeys and seven chickens, and on May 1 he noted that Lee, who apparently would not be accompanying the general to Chicago, "had his papers fixed up," a task that Crook undoubtedly helped him to complete.[3]

On April 24 Crook formally notified the adjutant general of his acceptance of the promotion to major general; and on May 1 he took the prescribed oath of office.[4] The good-byes continued for another three days, ending with a lavish banquet held in his honor at Omaha's Union Club on May 4. Crook thoroughly enjoyed the occasion, noting that "wine flowed freely" and "a lively time" was had by all. The festivities lasted well into the morning hours and must have had their sentimental moments, including the solemn presentation by Lee to his general of a handkerchief as a parting gift.[5] The following morning the general awoke, bleary-eyed, one would imagine, to a heavy rain. But the sky cleared in the afternoon, so that, he wrote, "we had a nice day to leave Omaha." Accompanied by Lieutenants Kennon and Green, who would continue to serve as his aides at his new post, and by his faithful striker, Andrew Peisen, and Peisen's wife and children, he boarded a special car put on for the occasion by the railroad. Amid the cheers of a crowd of military and civilian onlookers, the train pulled out of Omaha's Union Station on schedule, bearing its famous passenger to his new life.[6]

Crook's arrival in the Windy City marked a substantial change in his circumstances. Though he had visited Chicago often in the course of his career, chiefly to call on Sheridan at his headquarters, he had never resided in such a distinctly urban environment. Omaha had experienced considerable growth during the 1880s, but it was still basically a frontier town of perhaps thirty thousand residents. Chicago, on the other hand, was one of the fastest-growing cities in the world, boasting a population of over half a million souls in 1880, a number that would double by 1890. The Chicago Fire of 1871 had spurred the modernization of the city; with its huge labor pool and central location, it had become almost overnight the commercial and transportation hub of the Midwest. So the old campaigner and former Ohio farm boy, having spent most of his career on the frontier or in the field, must have found his new surroundings a bit daunting.[7]

He arrived on a Sunday morning and was met at the depot by one of his subordinates, Colonel Judson D. Bingham, the division's quartermaster. He spent the night at the Leland Hotel, a luxurious accommodation centrally located on Michigan Avenue with views of the lake. The next morning he inspected his offices at division headquarters in the Pullman Building. They were impressive, occupying the fifth and sixth floors of the edifice, an imposing, ten-story turreted structure. Built after the Great Fire, it had space for commercial establishments, offices, and, on its top floors, residential suites. As the army did not provide him with housing, Crook investigated the suites with an eye to perhaps taking rooms there. But he decided that despite the convenience of living and working at the same address, he preferred to stay at the more recently renovated Leland Hotel. He would remain there for some months before moving to the Calumet Club, and finally settle into more commodious quarters at the Grand Pacific Hotel, one of the most prominent hotels in the city, when Mary finally arrived from Oakland in November.[8]

Crook's social life in Chicago, at least as he recorded it in his diary, replicated in many respects the one that he had left in Omaha, but at a more exalted level. His new status and reputation afforded him access to the city's wealthy elite in both the private and public sectors. As befitted his new rank and Chicago's greater size and importance, his friends and associates were far wealthier and more prominent than those he had known in Nebraska. The names of many still resonate today in the history of American enterprise, among them Marshall Field and

John Wanamaker, department store magnates; Peter Studebaker, of the carriage trade; and the Armours, founders of the meatpacking empire. While he attended, and by his account enjoyed, social events at their homes and clubs, he appears to have felt most comfortable, particularly in Mary's absence, among friends from his recent past, many of whom came regularly to Chicago for visits. As he had always done, he also maintained close ties to members of his staff. His diary reflects firm friendships with Colonels Robert Williams and Henry Corbin, his assistant adjutant generals, and with his aides Lieutenants Kennon and Green. Childless and often alone, he drew pleasure from attending their family gatherings, at which he could play games with their children. He remained an ardent card player, attended the theater on occasion, and, of course, continued to fish and hunt with longtime companions like Webb Hayes and John Collins, though these outings now became more infrequent. Adapting to his urban environment, he took long rides almost daily for exercise and to explore his new surroundings. Either on horseback or by carriage he visited various parts of the city, particularly its numerous parks, often accompanied by Colonel Williams, after which the two men would repair to the colonel's home for a meal and a romp with the children.[9]

Within days after his arrival, Crook received a visit from General Sheridan. For several days the two men seem to have put aside their differences and socialized extensively. Together they attended a "magnificent affair" given by Marshall Field and others to honor the new major general. Crook recorded that twenty-three local luminaries attended who, he noted with perhaps a touch of envy, possessed a combined wealth of $40 million. Several days later he was present at a second function where he counted thirty-one attendees possessed of an aggregated wealth he estimated at $475 million. This was truly heady stuff for the son of a frontier farmer. These occasions surely challenged his modest, self-effacing personality. At one lavish entertainment held in his honor, he found himself seated at a table with several generals. Looking up, he saw, with some embarrassment, a huge bouquet of roses in the center of the table. Violets had been used to spell out "The Hero of the Apaches" on one side and on the other "Fisher's Hill," a reference to a Civil War victory.[10]

By introducing Crook to a world of great wealth and luxury, Chicago society exposed him to existing opportunities to amass great fortunes. His new friends took him to visit the Board of Trade, opening his eyes to possibilities for investment at a time when he continued to harbor concerns for Mary's security in the event he predeceased her. Over the years he had earned little beyond his modest pay as a soldier, and his few forays into private enterprise to augment his salary had yielded not much in the way of accumulated assets.[11] His attempts at ranching and mining investments had produced meager results. Now, as diary entries reveal, his attention turned to the commodities market, especially wheat and corn. Here, too, he appeared to have met with little success. On August 31, 1888, not long after his move to Chicago, he noted that he had "sold wheat at a sacrifice." That fall he observed a boom in both futures but made no mention whether he had profited from either. Judging from past performance, it is probable that he had sold out too soon.[12]

Neither his promotion nor occasional health problems curbed Crook's urge to travel. If anything, his new status afforded him the time, opportunity, and means to indulge his curiosity about a country that had changed greatly during his years on the frontier and to revisit places and individuals from his past. His duties as a division commander together with the developing rail system and his entitlement to free travel greatly facilitated such adventures. In his diary he recorded in loving detail his official travels, usually to inspect various facilities under his command. He also took excursions for pleasure, attending reunions of Civil War veterans and indulging his love of hunting. Sometimes he traveled for no apparent purpose other than to see the sights offered by the fast-growing nation.[13]

No longer were these trips burdensome journeys requiring many days jolting over dust-choked trails in rickety ambulances or crowded stagecoaches. Now he luxuriated in the comfort of Pullman cars that whisked him over unimaginable distances while he slept peacefully in his berth. Wherever his travels took him, his rank entitled him to almost royal treatment, which he seems to have taken in stride as the well-earned reward for long and difficult years of service.

In April 1889 the general made one of his most interesting trips. Accompanied by Mary, he traveled to New York City to represent the army at the celebration of the one hundredth anniversary of President Washington's inauguration. He described sidewalks lined with crowds so thick that the police were forced to use their clubs to keep them back; a Naval Review ("hundreds of vessels of all descriptions scattered along the line"); a grand ball ("6 to 10,000 people present"); a military parade ("a very credible affair"); and the fireworks ("very insignificant for such an occasion") filling the pages of his diary with untypically generous detail. President Cleveland was in attendance, and Crook, still in his favor, called on him during the festivities. He and Mary returned to Chicago exhausted but exhilarated by the experience.[14]

Despite the impression often created by Crook's diary entries, his days as a divisional commander were not all Pullman cars, wine, and roses. His promotion had elevated him to a position of broad responsibility over much of the trans-Mississippi West. He now found himself in a more sophisticated and powerful milieu, not only socially but also professionally, and it is very likely he was somewhat outside his comfort zone. Lieutenant Kennon had accompanied him to Chicago, and Captain Roberts would soon join them. But he surely missed the intellectual and urbane perspective that John Bourke had lent to his staff, and though he would never admit it, he undoubtedly missed the captain's comradeship. So he asked that he be reassigned to him in Chicago.

Unlike Roberts, however, Bourke had little interest in rejoining the general and refused the assignment. He held ambitions of his own that could not be satisfied by resuming his position as Crook's aide-de-camp, a posting that ensured that his superior would always overshadow his best efforts. During the years 1888 and 1889, Bourke, still a captain, had actively lobbied for a transfer to an assignment in the War Department that might earn him promotion to major. He fixed on a job in the inspector general's office. As commander in the Platte, Crook had vigorously championed Bourke's efforts while also promoting Captain Roberts in an ultimately unsuccessful campaign for an assignment to the judge advocate general's department. On Bourke's behalf, he had written a lengthy letter to President Cleveland lauding the captain's "brilliant and meritorious service." But despite Crook's strong endorsement, Bourke, like Roberts, failed to win the post. He had fallen out of favor, apparently, with both the president and his erstwhile supporter, General Sheridan, after criticizing the army's handling of the Chiricahua prisoners. The coveted appointment went to Captain Lawton, who, much to Bourke's annoyance, was touted as the "captor of Geronimo."[15] Bourke made two further attempts that year to transfer into the War Department bureaucracy, but these too came to nothing, again likely because he remained in disfavor with the Cleveland administration.

When Benjamin Harrison, a Republican, assumed the presidency in March 1889, Bourke renewed his efforts to obtain a transfer, this time to a position in the adjutant general's office. Unfortunately for Bourke, Captain Roberts applied for the same position. Both, of course, asked Crook for his endorsement, placing the general in the awkward position of having to choose between two longtime and valued aides. Crook chose to support Roberts's candidacy. Perhaps this was because the latter had served at his side off and on since the Civil War, much longer than Bourke. Or perhaps he was miffed by Bourke's refusal to join Crook's staff in Chicago. Whatever his reason, Bourke was deeply offended by Crook's decision.[16]

The general seemed oblivious to the upset he had caused. That spring, as the competition for the posting heated up, Crook arrived in Washington to preside over a court-martial. While in the city he called on Captain and Mrs. Bourke on at least two occasions, apparently behaving as though nothing was amiss. As he was about to depart on April 5, Crook visited Bourke a last time. The general omitted reference to the occasion in his diary, but Bourke described it in detail. When Bourke asked him point-blank for his support in filling the vacancy, Crook indicated his preference for Roberts, even as he admitted that he did not think the man stood "a ghost of a show." Bourke's wife then asked why the general preferred to support Roberts rather than her husband, as the latter had a better chance at getting the job. In Bourke's words, Crook "hemmed and hawed" and "squirmed like a drunken monkey." The next day Crook, who apparently continued to be insensible to the hurt he had caused, sent Kennon to borrow one of the captain's diaries for the general's use. Bourke reacted angrily, recording:

> After all my hard work under General Crook, I felt his treatment of me was ungrateful: therefore, as a matter of self-respect, I must withdraw from any efforts in his behalf—I didn't intend to become an enemy to Crook: the past was past: it could not come back again. . . . Crook was as much account to me as an old spittoon: he had no further use for me, I, no use for him.[17]

In the end neither Bourke nor Roberts won the desired appointment. It went to Arthur MacArthur (father of Douglas), a decision that Bourke bitterly attributed to politics rather than merit.[18] Roberts joined Crook's staff, but Bourke continued to steadfastly refuse. The relationship between Crook and Bourke, once so close, cooled perceptibly. For a period they were so estranged that rather than speak directly, they communicated through Lieutenant Kennon.

In a bizarre twist, following Crook's subsequent appointment to the Sioux commission (see chapter 26), Bourke contacted him, presumably through Kennon, to express an interest in an assignment for himself on the commission staff. The general wrote to Kennon that while he thought that "all of the work in the Commission will have to be done by myself individually, I will be glad to have Bourke go with the Commission." Bourke must then have asked Crook to intervene directly to request his detail to the commission. But the general did not think that he should directly involve himself in the process. To Kennon he wrote, "Tell Bourke that this being a civil commission and I only one of its members that it wouldn't be the correct thing for me to ask for anybody, but for him to see the Sec of War and ask to be sent in the same capacity as he went to the Apaches by Gen. Sheridan's orders."[19] Such punctiliousness was unusual in the Gilded Age. More likely Crook could not let go of his pique at Bourke's refusal to join his staff, a manifestation of his reluctance to part with old grudges. Else why would he pass up a chance to mend fences with the captain with this simple gesture? Looked at from another perspective, the incident also demonstrates Bourke's own shortcomings in his willingness to ask a favor of someone he felt had wronged him.[20] In the end Bourke proved to have the greater generosity of spirit, putting aside his disappointments to write *On the Border with Crook*, a work describing Crook's character and achievements in almost hagiographic terms. Recognized today as a classic, at the time of its publication it secured for the general a prominent place in the history of the western frontier.

CHAPTER TWENTY-SIX

The Sioux Commission

With perhaps the sole exception of the Apaches' imprisonment, the dominant issue for Crook during his tenure in Chicago was the matter of Indian land, particularly on the Great Sioux Reservation. Powerful forces, both political and economic, coveted this huge block of territory guaranteed to the tribe under the Fort Laramie Treaty of 1868. Though in 1876 the government had seized the Black Hills, a part of the reservation, Anglo-American lust for Lakota land had hardly been slaked.

The treaty and subsequent legislation in 1877 confirmed the Sioux nation's title to a vast landscape that sprawled over most of present-day western South Dakota, an entitlement that blocked commercial interests in the Black Hills from direct access to the Missouri River and commercial markets farther to the east. From the perspective of white settlers and land speculators, a mere 24,000 Indians occupied an area of 43,000 square miles and made scant use of it, at least in the opinion of those who sought to exploit it. To westerners the situation cried out for reform.

Efforts to chip away at Lakota lands predated the Sioux War. But the first comprehensive assault on the Great Sioux Reservation was made by Richard Pettigrew, a delegate to Congress from Dakota Territory. In 1882, backed by Dakota politicians and businessmen, he added last-minute language to an appropriations bill authorizing the creation of a commission to assess the tribes' willingness to part with a portion

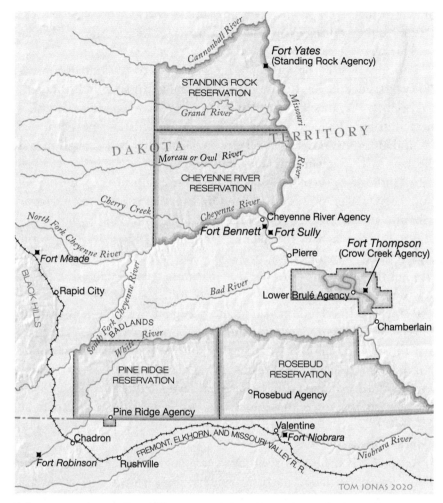

Lakota reservations at time of Sioux commission visit, 1889. Map by Tom Jonas.

of their lands. In return, he proposed that the Sioux nation receive confirmed legal title to five separate reserves carved out of the existing reservation. The tribesmen living on these reserves would receive allotments of land as their own private holdings: 320 acres for each family, supplemented by an additional 80 acres per child. In addition, the Sioux would receive the education and training to allow them to farm their new holdings. Any lands remaining within the reserves following the allotment process would then be opened to white settlement. Not incidentally, the boundaries of the new reserves would be drawn in such a way as to open up a broad corridor between eastern Dakota and the Black Hills and free up 17,000 square miles of Indian land for white settlement.[1]

The appeal of Pettigrew's plan to deed lands to the Indians in severalty extended beyond those greedy for the tribal land and its potential bounty. Private ownership of real property had an almost mystical attraction for nineteenth-century Americans, and reformers who led the Indian rights movement, fervent in their belief that capitalism was the key to the advancement of civilization, were no exception. As tribal authority rested in large measure on communal ownership of land, they viewed possession of land in severalty as a means to destroy tribalism and instill capitalist values among the new landowners. Placing title to the land in the hands of individual Indians would, in the eyes of the reformers, direct their interests toward themselves and their families rather than toward the welfare of the tribe. Their assimilation into white society would, they supposed, follow naturally.[2]

Reformers like Herbert Welsh also accepted the argument that the tribes now held more land than they could productively use. They saw that the government would inevitably appropriate the land it wanted. If instead the Indians could realize some funds from the seizures, they would be able to invest it to better themselves. Moreover, the reformers claimed that reducing the size of the reservations would force the Indians into closer proximity with the whites, promoting rapid assimilation.[3]

As for Crook, he was well aware of Anglo-Americans' insatiable desire for Indian lands and its inevitable impact on the reservations. While sympathetic to the plight of Native Americans, he was also a realist. Addressing the Lakota chiefs, he told them:

> The White men in the East are like birds. They are hatching out their eggs every year, and there is not room enough in the East, and they must go elsewhere, and they come out West, as you have seen them coming until they overrun all of this country; and you can't prevent it, nor can the President prevent it. Everything is decided in Washington by the majority, and these people come out West and see that the Indians have a big body of land that they are not using and they say, "we want the land."[4]

He also shared with his friends in the Indian reform movement the belief that many positive benefits to the Indians would accrue from Pettigrew's proposal. At least the Indians would get something for their lands. Moreover, he, too, thought that an allotment system would hasten the Indians' assimilation into white society, his own long-term solution to the so-called Indian problem. But while Crook saw land reform as an essential step in a process he believed would advance Indians up the ladder of civilization, it was not, he warned, a magic bullet. It must be implemented gradually: "We must not drive the Indian too fast in effecting these changes. We must not try to force him to take civilization immediately in its complete form." If properly introduced, however, he was optimistic that severalty would work, telling a Boston audience in 1887, "Under just laws guaranteeing to Indians equal civil laws, . . . the Indian question . . . will soon be a thing of the past."[5]

Crook's experiences in Arizona had given him an exaggerated confidence in the beneficent effects of land ownership. In 1886 he had written in glowing terms of the conversion of the once warlike Apaches at San Carlos into peaceful capitalists by their experiences on the land. "The Apache is becoming a property owner. It is his property, won by his own toil, and he thrills at once with the pride of acquisition, and the anxiety of possession. He is changing both inside and out: exteriorly he dresses in white man's garb, wholly or in part. Mentally he is counting the probable value of his steers and [is] interested in knowing how much of his crop the quartermaster may want next month."[6] Crook also found great appeal in the reformers' assertion that smaller land holdings would bring the Sioux into greater contact with the whites. Holding that the Indian "will be eventually absorbed by the whites," he believed that living in proximity would foster a "community of interest" between Indians and whites that would further promote the assimilation of the former into the latter's superior culture.[7]

The only obstacle to acquiring Sioux lands was the Fort Laramie Treaty's stipulation that approval by three quarters of the male members of the tribe was required to make any alterations in the reservation's boundaries. It was upon this rock that Pettigrew's proposal foundered. According to its enabling legislation, the Sioux commission was only supposed to "go among the Sioux and find out if the Indians were willing to sell their surplus lands."[8] But under the guidance of its chair, former Dakota governor and Yankton entrepreneur Newton Edmonds, the commissioners had no interest in exploring Indian attitudes. They only wished to make a deal. Ignoring their mandate, they set out to convince the Sioux leadership to assent to the purchase of about half the reservation lands in return for clearly inadequate compensation. In their zeal to obtain their objective, they used misinformation, coercion, and outright fraud. Despite blandishments and threats, however, they failed to secure the necessary signatures to win approval. Their lies and blatant efforts at bribery and extortion aroused opposition from the Indian rights groups and engendered deep suspicion in the minds of the Sioux, making the work of those who followed in Pettigrew's footsteps far more difficult. An embarrassed Congress ultimately disavowed the commission's work and shelved the entire project.[9]

Yet the concepts behind Pettigrew's initiative continued to mesmerize reformers and exert enormous political and economic appeal to Westerners. Ironically, the prime mover in carrying the plan forward was a reform-minded senator from Massachusetts, Henry L. Dawes, who was widely considered a friend of the Indians. Though an easterner, Dawes had long espoused interest in the West and its indigenous peoples. A veteran legislator, he served in the House of Representatives from 1856 to 1875 and then in the Senate until 1893. During the 1880s he developed a close relationship with the Boston Indian rights advocates and with Herbert Welsh and his IRA. In doing so, Dawes became an ardent advocate of their doctrine of assimilation, regarding the reservation system as nothing more than a training ground to bring Indians into white society. When the need for reservations had been fulfilled, he declared, they "will pass like snow in the springtime."[10] Impatient to see this occur quickly, Dawes ignored the reality of Sioux resistance to the idea of ownership of land in severalty.[11] As chair of the Committee on Indian Affairs in the Senate, he relentlessly pursued the concept as the true means to bring civilization to the Indians. Like Crook, he believed that unless he did so, growing political pressure would result in more draconian solutions that deprived the Indians of all reservation lands.[12]

In 1887 Dawes's efforts produced legislation that tested the limits of paternalism, turning the idea of severalty into a mandate to be imposed on the tribes for their own good. The General Allotment Act, popularly known as the Dawes Act, applied to all Indians in the United States with the exception of certain tribes, like the Cherokees, already deemed "civilized." The act was sweeping in scope, authorizing the president to survey any reservation at his discretion and then redistribute its lands in plots—in most cases 160 acres in size—to individual Indians as private property. Recipients of such acreage would become officially detribalized and consequently entitled to U.S. citizenship and the rights and protections it afforded. Land left over after distribution of individual holdings—and in many cases (most obviously the Great Sioux Reservation) that acreage would be substantial—would then be opened up for sale to white settlers under terms stipulated in the Homestead Act. The proceeds would be held in trust by the Interior Department "for the benefit of the tribe."[13]

The act was hailed as a long-overdue solution to the "Indian problem." Thousands of acres of what land promoters advertised as prime farming and grazing land would now be available for settlement, and the Indians would be brought into the American mainstream, all at one stroke. But more was to come. A year later, in 1888, Congress passed the Sioux Land Act. The citizens of the Dakota Territory grew ecstatic. Dawes's initial legislation had called for surveys at the outset, followed by allotments to the Indians. Only then would the surplus land be sold to settlers. Under the new law, however, fearing that the allotment process would delay land sales, Congress authorized the opening of Sioux lands to whites before the survey and allotment process had been completed.[14]

The act envisioned the immediate establishment of the separate smaller reserves Pettigrew had proposed, making available over nine million acres of so-called excess land that would be bought from the Sioux by the government for 50 cents an acre. This vast acreage would promptly be offered for resale to settlers at $1.60 an acre under the Homestead Act. Like its predecessor law, the Sioux Land Act stipulated that after deduction for "expenses," all proceeds from the sale of Sioux lands would go to the Interior Department to be held for the future benefit of the tribes. Interest earned on the amount would be used to provide the Sioux with "educational benefits" and livestock, seeds, and tools to help the new Indian farmers get started on their allotments.[15]

The only impediment to the implementation of the act was the same obstacle that had destroyed Pettigrew's initiative: the treaty requirement that three quarters of the adult male members of the tribe approve the alienation of Sioux lands. The Cleveland administration, as well as some in Congress, reluctant to ignore the treaty, believed that a sincere effort had to be made to sell the skeptical Sioux on the new plan.[16] Many politicians thought that Crook's intercession would be of great value in this regard, viewing his prestige among the Sioux as a key to convincing the tribe to part with much of their territory.[17] Perhaps this consideration had lurked in the shadows as an unspoken reason for his recent promotion. No one could gainsay that he had earned the rank after a lifetime of service and that his handling of Indian affairs had certainly helped U.S. western expansion, but another important consideration was the esteem, and in some cases fear, with which he was regarded by the western tribes and his consequent ability to influence them.

Predictably, another commission was created, and Crook was invited by Secretary Endicott to join it. At first, wary of committing to a course that might reflect poorly on his reputation with the Indians, he indicated cautiously that he would be willing to serve, but only if no other suitable officer could be found. When the secretary persisted, Crook declined, influenced by "recent information from Pine Ridge," which undoubtedly related to Sioux opposition to the allotment plan. Candidly, he told Endicott that if he chaired such a commission, "I should probably be held responsible for all its acts and for any trouble growing out of this new law. Such service would almost certainly destroy my usefulness in any future trouble which may arise with these Indians."[18] His reasoning would prove prescient.

Captain Richard H. Pratt was selected in his stead. Known for his interest in the welfare of the Indians, Pratt was the founder and main engine behind the Carlisle Indian School, and he was considered by the administration to be the ideal person to sell the Indians on Dawes's plan. Unfortunately, the Sioux viewed him in a different light. Already deeply suspicious of the allotment plan because of their experiences with the Edmunds commission, they saw Pratt as the man who had forcibly taken children from their families and removed them to the far-away Carlisle, Pennsylvania, Indian school, from which many never returned.[19] They were quick to rebuff his initiative.

At Standing Rock, one of the new reservations, the Hunkpapas (Sitting Bull's people) and the Yanktonais stonewalled for a month while Pratt cajoled, promised, and finally threatened. In the end only twenty-two Indians touched the pen. Lower Brulé and Crow Creek reservations produced better results, but the numbers still fell far short. Pine Ridge, Rosebud, and Cheyenne River were united in opposition to the agreement. Humiliated by their failure, the commissioners denounced Sioux obstinacy and recommended that the government implement the legislation without the tribes' consent. But under pressure from reformers, the administration refused to abandon the treaty requirement of Indian approval for the land grab.[20]

The subsequent election of Republican Benjamin Harrison to the White House left unchanged the commitment to abide by the treaty stipulation and actually strengthened the popularity of the legislation's concepts, now supported by an odd coalition of politicians, business interests, and reformers. Harrison appointee John W. Noble, the new secretary of the interior, and his commissioner of Indian affairs, Thomas J. Morgan, were both ardent assimilationists firmly in the reformers' camp on the issue of land severability. At the same time, the new administration was under considerable pressure from western Republican politicians to open up Sioux lands to whites. Dakota Territory was about to be admitted to the Union as North and South Dakota, and reservation acreage was a crucial issue for the territory's solidly Republican voters.

In March 1889 Congress passed a new Sioux act with additional inducements to bring the Indians around.[21] The price of the reservation land sold to whites was increased, as were the acreage to be allotted to each Indian family and the funds allocated for them to develop it. To neutralize opposition from many Lakotas reluctant to see the end of communal ownership of tribal lands, the act stipulated that the allotment program would not be implemented until a majority of the adult males had voted in favor of it. Finally, as a sweetener for the Pine Ridge Oglalas and Red Cloud, still one of the most influential chiefs and a vigorous opponent of the bill, the legislation included compensation for ponies that had been seized from his band during the Sioux War of 1876, an outstanding issue the government had neglected to resolve for more than a decade.[22]

Yet another Sioux commission was created to sell the new deal to the Sioux. Its members were instructed to submit the revised terms to the bands for an up or down vote. If rejected, then and only then were its members authorized to make further concessions to obtain the necessary consent.[23] Two of the three Harrison appointees to the commission were political appointees with no Indian experience. Charles Foster, its chair, was a former Republican governor of Ohio, while William Warner had been mayor of Kansas City, a Republican congressman from Missouri, and was now president of the Grand Army of the Republic, the powerful organization of Union war veterans. But it was Harrison's third appointment, Major General George Crook, who gave the body its substance. This time he accepted the assignment.[24]

Few questioned the choice. Respected and trusted by the Sioux, he was purported to "think like an Indian." His reputation for integrity would give comfort to the Indians and, to the reformers, lend credibility to the process. To these qualifications, a noted historian has added that "when [the Sioux] thought of him, they saw regiment on regiment of cavalry standing in their ranks, ready if he lifted his arm. Rightly or wrongly, the Sioux saw in the coming of Crook a threat." Truly, the Indians accorded the general more trust than they did most whites. But it was also undeniable that, whether in uniform or mufti, he certainly "revived unpleasant memories" among the Sioux.[25] For all these reasons, Three Stars (while the Apaches knew him as the Gray Fox, the Sioux called him by this name) was the only commission member familiar to the Indians and the only one who commanded their respect. Upon his shoulders would fall the burden of convincing them of the efficacy of the legislation.[26]

Why, after previously refusing, did Crook agree to take on this task? As usual, he did not make his reasons clear. Possibly he was motivated by the better terms offered under the new legislation or by the chance to curry favor with the new Republican administration. But his primary motivation was most likely that he viewed this bill as the last opportunity for the Sioux to realize some benefits from the inevitable loss of their lands. Whatever moved him, to his diary he merely confided that he received a telegram from Secretary Noble "wanting me to go on the Indian Commission."[27]

Less than a week after Crook's appointment, on April 12, Red Cloud and a delegation of Sioux leaders called on him in Chicago. What they talked about remains unknown. But as the chief was en route to Washington on a doomed mission to argue against the new legislation, it is fair to presume that the act was discussed, and the general was apprised of the tribe's continuing opposition to its terms. These conversations undoubtedly gave Crook much to think about. Later that month he traveled to Boston, intending to consult with reformers and possibly assuage doubts he may have had about involving himself in this enterprise. In this he was frustrated. The Boston people were unprepared to confer with him, having failed to receive the telegram announcing his visit. As a meeting of the association could not be arranged, he left the city the following day without the insights he might have been seeking.[28]

On May 27, almost two months after his appointment, Crook met for the first time with his fellow commissioners, Foster and Warner, in Chicago. During their meeting, probably at Crook's suggestion, it was decided that they should begin their work at the Rosebud agency, home of Spotted Tail's Brulés, who had remained aloof from the fighting during the Sioux War. Spotted Tail, a leading contributor to Crook's efforts to end the war and the man who arranged for the surrender of Crazy Horse, was now dead. But the tribe had reportedly remained well disposed toward the general.[29] Perhaps Crook thought that success at Rosebud was assured and might be important in winning over the other agencies, particularly Red Cloud's Oglalas. The commissioners seemed to get along well together, and the next day Crook and Chairman Foster bonded further during a ride through Chicago.[30]

Early on the evening of May 29, the three men embarked on their mission, ensconced in a special car furnished by the Northwestern Railroad. Accompanying them were Crook's aide, Major Roberts, and a disbursing officer to manage the $25,000 appropriation provided for the commission's expenses. A secretary, two clerks, and "a colored messenger" rounded out the staff. The general expressed pleasure at the accommodations afforded by the railroad, especially the fine cook and the plentiful food. After a convivial dinner, the commissioners played a few hands of whist and then retired to their Pullman bunks.[31] Traveling in such comfort, they arrived two days later at the rail depot in Valentine, Nebraska, and were greeted with solemn formality by columns of mounted Indian police lining both sides of the road, their carbines held rigidly at "inspection arms." Mounting buckboards with the police forming ranks about the wagon, the entourage set out for the Rosebud agency. There Crook was greeted warmly by old friends from the tribe, climaxing what the general declared a "perfect" day. In the month that followed, there would not be many such days.[32]

The Sioux commissioners at the outset of their visit to the Sioux agencies, 1889. Seated, left to right, George Crook, Charles Foster, William Warner. Author's collection.

Crook did not anticipate that the chiefs, whose power rested on the communal nature of tribal society, would support the bill, since its reforms were clearly intended to undermine their authority. For that reason, he hoped to bypass the traditional leadership and appeal directly to the rank and file. He began by "tuning up the Indians," by which he meant putting them in a proper mood to accept his overtures. To accomplish this, he demonstrated his knowledge of and sensitivity to their customs by arranging to temporarily lift the ban on traditional dancing imposed by missionaries since 1873. For a brief moment, the Brulés would be allowed to enjoy this long-denied but important aspect of their culture in order to entertain their guests in the traditional Lakota manner. Crook had also arranged for the purchase of beeves at commission expense so that the tribe could host a feast, an equally valued custom.

But Three Stars could see that there had been changes on the reservation since his departure from the Platte, and they were not for the better. The dancers lacked the old enthusiasm and spirit that he remembered from ten years before. And he was appalled by the Brulés' sad attempt to recreate their traditional buffalo hunts by riding down and shooting the cattle delivered to them as their beef ration. Most critically, despite his efforts to win the Brulé over, he found that oppo-sition ran far deeper than he had anticipated. The men showed "much unfriendliness to the bill" and became "undemonstrative and inclined to be a little sullen." Some even "threatened to kill" anyone who signed their approval. They impatiently waved away an explanation of the bill, asserting that they understood it fully, and resisted efforts to push them into a quick decision, quite reasonably asking for time to consider the measure amongst themselves.[33]

The reality was that the entire Sioux nation was keenly aware that they were being asked to approve legislation that would profoundly change their lives. Having been cheated and lied to over the years, they were deeply suspicious of both the government's motives and its com-mitment to fulfill the promises that were now being made to them. Moreover, such terms as "land ownership," "acreage," and "bound-aries" now bandied about by these white men were foreign to Lakota culture and hence were difficult abstractions and their ramifications hard to grasp. With this lack of understanding came fear—of the unknown and the unknowable. They had fundamental questions that needed to be addressed. How big was an acre? How much would they receive for their lands? And most importantly, how would they survive under the new system? A society that had supported itself on game and forage had seen its food resources destroyed and replaced by inadequate rations. Now it was being asked to sustain itself by farming, a concept that appeared dubious and even frightening given their experience try-ing to grow food in the harsh Dakota climate and on the poor lands allotted them. Would they continue to receive rations to ensure against starvation under these new conditions?[34]

Though he clearly understood their fears, Crook knew the Indians' fate was sealed. This was to be their lot, and he knew they could expect nothing better. He would work hard to make the government live up to its promises, but for now, for him, the overriding imperative was to ensure that they approved the bill lest they suffer consequences more dire than those promised by Senator Dawes's legislation.

His strategy was to profess impatience with their intransigence. He was in a hurry, he declared. He had the other agencies to visit and wanted to get on with it. Part of this professed urgency was real, as was the professed irritability. He did, indeed, have much to do and not a great deal of time to do it in. In addition, he had developed a sore throat and stomach issues, and the discomfort of a dusty and increasingly sweltering prairie spring was beginning to tell on him. But much of his apparent impatience was bluff, driven by his concern that the longer the Indians considered the reforms, the less likely they were to accept them. He also feared the influence of a few white reformers who now worked among the Indians stirring opposition to the bill, believing that their efforts ran counter to the tribe's best interests.[35]

Feigning indifference, a technique that had served him well in past negotiations, he told the assembled Indians that he and his fellow commissioners had no personal stake in the outcome of the vote. As they had much work to do elsewhere, if the Brulés were not prepared to sign immediately, the delegation would consider their inaction as opposition and move on to other agencies. He left his listeners to ponder what would happen to them should the bill be approved by the other Lakota bands without Brulé participation.

Using an alliance of friendly progressives—the term applied to those full-blooded Indians who favored accommodation with the government—and mixed-race men and "squaw men" (whites who had taken Indian wives and lived on the reservation), Crook labored to undermine the resistance of the traditional leadership. To diminish the chiefs' influence, these men went among their neighbors sowing fear that a failure to approve the bill would exclude them from the benefits offered, and they would wind up with nothing. Their lobbying ultimately exacerbated divisions in Sioux society and set the stage for future factional conflict. But in the short run, it had the desired impact, at least at Rosebud. Gradually, a combination of incessant jawboning, more feasting, and the fear of being left out in the cold created momentum for approval. Increasing numbers of Indians began stepping forward to touch the pen, though clearly many who did so remained confused and uncertain as to the nature and future effects of the agreement. On June 12 the commission announced that it had received the requisite three-quarters majority needed for approval.[36] It was time to move on to Pine Ridge. There they would follow the same strategy but with different results.

Despite Red Cloud's age and declining capacity, Pine Ridge was still very much his political bailiwick. A shrewd and adamant traditionalist, he remained a respected and powerful leader among the Oglala, and he had the advantage of support from at least one faction in white society, the National Indian Defense Association (NIDA), the reformers who had worried Crook at Rosebud.

Almost alone among Indian reform groups, NIDA opposed severalty, particularly the program outlined in the Dawes legislation. Led by Dr. Thomas A. Bland, the fiery Quaker publisher of the Indian rights paper *Council Fire,* the organization mounted a vigorous campaign against the bill, believing that it was nothing but an unethical land grab and that Congress's haste to open Indian land to white settlement laid the basis for the destruction of tribal society without replacing it with a viable alternative. To Bland the Dawes Act was simply a law intended to impose the views of certain reformers on what was best for the Indians. The tribes ought not be stampeded into giving up their communal lands and accepting white social values and culture. Rather, they should be allowed to proceed toward assimilation at their own pace. Bland's fulminations against the act filled *Council Fire's* pages, resulting in the wide dissemination of his views both on and off the reservation. Though Crook had previously warned of the very dangers of pushing the Indians into the white world too fast, now, as a commissioner, he opposed NIDA for trying to sabotage the commission's work. And at Pine Ridge he certainly had every reason to worry. NIDA's support undoubtedly stiffened opposition to the bill at the Oglala agency.[37]

The Pine Ridge agency, situated on the banks of White Clay Creek in the southwestern corner of the reservation, was about a hundred miles west of Rosebud, a two-day journey by rail and wagon. At the time of the commission's arrival, spring rains had turned the plain surrounding the agency a lush green, giving the place a deceptively bucolic and fertile appearance. But the scenery did not beguile Crook. Troubled by stomach problems, his discomfort was hardly relieved when a host of painted warriors, mounted and in full battle regalia, rode out to meet him, a welcome arranged by Red Cloud to underscore opposition to the bill. The chief's message rang loud and clear. Crook did not like it and told the chiefs so.[38]

Over the next several days, the intransigency of the Oglalas, persistent stomach pains, and the pervasive dust and gathering heat conspired to blacken Three Star's mood. Discussions with the tribe began on June 15. Crook was too ill to attend, leaving his fellow commissioners to face seven hundred Oglalas by themselves. Seated beneath a canvas awning erected to shade the white men from the blazing sun, Chairman Foster extolled the bill's promise to enable the Sioux to stand up as free and equal participants in American society. Though he tried to present his case in positive terms, he made no attempt to sugarcoat the alternative. When Dakota territory joined the Union as two states, the white citizens would no longer tolerate the presence of the Great Sioux Reservation in their midst. If the Sioux did not accept the bill and the money paid pursuant to it, Dakota politicians would find a way to take the land, one way or another.[39]

Two days later the commissioners, now joined by a recovered Crook, again met with the assembled Indians and quickly learned that, like the Brulé, the Oglalas were fearful of the leap into the unknown offered by the white man. Red Cloud opened the discussion, articulating the tribe's skepticism. Referring to the previous treaty of 1868, the chief pointed out that many of the commitments contained in it still remained unfulfilled. Using an analogy that tickled his fellow Indians, he recalled that when he went to the reservation store with an unpaid bill, "these storekeepers want that paid before he [sic] gets any more."[40] Such talk of unkept promises angered the commissioners. Warner indignantly berated the Indians. The Great Father had watched over his children, yet "today you come here and slap [him] in the face."[41]

While the Indians were still considering this outburst, Crook rose to speak. Convinced that he could work his way on individuals in private, he did not waste much time on this public gathering. He was speaking to a defeated people and he knew it. His words were abrupt and to the point. "It is certain that you will never get any better terms than are offered in this bill, and the chances are that you will not get so good. And it strikes me that instead of complaining of the past, you had better provide for the future. . . . And that when you can't get what you like best you had better take what is the best for you."[42]

But what was being offered? Like the Brulé, the Oglalas found the concepts and terminology alien and difficult to comprehend.[43] Red Cloud, ill and dispirited, retired to the background, allowing a fellow chief, American Horse, to come forward in his place.[44] The latter, an articulate and cosmopolitan leader, had fought the whites during Red Cloud's war but had also ridden in Buffalo Bill's Wild West Show. He was no traditionalist, but his eyes were open to the flaws in the bill. He spoke for three days, dominating the agenda and covering a wide range of topics in speeches heavily critical of the government's past failure to deal fairly with his people. He was so effective that Crook was forced to admit that he "was a better speaker than any of us" and allowed that he was "too much for the Commission."[45] But eventually, despite his critical stance, after talking privately with Crook, American Horse became one of only two Oglala headmen to sign the agreement. But his public capitulation persuaded few to follow his lead, and perhaps that had been his real objective all along.

Despite the feasts, cajoling, and a desperate and discreditable last-minute effort to bribe the opposition's leadership, the commissioners failed to move the tribe.[46] They departed Pine Ridge on June 24, their mission a failure. Of the 1,336 men said to be eligible to sign at the agency, only 684 actually touched the pen, far short of the three-quarter majority needed for approval. Among the signatories, the full-blooded Sioux numbered far fewer than the mixed-race men, squaw men, and Cheyennes, the latter indifferent to the outcome as they hoped to soon have their own reservation in Montana.[47]

The commissioners next proceeded to the smaller Lower Brulé and Crow Creek agencies. Dispirited by failure, a chill rain, and the sad news that Lucy Hayes, the former president's wife, had passed away, Crook and his fellow commissioners were delivered by their special rail car to the town of Chamberlain on June 30. The small town, perched on a bluff overlooking the Missouri, afforded them a firsthand look at the public hunger for Sioux land that had been the impetus for the bill. The hamlet was thronged with wagons packed with settlers impatiently awaiting word that reservation lands were open for settlement. Bypassing the restless crowd, the commission embarked in rowboats for the short journey downriver to Lower Brulé.

The Indians living at both Lower Brulé and Crow Creek knew that their relatively good land and its proximity to the Missouri River exposed them to the greed of whites like those who lined the streets of Chamberlain. They were fearful that boundary adjustments promised by the bill would wipe out their holdings.[48] Crook tried to reassure them that this was not the case, but he could not allay their doubts. At Lower Brulé, he eventually swayed the chiefs with his personal pledge that if their lands were taken, they would be resettled on equally good acreage at Rosebud where the remainder of their fellow tribesmen were now living.

438 AN HONEST ENEMY

That pledge was but one of several that Crook made in order to win over the Indians. George C. Hyde, a noted chronicler of Sioux history, characterized these promises as bribery, effective because "many of the chiefs knew him and had strong faith in his honesty." He criticized the general for making commitments that he knew or should have known neither the administration nor Congress was likely to honor.[49] His point appears well taken. The sad truth seems to have been that as the weather grew hotter and dustier and the Indians became more anxious and obdurate, Crook became increasingly frustrated and impatient about the pace of events. He wanted the Indians to approve the bill, and he wanted it done quickly. In desperation, he made promises without any certainty they would be met. Yet he valued his reputation for integrity so greatly and held his honor in such esteem that there can be little doubt that he fully intended to do his utmost to see that each commitment would be fulfilled.[50]

Crook's blandishments succeeded in winning a slim plurality at both agencies, and on July 12 the commissioners moved on to Pierre, then a small but growing settlement destined to become the capital of South Dakota. Pierre's citizenry saw the Dawes legislation as a bonanza that would cause the town's economy to boom. Accordingly, they greeted the commissioners with much fanfare. But Crook was in a hurry, and at his urging the delegation embarked the same day they arrived, traveling upriver to the Cheyenne River agency, home of the Miniconjou, Sans Arc, Two Kettle, and Blackfeet Sioux. These Indians, many of whom had accompanied Sitting Bull into Canada, were traditionalists who had made little effort to adapt to reservation life since their surrender six years before. Most vehemently opposed the bill. They followed Hump, a militant Miniconjou who was the only chief on the Great Sioux Reservation to keep a Soldier Lodge, which Lakota chiefs had traditionally used to maintain their authority. Anticipating that Hump would cause trouble, Crook had sent word for Major George M. Randall at Fort Bennett to meet the commissioners at the agency, hoping that the presence of a uniformed officer would help quiet the Indians.[51]

The Indians listened silently for two days while the bill was explained to them, after which Crook called for signers. Hump's faction then rose to express their opposition. Intending to physically bar anyone from coming forward, one warrior leaped to the front, wielding his war club in a threatening manner. Crook looked around the room for a weapon.

Finding none, he grabbed a chair, planning to brain the man if he attacked. Fortunately for the commission's decorum, the Indian police intervened and hustled the protesting Indian to the guardhouse.[52] Some signed that day, but only after Crook angrily warned that, if necessary, he would order in the military to protect the signers.

His words quieted Hump's faction, and all went well for a short while. But four days later, at an afternoon council, the chief and his followers descended on the pavilion in which the talks were being held, mounted and singing their war chants. The arrival of two hundred restive Indians (by Crook's estimation) completely disrupted the proceedings and infuriated Crook. The next day the general tore aside his mask of bland indifference and lambasted the Indians for their conduct. Dismissing their spokesman's assertion that they had accorded the commissioners "gentlemanly treatment" as "humbug," he assured the cowed assemblage that if any harm came to the signers or their property, he would see to it that the miscreants' rations were assessed for the damages. He then announced that he was leaving the agency and that Major Randall, who had arrived in the interim, and the Indian agent would supervise the remainder of the signings.[53] The three commissioners then abruptly departed for Standing Rock, the northernmost and final agency on their schedule, home to Sitting Bull and his unreconstructed Hunkpapas.[54] Crook's precipitous withdrawal from Cheyenne River proved a successful ploy. Within two weeks of their departure, using means that remain unrecorded, the agent and Major Randall had secured the signatures of 620 of the 750 eligible males on the reservation, including that of the diehard, Hump.[55]

The Standing Rock agency stood on a bluff over the Missouri on the remote eastern edge of the Great Sioux Reservation under the watchful eye of four companies of infantry and two troops of cavalry garrisoned at adjacent Fort Yates. Here Crook had supposed he would have the support of at least the moderate faction of the Hunkpapas, who were led by John Grass, a highly articulate and intelligent chief known for his accommodation to white interests in the past. Yet the commissioners found that the entire tribe, including Chief Grass, stood united in their determination to sell none of their land and had pledged to not even discuss the matter.

Like the Indians at Cheyenne River, the Hunkpapas listened in attentive silence for two days while the commissioners explained the bill. Sitting Bull and his followers deliberately absented themselves from the council, signaling their disapproval by remaining in their lodges several miles away.[56] On July 29 Chief Grass rose to present the Hunkpapas' case. There was plenty of land available across the Missouri for whites, he declared. Let them take that land and stay off the reservation. There was nothing in the agreement that made sense from the Sioux's perspective, and they would not sign it. Despite Grass's position, Crook admired his presentation, confiding to his diary that the chief demonstrated a thorough understanding of the terms of the bill and that his remarks "had more sense in them than we have heard from all the Indians since engaged in this duty."[57] Though impressed, the general had no intention of changing his position and immediately set to work softening the dissenters with gifts of cattle for a feast and sending their agent, James McLaughlin, "amongst the Indians tuning up John Grass and others."[58]

McLaughlin had been at Standing Rock since 1881, having retained his politically vulnerable position through several administrations due to his extraordinary competence. Married to a Lakota woman, he was sympathetic toward and very knowledgeable about the Standing Rock community. Yet he was paternalistic and had no compunction about ruthlessly using the powers of his office to further policies that he considered in the best interest of his charges. With respect to the Sioux, he was probably Crook's equal or superior in understanding the psychology necessary to sway them. Now, privately and discreetly, he set about persuading the more moderate factions in the tribe to change their positions by underscoring the dangers of rejecting the bill.[59] Using the fact that Standing Rock was the last agency visited by the commission, he and the commissioners misrepresented the support the bill had received elsewhere. Telling the chiefs that all the other agencies had approved the measure, he later admitted in his memoirs that he told Grass that "if he and his people did not sign, Congress would take all their land and they would get no compensation." Such threats wore Grass down, and he finally conceded to Crook that the commissioners "were too much for him."[60]

On August 3 the commission announced that it was time for the Indians to come forward to sign. As they approached, John Grass in the lead, Sitting Bull, who up to this time had not attended one meeting, suddenly arrived with twenty of his adherents. They rode into the crowd of Indians, attempting to drive them away from the door of the warehouse where the document was to be signed. But McLaughlin was prepared for such a disruption and had his Indian police on hand. As Crook triumphantly recorded in his diary, "Sitting Bull tried to speak after the signing commenced but I stopped him. Then he tried twice to stampede the Indians away from the signing, but his efforts failed and he flattened out. His wind bag was punctured and several of his followers have already deserted him. We obtained 279 signers today." By the time the commissioners departed four days later, Crook tallied a total of 673 signatures on the document.[61]

On August 7 the weary commissioners boarded a train that would return them to Chicago. In the comfortable privacy of their rail car, they counted the number of signatories from each agency. To their chagrin, they found that they were short of the three-fourths majority needed for approval of the bill. Undeterred, they wired Agent McLaughlin, who soon secured enough signatures and more to make up the deficit from among the browbeaten Hunkpapas.[62]

Crook arrived back in Chicago exhausted from three months of unremitting and stressful labor in the heat and dust of a northern plains summer. At sixty-one years of age and in uncertain health, he badly needed rest. So after a cursory visit to his headquarters, he rushed off to join Mary at her family home in the Maryland panhandle where they were constructing what they planned to be their home in retirement.[63] His stay was brief, and he returned to Chicago two weeks later, only to receive the stunning news that Indian Commissioner Thomas Morgan had slashed the Sioux's beef ration by one million pounds at Pine Ridge and by twice that amount at Rosebud and had ordered similar cuts for the other agencies. It seems that an audit of the populations at the various agencies disclosed that the tribes had been padding their ration rolls, a deception they had resorted to in order to avoid widespread starvation following previous congressional reductions in their annual appropriations. Though Interior Department bureaucrats could hardly have been ignorant the Sioux's dilemma, they seemed indifferent to it. Nor did they stop to consider the devastating impact the timing of these reductions would have, coming on the heels of a severe drought that had cost the Sioux their crops for the past two years, and after having to abandon their current crop in mid-season to attend the councils called by the Sioux commission. This confluence of circumstances now left them without reserves in the face of these recent reductions.[64]

Crook and the other commissioners were sickened by Morgan's decision. As part of their effort to convince the Sioux to agree to the allotment bill, they had repeatedly reassured the Indians that their assent would in no way affect their ration entitlements, a major concern raised at all the agencies. Upon learning of Morgan's ruling, Crook had immediately pointed out to Governor Foster that "the effect will of course be bad, coming so soon after the visit of the Commission and it will be impossible to convince [the Sioux] that it is not one result of their signing."[65] More immediately, it threatened the Sioux nation's very survival. As a body, the commissioners wrote to Secretary of the Interior Noble asking if there was "any way that can be devised to remedy the (in our opinion) grave error. . . . We most earnestly urge such action as will result in its speedy correction." Stating the obvious, they pointed out: "It is an act of injustice closely approaching cruelty."[66]

As the commissioners feared, the decision stirred unrest and divisiveness on the reservation, turning many against the Sioux leaders who had urged them to sign the approval documents. In the hope of quieting this turmoil and perhaps restoring the rations, the commissioners arranged for a delegation of chiefs to visit Washington, D.C., to underscore the gravity of the situation. The delegation, accompanied by the commissioners and Crook aides Kennon and Roberts, arrived in the capital in early December. But a meeting with Secretary Noble and the president failed to alter the Interior Department's decision. Rations remained at the levels Morgan had set for them. The people grimly tightened their belts, convinced of the commission's perfidy. Other disappointments would follow.

Three months later, on February 10, 1890, instead of fulfilling the legal requirement of first surveying the land and distributing parcels to the tribespeople, President Harrison gave in to pressure from land-hungry whites and declared the unallotted lands immediately open to white settlement. Boomers flooded across the Missouri hauling wagonloads of building supplies and farm equipment to occupy the 9,274,669 acres of prairie now available to them under the terms of the Homestead Act. The Sioux could do nothing but helplessly watch the usurpation of their lands.

Perhaps as a sop to the Indians, the president also submitted a draft bill to Congress that would meet all the commitments that the commission had made to the Sioux. But Crook's death in March deprived the Sioux nation of one their few advocates in government and perhaps their most influential one. Though the bill was successfully shepherded through the Senate by Senator Dawes, it died in the House without the general's prestige to support it. Adding insult to injury, the House then delayed passage of the appropriations legislation for 1891 so that annuities, which included warm clothing, did not reach the Indians until mid-winter. And the funds eventually appropriated were insufficient to provide the Sioux their full rations that year.[67]

Ironically, the opening of the Sioux lands to white settlement failed to meet the expectations of its white boosters. Though Harrison's action had initially precipitated a rush for reservation land, demand dried up in the face of a disastrous multiyear drought and the realities of farming the arid, wind-whipped South Dakota plains. As funds realized from the sale of the land failed to materialize, so did the necessary inputs for the purchase of equipment and supplies needed to farm the Indian allotments. Consequently, it became almost impossible to produce crops or raise livestock under prevailing conditions. Life on the reservation sank to a new low. Game, formerly a vital source of food for the Plains Indians, had long been hunted out. Tribespeople, unable to grow food on the parched land, had to rely solely on the inadequate rations authorized by Congress. The resulting malnutrition rendered the Indians vulnerable to European diseases that now swept through the tribe—influenza, whooping cough, and measles, followed by pneumonia and tuberculosis killed many.[68]

Hardships such as those suffered by the Sioux in 1889 and 1890 sometimes unite a community in the face of adversity. The Sioux were denied even this beneficial crumb. The commission's work had exacerbated the split between the traditionalists and those who wished to accommodate to the whites, widening a schism that dated back to the early days of the tribes' confinement to the reservation. Any tribal structure and discipline that might have helped reunify the Sioux was further undermined by the government's persistent and impatient efforts to eliminate all traces of native culture, and its failure to replace it with a viable alternative.

The promises the general and his fellow commissioners had made in order to secure support for the allotments gave the Sioux hope, a precious commodity for such a beset people. Crook's death, the invasion of white settlers, the cut in rations, and a delay in the allotment of Indian lands, seemed to seal their fate. On hearing of Crook's demise, Red Cloud is reputed to have said, "Then General Crook came: he, at least, never lied to us. His words gave our people hope. He died. Then hope died. Despair came again."[69] Another tribesman summed up the Sioux's reaction with weary cynicism: "They made us many promises, more than I can remember, but they never kept but one; they promised to take our land and they took it."[70]

CHAPTER TWENTY-SEVEN

End of Days

Following his return from Oakland and his initial efforts to convince the Interior Department to restore the Sioux's rations, Crook sought temporary refuge from this painful matter in his annual fall hunt, conveniently scheduled to follow on the heels of an inspection trip to Fort Robinson in western Nebraska. That year the expedition would travel deep into the primitive wilderness north of Casper, Wyoming. The general's health was in a precarious state following his stint with the Sioux commission, and having hunted in the Wyoming wilderness as a younger man, he had to have known that the difficult terrain and the weather at that time of year would make the trip dangerously taxing. Yet such was his love of these annual outings and so strong was his confidence in his own abilities, he seems hardly to have given the matter a second thought.

As he confided to his diary, Crook's body, after sixty-one years of exceptionally hard use, had been exhibiting unmistakable signs of deterioration since his departure from Arizona. Episodes of shortness of breath and indigestion during his time in Omaha were indications that today might have led to follow-up examinations to determine whether he suffered from hardening of the arteries. Now known as atherosclerotic cardiovascular disease (CAD), the condition, caused by the build-up of plaque and calcium beneath the lining of the arteries, reduces the flow of oxygen-enriched blood to one or more vital organs. It is often accompanied by angina pectoris, a pain in the heart muscle caused by oxygen deprivation during periods of increased workload brought on by stress, exertion, strong emotion, or even a heavy meal. In addition to chest pains, angina can also cause abdominal distress, which is often dismissed as indigestion. In his diary over the last two years, Crook indicated that he had suffered from chest pains on several occasions, as well as bouts of indigestion, though admittedly, the latter condition could have equally been the result of unhygienic food preparation or improper storage common at that time.

Soon after the general arrived in Chicago in May 1888, a physician had examined him. Crook noted at the time that the doctor "could find no organic trouble that need cause any alarm." Yet the man was apparently concerned enough to take the general's pulse the following day, finding "a great difference in the beating of my two wrists," a further indication of coronary artery disease.[1]

Then, on August 26, only two days before he was to leave on the hunt, Crook suffered what by his own account were "the worst chest attacks . . . yet [while] coming home after dinner" at the end of a hot and active summer day.[2] As a heavy meal could bring on an attack of angina, this could well have been yet another warning of progressive arterial sclerosis. But he chose to ignore the discomfort and departed on schedule for Fort Robinson and the fall hunt.[3]

Fort Robinson had held annual encampments since 1885 as training exercises for the post's garrison. The troops engaged in various field exercises for a month while housed some miles from the fort at campsites named for well-known generals. Crook arrived in the midst of that year's exercise, which was said to involve the largest body of regulars assembled since the Civil War.[4] He must have been gratified to learn that the post commander had named this year's site "Camp George Crook," although he did not mention the fact in his diary. For eleven days he witnessed various exercises and drills and pronounced himself "favorably impressed" with the quality of the training and the efficiency and discipline of the troops.[5] Then, on September 10, he boarded a train for Casper, where a small detachment of cavalry and infantry awaited to transport him to the hunters' base camp and then to serve as escorts and logistical support for the sportsmen.

Like the general's previous annual hunts, this was not some slapdash affair but a carefully prepared expedition organized along the lines of an army operation. But unlike the personnel on many of Crook's military campaigns, the hunters did not travel light. Four wagons with six-mule teams and sixteen additional pack mules managed by eight packers would transport what Crook was pleased to call his "plunder" (mountain man terminology for baggage), and the game they harvested. Little Bat (Baptiste Garnier), one of Crook's most accomplished scouts during the Sioux War, and four Brulé warriors from Rosebud agency would serve as guides and trackers, while three Sioux women and their children came along to skin and dress the game. To transport all the personnel involved, Crook had commandeered sixty-five horses and mules, the latter said to include Apache, the mule he had ridden in his Arizona days.[6]

Crook did not loiter about Casper but immediately departed with his escort for his hunting camp some miles out of town, incidentally bagging ten antelope on the way. Joined by Webb Hayes, John Collins, and the pack train several days into the hunt, the general spent the next four weeks happily stalking, killing, and carefully tallying large numbers of deer, antelope, mountain sheep, and eagerly-sought-after but elusive bear.

Winter comes early in that part of the country, and, not unexpectedly, as September faded into October, the general recorded chill temperatures, snow, and hail in his diary. Undeterred, he faithfully tabulated a daily slaughter that greatly exceeded the party's need for meat, until on the evening of September 29, apparently sated, he recorded that he "could have killed some fine bucks, but didn't want them." On October 1 he wrote of receiving word that his old hunting companion, Albert Touzalin, a regular participant who Crook had hoped would join this year's hunt, had died. Perhaps hoping to keep these sad tidings from touching him too deeply, he only briefly mentioned the tragic event in his diary, following it immediately with the news that "Wright Killed a porcupine," a piece of intelligence that Touzalin would surely have found edifying.[7]

The hunt continued unabated until October 4, when another tragedy intruded—one of profound and immediate impact on the hunters. A soldier assigned to escort the hunters accidentally shot a comrade, destroying his jaw and half of his face and leading him to die in agony half an hour later. The incident so shocked the participants that they abruptly terminated the hunt. Packing up their gear, they headed back to the railhead, carrying the body of the unfortunate soldier on one of the wagons. Although burdened by grief and a full load of dressed meat and skins, they nevertheless managed to kill an additional forty-three antelope and six sage hens en route.[8]

If his diary is to be credited, upon his return to Chicago on October 11, Crook immediately plunged back into the busy routine of official and social activities that had been his lot since he had first arrived in the Windy City. His first order of business, as usual, involved responding to the correspondence that had accumulated in his absence. On this occasion his in-box, or whatever served as one, included a letter from the Woman's Christian Temperance Union on the question of prohibition. Instead of the preachy and dogmatic response one might expect from an elderly teetotaler, his answer is pragmatic and surprisingly modern, reflecting an insight and tolerance acquired over years of military service. Though freely acknowledging the evils of alcohol and the desirability of preventing its use, his experience with efforts to ban liquor in the army had shown, he wrote, that appetites "cannot be controlled by legislation." Only education, marshaling the forces of public opinion against the evil, would, he opined, do the trick.[9]

In another response, he again demonstrated his apparently newfound tolerance for human frailty, this time in a letter to the adjutant general of the army asking for clemency for Lieutenant Colonel George A. Forsyth, known for his heroic leadership in the battle at Beecher's Island in 1868. Forsyth, who had served with Crook during the Civil War and had spent many years on Sheridan's staff, had been found guilty by court-martial of financial irregularities and was about to be sentenced. In arguing that his punishment be mitigated, Crook made an unusually modern and, for the time, novel argument in defense of the colonel. He observed that Forsyth's conduct had likely resulted from a bullet wound to the head that had impaired his judgment. Hence, "he was not morally responsible" for his misdeeds and should therefore have his sentence remitted and the promotion denied him as a consequence, reconsidered.[10]

After only two weeks in Chicago and still recovering from the exertions of his hunt, the peripatetic general once more boarded a train, this time for a weeklong inspection tour in Colorado and Nebraska. Upon his return to Chicago in early November, after preparing for a brief visit by President Harrison to the city, he again turned to the matter Sioux rations, organizing and, with his aides, accompanying the del-

END OF DAYS   449

egation of Sioux chiefs to Washington, D.C., described in the previous chapter.[11] While the delegation failed to achieve its purpose, the sojourn in the capital afforded Crook an opportunity to travel to make a brief foray into nearby Virginia to revisit some of the scenes of his Civil War service. Since his promotion to major general, he had been increasingly drawn to re-examine his role in the war, probably moved by the nostalgia that commonly affects the aging, but also motivated to refresh his recollections for the memoir, which he was now working on.

Reawakened memories had revived old grievances, and with them came the desire to right old wrongs. For some time he had considered publication of an article or paper on the Shenandoah campaign of 1864 that would, he hoped, garner the recognition for his contributions to the fighting that he believed General Sheridan had deprived him of during the war. It is likely this idea figured in his decision to appoint Lieutenant Kennon, a skilled researcher and author of historical studies, to his staff. The previous spring, in preparation for the article, he had sent Kennon to Lynchburg, Virginia, to interview Jubal Early, the Confederate general who had led the forces that opposed Sheridan in the Shenandoah.[12] Kennon's conversations with Early were followed by several additional interviews that he conducted at Crook's behest with other senior officers who had participated on both sides in the Shenandoah campaign.[13] Just prior to their departure for Washington, Crook had introduced him to Brigadier General William H. Powell, a cavalry commander under Crook during the campaign. Powell was highly regarded by the general, and he evidently hoped the old cavalry officer would supply Kennon with additional information about Crook's performance in the Shenandoah.[14]

Even Kennon's presence in the capital now seemed partially related to the project. While there, though their days were occupied lobbying on behalf of the Sioux, Crook and Kennon spent their evenings socializing with more of the general's old wartime comrades. On at least three occasions they visited the McKinleys. As a young lieutenant, William McKinley had served as an aide to Crook in the Shenandoah. Now a prominent Ohio congressman, he had advanced rapidly through the ranks of the Republican Party on a trajectory that would ultimately carry him to the presidency. With Kennon listening attentively, the old general and the congressman undoubtedly exchanged campaign reminiscences. On another occasion, Crook took Kennon to see Robert C. Schenck, the former congressman who had nominated Crook to West Point. Schenck had kept in close touch with the general throughout his career, a longtime association that made him a valuable, and laudatory, resource in any study of Crook's contribution to the war effort.[15]

On Christmas Day, having completed his work on the final report of the Sioux land commission and delivered it to the secretary of war, Crook left the city to tour the Shenandoah Valley in the company of Roberts and Kennon. For two days he walked the battlefields of the campaign—Opequon, Winchester, Fisher's Hill, and Cedar Creek—examining the terrain and recalling the details of these struggles. Though much of the landscape had changed, as he climbed Fisher's Hill and walked the ground at Cedar Creek, vivid memories overwhelmed him. The recollections that washed over him brought with them a tide of lingering bitterness, and he once more experienced the anger he had felt at General Sheridan's claim of exclusive credit for the victories in these engagements, both during the war and afterwards. Unable to contain his emotions and in a rare loss of self-control, he allowed the acrimony to spill out on the pages of his diary:

> After examining the grounds and the positions of the troops after the 25 years which have elapsed[,] and in light of subsequent events, it renders Sheridan's claims[,] and his subsequent actions in allowing the general public to remain under impressions regarding his part in these battles, when he knew they were fiction[,] all the more contemptible. The adulations heaped on him by the grateful nation for his supposed genius turned his head which, added to his natural disposition, caused him to bloat his little carcass with debauchery and dissipation, which carried him off prematurely.[16]

Returning to Washington two days later, his anger apparently purged by his outburst, he spent an evening vicariously enjoying the peaceful home life of an old army comrade. Frolicking with the man's children, he confided to his diary that he did not know when he had enjoyed himself so much.[17] The next day he boarded a train once more, Kennon at his side. This time, in the company of Senator Dawes, he was bound for North Carolina to inspect a proposed new home for the

Chiricahuas on Cherokee lands. He reviewed the site and then traveled to Alabama to call on the tribe briefly at their Mount Vernon reservation and bask in the warmth of their fond greeting.[18]

Traveling from North Carolina to Washington, the train in which the two officers were riding was involved in a collision at Lynchburg. They were uninjured but were left stranded in the town overnight. Perhaps at Kennon's suggestion, they took the opportunity to call on Jubal Early, who lodged in shabby rooms in the town. The old man greeted them warmly. He had good feelings for Crook, regarding him as among the few generals of any worth who had opposed him. Crook, however, was less generous in his appraisal of his old adversary. He saw in Early a man "stooped and enfeebled and as bitter and virulent as an adder." Ignoring his own emotional baggage from the war, Crook uncharitably wrote that the Confederate general "had fought his battles over so many times that he had worked himself into the belief that many of the exaggerated and some ridiculous stories he tells are true."[19]

The constant travel over the past several months had tired Crook, but there was more in the offing. He only spent a couple of days in Washington before returning to his Chicago headquarters on January 8. There he found a request from the president asking that he go immediately to Indian Territory to inspect the Fort Sill site the general had promoted as the final homeland for the Chiricahuas. Obediently, he boarded yet another train, this time for Oklahoma. Although winter was upon the land, giving the place a rather bleak appearance, his brief tour of the area convinced him that the country adequately met the Apaches' needs.

After finishing his inspection, and despite the raw and cold weather, when invited on a hunt for quail on the nearby Canadian River, the inveterate sportsman was unable to resist. It was a serious error in judgment. The chill temperatures and icy north winds penetrated the thin clothing he had brought with him and made him increasingly uncomfortable. When a fellow hunter worried about his health, he dismissed his concern as "only a little of the grippe." Yet by the end of each day, he was "thoroughly exhausted."[20] He continued to brave the elements for about five days until, one morning, he awoke with pains under his shoulder blade, quite probably an angina attack triggered by exposure to cold. In acute discomfort, he retired to a rail car used by the hunters as sleeping quarters, where he remained for two days. But the condition persisted, and he reluctantly decided to abandon the hunt.[21] On February 16, after a two-day train ride, he arrived back at his Chicago headquarters, where he confided to his diary that he still felt "fairly sick." A week later, the weather gloomy and cold, he complained of being unable to regain his strength and, the next day, of still being "under the weather."[22] For the remainder of that month and into March, despite his claims to feeling better, his diary reflected a marked decline in his activity level, though he still managed to campaign by letter for passage of the Senate bill authorizing the resettlement of the Chiricahuas at Fort Sill. Major Ely McClellan, the post surgeon attached to Crook's headquarters staff, attended the general during this period and, for a time, believed that he was improving. But in the third week of March, his condition again increased in severity, though he continued to display some of his old resilience and appeared to rally.

During the week of March 17, he cheerfully welcomed a visit from Captain Charles King, an ardent and loyal admirer whose friendship with Crook dated back to the Sioux War.[23] Now King called on the general to discuss plans they had previously made to publish an account of Crook's experiences with the Indians that the captain intended "to be magnificently illustrated from the Smithsonian collection." As King later recalled, Crook hoped to produce the work as a means of earning sufficient funds to discharge an onerous debt that he had assumed some time before on behalf of a "no-account nephew." In furtherance of that effort, the two men had assembled the general's personal papers, intending that they would serve as "the basis of a work on the Indians of the U.S." During this visit, King related, he had informed Crook that he, King, had received a contract offer from a "wealthy Eastern publisher" to print the book. On hearing the news, King said that Crook exclaimed to his wife, "I am the happiest man on Earth, Mary."[24]

On March 20 the general went to his office and performed his duties as usual. To his staff he seemed in a "happy frame of mind, and wore his old-time smile as he greeted his friends." That evening, however, while he attended the theater with Mary and her sister, an aide, Major Randall, thought he looked unwell and asked him whether he was in pain. The general responded in the negative and was later seen in the corridors of the Grand Pacific Hotel, cheerfully greeting old friends. The next morning, he was dead.[25]

John S. Drake, the proprietor of the Grand Pacific and by now a friend of the general's, provided for reporters what appears to be an authoritative account of the circumstances:

> General Crook arose shortly before 7 o'clock yesterday morn-ing [March 21] apparently in his usual health and, in accor-dance with his custom, began exercising with the weights and pulleys connected with an apparatus for the purpose, which he kept in the room. After exercising for a few minutes he stopped and went and lay down on a lounge, saying that he felt a difficulty in breathing. A few moments later he called out to his wife: "Oh, Mary, Mary, I need some help. I can't get my breath." Dr. [Vincent L.] Hurlbut, who lives nearby, was sent for. Everything that could be done was done, but he failed to rally and died at 7:15. Mrs. Crook and her sister, Mrs. [Fanny] Reid were the only members of the family present at his bed-side when he passed away.[26]

Dr. Hurlbut reported that he arrived on the scene "only four or five minutes before death supervened." He discovered the general was "suf-fering from irregular action of the heart and his lungs or chest seemed to be filled up." He made some efforts, using the medical knowledge of the time. These included "hot applications with sinapisms [mustard plasters], hot bags to his feet, etc.," but the general was in what the doctor termed *articule mortis,* and it was too late to revive him. From the symptoms he observed, Dr. Hurlbut later surmised that Crook had died of heart fail-ure, a diagnosis that he cautiously qualified, warning that he had never attended him before. He added his speculation that there may have been some "stomachic complications." Crook's aide, Major Roberts, and oth-ers who knew him well thought that a contributing factor was "his great worry over the Indian prisoners at Mount Vernon and his desire to have justice shown them." To any list of stresses that the general was subject to at the time, the major might have also added Crook's concern for the fate of the Sioux following the work of the land commission.[27]

Doctor Hurlbut's description of the general's symptoms leaves little doubt that Crook died of a heart attack, its immediate cause prob-ably the vigorous exercise in which he had engaged that morning. His clogged arteries were unable to supply sufficient oxygen needed to meet the extra workload on the heart, bringing on a fatal arrhythmia that resulted in heart failure, accompanied, as the doctor noted, by congestion of the lungs and, ultimately, death.

Mrs. Crook's popularity in Prescott during the general's tenure in Arizona moved the town's leading newspaper, the *Prescott Courier* to provide greater detail regarding the impact of his death upon her than appeared in other papers of the day. The general's sudden demise was a great shock to her, all the more so as he likely took pains to conceal his health issues from her. The *Courier* reported that it was only with great difficulty that she could be persuaded to leave his deathbed and that her sister had to return with her several times during the day to view his body in order to convince her that he had, indeed, passed away. The most difficult time for her, according to the paper's account, was at five o'clock on the evening he passed, the hour when the general usually returned to their quarters from his office. As Mary entered the room to view the body at that critical moment, the guards on duty discretely departed to allow her to spend this time alone with her lifeless husband. It must have been at that moment that she grasped the extent of her loss, for she reportedly collapsed in a state of nervous prostration.[28] Attended by Major McClellan and Mrs. Reid, she soon revived, and by the following morning she had recuperated sufficiently to decisively make known her wish that the general be buried beside her father and brother in the family plot in Oakland, her Maryland home. Two of Crook's brothers, Charles and Walter, had come to Chicago at news of their brother's death. They apparently expressed the hope that the general would be interred at the Crook homestead in Dayton, Ohio. But Mary's decision carried the day.[29]

Before she could return her husband's body to Oakland, Mary first had to endure a public viewing and funeral service in Chicago, arranged so that friends, fellow officers, and the public had an opportunity to bid the general a ceremonial last farewell. Contemporary accounts judged that the affair was conducted with fitting solemnity and an underlying sadness that reflected the love and esteem in which his friends and admirers held him. The day following his demise, his body rested in a room at the Grand Pacific, encased in a flag-draped casket on which his sword and belt had been placed, along with his plumed helmet and a profusion of palm leaves and flowers. He was clad in his rarely worn full-dress uniform with medals from the Loyal Legion. A pin denoting his membership in his beloved Army of West Virginia had been fastened to the lapel of his coat. The general's upper body was visible beneath a glass plate in the coffin lid, and newspaper accounts described him as completely natural and peaceful in appearance.[30]

Among the mourners was Major Roberts, his longtime aide, accompanied by the major's young daughter, Laura, a favorite of the general's. Separated by the thick glass from the man who had been almost a surrogate grandfather, she turned to her father and asked something in a whisper. When her wishes became known, the honor guard slid the glass panel aside and allowed her to tearfully slip a bunch of violets, the general's favorite flower, into the coffin. Attached was a small card on which she had neatly printed in her childish hand: "LAURA TO COOKIE WITH LOVE." A reporter present noted that "her innocent display of grief unleashed a flood of emotion among those who witnessed it."[31]

The funeral was held the next day, March 23. The religious arrangements were somewhat eccentric, somehow fitting for a man raised in the strict confines of Methodist dogma but who eschewed organized religion in his adult years.[32] The service was held in Chicago's Grace Episcopal Church, officiated by a cluster of three Presbyterian and two Episcopal preachers. The eulogy was delivered by Professor David Swing, a Presbyterian minister much loved in Chicago, who had been expelled from his church as a heretic a decade before for, among other sinful beliefs, "unduly countenancing Unitarianism."[33]

After a short but moving ceremony, a coterie of honorary pallbearers carried the casket on its path from the church to the hearse that bore it through the streets of Chicago to the Baltimore and Ohio depot for its final journey to Oakland. The pallbearers were drawn from among the general's friends and represented the varied aspects of Crook's life— aides and comrades from his military career, hunting companions, and elite members of society with whom he associated during in his later years. Among them were President Hayes, Thaddeus Stanton, John Collins, Marshall Field, Peter Studebaker, and Governor Foster from the Sioux commission. Under the gaze of "tens of thousands" of people who lined the way, silently paying their respects, the hearse proceeded down Michigan Avenue followed by an escort provided by the Chicago Police, several military regiments, and veterans from the Loyal Legion and the Grand Army of the Republic.[34]

At the depot a train with a special Pullman car draped in black crepe awaited the general. At two that afternoon, it departed the station. On board were Mary and her sister, Mrs. Reid, and the two Crook brothers (Charles and Walter), the only siblings to attend the funeral. Members of Crook's headquarters staff and Paymaster Thaddeus Stanton joined them for the sad journey. President Hayes had elected to return to his home in Ohio after the Chicago service, but his son, Webb, boarded the Oakland-bound train. John Bourke did not. He journeyed directly from Washington, D.C., to Western Maryland after Mary requested his presence at the interment.[35]

On Monday, March 24, Crook was laid to rest in Oakland's Odd Fellows cemetery, not far from Crook Crest, the unpretentious but spacious retirement home that the general would never occupy. Though Mary had asked that the funeral be small and private, many old friends and comrades flooded the town to pay their last respects, and Oakland residents, who had come to know the general over the years, turned out en masse. Once more the grieving widow endured a public viewing, this time at the Oakland depot. It was followed by a funeral procession that wound through the town streets, past shuttered shops draped in black, to the cemetery. There, the general was interred beside the graves of Mary's kin, the Daileys. Among her family members buried on that hillside was Mary's brother, James, a member of a detachment of Confederate guerillas who had kidnapped the general in nearby Cumberland in the winter of 1865. Others of that band now stood respectfully at the graveside.[36]

But the general's body did not remain long in the Maryland hills. Soon after the funeral, it was decided that Crook's importance merited the significance of a burial site at Arlington National Cemetery. Accordingly, on November 11, seven months after his death, his body was disinterred and transported by rail to Washington, this time accompanied only by a small cadre of close friends: Lyman Kennon, John Bourke, Thaddeus Stanton, and Webb Hayes. The following day his body was escorted by two troops of cavalry to the cemetery. Only those who had come with him from Oakland and a few others—most notably Major General Schofield, commander of the army—were in attendance. Accounts of the service do not list Mary as being among them, possibly because she objected to removing the body from Oakland. The ceremony was brief and simple. The coffin was lowered into

Crook Crest, Oakland, Maryland, as it appears today. Author's photo.

the earth and an honor guard fired the traditional three volleys over the grave. Then, as the sound of taps reverberated through the chill winter air, the mourners departed.[37]

Two years later, with money raised by Webb and President Hayes, a monument was erected to mark the site, an imposing rectangular granite block with the general's name, rank, and the places and dates of his birth and death inscribed on one side. (The date of his birth is given as September 9, 1830, one of many dates given for that event and certainly not the correct one.[38]) Below the dates are the words "Society of the Army of West Virginia," possibly in recognition of that organization's contribution to the monument's cost. On the block's opposite face is affixed a 3 x 6 ft. bronze bas relief depicting a scene memorializing Crook's Sierra Madre campaign, considered by Hayes and others his most memorable military action against an Indian foe. As no photos were taken during that expedition, the scene on the plaque is based on the famous Fly photograph of the general's meeting with Geronimo at the Cañon de los Embudos, an entirely separate event occurring three years later and at a different location. The basis for the artist's work was a copy of the Fly photo owned by Lieutenant Gatewood and borrowed by Webb Hayes. Using artistic license, the sculptor sought to capture the spirit of the moment and at the same time honor the principle actors in the Geronimo campaign, both white and Indian. In doing so, he included individuals who had not been in the original 1886 photo. In the years that followed, some criticized the work for this historical inaccuracy. To that charge both Webb Hayes and Charles Gatewood, the son of the late lieutenant, angrily replied that no one was portrayed in bronze that did not deserve honor and recognition for his part in the campaign.[39]

The choice of the Sierra Madre campaign as the signal achievement of Crook's career may be questioned. Yet once the selection had been made, Gatewood and Hayes's decision to recognize those who were depicted seems entirely appropriate. All played their part in Crook's Arizona campaigns. Foremost among them is, of course, the general, wearing his readily identifiable Japanese hat. By his side is his loyal aide John Bourke. Scattered throughout the wooded glen in which the meeting took place are those military figures who contributed their efforts, and in some cases their lives, to one of the most dangerous and arduous conflicts in the history of Indian warfare. They include Captain Crawford, whose tragic death occurred some time before the Fly photo was taken; the intrepid chief of scouts Al Sieber; Lieutenant Gatewood; and a number of other junior officers who served Crook in Arizona. Seated with the whites or standing in the background are the most prominent of the Apache scouts, without whom the campaign could not have succeeded: Chatto, the scout whom Crook seems to have most admired; and Peaches, who led the army to the Chirica-huas' mountain hideout. Alchesay, the White Mountain scout who faithfully fought by the general's side in the 1870s and again during the Geronimo campaign, is also deservedly present. Fittingly, the artist also chose to portray some of those who fought against the Gray Fox, as they, too, had contributed to the story. Included are Geronimo, the proud Chihuahua, Benito, and the unwilling accomplice, old Loco.[40]

The monument stands today in a shaded grove of pines where its size dominates the smaller gravesites of other military figures buried in its vicinity. It can be reached by following a short boxwood-lined cement path named Crook Walk that intersects Lee Avenue, not far from the entrance to the cemetery. It may be a somewhat immodest marker for such a self-effacing man, but it is one certainly merited by his achievements.

Crook's gravesite, Arlington National Cemetery. Author's photograph.

The evening of the day Crook died, General Miles, attending a dinner party, could not be reached for comment. But a friend, speaking to the press in his behalf, allowed that the general "had great respect for Crook, and was very much shocked by his sudden death."[41] Others were considerably more effusive. Crook's demise prompted a flood of accolades, many framed, as one might expect, in the hyperbolic and flowery language of the day. Naturally, they extolled his soldierly virtues, his battle-tested courage, his patriotism "unsullied by any thought of personal aggrandizement," and his brilliance as a tactician. The War Department was moved to honor him by naming the new military post at Omaha in his honor: Fort Crook.[42]

But military prowess was not foremost in the minds of all who marked his passing. Several chose to emphasize other human and humanitarian qualities that distinguished him from a number of his army contemporaries: his essential simplicity, his directness, his disdain for cant and pretense, and, above all, his commitment to integrity, truth, and honor. It may have been something of an overstatement to resolve, as the city council of Prescott did, that "he never made a promise to white man or Indian that was not literally fulfilled."[43] Yet there was almost universal recognition of his lifelong striving toward that goal. The *New York Times* captured this virtue in its lead to an article announcing his passing—"An Honorable Life Ended."[44]

The Illinois unit of the Loyal Legion, one of a number of Civil War veterans' organizations that venerated Crook, elected to remember his humanity: "Firm as the ideal soldier, he had withal, that generous consideration of the rights of others which characterizes the spirit of the truly just; and no success, however distinguished, over-shadowed the modesty and kindliness of his daily life."[45] To which former President Hayes added, "General Crook has gone beyond most and perhaps beyond all others in his humanity and in the attainment of beneficent results in his dealings with the Indian tribes." With a rhetorical flourish, he added, "He also achieved the pure fame which belongs to him who, taking the part of a weak, injured and almost friendless people, has had the supreme satisfaction of giving to them a fair start and equal chance in the race of life."[46]

General Howard, noted himself for good works, focused on the humanitarian aspects of Crook's character in a eulogy published in the *Chatauquan* two months after the general's death. The two men had crossed swords on several occasions.[47] Yet Howard thought that in recent years Crook had abandoned the severity that characterized his pursuit of the Indians earlier in his career: "The sternness of his nature gave way, and some years back there came in upon him a strong desire to build up the lowly, those who had few friends and no efficient helpers." Noting as an example Crook's battle on behalf of the imprisoned Chiricahuas, Howard wrote: "His whole course toward these Indians exhibited a decided and unique character. Some of them had been his scouts, and he thought they had been treated with injustice; some . . . had been fierce, though wretched enemies; he thought these had been subdued and should be forgiven."[48]

The Indian Rights Association agreed with Howard's assessment. "The character of General Crook in dealing with the Indians was that of a soldier and a gentleman. While he was frequently obliged to exercise great severity toward them, his dealings were just, wise, and in accordance with his promises." They further recognized that Crook's name "was a tower of strength to all who labored for Indian civilization and who sought to turn the tide of popular sentiment in his favor.

To quote Gen. Crook was sufficient at least to silence sneers and to secure a fair hearing for the facts of the Indian cause."[49]

John Bourke, serving as an attaché to the Pan-American Congress, then in session, had been shocked by the suddenness of Crook's demise, though he allowed in a press interview that it was not unexpected. He observed that in recent years, the general had seemed at times on the verge of physical breakdown, complaining often of heartburn, which, in retrospect, was more likely angina. Bourke's praise for his former commander was unstinting, showing no hint of the breach that had developed between them. While he, too, dwelled on Crook's military achievements, he saw his administration of Indian affairs as "the brightest and most honorable chapter in the history of our relations with the American aborigines." And he, like others, ascribed the general's success to "his integrity. George Crook never lied to mortal man."[50] To a reporter he said, "[Crook] was recognized as the best friend the Indians ever had in this country." And, as one who had spent most of his career working closely with the general in Indian affairs, he described his commander's philosophy in terms that Crook himself might have used. "'If you don't behave yourself, I'll follow you up and whip you till you do, but if you do behave, I'll be your friend, allow no one to lie to you[,] to steal from you[,] nor to abuse you[,] and I'll find you the means to work for a living as white men have to do.'"[51]

Perhaps most apt were the words uttered by Professor David Swing at the general's Chicago funeral. In a single paragraph, he tried to reconcile the several apparently conflicting threads that composed Crook's personality.

> The life of General Crook when it shall be written will be the true portrait of the soldier. It will show the line between cruelty and war. It will point out places where on the battlefield courage and mercy met. It will harmonize the camp of the general and the closet of the philanthropist. It will show how a foe is also a friend. It will be the picture of a hero, of a friend— a man, a child, a thinker, a citizen, a soldier.[52]

Following Crook's death, Mary dealt courageously with her overwhelming grief and the reality of a future without her beloved husband. It has been noted that the general had not accumulated many assets during his career. But what he had, he left entirely to her under a will executed in February 1876 at the outset of the Sioux War. As it seems never to have been updated or superseded, Mary must have been referring to it in a letter to Captain Bourke following Crook's death, in which she noted without regret that the general had left relatively little property behind. According to Arizona probate court records, Crook owned a share in ranchland and livestock in Yavapai County, from which Mary realized about $9,000 when sold.[53] Other than that, though, when Lyman Kennon, as one of his last duties as Crook's aide, scoured the West for other properties, there is no record that he discovered any.

Crook Crest seemed to be the only other asset of substance. Mary referred to the couple's Oakland retirement home in another letter to Bourke. Bourke must have suggested that she apply for a pension as the general's widow. For she replied: "I rather shrink from [the idea]. I rather hope that God will not give me a longer life. I shall gladly welcome the hour that will take me to my noble dead. My wants here will be very few and I shall live in the simplest and plainest manner, but I hope to have a home where I can welcome my friends." To Mary, at least, the dwelling was her husband's most valued legacy.[54]

But Congress, untroubled by the suffering and poverty to which its indifference had consigned the Indians, was unwilling to see the widow of General Crook sink into penury. In June 1890 it passed legislation providing her with the modest pension of $1,200 a year (about $30,000 in today's dollars).[55] This sum, in addition to the funds received from Crook's estate, was sufficient for her to live on and also to allow her and her sister Fanny to travel to Europe in December 1892. She provided a commentary on her tour that was published in the *Omaha Bee* that revealed her as an intelligent, well-read, and sprightly tourist who, despite her grief, was still able to enjoy the novelty of her first and only visit to foreign shores.[56]

Mary was not long in fulfilling her wish to join her "noble dead." Like George, she, too, suffered from heart disease. She died only three years following her return from Europe. Her funeral was held in Washington, D.C. Thaddeus Stanton and Lieutenant Kennon, loyal friends, joined a few others at her graveside, laying her to rest beside her husband at Arlington National Cemetery on September 27, 1895.[57]

CHAPTER TWENTY-EIGHT

Summing Up

In many ways, throughout his life George Crook remained the simple, unpretentious person he had been in his youth. But for happenstance, he likely would have followed the path set by his father, a prosperous and respected farmer and country squire in rural Ohio. But fate intervened and he found himself pursuing a military career that earned him fame, prestige, and a place in history that as a boy he never imagined or aspired to.

From childhood, Crook's first love had not been books or military matters but the untamed wilderness, a passion that only grew stronger during his postings in the West. A throwback to the generation of border rangers who preceded his family into the Ohio River country, he sought out the untrammeled frontier and the freedom, mysteries, and even the dangers that it embodied. He had a boundless interest in wildlife, plants, and geography, and like his frontier antecedents, his fascination extended to the Indians who inhabited the natural world and shared his affinity for it.

Though he ultimately spent his life soldiering, he did not come to the profession easily. His difficulties in adapting to academic life and the stultifying discipline of West Point were ultimately reflected in his class standing upon graduation, the lowest of any West Pointer to become a major general.[1] Thereafter, he never fit comfortably into the traditional mold of military dress, ceremony, and social caste expected of an officer. Yet once in the field, he won plaudits, especially for innovations in guerilla warfare still relevant in the modern age.[2] His skills as an Indian fighter were grounded in his early interest and empathy for the tribes and in his deep knowledge of wilderness lore, both of which gave him an uncanny understanding of Indian culture and mentality and of their environment. Not only skilled at predicting and countering the actions of Indians in pursuit and combat, when the need arose he could turn them into loyal and effective allies, a rare ability that brought him success when many of his fellow officers failed. His talents resulted in his being credited with bringing peace to significant portions of the frontier and thus accelerating the pace of westward expansion.

But Crook had another side to his personality, one that strongly draws people to him today—his humanitarianism. His benevolence seems to have been instinctive. From childhood he was said to have exhibited a reflexive intolerance for injustice and a sympathy for the weak or oppressed. A friend who knew him as a youth described him as like "a big Newfoundland dog among a lot of puppies. He would never permit injustice or bullying of smaller boys."[3] In the latter period of his life, as the Indian wars drew to a close, Crook's concern for the welfare of his former foes—always present but until then subverted to his duties as a military officer—came to the fore. By the late 1880s it must have become apparent to him that his successes had contributed to the tragic destruction of a people and a way of life that he had come to know and admire. A more intellectual and introspective individual might have been overwhelmed or embittered by this irony. But Crook was not a man who pondered life's unfortunate paradoxes. Of a more pragmatic bent, rather than being crushed by the weight of responsibility for the fate of the Indians, he threw his energy into reforms that might achieve justice and equity for the tribes, an unpopular cause that could have jeopardized his military career.

Instead, he managed to turn his humanitarian instincts into an asset. For the Indians, his willingness to oppose inequity and his reputation for keeping his word earned him their respect and trust. Their regard became a resource, according to one contemporary observer, "almost as important a factor in [his] success as his matchless knowledge of [Indian] traits."[4] It enabled him to resolve conflicts and win concessions from the tribes, drawing approbation from his superiors and advancing his career.

But Crook's empathy for the Indians was a two-edged sword. While his influence with the tribes increased, and with it, his usefulness to the army, in later years his outspoken advocacy of reform put him out of step with government policy and the popular mood, irritating superiors and powerful political and economic interests, especially in the West. Ambitious and sensitive to public criticism, the outwardly stoic general was often deeply stung by the disparagements that greeted his efforts. Furthermore, since many of Crook's causes were unpopular, more often than not they met with rejection, adding frustration to his emotional burdens. His oft-stated opinion that the Indians, a people regarded by most of his contemporaries as Stone Age savages, could be integrated into the fabric of nineteenth-century white America was widely regarded as Quixotic at best.

The successful realization of Crook's aspirations for the Indian peoples depended on a national consensus on the desirability of assimilation and a willingness to devote substantial resources to the effort. Neither precondition seemed to exist during his lifetime and may not even exist today. Viewing the Indians with a mixture of fear and contempt, most of his contemporaries simply wanted them gone. Some advocated extermination. The more progressive favored removal to remote locations well away from white America. With a few notable exceptions, the nation's leaders and politicians followed the herd, particularly in the West, where open hostility toward the Indians, coupled with an insatiable hunger for their land, were the norms. Instead of adopting policies directed toward easing the tribes' transition into white society, the government's program became one of neglect compounded by corruption and mismanagement. Under these circumstances, it is not surprising that while Crook won most of his battles against the Indians in the field, his struggles in defense of their rights often became frustrating exercises in futility.

That is not to say that Crook's exertions were for naught. His efforts in the Ponca case, for example, laid the legal groundwork for the protection of Indian rights in the U.S. court system. And more than a few of his interventions in behalf of the Apaches, Utes, and Sioux avoided potentially bloody conflict and in some cases succeeded, at least temporarily, in fending off the usurpation of Indian lands. Perhaps of equal importance, as pointed out by the Indian Rights Association, in his later years his prominent advocacy on behalf of the tribes lent credibility to many of the policies dear to reformers.

Today, Crook's aspirations for the Indians are not viewed with the same degree of admiration as enlightened thinkers accorded them in his era. Many of the concepts that he and his fellow reformers espoused, including those emphasizing assimilation through the destruction of Indian culture, are now seen as ethnocentric and paternalistic. Yet given the ethos that prevailed at the time, they represented the most progressive thinking of the period.

In sum, the central irony in Crook's life, the inherent conflict between his regard and empathy for the Indians and his role in their destruction, was compounded by his inability to ameliorate the damage he had helped to inflict because of the unpopularity of the causes he espoused. Even the most fundamental of preconditions for assimilation of the Indians, his most cherished goal—citizenship—would be denied to them until thirty-four years after his death. At least death spared him awareness of the final, cruel twist of fate: that his passing deprived the Sioux and the Apaches, the tribes for whom he had the greatest regard, of their most effective advocate at a time when his voice was so urgently needed. But the irony and ambiguity implicit in Crook's life should not obscure its salient truth. He was a man of honor who shown light on inequity and strove to correct it. Who among us would not accept that much as evidence of a life well lived?

Notes

LIST OF ABBREVIATIONS

AG	Adjutant General
AAG	Assistant Adjutant General
AGO	Office of the Adjutant General
AHEC	U.S. Army Heritage and Education Center, Carlisle, Penn.
AHS	Arizona Historical Society, Tucson
ARSW	*Annual Report of the Secretary of War* (followed by year)
DA	Military Department of Arizona
DP	Military Department of the Platte
LC	Library of Congress
LR/LS	Letters Received/Letters Sent
NARA	National Archives and Records Administration, Washington, D.C.
NSHS	Nebraska State Historical Society, Lincoln
RG	Record Group

INTRODUCTION

1. Minnesota Climatology Working Group, *Minnesota's "Year without Winter, 1877–1879,"* accessed May 29, 2019, http://climate.umn.edu/doc/journal/wint77_78.html.

2. Regarding the death of Crazy Horse and the removal of the Sioux to the Missouri, see Magid, *Gray Fox*, ch. 31, "Death of Crazy Horse," and ch. 32, "Removal." For a detailed accounting of the defections of the Northern Sioux during the removal, see Bray, "We Belong to the North."

3. For more on these aspects of Crook's career, see Magid, *Gray Fox*, ch. 20, "The Rosebud Revisited."

4. *Omaha Republican*, Dec. 23, 1877; ibid., Jan. 1, 1878.

5. (Salt Lake) *Deseret News*, Jan. 9, 1878; J. J. Dickey to Robert Williams, AAG, Dec. 14, 1877, NARA, Dept. of the Platte, Letters Received, RG 393 (hereafter cited as NARA, DP, LR, RG 393); Bourke, *Diaries*, 3:356.

6. "Probability that the Bannocks Will Cause Trouble," *Omaha Republican*, Dec. 25, 1877.

CHAPTER 1. IT IS AN OUTRAGE

1. "The Hostile Indians," *New York Times*, Mar. 30, 1878.

2. *Annual Report of the Commissioner of Indian Affairs*, 1864, p. 155.

3. John Owen to Geary Flathead agency, Washington Territory, Feb. 13, 1861, in Dunbar and Phillips, *Journals and Letters of Major John Owen*, 2:243, quoted in Madsen, *Bannock of Idaho*, 125.

4. For details of the engagement, see Madsen, *Bannock of Idaho*, 63–83, 118–29.

5. Per General Order No. 65, series of 1875, quoted in Sheridan, *Records of Engagements, 1868 to 1882*, 5.

6. Brimlow, *Bannock Indian War*, 42–44.

7. For details of the treaty, see Madsen, *Bannock of Idaho*, 162–66.

8. See Brimlow, *Bannock Indian War*, 34–48.

9. Madsen, *Bannock of Idaho*, 207–9.

10. Brimlow, *Bannock Indian War*, 43–44.

11. In a highly critical analysis of the discontent prevalent on the Bannock reservation, the *Army and Navy Journal*, certainly no advocate for Indian rights, pointed out that the amount available to feed one member of the tribe amounted to about fifteen dollars a year or four cents a day; rations meant to last a week were usually exhausted after the fourth day. *U.S. Army and Navy Journal and Gazette* 15, no. 48 (1878): 776.

12. Greene, *Nez Perce Summer* 159.

13. An article in the *Idaho Weekly Statesman*, Nov. 25, 1877, identified Tambiago as a brother of the prisoner, quoted in Brimlow, *Bannock Indian War*, 62. Madsen described him as a friend. *Bannock of Idaho*, 204.

14. Bainbridge to Crook, Nov. 26, 1877, NARA, DP, LR, microfilm.

15. Bainbridge to AAG, Nov. 26, 1877, NARA, DP, Bannock War, 1877–78, M666. Both Crook and John Bourke, his aide, spell the agent's name "Danielson." See Bourke, *Diary*, 2:368; Crook to AAG, Div. of the Missouri, July 27, 1878, Crook Letterbook, 374, Hayes Library.

16. Bainbridge to AAG, Dec. 6, 1877, NARA, DP, LR, RG 393.

17. See Smith to AAG, Dec. 25, 1877, ibid.

18. Smith to AAG, Dec. 25 and 26, 1877, ibid. Crook to Sheridan, Jan. 3, 1878, NARA, DP, Telegrams Received, Bannock War, M666; Sheridan to Crook, Dec. 4, 1877, Jan. 4, 1878, NARA, DP, Telegrams Received, RG 393.

19. Smith to Crook, Jan. 12, 1878, NARA, DP, Telegrams Received, RG 393.

20. Crook to Sheridan, ibid.

21. *Army and Navy Journal* 15, no. 24 (Jan. 19, 1878): 373; Crook to Townsend AAG, Jan. 19, 1878, NARA, DP, Telegrams Sent, RG 393; Brimlow, *Bannock Indian War*, 65.

22. See Brimlow, *Bannock Indian War*, 61–65, 69.

23. For the source of the Royall-Crook discord, see Magid, *Gray Fox*, 248–50.

24. Brimlow, *Bannock Indian War*, 73–74.

25. Bourke, *Diaries*, 2:365.

26. Ibid., 2:361.

27. Ibid., 2:368–70.

28. See exchange of correspondence between the secretaries of war and the interior and their respective subordinates, Jan.–Mar. 1878, NARA, DP, LR, RG 393.

29. Brimlow, *Bannock Indian War*, 212.

30. Bourke, *Diaries*, 2:368–71.

31. Crook to Sheridan, Apr. 2. 1878, NARA, DP, Bannock War, M666; Crook to AG, Mil. Div. of the Missouri, Apr. 3, 1878, Crook Letterbook, Hayes Library, 412–13.

32. First endorsement to Crook's recommendation dated Apr. 4, 1878, NARA, DP, Bannock War, M666.

33. Ruby and Brown, *Indians of the Pacific Northwest*, 250; Brimlow, *Bannock Indian War*, 79.

34. Sadly, the active participants in the breakout were not the only Indians to suffer. The Lemhi Bannocks, though they had refused to join their Fort Hall brothers on the warpath, received hardly better treatment. Pressured by local settlers who coveted the tribe's land, the government began a campaign to remove them from their reservation. It took thirty years, but the Lemhi were ultimately forced from their homes in the Salmon River country and crowded on to the Fort Hall reservation. Madsen, *Bannock of Idaho*, 217.

35. Crook to AAG, July 27, 1878, Crook Letterbook, Hayes Library.

36. The inaccuracy of Crook's estimate seems evident because in February of the next year, he reported that in his department alone, 131 Bannocks were being held as prisoners of war. In a census taken at Fort Hall in December 1878, an additional 50 tribesmen had been reported killed or captured by General Miles, and 349 were still unaccounted for out of a total of 672 Bannocks on the reservation. Thus, if one includes all of those unaccounted for, though an unlikely scenario, it would appear that 530 Indians had been involved in the outbreak, in one way or another. Brimlow, *Bannock Indian War*, 189–91.

37. Madsen, *Bannocks of Idaho*, 220–21.

38. Ruby and Brown, *Indians of the Pacific Northwest*, 253. During the winter of 1877, despite Crook's vehement opposition, the Interior Department ordered the forced removal of the Oglalas and Brules from their home reservation on the Nebraska border to the malarial country adjacent to the Missouri River. For details and Crook's role, see Magid, *Gray Fox*, ch. 32, "Removal."

39. Crook to Rutherford Hayes, Oct. 14, 1871, Crook Letterbook, Hayes Library, quoted in King, "A Better Way," 241.

40. *Army and Navy Journal* 15, no. 47 (June 29, 1878): 758.

41. *Annual Report of the Secretary of War*, Sept. 23, 1878, NARA, M997. Crook and his contemporaries often used the term "savage" not as a pejorative but as descriptive of societies that they believed did not have the "benefit" of the civilizing influences of western culture.

42. Crook to Mrs. Lucy Hayes, June 7, 1878, quoted in Juarez, *Tarnished Saber*, 80.

43. General Order No. 8, Omaha Barracks, NE, July 17, 1878, in Bourke Papers, NSHS, RG 2955, Box 11-4.

44. Crook to Hayes, Oct. 21, 1878, quoted in Juarez, *Tarnished Saber*, 81.

45. Ibid., 84.

46. Porter, foreword to Schmitt, *General George Crook*, xiii.

47. For a detailed discussion of the whole affair, see Juarez, *Tarnished Saber*, 98–109. For Crook's allegations concerning Nickerson at the Rosebud, see Kennon diary, Aug. 7,

1886, Crook/Kennon Papers, AHEC; Crook, *Autobiography*, 196. See also this work, ch. 23, "Campaigning for Indian Rights."

CHAPTER 2. BLOOD ON THE SNOW

1. Email to the author from Carolyn Lawton, a Crook descendant, Jan. 19, 2007, quoting a newspaper clipping found taped inside the family's copy of Bourke's memoir, *On the Border with Crook*.

2. Proceedings, *Annual Reunion of the Society of the Army of West Virginia*, Daily News Print, Office and Bindery, Cumberland, MD, 1880.

3. Magid, *George Crook*, 264, 284.

4. *Bourke Diaries* 3:117–18.

5. Webb Hayes to Crook, Aug. 30, 1878, Executive Mansion Telegrams, Webb Hayes Papers, and Letter from Crook to Hayes, Sept. 14, 1878, Webb Hayes Papers, Rutherford B. Hayes Presidential Library, Freemont, Ohio (hereafter cited as Hayes Library).

6. Magid, *Gray Fox*, 365–66.

7. Collins, *Experiences in the West*, 194. Collins would later recall that on one typical hunt, they "killed three bear, three mountain sheep (the last of the race on this range), one bull elk (also the last of his kind in the vicinity), and a wagonload of black tail deer." Ibid., 214.

8. Crook to Webb Hayes, Sept. 14, 1878, Crook Papers, Hayes Library.

9. Lieker and Powers, *Northern Cheyenne Exodus*, 21.

10. Grinnell, *Fighting Cheyennes*, 400.

11. See Monnett, *Tell Them We Are Going Home*, 20–21.

12. Sheridan to Townsend, AAG, Feb. 27, 1879, Sheridan Papers, Library of Congress, Washington, D.C. (hereafter cited as LC).

13. Wild Hog's testimony, Senate Committee on Indian Affairs, Select Committee on the Removal of the Northern Cheyennes: Testimony Submitted to the Committee, SR 708, 46th Cong., 2d sess. (Serial 1899), 160 (hereafter cited as Committee on the Removal of the Northern Cheyennes), quoted in Monnett, *Tell Them We Are Going Home*, 23–24.

14. Monnett, *Tell Them We Are Going Home*, 23.

15. Crook to Senator S. S. Kirwood, Committee Chairman, Fort Omaha, Feb. 22, 1880, Crook Letterbook, Hayes Library. But see testimony by Indian agent John Miles, reporting Cheyennes as claiming they only went south on a trial basis and under great pressure. Committee on the Removal of the Northern Cheyennes, quoted in Monnette, *Tell Them We Are Going Home*, 23.

16. J. K. Mizner (commanding officer at Fort Reno) to AAG, Sept. 19, 1878, NARA, Office of the Adjutant General, Letters Received, Record Group 94 (hereafter cited as AGO, LR, RG), Microfilm. The slaughter of the buffalo may have been deliberate policy. See, for example, Sheridan's statement regarding the slaughter: "The white hide hunters have done more in the last two years to settle the vexing Indian question than the entire regular army has done in the past thirty years. They are destroying the Indians' commissary. For the sake of a lasting peace, let them kill, skin and sell until the buffalo are exterminated. Then your prairies can be covered with speckled cattle and the festive cowboy." Starita, *Dull Knifes*, 57. Regarding starvation on the reservation, see N. Lewis to AG, Sept. 15, 1878, quoted in ibid.

17. "The Cheyenne Outbreak," *New York Times*, Sept. 24, 1878.

18. John Miles to Mizner, Sept. 20, 1878, NARA, AGO, LR, RG 94. For further discussion of the reasons for the breakout see *Final Report of the Board of Officers*, Feb. 26, 1879, Dept. of the Platte (hereafter cited as DP), in ibid.; see also Starita, *Dull Knifes*, 40. For a thorough, contemporary analysis of the causes, see Leiker and Powers, *Northern Cheyenne Exodus*, 38–48.

19. Mizner to Pope, undated telegram, NARA, AGO, LR, RG 94, Microfilm.

20. John Miles to Mizner, Sept. 20, 1879, quoted in Monnett, *Tell Them We Are Going Home*, 42.

21. Ibid. For additional details, see ibid., 44–77.

22. Sheridan to Crook, Sept. 19, 1878, NARA, DP, RG 393.

23. Crook to Thornburgh, Sept. 13 and 19, 1878, quoted in Buecker, *Fort Robinson*, 129–30. See also Bronson, "Finish Fight for a Birthright," in Cozzens, *Eyewitnesses*, 4:489.

24. Bourke, *Diaries*, 3:118.

25. In addition to the Fourth, detachments of the Ninth and Fourteenth Infantries were present, as well as one company of the Fifth Cavalry and smaller units from the Seventh and Third. Bourke, *Diaries*, 3:125–26.

26. Ibid.

27. Sheridan to Pope, Sept. 18, 1878, NARA, DP, LR, RG 393.

28. Bourke, *Diaries*, 3:127.

29. Bronson, "Finish Fight for a Birthright," in Cozzens, *Eyewitnesses*, 4:491.

30. Dodge, *Indian Territory Journals*, 96n55.

31. Bourke, *Diaries*, 3:123.

32. Ibid., 3:124–25.

33. Ibid., 3:127.

34. Robinson, *Crook and the Western Frontier*, 222.

35. Sheridan to Pope, Oct. 4, 1878, NARA, Special Files, "The Cheyenne Outbreak, 1878–79," Microfilm (hereafter cited as NARA, Special Files, "Cheyenne Outbreak").

36. Sheridan to Townsend, Feb. 26, 1879, ibid.

37. For more on this issue, see Grinnell, *Fighting Cheyennes*, 413; Monnett, *Tell Them We Are Going Home*, 98n51; Leiker and Powers, *Northern Cheyenne Exodus*, 66. Monnett names the author Mari Sandoz as a primary proponent of the idea that the raids were an act of revenge for the Sand Creek massacre (93).

38. Monnett, *Tell Them We Are Going Home*, 79. For an extended discussion of the significance of the rapes, see Leiker and Powers, *Northern Cheyenne Exodus*, 59–62.

39. "The Trail of the Cheyennes," *New York Herald*, Oct. 5, 1878.

40. Sheridan to Williams, Oct. 5, 1878, NARA, HQ, Div. of Missouri, Telegrams Sent.

41. Sheridan to Sherman, Oct. 5, 1878, ibid.

42. Sheridan to Williams, Oct. 5, 1878, ibid.

43. For details of struggle over Reconstruction and its relationship to the frontier, see Utley, *Frontier Regulars*, 93–95.

44. Waltman, "Interior Department, War Department," 277–308.

45. For a complete report on the committee's investigations, see *Report of Testimony Taken by the Joint Committee Appointed to take into Consideration the Expediency of Transferring the Indian Bureau to the War Department* (hereafter *Report of Testimony Taken*); see also Crook, *Autobiography*, 228–30. The latter incorrectly assumed that the hearings were held

in October 1879, since the committee was authorized in the 1879 army appropriations legislation, which was actually passed in June 1878.

46. Camp Robinson was so named in 1874 after Lieutenant Levi Robinson of the Fourteenth Cavalry was killed by Indians that year. It was redesignated Fort Robinson in December 1878, prior to the Cheyenne crisis. Buecker, *Fort Robinson*, 20, 123.

47. *Report of Testimony Taken*, 118.

48. Ibid., 119.

49. For a detailed explanation of the history and politics of the transfer movement during this period, see Waltman, "Interior Department, War Department."

50. Crook to Sheridan Oct. 15, 1878, NARA, Special File, "Cheyenne Outbreak."

51. Sheridan to Townsend, Oct. 21, 1878, ibid.

52. Sheridan to Sherman, Oct. 14, 1878, ibid.

53. Crook to Sheridan, Oct. 26, 1878, NARA, DP, RG 393.

54. Buecker, *Fort Robinson*, 134–35; Monnett, *Tell Them We Are Coming Home*, 112–13.

55. See "Proceedings of a Board of Officers," NARA, Special File, "Cheyenne Outbreak."

56. Crook to Sheridan, Oct. 26, 1878, ibid.

57. "The Indian Commission," (Salt Lake) *Deseret News*, Oct. 23, 1878.

58. See "An Interview with General Crook," *New York Herald*, Jan. 31, 1879; Crook's report, Sep. 7, 1879, in *Annual Report to Secretary of War, 1879* (hereafter cited as *ARSW*, followed by year), Crook Letterbook, Hayes Library.

59. See Crook to Carlton, Oct. 29–30, 1878, NARA, Special File, "Cheyenne Outbreak."

60. Crook to AAG, Div. of Missouri, Jan. 22, 1879, Crook Letterbook, Hayes Library.

61. Crook to Sheridan, Nov. 1, 1878, NARA, Special File, "Cheyenne Outbreak."

62. Sheridan to AG, Nov. 5, 1878, ibid.

63. Sec. of interior to sec. of war, Nov. 22, 1878, ibid.

64. Crook to Sheridan, Dec. 20, 1878; Sheridan to AG, Dec. 20, 1878, ibid.

65. Whipple to Crook, Dec. 21, 1878, ibid.

66. Crook to AAG, Dec. 24, 1878, ibid.

67. AAG to Crook, Dec. 24, 1878, ibid.

68. Crook to Wessells, Dec. 28, 1878, ibid.; Crook to AAG, Report on Breakout, Jan. 22, 1879, Crook Letterbook, Hayes Library. On the matter of Crook's health during this period, see "General Crook Eliciting Facts as to Who Is Responsible," *New York Herald*, Jan. 21, 1879; "Gen. Cook has been suffering many weeks from a severe cold, with an attack of malarial fever"; and "Still Chasing the Cheyennes," *New York Times*, Jan. 13, 1879, quoting report of Jan. 9 to the effect that General Crook had been sick for several weeks.

69. Wessells's testimony in "Proceeding of Board of Officers," NARA, Special File, "Cheyenne Outbreak."

70. Wessells to Crook, Jan. 5, 1879, ibid.

71. Crook to AG, Washington, Jan. 7, 1878, ibid.

72. Crook to Sheridan, Jan. 7, 1879, ibid.

73. Wessells to Crook, Jan. 7, 1879, ibid.

74. Grinnell, *Fighting Cheyennes*, 419; "Proceedings of Board of Officers," NARA, Special File, "Cheyenne Outbreak."

75. "Proceedings of Board of Officers," NARA, Special File, "Cheyenne Outbreak."

76. Wessells's testimony, ibid.

77. Ibid., 3. These figures have been disputed by historians. Another source estimated five long guns and eleven pistols (Grinnell, *Fighting Cheyenne*, 420); based on newspaper accounts, Hoig reported fifteen rifles and two revolvers. Hoig, *Perilous Pursuit*, 169.

78. For a detailed account of the fight and pursuit, see Grinnell, *Fighting Cheyenne*, 420–26; "Proceedings of Board of Officers," NARA, Special File, "Cheyenne Outbreak."

79. Wessells to Crook, Jan. 10, 1879, ibid.

80. Crook to Wessells, Jan 10, 1879, ibid.

81. "Massacre of Cheyennes," *New York Herald*, Jan. 11, 1879.

82. Crook relayed that information to Sheridan, and it was later confirmed in a report to the assistant adjutant general of the Division of the Missouri. "Proceedings of Board of Officers," NARA, Special File, "Cheyenne Outbreak"; Crook to AAG, Div. of Missouri, Sept. 22, 1879, Crook Letterbook, Hays Library. For a firsthand account, see DeWitt, "Surrender of Chief Dull Knife," quoted in Greene, *Indian War Veterans*, 161–62.

83. Crook to Wessells, Jan. 11, 1879, NARA, Special File, "Cheyenne Outbreak."

84. See Wessells to Crook, Jan. 12; Crook to Sheridan, Jan. 23, 1879, ibid.

85. Monnett, *Tell Them We Are Going Home*, 134–35.

86. Examples of the injuries sustained include "Short Woman, GSW [gunshot wound] R. Hand, Head and cheek and back, thigh fractured; . . . Medicine Woman, GSW head, R. eye shot out; . . . Little girl 5 years, penetrating wound of abdomen died 12 hours after; . . . Baby (girl) one year fracture both thighs upper third, died one hour after being brought in, Baby (girl) 6 mos. Fracture L Thigh Died January 12, '79, morning." Surgeons' report quoted in Monnett, *Tell Them We Are Going Home*, 139. The board of inquiry (see below) later found that when the bodies of the Indians were collected on January 10, more than a dozen had been scalped. The board inferred that these acts were perpetrated by civilians who were seen "examining the dead." The board members recorded no evidence that soldiers were involved in these deeds. "Proceedings of Board of Officers," NARA, Special File, "Cheyenne Outbreak."

87. Crook to Sheridan, Jan. 10, 1879, NARA, Special File, "Cheyenne Outbreak."

88. Townsend, AG, to Sheridan, Jan. 10, 1879, ibid.

89. Sheridan to Crook, Jan. 13, 1879, ibid.

90. "General Sherman on the Outbreak at Fort Robinson—the Conduct of the Military Approved," *New York Herald*, Jan. 16, 1879; Sherman to Sheridan, Jan. 21, 1879, NARA, Special File, "Cheyenne Outbreak."

91. Crook to Sheridan, Jan. 12, 1879, ibid.

92. "Lieutenant Schuyler's Mission," *New York Herald*, Jan. 18, 1879.

93. Crook to Sheridan, Jan. 14, 1879; Sheridan to Crook, Jan. 15, 1879, NARA, Special File, "Cheyenne Outbreak."

94. *New York Herald*, Jan. 16, 1879.

95. Crook to Wessells, Jan. 14, 1879, NARA, Special File, "Cheyenne Outbreak."

96. Crook to Evans, Jan. 15, 1879, ibid.

97. "A Court of Inquiry Ordered by General Crook," *New York Herald*, Jan. 21, 1879; Sheridan to Crook, Jan. 23, 1879, NARA, Special File, "Cheyenne Outbreak."

98. Sheridan to Crook, Jan. 18, 1879, ibid.

99. Crook to Sheridan, Jan. 18, 1879, ibid.

100. "Cheyenne Widows and Orphans to be Delivered to Red Cloud," *New York Herald*, Jan. 19, 1879.

101. Crook to Wessells, Jan. 17, 1879, NARA, Special File, "Cheyenne Outbreak"; "Red Cloud Reluctant to Have His Young Men Used in Their Capture," *New York Herald*, Jan 19, 1879.

102. Sherman to Sheridan, Jan. 19, 1879, NARA, Special File, "Cheyenne Outbreak".

103. Hoig, *Perilous Pursuit*, 185, 188–93; Evans to Crook, Jan. 23, 1879, NARA, Special File, "Cheyenne Outbreak"; Crook to Sheridan, Jan. 23, 1879, ibid.

104. Hoig, *Perilous Pursuit*, 193.

105. "Proceedings of Board of Officers," NARA, Special File, "Cheyenne Outbreak"; "The Cheyenne Fight," *New York Herald*, Jan. 24, 1879. This article also listed twenty-three Indian dead, including seventeen warriors, and nine survivors, including one man and five women wounded and the remaining three women unhurt.

106. Monnett, *Tell Them We Are Going Home*, 156–57.

107. Crook to Evans, Jan. 23, 1879, NARA, Special File, "Cheyenne Outbreak."

108. Crook to AAG, Div. of Missouri, Jan. 23, 1879, ibid.

109. AAG, Div. of the Missouri, to Crook, Jan. 23, 1879, ibid.

110. Crook to Sheridan, Jan 23, 1879, ibid.; Crook to Sheridan, Jan. 25, 1879, ibid.

111. "Removal of the Widows and Orphans to Red Cloud," *New York Herald*, Feb. 1, 1879.

112. Letter from Kansas governor George T. Anthony to sec. of war, Nov. 11, 1878. For a detailed discussion of the depredations, see Leiker and Powers, *Northern Cheyenne Exodus*, 61–64, 75. The authors support Anthony's contention that at least forty civilians died, and "perhaps as many as a dozen" women and children were victims of rape.

113. Grinnell, *Fighting Cheyennes*, 412.

114. Starita, *Dull Knifes*, 68.

115. Crook to AAG, Div. of Missouri, Sept. 27, 1879, Crook Letterbook, Hayes Library.

116. Crook to AAG, Div. of Missouri, ibid.

117. Prucha, *Great Father*, 186.

118. Committee on the Removal of the Northern Cheyennes, quoted in ibid., 186.

CHAPTER 3. I AM A MAN

1. Dando-Collins, *Standing Bear*.

2. Other than the participants, there were no witnesses to this visit, and its only recorded mention is in two books by Tibbles. In an early account of the Ponca case, *Ponca Chiefs*, published in 1889 as part of a national effort to transform government Indian policy, Tibbles does not mention Crook's presence on the night of March 29. Instead, according to Tibbles, the *Herald's* city editor entered the journalist's office at eleven o'clock that evening with the news that a band of Ponca Indians had been arrested and were being held at Fort Omaha, charged with leaving their reservation in Indian Territory without permission. This, Tibbles wrote, caused him to go the fort the next morning to interview the prisoners and hence involve himself in the case. Tibbles, *Ponca Chiefs*, 18. In his memoir, written in 1905 (fifteen years after Crook's death), Tibbles admitted that the general appeared at his door, though in this account he omits mention of the presence of the two Omahas. King, "A Better Way," 244; Tibbles, *Buckskin*

and Blanket, 193. However, Dando-Collins makes a persuasive case that the chief and his daughter accompanied Crook that night, and I have accepted the logic of his position. Dando-Collins, *Standing Bear*, 53–54, 240–41nn73,74. Tibbles failure to mention Crook in *Ponca Chiefs* was apparently a deliberate effort to protect the general's military career by concealing his involvement in the case. By the time Tibbles published his subsequent memoir, circumstances had changed. The revelation of Crook's connection was no longer harmful and, on the contrary, redounded to the general's credit. Tibbles's failure to mention the Omahas may have also been an effort to protect them. The fact that he subsequently married the young woman would seem to lend credibility to this reasoning. See "Note on the Text," *Ponca Chiefs*, 141–42.

3. Dando-Collins, *Standing Bear*, 53. Tibbles thought that the two men were unique among whites in being so honored. Tibbles, *Buckskin and Blanket*, 193.

4. Tibbles, *Buckskin and Blanket*, 190–92; Magid, *Gray Fox*, 393.

5. See ch. 2, "Blood on the Snow," in this work; and King, "A Better Way," 243.

6. "Nebraska Sentiment about the Cheyenne Massacre," *Omaha Daily Herald*, Jan. 17, 1879, reprinted in *New York Herald*, Jan. 22, 1879.

7. Dando-Collins, *Standing Bear*, 51. Most surviving photos show Tibbles clean shaven and with gray hair.

8. The story of Tibbles's induction into the Soldier Lodge secret society and other adventures is told in Tibbles, *Buckskin and Blanket*, chs. 1–20.

9. Grinnell, *Fighting Cheyennes*, 412.

10. Sec. of interior to War Dept., Mar. 7, 1879, NARA, DP, LR, RG 98.

11. Bourke, *Diaries*, 3:180

12. One Ponca woman was, in fact, too ill to travel and so remained with the Omahas. King to AAG, Mar. 26, 1879, quoted in Tibbles, *Ponca Chiefs*, 41.

13. Tibbles, *Buckskin and Blanket*, 195; Bourke, *Diaries*, 3:180.

14. Dando-Collins, *Standing Bear*, 5.

15. Ibid., 8.

16. Bourke, *On the Border*, 426.

17. Tibbles, *Ponca Chiefs*, 6.

18. Ibid., 7.

19. Dando-Collins, *Standing Bear*, 15–23.

20. Standing Bear's account of the journey is found in Tibbles, *Ponca Chiefs*, 7–8. See also "Ponca Trail of Tears," Nebraskastudies.org.

21. Tibbles, *Ponca Chiefs*, 12.

22. "Ponca Trail of Tears."

23. Dando-Collins, *Standing Bear*, 38–39.

24. *Annual Report of the Commissioner of Indian Affairs, 1877*, quoted in Tibbles, *Ponca Chiefs*, 123.

25. Standing Bear quoted in Tibbles, *Ponca Chiefs*, 14. See also Bourke, *Diaries*, 3:182.

26. Tibbles, *Ponca Chiefs*, 14.

27. Ibid., 25.

28. Ibid., 15.

29. Bourke, *On the Border*, 427.

30. Vore to Schurz, Mar. 4, 1879, quoted in Tibbles, *Ponca Chiefs*, 43.

31. Dando-Collins, *Standing Bear*, 49–50.

32. Tibbles, *Buckskin and Blanket*, 192.

33. Ibid., 195.

34. Ibid., 195–96.

35. Ibid., 196.

36. Bourke, *Diaries*, 3:179.

37. Tibbles, *Buckskin and Blanket*, 180–81.

38. In contrast, Tibbles describes Crook as saying, "I am a soldier and must obey orders," but has him add, "I will do all I can to have the orders . . . countermanded." Ibid., 198.

39. Bourke, *Diaries*, 3:184.

40. Ibid., 3:184–85.

41. Tibbles, *Ponca Chiefs*, 32–33.

42. Dando-Collins, *Standing Bear*, 27–29.

43. "A Talk with Sec. Schurz about the Ponca Indians," *Chicago Tribune*, Aug. 23, 1879, quoted in Mathes and Lowitt, *Standing Bear Controversy*, 114. For a detailed discussion of Schurz's policies, see ibid., 107–11.

44. Tibbles, *Ponca Chiefs*, 34; Tibbles, *Buckskin and Blanket*, 198–99.

45. Webster was so well regarded that he had recently been selected to preside over Nebraska's constitutional convention. Tibbles, *Ponca Chiefs*, 34.

46. Ibid.

47. Ibid.

48. Ibid., 35; Tibbles, *Buckskin and Blanket*, 199. For more on Poppleton's career see, Morton, "Biographical Sketch of Andrew Jackson Poppleton," 324.

49. Poppleton made this assertion in a pamphlet entitled *Reminiscence*, published June 11, 1915, quoted in Mathes and Lowitt, *Standing Bear Controversy*, 55, 60n45.

50. Latin translation from *American College Dictionary*.

51. Mathes and Lowitt, *Standing Bear Controversy*, 56.

52. Dando-Collins, *Standing Bear*, 84.

53. Tibbles, *Buckskin and Blanket*, 199.

54. The petition and other documents related to the case are set forth in Tibbles, *Ponca Chiefs*, 36–45.

55. Ibid.; Mathes and Lowitt, *Standing Bear Controversy*, 57; Dando-Collins, *Standing Bear*, 88.

56. Hayt to sec. of interior, Apr. 10, 1879, quoted in Tibbles, *Ponca Chiefs*, 46–48. Though Crook held his tongue as required by his rank, he had little regard for either Schurz or Hayt. Writing in his diary, however, John Bourke was less constrained. Less than a year after the Ponca case had been decided, he read of Hayt's dismissal as the result of a silver mine scandal. Remarking on the disgraced commissioner, he wrote, "It will be impossible to find a more thorough rascal." Bourke, *Diaries*, 3:353. He had previously written off Schurz as "a spindleshanked Mephistopheles." Ibid., 3:68.

57. Tibbles, *Ponca Chiefs*, 49–52.

58. Ibid., 53–61.

59. Dando-Collins, *Standing Bear*, 93–94.

60. In *Ponca Chiefs* Tibbles gives the opening date of the trial as April 30, but the *Daily Herald* and the *Lincoln Daily State Journal* both indicated that the proceedings commenced the next day. See "Notes on the Text," *Ponca Chiefs*, 140.

61. Tibbles, *Buckskin and Blanket*, 200.

62. See editor's note, *Ponca Chiefs*, 93, and Petition for the writ of Habeas Corpus in ibid., 36–38.

63. Dando-Collins, *Standing Bear*, 105.

64. Ibid., 84–85, 105–10; Mathes and Lowitt, *Standing Bear Controversy*, 65; Starita, "Case of Standing Bear," 4–11; Starita, "*I Am a Man*," 139–40.

65. Starita, "Case of Standing Bear," 4.

66. Dando-Collins, *Standing Bear*, 107.

67. Starita, "Case of Standing Bear," 5.

68. Dando-Collins, *Standing Bear*, 110.

69. *Omaha Daily Herald*, May 2, 1880; Dando-Collins, *Standing Bear*, 111; King, "A Better Way," 239–56, 248.

70. Dando-Collins, *Standing Bear*, 112.

71. Tibbles, who reported Webster's remarks almost verbatim in both his newspaper and in his book *Ponca Chiefs*, paid only cursory attention to Lambertson's argument, leaving little of its detail to posterity. See editor's note in Tibbles, *Ponca Chiefs*, 92–93.

72. Tibbles, *Buckskin and Blanket*, 200; King, "A Better Way," 8; Dando-Collins, *Standing Bear*, 120–23.

73. Tibbles, *Buckskin and Blanket*, 200.

74. Dando-Collins, *Standing Bear*, 126.

75. Ibid., 126–27.

76. See "Editor's Note on Text," in Tibbles, *Ponca Chiefs*, 140–41.

77. Tibbles, *Buckskin and Blanket*, 201.

78. *Omaha Daily Herald*, May 2, 1879; Tibbles, *Buckskin and Blanket*, 201–2; *Ponca Chiefs*, 93; Dando-Collins, *Standing Bear*, 127–29.

79. All quotes from Dundy's opinion come from *United States ex rel. Standing Bear v. Crook*, quoted in Tibbles, *Ponca Chiefs*, 99–102.

80. Section 2149, *Revised Statutes of the United States*, as quoted in Dundy's opinion, quoted in pertinent part in Dando-Collins, *Standing Bear*, 135.

81. Judge Dundy's opinion can be found in its entirety in Dillon, *Cases Determined in the Circuit Court for the Eight Circuit*, 453; *Arkansas City Traveler* (Kan.), May 21, 1879, quoted in Dando-Collins, *Standing Bear*, 137.

82. For summary of national reaction, see Dando-Collins, *Standing Bear*, 140–41; and Mathes and Lowitt, *Standing Bear Controversy*, 70–71.

83. *Omaha Daily Herald*, May 15, 1879, quoted in Dando-Collins, *Standing Bear*, 140.

84. Quoted in Dando-Collins, *Standing Bear*, 135; see also page 151.

85. "Gen. Sherman and the Indians," *New York Times*, Dec. 3, 1878; "Sheridan and Shurz," *New York Times*, Jan. 2, 1879.

86. On Sherman and the Poncas, see Sherman to McCrary, May 20, 1879, included in Testimony Relating to Removal of the Ponca Indians, quoted in Mathes and Lowitt, *Standing Bear Controversy*, 69.

87. Sherman to Sheridan, May 22, 1879, 46th Cong. 3rd Sess. Sen. Ex. Doc., 14.

88. Dando-Collins, *Standing Bear*, 149; Mathes and Lowitt, *Standing Bear Controversy*, 69.

89. Schurz to Helen Hunt Jackson, Jan. 17, 1880, quoted in Jackson, *A Century of Dishonor*, 361–62.

90. Ibid., 365.

91. Tibbles, *Buckskin and Blanket*, 203.

92. Ibid.; Starita, "*I Am a Man,*" 166–67.

93. Dando-Collins, *Standing Bear*, 151; Mathes and Lowitt, *Standing Bear Controversy*, 73.

94. Dando-Collins, *Standing Bear*, 164.

95. Mathes and Lowitt, *Standing Bear Controversy*, 74.

96. Tibbles, *Buckskin and Blanket*, 204.

97. Crook to Tibbles, June 19, 1879. The letter was reproduced by Bourke in his diary and can be found in *Diaries*, 3:197–201. It was also published under the heading, "The Indian Problem, Letters from Thomas H. Tibbles and General Crook," *New York Times*, Oct. 10, 1879.

98. King, "A Better Way," 250.

99. Porter, foreword to Schmitt, *General George Crook: His Autobiography*, 69.

100. Crook, *Autobiography*, 73.

101. Crook letter, Bourke, *Diaries*, 3:199.

102. Ibid., 200.

103. Ibid., 201.

CHAPTER 4. THE PONCA COMMISSION

1. Editor's commentary in Bourke, *Diaries*, 4:65.

2. See ch. 6, "Cowboys and Indians," in this work for events leading to the tribe's removal from Colorado.

3. Crook to AAG, Div. of Missouri, Aug. 8, 1880, reproduced in Bourke, *Diaries*, 4:62.

4. Bourke, *Diaries*, 4:480; Crook, *Autobiography*, 117n6.

5. See Bourke, *Diaries*, 4:29–37, and ch. 7 of this work on Crook's involvement with the Murchie mine.

6. Bourke, *Diaries*, 4:60.

7. Ibid., 4:66–67. For a description of Stanton and his friendship with Crook, see Magid, *Gray Fox*, 89–90.

8. Bourke, *Diaries*, 3:409, 351.

9. Ibid., 4:84, 94.

10. Ibid., 4:74, 75, 85. For more on Tom Moore, see Magid, *Gray Fox*, 81–82, 410n29.

11. Crook to AAG, HQ, Div. of Missouri, Aug. 27, 1880, reproduced in Bourke, *Diaries*, 4:102.

12. Janetski, *Indians in Yellowstone National Park*, 101, 105.

13. Bourke, *Diaries*, 4:96–103.

14. For a clear summary of Schurz's shifting positions regarding the Poncas, see ch. 6, "Schurz Defines in Position and Dawes Disagrees," in Mathes and Lowitt, *Standing Bear Controversy*.

15. Ibid., 127.

16. President's transmittal letter, *Report of Special Commission to the Poncas*, 1, reproduced in Bourke, *Diaries*, 4:200–221.

17. Hayes, *Diary and Letters*, entry of Dec. 18, 1880.

18. Hayes to Hoar, Dec. 16, 1880, ibid., 631; Wikipedia, s.v. "George Frisbie Hoar."

19. President's transmittal letter, *Report of Special Commission to the Poncas*, 3, reproduced in Bourke, *Diaries*, 4:200–221.

20. On December 22, 1880, the Oklahoma chiefs sent a petition confirming their position to Schurz; see *Report of Special Commission to the Poncas*, 18. For further details of

the events leading to the creation of the Ponca Commission, see ch. 7, "Expanding the Parameters," in Mathis and Lowitt, *Standing Bear Controversy*.

21. R. C. Drum to Crook, Dec. 10, 1880; and Executive Mansion to Crook, Dec. 11, 1880, NARA, George Crook, Appointments File, Telegrams, MR1395.

22. Bourke, *Diaries*, 4:158–60; Hayes, *Diary and Letters*, Dec. 15, 1880.

23. Hayes to Hoar, Dec. 16, 1880, Hayes, *Diary and Letters*, 631.

24. Bourke, *Diaries*, 4:161.

25. For relationship between Hayes and Crook, see Magid, *George Crook*, 7, 264, 284.

26. For more on the rivalry between Crook and Sherman, see Magid, *Gray Fox*, 342–44.

27. Bourke, *Diaries*, 4:216.

28. Ibid.

29. Jackson to Dawes, Dec. 1880, Dawes Papers, LC, quoted in Mathes, *Helen Hunt Jackson*, 35.

30. Bourke, *Diaries*, 4:172–89.

31. Ibid., 4:179.

32. *Report of Special Commission to the Poncas*, 17; Bourke, *Diaries*, 4:188.

33. Bourke, *Diaries*, 4:188.

34. Ibid., 4:194.

35. Ibid.

36. Ibid., 4:196.

37. Bourke, *Diaries*, 4:218.

38. Ibid., 4:234.

39. Ibid., 4:236–37.

40. Ibid., 4:273–74.

41. The report is reprinted in Bourke, *Diaries*, 4:279–83.

42. Ibid., 4:283.

43. Ibid., 4:280.

44. Ibid., 4:283.

45. Mathes and Lowitt, *Standing Bear Controversy*, 141–45.

46. Ibid., 151.

47. Ibid., 153–58.

48. Congressional Record, Mar. 3, 1881, 2381–85, quoted in Mathes and Lowitt, *Standing Bear Controversy*, 163.

49. Ibid., 181. For more on the Sioux commission, see ch. 26 of this work. For a detailed description of the Poncas' fate following the passage of the 1881 appropriations legislation, see Mathes and Lowitt, *Standing Bear Controversy*, 161–82.

CHAPTER 5. CROOK HOUSE

1. Sharp, "Fort Omaha," 18–19, 22.

2. Mattes, *Indians, Infants, and Infantry*, 238.

3. Sharp, "Fort Omaha," 20.

4. Bourke, *Diaries*, 4:209.

5. Greguras, "History of the Post of Omaha," 2.

6. The fort had been renamed in December 1878, as it now housed the headquarters for the military department. Sharp, "Fort Omaha," 79. For the locations of Crook's

headquarters and residences, see Wolfe, *Omaha Directory for 1876–77* and *1878–79*, pp. 81 and 16, respectively.

7. Andreas, *History of Nebraska*, 1:768.

8. *Crook House Museum Tour Guide*.

9. George W. Parker to Crook, Lyons, Iowa, Oct. 29, 1878, Douglas County Historical Society Archives, Omaha.

10. Greguras, "History of the Post of Omaha," note 34, n.p.

11. J. H. Lindt, "Brief History of Crook House," Dec. 1930, unpublished memorandum quoted in Sharp, "Fort Omaha," 83.

12. Ruhling, "Wallpaper in the General Crook House."

13. Burkley, *Faded Frontier*, 167.

14. Where not otherwise noted, much of the information about the layout and construction of the house can be found in *General Crook House Museum Tour Guide* and in a booklet entitled *Docent Training for the Douglas County Historical Society*, provided to the author by the society.

15. Burkley, *Faded Frontier*, 388–89.

16. Sharpe, "Fort Omaha," 91; Mattes, *Indians, Infants, and Infantry*, 239.

17. "Tour Information," undated and anonymous one-page typescript in the archives of the Douglas County Historical Society, Crook House, Omaha, Neb.; Burkely, *Faded Frontier*, 336; Bourke, *Diaries*, 3:342.

18. *Omaha Bee*, Sept. 2, 1880.

19. "The Presidential Party Arrives in Omaha, Take In the Town and Leave for the West," *Omaha Bee*, Sept. 4, 1880.

20. Broadfield, *Stories of Omaha*, 108.

21. "Presidential Party Arrives," *Omaha Bee*, Sept. 4, 1880; "Hayes-Sherman," *Omaha Daily Herald*, Sept. 4, 1880; "The Nation's Chief Executive," *Omaha Daily Republican*, Sept. 4, 1880.

22. Crook to Commanding General, Mar. 11, 1880, NARA, DP, LS, RG 393; Wolfe, *Omaha Directory*, 1881, 1882, 1887, and 1888.

CHAPTER 6. COWBOYS AND INDIANS

1. For more on Posse Comitatus and statutory authorities, see Doyle and Elsea, "Posse Comitatus Act"; Tom Head, "The Posse Comitatus Act of 1878," ThoughtCo, Nov. 1, 2017, thoughtco.com/the-posse-comitatus-act-of-1878–721707.

2. For an account of Olive's life and character, see Chrisman, *Ladder of Rivers*.

3. Bourke, *Diaries*, 3:186. There is general agreement that Print hanged the men, but the burning of the bodies has been variously attributed to a deliberate attempt ordered by him to destroy evidence. Mattes, *Indians, Infants, and Infantry*, 240. More likely, as the act of two drunken Olive employees after Print left the scene. Chrisman, *Ladder of Rivers*, 255.

4. Chrisman, *Ladder of Rivers*, 263–71.

5. Quoted ibid., 272.

6. Magid, *George Crook*, 337–42.

7. Crook to AAG, Div. of Missouri, Apr. 14, 1879, Crook Letterbook, Hayes Library.

8. McCrary to Nance, Apr. 12, 1879, quoted in Laurie and Cole, *Role of Federal Military Forces*, 74.

9. Thurston quoted in Mattes, *Indians, Infants, and Infantry*, 240–41; and Sharpe, "Fort Omaha," 86. In a note Sharpe points out that only two companies of infantry were stationed at Fort Omaha, and the returns of the second company do not mention being sent to Hastings for the Olive trial. Thus he concluded that Burt had only one company with him. Ibid.

10. The defense raised this point in their summation. Chrisman, *Ladder of Rivers*, 294. After spending twenty months in prison, Print was released when his conviction was overturned on a technicality. Retried in a court on his home turf, he was acquitted and set free. He was later shot down while entering a saloon in Trail City, Colorado. In one of those ironies of fate, his murderer too, was tried, convicted, released on a technicality, and ultimately tried again and acquitted. Myers, "I. P. Print Olive."

11. Laurie and Cole, *Role of Federal Military Forces*, 74–75.

12. Marsh, *People of the Shining Mountains*, 79–80.

13. *Annual Report of the Commissioner for Indian Affairs, 1878*, quoted in *Annual Report of the Commissioner*, 1879, xxxiv. Colorado was admitted to the Union on Aug. 1, 1876.

14. Santala, "Ute Campaign of 1879," 56; Marsh, *People of the Shining Mountains*, 3.

15. For Ute John at Slim Buttes, see Greene, *Slim Buttes*, 80. For more on Crook at the battle, see Magid, *Gray Fox*, ch. 26, "Slim Butte."

16. Bourke, *Diaries*, 2:48; see also Emmitt, *Last War Trail*, 197.

17. For more background on the Utes, see "The Betrayal of Jack," in Emmitt, *Last War Trail*, 300–304; Santala, "Ute Campaign of 1879," 55–62; and Marsh, *People of the Shining Mountains*, generally.

18. Pitkin quoted in Emmitt, *Last War Trail*, 26. See also ibid., 23; and Marsh, *People of the Shining Mountains*, 79.

19. *Annual Report of the Commissioner for Indian Affairs, 1877*, quoted in *Report of the Commissioner, 1879*, xxxvi.

20. Santala, "Ute Campaign of 1879," 67.

21. See Hayt to Meeker, Aug. 15, 1879: "You are directed to adopt without delay, decisive measures to put a stop to these roaming habits of your Indians. Office instructions . . . in regard to their being treated as hostile Indians and liable to arrest if they are found outside of their reservations without passes, should be enforced, and you should also give them to understand that their annuities will be withheld from them if they do not comply." *Annual Report of the Commissioner for Indian Affairs, 1879*, xxvi.

22. Ibid., xviii.

23. See Emmitt, *Last War Trail*, 307–8.

24. *Annual Report of the Commissioner for Indian Affairs, 1879*, xxi.

25. Emmitt, *Last War Trail*, 307–8.

26. Ibid., 95–96.

27. Lieutenant Bourke, who had attended West Point with Thornburgh, noted in his diary that he personally "bore [the major] very warm and kindly feelings," undoubtedly a reflection of Crook's own regard for the man. *Diaries*, 3:100, 104, 301.

28. Thornburgh to Crook, July 27, 1879, quoted in *Annual Report of the Commissioner of Indian Affairs, 1879*, xxiii.

29. Thornburgh to Crook, July 20, 1879, quoted in Emmitt, *Last War Trail*, 96–101.

30. Crook to Sheridan, Fort Omaha, Aug. 4, 1879, quoted *Annual Report of the Commissioner of Indian Affairs, 1879*, xxii–xxiii.

31. Bourke, *Diaries*, 3:288.

32. In November 1864 Colorado militia, led by Colonel John M. Chivington, had fallen on the sleeping families of Black Kettle's Cheyenne village at Sand Creek, slaughtering its occupants. See Hoig, *Peace Chiefs*, 64–66, among a great many other sources.

33. The delay in receiving the annuities was not Meeker's fault but can be attributed to the Interior Department. The supplies were being held in a Union Pacific warehouse as the department had as yet not paid for their shipment. Emmitt, *Last War Trail*, 309.

34. *Report of the Commissioner of Indian Affairs, 1879*, xxix.

35. Ibid., xxix.

36. For an apparently unbiased account of the confrontation, see Emmitt, *Last War Trail*, 150–54.

37. *Report of the Commissioner of Indian Affairs, 1879*, xxx.

38. Crook to Williams, Sept. 15, 1879, NARA, Special File, "White River Utes, 1879," Microfilm.

39. Santala, "Ute Campaign of 1879," 77.

40. Thornburgh to Williams, Sept. 16, 1879, NARA, Special File, "White River Utes."

41. Williams to Thornburgh, Sept. 17, 1879, ibid.

42. Williams to Thornburgh, Sept. 23, 1879, ibid.

43. Meeker to Thornburgh, Sept. 27, 1879, *Annual Report of the Commissioner of Indian Affairs, 1879*, xxxi.

44. Thornburgh to Williams, Sept. 26, 1879, NARA, Special File, "White River Utes."

45. Thornburgh to Meeker, Sept. 28, 1879, ibid.

46. *Annual Report of the Commissioner of Indian Affairs, 1879*, xxxiii.

47. Ibid., xxxiii; Santala, "Ute Campaign of 1879," 79–84. For a firsthand account of the fight, see Sumner, "Besieged by the Utes," 12–22.

48. *Annual Report of the Commissioner of Indian Affairs, 1879*.

49. Bourke, *Diaries*, 3:294; Williams to James Francis, Oct. 1, 1879, copied into ibid., 3:298.

50. Ibid., 3:300. General Pope's opinion of the White River Utes was similar to Sheridan's. He described them as "worthless idle vagabonds who are no more likely to earn a living where they are by manual labor than by teaching metaphysics." Pope to Sheridan, Sept. 13, 1879, NARA, Special File, "White River Utes."

51. Bourke, *Diaries*, 3:301.

52. Ibid., 3:312.

53. Ibid., 3:341.

54. Ibid., 3:339.

55. Emmitt, *Last War Trail*, 315–20.

56. Crook Annual Report, Sep. 30, 1880, Crook Letterbook, Hayes Library; see also Bourke, *Diaries*, 3:347, in which Bourke echoes Crook's anger, railing that "no effort has been made to have justice dealt out to those who so treacherously attacked Thornburgh and his command." Legislation to confer brevet recognition to Indian War veterans was not passed until 1890. Utley, *Frontier Regulars*, 22.

57. Finerty, *War-Path and Bivouac*, 192; Emmitt, *Last War Trail*, 96. As scalping was not part of the Ute tradition, Nicaagat may have picked up the practice from other tribes while serving in Crook's command during the Sioux War.

CHAPTER 7. INVESTING IN THE FUTURE

1. Utley, *Frontier Regulars*, 20. But see Adams, *Class and Race in the Frontier Army*, 23, which states to the contrary that officers' salaries exceeded those of 90 percent of American families.

2. Soule, *United States Blue Book, 1877*, 85.

3. For accounts of frontier officers who availed themselves of entrepreneurial opportunities, some successful, many not, see Tate, *Frontier Army in the Settlement of the West*, 199, 282–303.

4. Magid, *George Crook*, 56.

5. In September 1881 Crook happily reported that "the Indians throughout the Department have been unusually quiet and there have been no depredations committed by them. They are in my opinion gradually improving in knowledge of civilized life and are paying more attention to agriculture than ever before and, I am informed, with good results." Crook to AAG, Annual Report, Sept. 29, 1881, Div. of the Missouri, Crook Letterbook, Hayes Library.

6. Bourke, *Diaries*, 3:347.

7. Crook, *Autobiography*, 238n14. According to Crook's editor Martin Schmitt, efforts to make the mine pay continued long after Crook had disengaged from ownership. By 1935 mine excavations had reached the level of 1,600 feet when Murchie was operated as one of a number of mines under the control of Empire-Star Mines. Ibid., 238n13. The mine was eventually shut down during World War II and in 1975 was purchased by the State of California, which now runs it as a historical site and state park. "California's Gold History Lives."

8. Crook, 237–40; Crook to Schuyler, Mar. 11, 1880, Schuyler Papers, Huntington Library, San Marino, Calif.

9. For more on Fort Terwaw, see Magid, *George Crook*, 87–92.

10. Magid, *Gray Fox*, 289. King was to become a close friend of the general's and author of a book that contributed to the general's fame, *Campaigning with Crook*. For a brief biography of King, see the introduction by Don Russell in the 1964 reprint published by the University of Oklahoma Press. For a more complete study of King's life and career, see Russell, *Campaigning with King*.

11. Bourke, *Diaries*, 3:248; Crook, *Autobiography*, 238.

12. Crook to Schuyler, Jan. 18, 1880, Schuyler Papers, Huntington Library.

13. Crook to Schuyler, ibid.; Crook, *Autobiography*, 238.

14. Crook to Schuyler, Apr. 18, 1880, Schuyler Papers, Huntington Library.

15. Crook to Schuyler, Mar. 11, 1880, ibid.

16. Sackett to Crook Mar. 18, 1880, ibid.

17. Crook to Schuyler, Apr. 10, 1880, ibid.

18. Crook to Schuyler, Apr. 28, 1880, ibid.

19. Crook, *Autobiography*, 239.

20. Crook to Schuyler, June 26, 1880, Schuyler Papers, Huntingdon Library.

21. Crook, *Autobiography*, 240.

22. Ibid.

23. Crook to Schuyler, Dec. 31, 1881, Schuyler Papers, Huntington Library.

24. Schmitt, in Crook, *Autobiography*, 240.

25. Magid, *George Crook*, 112–16.

26. Crook, Appointments, Commissions File, NARA, MI395. See also Magid, *Gray Fox*, 118.

27. Crook, Appointments, Commissions File, NARA, MI395.

28. Crook to Webb Hayes, Dec. 4, 1881, Crook Letterbook, Hayes Library.

29. Crook to Webb Hayes, Dec. 11, 1881, ibid. Jay Gould was at the time a speculator in railroad stock. How Crook knew him or what he might do to help in promotion to major general is mystery. Regarding McKinley's Civil War service on Crook's staff, see Magid, *George Crook*, 250.

30. Crook to Webb Hayes, Dec. 14, 1881, Crook Letterbook, Hayes Library.

31. Breth, "Analysis and Comparison of the Military Retirement System."

32. Crook to Webb Hayes, Dec. 14, 1881, Crook Letterbook, Hayes Library.

33. Magid, *Gray Fox*, 353–54.

34. Crook to Rutherford Hayes, Dec. 18, 1881, Crook Letterbook, Hayes Library.

35. Crook to Webb Hayes, Jan. 17, 1882, ibid.

36. Anonymous Petition to President Chester Arthur, Mar. 29, 1882, NARA, Appointments, Commissions File, MI395.

37. Magid, *Gray Fox*, 258.

38. Anonymous Petition to President Chester Arthur, Mar. 29, 1882, NARA, Appointments, Commissions File, MI395.

39. Official Army Register for 1883, AGO, Washington, D.C., 1883.

CHAPTER 8. RETURN TO APACHERIA

1. Fort Apache began as Camp Ord in July 1870. Renamed Camp Mogollon in August of that year, it then became Camp Thomas and finally Camp Apache in 1871. In 1879 the army camps were all designated forts. Walker and Bufkin, *Historical Atlas of Arizona*, 37.

2. Barnes, *Apaches and Longhorns*, 91.

3. "General George Crook," *Boston Daily Advertiser*, Sept. 1, 1882.

4. McChristian, *Fort Bowie, Arizona*, 175.

5. The appointment was made pursuant to General Orders No. 78, July 14, 1882, Sherman to sec. of war, Aug. 2, 1882, quoted in C. Collins, *Apache Nightmare*, 210–11.

6. Crook to Welsh, July 16, 1884, quoted in Thrapp, *Sierra Madre Adventure*, 177.

7. Thrapp, foreword to *Indeh*, xvi.

8. Ball, *Indeh*, 112n2.

9. Ibid., 125.

10. Bourke *On the Border*, 434.

11. Radbourne, *Mickey Free*, 83.

12. Crook to AAG, Div. of Pacific, Sept. 6, 1882, Crook Letterbook, Hayes Library.

13. Ibid., Sept. 28, 1882.

14. Magid, *Gray Fox*, 71.

15. Bourke, *On the Border*, 435; Thrapp, *Encyclopedia of Frontier Biography*, 2:983; C. Collins, *Apache Nightmare*, 212.

16. Cruse, *Apache Days and After*, 179.

17. Polygamy was practiced to some extent among the Apaches. But, as in Cooley's case, if a man took more than one wife, the second woman was usually the sister or relative of the other. For a full discussion of polygamy among the Apaches, see Opler, *Apache Life-way*, 416–20.

18. Barnes, *Apaches and Longhorns*, 92; Thrapp, *Encyclopedia of Frontier Biography*, 3:1289.

19. Bourke, *Diaries*, 5:420–21.

20. Ibid.; see also Carr's Report to AAG, Nov. 4, 1881, app. K, quoted in Thrapp, *Sierra Madre Adventure*, 13.

21. Bourke, *Diaries*, 5:420–21.

22. Bourke diaries, 45:2070, quoted in C. Collins, *Apache Nightmare*, 30–31; Trial of Enlisted Men at Fort Grant, A.T., 1881, Trial of Private no. 15, quoted in ibid., 30–31. *Author's note:* The published editions of Bourke's diaries, edited by Charles Robinson (in five volumes), end with Bourke's arrival at Fort Apache on August 25, 1881, prior to his visit to Pedro's camp. Diary entries after that date can be found at the Nebraska State Historical Society (hereafter cited as NSHS), as well as several other locations, including the West Point library collections. The entries here from the published diaries are cited as "Bourke, *Diaries*." Citations from the unpublished diaries appear as "Bourke diaries."

23. Porter, *Paper Medicine Man*, 72–145.

24. Crook to AG, Apr. 10, 1874, Crook Letterbook, Hayes Library.

25. Crook to AAG, Div. of the Missouri, Aug. 31, 1874, *ARSW*, 1873–74.

26. Ibid.; Magid, *Gray Fox*, 126.

27. Bourke, *On the Border*, 434, 441.

28. Barnes, *Apaches and Longhorns*, 92.

29. Bourke, *On the Border*, 435–36.

30. Ibid., 436–41.

31. Mose's statement is quoted in C. Collins, *Apache Nightmare*, 214.

32. Thrapp, *Victorio*, 172.

33. Ibid., 165.

34. Thrapp, *Conquest of Apacheria*, 111; Ogle, *Federal Control of the Western Apaches*, 124–25.

35. Cruse, *Apache Days and After*, 31.

36. Ball, *Induh*, 37.

37. For details of the removal of the Yavapais and Tontos to San Carlos, see Magid, *Gray Fox*, 130–32. For a contemporary account, see Corbusier, *Verde to San Carlos*, ch. 16.

38. Ogle, *Federal Control of the Western Apaches*, 152; Thrapp, *Conquest of Apacheria*, 167; Clum, *Apache Agent*, 161.

39. Sweeney, *Cochise to Geronimo*, 41; C. Collins, *Apache Nightmare*, 11.

40. Magid, *Gray Fox*, 99, 117.

41. Magid, *Gray Fox*, 99–100; Sweeney, *Cochise to Geronimo*, 15; Thrapp, *Conquest of Apacheria*, 168; Lockwood, *Apache Indians*, 112–21.

42. Thrapp, *Victorio*, 173; Sweeney, *Cochise to Geronimo*, 47–59.

43. Quoted in Sweeney, *Cochise to Geronimo*, 62.

44. Thrapp, *Victorio*, 170.

45. Sweeney, *Cochise to Geronimo*, 64; Worcester, *The Apaches*, 213.

46. Thrapp, *Conquest of Apacheria*, 182–210, and *Victorio*, 301–4; Sweeney, *Cochise to Geronimo*, 165.

47. Thrapp, *Conquest of Apacheria*, 165.

48. For more on John Clum, see Clum, *Apache Agent*.

49. At least one source claims that Chaffee was relieved at his own request, "unable to cope with the dishonest contractors with their political backing, and with the Indian Bureau." See Fieberger, "Crook's Campaign in Old Mexico," 16–24, 18–19.

50. Ogle, *Federal Control of Western Apaches*, 336; Goodwin, *Western Apaches*, 16–18.

51. C. Collins, *Apache Nightmare*, 10–11.

52. Thrapp, *Conquest of Apacheria*, 217.

53. Ibid.

54. Cruse, *Apache Days and After*, 93.

55. Debo, *Geronimo, the Man*, 127–30.

56. Cruse, *Apache Days and After*, 94; Bourke, *Diaries*, 5:421.

57. Cruse, *Apache Days and After*, 96.

58. C. Collins, *Apache Nightmare*, 22.

59. Carr to Willcox, Aug. 6, 1881, quoted in C. Collins, *Apache Nightmare*, 20, and Lockwood, *Apache Indians*, 236.

60. Willcox to Carr, Aug. 7, 1881, quoted in C. Collins, *Apache Nightmare*, 23.

61. During the Civil War Tiffany was hired as a purchasing agent for the army and, when the war ended, was the subject of an investigation into his practices. Then, too, no prosecution ensued. Thrapp, *Sierra Madre Adventure*, 6n5. For Tiffany's tenure at San Carlos, see Harte, "Strange Case of Joseph C. Tiffany," 385. Harte argues that Tiffany's reputation was undeserved.

62. See Thrapp, *Sierra Madre Adventure*, 5–6; Ogle, *Federal Control of the Western Apaches*, 201–2; Bourke, *On the Border*, 442.

63. Cruse, *Apache Days and After*, 97.

64. Tiffany to Carr, Aug. 14, 1881, quoted in C. Collins, *Apache Nightmare*, 21.

65. For a vivid firsthand account of the fight, see Cruse, *Apache Days and After*, 117–18.

66. Cruse, *Apache Days and After*, 125. See also *Arizona Weekly Star*, Sept. 8, 1881, quoting Mickey Free, "an Indian" who was said to be "at the fight." Free, the article claimed, described a massacre in which few soldiers surviving the fighting. Actually, Free was not present at the fight and, if correctly quoted, must have gotten his information second- or third-hand. Article quoted in Radbourne, *Mickey Free*, 76.

67. C. Collins, *Apache Nightmare*, 88.

68. AG to McDowell, Sept. 7–11, 1881, quoted in C. Collins, *Apache Nightmare*, 102.

69. Ibid.

70. For a detailed discussion of this aspect of military operations, see ibid., 138–77.

71. Ibid., 95.

72. Ibid., 12.

73. Ibid., 88–91.

74. Only one Chiricahua, George, a Chokonen married to a Coyotero woman, had actually taken part at Cibicue. A second Apache, Benito (or Bonito), whom General Willcox regarded as Chiricahua but who may actually have been White Mountain, had allied himself and his followers with George's band. See Debo, *Geronimo, the Man*, 131.

75. Sweeney, *Cochise to Geronimo*, 178–79.

76. Ibid., 180–83; Thrapp, *Conquest of Apacheria*, 231–32.

77. Lockwood, *Apache Indians*, 242–43.

78. C. Collins, *Apache Nightmare*, 97.

79. Ibid., 201–3.

80. Cruse, *Apache Days and After*, 139.

81. Report of O. O. Willcox, Aug. 31, 1882, in *ARSW*, 1882, 1:146.

CHAPTER 9. THERE IS NOT NOW A HOSTILE APACHE IN ARIZONA

1. Cruse, *Apache Days and After*, 179–81.

2. Bourke, *On the Border*, 440.

3. Crook to AAG, Div. of Pacific, Sept. 28, 1882, Crook Letterbook, Hayes Library.

4. Bourke, *On the Border*, 441.

5. C. Collins, *Apache Nightmare*, 221; Lockwood, *Apache Indians*, 257; Crook to AAG, Div. of Pacific, Sept. 28, 1882, Crook Letterbook, Hayes Library.

6. The minutes of Crook's meeting with the Apaches, including this quote and the Indians' testimony, is found in Crook to AG, Sept. 28, 1882, Div. of Pacific, NARA, Bureau of Indian Affairs, Letters Received, 1882. Much of this dialogue, including Crook's response quoted above, is reproduced in C. Collins, *Apache Nightmare*, 215–20.

7. Crook report, Sept. 27, 1883, in *ARSW*, 1883, 1:159–61.

8. Crook to AAG, Div. of Pacific, Sept. 28, 1882, Crook Letterbook, Hayes Library.

9. Ibid.

10. Ibid.

11. Ibid.

12. Ibid.

13. Dept. of Arizona (hereafter cited as DA), General Orders No. 43, Oct. 5, 1882, quoted in Bourke, *On the Border*, 443.

14. Crook to Zabriskie, USDA for A.T., Oct. 8, 1882, Crook Letterbook, Hayes Library.

15. C. Collins, *Apache Nightmare*, 224.

16. Crook to AAG, Div. of Pacific, May 24, 1884, NARA, DA, LS, RG 98; Army Special Order 142, June 19, 1884, quoted in C. Collins, *Apache Nightmare*, 224.

17. In an ironic twist, the ranking NCO in the last contingent of scouts to serve, a sergeant named Sinew Riley, was the grandson of Dead Shot, one the three scouts hanged for their participation in Cibicue. Thrapp, *Encyclopedia of Frontier Biography*, 3:1,222.

18. Crook to AAG, Div. of Pacific, Crook Letterbook, Hayes Library.

19. Lt. William Weigel, "Notes on the Apaches," in Carroll, *Unpublished Papers of the Indian Wars*, 6:12–14.

20. Ibid.; Crook, *Autobiography*, 244.

21. Crook report, *ARSW*, 1882.

22. Crook report, *ARSW*, 1883, 7.

23. Davis, *Truth about Geronimo*, 34; Lockwood, *Apache Indians*, 259.

24. Ogle, *Federal Control of the Western Apaches*, 217.

25. Harte, "Strange Case of Joseph Tiffany," 393.

26. Harte, "Conflict at San Carlos," 27–44, 33; Lockwood, *Apache Indians*, 259.

27. Davis, *Truth about Geronimo*, 34.

28. "An End to Indian Outbreaks," *Denver Tribune*, Nov. 2, 1882, in Cozzens, *Eyewitnesses*, 1:321–23.

29. Crook to AG, NARA, Files of AGO, 1883, M1066; Crook report, in *ARSW,* 1885; Harte, "Conflict at San Carlos," 34.

30. Crook, *Autobiography,* 244.

31. Harte, "Conflict at San Carlos," 34; Davis, *Truth about Geronimo,* 39–40.

32. Davis, *Truth about Geronimo,* 31; Corbusier, *Verde to San Carlos,* 159.

33. Davis, *Truth about Geronimo,* 31–32.

34. Utley, introduction to Davis's *Truth about Geronimo,* vi.

35. Kraft, *Gatewood and Geronimo,* 221.

36. Ibid., 22; Davis, *Truth about Geronimo,* 32; Cruse, *Apache Days and After,* 226.

37. Thrapp, *Conquest of Apacheria,* 304.

38. Crook to AAG, Div. of Pacific, Sept. 27, 1883, app. C, Memorandum of a Council at San Carlos, Arizona, Nov. 2, 1882 on the White River Reservation, in *ARSW,* 1883; Gatewood Papers, Arizona Historical Society (hereafter cited as AHS); Crook, *Autobiography,* 244.

39. Crook to AAG, Div. of Pacific, Sept. 27, 1883, *ARSW,* 1883.

40. Ibid.

41. *ARSW,* 1883.

42. Bourke, *On the Border,* 445; *ARSW,* 1883.

43. Davis, *Truth about Geronimo,* 34.

44. Ibid., 42–43.

45. Ibid., 41–42.

46. Davis, *Truth about Geronimo,* 44–45.

47. Ibid., 31.

48. Ibid., 31, 46.

49. Crook to Teller, Feb. 23, 1883, Crook Letterbook, Hayes Library; Ogle, *Federal Control of the Western Apaches,* 221.

CHAPTER 10. PREPARATIONS FOR A CAMPAIGN

1. Crook to AAG, Div. of Pacific, Sept. 6, 1882, Crook Letterbook, Hayes Library.

2. For details of the Tonto campaign, see Magid, *Gray Fox,* ch. 9, "The Tonto Campaign," 101–19; Radbourne, *Mickey Free,* 101; For an excellent biography of Al Sieber, see Thrapp, *Al Sieber.*

3. For more on McIntosh, see Thrapp, *Encyclopedia of Frontier Biography,* 2:908–9; Magid, *Gray Fox,* 16, 18. For additional information on Bowman, see Davis, *Truth about Geronimo,* 36; Thrapp, *Sierra Madre Adventure,* 12n25.

4. Horn, *Life of Tom Horn,* 25.

5. Connell, "The Apaches," unpublished manuscript, quoted in Radbourne, *Mickey Free,* 17.

6. For the details of Free's fascinating early life, I refer readers to Radbourne, *Mickey Free*; and Hutton, *The Apache Wars.*

7. Ibid., chs. 1–4.

8. Davis, *Truth about Geronimo,* 38.

9. Ibid.

10. General Orders No. 13, Apr. 8, 1873, NARA, DA, General Orders, 1870–93, RG 393.

11. Crook to sec. of interior, Mar. 26, 1883, Crook Letterbook, Hayes Library.

12. Magid, *Gray Fox*, 117.

13. Crook to AAG, Div. of Pacific, Annual Report, Sept. 28, 1871, Crook Letterbook, Hayes Library.

14. Crook to AAG, Div. of Pacific, Feb. 11, 1873, ibid.

15. July 7, 1873, ibid.

16. Annual Report, Aug. 31, 1874, ibid.

17. Mar. 7, 1883, ibid.

18. Secretary of State Frederick T. Frelinghuysen, Memorandum of Agreement between the United States and Mexico, July 29, 1882, reprinted in Cozzens, *Eyewitnesses*, 1:343–45; Bourke, *Apache Campaign*, 34–35.

19. Crook to AAG, Div. of Pacific, Sept. 28, 1882, Crook Letterbook, Hayes Library; Thrapp, *Sierra Madre Adventure*, 114.

20. Thrapp, *Sierra Madre Adventure*, 114.

21. Crook to AAG, Div. of Pacific, Mar. 28, 1883, Crook Letterbook, Hayes Library.

22. Lockwood, *Apache Indians*, 42.

23. Crook to AAG, Div. of Pacific, Crook Letterbook, Hayes Library.

24. Sweeney, *Cochise to Geronimo*, 283.

25. Crook to AAG, Div. of Pacific, Crook Letterbook, Hayes Library.

26. Ibid.; Bourke, *Apache Campaign*, 25.

27. Crook to AAG, Div. of Pacific, Crook Letterbook, Hayes Library; Thrapp, *Sierra Madre Adventure*, 108–110; Sweeney, *Cochise to Geronimo*, 283.

28. "General Crook's Apache Campaign," *New York Semi-Weekly Evening Post*, June 15, 1883.

29. Extract from Report of General Crook, Sept. 27, 1883, *ARSW*, 1883; Crook to AAG, Div. of Pacific, Mar. 28, 1883, ibid.; Davis, *Truth about Geronimo*, 55; Bourke, *Apache Campaign*, 26.

30. Simmons, *Massacre on the Lordsburg Road*, 82.

31. Betzinez, *I Fought with Geronimo*, 97; Sweeney, *Cochise to Geronimo*, 283.

32. Sweeney, *Cochise to Geronimo*, 286–87.

33. Betzinez, *I Fought with Geronimo*, 102; Sweeney, *Cochise to Geronimo*, 288.

34. Crook to AAG, Div. of Pacific, Mar. 28, 1883, Crook Letterbook, Hayes Library.

35. Thrapp, *Sierra Madre Adventure*, 118.

36. Sweeney, *Cochise to Geronimo*, 290, Simmons, *Massacre on the Lordsburg Road*, 84–87.

37. Betzinez, *I Fought with Geronimo*, 107; House Exec. Doc. 1, 48th Cong., 1st sess., Part 2, quoted in Radbourne, *Mickey Free*, 103.

38. *Arizona Star*, Mar. 27, 1883, which includes the comments from the *Epitaph* and *Herald*, quoted in Thrapp, *Conquest of Apacheria*, 269.

39. Simmons, *Massacre on the Lordsburg Road*, 116; Goodwin, "Experiences of an Indian Scout," 154.

40. Porter, *Paper Medicine Man*, 148–49; Simmons, *Massacre on the Lordsburg Road*, 141–42.

41. Crook to Teller, Mar. 26, 1883, Crook Letterbook, Hayes Library.

42. Bourke likened the effort to "catching so many fleas" in *Apache Campaign*, 27–28; Simmons, *Massacre on the Lordsburg Road*, 130. Thrapp describes the troop movements ordered by Crook in *Dateline Fort Bowie*, 102.

43. Loomis, "Bloody Raid of Geronimo's Band," *Los Angeles Times*, Apr. 25, 1886, quoted in Thrapp, *Dateline Fort Bowie*, 103.

44. Schofield to Crook, Mar. 31, 1883, quoted in Thrapp, *Dateline Fort Bowie*.

45. Bourke, *Apache Campaign*, 28; Simmons, *Massacre on the Lordsburg Road*, 131.

46. Davis, *Truth about Geronimo*, 56–57.

47. Crook gave his Apache name as Pe-nal-tishn, which Bourke renders as Pa-nayo-tishn (Coyote Saw Him) in *Apache Campaign*, 31; Crook's report, app. E, *ARSW*, 1883.

48. That was Tzoe's story, but the circumstances under which he had left the raiders, whether voluntarily or under cloak of darkness, remain murky. Betzinez, who was a cousin of Beneactiney and was with Geronimo at the time, said that Peaches, grief-stricken by the death of his friend, told the others in the raiding party that he could not go on and would return to his family. According to Betzinez, the other Indians did not attempt to dissuade him and gave him supplies for the journey. Betzinez, *I Fought with Geronimo*, 116–17. Bourke, on the other hand, recorded that Peaches told Crook that he had joined the raiding party under duress and that he had been "forced to steal away in the night." Bourke diary, 66:20–31, quoted in Thrapp, *Sierra Madre Adventure*, 121. For his part, Davis quotes Peaches as simply saying that "he had left the hostiles near the eastern edge of the Reservation." Davis, *Truth about Geronimo*, 57–59.

49. Davis, *Truth about Geronimo*, 58–59.

50. Thrapp, *Sierra Madre Adventure*, 121–23.

51. Bourke, *Apache Campaign*, 33.

52. Fiebeger, "Crook's Campaign in Old Mexico," 16–24.

53. Crook to Topete, Mar. 28, 1883, Crook Letterbook, Hayes Library.

54. Crook's report, July 23, 1883, app. E, in *ARSW*, 1883

55. Thrapp, *Sierra Madre Adventure*, 124–25.

56. Bourke diary, 65:36–96, 66:1–17, quoted in Thrapp, *Sierra Madre Adventure*, 124–25. Fiebeger had a different recollection of the order of travel. According to him, Crook traveled first to Guaymas and Hermasillo, then to Arizona to consult with Mackenzie, and finally from there to Chihuahua via El Paso. Fiebeger, "Crook's Campaign in Old Mexico," 197.

57. Crook to AG, Apr. 18, 1883, Crook Letterbook, Hayes Library.

58. Sherman to Crook, Apr. 28, 1883, ibid.

59. Bourke, *Apache Campaign*, 36.

60. Crook to AG, Apr. 30, 1883, Crook Letterbook, Hayes Library.

61. Thrapp, *Sierra Madre Adventure*, 127.

62. Crook to AG, Apr. 30, Crook Letterbook, Hayes Library.

CHAPTER 11. INTO THE SIERRA MADRE

1. There is no lack of primary sources providing a variety of perspectives on the campaign. First and foremost was the account of its leader, General Crook, found in his official report and in appendix E to that report. Crook to AG, Div. of Pacific, Sept. 4, 1883, Gatewood Papers, AHS (hereafter cited as Crook, Sierra Madre Report, AHS; in the AHS reprint of this report, page numbers have been added in the apparently retyped appendixes, and they are cited here). Crook also provided an informal account in an interview with the *New York Herald* reporter A. Franklin Randall, who accompanied the expedition. "Apache Affairs: An Interview with General Crook," *New York Herald*, July 9, 1883, reprinted in Cozzens, *Eyewitnesses*, 1:396–404. For a timeline of the column's

movements, vivid descriptions of the terrain and daily life on the trail, and numerous details about Apache lifeways garnered from the scouts, see Bourke's diaries. The relevant portions are in vols. 66–68, reprinted as "With Crook in the Sierra Madre," in Cozzens, *Eyewitnesses*, 1:346–84 (hereafter cited as Bourke, "With Crook"). In addition, he later turned his diary entries into a series of articles ultimately published in book form as *An Apache Campaign in the Sierra Madre*. In addition to Bourke's work, see Fiebeger, "Crook's Campaign in Old Mexico," and Randall, "In the Heart of the Sierra Madre," in Cozzens, *Eyewitnesses*, 1:394–95. For a scout's perspective, the recollections of White Mountain Apache John Rope are invaluable. See Goodwin, "Experiences of an Indian Scout," and "John Rope," the latter in *Western Apache Raiding and Warfare*, 93–186. I have relied on accounts by Geronimo and his nephew Betzinez for the Chiricahua point of view. See Barrett, *Geronimo's Story of His Life*, 137–38, and Betzinez, *I Fought with Geronimo*, 110–20. Tom Horn, mule skinner and packer, wrote his own account. Among his many talents was his mastery of the frontier art of the tall story. As befitted the genre, he often exaggerated and frequently lied about events. His account, found in an autobiography that he wrote in jail while he awaited execution for murder, is widely regarded as unreliable because it does not accord with most other narratives of the campaign in many respects. His version cast him in a central role in events in which he may or may not have participated. Though his limitations as an eyewitness must be taken into account, Horn's tale is a fascinating and colorful story of the expedition told from a civilian perspective. Horn, *Life of Tom Horn*, chs. 14–16, and prologue, xxi–xxx.

2. Bourke, *Apache Campaign*, 37, 54.

3. Crook to AG, Apr. 30, 1883, Crook Letterbook, Hayes Library.

4. Goodwin, "John Rope," 154; Bourke, *Apache Campaign*, 57.

5. Bourke, *Apache Campaign*, 39–40.

6. Ibid.; Goodwin, "John Rope," 154; Opler, *Apache Life-way*, 260–61.

7. Goodwin, "John Rope," 154.

8. Thrapp describes Free as speaking "present-tense Spanish." *Sierra Madre Adventure*, 154.

9. Goodwin, "John Rope"; Thrapp, *Sierra Madre Adventure*, 129–30.

10. John Rope would later comment, "I think he was telling us the truth all right because all of us scouts are now drawing pensions." Goodwin, "John Rope," 154; Thrapp, *Sierra Madre Adventure*, 128; Thrapp, *Dateline Ft. Bowie*, 105; Crook, *Autobiography*, 247.

11. Smith, "White Eyes, Red Heart," 214. Sieber remarked to John Rope that he knew Geronimo had slain the scout's father, perhaps hoping to motivate Rope to avenge himself on the Chiricahuas. Goodwin, "John Rope," 147–48. One scout apparently decided that he had no personal grudge against the Chiricahuas and therefore declined to join the expedition. Thrapp, *Sierra Madre Adventure*, 129.

12. Goodwin, "John Rope," 154, 312n81; Opler, *Apache Life-way*, 336.

13. Bourke, *Apache Campaign*, 37–38, 42.

14. Crook, Sierra Madre Report; Fiebeger, "Hunting Hostile Indians," *New York Times*, Apr. 29, 1883.

15. Randall, "Apache Affairs," 404.

16. Cook, *Autobiography*, 247. Loomis quotes Crook as saying he had 350 mules. Thrapp, *Dateline Fort Bowie*, 104–5. Thrapp, *Sierra Madre Adventure*, 128; Fiebeger, "Crook's Campaign," 198; Bourke, *Apache Campaign*, 55–56; Sweeney, *Cochise to Geronimo*, 304.

17. Thrapp, *Sierra Madre Adventure*, 131–32.

18. "A Rumor about Crook," May 26, 1883, unidentified clipping, Gatewood File, AHS; "Schofield," *Chicago Times*, May 24, 1883. See also *Tucson Arizona Citizen*, May 25, 1883; *Omaha Herald*, May 7, 1883. The latter three articles are reproduced in "Where Is Crook?," in Cozzens, *Eyewitnesses*, 1:388–90.

19. "Hunting Hostile Indians," *New York Times*, Apr. 29, 1883.

20. Ibid.

21. Randall, "Apache Affairs," 398.

22. Crook, Sierra Madre Report, AHS, app. E, 17; Bourke, "With Crook," 356; Bourke, *Apache Campaign*, 61, 64–65; Thrapp, *Dateline Fort Bowie*, 106; Fiebeger, "Crook's Campaign," 198.

23. Crook, Sierra Madre Report, AHS; Goodwin, "John Rope," 156.

24. Crook, Sierra Madre Report, AHS.

25. Bourke, "With Crook," 353–54; Goodwin, "John Rope," 156; Fiebeger, "Crook's Campaign," 16–24.

26. Bourke, "With Crook," 353–54.

27. Ibid., 356.

28. Opler, *Apache Life-way*, 229.

29. Bourke, *Apache Campaign*, 74, and "With Crook," 357.

30. Bourke, "With Crook," 360.

31. Bourke, *Apache Campaign*, 74.

32. Bourke, "With Crook," 361.

33. Ibid., 358, 361–63.

34. Crook, Sierra Madre Report, AHS, app. E, 18.

35. Bourke, "With Crook," 362–63.

36. Bourke, "With Crook," 364.

37. The contents of Crawford's correspondence with Crook on May 14 and 15, 1883, quoted in Thrapp, *Sierra Madre Adventure*, 142–45.

38. Crook, Sierra Madre Report, AHS, app. E, 18; Bourke, *Apache Campaign*, 87–93, and "With Crook," 368.

39. Betzinez, *I Fought with Geronimo*, 118. Quite a different account of the boy's death was provided by Ruey Darrow to Eve Ball many years later. Darrow's mother and grand-mother, she said, had been in the camp at the time of the raid. They recounted that the boy, wounded by a stray bullet, was left to die because any attempt to save him would have endangered the Chiricahua warriors. This story is hearsay and somewhat self-serv-ing, but it cannot be entirely discounted. Ball, *Indeh*, 51.

40. Bourke, "With Crook," 370.

41. Bourke, *Apache Campaign*, 92–95.

42. Crook, Sierra Madre Report, AHS, app. E, 19.

43. Betzinez, *I Fought with Geronimo*, 112; Crook, Sierra Madre Report, AHS, app. E, 19; Bourke, "With Crook," 371; Thrapp, *Sierra Madre Adventure*, 139.

44. Goodwin, "John Rope," 163. Goodwin notes that providing a fine horse and tobacco were examples of Crook's talent for Indian diplomacy; doing anything less might have been taken as an insult and given the subchief an excuse to spurn further negotiations.

45. Bourke, "With Crook," 375; Crook, Sierra Madre Report, AHS, app. E, 19; Goodwin, "John Rope," 163–64.

46. Goodwin, "John Rope," 165.

47. Bourke, "With Crook," 374.

48. Crook, Sierra Madre Report, AHS, app. E, 20; Bourke, *Apache Campaign*, 98–99.

49. Bourke, "With Crook," 375–76.

50. Goodwin, "John Rope," 165; Thrapp, *Sierra Madre*, 154.

51. Goodwin, "John Rope," 165.

52. Bourke, *Apache Campaign*, 99–100; Thrapp, *Sierra Madre Adventure*, 154.

CHAPTER 12. GERONIMO—HUNTER AND PREY

1. See Opler, *Apache Life-way*, 200; Perico, quoted in Utley, *Geronimo*, 21.

2. Betzinez, *I Fought with Geronimo*, 15.

3. Sweeney, *Cochise to Geronimo*, 288.

4. Demings (N. Mex.) *Tribune*, ca. Oct. 4, 1883, quoted in Roberts, *Once They Rode*, 242, 251.

5. Utley, *Geronimo*, 245.

6. Barrett, *Geronimo's Story*, xi.

7. Utley, *Geronimo*, 260; Debo, *Geronimo, the Man*, 4–5.

8. In his autobiography the shaman claimed to have been born in 1829. Barrett, *Geronimo's Story*, 17. Modern historians believe he confused the dates and think he was born in 1823, since he had a wife and three children by 1850. Debo, *Geronimo, the Man*, 7; Utley, *Geronimo*, 6–7.

9. Utley, *Geronimo*, 9–10.

10. Barrett quotes Geronimo as saying he was but a young boy at the time of his father's death. *Geronimo's Story*, 36. This may be yet another error. Debo attributes the statement to a mistranslation, as the boy was old enough to support his mother at the time. *Geronimo, the Man*, 26.

11. Geronimo and Betzinez give the date as 1858, but Debo concluded that this date, too, was erroneous, another example of the Apaches' difficulties with the European calendar. Barrett, *Geronimo's Story*, 43; Debo, *Geronimo, the Man*, 35.

12. Barrett, *Geronimo's Story*, 43–45; Debo, *Geronimo, the Man*, 34–35; Betzinez, *I Fought with Geronimo*, 3. In contrast to the Mexicans and some American frontiersmen, though Apaches sometimes tortured their victims, they seldom scalped an enemy. If they did the scalp was quickly destroyed, as it was regarded as the repository of the dead man's spirit. Debo, *Geronimo, the Man*, 5; Ogle, *Federal Control of the Western Apaches*, 349–50.

13. Barrett, *Geronimo's Story*, 43–50; Betzinez, *I Fought with Geronimo*, 17.

14. The story of death of Mangas has been told many times. For a recent example, see Utley, *Geronimo*, 53; and for earlier accounts, Thrapp's version in *Conquest of Apacheria*, 21–23, and *Victorio*, 82–83. Mangas's body was decapitated after his death and his head was sent East to a phrenologist who pronounced its brain cavity to be equal in size to that of Daniel Webster. Thrapp, *Conquest of Apacheria*, 23, and *Victorio*, 83.

15. Debo, *Geronimo, the Man*, 33; Utley, *Geronimo*, 9–10, 260–61; Thrapp, *Encyclopedia of Frontier Biography*, 2:935.

16. Barrett, *Geronimo's Story*, 119; Debo, *Geronimo, the Man*, 33; Thrapp, *Conquest of Apacheria*, 22.

17. Debo, *Geronimo, the Man*, 98–99.

18. Barrett, *Geronimo's Story*, 142; for one of Clum's versions of his arrest of Geronimo, see Clum, *Apache Agent*, 215–36; for an analysis, see Utley, *Geronimo*, 89–92.

19. Sweeney, *Cochise to Geronimo*, 182.

20. Foreword by W. S. Nye, in Betzinez, *I Fought with Geronimo*; Utley, *Geronimo*, 261.

21. Betzinez, *I Fought with Geronimo*, 113–15.

22. Thrapp, *Conquest of Apacheria*, 289.

23. Bourke, *Apache Campaign*, 102.

24. Bourke, "With Crook," 377.

25. Bourke, *Apache Campaign*, 101.

26. Betzinez, *I Fought with Geronimo*, 116; Debo, *Geronimo, the Man*, 182. Bourke says the messengers were "a couple of squaws." Bourke, "With Crook," 377.

27. Bourke, "With Crook," 377.

28. Goodwin, "John Rope," 167; Betzinez, *I Fought with Geronimo*, 120; Bourke, "With Crook," 376.

29. Crook to Schofield, June 19, 1883, Crook Letterbook, Hayes Library.

30. Feibeger, "Crook's Campaign," 200.

31. Crook, Sierra Madre Report, AHS, app. E, 20.

32. Bourke, "With Crook," 377–78.

33. Fiebeger, "Crook's Campaign," 200.

34. Barrett, *Geronimo's Story*, 137–38.

35. Goodwin, "John Rope," 167. While no one else mentioned this incident, Bourke, in a diary entry dated May 21, the day *after* the chiefs entered the camp, recorded that Crook went on "a bird shooting walk along the camp lines." Bourke, "With Crook," 383.

36. Goodwin, "John Rope," 166–67; Bourke, "With Crook," 380; Debo, *Geronimo, the Man*, 182; Thrapp, *Sierra Madre Adventure*, 155.

37. *Chicago Times*, Oct. 1883, quoted in Thrapp, *Sierra Madre Adventure*, 156–57.

38. Thrapp, *Sierra Madre Adventure*, 157–58. For Crook hunting in Indian country, see Magid, *Gray Fox*, 266, 269, 271.

39. Thrapp, *Sierra Madre Adventure*, 158.

40. Bancroft, *History of Arizona*, 571.

41. "The Renegades, What Shall We Do with Them," *Arizona Weekly Citizen*, June 30, 1883.

42. G. Gordon Adam, "Resolution Adopted at Meeting of Residents of Cochise County, Arizona, Regarding Outbreak of Indians from San Carlos Reservation," Tombstone, June 15, 1883, reprinted in Cozzens, *Eyewitnesses*, 1:414.

43. For an example of Crook's negotiating technique, see Magid, *Gray Fox*, 45.

44. Crook, Sierra Madre Report, AHS, app. E, 21. In magazine articles written well after the fact, Bourke described Crook's language in very similar terms. However, as he was not present, he undoubtedly relied on his commander's accounts for their content. Bourke, *Apache Campaign*, 102–3, 111–13.

45. Horn, *Life of Tom Horn*, 182–86.

46. Thrapp, *Sierra Madre Adventure*, 159.

47. Bourke, "With Crook," 383.

48. Crook, Sierra Madre Report, AHS, app. E, 21–22.

49. Bourke, *Apache Campaign*, 11.

50. Utley, *Geronimo*, 140–41; Bourke, *Apache Campaign*, 102.

51. Crawford to Crook, March 21, 1884, quoted in Sweeney, *Cochise to Geronimo*, 309.

52. Horn, *Life of Tom Horn*, 184–86.

53. Goodwin, "Experiences of an Indian Scout," 31–72, and esp. 68–69.

54. Goodwin, *Western Apache*, 168–69.

55. Sweeney, *Cochise to Geronimo*, 309; Thrapp, *Sierra Madre Adventure*, 161–62; Goodwin, *Western Apache*, 168–69; Horn, *Life of Tom Horn*, 176.

56. Bourke, "With Crook," 383.

57. Crook, Sierra Madre Report. app. E, 22.

58. Sweeney, *Cochise to Geronimo*, 309.

59. "Apache Affair," reprinted in Cozzens, *Eyewitnesses*, 1:404.

60. Crook, Sierra Madre Report, AHS, app. E, 24.

61. Ibid.

62. Thrapp, *Sierra Madre Adventure*, 162, and *Conquest of Apacheria*, 291; Bourke, *Apache Campaign*, 113.

63. Shapard, *Chief Loco*, 199. Thrapp says Loco came in at dusk on May 25. *Sierra Madre Adventure*, 162. This is an example of the confusion of dates that characterizes not only contemporary narratives but also those of modern historians. The imprecision pervades the descriptions of many of the events that occurred between May 22 and the column's departure from the camp on May 24. Apparently there was a lot of coming and going by individuals. Crook's report is little help as he gives no dates whatsoever.

64. Thrapp, *Al Sieber*, 283.

65. Bourke, *Apache Campaign*, 115; Bourke, "With Crook," 385.

66. Thrapp says Chatto came in on May 25. *Sierra Madre Adventure*, 162–63.

67. Crook, Sierra Madre Report, AHS, app. E, 22; Bourke, *Apache Campaign*, 112–13.

68. Crook to AAG, Div. of Pacific, June 12, 1883, quoted in Thrapp, *Sierra Madre Adventure*, 165.

69. Bourke, *Apache Campaign*, 115–16.

70. Thrapp, *Sierra Madre Adventure*, 162; Bourke, *Apache Campaign*, 115.

71. Bourke, *Apache Campaign*, 115–21.

72. Crook, Sierra Madre Report, AHS, app. E, 22.

73. Ibid.; Horn, *Life of Tom Horn*, 198.

74. Crook, Sierra Madre Report, AHS, app. E, 22.

75. Bourke diaries, 67:20–21, quoted in Thrapp, *Sierra Madre Adventure*, 163.

76. Thrapp, *Sierra Madre Adventure*, 166; *Arizona Weekly Citizen*, June 23, 1883.

77. Sources do not agree on the date, but it was before Crook resumed his trek to the border. Sweeney, *Cochise to Geronimo*, 311; Bourke *Apache Campaign*, 121.

78. Fiebeger, "Crook's Campaign," 23; Bourke, *Apache Campaign*, 121; Bourke diaries, quoted in Thrapp, *Sierra Madre Adventure*, 168.

79. Thrapp, *Sierra Madre Adventure*, 168.

80. Sweeney, *Cochise to Geronimo*, 331–32.

81. Bourke, *Apache Campaign*, 125–26.

82. Ibid., 124.

83. Bourke diaries, quoted in Thrapp, *Sierra Madre Adventure*, 168.

84. Ibid., 175.

85. Sweeney, *Cochise to Geronimo*, 311; Davis, *Truth about Geronimo*, 69; Thrapp, *Conquest of Apacheria*, 292.

86. Crook was addressing Biddle using his Civil War rank in the volunteer army.

87. Randall, "General Crook's Modesty," *New York Herald*, June 13, 1883.

88. Crook to Schofield, Jun. 11, 1883, quoted in full in "Gen. Crook's Victory," *New York Times*, June 13, 1883.

89. "General Crook's Prisoners," *New York Daily Tribune*, June 14, 1883.

90. "Gen. Crook's Victory."

91. "Punish the Apaches," editorial, *San Francisco Tribune*, June 16, 1883.

92. "General Crook's Victory(!)," *Arizona Silver Belt*, June 30, 1883.

93. Bourke, *Apache Campaign*, 127; Debo, *Geronimo, the Man*, 191.

94. *Chicago Tribune*, June 13, 1883.

CHAPTER 13. FIRE IN MY REAR

1. "The Raid on the Apaches," *New York Times*, June 1, 1883.

2. Harte, "Conflict at San Carlos," 36; Sweeney, *Cochise to Geronimo*, 313.

3. For a detailed account of Wilcox's obstructionism, see Sweeney, *Cochise to Geronimo*, 311–15.

4. Ibid., 304.

5. Crook, Sierra Madre Report, AHS, 171.

6. Sweeney, *Cochise to Geronimo*, 312; Cook, *Autobiography*, 248–49.

7. Teller to Lincoln, June 14, 1883, quoted in "The Hostiles," *Chicago Tribune*, June 14, 1883.

8. *Cleveland Herald*, July 8, 1883.

9. Harte, "Conflict at San Carlos," 36.

10. Crook to AG, June 26, 1883, Crook Letterbook, Hayes Library.

11. Goodwin, *Western Apache*, 171; Crook, Sierra Madre Report, AHS, app. E, 26.

12. Crook to Schofield, June 19, 1883, Crook Letterbook, Hayes Library.

13. Schofield to Sherman, June 17, 1883, quoted in Sweeney, *Cochise to Geronimo*, 314.

14. "Banquet in Honor of General George Crook," *Arizona Weekly Citizen*, June 23, 1883.

15. "General Crook Interviewed," *Arizona Weekly Citizen*, June 23, 1883.

16. Davis later estimated that about two hundred Apaches, including the tribe's fighting men, remained in Mexico. Davis, *Truth about Geronimo*, 69.

17. "Crook Interviewed."

18. Ibid.

19. Harte, "Conflict at San Carlos," 37.

20. Betzinez, *I Fought with Geronimo*, 122.

21. Goodwin, "John Rope," 172; Davis, *Truth about Geronimo*, 70–71; Sweeney, *Cochise to Geronimo*, 315; Thrapp, *Sierra Madre Adventure*, 174–75, and *Conquest of Apacheria*, 292–93; Betziniz, *I Fought with Geronimo*, 122.

22. Goodwin, "John Rope," 172.

23. Drum to Crook, June 25, 1883; Crook to Drum, June 26, 1883, quoted in "Drum and Crook, Their Correspondence on the Captured Apache Problem," *Cleveland Herald*, June 27, 1883.

24. Crawford to Crook, June 26, 1883, Gatewood Papers, AHS.

25. "What Will We Do with Them?," *New York Times*, June 18, 1883.

26. "General Crook Confers with Government Officials," *Cleveland Herald*, July 6, 1883; Thrapp, *Conquest of Apacheria*, 296–97; Sweeney, *Cochise to Geronimo*, 319.

27. "The Apache Question Settled," *New York Daily Tribune*, July 7, 1883; Thrapp, *Conquest of Apacheria*, 296–97; Sweeney, *Cochise to Geronimo*, 319.

28. "Our Indian Policy," *New York Herald*, July 7, 1883.

29. Porter, *Paper Medicine Man*, 201–2.

30. Ibid.; Crook to unknown, Feb. 5, 1884, Bourke Papers, NSHS, quoted in ibid., 202; Crook to Bourke, July 9, 1883, ibid.; *Omaha Bee*, July 27, 1883.

CHAPTER 14. SETTLING DOWN THE CHIRICAHUAS

1. Ogle, *Federal Control of the Western Apaches*, 222; Lockwood, *The Apache Indians*, 274.

2. Davis, *Truth about Geronimo*, 31; Weigel, "Notes on the Apaches."

3. Elliot, "Indian Reservation," reprinted in Cozzens, *Eyewitnesses*, 1:405–6.

4. Davis, *Truth about Geronimo*, 72.

5. Ibid., 69.

6. *Arizona Weekly Citizen*, Nov. 24, 1883.

7. *Arizona Silver Belt*, Dec. 1, 1883.

8. Crook, Sierra Madre Report, AHS, app. E, 27.

9. "More Apache Trouble," *New York Times*, July 20, 1883; Davis, *Truth about Geronimo*, 73, 75, 77; Elliot, "Indian Reservation," reprinted in Cozzens, *Eyewitnesses*, 1:405.

10. "Work of Apaches in Sonora," *Arizona Weekly Citizen*, Sept. 15, 1883.

11. Bourke, *Apache Campaign*, 127.

12. Crook to Wright, Oct. 22, 1883, reprinted in *Weekly Phoenix Herald*, Nov. 15, 1883.

13. Crook to AAG, Div. of Pacific, Nov. 24, 1883, Crook Letterbook, Hayes Library.

14. Sweeney, *Cochise to Geronimo*, 342.

15. Ibid., 329.

16. Ibid., 329–35.

17. See, for example, "Gen. Crook's Positions," *Arizona Silver Belt*, Sept. 15, 1883; see also Crook to Topete, Nov. 22, 1883, Crook Letterbook, Hayes Library.

18. Davis, *Truth about Geronimo*, 75.

19. Ibid., 77.

20. Sweeney, *Cochise to Geronimo*, 325.

21. Crook to AG, Aug. 7, 1883, Crook Letterbook, Hayes Library; Sweeny, *Cochise to Geronimo*, 323; Davis, *Truth about Geronimo*, 75, 77.

22. Crook to AG, Sept. 30, 1883, Crook Letterbook, Hayes Library.

23. June 26, 1883, ibid.

24. Ware to sec. of state, Aug. 31, 1883, quoted in Sweeney, *Cochise to Geronimo*, 325–26.

25. Sweeney, *Cochise to Geronimo*, 325–26.

26. *Weekly Phoenix Herald*, Nov. 15, 1883; see also Sweeney, *Cochise to Geronimo*, 326, who cites the (N. Mex.) *Southwest Sentinel*, Nov. 3, 1883, as his source.

27. Crook to AAG, Div. of Pacific, Nov. 24, 1883, Crook Letterbook, Hayes Library; Davis, *Truth about Geronimo*, 77–78; Sweeney, *Cochise to Geronimo*, 327.

28. Rafferty to Roberts, Oct. 26, 1883, NARA, Records of the AGO, RG 94 (hereafter cited as NARA, Rafferty Report), reprinted in *Arizona Weekly Citizen*, Nov. 17, 1883; Davis, *Truth about Geronimo*, 79–80; see also Sweeney, *Cochise to Geronimo*, 337–39.

29. Thrapp, *Conquest of Apacheria*, 306; NARA, Rafferty Report.

30. Newspapers hostile to Crook would attribute the warriors' decision to return to the reservation to their supposed defeat in an engagement with Mexican troops at Casas Grandes. As the newspapers told it, "The Indians were reported routed [chased to the border] with considerable slaughter, and again over-taken on American soil." One paper composed a bit of doggerel to commemorate the supposed occurrence. "Little Crook peep lost his Indian sheep, / And didn't know where to find them; / So he left them alone, and they came home, / With the Mexican troops behind them." In reality the Indians had escaped unscathed from a planned Mexican ambush at Casa Grande. The papers distorted the event either in a deliberate attempt to discredit Crook or because some chose to accept and reprint the Mexican government's self-serving description of the incident. "Mexican Troops Again Victorious," *Arizona Silver Belt*, Oct. 27, 1883. In contrast, see Captain Rafferty's report containing the Chiricahua's version of the incident in "Full Text of Captain Rafferty's Report," *Arizona Weekly Citizen*, Nov. 17, 1883. For analysis, see Sweeney, *Cochise to Geronimo*, 335–36.

31. NARA, Rafferty Report.

32. Sweeney, *Cochise to Geronimo*, 339. In writing of the event years later, Davis demonstrated that he knew about the raids, commenting that the returnees seemed well supplied with Mexican ponies. *Truth about Geronimo*, 79.

33. Davis, *Truth about Geronimo*, 73.

34. Sweeney, *Cochise to Geronimo*, 340.

35. Ibid., 338.

36. Crook to Judge Wright, Nov. 9, 1883, reprinted in *Arizona Weekly Citizen*, Nov. 17, 1883; Sweeney, *Cochise to Geronimo*, 340, Crawford to Crook, Nov. 14, 1883, Crook Letterbook, Hayes Library.

37. Crawford to Crook, Nov. 22, 1883, Crook Letterbook, Hayes Library.

38. Crook to AAG, Div. of Pacifc, Nov. 24, 1883, ibid.

39. Ibid.

40. Debo, *Geronimo, the Man*, 196; Thrapp, *Sierra Madre Adventure*, 176. Davis reported that Chatto arrived with a "band of fifty or sixty," but he may have confused his arrival with that of the earlier group. *Truth about Geronimo*, 80.

41. Davis, *Truth about Geronimo*, 84.

42. Davis to AAG, DA, Feb. 26, 1884, included with Crook's letter to AG, Mar. 20, 1884, NARA, Records of the Adjutant General's Office, RG 94.

43. For a full account of the adventures encountered by Davis on this trip, see Davis, *Truth about Geronimo*, 88–101; Crawford to Crook, Mar. 24, 1884, Crook Letterbook, Hayes Library; Debo, *Geronimo, the Man*, 202; Thrapp, *Conquest of Apacheria*, 293–94; *Arizona Weekly Citizen*, Mar. 15, 1884.

44. Geronimo related his tale in Barrett, *Geronimo's Story*, 135–36.

45. Crawford to Crook, March 24, 1884, Crook Letterbook, Hayes Library.

46. Crook's report, *ARSW*, 1884, app. A.

CHAPTER 15. MOVE TO TURKEY CREEK

1. Crook to AAG, Div. of Pacific, Nov. 3, 1883, Crook Letterbook, Hayes Library.

2. Ibid.

3. Crawford to Crook, Nov. 20, 1883, ibid.; Betzinez, *I Fought with Geronimo*, 122–23.

4. Crook to AAG, Nov. 3, 1883, Crook Letterbook, Hayes Library.

5. Crook to AG, Nov. 22, 1883, ibid.

6. Davis, *Truth about Geronimo*, 45–46.

7. Crawford to Crook, Nov. 20, 1883, and Nov. 22, 1883, Crook Letterbook, Hayes Library.

8. Crook to AG, Mar. 19, 1884, ibid.

9. Teller to Wilcox, Feb. 23, 1883, NARA, DA, LR, RG 393; "The Deer Creek Coal Fields," *Arizona Weekly Citizen*, June 21, 1884; *Arizona Sentinel*, Mar. 8, 1884.

10. Crook to AG, Mar. 19, 1884, Crook Letterbook, Hayes Library. According to Britton Davis, Crook's efforts succeeded in keeping the miners off the reservation for the remainder of his tenure in Arizona. *Truth about Geronimo*, 52. But upon his departure coal operations resumed and continued well into the next century. These depredations continue even today, as legislation was passed to mine copper on land sacred to the San Carlos Apaches and was only temporarily blocked at this writing by declaring the area a national historic site. Tony Dokoupil, "A Battle over Land Sacred for Apaches and Lucrative for a Mining Company," msnbc.com, Mar. 31, 2015; Jessica Swarner, "Did Obama Just Block the Sale of Sacred Apache Land to a Foreign Mining Company? Well. . . ." indiancountrytodaymedianetwork.com, Mar. 17, 2016.

11. Crawford to Crook, Mar. 24, 1884, Crook Letterbook, Hayes Library.

12. Ibid.

13. Despite these advantages Geronimo objected to Turkey Creek, insisting that mescal, basic to the Apache diet, did not grow there. However, the rest of the leadership overruled him as they favored the move. Sweeney, *Cochise to Geronimo*, 365.

14. Betzinez, *I Fought with Geronimo*, 122–25; Thrapp, *Conquest of Apacheria*, 306–7.

15. Magid, *Gray Fox*, 71–72, 115, 409n32.

16. Elliot, "Indian Reservation," reprinted in Cozzens, *Eyewitnesses*, 1:408.

17. Davis, *Truth about Geronimo*, 145.

18. Elliot, "Indian Reservation," 408–9.

19. Davis, *Truth about Geronimo*, 122–23.

20. Ibid., 123; Crawford to Crook, Mar. 24, 1884, Crook Letterbook, Hayes Library. Surprisingly, Chatto, the leader of the raid that precipitated Crook's campaign into the Sierra Madre, had joined the scouts and was now highly regarded by the military for his loyalty and reliability, though equally despised for that reason by the more hardcore resisters. Debo, *Geronimo, the Man*, 222; Ball, *Indeh*, 83.

21. Crawford to AAG, DA, in Crook's report, *ARSW*, 1884, app. A; Betzinez, *I Fought with Geronimo*, 126.

22. Davis, *Truth about Geronimo*, 123–30. Eve Ball wrote an account of this incident blaming Chatto for Ka-ya-ten-nae's arrest. Ball and Kaywaykla, *In the Days of Victorio*, 162–67. But Sweeney asserts that there were so many discrepancies in the story Ball was told by her informants—and Chatto was so widely disliked by them—that Davis's account appears the more credible. Sweeney, *Cochise to Geronimo*, 375.

23. Sweeney, *Cochise to Geronimo*, 376–77.

24. Crawford to Crook, June 28, 1884, quoted in ibid., 378.

25. Crook to Crawford, July 11, 1884, Crook Letterbook, Hayes Library.

26. Crook to AAG, Div. of Pacific, May 24, 1884, ibid.

27. Crook to AAG, Div. of Pacific, Aug. 2 and Oct. 30, 1884, ibid.; Bourke, *On the Border*, 473.

28. Sweeney, *Cochise to Geronimo*, 247.

29. At least one witness identified Dutchy after he returned to San Carlos, claiming that he knew enough to "hang" the scout. Ibid., 247, 290; Crawford to Crook, Nov. 22, 1883, quoted in ibid.

30. Davis, *Truth about Geronimo*, 116.

31. Ibid.

32. Crawford to Crook, Nov. 14, 1883, Crook Letterbook, Hayes Library; Thrapp, *Conquest of Apacheria*, 309–10.

33. Tidball to Crook, Nov. 25, 1883, NARA, Records of the AGO, RG 94, Microfilm.

34. Crook to AG, endorsement, Nov. 28, 1883, ibid.

35. Teller to Crook, Dec. 20, 1883, ibid.

36. Crook to AG, May 25, 1884, ibid.

37. Tidball to Crook, Nov. 18, 1884, ibid.

38. Ibid.; Crook to AG, Nov. 24, 1884, ibid.

39. Thrapp, *Conquest of Apacheria*, 310; Sweeney, *Cochise to Geronimo*, 581.

40. Crook to AAG, Div. of Pacific, July 11, 1884, Crook Letterbook, Hayes Library.

41. Sweeney, *Cochise to Geronimo*, 393.

42. Ibid.

43. Crook to AG, Apr. 7, 1885, Crook Letterbook, Hayes Library.

44. Sweeney, *Cochise to Geronimo*.

45. Crook's report, *ARSW*, 1884, 134.

46. Magid, *Gray Fox*, 54.

47. Lyon, "Archie McIntosh," 115, 121.

48. Ibid., 117; Crook to Crawford, Apr. 4, 1884, Crook Letterbook, Hayes Library; Sweeney, *Cochise to Geronimo*, 367.

49. Sweeney, *Cochise to Geronimo*, 367.

CHAPTER 16. MORE FIRE FROM THE REAR

1. Crook to AAG, Div. of Pacific, May, n.d., 1884, Crook Letterbook, Hayes Library.

2. Crook recounted the entire history of his relations with Wilcox and the Interior Department from his arrival in 1882 in his annual report to the secretary of war, Sept. 9, 1885, Gatewood File, AHS. See also Sweeney, *Cochise to Geronimo*, 319–21, 349–54; Harte, "Conflict at San Carlos," 34–35; and ch. 13 of this work.

3. Crook to AG, Apr. 12, 1884, NARA, Records of the AGO, RG 94, Microfilm.

4. Crook to Teller, Feb. 23, 1883, Crook Letterbook, Hayes Library.

5. Wilcox to Crook, Feb. 27, 1883, NARA, DA, LR, RG 393.

6. Harte, "Conflict at San Carlos," 35–36.

7. Wilcox to Crook, May 18, 1883, NARA, DA, LR, RG 393.

8. Lummis, *Crook and the Apache Wars*, 15.

9. Ibid., 171–72.

10. Crook's report, *ARSW*, 1885.

11. Crook to Lincoln, Sept. 5, 1883, NARA, Records of the AGO, RG 94.

12. Thrapp, *Conquest of Apacheria*, 296; "Gen. Crook's Return," *New York Times*, June 18, 1883.

13. "Gen. Crook's Return"; *Philadelphia Press*, July 18, 1883, quoted in Thrapp, *Conquest of Apacheria*, 297.

14. *Philadelphia Press*, July 17, 1883, quoted in Thrapp, *Conquest of Apacheria*, 296–97.

15. Ibid., 297.

16. *Omaha Daily Bee*, July 23, 1883.

17. Writing in 1889 Bancroft noted: "There is extant in Arizona a theory that . . . General Crook, through placing too much confidence in his scouts, found himself really in the power of the Chiricahuas, and was obliged to accept Geronimo's terms. I have not attached much importance to this theory, though the events of 1885–6 tend somewhat to give it plausibility." Bancroft, *History of Arizona*, 572n. Historian James McClintock resurrected the story in his 1916 history of Arizona. McClintock, *Arizona, Prehistoric*, quoted in Thrapp, *Conquest of Apacheria*, 299. Thrapp devoted an entire chapter (entitled "Who Captured Whom—or, Did Geronimo Take Crook?") to the capture story in *Conquest of Apacheria*. He described McClintock's description of his meeting with the Chiricahuas as "heavily inaccurate and slipshod" (295–302).

18. Teller to Wilcox, July 7, 1883; Wilcox to Teller, Sept. 12, 1883; Wilcox to Crawford, Dec. 3, 1883, all in NARA, Records of the AGO, RG 94; Investigation and Trial of Emmet Crawford, July 1884, NARA, RG 153, File RR 44.

19. Sweeney, *Cochise to Geronimo*, 349.

20. Harte believed that another reason why Crook sided with Crawford on this matter was his "fundamental premise . . . that once the military had assumed a duty, the responsibility should never be surrendered lest the Indians think its loss a sign of weakness." "Conflict at San Carlos," 39. In his report included in the *ARSW*, 1885, Crook spells out this premise.

21. Crawford to AAG Whipple, undated letter written in the spring of 1884, NARA, Records of the AGO, RG 94.

22. Harte, "Conflict at San Carlos," 39.

23. Crawford to Crook, Aug. 14 and Sept. 23, 1883, quoted in Sweeney, *Cochise to Geronimo*, 349.

24. Teller to Lincoln, Feb. 2, 1884; Crawford to AAG, Fort Whipple, Mar. 6, 1884; Gen. Orders No. 13, July 14, 1884, all in NARA, Records of the AGO, RG 94; Sweeney, *Cochise to Geronimo*, 350.

25. Wilcox to Crawford, Dec. 3, 1883; Crawford to Wilcox, Dec. 3, 1883; Price to Teller, Feb. 14, 1884, all in NARA, Records of the AGO, RG 94.

26. Crawford to Wilcox, Dec. 3, 1883; Crawford to AAG, Jan. 6, 1884, both in NARA, Records of the AGO, DA, RG 94; Sweeney, *Cochise to Geronimo*, 351.

27. Crawford to AAG, Div. of Pacific, Dec. 29, 1883, NARA, Records of the AGO, RG 94.

28. Sweeney, *Cochise to Geronimo*, 352–53.

29. Wilcox to Price, Feb. 9, 1884, NARA, Records of the AGO, RG 94.

30. Ibid.

31. Crook to AAG, Div. of Pacific, Apr. 12, 1884, NARA, Records of the AGO, RG 94.

32. Ibid.

33. See Magid, *Gray Fox*, 116.

34. Crook to AAG, Div. of Pacific, Apr. 12, 1884, NARA, Records of the AGO, RG 94.

35. General Orders No.13, July 14, 1884, Whipple Barracks, Prescott, Investigation and Trial of Emmet Crawford, July 1884, NARA, RG 153, File RR 44.

36. Endorsement on Statement of Captain Emmet Crawford in reply to charges brought against him by Agent Wilcox, Apr. 29, 1884, NARA, Files of the AGO, RG 94.

37. Crook to Pope, Endorsement to Crawford Report re Rationing of Indians, Oct. 4, 1884, NARA, DA, LS, RG 393.

38. AAG, Div. of the Pacific to AG, Aug. 2, 1884; Stevens, CIA, to sec. of interior, Aug. 14, 1886, both in NARA, DA, LR, RG 393.

39. Crawford to AAG, Whipple, Sept. 23, 1884; Sheridan to Crook, Oct. 28, 1884, both in ibid.; Beaumont to Wilcox, June 20, 1884, quoted in Ogle, *Federal Control of Western Apaches*, 228.

40. Ogle, *Federal Control of Western Apaches*, 228–29.

41. Harte, "Conflict at San Carlos," 41; Sweeney, *Cochise to Geronimo*, 386; Robinson, *Crook and the Western Frontier*, 270.

42. Sweeney, *Cochise to Geronimo*, 387.

43. Ibid., 389; Crawford to Crook, Feb. 27, 1885, quoted in Harte, "Conflict at San Carlos," 41.

44. Harte, "Conflict at San Carlos," 41.

45. Ford to CIA, Jan. 18, 1885, quoted in Sweeney, *Cochise to Geronimo*, 388; Crook, *Autobiography*, 252; Harte, "Conflict at San Carlos," 41.

46. Crook to AG, Feb. 19, 1885, quoted in Crook's report, *ARSW*, 1885, 8–9; Pope, First Endorsement to Crook's Letter, Feb. 24, 1885, ibid.; Harte, "Conflict at San Carlos"; Bourke, *On the Border*, 41; Sweeney, *Cochise to Geronimo*, 389.

47. Sweeney, *Cochise to Geronimo*, 389.

48. Ogle, *Federal Control of Western Apaches*, 229–30; Harte, "Conflict at San Carolos," 41–2; Sweeney, *Cochise to Geronimo*, 389–90.

49. General Orders No. 7, Feb. 27, 1885, quoted in Sweeney, *Cochise to Geronimo*, 390.

50. Sweeney, *Cochise to Geronimo*, 391; Cruse, *Apache Days and After*, 205.

51. Sweeney, *Cochise to Geronimo*, 391; Harte, "Conflict at San Carlos," 42.

52. Endicott to Lamar, Mar. 28, 1885, quoted in Crook's report, *ARSW*, 1885, app. F, 29.

53. For more on Lamar, see Mayes, *Lucius Q. C. Lamar*, 493.

54. Ogle, *Federal Control of Western Apaches*, 230–31.

55. For the story of the visit to the Supais, I am indebted to Frank Casanova, editor of *Arizona and the West*, for providing background material on the Havasupai and copious quotes from Bourke's diary, vols. 74 and 75, the only known contemporary account of the expedition. Casanova, "Crook Visits the Supais," 253–78.

56. For a description of Crook's visit to the Moqui, see "Final Days in Arizona," in Magid, *Gray Fox*, 133–37.

CHAPTER 17. BREAKOUT

1. Crook to AAG, Div. of Pacific, Feb. 19, 1885, quoted in Sweeney, *Cochise to Geronimo*, 392.

2. Pierce's report is reprinted in Bourke, *On the Border*, 465–66.

3. Ibid.; Betzinez, *I Fought with Geronimo*, 125; Davis, *Truth about Geronimo*, 137.

4. Betzinez, *I Fought with Geronimo*, 125; Davis, *Truth about Geronimo*, 136–37.

5. Davis, *Truth about Geronimo*, 136; Pierce to Roberts, Aug. 4, 1885; Ford to CIA, June 24, 1885, both quoted in Sweeney, *Cochise to Geronimo*, 395–96.

6. Davis, *Truth about Geronimo*,139. To these theories a modern observer might also add another compelling reason for the spousal abuse and alcoholism. These are problems commonly associated with societies sunk in hopelessness and despair as the consequence of economic and social dislocation such as that experienced by the Apaches at San Carlos in the 1880s and on reservations today.

7. See Gatewood, *Lt. Charles Gatewood*, 7–8.

8. Sweeeny, *Cochise to Geronimo*, 394–95; Elliot, "Geronimo Campaign of 1885–1886," in Cozzens, *Eyewitnesses*, 1:427–46, 428.

9. Davis, *Truth about Geronimo*, 137–38.

10. Davis drew this conclusion and described the ensuing events in detail in Davis to AAG, Sept. 15, 1885, quoted in Crook's report, *ARSW*, 1885, app. H.

11. Opler, *Apache Life-way*, 369–70.

12. Sweeney, *Cochise to Geronimo*, 397.

13. Davis, *Truth about Geronimo*, 140; Cruse, *Apache Days and After*, 206.

14. Davis, *Truth about Geronimo*, 139.

15. Sweeney, *Cochise to Geronimo*, 397–98; Davis, *Truth about Geronimo*, 142.

16. Ball, *Indeh*, 50; Davis, *Truth about Geronimo*, 146; Sweeney, *Cochise to Geronimo*, 394; Betzinez, *I Fought with Geronimo*, 129. See also Geronimo to Crook, at Cañon de los Embudos, Mar. 25, 1886, Sen. Exec. Doc. No. 88, 51st Cong., 1st sess., 11.

17. Davis, *Truth about Geronimo*, 144–46.

18. Ibid.

19. Ibid.

20. Ibid., 146–48. The entire text of the telegram is quoted in Thrapp, *Conquest of Apacheria*, 313, citing the appendix of Crook's report on Apache operations in the field, Fort Bowie, Apr. 10, 1886.

21. Davis, *Truth about Geronimo*, 149; Sweeney, *Cochise to Geronimo*, 395–400; Thrapp, *Al Sieber*, 294.

22. Thrapp, *Conquest of Apacheria*, 311; Sweeney, *Cochise to Geronimo*, 402.

23. Geronimo dispatched two of his relatives who served as scouts to carry out this mission, which Davis inadvertently foiled. Just prior to taking the trail in pursuit of Geronimo, the lieutenant had assembled his scouts with their weapons. Suspecting possible disloyalty among them, he ordered Chatto and Dutchy, whom he trusted implicitly, to shoot anyone who attempted to raise his weapon from the ground. Thinking that Davis had been alerted to the plan, the would-be assassins slipped hurriedly away into the brush. Davis, *Truth about Geronimo*, 150–51; Sweeney, *Cochise to Geronimo*, 402.

24. Thrapp, *Conquest of Apacheria*, 314.

25. For a participant's account, see Parker, *The Old Army*, 152–60. See also Crook to AG, Div. of Pacific, May 26, 1885, Crook Letterbook, Hayes Library; Davis, *Truth about Geronimo*, 149–51; Lockwood, *Apache Indians*, 281.

26. In the months that followed, a number of people, including officers on Crook's own staff, were unaware that the general had not received Davis's wire and unjustly blamed him for not reacting quickly to the crisis. Thrapp, *Conquest of Apacheria*, 313n6. Davis later speculated that if Crook had received his message, the general would have taken decisive action. Davis, *Truth about Geronimo*, 149; Sweeney, *Cochise to Geronimo*, 400. Crook himself sought to remove any misapprehension concerning the telegram.

In December 1886, in a lengthy treatise defending his use of Apache scouts, he wrote in passing that "I am firmly convinced that had I known of the occurrences reported in Lt. Davis' telegram on May 15, 1885, which I did not see until months afterwards, the outbreak of Mangas and Geronimo a few days later would not have occurred." Crook, *Resumé of Operations*, 11–12. Several years later he again referred to the telegram in a conversation with Davis, repeating that he never received it. If he had, he told his former lieutenant, "the outbreak would probably never have occurred." He then added with a touch of bravado, "If it had occurred, the Indians would never have reached Mexico but would have been taught a lesson they would never have forgotten." Davis professed to agree with Crook's assessment. Davis, *Truth about Geronimo*, 148–49.

27. Sweeney, *Cochise to Geronimo*, 408.

28. *Clifton* (Ariz.) *Clarion*, June 3, 1885.

29. *Arizona Weekly Citizen*, June 13, 1884.

30. As an example, see G. Gordon Adam, "Resolution Regarding Outbreak of Indians from San Carlos Reservation," June 15, 1885, in Cozzens, *Eyewitnesses*, 1:414–24.

31. Crook to AAG, Div. of Pacific, June 5, 1885, Crook Letterbook, Hayes Library; Sweeney, *Cochise to Geronimo*, 430–31.

32. Crook's report, in *ARSW*, 1885.

33. Pope to AG, July 27, 1885; Lamar to Endicott, July 31, 1885; Pope to AG, Aug. 1, 1885, all quoted in Sweeney, *Cochise to Geronimo*, 465. See also Harte, "Conflict at San Carlos," 41–42.

34. Sweeney, *Cochise to Geronimo*, 405–7.

35. Crook's report, *ARSW*, 1885, 13–15.

36. Crook to Davis, May 21, 1885, Crook Letterbook, Hayes Library; Sweeney, *Cochise to Geronimo*, 411; Thrapp, *Conquest of Apacheria*, 316.

37. Crook to AAG, Div. of Pacific, May 21, 1885, Crook Letterbook, Hayes Library.

38. Debo, *Geronimo, the Man*, 241.

39. Crook to AAG, Div. of Pacific, Apr. 7, 1885; Crook to AAG, May 7, 1885; Crook to AAG, May 19, 1885, all in Crook Letterbook, Hayes Library.

40. Crook to AAG, Div. of Pacific, May 20, 1885, ibid.; Davis, *Truth about Geronimo*, 152. Sweeney reckoned that 42 men and boys and 102 women and children accompanied Geronimo, a difference accounted for by the author's decision to count one of the boys as a child not old enough to bear arms. Sweeney, *Cochise to Geronimo*, 404–6.

41. Thrapp, *Conquest of Apacheria*, 315; Utley, *Geronimo*, 160.

42. Crook to AAG, Div. of Pacific, May 21, 1885; Crook to Davis, May 21,1885, Crook Letterbook, Hayes Library.

43. Davis to Crook, May 20, 1885; Crook to Davis, May 21, 1885, both in ibid.

44. Crook to AAG, Div. of Pacific, June 2, 1885, ibid.

45. Crook to AAG, Div. of Pacific, May 27 and 29, 1885; Crook to Pierce, May 20, 1885; Crook to Bradley, May 27, 1885; all in Crook Letterbook, Hayes Library; Thrapp, *Conquest of Apacheria*, 321; Sweeney, *Cochise to Geronimo*, 411–12.

46. Crook to CO, Fort Bowie, May 29, 1885; Crook to AAG, Div. of Pacific, May 31, 1885, Crook Letterbook, Hayes Library; Sweeney, *Cochise to Geronimo*, 429.

47. Debo, *Geronimo, the Man*, 241; Thrapp, *Conquest of Apacheria*, 317–18.

48. Crook to AAG, Div. of Pacific, May 31, 1885, Crook Letterbook, Hayes Library.

49. Davis, *Truth about Geronimo*, 166.

50. Crook to Davis, May 21, 1885, Crook Letterbook, Hayes Library.

51. The local papers were quick to resurrect old rumors about the scouts betraying Crook in the Sierra Madre. For example, the June 13, 1885, edition of the *Arizona Weekly Citizen* editorialized, "Crook has trusted scouts before and they were faithful, but that time in the Sierra Madre, they betrayed him.".

52. Greene, "The Crawford Affair," 143.

53. Crook to AAG, Div. of Pacific, June 5, 9, 10, and 13, 1885, Crook Letterbook, Hayes Library.

54. Sweeney, *Cochise to Geronimo*, 440.

55. Ibid., 441.

56. Crook, *Resumé of Operations*, 22; Crook's report, *ARSW*, 1886, 4–5; Daly, "Geronimo Campaign," in Cozzens, *Eyewitnesses*, 1:447–87, 450; Porter, *Paper Medicine Man*, 172; Thrapp, *Conquest of Apacheria*, 326–27.

CHAPTER 18. PURSUIT INTO MEXICO

1. Roberts, "Notes on the Service of Cyrus Swan Roberts."

2. Sheridan to Crook, June 9, 1885, attachment, Crook's report, *ARSW*, 1886, 4–5, 19; Sweeney, *Cochise to Geronimo*, 431; Thrapp, *Conquest of Apacheria*, 328; Crook, *Autobiography*, 255.

3. See chapter 27 in this work.

4. Magid, *George Crook*, 9.

5. Crook diary, vol. 1, Crook/Kennon Papers, U.S. Army Heritage and Education Center, Carlisle, Penn (hereafter cited as Crook diary, Crook/Kennon Papers, AHEC).

6. Crook, *Autobiography*, 255–56.

7. Crook's report, *ARSW*, 1886, 3; Davis, *Truth about Geronimo*, 152; Daly, "Geronimo Campaign," in Cozzens, *Eyewitnesses*, 1:449–50; Sweeney, *Cochise to Geronimo*, 431.

8. Davis, *Truth about Geronimo*, 161.

9. See ibid., 160–61. Ironically, in the present instance, Davis would later learn that the White Mountain warriors were killed by an American rancher living in Mexico who assumed the scouts were hostile Apaches threatening his herd. Ibid., 164. See also Elliot, "Geronimo Campaign," in Cozzens, *Eyewitnesses*, 1:427–46.

10. Crawford to Crook, June 25, 1885, quoted in Elliot, "Geronimo Campaign," in Cozzens, *Eyewitnesses*, 1: 433–34; Ball, *Indeh*, 98–99; Sweeney, *Cochise to Geronimo*, 434–35; Davis, *Truth about Geronimo*, 166–68.

11. Davis, *Truth about Geronimo*, 172–73.

12. Elliot, "Geronimo Campaign," in Cozzens, *Eyewitnesses*, 1:434–36. Elliot's piece also contains extracts from General Crook's report on the campaign as well as Crawford's. For Crook's, see 431; for Crawford's, 433.

13. Ibid., 438.

14. Davis, *Truth about Geronimo*, 172–73; Daly, "Geronimo Campaign," in Cozzens, *Eyewitnesses*, 1:452.

15. Davis, *Truth about Geronimo*, 174–75; Sweeney, *Cochise to Geronimo*, 440.

16. Crook to AAG, Div. of Pacific, Aug. 17, 1885, Crook Letterbook, Hayes Library.

17. Debo, *Geronimo, the Man*, 244.

18. Despite a life lived precariously on the edge, the old chief survived to the age of about ninety-six, dying in 1894 of natural causes at Fort Sill, Oklahoma. Thrapp,

Encyclopedia of Frontier Biography, 2:1039. Chapo, too, was unharmed, but he tragically contracted tuberculosis at Carlisle Indian School while still young. He died attended by his family at Mount Vernon Barracks, a prisoner of war. Utley, *Geronimo*, 249.

19. Barrett, *Geronimo's Story*, 136. Crook recorded the engagement in his diary. Crook diary, vol. 1, Aug. 17, 1885, Crook/Kennon Papers, AHEC. See also Davis, *Truth about Geronimo*, 174–76; Daly, "Geronimo Campaign," in Cozzens, *Eyewitnesses*, 1:452; Thrapp, *Conquest of Apacheria*, 330. *The Chronological List of Actions, etc., with Indians from January 15, 1837, to January 1891*, dates this engagement as occurring on Aug. 7, 1885, and lists five Indians killed and fifteen captured, possibly based on Crook's initial report. Quoted in Cozzens, *Eyewitnesses*, 1:672n8. For the Indian perspective, see Debo, *Geronimo, the Man*, 244; and Ball, *Indah*, 154.

20. Crook to AAG, Div. of Pacific, Aug. 18, 1885, Crook Letterbook, Hayes Library.

21. Crawford had authorized the to slaughter cattle for food along the route, paying for them with receipts to be honored at a later date by the army, a form of compensation that would have had little meaning to a poor, desert-dwelling Mexican peasant. Elliot, "Geronimo Campaign," in Cozzens, *Eyewitnesses*, 1:437.

22. Ibid., 1:439; Davis, *Truth about Geronimo*, 183–88.

23. Utley, *Frontier Regulars*, 393.

24. Crook diary, Sept.1–4, 1885, Crook/Kennon Papers, AHEC; Faulk, *Geronimo Campaign*, 69; Sweeney, *Cochise to Geronimo*, 464–65.

25. Crook to AAG, Div. of Pacific, Sept. 6, 1885, Crook Letterbook, Hayes Library; Sweeney, *Cochise to Geronimo*, 460.

26. Davis, *Truth about Geronimo*, 185–95; Crook diary, Sept. 6 and 12, 1885, Crook/Kennon Papers, AHEC; Elliot, "Geronimo Campaign," in Cozzens, *Eyewitnesses*, 1:437; Crook to AAG, Div. of Pacific, Sept. 6, 1885, Crook Letterbook, Hayes Library; Sweeney, *Cochise to Geronimo*, 460.

27. Crook, *Autobiography*, 258.

28. Sweeney, *Cochise to Geronimo*, 461; Utley, *Geronimo*, 172; Debo, *Geronimo, the Man*, 246.

29. Sweeney, *Cochise to Geronimo*, 461–63.

30. Crook to AAG, Div. of Pacific, Sept. 22, 1885, Crook Letterbook; Utley, *Geronimo*, 173; Sweeney, *Cochise to Geronimo*, 470; Crook diary, Sept. 23, 1885, Crook/Kennon Papers, AHEC.

31. Crook's report, *ARSW*, 1886, 5; Sweeney, *Cochise to Geronimo*, 450–52; Thrapp, *Conquest of Apacheria*, 332; Utley, *Geronimo*, 172.

32. Crook diary, Sept. 28, 1885, Crook/Kennon Papers, AHEC.

33. For a full account of Captain Wirt Davis's first expedition into Mexico, see his Report to Captain C. S. Roberts, Seventeenth Infantry, Fort Bowie, Mar. 10, 1886, app. F, in Crook's report, *ARSW*, 1886.

34. Crook to Pierce, Nov. 14, 1885, NARA, DA, Letters Sent, RG 393; Crook diary, Nov. 13, 1885, Crook/Kennon Papers, AHEC.

35. Magid, *Gray Fox*, 125–26.

36. Roberts to Gatewood, Sept. 30, 1885, quoted in Sweeney, *Cochise to Geronimo*, 473.

37. Crook's report, *ARSW*, 1886; Thrapp, *Conquest of Apacheria*, 332–33; Lockwood, *Apache Indians*, 283; Sweeney, *Cochise to Geronimo*, 475.

38. Utley, *Geronimo*, 173.

39. Sweeney, *Cochise to Geronimo*, 479–80; Utley, *Geronimo*, 173; Thrapp, *Conquest of Apacheria*, 334–8; Roberts, *Once They Moved Like the Wind*, 263.

40. Crook to AAG, Div. of Pacific, Nov. 14, 1885, Crook Letterbook, Hayes Library.

41. "The Apaches, Some of Their More Recent Depredations and Bloody Work," *Las Vegas Daily Gazette*, Dec. 30, 1885; Utley, *Geronimo*,173.

42. Crook diary, Nov. 26, 1885, Crook/Kennon Papers, AHEC; Sweeney, *Cochise to Geronimo*, 487–89.

43. Sweeney, 487–89, 507–9; Crook to AAG, Div. of Pacific, Nov. 25 and 27, 1885, Crook Letterbook, Hayes Library; *Las Vegas Daily Gazette*, Dec. 30, 1885.

44. Crook's report, *ARSW*, 1886.

45. Crook to AAG, Div. of Pacific, Sept. 17, 1885, quoted in Sweeney, *Cochise to Geronimo*, 467.

46. Sheridan to secretary of war, *ARSW*, 1885, 61–62; Hutton, *Sheridan and His Army*, 364.

47. Sweeney, *Cochise to Geronimo*, 466–69; Sheridan to Endicott, Sept. 30, 1885, quoted in ibid., 468.

48. Crook diary, Nov. 19, 1885, Crook/Kennon Papers, AHEC.

49. Crook to Sheridan, Nov. 19, 1885, Crook Letterbook, Hayes Library.

50. Hutton, *Sheridan and His Army*; McChristian, *Fort Bowie*, 197.

51. Crook diary, Nov. 21, 1885, Crook/Kennon Papers, AHEC; Wirt Davis to Roberts, Mar. 11, 1886, Crook's report, app. G, *ARSW*, 1886.

52. Crook diary, Nov. 26, 1885, Crook/Kennon Papers, AHEC; Crook to AAG, Div. of Pacific, Nov. 25, 1885, Crook Letterbook, Hayes Library.

53. See, for example, the general's use of Colonel Rutherford Hayes to present his plan to Sheridan for the taking of Fisher's Hill during the Shenandoah campaign in 1864. Magid, *George Crook*, 258–59.

54. Charles Roberts, son of Crook aide Cyrus Roberts, kept a diary at the time. He recorded that Crawford had departed from the post the day prior to Sheridan's arrival, making the described meeting between the two men unlikely. However, Shipp, an officer present, wrote that Sheridan had inspected Crawford's scouts during his visit, indicating that the young man's recollection was inaccurate. See Charles Roberts, diary entry, Nov. 29, 1885, in "Memoirs of the Apache Wars," in Carroll, *Unpublished Papers of the Order of the Indian Wars*, no. 8, n.p.; Shipp, "Crawford's Last Expedition," in Cozzens, *Eyewitnesses*, 1:520.

55. Crawford's skills as an advocate can better be appreciated in light of Sheridan's longstanding opposition to the use of scouts. A year before he had presented testimony on a proposed military school for Indians in which he had opined to the Congressional Committee on Indian Affairs that "the [Indians] do not possess stability or tenacity of purpose. . . . They cannot appreciate responsibility or the sacredness of an oath . . . [They are] a race so distinctive from that governing this country that it would be neither wise nor expedient to recruit our army from their ranks." Though Crawford convinced Sheridan to allow the use of the scouts against Geronimo, as will become apparent, his presentation did not alter the lieutenant general's prejudice against the use of scouts or his attitude toward the Chiricahuas in general. See Sheridan to Robert Lincoln, Sec. of War, *Report of the Committee on Indian Affairs on the Advisability of a Military School for Indians*, quoted in Dunlay, *Wolves for the Blue Soldiers*, 66.

56. Crook to AAG, Div. of Pacific, Dec. 1, 1885, Crook Letterbook, Hayes Library.

57. For background on the rivalry between the two officers, see Magid, *Gray Fox*, 342–43, 346, 348, 355–56; Wooster, *Nelson A. Miles*, 140.

58. Wooster, *Nelson A. Miles*, 131; Amchan, *Most Famous Soldier*, 62.

59. Wooster, *Nelson A. Miles*, 141; Miles to AAG, Div. of the Missouri, Nov. 10, 1885, NARA, RG 94, M689; Schofield to AG, Nov. 12, 1885, quoted in Sweeney, *Cochise to Geronimo*, 483.

60. Miles to Long, Nov. 2, 1886, Long Papers, Huntington Museum, quoted in Wooster, *Nelson A. Miles*, 141.

61. Miles, *Personal Recollections*, 476; Miles to Sherman, Jan. 6, 1886, Sherman Papers, LC, quoted in Wooster, *Nelson A. Miles*, 142; *New York Times*, Sept. 27, 1885, quoted in Amchan, *Most Famous Soldier*, 68.

62. Bourke diary entries from January to March 1886 quoted in Shepard, "Miles-Crook Controversy," 43–49.

63. *New York Times*, Jan. 10, 1886, quoted in ibid., 46.

64. *San Franciscan*, Jan. 10, 1886, quoted in ibid.

65. Lamar, "Edmund G. Ross as Governor," 197–98; Porter, *Paper Medicine Man*, 174; Amchan, *Most Famous Soldier*, 69; Wooster, *Nelson A. Miles*, 141; Llewellyn to Crook, Jan. 30, 1886, quoted in Shepard, "Miles-Crook Controversy," 50–51.

66. Barlow to unknown addressee, Feb. 3, 1886, Miles Papers, quoted in Amchan, *Most Famous Soldier*, 68.

67. Magid, *Gray Fox*, 355–57.

68. Bourke diary, vol. 89, quoted in Porter, *Paper Medicine Man*, 174; Sonnichsen, *Mescalero Apaches*, 231–33.

69. Crook to AAG, Div. of Pacific, Sept. 19, 1885, Crook Letterbook, Hayes Library.

70. Amchan, *Most Famous Soldier*, 67; Wooster, *Nelson A. Miles*, 142.

CHAPTER 19. A TRAGIC LOSS

1. Crook to Sheridan, Dec. 24, 1885, Crook Letterbook, Hayes Library.

2. Crook to Bradley, Dec. 6, 1885, ibid.

3. Crook to Sheridan, Dec. 24, 1885, ibid.; Sweeney, *Cochise to Geronimo*, 475–76; Faulk, *Geronimo Campaign*, 70.

4. Sweeney, *Cochise to Geronimo*, 475–76.

5. Ibid., 509–10; Crook diary, Dec. 6–23, 1885, Crook/Kennon Papers, AHEC.

6. Crook diary, Dec. 7 and 14–15, 1885, Crook/Kennon Papers, AHEC.

7. Crook diary, Jan. 4 and 5, 1886, Crook/Kennon Papers, AHEC; Crook to Sheridan, Dec. 30, 1885; and Crook to AAG, Div. of Pacific, Jan. 5, 1885, both in Crook Letterbook, Hayes Library; Beck to Viele, Cave Canyon Camp, Jan. 8, 1886; Viele to Roberts, Jan. 8, 1886, both in NARA, DA, LR, RG 393.

8. Crook diary, Dec. 26 and 30, 1885, Crook/Kennon Papers, AHEC; Crook, *Autobiography*, 259; Sweeney, *Cochise to Geronimo*, 512; Crook to Sheridan, Dec. 24 and 30, 1885, Crook Letterbook, Hayes Library.

9. Crook to AG, Washington, D.C., Jan. 27, 1886, Crook Letterbook, Hayes Library.

10. Daly, "Scouts—Good and Bad," 69.

11. Sweeney, *Cochise to Geronimo*, 485–86; Shipp, "Crawford's Last Expedition," in Cozzens, *Eyewitnesses*, 1:518; Thrapp, *Dateline Fort Bowie*, 69, 183.

12. Thrapp, *Al Sieber*, 312.

13. Thrapp, *Encyclopedia of Frontier Biography*, 960; Sweeney, *Cochise to Geronimo*, 485–6; Horn, *Life of Tom Horn*, 255; Daly, "Scouts—Good and Bad," 69; Crook to AAG, Div. of Pacific, Dec. 1, 1885, Crook Letterbook, Hayes Library; Crook's report, *ARSW*, 1886, 71; Maus to C. S. Roberts, Feb. 23, 1886, app. L, ibid.; Dunlay, *Wolves for the Blue Soldiers*, 178–79; McChristian, *Fort Bowie*, 197.

14. Hanna, "With Crawford in Mexico," in Cozzens, *Eyewitnesses*, 1:514; Shipp, "Crawford's Last Expedition," in ibid., 518–19.

15. Hooker, *Child of the Fighting Tenth*, 183–84, quoted in Sweeney, *Cochise to Geronimo*, 493.

16. Greene, "Crawford Affair," 143–153, 145; "Maus' Narrative," in Miles, *Personal Recollections*, 2:450–471, 450–51.

17. Sweeney, *Cochise to Geronimo*, 495; Maus to Roberts, Feb. 23, 1886, *ARSW*, 1886, 48.

18. Shipp, "Crawford's Last Expedition," in Cozzens, *Eyewitnesses*, 1:523; "Maus' Narrative" in Miles, *Personal Recollections*, 2:455.

19. Shipp to Maus, Jan. 20, 1886, from Camp on Virgo River, in Crook's report, app., *ARSW*, 1886, 64.

20. Shipp, "Crawford's Last Expedition," in Cozzens, *Eyewitnesses*, 1:525; Sweeney, *Cochise to Geronimo*, 498; Utley, *Geronimo*, 179.

21. Crook later maintained that had Crawford met with Geronimo, almost every dissident in Mexico would likely have surrendered at the time. Crook report to AAG, Div. of Pacific, Apr. 10, 1886, Crook Letterbook, Hayes Library.

22. Horn, *Life of Tom Horn*, 280; Maus to Roberts, Feb. 23, 1886, Crook's report, *ARSW*, 1886.

23. Shipp, "Crawford's Last Expedition," in Cozzens, *Eyewitnesses*, 1:526.

24. Henry Daly, not present at the time, claimed that it was not a Mexican but Dutchy, who was by Crawford's side, who killed Crawford and then robbed him. Daly's allegation is suspect given his dislike and distrust of the scout and the fact that none of the accounts of officers who witnessed the shooting provided any evidence or voiced suspicion of Dutchy's involvement. Daly, "Scouts—Good and Bad," 70.

25. Maus to Roberts, Feb. 23, 1886, Crook's report, *ARSW*, 1886.

26. Crook interview with Lummis, *Los Angeles Times*, May 16, 1886, quoted in Thrapp, *Dateline Fort Bowie*, 184; Crook's report, *ARSW*, 1886; Greene, "Crawford Affair," 150.

27. Daly, "Geronimo Campaign," in Cozzens, *Eyewitnesses*, 1:462.

28. "Maus' Narrative," in Miles, *Personal Recollections*, 2:458.

29. Greene, "Crawford Affair," 148.

30. "Maus's Narrative," in Miles, *Personal Recollections*, 2:463.

31. Maus to Roberts, Jan. 21, 1886, Crook's report, app. K, *ARSW*, 1886; Maus to Roberts, Feb. 6, 1886, Crook Letters, Special Collections and Archives, University of Oregon; "Maus's Narrative," in Miles, *Personal Recollections*, 2:463.

32. Sweeney, *Cochise to Geronimo*, 505. Daly wrote that Geronimo chose the site for the meeting with Crook at this time. However, Sweeney argues compellingly that, based on Maus's communication to Crook on March 19, the site was not chosen until later. Ibid., 519; Daly, "Geronimo Campaign," in Cozzens, *Eyewitnesses*, 1:465.

33. "Maus's Narrative," in Miles, *Personal Recollections*, 2:464.

34. Ibid., 2:466.

35. Maus to Roberts, Jan. 21, 1886, Crook's report, *ARSW*, 1886.

CHAPTER 20. CAÑON DE LOS EMBUDOS

1. Crook diary, Jan. 11, 1886, Crook/Kennon Papers, AHEC.

2. Crook to Torres, Jan. 11, 1886, Crook Letterbook, Hayes Library.

3. Crook voiced this concern in his annual report, *ARSW*, 1886, 9.

4. Crook diary, Jan. 25, 1885, Crook/Kennon Papers, AHEC.

5. Crook to AG, Jan. 27, 1886, Crook Letterbook, Hayes Library; Crook diary, Jan./Feb. 1886, Crook/Kennon Papers, AHEC.

6. Bigelow, *On the Bloody Trail*, 125; Crook diary, Jan. 27 and 28, Feb. 7, 1886, Crook/Kennon Papers, AHEC.

7. Crook diary, Jan. 30, Feb. 2, 3, 8, and 10, 1886, Crook/Kennon Papers, AHEC; Thrapp, *Dateline Fort Bowie*, 66.

8. Barber to Crook, Feb. 8, 1886, NARA, DA, LR, RG 393; Crook diary, Feb. 16, 1886, Crook/Kennon Papers, AHEC; Crook to AG, Feb. 17, 1886, Crook Letterbook, Hayes Library.

9. Crook to Ramon Carral, Feb. 22, 1886, Crook Letterbook, Hayes Library.

10. Crook to Z. T. Crawford, Feb. 26, 1886, ibid.; Crook diary, Feb. 28, 1886, Crook/Kennon Papers, AHEC.

11. Sheridan to Crook, Feb. 1, 1886, Crook Letterbook, Hayes Library.

12. Crook to AAG, Div. of Pacific, Jan. 30, 1886; Drum to Crook, Feb. 1, 1886, both in ibid.

13. Crook to AAG, Div. of Pacific, Feb. 10, 1886, ibid.

14. Crook to AAG, Div. of Pacific, Feb. 19, 1886, ibid.

15. Crook to AAG, Div. of Pacific, Feb. 24 and 26, 1886; Crook to Sheridan, Mar. 12, 1886, ibid.

16. Maus to Roberts, Mar. 14, 1886, quoted in Sweeney, *Cochise to Geronimo*, 518–19.

17. Bourke, *On the Border*, 473.

18. Maus to Roberts, Mar.14 and 19, 1886, quoted in Sweeney, *Cochise to Geronimo*, 518–19; Crook to Sheridan, Mar. 16, 1886, Crook Letterbook, Hayes Library; Thrapp, *Conquest of Apacheria*, 342–43.

19. Crook diary, Mar. 22, 1886, Crook/Kennon Papers, AHEC; Thrapp, *Conquest of Apacheria*, 342–43.

20. Sweeney, *Cochise to Geronimo*, 519–20; Thrapp, *Conquest of Apacheria*, 342–43; Daly, "Geronimo Campaign," 466; "Reminiscences of James B. Glover," 1928, Glover Papers, AHS.

21. Daly, "Geronimo Campaign," 466; Charles D. Roberts, "Memories of Apache Wars" (extracts from his diary; hereafter cited as Roberts diary), in Carroll, *Unpublished Papers of the Indian War*, no. 8, n.p.; Bourke, *On the Border*, 473–74. Visiting the camp during the ensuing talks, Bourke found it located "upon the apex of an instinct [extinct?] crater" and so well fortified that "a full brigade could not drive out that little garrison." Ibid., 477.

22. Bourke put Charlie's age at ten, while the reporter Lummis, thought he was eleven. But he was born in June 1873, making him twelve at the time. In later years Charlie would follow his father into the army and have his own successful career. As a young second lieutenant in Cuba, he received the Medal of Honor. Advancing to major general and commanding two divisions in the AEF during World War I, he went on to win the Distinguished Service Medal, as well as the Croix de Guerre and the Belgian Order of Leopold, for military operations in France. See Thrapp, *Dateline Fort Bowie*, 28; Bourke,

On the Border, 474; and Bell, "West of Charles Roberts," 2–8. Regarding the packers, see Glover, "Reminiscences," Glover Papers, AHS.

23. Fly's studio was adjacent to the site of the famous shootout at the OK Corral, which he had personally witnessed. He supposedly disarmed one of Clantons following the shootout. Weiser, "Camillus Sidney [*sic*] Fly."

24. Crook to Haynes, undated telegram quoted in Thrapp, *Dateline Fort Bowie,* 6.

25. Crook's diary indicates that it was at Contraband Springs, rather than Mud Springs, that they were joined by the pack train. Crook diary, Mar. 24, 1886, Crook/ Kennon Papers, AHEC; see also Bourke, *On the Border,* 473; Roberts diary, Mar. 24, 1886, in "Memoirs of the Apache Wars," in Carroll, *Unpublished Papers of the Order of the Indian Wars,* no. 8.

26. Bourke, *On the Border,* 473; Roberts diary, Mar. 25, 1886.

27. Daly, "Geronimo Campaign," in Cozzens, *Eyewitnesses,* 1:467; Glover, "Reminiscences," Glover Papers, AHS, 2.

28. Evidently there was more than one Tribolet. Daly thought it had been a brother named Charles who sold the liquor to Geronimo. Thrapp believed it was Robert, another sibling. See Thrapp, *Dateline Fort Bowie,* 21n17, 21; Daly, "Geronimo Campaign," in Cozzens, *Eyewitnesses,* 1:467; Bourke, *On the Border,* 480; Sweeney, *Cochise to Geronimo,* 519–20.

29. Glover, "Reminiscences," Glover Papers, AHS, 2.

30. Bourke, *On the Border,* 474, 477; Crook to Sheridan, Mar. 28, 1886, Crook Letterbook, Hayes Library.

31. Bourke, *On the Border,* 474.

32. Daly, "Geronimo Campaign," in Cozzens, *Eyewitnesses,* 1:469; Bourke, *On the Border,* 475–76.

33. Roberts diary, Mar. 25, 1886; Bourke, *On the Border,* 475–76.

34. Roberts diary, Mar. 25, 1886; Sweeney, *Cochise to Geronimo,* 522.

35. Bourke, *On the Border,* 476.

36. Crook to Sheridan, Mar. 28, 1886, Crook Letterbook, Hayes Library.

37. Crook's report, *ARSW,* 1886, 153.

38. Sweeney, *Cochise to Geronimo,* 523; Crook, *Resumé of Operations,* 14.

39. Crook to Sheridan, Mar. 26, 1886, Crook Letterbook, Hayes Library; Bourke, *On the Border,* 478; Roberts diary, Mar. 26, 1886; Crook diary, Mar. 26, 1886, Crook/ Kennon Papers, AHEC.

40. Bourke, *On the Border,* 478.

41. Daly, "Geronimo Campaign," in Cozzens, *Eyewitnesses,* 1:471; Bourke, *On the Border,* 478–79.

42. "Report of Conference between General Crook and the Hostiles, El Canon de los Embudos," quoted in Davis, *Truth about Geronimo,* 210, 211.

43. Crook to Sheridan, Mar. 29, 1886, reprinted in *Resumé of Operations,* 14; Bourke, *On the Border,* 479.

44. Crook to Sheridan, reprinted in *Resumé of Operations,* 14; Bourke, *On the Border,* 479.

45. Crook's report, *ARSW,* 1886, 154.

46. Roberts diary, Mar. 27, 1886.

47. Daly, "Geronimo Campaign," in Cozzens, *Eyewitnesses,* 1:472; Bourke, *On the Border,* 481.

CHAPTER 21. TOO WEDDED TO MY VIEWS

1. Daly, "Geronimo Campaign," in Cozzens, *Eyewitnesses*, 1:471–72; Bourke, *On the Border*, 481.

2. Crook' report, *ARSW*, 1886, 153–54; Bourke, *On the Border*, 480; Maus to Roberts, Apr. 18, 1886, Att. I, in Crook' report, *ARSW.*

3. Maus to Roberts, Apr. 18, 1886, Att. I, in Crook' report, *ARSW*, 1886.

4. At least one historian hypothesized that Tribolet had been hired by the Tucson Ring to disrupt the talks and prevent the Apaches from returning to Arizona in the hope of continuing hostilities and the consequent benefits of continued military presence to the Arizona business community. See Thrapp, *Conquest of Apacheria*, 346–47; Crook' report, *ARSW*, 1886; Bourke, *On the Border*, 481; Thrapp, *Dateline Fort Bowie*, 50.

5. Crook's report, *ARSW*, 1886.

6. Maus to Roberts, Apr. 18, 1886, ibid. Crook in his report to Sheridan initially put the number of warriors with Chihuahua at twelve, including Nana and Ulzana. Crook to Sheridan, Mar. 30, 1886, Crook Letterbook, Hayes Library. He later increased the number to fourteen to include two additional warriors who, after sobering up, joined the cavalcade to Bowie. Crook' report, *ARSW*, 1886, 154; Thrapp, *Dateline Fort Bowie*, 75.

7. Thrapp, *Dateline Fort Bowie*, 20; Sheridan to Crook, Mar. 31, 1886, *ARSW*, 1886.

8. See, for example, Magid, *Gray Fox*, 259, 323–24, 397.

9. Crook to Sheridan, Mar. 31, 1886, reprinted in *Resumé of Operations*, 16.

10. Sheridan to Crook, Mar. 29, 1886; Sheridan to Crook, Mar. 30, 1886, both in ibid.

11. Crook to Sheridan, Mar. 31, 1886, ibid., 18.

12. Sheridan to Crook, Apr. 1, 1886, ibid.

13. Crook to Sheridan, Apr. 1, 1886, ibid., 19.

14. "The Apache Captives," *Los Angeles Times*, Apr. 3, 1886, quoted in Thrapp, *Dateline Fort Bowie*, 33; "A Bowie Budget," *Los Angeles Times*, Apr. 10, 1886, quoted in ibid., 61.

15. Crook to Sheridan, Apr. 2, 1886, Crook, *Resumé of Operations*, 19.

16. Crook to Sheridan, ibid.; Crook, *Autobiography*, 265; Sweeney, *Cochise to Geronimo*, 530.

17. Thrapp, *Dateline Fort Bowie*, 33.

18. Sheridan to Crook, Apr. 5, 1886, Crook Letterbook, Hayes Library.

19. Bourke diary, 81:155, quoted in Porter, *Paper Medicine Man*, 204, 209–11.

20. Crook diary, Apr. 2, 1886, Crook/Kennon Papers, AHEC.

21. Ibid.; Thrapp, *Dateline Fort Bowie*, 33; "Crook and Miles Among the Indians on the Border," *Los Angeles Times*, Apr. 12, 1886, quoted in Thrapp, *Dateline Fort Bowie*, 69.

22. Crook diary, Apr. 2, 1886, Crook/Kennon Papers, AHEC; "Escaped, Geronimo Gives his Captors the Slip," *Los Angeles Times*, Mar. 31, 1886, quoted in Thrapp, *Dateline Fort Bowie*, 69; "On the Trail, Another Party Pursuit of Geronimo," *Los Angeles Times*, Apr. 5, 1886. quoted in ibid., 34.

23. The paper changed its name to the *Los Angeles Times* in 1886; see Wikipedia, s.v. "Los Angeles Times."

24. Thompson, *American Character*, 5–18.

25. Ibid. 19.

26. Ibid., 47–59.

27. *Los Angeles Times*, Mar. 29, 1886, quoted in Thrapp, *Dateline Fort Bowie*, 9.

28. "At Fort Bowie, the Apache Matter as Seen on the Ground," *Los Angeles Times*, Apr. 6, 1886, quoted in ibid., 26–27.

29. Ibid., 27.

30. "Army Changes, General Crook Removed from Department of Arizona," Apr. 3, 1886; "Lieut. Maus Compelled to Abandon the Pursuit of Geronimo," Apr. 4, 1886, both in *Los Angeles Times*, quoted in Thrapp, *Dateline Fort Bowie*, 33–34.

31. Ibid., 35–36; Sheridan to Crook, Apr. 3, 1886, reprinted in Crook, *Resumé of Operations*, 20. One historian concluded that Cleveland had selected Fort Marion to justify his request to Congress for funds to repair the fort, an issue that had been languishing in Congress for some time. Stockel, *Shame and Endurance*, 11.

32. Thrapp, *Dateline Fort Bowie*, 36.

33. Ibid., 64. Eugene Chihuahua, the chief's son who was aboard the train to Florida, later recalled that to soothe the people during the trip, Nana would go among them and tell them that "though our land and homes had been stolen from us, now families could be together, and that in two years we could go back home." Chihuahua reassured them that "Nantan Lupan did not speak with a forked tongue, and we could rely upon [his word]." Ball, *Indah*, 125.

34. Roberts diary, Apr. 5 and 7, 1886; "The Apaches, The Prisoners to be sent to Fort Marion, Fla.," *Los Angeles Times*, Apr. 7, 1886, reprinted in Thrapp, *Dateline Fort Bowie*, 36.

35. Crook diary, Apr. 7, 1886, Crook/Kennon Papers, AHEC; Sweeney, *Cochise to Geronimo*, 532.

36. *Los Angeles Times*, Apr. 7, 1886, quoted in Stockel, *Shame and Endurance*, 9; "Bowie Budget, Reason Why General Crook was Relieved," *Los Angeles Times*, Apr. 10, 1886, reprinted in Thrapp, *Dateline Fort Bowie*, 65.

37. *Florida Times-Union*, Apr. 14, 1886, quoted in Stockel, *Shame and Endurance*, 11–12.

CHAPTER 22. CHANGING OF THE GUARD

1. "Bowie Budget," quoted in Thrapp, *Dateline Fort Bowie*, 60, 63.

2. Popular opinion in Arizona was perhaps typified by the headline in Tombstone's daily paper, the *Epitaph*—"Gone Where They Belong," *Daily Tombstone Epitaph*, Apr. 21, 1886, referring to the departure of the Chiricahuas for Florida.

3. "Bowie Budget," quoted in Thrapp, *Dateline Fort Bowie*, 65. The author has been unable to confirm that Crook followed through on this commitment.

4. Miles, *Personal Recollections*, 2:476.

5. Ibid.; Wooster, *Miles and the Twilight*, 143.

6. "Crook and Miles among the Indians on the Border," *Los Angeles Times*, Apr. 12, 1886, quoted in Thrapp, *Deadline Fort Bowie*, 67; Sweeney, *Cochise to Geronimo*, 533.

7. General Field Orders Nos. 3 and 4, Apr. 11, 1886, quoted in Thrapp, *Dateline Fort Bowie*, 67.

8. Johnson, *Unregimented General*, 230.

9. "Crook and Miles among the Indians," in Thrapp, *Dateline Fort Bowie*, 68.

10. Roberts would rejoin his old regiment, the Seventeenth Infantry, at Fort Russell, Wyoming, and remain there until Crook was appointed major general, when he

agreed to be reassigned to Chicago to once again serve as Crook's aide, a position he continued to hold until Crook's death in 1890. Thrapp, *Dateline Fort Bowie*, 70; Roberts diary.

11. Miles to Mary Miles, Apr. 12, 1886, quoted in Johnson, *Unregimented General*, 231.

12. Crook, *Autobiography*, 266.

13. Legislative Assembly of the Territory of Arizona, *Joint Resolution Conveying the Thanks of the Thirteenth Legislative Assembly of Arizona*, Tucson, Dec. 17, 1885; Bourke diary, Jan.–Mar. 1886, quoted in Shepard, "Miles-Crook Controversy," 46–47.

14. *Tucson Weekly Citizen*, Apr. 24, 1886.

15. *Tombstone Epitaph*, Apr. 16, 1886.

16. Davis, *Truth about Geronimo*, 219.

17. Ibid.; Thrapp, *Conquest of Apacheria*, 350.

18. Drum to Miles, Apr. 2, 1886, quoted in Wooster, *Miles and the Twilight*, 145; see also Thrapp, *Dateline Fort Bowie*, 71n8.

19. Thrapp, *Conquest of Apacheria*, 350.

20. For Miles's use of heliographs, see McChristian, *Fort Bowie*, 201; Thrapp, *Conquest of Apacheria*, 351; Wooster, *Miles and the Twilight*, 147; Miles, *Personal Recollections*, 2:482–85.

21. Davis, *Truth about Geronimo*, 219; General Field Order No. 7, Apr. 20, 1886, quoted in Miles's report, *ARSW*, 1886, 166.

22. Miles's *Personal Recollections*, 2:487; Lockwood, *The Apache Indians*, 295.

23. Lockwood, *The Apache Indians*, 295; Wooster, *Miles and the Twilight*, 148.

24. For details of the activities of Geronimo and Naiche during this period, see Sweeney, *Cochise to Geronimo*, 535–56.

25. Sweeney, *Cochise to Geronimo*, 543. In his book Britton Davis claimed that this deserter would later volunteer as a scout to guide an expedition into Mexico to talk Geronimo into surrendering. However, the Chiricahua deserter and the scout who volunteered were different individuals. See Kraft, *Lt. Charles Gatewood*, 236; Davis, *Truth about Geronimo*, 220.

26. For a day-to-day description of Lawton's campaign, see Lane, *Chasing Geronimo*.

27. Sweeney, *Cochise to Geronimo*, 553–55.

28. Utley, *Geronimo*, 200.

29. Sweeney, *Cochise to Geronimo*, 544; Miles to Pierce, May 24, 1886, quoted in ibid., 544.

30. Ibid.

31. Sweeney, *Cochise to Geronimo*, 557; "Interview with George Martine," in Ball, *Indah*, 109.

32. Utley, *Geronimo*, 200; Ball, *Indah*, 109.

33. Kraft, *Lt. Charles Gatewood*, 134.

34. Parker, *The Old Army*, 178.

35. Utley, *Geronimo*, 205–9.

36. Gatewood's own account is found in an unpublished, undated manuscript, "Gatewood on the Surrender of Geronimo," Charles Bare Gatewood Collection, AHS. It is reprinted in part in Kraft, *Lt. Charles Gatewood*, 136–43. Good secondary accounts are found in Thrapp, *Conquest of Apacheria*, 353–63; Utley, *Geronimo*, 209–12; Sweeney, Cochise to Geronimo, 562–64, among other works. For those inclined to a more visual—but less accurate—presentation, there is the entertaining movie *Geronimo*,

starring, among others, Wes Studi (Geronimo), Gene Hackman (Crook), Matt Damon (Britton Davis), and Robert Duval (Sieber).

37. Sweeney, *Cochise to Geronimo*, 564. In Gatewood's account, Geronimo asked the lieutenant for thorough description of Miles's character, which Gatewood "did my best to answer truthfully & without exaggeration." Quoted in Kraft, *Lt. Charles Gatewood*, 142.

38. Miles wrote to his wife, Mary, after a visit to San Carlos that he was convinced (with little to support it) that the reservation Chiricahuas, "although not on the war path, are to some extent in sympathy with the hostiles and liable to go out at anytime." Quoted in Johnson, *Unregimented General*, 240–42.

39. Crook, *Resumé of Operations*, 10–11.

40. Miles, *Personal Recollections*, 2:494; Wooster, *Miles and the Twilight*, 149.

41. Goodman, "Apaches as Prisoners of War," 11, 28n45.

42. Porter, *Paper Medicine Man*, 212.

43. Sheridan to sec. of war, July 7, 1886, quoted in Goodman, "Apaches as Prisoners of War," 12.

44. Miles, *Personal Recollections*, 2:496–97; Sweeney, *Cochise to Geronimo*, 556.

45. Miles to Mary, Apr. 11, 1886, quoted in Johnson, *Unregimented General*, 243–44; Davis, *Truth about Geronimo*, 234.

46. Wooster, *Miles and the Twilight*, 149; Porter, *Paper Medicine Man*, 213; Johnson, *Unregimented General*, 242. For a thumbnail biography of Dorst, see Goodman, "Apaches as Prisoners of War," 29n53.

47. Miles, *Personal Recollections*, 2:497; stenographer's notes of conference between William Endicott, Secretary of War, and Chatto, July 26, 1886, Bourke File, NSHS; Porter, *Paper Medicine Man*, 215.

48. Goodman, "Apaches as Prisoners of War," 13–15.

49. Ibid., 16–17.

50. Bourke diary, 82:110, quoted in Porter, *Paper Medicine Man*, 216.

51. Miles, *Personal Recollections*, 2:498.

52. Debo, *Geronimo, the Man*, 276–77; Miles, *Personal Recollections*, 2:498; Goodman, "Apaches as Prisoners of War," 20–21.

53. Chatto to Crook, in *Message from the President of the United States*, Senate Exec. Doc. 35 (51-1) 34, quoted in Stockel, *Shame and Endurance*, 18.

54. Miles, *Personal Recollections*, 2:503–4; Goodman, "Apaches as Prisoners of War," 55; Wooster, *Miles and the Twilight*, 151; Davis, *Truth about Geronimo*, 233. The Indians remembered the event slightly differently. Eugene Chihuahua, Chihuahua's son, said that the warriors were ordered to report to the post without their weapons, where they were then surrounded by troops and herded into the quartermaster's building. Then they were told that they, together with their families, were going to Washington to meet the Great White Father. After their families had joined them, Colonel Wade announced their true destination and ordered the women to return to camp to gather their belongings. Ball, *Indah*, 113–14. Neither scenario reflects well on the army.

55. Utley, *Geronimo*, 213; Parker, *The Old Army*, 183.

56. Utley, *Geronimo*, 213.

57. Of course, this recommendation was never carried out. Parker, one of Lawton's lieutenants, ascribed it to other junior officers in Lawton's command and wrote that he vigorously argued against such a course of action, telling Lawton it would ruin his career. Lawton, according to Parker, agreed. Parker, *The Old Army*, 184–85. Miles himself only

admitted to uneasiness regarding the welfare of his men. He wrote that he feared the Apaches might seize them and hold them for ransom or kill them. Miles, *Personal Recollections*, 2:520.

58. Wooster, *Miles and the Twilight*, 151; Utley, *Geronimo*, 213–18; Thrapp, *Conquest of Apacheria*, 362; Ball, *Indah*, 108–9; Miles, *Personal Recollections*, 2:520; Goodman, "Apaches as Prisoners of War," 37–39.

59. Undated dispatch from Drum to Crook, reprinted in *Resumé of Operations*, 13.

60. For Gatewood's words to Geronimo, see Davis, *Truth about Geronimo*, 225–26, 233; For Miles's own words, see *Personal Recollections*, 2:522.

61. Sheridan to Cleveland, Sept. 7, 1886; Cleveland to Sheridan, Sept. 8, 1886, quoted in Lockwood, *The Apache Indians*, 308.

62. Miles, *Personal Recollections*, 2:528.

63. Sheridan to Miles, Sept. 7, 1886; Miles to Sheridan, Sept. 7, 1886, both in *Correspondence with Gen. Miles Relative to the Surrender of Geronimo*, quoted in Stockel, *Shame and Endurance*, 33–34.

64. Cleveland to Miles, Sept. 8, 1886, quoted in ibid.

65. Miles would insist that he never received the wire because he had left Bowie the same day as the prisoners and so had missed it. Leonard Wood later claimed that one of Miles's aides bragged to him that he had deliberately "pigeon holed" the president's message so that Miles would not be embarrassed by having to renege on his promise to Geronimo. Lane, ed., *Chasing Geronimo*, 114; Lockwood, *The Apache Indians*, 308–9; Thrapp, *Conquest of Apacheria*, 365; Wooster, *Miles and the Twilight*, 152–54; Miles, *Personal Recollections*, 2:528; Goodman, "Apaches as Prisoners of War," 43.

66. Miles, *Personal Recollections*, 2:528; Shepard, "Miles-Crook Controversy," 63–64, 85; Johnson, *Unregimented General*, 252; Davis, *Truth about Geronimo*, 227.

67. Goodman, "Apaches as Prisoners of War," 43. Their achievements unrecognized, the two scouts endured confinement and exile with their fellow Chiricahuas. It was only some forty years later that, with the aid of Gatewood's son, their contribution was finally acknowledged, and they received a small pension from the government. Ball, *Indah*, 109, 111.

68. Miles to Mary, Sept. 7, 1886, quoted in Johnson, *Unregimented General*, 250.

69. Cleveland to sec. of war, Sept. 8, 1886, quoted in Stockel, *Shame and Endurance*, 33. For the prisoners' reaction, see ibid., 34–35; Goodman, "Apache Prisoners of War," 52.

70. Goodman, "Apache Prisoners of War," 61–62.

71. Lockwood, *The Apache Indians*, 309; Wooster, *Miles and the Twilight*, 152–54; Johnson, *Unregimented General*, 253; Stockel, *Shame and Endurance*, 162.

72. Wooster, *Miles and the Twilight*, 155.

73. Due to his own behavior, Gatewood's appointment to Miles's staff never paid the dividends he had anticipated. Unfortunately embittered by Miles's refusal to give him credit for his actions, after some months on the job the lieutenant, in an alcoholic rage, alienated the general by publicly denigrating Miles's role in the surrender. Removed from Miles's staff as a result, he was returned to his old regiment then stationed in Wyoming, where he was severely injured in a barracks fire. Disabled and retired at half pay, Gatewood died in 1896, leaving a widow and two small children to survive on the meager pension of $17 a month. Davis, *Truth about Geronimo*, 235, Wooster, *Miles and the Twilight*, 156; Kraft, *Gatewood and Geronimo*, 210–12.

CHAPTER 23. CAMPAIGNING FOR INDIAN RIGHTS

1. "Feted for his Laurels, Crook in the Heart of Omaha," *Omaha Daily World*, Apr. 29, 1886; *Washington Post*, Apr. 29, 1886, both quoted in Crook, *Resumé of Operations*, 2.

2. *Army and Navy Journal*, June 12, 1886, quoted in ibid.

3. Crook, *Autobiography*, 291; See also Crook to Bourke, Oct. 1, 1886, Bourke File, NSHS.

4. "From the Apache Land, Col. Royall and the Campaign," *Omaha Daily World*, Apr. 6, 1886.

5. Kennon diary, Aug. 7, 1886, Crook/Kennon Papers, AHEC.

6. Sheridan to sec. of war, Oct. 10, 1886, in *ARSW*, 1886, quoted in Crook, introduction to *Resumé of Operations*, 3.

7. Magid, *George Crook*, 248, 281–82.

8. A copy of Crook's report with missing appendices is also in Bourke's diary, vol. 82. Crook, *Resumé of Operations*, 7n12. According to the editor, the omitted appendices covered a total of seventy pages. It was not unusual for such lengthy appendices to be omitted from the published version of the secretary of war's annual reports.

9. Crook, "The Apache Problem," 266–69.

10. Crook to AG, Feb. 10, 1887; AAG Kelton to Crook, Mar. 8, 1887; Crook to AG, Mar. 16, 1887, all reprinted in Crook, *Resumé of Operations*, 4–5; Crook to Bourke, Apr. 25, 1887, Bourke File, NSHS.

11. Crook, foreword to *Resumé of Operations*, 5.

12. Crook to Bourke, Oct. 1, 1886, Bourke File, NSHS.

13. Crook to Bourke, Jan. 18, 1877, ibid.

14. See Turcheneske, "Arizonans and the Apache Prisoners," 198.

15. Crook to Bourke, Oct. 1, 1886, Bourke File, NSHS.

16. Magid, *Gray Fox*, 78.

17. Ibid.

18. Hagan, *Indian Rights Association*, 4.

19. Ibid., 7, 9.

20. Ibid., 1–14. In his annual report to the secretary of war in 1884, Crook wrote that "to issue rations and not place the Hualapais at work is no great favor. Life may be prolonged but the debauchery of men and women is increased, not averted." Crook's report, *ARSW*, 1884.

21. Hagan, *Indian Rights Association*, 31–32.

22. Magid, *Gray Fox*, 105–7, 128–29.

23. Executive committee minutes, June 5, 1883, IRA Papers, quoted in Hagan, *Indian Rights Association*, 31.

24. Hagan, *Indian Rights Association*, 31; Porter, *Paper Medicine Man*, 212.

25. Welsh, "An Interview with General Crook," clipping dated Sept. 24, 1884, in Crook Scrapbook, AHEC; Robert Frazer, *Apaches of the White Mountain Reservation*, quoted in Hagan, *Indian Rights Association*, 32.

26. For the battle at Salt River Cave, see Magid, *Gray Fox*, 111–13.

27. *Alta California*, Dec. 24, 1885.

28. Crook to Welsh, Jan. 3, 1885, reprinted by IRA as *Letter from General Crook on Giving the Ballot to the Indians*, LC, Indian Rights Association, microfilm.

29. Bourke to Welsh, May 18, 1886, quoted in Porter, *Paper Medicine Man*, 212.

30. Bourke to Welsh, Sept. 22, 1886, quoted in ibid., 225.

31. Hagan, *Indian Rights Association*, 94; Stockel, *Shame and Endurance*, 19–20; Porter, *Paper Medicine Man*, 224.

32. Crook diary, Feb. 23, 1886, Crook/Kennon Papers, AHEC; Mathes and Lowitt, *Standing Bear Controversy*, 74; Crook to Bourke, Mar. 23, 1887, Bourke File, NSHS.

33. Boston Indian Rights Citizenship Committee to Crook, Feb. 3, 1887, Crook/Kennon Papers, AHEC.

34. Kennon, a Rhode Islander, joined Crook's staff as aide de camp on July 1, 1886, following service with the Sixth Infantry in Utah. Collum, *Biographical Register of Officers*, 351; Kennon diary, Feb. 23, 1887, Crook/Kennon Papers, AHEC.

35. Crook diary, Feb. 23, 1887, Crook/Kennon Papers, AHEC.

36. Crook diary, Feb. 28–Mar. 6, 1887, Crook/Kennon Papers, AHEC; Crook, *Autobiography*, 260–71; "General Crook's Address at Memorial Church, Boston," *Boston Post*, Feb. 28, 1887, quoted in Crook, *Autobiography*, 271.

37. Crook diary, Mar. 2, 1887, Crook/Kennon Papers, AHEC; Crook to Bourke, Mar. 6, 1887, Bourke File, NSHS.

38. Crook to Bourke, Mar. 6 and June 4, 1887, ibid.

39. Porter, *Paper Medicine Man*, 226–27.

40. "The Apaches in Florida, Their Treatment at Fort Marion," *New York Tribune*, Mar. 21, 1887.

41. Goodman, "Apaches as Prisoners of War," 88–91; Sweeney, *Cochise to Geronimo*, 576–77, Welsh Report, in Stockel, *Shame and Endurance*, 22–23; Hagan, *Indian Rights Association*, 94; "Apaches in Florida"; Bourke diary 85:8–12, quoted in Porter, *Paper Medicine Man*, 228–29.

42. "Apaches in Florida," *New York Tribune*.

43. Tibbles to Bourke, Mar. 16 and 22, 1887, Bourke File, NSHS.

44. Crook to Welsh, Apr. 28, 1887, quoted in Goodman, "Apaches as Prisoners of War," 119; Crook to Bourke, Mar. 29, 1887, Bourke File, NSHS.

45. Welsh, *Apache Prisoners at Fort Marion*, quoted in Stockel, *Shame and Endurance*, 160n35; Hagan, *Indian Rights Association*, 22–23, 94; Porter, *Paper Medicine Man*, 236–38.

46. Gatewood, *Army and Navy Register*, Apr. 27, 1887, quoted in an excerpt of Welsh Report in Porter, *Paper Medicine Man*; 52–53, 236; Crook to Welsh, Apr. 16, 1887, quoted in Porter, *Paper Medicine Man*, Goodman, "Apaches as Prisoners of War," 110.

47. Ayres to Sheridan, Mar. 25, 1887, Bourke File, NSHS; Porter, *Paper Medicine Man*, 228, 232.

48. Ibid., 234.

49. Ibid., 232; Bourke to AG, Apr. 19, 1887, Bourke File, NSHS.

50. Bourke to AG, Apr. 19, 1887, Bourke File, NSHS; Porter, *Paper Medicine Man*, 238; Stockel, *Shame and Endurance*, 49.

51. Porter, *Paper Medicine Man*, 235; Stockel, *Shame and Endurance*, 41; Goodman, "Apaches as Prisoners of War," 108.

52. Ball, *Indah*, 152–53.

53. Goodman, 121–22; Report by General Howard to AG, Dec. 23, 1889, in *Message from the President of the United States*, quoted in Stockel, *Shame and Endurance*, 72; Ball, *Indah*, 158.

54. Mary Sherman Miles to William T. Sherman, May 15, 1887, quoted in Wooster, *Miles and the Twilight*, 167.

55. Hayes letters to supporters and to Fuller, Mar. 20, 1888, Hayes diary, vol. 4, rbhayes.org; Crook, *Autobiography*, 177. See also Wooster, *Miles and the Twilight*, 166–68; Robinson, *Crook and the Western Frontier*, 294.

56. Crook diary, vol. 2, Apr. 6, 1888, Crook/Kennon Papers, AHEC; Hayes diary, vol. 4, rbhayes.org. Recall that Canby died at the hands of the Modoc chief Captain Jack in April 1873.

57. Crook, *Autobiography*, 279; Robinson, *Crook and the Western Frontier*, 294; Oath of Office, May 1, 1888, NARA, Crook ACP File, Microfilm; Crook diary, vol. 2, May 1, 1888, Crook/Kennon Papers, AHEC.

58. Crook to Welsh, June 29, 1888, quoted in Goodman, "Apaches as Prisoners of War," 131.

59. Ibid., 125–34.

60. Ibid., 175.

61. Kennon diary, Jan. 2, 1890, quoted in Crook, *Autobiography*, 292–94; and "Notes of an Interview between Maj. Gen. George Crook, U.S. Army, and Chatto, Kae-te-na, Noche and other Chiricahua Apaches," quoted in Goodman, "Apaches as Prisoners of War," 176–77; Crook diary, Jan. 2, 1890, Crook/Kennon Papers, AHEC; Crook to sec. of war, Jan. 6, 1890, Crook Letterbook, Hayes Library.

62. "Story of a Great Wrong," *Washington Post*, Jan. 8, 1890. The article is discussed in Goodman, "Apaches as Prisoners of War," 177–79.

63. Crook to sec. of war, Jan. 6, 1890, Crook Letterbook, Hayes Library.

64. Crook to AG, Feb. 20, 1890, ibid.; Crook diary, vol. 2, Feb. 8, 1890, Crook/Kennon Papers, AHEC.

65. Crook to sec. of war, Jan. 6, 1890, Crook Letterbook, Hayes Library; Proctor to Harrison, Jan. 13, 1890, referenced in Goodman, "Apaches as Prisoners of War," 179.

66. Goodman, "Apaches as Prisoners of War," 179–80.

67. *Arizona Daily Star* (Tucson), Jan. 25, 1890, quoted in Turcheneske, "Arizonans and Apache Prisoners," 204.

68. *Arizona Weekly Citizen*, Jan. 18, 1890, quoted in ibid., 200.

69. *Tombstone Epitaph*, Jan. 11, 1890, quoted in ibid.

70. *Washington Post*, Jan. 28, 1890, quoted in ibid., 206.

71. *New York Herald*, Feb. 16, 1890, quoted in ibid., 206–7. Crook and the *Herald* had a long history of enmity dating back to the Sioux War; see Magid, *Gray Fox*, 224, 259–60.

72. Testimony of General Nelson A. Miles, Feb. 15, 1890, "Removal of Apache Indians from Mount Vernon, Alabama to Fort Sill, Indian Territory," quoted in Turcheneske, "Arizonans and Apache Prisoners," 212–14. See also Miles, *Personal Recollections*, 2:496–97.

73. See, for example, *Arizona Silver Belt*, Mar. 22, 1890, detailing rumors of Apache raiding on the border.

74. *Arizona Daily Star*, Mar. 9, 1890, quoted in Turcheneske, "Arizonans and Apache Prisoners," 219–20.

75. *Prescott Weekly Courier*, Feb. 28, 1890, quoted in ibid., 217.

76. Crook to Howard, Feb. 27, 1890, Crook Letterbook, Hayes Library. In the same vein, see Crook's letter to Kennon: "From here, it looks as if M's change of heart about the Indians going to I.T. was 'anything to beat me.'" Crook to Kennon, Mar. 7, 1890, quoted in Crook, *Autobiography*, 296.

77. Crook to Kennon, Mar. 5, 1890, quoted in Crook, *Autobiography*, 298.

78. Goodman, "Apaches as Prisoners of War," 189.

79. Crook to Mrs. Stephen Bullard, Mar. 10, 1890, Crook Letterbook, Hayes Library.

80. Goodman, "Apaches as Prisoners of War," 224; Utley, *Geronimo*, 269–70.

81. Debo, *Geronimo, the Man*, 448–50.

82. Utley, *Geronimo*; Debo, *Geronimo, the Man*, 430–31; Stockel, *Shame and Endurance*, 124–29.

83. Utley, *Geronimo*, 262; Debo, *Geronimo, the Man*, 440–42.

CHAPTER 24. OMAHA SOJOURN

1. Crook diary, vol. 1, Apr. 28, 1886, Crook/Kennon Papers, AHEC.

2. Ibid., entries for 1886 and 1887; Crook, *Autobiography*, 267–74.

3. Crook diary, vol. 2, Dec. 21, 1887, Jan. 2, 1888, Crook/Kennon Papers, AHEC. An announcement in the *Army and Navy Journal* that Jennie married Second Lieutenant Hiram Powell in 1895 seems to confirm her youth in the 1880s. *United States Army and Navy Journal and Gazette* 33 (Sept. 21, 1895): 37.

4. Collins, *My Experiences in the West*, v–vi, 179; Fusco, "The Last Hunt," 36–40, 38; for examples of letters to Webb, see Crook to Webb Hayes, Aug. 12, 1889, Crook Letterbook, Hayes Library.

5. Crook diary, vol. 1, Nov. 14 and 19, 1886, June 11, 1887, Crook/Kennon Papers, AHEC.

6. See, for example, the following diary entries for 1886: May 23 (Lewisburg); May 2 (visit from Confederate General Heth); June 17 (Rosebud); and 25 (Custer battle). Crook diary, vol. 1, Crook/Kennon Papers, AHEC.

7. Ibid., entries for Sept. 6–8, 1886; addresses by Hayes at eighth and ninth reunions of the Society of the Army of West Virginia, Sep. 2, 1864, Sep. 16, 1885; Speeches and Messages of Rutherford B. Hayes, www.rbhayes.org/hayes/speeches.

8. Crook diary, vol. 1 Sept. 6–8, 1886, Aug. 19, 1887, Crook/Kennon Papers, AHEC.

9. Ibid., May 5, 23–24, 1886.

10. See ibid., Crook diary entries for May 16, June 28–July 3, and July 15–22, 1887 (malaria); Jan. 2, 1887 (laryngitis); Jan. 5–6, 1887, and Apr. 3, 1888 (vol. 2) (heart disease).

11. Crook diary, vol. 2, Apr. 18–26, 1888, Crook/Kennon Papers, AHEC; westernmininghistory.com.

12. "Outline of the Military History of Colonel L. W. V. Kennon, Ninth Infantry," Crook/Kennon Papers, AHEC; Obituary, "Col. L. W. V. Kennon, USA," *Charlotte Observer*.

13. General Orders No. 7, July 1, 1886, Kennon diary, July 1, 1886, Crook/Kennon Papers, AHEC.

14. Annual Report, DP, Aug. 27, 1887, Crook Letterbook, Hayes Library.

15. Magid, *George Crook*, 116–18.

16. Annual Report, DP, Aug. 27, 1887, Crook Letterbook, Hayes Library.

17. For background on Ute removal from Colorado, see chapter 6 of this work. For a history of the Ute Tribe, see Marsh, *People of the Shining Mountains*.

18. Crook diary, Aug. 9–26, 1886; Kennon diary, Aug. 9–26, 1886, both in Crook/Kennon Papers, AHEC; Huetter, "History of Fort Duchesne," 28.

19. Huetter, "History of Fort Duchesne," 28–29; Crook diary, Aug. 20, 1886, Crook/Kennon Papers, AHEC.

20. Huetter, "History of Fort Duchesne," 28–29.

21. Ibid.

22. Ibid.; Crook diary, Kennon diary, both in Crook/Kennon Papers, AHEC; Annual Report, DP, Aug. 27, 1887, Crook Letterbook, Hayes Library.

23. Crook, *Autobiography*, 174–75; Crook Report on Ute Indian Troubles to AAG, Div. of the Missouri, Sept. 15, 1887, Crook Letterbook, Hayes Library.

24. Crook Report on Ute Troubles, Crook Letterbook, Hayes Library.

25. Ibid.; Crook, *Autobiography*, 274–76; Crook's report, *ARSW*, 1888, 1: 171–72.

26. Crook Report on Ute Troubles, Crook Letterbook, Hayes Library; Crook diary, vol. 2, Aug. 29–Sept. 2, 1887, Crook/Kennon Papers, AHEC.

27. Crook Report on Ute Troubles, Crook Letterbook, Hayes Library. Crook's use of quotation marks around the term "buck" perhaps indicates a growing awareness of the inappropriateness of this pejorative term applied freely by many whites, including himself in past instances, to adult male Indians.

28. Ibid.

CHAPTER 25. CHICAGO

1. Crook, *Autobiography*, 280.

2. Crook diary, vol. 2, Apr. 13, 1888, Crook/Kennon Papers, AHEC.

3. Ibid., Apr. 219, 1888. The reference to Lee's paperwork may have been related to the Chinese Exclusion Act of 1882, which imposed a ten-year moratorium on the importation of labor from China and was amended in 1888 to prohibit all future immigration of Chinese nationals into the United States. Crook probably assisted Lee in completing documents intended to demonstrate that Lee had been in this country prior to the passage of the recent amendment and hence could remain and work here. Wikipedia, s.v. "History of Chinese Americans."

4. Crook diary, vol. 2, Apr. 24, 1888, Crook/Kennon Papers, AHEC; Crook to AG, Apr. 24,1888, NARA, Crook ACP File, Oath of Office.

5. Crook diary, vol. 2, May 4, 1888, Crook/Kennon Papers, AHEC.

6. Ibid., May 4–5.

7. Crook, *Autobiography*, 279.

8. Crook diary, May 5–8, Nov. 6, 7, 1888, Crook/Kennon Papers, AHEC; Crook, *Autobiography*, 279. For more on the Pullman Building, see "The Pullman Building," Pullman-Museum.org.

9. Crook diary, various dates, 1888–89, Crook/Kennon Papers, AHEC.

10. Ibid., May 9–June 5, 1888. For details on battle of Fisher's Hill, see "Victory at Fisher's Hill," in Magid, *George Crook*.

11. For an example, see ibid., 56.

12. Crook diary, vol. 2, Aug. 31, Sept. 27, Oct. 3, 1888, Crook/Kennon Papers, AHEC.

13. Ibid., Sept. 12–14, 1888, Jan. 11–25, 1889, Apr. 10–12, 1889.

14. Ibid., Apr. 28–May 2, 1889.

15. Crook to Cleveland, Jan. 24, 1888, Crook Letterbook, Hayes Library; Porter, *Paper Medicine Man*, 249–51.

16. My evidence for this conclusion is the uncharacteristic bitterness shown in Bourke's diary entry of Apr. 6, 1889, that follows.

17. Bourke diary, Apr. 6, 1889, vol. 24, quoted in Porter, *Paper Medicine Man*, 251–52.

18. Ibid., 252.

19. Crook to Kennon, May 14 and 30, 1889, "Letters of General Crook, 1863–1890," Special Collections, University of Oregon Libraries, Eugene.

20. Porter, in his insightful biography of Bourke, wrote that Crook "insisted" that Bourke serve on the Sioux commission but that the captain had turned him down. The correspondence quoted above does not seem to support that conclusion, though such a scenario seems consistent with the personalities of the two men. *Paper Medicine Man*, 252.

CHAPTER 26. THE SIOUX COMMISSION

1. Greene, *American Carnage*, 31–32; Hyde, *Sioux Chronicle*, 110.

2. Hagan, *Indian Rights Association*, 40.

3. Ibid.

4. Quoted in Crook, *Autobiography*, 281.

5. "General Crook's Address at Memorial Church," *Boston Post*, Feb. 28, 1887, quoted in Crook, *Autobiography*, 271.

6. Crook, "The Apache Problem," quoted in Crook, *Autobiography*, 283.

7. "Indians as Fighters, Gen. Crook's Interesting Talk," *Chicago Herald*, undated clipping, Crook/Kennon Papers, AHEC.

8. Hyde, *Sioux Chronicle*, 110.

9. This sordid tale is related in detail by Hyde, ibid., 110–44; see also Utley, *Last Days*, 41–2; Greene, *American Carnage*, 30–32. See also Hagan, *Indian Rights Association*, 41, for the association's view.

10. Dawes speech at Lake Mohonk conference in 1887, quoted in Larson, *Red Cloud*, 242.

11. Hyde, *Sioux Chronicle*, 155.

12. Larson, *Red Cloud*, 241–44; Hyde, *Sioux Chronicle*, 184–87.

13. *Annual Report of the Commissioner of Indian Affairs*, 1887; Utley, *Last Days*, 44.

14. Utley, *Last Days*, 44.

15. Ibid., 44–45.

16. Ibid.; Crook, *Autobiography*, 283; Greene, *American Carnage*, 33.

17. Utley, *Last Days*, 42; Greene, *American Carnage*, 30–31.

18. Crook to sec. of war, June 8 and 11, 1888, Crook Letterbook, Hayes Library.

19. Hyde, *Sioux Chronicle*, 189.

20. Utley, *Last Days*, 46–47.

21. Hyde, *Sioux Chronicle*, 198.

22. Utley, *Last Days*, 48–49. For the circumstances surrounding the pony seizure, see Olson, *Red Cloud and the Sioux Problem*, 228–33; Magid, *Gray Fox*, 321–24.

23. Hyde, *Sioux Chronicle*, 198–99; Utley, *Last Days*, 48–49.

24. Olson, *Red Cloud and the Sioux Problem*, 313; Greene, *American Carnage*, 39–40; Larson, *Red Cloud*, 25; Utley, *Last Days*, 49, Crook, *Autobiography*, 284. Hyde mistakenly identified Crook as the chair of the commission. *Sioux Chronicle*, 199–200.

25. Hyde, *Sioux Chronicle*, 199–200; Utley, *Last Days*, 4.

26. Utley, *Last Days*, 4, 49; Greene, *American Carnage*, 40. Regarding Crook's reputation among the Sioux for integrity, Colonel Hatch, commander of Fort Robinson near Pine Ridge, reported that prior to the commission's visit, "between two and three hundred Sioux" visited the post to ask about rumors concerning the Sioux act. They stated that they would not be satisfied by any explanation from anyone other than General Crook, "in whose words they have unbounded confidence." Hatch to AAG, DP, Mar. 4, 1889, quoted in Olson, *Red Cloud and the Sioux Problem*, 31n26.

27. Crook diary, vol. 2, Apr. 9, 1889, Crook/Kennon Papers, AHEC.

28. Ibid., Apr. 12, 1889 (Red Cloud visit); Apr. 25–27, 1889 (Boston trip).

29. For Spotted Tail's role in the Sioux peace negotiations, see Magid, *Gray Fox*, 349–50. For a thorough review of the reasons the commission chose the Rosebud agency and other aspects of the commission's work, see Greene, "Sioux Land Commission of 1889," 41–72, 49.

30. Crook diary, vol. 2, May 28, 1889, Crook/Kennon Papers, AHEC.

31. Ibid., May 29, 1889.

32. Ibid., May 31, 1889.

33. Ibid., June 2, 3, and 5, 1889.

34. Utley, *Last Days*, 50–53.

35. Crook diary, vol. 2, June 1–11, 1889, Crook/Kennon Papers, AHEC.

36. Ibid.; Hyde, *Sioux Chronicle*, 202–12; Greene, *American Carnage*, 43.

37. Crook diary, June 7, 1889, Crook/Kennon Papers, AHEC; Hyde, *Sioux Chronicle*, 212–13.

38. Crook diary, June 12 and 14, 1889, Crook/Kennon Papers, AHEC; Hyde, *Sioux Chronicle*, 212–13.

39. Olson, *Red Cloud and the Sioux Problem*, 314.

40. *Annual Report of Commissioner of Indian Affairs*, 1889, quoted in Olson, *Red Cloud and the Sioux Problem*, 315.

41. Ibid., 316.

42. *Report of the Sioux Commission of 1889*, quoted in Utley, *Last Days*, 50.

43. Ibid., 51.

44. Olson, *Red Cloud and the Sioux Problem*, 316.

45. Crook diary, June 19, 1889, Crook/Kennon Papers, AHEC.

46. Olson, *Red Cloud and the Sioux Problem*, 316–17; Hyde, *Sioux Chronicle*, 214–15; Crook confessed his attempt to bribe Red Cloud, Little Wound, and Young Man Afraid of His Horse in an Aug. 27, 1889, letter to Foster. Crook, *Autobiography*, 288n11.

47. Hyde, *Sioux Chronicle*, 219; Olson provides somewhat different numbers, but they did not alter the final result. *Red Cloud and the Sioux Problem*, 319.

48. Hyde, *Sioux Chronicle*, 219, Crook, *Autobiography*, 287.

49. Hyde, *Sioux Chronicle*, 219. Jerome Greene notes that Crook promised congressional action. *American Carnage*, 44–45.

50. Hyde, *Sioux Chronicle*, 219; Crook diary, June–July 1889, Crook/Kennon Papers, AHEC.

51. Hyde, *Sioux Chronicle*, 220–21.

52. Crook diary, July 18, 1889, Crook/Kennon Papers, AHEC.

53. Ibid., July 13–23.

54. Greene, *American Carnage*, 46–48.

55. Hyde, *Sioux Chronicle*, 225.

56. Utley, *Lance and Shield*, 278.

57. Crook diary, July 29, 1889, Crook/Kennon Papers, AHEC; Greene, *American Carnage*, 46–47.

58. Crook diary, July 31, 1889, Crook/Kennon Papers, AHEC.

59. Utley, *Lance and Shield*, 249.

60. McLaughlin, *My Friend the Indian*, 284–86, quoted in Hyde, *Sioux Chronicle*, 226; Crook diary, July 31, 1889, Crook/Kennon Papers, AHEC.

61. Crook diary, Aug. 3–7, 1889, Crook/Kennon Papers, AHEC; Utley, *Last Days*, 279.

62. Hyde, *Sioux Chronicle*, 228.

63. Crook diary, Aug. 13–24, 1889, Crook/Kennon Papers, AHEC.

64. Hyde, *Sioux Chronicle*, 226; Greene, *American Carnage*, 49.

65. Crook to Foster, Aug. 27, 1889, Crook Letterbook, Hayes Library.

66. *Reports Relative to the Proposed Division of the Great Sioux Reservation*, quoted in Greene, *American Carnage*, 434.

67. See the following sources for more detailed, moving accounts of the government's betrayal of the Sioux and the commission's promises: Utley, *Last Days*, 55–59; Greene, *American Carnage*, 51–53; Hyde, *Sioux Chronicle*, 229–33.

68. Greene, *American Carnage*, 57–60.

69. Bourke, *On the Border*, 486.

70. *Ninth Annual Report of the Indian Rights Association*, 1891, quoted in Utley, *Last Days*, 59.

CHAPTER 25. END OF DAYS

1. Crook diary, vol. 2, May 10 and 11, 1888, Crook/Kennon Papers, AHEC.

2. Ibid., Aug. 26, 1889.

3. I am indebted to Dr. Everett K. Spees, MD, PhD, for the information on CAD and for developing the connection between the diary entries concerning Crook's health and the possible presence of CAD. Dr. Spees retired after a distinguished career as medical officer in the U.S. Army as a heart surgeon and is currently an avid student and chronicler of military history.

4. Fifty-eight companies participated from eleven different posts, training 102 officers and 2,155 enlisted men. Grange, *Fort Robinson*, 227.

5. Buecher, *Fort Robinson and the West*, 154; Crook diary, vol. 2, Aug. 30–Sept. 9, 1889, Crook/Kennon Papers, AHEC.

6. Fusco, "The Last Hunt," 36–40.

7. Crook to Webb Hayes, Aug. 21, 1889, Crook Letterbook, Hayes Library; Crook diary, vol. 2, Oct. 2, 1889, Crook/Kennon Papers, AHEC. Fusco, in his detailed account of the hunt, seems to believe that Touzalin was present and identifies one of the subjects of a photo of the hunters that accompanies the article as Touzalin. But his conclusion does not accord with Crook's diary entry and subsequent events. Further, on the back of one copy of that photo, believed to have belonged to Thaddeus Stanton, also on the hunt, and provided to the author by Mark Kasal, was a notation that the picture was taken on a similar hunt in 1886. Fusco, "The Last Hunt," 36–39.

8. Crook diary, vol. 2, Oct. 5–7, 1889, Crook/Kennon Papers, AHEC; Fusco, "The Last Hunt," 36–39.

9. Crook to Sarah A. McClees, WCTU, Oct. 14, 1889, Crook Letterbook, Hayes Library.

10. Crook to AG, Dec. 3, 1889, ibid.

11. Crook diary, vol. 2, Oct. 11–Dec. 13, 1889, Crook/Kennon Papers, AHEC.

12. Kennon diary, Mar. 3, 1889, ibid.

13. Eventually, Kennon's research resulted in his producing a paper on the campaign that was published by the Massachusetts Military Historical Society and hailed by those who had taken part as a "truthful, just, and clear account of the problems, mistakes, and results of that campaign." "Col. Lyman Kennon, Camp Commandant, Has Record of Brilliant Achievements," *New York Times*, undated article, Crook/Kennon Papers, AHEC. The article itself can be found under the title "The Valley (Sheridan's) Campaign of 1864," in the *Proceedings of the Mass. Military Historical Society*, vol. 6, 1907.

14. Crook diary, vol. 2, Dec. 13, 1889, Crook-Kennon Papers, AHEC.

15. Ibid., Dec. 15–16. For Mckinley, see Magid, *George Crook*, 250; for Schenck, see ibid., 21–22, 131.

16. Crook diary, vol. 2, Dec. 26, 1890, Crook/Kennon Papers, AHEC. For descriptions of the actions to which Crook referred in this outburst, see chapters 26–29 in Magid, *George Crook*. For a detailed account of the battle, see Hedren, *Rosebud*.

17. Crook diary, vol. 2, Dec. 28, 1889, Crook/Kennon Papers, AHEC.

18. Ibid., Dec. 28, 1889–Jan. 1, 1890.

19. Ibid., Jan. 4, 1890.

20. Howard, "Major General George Crook," 326–30.

21. Crook diary, vol. 2, Feb. 16, 1890, Crook/Kennon Papers, AHEC.

22. Ibid., Feb. 18–24, 1890.

23. For an account of King's role in the Sioux War, see King, *Campaigning with Crook*.

24. King to Gatewood, Nov. 5, 1927, Gatewood File, ASHA.

25. "General Crook Is Dead," *Omaha Bee*, Mar. 22, 1890.

26. "Death of General Crook," *Prescott Courier*, Mar. 22, 1890. The *Cincinnati Enquirer* and many other papers carried the identical article the same day.

27. *Cincinnati Enquirer*, Mar. 22, 1890; Roberts diary, quoted in Crook, *Autobiography*, 300.

28. "Death of General Crook."

29. "General Crook Lying in State," *Omaha Bee*, Mar. 23, 1890.

30. "Death of General Crook," *Prescott Courier*, Mar. 23, 1890. See also description of the body in "Gen. Crook Lying in State."

31. "Death of General Crook."

32. For more on Crook's religious beliefs, see Magid, *George Crook*, 16.

33. Wikipedia, s.v., "David Swing."

34. "Death of Gen. Crook," *Prescott Courier*, undated clipping, Crook File, Sharlot Hall Museum Library and Archives Research Center, Prescott.

35. Clipping, ibid.; Mary Crook to John Bourke, Apr. 23, 1890, John Bourke Papers, NSHS.

36. For further details of the kidnapping and funeral, see Magid, *George Crook*, preface and ch. 31.

37. Bourke, *On the Border*, 491; "Last Honors to General Crook," *Washington Star*, Nov. 12, 1890.

38. For the various dates given as the day of Crook's birth, see Magid, *George Crook*, 350n1. The confusion surrounding Crook's birth date is further exacerbated by the gen-

eral's diary entry of Sept. 8, 1889, which referred to his birth on that day sixty-one years before. Crook diary, vol. 2, Sept. 8, 1889, Crook/Kennon Papers, AHEC.

39. Charles Gatewood to the editor, *American Legion Monthly*, Jan. 26, 1927, AHS; Webb Hayes to May C. McIlvaine, May 29, 1906, Crook File, Hayes Library.

40. Gatewood to the editor, *American Legion Monthly*, Jan. 26, 1927, AHS; Webb Hayes, to McIlvaine, May 29, 1906, Crook File, Hayes Library.

41. "Death of General Crook," *New York Times*, Mar. 22, 1890.

42. In 1918 a balloon company was stationed at Fort Crook. An airfield was subsequently constructed on the site, which became Offutt Field. In 1948 Fort Crook was redesignated Offutt Air Force Base, an element in the Strategic Air Command. Wikipedia, s.v. "Offutt Air Force Base."

43. "General Crook's Memory Honored in Arizona," *Prescott Courier*, Apr. 5, 1890.

44. "Death of Gen. Crook."

45. "In Memoriam, Companion Major General George Crook."

46. "General Hayes Tribute to General Crook," *New York Tribune*, Mar. 22, 1890.

47. Magid, *Gray Fox*, 92–93, 95, 97.

48. Howard, "Major-General George Crook," 329.

49. Indian Rights Association, Apr. 2, 1890, Bourke Papers, NSHS.

50. Bourke, "George Crook."

51. "Bourke Reminiscences," unidentified newspaper clipping in Bourke Papers, NSHS.

52. "Death of Gen. Crook," *Prescott Courier*, Mar. 23, 1890.

53. Records of the Probate Court of the County of Yavapai, Territory of Arizona, Mar. 1891–Jan. 1892, Crook File, Sharlot Hall Museum, Prescott.

54. Mary Crook to John Bourke, Apr. 5, 1890, Bourke Papers, NSHS.

55. 51st Cong., Recommendation from Committee on Pensions, Report No. 1422, Jun. 28, 1890, Sen. Bill 3257, Mar. 25, 1890.

56. "Normandy Seen through the Eyes of Mrs. Crook," *Omaha Bee*, Dec. 28, 1892, reprinted in *The Connection*, Douglas County Historical Society, Issue 1, 2017.

57. "The Funeral of Mrs. George Crook," *New York Times*, Sept. 27, 1895.

CHAPTER 28. SUMMING UP

1. Magid, *General Crook*, 30.

2. For a description of Crook's innovations in this guerilla warfare, see Greene, "Military Innovation"; Greenberg, "Crook and Counterinsurgency Warfare"; Pirkle, "Crook's Use of Counterinsurgency Warfare."

3. Crook, *Autobiography*, xxii.

4. Lummis, *Crook and the Apache Wars*, 27.

Bibliography

MANUSCRIPTS AND ARCHIVAL SOURCES

Arizona Historical Society Library, Tucson
    Gatewood Papers
        Crook to AG, Div. of Pacific, Sept. 4, 1883 (Sierra Madre Report)
    Glover Reminiscences
    Kitt, Mrs. George F. "Reminiscences of James B. Glover," 1928.
Douglas County Historical Society Archives, Omaha
Henry E. Huntington Library and Art Gallery, San Marino, Calif.
    Walter Scribner Schuyler Papers, 1871–1932
Library of Congress, Washington, D.C.
    Phillip Sheridan Papers
    Papers of the Indian Rights Association
National Archives and Records Administration, Washington, D.C.
    Crook, George. Appointments, Commissions, and Personnel (ACP) File. Microfilm
        Records, M1395.
    Department of Arizona. General Orders, Circulars, and Court-Martial Orders, 1870–
        1893, RG 393.
    Department of the Platte. Letters Sent. Records of the U.S. Army Continental Com-
        mands, RG 393.
    Department of the Platte. Letters Received. Records of the U.S. Army Continental
        Command, RG 393.
    Department of the Platte. Telegrams. Records of the U.S. Army Continental Com-
        mand, RG 393.
    Records of the Adjutant General's Office, RG 94.
        Investigation and Trial of Captain Emmet Crawford
    Special File. "The Cheyenne Outbreak, 1878–79," Microfilm Records.
    Special File. "White River Utes, 1879." Microfilm Records.

Nebraska State Historical Society, Lincoln
    Bourke, John. Papers, RG 2955.
Rutherford B. Hayes Library, Rutherford B. Hayes Presidential Center, Fremont, Ohio
    George Crook Collection
        Biographic File
        Letterbooks
Sharlot Hall Museum Library and Archives Research Center, Prescott, Ariz.
    George Crook File
Special Collections and Archives, University of Oregon Libraries, Eugene
    Crook, George. Letters, 1863–1890.
U.S. Army Heritage and Education Center, Carlisle, Penn.
    Crook/Kennon Papers
        George Crook Diary. 2 vols.
        Lyman W. V. Kennon Diary

GOVERNMENT DOCUMENTS

Annual Report of the Commissioner of Indian Affairs, 1864. Washington, D.C.: GPO, 1864.
Annual Reports of the Commissioner of Indian Affairs for 1879, 1887. Washington, D.C.: GPO, 1879.
Annual Reports of the Secretary of War, 1878–1886, Washington, D.C.: GPO, 1882.
Final Report of the Board of Officers convened by General Crook to examine and report the facts attending the arrest, confinement, disarmament, escape and recapture of the Cheyenne Indians at Fort Robinson, NE, Feb. 7, 1879, attached to letter from Sherman to Sheridan, Mar. 14, 1879, in Huntington Library, Pasadena, Calif.
Official Army Register for 1883, U.S. Adjutant General's Office, Washington, D.C., 1883.
"Proceedings of a Board of Officers Convened by Virtue of the Following Special Order: Headquarters Department of the Platte, Fort Omaha, Nebraska, January 21, 1879, Special Orders No. 8," NARA, Special File, "The Cheyenne Outbreak," Microfilm.
Report of Testimony Taken by the Joint Commission Appointed to Take into Consideration the Expediency of Transferring the Indian Bureau to the War Department, 45th Cong., 3rd sess., Sen. Doc. 53, 1878–1879, Washington, D.C.: GPO, 1879.
Report of Special Commission to the Poncas. 46th Cong., 3rd sess., S. Ex. Doc. No. 30, Serial 1941. Washington, D.C., GPO, 1881.

NEWSPAPERS

Arizona Daily Star
Arizona Silver Belt
Arizona Weekly Citizen
Arizona Weekly Star
Boston Daily Advertiser
Boston Post
Charlotte Observer
Chicago Herald
Cincinnati Enquirer
Cleveland Herald

Clifton (Arizona) Clarion
Los Angeles Times
Las Vegas (NM) Daily Gazette
New York Daily Tribune
New York Herald
New York Semi-Weekly Evening Post
New York Times
Omaha Bee
Omaha Daily Herald
Omaha Republican
(Salt Lake) Deseret News
Prescott Weekly Courier
San Franciscan
Tombstone Epitaph
United States Army & Navy Journal and Gazette
Washington Post
Washington Star
Weekly Phoenix Herald

UNPUBLISHED SECONDARY SOURCES

Breth, Bruce R. "An Historical Analysis and Comparison of the Military Retirement System and the Federal Employee Retirement System." Master's thesis, Naval Post Graduate School, Monterey, Calif., 1998.

Goodman, David Michael. "Apaches as Prisoners of War, 1886–1894." PhD diss., Texas Christian University, Fort Worth, 1968.

Greenberg, William L. "General Crook and Counterinsurgency Warfare." Master's thesis, U.S. Army Command and General Staff College, Fort Leavenworth, Kans., 2001.

Greene, Jerome A. "Military Innovations and Tribal Acculturation on the Frontier: The Indian Control Policies of General George Crook." Typescript provided by Mr. Greene to the author.

Greguras, Fred M. "The History of the Post of Omaha, Fort Omaha, Fort Crook and the Quartermaster Depots." Accessed May 27, 2019. http://www.usgennet.org/usa/ne/topic/military/omaha_mil_history/pg1.htm.

Huetter, Robert A. "A History of Fort Duchesne, Utah, and the Role of its First Commanding Officer, Fredrick W. Benteen." Master's thesis, Brigham Young University, Provo, Utah, 1990.

Pirkle, Wesley M. "Major General George Crook's Use of Counterinsurgency Compound Warfare During the Great Sioux War of 1876–77." Master's thesis, U.S. Army Command and General Staff College, Fort Leavenworth, Kans., 2008.

Santala, Russel D. "The Ute Campaign of 1879: A Study in the Use of the Military Instrument." Master's thesis, US Army Command and General Staff College, Fort Leavenworth, Kans., 1993.

Sharp, Walter C. "Fort Omaha and the Winning of the West." Master's thesis, University of Omaha, Neb., 1967.

Shepard, Katherine. "The Miles-Crook Controversy." Master's thesis, University of New Mexico, Albuquerque, 1936.

Smith, Victoria, A. O. "White Eyes, Red Heart, Blue Coat: The Life and Times of Mickey Free." PhD diss., Arizona State University, Tempe, 2002.

Waltman, Henry George. "The Interior Department, War Department, and Indian Policy, 1865–1887." PhD diss., University of Nebraska, Lincoln, 1962.

ARTICLES AND PAMPHLETS

Bell, William G. Bell, William G. *John Gregory Bourke: A Soldier-Scientist on the Frontier.* Great Western Series No. 14. Washington, D.C.: Potomac Corral, The Westerners, 1978.

———. "The West of Charles Roberts." *Corral Dust: Potomac Corral of the Westerners* 10, no. 2 (Spring 1965): 2–8.

Bourke, John G. "George Crook." *Journal of the Association of the Graduates of the United States Military Academy,* June 1, 1890.

———. "With Crook in the Sierra Madre." Reprinted in Cozzens, *Eyewitnesses to the Indian Wars,* vol. 1, *Struggle for Apacheria,* 346–84.

Bray, Kingsley. "'We Belong to the North': The Flight of the Northern Indians from the White River Agencies, 1877–78." *Montana Magazine* 55, no. 3 (Spring 2005).

Carroll, John M., ed. *Unpublished Papers of the Order of the Indian Wars.* 8 numbered pamphlets. New Brunswick, NJ: Privately printed, 1977.

Casanova, Frank, ed., "General Crook Visits the Supais as Reported by John G. Bourke." *Arizona and the West* 10, no. 3 (Autumn 1963): 253–78.

Crook, George. "The Apache Problem." *Journal of the Military Service Institution of the United States* 7, no. 27 (Oct. 1886): 257–69.

———. "Letter from General Crook on Giving the Ballot to the Indians." Philadelphia. Indian Rights Association, 1885.

———. *Resumé of Operations against the Apache Indians, 1882 to 1886.* Notes and Introduction by Barry C. Johnson. London: Johnson-Taunton Military Press, 1971.

Daly, Henry W. "The Geronimo Campaign." *Winners of the West* 11, no. 1 (Dec. 1933). Reprinted in Cozzens, *Eyewitnesses to the Indian Wars,* vol. 1, *Struggle for Apacheria,* 447–87.

———. "Scouts—Good and Bad." *American Legion Monthly* 5, no. 2 (Aug. 1928): 24, 68–70.

Dillon, John. *Cases Determined in the Circuit Court for the Eight Circuit.* Vol. 5. Davenport, Iowa: Egbert, Fidlar & Chambers, 1880.

Doyle, Charles, and Jennifer K. Elsea. "The Posse Comitatus Act and Related Matters: The Use of the Military to Execute Civil Law." Congressional Research Service, CRS 7–5700, R42659, Washington, D.C., 2012.

Elliot, Charles P. "The Geronimo Campaign of 1885–1886." *Journal of the United States Cavalry Association* 21, no. 80 (September 1910): 211–36. Reprinted in Cozzens, *Eyewitnesses to the Indian Wars,* vol. 1, *Struggle for Apacheria,* 427–46.

———. "An Indian Reservation under General George Crook." *Military Affairs* 12, no. 2 (1948): 91–102. Reprinted in Cozzens, *Eyewitnesses to the Indian Wars,* vol. 1, *Struggle for Apacheria,* 405–13.

Fiebeger, Gustav J. "George Crook's Campaign in Old Mexico in 1883: Events Leading Up to It and Personal Experiences in the Campaign." *By Valor and Arms: Journal of American Military History* 1, no. 3 (Spring 1975): 16–24.

Fusco, Eugene M. "The Last Hunt of George A. Crook." *Montana Magazine* 21, no. 4 (Autumn 1962): 36–40.

The General Crook House Museum Tour Guide. Omaha, Neb.: Douglas County Historical Society, 2001.

Goodwin, Grenville. "Experiences of an Indian Scout: Excerpts from the Life of John Rope." *Arizona Historical Review* 7, nos. 1, 2 (Jan., Apr. 1936): 31–68, 31–72.

———. "John Rope." In *Western Apache Raiding and Warfare*, by Grenville Goodwin, edited by Keith H. Basso, 93–186. Tucson: University of Arizona Press, 1971.

Greene, Jerome A. "The Crawford Affair: International Implications of the Geronimo Campaign." *Journal of the West* 21, no. 1 (January 1972): 143–53.

Hanna, Robert. "With Crawford in Mexico." *Overland Monthly* 8, 2nd ser. (July 1886): 78–83. Reprinted in Cozzens, *Eyewitnesses to the Indian Wars,* vol. 1, *Struggle for Apacheria,* 514.

Harte, John Bret. "Conflict at San Carlos." *Arizona and the West* 15 (Spring 1973): 27–44.

———. "The Strange Case of Joseph C. Tiffany: Indian Agent in Disgrace." *Journal of Arizona History* 16, no. 4 (Winter 1975): 383–403.

Howard, Oliver O. "Major-General George Crook, U.S.A." *Chautauquan* 40, no. 3 (June 1890): 325–30.

"In Memoriam, Companion Major General George Crook." In *Military Order of the Loyal Legion of the United States,* Circular No. 5, Series of 1890, Whole No. 132, Chicago, April 25, 1890.

Kennon, Lyman W. V. "The Valley (Sheridan's) Campaign of 1864." *Proceedings of the Mass. Military Historical Society,* vol. 6, 1907.

King, James T. "A Better Way: General Crook and the Ponca Indians." *Nebraska History* 50, no. 3 (Fall 1969): 239–56.

Lamar, Howard, R. "Edmund G. Ross as Governor of New Mexico Territory: A Reappraisal." *New Mexico Historical Review* 36, no. 3 (July 1961): 197–98.

Lyon, Juana Fraser. "Archie McIntosh, the Scottish Indian Scout." *Journal of Arizona History* 7, no. 3 (Autumn 1966): 103–22.

McGeary, George D. "My Search for General George Crook: The Interrupted Autobiography and the Mystery of the Missing Papers." *Journal of Arizona History* 41 (Autumn 2000): 289–306.

Myers, Roger. "I. P. Print Olive, One Tough Hombre." *Wild West Magazine,* December 2002.

Porter, Joseph C. Foreword to *General George Crook: His Autobiography.* Edited by Martin F. Schmitt. Norman: University of Oklahoma Press, 1986.

Randall, A. Franklin. "Apache Affairs: An Interview with General Crook." Reprinted in Cozzens, *Eyewitnesses to the Indian Wars,* vol. 1, *Struggle for Apacheria,* 396–404.

———. "In the Heart of the Sierra Madre." Reprinted in Cozzens, *Eyewitnesses to the Indian Wars,* vol. 1, *Struggle for Apacheria,* 394–95.

Roberts, Charles D. "Notes on the Service of Cyrus Swan Roberts with Particular Reference to the Indian War." In *Unpublished Papers of the Order of the Indian Wars,* no. 4, edited by John M. Carroll. New Brunswick, N.J.: Privately printed, 1977.

Ruhling, Nancy A. "Wallpaper in the General Crook House." *Victorian Homes.* n.d. General Crook Biographic File, Hayes Presidential Library, Fremont, Ohio.

Shipp, William E. "Captain Crawford's Last Expedition." *Journal of the United States Cavalry Association* 5, no. 19 (Dec. 1892): 343–61. Reprinted in Cozzens, *Eyewitnesses to the Indian Wars,* vol. 1, *Struggle for Apacheria,* 520.

Starita, Joseph. "The Case of Standing Bear: Establishing Personhood under the Law." *Court Review: Journal of the American Judges Association* 45 (2009): 4–11.

Sumner, E. V. "Besieged by the Utes: The Massacre of 1879." *By Valor and Arms: Journal of American Military History* 2, no. 1 (Fall 1975): 12–22.

Thrapp, Dan L. Foreword to *Indeh, An Apache Odyssey*, by Eve Ball. Reprint, Norman: University of Oklahoma Press, 1988.

Turcheneske, John A. "Arizonans and the Apache Prisoners at Mount Vernon Barracks, Alabama: 'They Do Not Die Fast Enough.'" *Military History of Texas and the Southwest* 11, no. 3 (1973): 197–226.

Weigel, William. "Notes on the Apaches." In *Unpublished Papers of the Order of the Indian Wars,* edited by John M. Carroll. New Brunswick, N.J.: Privately printed, 1977.

BOOKS

Adams, Kevin. *Class and Race in the Frontier Army: Military Life in the West, 1870–1890.* Norman: University of Oklahoma Press, 2009.

Amchan, Arthur J. *The Most Famous Soldier in America: A Biography of Maj. Gen. Nelson A. Miles.* Alexandria, Va.: Amchan Publications, 1989.

Andreas, A. T., comp. *History of Nebraska.* Vol. 1, 1882. Facsimile ed. 768, Evansville, Ind.: Unigraphic, Inc., 1975.

Ball, Eve. *Indeh, An Apache Odyssey.* 1980. Reprint, Norman: University of Oklahoma Press, 1988.

Ball, Eve, and James Kaywaykla. *In the Days of Victorio: Recollections of a Warm Springs Apache.* Tucson. University of Arizona Press, 1970.

Bancroft, Hubert H. *A History of Arizona and New Mexico, 1530–1888.* Vol. 17 of *The Works of Hubert Howe Bancroft.* San Francisco: History Co., 1889.

Barnes, Will C. *Apaches and Longhorns: The Reminiscences of Will C. Barnes.* 1941. Facsimile ed., Tucson: University of Arizona Press, 1982.

Barrett, S. M., ed. *Geronimo's Story of His Life.* 1906. Reprint, Harrisburg, Penn.: National Historical Society, 1994.

Betzinez, Jason. *I Fought with Geronimo.* New York: Bonanza Books, 1959.

Bigelow, John Jr. *On the Bloody Trail of Geronimo.* Tucson, Ariz.: Westernlore Press, 1986.

Bourke, John G. *An Apache Campaign in the Sierra Madre.* 1886. Reprint, New York: Charles Scribner's Sons, 1958.

———. *The Diaries of John Gregory Bourke.* Vols. 2–5. Edited and annotated by Charles M. Robinson. Denton: University of North Texas Press, 2003–13.

———. *On the Border with Crook.* 1891. Reprint, New York: Time-Life Books, 1980.

Brimlow, Francis. *The Bannock Indian War of 1878.* Caldwell, Idaho: Caxton Printers, 1938.

Broadfield, William E., comp. *Stories of Omaha: Historical Sketches of the Midland City.* 1898. Reprint, London: British Library Historical Print Editions, 2011.

Buecker, Thomas R. *Fort Robinson and the American West, 1874–1899.* Norman, University of Oklahoma Press, 1999.

Burkley, Frank J. *The Faded Frontier.* Omaha, Neb.: Burkley Envelope and Printing Co., 1935.

Chrisman, Harry. *The Ladder of Rivers: The Story of I. P. Olive.* Denver, Colo.: Sager Books, 1962.

Clum, Woodworth. *Apache Agent: The Story of John P. Clum*. Lincoln: University of Nebraska Press, 1978.

Collins, Charles. *Apache Nightmare: The Battle at Cibicue Creek*. Norman: University of Oklahoma Press, 1999.

Collins, John S. *My Experiences in the West*. 1911. Reprint, Chicago: Lakeside Press, R. R. Donnelly & Sons, 1970.

Collum, George W. *Biographical Register of the Officers and Graduates of the U.S. Military Academy at West Point, New York: 1802–1890*. Vol. 4. Boston: Houghton Mifflin, 1901.

Corbusier, William T. *Verde to San Carlos: Recollections of a Famous Army Surgeon and His Observant Family on the Western Frontier, 1869–1886*. Tucson, Ariz.: Dale Stuart King, Publisher, 1969.

Cozzens, Peter, ed. *Eyewitnesses to the Indian Wars, 1865–1890*. Vol. 1, *The Struggle for Apacheria*. Mechanicsburg, Penn.: Stackpole Books, 2001.

———, ed. *Eyewitnesses to the Indian Wars, 1865–1890*. Vol. 4, *The Long War for the Northern Plains*. Mechanicsburg, Penn.: Stackpole Books, 2004.

Crook, George. *General George Crook: His Autobiography*. Edited by Martin F. Schmitt. Norman: University of Oklahoma Press, 1946, 1960.

Cruse, Thomas. *Apache Days and After*. 1941. Reprint, Lincoln: University of Nebraska Press, First Bison Printing, 1987.

Dando-Collins, Stephen. *Standing Bear Is a Person: The True Story of a Native American's Quest for Justice*. Cambridge, Mass.: Da Capo, 2005.

Davis, Britton. *The Truth about Geronimo*. 1929. Reprint, Lincoln: University of Nebraska Press, Bison Edition, 1976.

Debo, Angie. *Geronimo, the Man, His Time, His Place*. 4th ed. Norman: University of Oklahoma Press, 1976.

Dillon, John. *Cases Determined in the Circuit Court for the Eight Circuit*. Vol. 5. Davenport, Iowa: Egbert, Fidlar & Chambers, 1880.

Dunbar, Seymour, and Paul C. Phillips, eds. *Journals and Letters of Major John Owen, Pioneer of the Northwest, 1850–1871*. Vol. 2. New York: Edward Eberstadt, 1927.

Dunlay, Thomas W. *Wolves for the Blue Soldiers: Indian Scouts and Auxiliaries with the United States Army, 1860–90*. Lincoln: University of Nebraska Press, 1982.

Emmitt, Robert. *The Last War Trail: The Utes and the Settlement of Colorado*. 1954. Reprint, Boulder: University Press of Colorado, 2000.

Faulk, Odie B. *The Geronimo Campaign*. New York: Oxford University Press, 1969.

Finerty, John F. *War-Path and Bivouac, or the Conquest of the Sioux*. 1890. Reprint, Norman: University of Oklahoma Press, 1977.

Gatewood, Charles. *Lt. Charles Gatewood: His Apache Wars Memoir*. Edited and with additional text by Louis Kraft. Lincoln: University of Nebraska Press, 2005.

Goodwin, Grenville. *Western Apache Raiding and Warfare*. Edited by Keith H. Basso. Tucson: University of Arizona Press, 1971.

Grange, Robert T. *Fort Robinson, Outpost on the Plains*. Lincoln: Nebraska State Historical Society, 1958.

Greene, Jerome A. *American Carnage*. Norman: University of Oklahoma Press, 2014.

———. *Indian War Veterans: Memories of Army Life and Campaigns in the West, 1864–1898*. New York: Savas Beatie LLC, 2007.

———. *Nez Perce Summer, 1877*. Helena: Montana Historical Society, 2000.

———. *Slim Buttes, 1876: An Episode of the Great Sioux War*. Norman: University of Oklahoma Press, 1982.

Grinnell, George Bird. *The Fighting Cheyennes*. 1915. Reprint, Norman: University of Oklahoma Press, 1983.

Hagan, William T. *The Indian Rights Association: The Herbert Welsh Years, 1882–1904*. Tucson: University of Arizona Press, 1985.

Hayes, Rutherford B. *Diary and Letters of Rutherford Birchard Hayes, Nineteenth President of the United States*. Vol. 3, 1865–1881. Edited by Charles R. Williams. Columbus: Ohio State Archeological and Historical Society, 1924.

Hedren, Paul L. *Rosebud, June 17, 1876: Prelude to the Little Big Horn*. Norman: University of Oklahoma Press, 2019.

Hoig, Stan E. *Perilous Pursuit: The United States Cavalry and the Northern Cheyenne*. Boulder: University Press of Colorado, 2002.

———. *Peace Chiefs of the Cheyenne*. Norman: University of Oklahoma Press, 1980.

Horn, Tom. *Life of Tom Horn, Government Scout and Interpreter*. 1904. Reprint, Chicago: R. R. Donnelly & Sons, 1987.

Hutton, Paul A. *The Apache Wars: The Hunt for Geronimo, the Apache Kid, and the Captive Boy Who Started the Longest War in American History*. New York: Crown, 2016.

———. *Phil Sheridan and His Army*. Lincoln: University of Nebraska Press, 1985.

Hyde, George E. *A Sioux Chronicle*. 1937. Rev. ed. Norman: University of Oklahoma Press, 1956.

Jackson, Helen Hunt. *A Century of Dishonor: A Sketch of the United States Government's Dealings with Some of the Indian Tribes*. New York: Harper & Brothers, 1881.

Janetski, Joel C. *Indians in Yellowstone National Park*. Salt Lake City: University of Utah Press, 2002.

Johnson, Virginia W. *The Unregimented General: A Biography of General Nelson A. Miles*. Cambridge, Mass.: Riverside Press, 1962.

Juarez, Angelo D. *The Tarnished Saber: Major Azor Howett Nickerson, USA, His Life and Times*. Chatham, Mass.: Nickerson Family Association, 1993.

Kime, Wayne R., ed. *The Indian Territory Journals of Colonel Richard Irving Dodge*. Norman: University of Oklahoma Press, 2000.

King, Charles. *Campaigning with Crook*. 1890. Reprint, with an introduction by Don Russell, Norman: University of Oklahoma Press, 1964.

Kraft, Louis. *Gatewood and Geronimo*. Albuquerque: University of New Mexico Press, 2000.

Lane, Jack C., ed. *Chasing Geronimo: The Journal of Leonard Wood, May–September 1886*. 1970. Reprint, Lincoln: University of Nebraska Press, 2009.

Larson, Robert W. *Red Cloud, Warrior-Statesman of the Lakota Sioux*. Norman: University of Oklahoma Press, 1997.

Laurie, Clayton D., and Ronald H. Cole. *The Role of Federal Military Forces in Domestic Disorders, 1877–1945*. Washington, D.C.: Center of Military History/U.S. Army, 1997.

Leiker, James N., and Ramon Powers. *The Northern Cheyenne Exodus in History and Memory*. Norman: University of Oklahoma Press, 2011.

Lockwood, Frank C. *The Apache Indians*. Lincoln: University of Nebraska Press, 1938; First Bison Press Printing, 1987.

Lummis, Charles R. *General Crook and the Apache Wars*. 1966. Reprint, Flagstaff, Ariz.: Northland Press, 1985.

Madsen, Brigham D. *The Bannock of Idaho*. Moscow: University of Idaho Press, 1996.

Magid, Paul. *George Crook: From the Redwoods to Appomattox*. Norman: University of Oklahoma Press, 2011.

———. *The Gray Fox: George Crook and the Indian Wars*. Norman: University of Oklahoma Press, 2015.

Marsh, Charles S. *People of the Shining Mountains*. Boulder, Colo.: Pruett Publishing, 1982.

Mathes, Valerie Sherer. *Helen Hunt Jackson and Her Indian Reform Legacy*. Austin: University of Texas Press, 1990.

Mathes, Valerie Sherer, and Richard Lowitt. *The Standing Bear Controversy: Prelude to Indian Reform*. Urbana: University of Illinois Press, 2003.

Mattes, Merrill J. *Indians, Infants, and Infantry: Andrew and Elizabeth Burt on the Frontier*. 1960. Reprint, Lincoln: University of Nebraska Press, Bison Edition, 1988.

Mayes, Edward. *Lucius Q. C. Lamar: His Life, Times, and Speeches, 1825–1893*. Nashville: Methodist Episcopal Church, South, 1895.

McChristian, Douglas C. *Fort Bowie, Arizona: Combat Post of the Southwest, 1858–1894*. Norman: University of Oklahoma Press, 2005.

Miles, Nelson A. *Personal Recollections and Observations of General Nelson A. Miles*. Vol. 2, 1896. Reprint, Lincoln: University of Nebraska Press, 1992.

Monnett, John H. *Tell Them We Are Going Home: The Odyssey of the Northern Cheyennes*. Norman: University of Oklahoma Press, 2001.

Morton, J. Sterling, ed. *Illustrated History of Nebraska*. Lincoln, Neb.: Western Publishing and Engraving Co., 1911.

Ogle, Ralph Hedrick. *Federal Control of the Western Apaches, 1848–1886*. 1940. Reprint, Albuquerque: University of New Mexico Press, 1970.

Olson, James C. *Red Cloud and the Sioux Problem*. Lincoln: University of Nebraska Press, 1965.

Opler, Morris, E. *An Apache Life-way*. New York: Cooper Square Publishers, 1965.

Parker, James. *The Old Army: Memories, 1872–1918*. 1929. Reprint, Mechanicsburg, Penn.: Stackpole Books, 2003.

Porter, Joseph C. *Paper Medicine Man: John Gregory Bourke and His American West*. Norman: University of Oklahoma Press, 1986.

Prucha, Francis Paul. *The Great Father: The United States Government and the American Indian*. Abridged ed. Lincoln: University of Nebraska Press, 1984.

Radbourne, Allan. *Mickey Free: Apache Captive, Interpreter, and Indian Scout*. Tucson: Arizona Historical Society, 2005.

Roberts, David. *Once They Rode Like the Wind*. New York: Simon & Schuster, 1993.

Robinson, Charles M. *General Crook and the Western Frontier*. Norman: University of Oklahoma Press, 2001.

Ruby, Robert H., and John A. Brown. *Indians of the Pacific Northwest: A History*. Norman: University of Oklahoma Press, 1988.

Russell, Don. *Campaigning with King: Charles King, Chronicler of the Old Army*. Lincoln: University of Nebraska Press, 1991.

Sandoz, Mari. *Cheyenne Autumn*. New York: McGraw-Hill, 1953.

Shapard, Bud. *Chief Loco: Apache Peacemaker*. Norman: University of Oklahoma Press, 2010.

Sheridan, Lt. Gen. P. H. *Records of Engagements with Hostile Indians within the Military Division of the Department of Missouri from 1868 to 1882*. Washington, D.C.: GPO, 1882.

Simmons, Marc. *Massacre on the Lordsburg Road*. College Station: Texas A&M University Press, 1997.

Sonnichsen, C. L. *The Mescalero Apaches*. Norman: University of Oklahoma Press, 1958.

Soule, J. H., ed. *United States Blue Book: A Register of Federal Offices and Employments in Each State and Territory and the District of Columbia with Their Salaries and Emoluments, 1877*. New York: J. H. Soule Publisher, 1877.

Starita, Joe. *The Dull Knifes of Pine Ridge: A Lakota Odyssey*. New York: G. F. Putnam's Sons, 1995.

———. *"I Am a Man": Chief Standing Bear's Journey for Justice*. New York: St. Martin's Press, 2008.

Stockel, Henrietta H. *Shame and Endurance: The Untold Story of the Chiricahua Apache Prisoners of War*. Tucson: University of Arizona Press, 2004.

Sweeney, Edwin. *From Cochise to Geronimo: The Chiricahua Apaches, 1874–1886*. Norman: University of Oklahoma Press, 2010.

Tate, Michael L. *The Frontier Army in the Settlement of the West*. Norman: University of Oklahoma Press, 1999.

Thompson, Mark. *American Character: The Curious Life of Charles Fletcher Lummis and the Rediscovery of the Southwest*. New York: Arcade, 2001.

Thrapp, Dan L. *Al Sieber: Chief of Scouts*. 1964. Reprint, Norman: University of Oklahoma Press, 1995.

———. *The Conquest of Apacheria*. Norman: University of Oklahoma Press, 1967.

———. *Encyclopedia of Frontier Biography*. Vols. 2–3. Lincoln: University of Nebraska Press in association with Arthur H. Clarke Co., 1988.

———. *General Crook and the Sierra Madre Adventure*. Norman: University of Oklahoma Press, 1972.

———. *Victorio and the Mimbres Apaches*. Norman: University of Oklahoma Press, 1974.

Thrapp, Dan L., ed. *Dateline Fort Bowie: Charles Fletcher Lummis Reports on an Apache War*. Norman: University of Oklahoma Press, 1979.

Tibbles, Thomas H. *Buckskin and Blanket Days*. 1905. Reprint, Garden City, N.Y.: Doubleday, 1957.

———. *Ponca Chiefs: An Indian's Attempt to Appeal from the Tomahawk to the Courts*. 1880. Reprint, Lincoln: University of Nebraska Press, Bison Book, 1970.

Utley, Robert M. *Frontier Regulars: The United States Army and the Indians, 1866–1890*. New York: Macmillan, 1973.

———. *Geronimo*. New Haven, Conn.: Yale University Press, 2012.

———. *The Lance and the Shield: The Life and Times of Sitting Bull*. New York: Ballantine Books, 1993.

———. *The Last Days of the Sioux Nation*. New Haven, Conn.: Yale University Press, 1963.

Walker, Henry P., and Don Bufkin. *Historical Atlas of Arizona*. Norman: University of Oklahoma Press, 1979.

Wolfe, J. M. *Omaha Directory for 1876, 1878, 1879, 1881*. Omaha, Neb.: J. M. Wolfe, 1876, 1878, 1879, 1881.

Wooster, Robert. *Nelson A. Miles and the Twilight of the Frontier Army*. Lincoln: University of Nebraska Press, 1993.

Worcester, Donald E. *The Apaches: Eagles of the Southwest*. Norman: University of Oklahoma Press, 1979.

ONLINE SOURCES

"California's Gold History Lives in Empire Mine State Historical Park." California Department of Parks and Recreation. Accessed June 7, 2019. https://www.parks.ca.gov/pages/24317/files/empiremineshp.pdf.

"Charles Duval Roberts." Find a Grave. Accessed May 28, 2019. https://www.findagrave.com/memorial/7866876/charles-duval-roberts.

"Cyrus Swan Roberts." Arlington National Cemetery. http:www.arlingtoncemetery.net/csroberts.htm.

"David Swing." Wikipedia. Accessed May 28, 2019. www.wikipedia.org/wiki/David_Swing.

Diaries and Letters. Rutherford B. Hayes Presidential Library and Museums. Accessed May 28, 2019. www.rbhayes.org/research/diary-and-letters-of-rutherford-b.-hayes.

"George Frisbie Hoar." Wikipedia. Accessed May 28, 2019. www.wikipedia.org/wiki/George_Frisbie_Hoar.

Greguras, Fred M. "The History of the Post of Omaha, Fort Omaha, Fort Crook, and the Quartermaster Depots." NEGenWeb. Accessed June 4, 2019. http://www.usgennet.org/usa/ne/topic/military/omaha_mil_history/pg1.htm.

"History of Chinese Americans." Wikipedia. Accessed May 28, 2019. https://en.wikipedia.org/wiki/History_of_Chinese_Americans.

"Offutt Air Force Base." Wikipedia. Accessed May 28, 2019. www.wikipedia.org/wiki/Offutt_Air_Force_Base.

"The Ponca Trail of Tears." Nebraskastudies.org. Accessed June 2, 2019. http://nebraskastudies.org/1875-1899/the-trial-of-standing-bear/the-ponca-trail-of-tears/.

"Posse Comitatus Act and the US Military on the Border: What the National Guard Can and Cannot Do." ThoughCo. Accessed May 28, 2019. www.thoughtco.com/the-posse-comitatus-act-of-1878–721707.

"The Pullman Building." Pullman Museum. Accessed May 28, 2019. http://www.pullman-museum.org/theCompany/pullmanBuilding.html.

Speeches. Rutherford B. Hayes Presidential Library and Museums. Accessed May 28, 2019. www.rbhayes.org/hayes/speeches.

Weiser, Katherine. "Camillus Sidney [sic] Fly—Photographer and Lawman." Legends of America. Accessed May 28, 2019. https://www.legendsofamerica.com/law-camillusfly.

Index

References to illustrations appear in italic type.

Adams, Alva, 412–13
Adams, Charles, 109–10
African Americans: freedman "uprising," 100; as soldiers, 410; troopers killed by Indian scout, 318; voting rights and, 381
Alchesay, *124*, 128, 131, 332, 338, 339, 356, 458
Allen, Walter, 83, 84–85, 86
allotment system, 422–24. *See also* land reform and ownership
Alta California, 381
American Horse, 436–37
Anthony, George T., 42, 474n112
Apache (Crook's mule), *124*, 127, 272, 275, 447
Apache Campaign in the Sierra Madre, An (Bourke), 180
Apache prisoners of war, 226, 307, 348, 351, 367–69, 387, 398
Apache Reservation: agricultural production on, 276–77, 381; army control over, 149–50; consolidation policy on, 132–34, 148–49, 151; headcounts, 151, 157, 165; identification tags, 151, 157, 165, 247; Indian courts on, 278; Indian

employment on, 159; interagency agreement concerning control of, 227, 230, 255; tiswin consumption on, 157, 247, 249, 279–82; white incursion on, 158, 244–45, 267. *See also* San Carlos Reservation
Apaches: consolidation policy impact on, 133–34; feuds between bands, 134–35, 137–38; land ownership and, 425; oral histories on Crook, 126; polygamy among, 484n17; removal to San Carlos, 135; revenge culture of, 184; scalping and, 493n12; spousal abuse among, 503n6; transition to reservation life, 130–31
Apaches, Aravaipa, 162
Apaches, Bedonkohe Chiricahua, 135, 136, 141, 198
Apaches, Chihenne Chiricahua, 136, 198, 237. *See also* Apaches, Mimbre; Apaches, Warm Springs
Apaches, Chiricahua: as agriculturalists, 276–77; civilian/military management struggle impact on, 277–78; Crook's advocacy for, 391–92, 396–97;

539

Apaches, Chiricahua (*continued*)
Crook's attitude toward, 164–65; feuds between bands, 135; memorandum of understanding regarding resettlement of, 227, 230, 255; plot to murder scouts, 210; as prisoners of war, 226, 307, 348, 351, 367–69, 387, 398; public opinion concerning, 206–7, 232–33, 370; relocation to Florida, 346, 351–52, 362–67, 369, 376–77, 513n33; relocation to Fort Sill, 397–98; relocation to Indian Territory as option for, 364–65; relocation to Mount Vernon Barracks, 388–89, 391; relocation to Texas, 369–70; relocation to Turkey Creek, 246, 363–64; resettlement at San Carlos following breakout, 219–28; retrieval of family members from Mexico, 234; warriors' skills, 167–68. *See also Geronimo campaign entries; San Carlos breakout entries*
Apaches, Chokonen Chiricahua, 135
Apaches, Cibicue, 129, 134, 137, 139–40, 141, 149
Apaches, Mescalero, 314
Apaches, Mimbre, 136, 286
Apaches, Nedni Chiricahua, 135, 136, 141
Apaches, San Carlos, 181, 184, 186, 231, 308
Apaches, Tonto, 134–35, 138, 181, 186, 308
Apaches, Warm Springs, 136, 142, 170, 198, 219, 286, 397–98
Apaches, Western, 137, 246; Ghost Dance movement and, 138–39; as jurors, 249; as scouts, 148, 186. *See also* Apaches, Tonto; Apaches, White Mountain
Apaches, White Mountain, 134, 137, 141, 149, 162, 184, 231, 246; as agriculturalists, 276; as scouts, 128, 157, 181, 293–94, 296; success on reservation, 243; Ulzana massacre of, 305
Apache scouts: in Arizona, 127; on Cibicue mutiny, 145–46; clothing and equipment, 183; Crook on, 186, 344, 374–77, 393; in Crook's strategy, 374–75; Davis on, 290; in Ghost Dance movement, 138–39; as intelligence gatherers, 164; Mexican complaints concerning, 327; Miles on use of, 312, 354, 357–58; plot to murder, 210; red headbands of, 174; San Carlos Reservation force, 127; scout charged with murder, 251–52; in second Geronimo campaign, 290, 293–94, 308, 320; Sheridan on use of, 309, 318, 374, 507n55; in Sierra Madre expedition, 148, 161–64, 181, 183; whites' distrust of following Cibicue mutiny, 125, 174, 186. *See also* Cibicue mutiny
Arapahos, 3, 103
Arizona: animosity toward Apaches in, 243; Apache raiding in, 359; Indian scouts in, 127; non-Indian population in 1880, 125; whites' resistance to Apache return to, 394–97
Arizona General Assembly, 356
Arizona Rangers, 225
Arizona Silver Belt, 217, 232, 233
Arizona Star, 174
Arizona Weekly Citizen, 135–36, 206, 222, 232, 283–84
Arlington National Cemetery, 338, 456, 458
Armour family, 417
Army and Navy Journal, 15, 468n11
Army and Navy Register, 386–87
Arthur, Chester, 121, 142, 226–27, 260
assimilation, 75–76, 465; Crook on, 28, 164, 256, 271, 384, 425; Dawes on, 426; land ownership in, 370–80, 384, 424
Atlantic & Pacific Telephone Company, 5
Ayres, Romeyn B., 387

Bainbridge, A.H., 9, 11
Ball, Eve, 126
Bancroft, Hubert, 206

Bannocks, 5–6; Crook's advocacy for, 48; Lemhi, 469n34; ration entitlement, 468n11; treaty with, 8

Bannocks, Lemhi, 469n34

Bannock scouts, 8–9

Bannock uprising: conflict over resources in, 13–14; Crook on, 12–13, 14, 15–16; number involved in, 469n36; precipitating factors in, 7–10

Barlow, Francis, 314

Barnes, Will C., 123

Barrett, S.M., 197, 203

Basaraca, Mexico, 187

Battle of Big Dry Wash, 142–43

Battle of Cedar Creek, 450

Battle of Fisher's Hill, 417, 450, 507n53

Battle of Hat Creek, 40

Battle of Little Big Horn, 4

Battle of Milk River, 107–9, 110

Battle of Opequon, 450

Battle of Powder River, 122

Battle of Salt River Cave, 381

Battle of the Rosebud, 4, 8, 17, 31, 122, 123, 125, 328, 373–74

Battle of Tres Castillos, 136

Battle of Winchester, 450

Battle of Wounded Knee, 138

"Battle Tactics of Infantry" (Kennon), 406–7

Bavispe, Mexico, 187

Bear Shield, 54

Beaumont, Samuel B., 150, 158–59

Beneactiney, 171, 174, 176

Benito, 171, 486n74

Benteen, Frederick, 410–11

Betzinez, Jason, 191, 199–200, 224, 246, 276, 490n48

Biddle, James, 185, 216

Bingham, Judson D., 416

Blackfoot, 80

Black Kettle, 482n32

Bland, Thomas A., 435

Board of Indian Commissioners, 83

Bonito, 215, 235, 237, 238, 305

Bonito, daughter of, 191, 192, 193

Boston Indian Citizenship Committee, 383, 384, 386, 426

Bourke, John G., 11, 19; *An Apache Campaign in the Sierra Madre*, 180; Apaches and, 126, 128–29, 210, 383; Bannocks and, 24–25; on Bright Eyes, 51; on Chiricahua return to San Carlos, 233; on Chiricahuas removal to Florida, 365; on Cibicue mutiny investigation, 144; on Crook, 78, 461; Crook promotion efforts and, 122; Crook's death and, 456, 458; on Ezra Hayt, 476n56; on Grover Cleveland, 366; illness, 228; in investigation of Fort Marion conditions, 384–85, 387, 388; John Welsh and, 382–83; on Ka-ya-ten-nae, 251, 332; marriage of, 228–29; Mickey Free and, 162; on Miles's rivalry with Crook, 312–13; mining investment, 113–15; on Nana, 212; on Nicaagat, 103; *On the Border with Crook*, 131, 421; on Omaha, Nebraska, 90; at peace talks, 335, *336*, 337; Ponca Commission and, 83, 84, 86, 87; Poncas and, 55, 57, 59, 61, 64; promotion efforts of, 419–21; on racial differences, 74; on Schurz, 79; on Sidney Barracks soldiers, 23; Sierra Madre expedition and, 178, 180, 181, 185, 187, 189, 194, 201, 202, 203, 209, 214, 217; Sioux Commission and, 421, 522n20; at Smithsonian, 347, 365, 384; on Utes, 109; visit to Havasupai, 272–75

Bowman, Sam, 162

Bradley, Luther, 289, 301, 308, 316–17

Bright Eyes, 47, 51, 55, 68, 384

Buffalo Horn, 8, 13, 14

buffalo slaughter, 470n16

Buffalo Soldiers, 410

Burkley, Frank, 94

Burnham, Horace B., 64, 66

Burns, Mike, 381

Burt, Andrew S., 5, 101–2

camas root, 8, 13
Camp Apache, 484n1
Camp Goodwin, 134, 136
Camp Medicine Butte, 408
Camp Mogollon, 484n1
Camp Robinson, 29, 31, 472n46. *See also*
    Fort Robinson
Camp Supply, 215, 221
Camp Thomas, 484n1
Canadian North-West Mounted Police, 4
Canby, Edward, 328
Cañon de los Embudos peace talks:
    amnesty implied in, 338; Chihuahua's
    surrender at, 339–40, 343; Geronimo's
    demands for attending, 327–28,
    331–32; Geronimo's escape from, 343;
    Geronimo's surrender at, 340; photo-
    graphs taken at, 333–34, *336*; physical
    location, 332–33; surrender terms,
    335–41, 340–41; surrender terms,
    Crook on, 344–45. *See also* Geronimo
    campaign, second
Captain Jack, 328
Carbo, Guillermo, 177–78
Carlisle Indian School, 262, 366, 385,
    389, 398, 428
Carpenter, William L., 51, 55
Carr, Eugene, 129, 138–40, 310–11
Chaffee, Adna R., 137, 185, 486n49
Chamberlain, Dakota Territory, 437
Chapo, 239, 298, 505n18
Charley (scout), 263–64
Chatauquan, 460
Chatto, 241, 253, 280, 282, 296, 297, 320,
    339, 383, 386, 458, 499n20; death of,
    398; at Mount Vernon Barracks, 392–
    93; in peace talks, 212, 214, 234; pursuit
    of fleeing Apaches by, 287–88; raiding
    in the Sierra Madre, 170–71, *172*, 174,
    175, 176, 232, 251; removal to Florida,
    365–66; return to the reservation, 223,
    237, 239; Ulzana revenge on, 304–5
Cheyenne, Northern, 3, 103; Bannocks
    and, 8; danger of mass suicide by,

32, 33; factions among, 30; ration
    shortages and, 21–22; resettlement of,
    20–21; women and children taken in
    by Sioux, 39, 41–42
Cheyenne, Northern, breakout: Crook
    on reasons for, 25, 29, 32, 41–42;
    Crook on rules of engagement, 36–37;
    Crook's pursuit following, 22–23, 39;
    from Darlington, 20, 36; from Fort
    Robinson, 35, 40–41; inquiry into,
    43–44, 46; public opinion concerning,
    41, 48; raids against settlers following,
    26; Sheridan on, 22–23, 25
Cheyenne, Southern, 20, 25
Cheyenne Dog Soldiers, 35
Cheyenne River agency, 429, 438
Cheyenne scouts, 24
Chicago, Burlington, and Northern
    Railroad, 402
Chicago, Ill., 414, 416–18
Chicago Fire of 1871, 416
Chicago Times, 204
Chihuahua, 170, *173*, 174, 191, 212, 214,
    237, 279; arrest warrant for, 348; death
    of, 398; Geronimo's resentment of,
    341; at Mount Vernon Barracks, 392;
    in peace negotiations, 193–94, 207,
    337, 338, 339; relocation to Florida,
    346–47, 351–52; in second breakout,
    286, 289, 297, 302, 303–4; surrender
    of, 339–40, 343; in tiswin-drunk inci-
    dent, 279, 280, 281, 282
Chihuahua, Eugene, 126, 389, 513n33
Chinese Exclusion Act, 521n3
Chivington, John M., 482n32
Cibicue mutiny, 125; Crook's investiga-
    tion of, 144–47, 256; Crook's nego-
    tiations following, 131–32; Crook's
    policies following, 147–48; execution
    of mutineers, 142, 487n17; Ghost
    Dance movement and, 139–40; scouts'
    version of events leading to, 145–46;
    whites' distrust of scouts resulting
    from, 186

Cleveland, Grover, 270–71, 285, 314–15, 318, 338, 344–45, 351, 364, 365–66, 368–69, 370, 385, 388, 390, 392, 419

Clifton Clarion, 283

Clum, John, 136–37, 149

coal mining, 245, 499n10

Cochise, 135, 162, 164, 171, 196, 199, 339

Cole, Ronald, 102

Collins, John S., 20, 23, 402, *403*, 415, 417, 447, 455, 470n7

Colorow, 411, 413

Colyer, Vincent, 165, 377

Committee on Indian Affairs, 27, 426

consolidation policy: Crook's opinion of, 148–49; impact on Apaches, 132–34; impact on Poncas, 53

Contraband Springs, 334

Cooley, Corydon, 128, 131

Cooper, James Fenimore, 377

Corbin, Henry, 417

Council Fire, 435

Cowarrow, 272, 274

Crawford, Emmet, *153*, 209, 221, 278; annuity issue and, 268–69; in arrest and trial of Ka-ya-ten-nae, 249–51; background, 152; on Chiricahua removal to Florida, 308–9; on Chiricahua retrieval of family members, 234–35; Crook's response to death of, 327–31, 347; death of, 319–23, 323, 397; depiction of on Crook's Monument, 458; Dutchy and, 251, 263; funeral escort for, 347; Indian spy network and, 164; on Ka-ya-ten-nae, 244; as military commander of San Carlos, 230; overreach of authority by, 269–70; rations shortage investigated by, 158–59; in second breakout pursuit, 291–92, 296, 297, 298, 299, 301, 303, 316, 319; in Sierra Madre expedition, 161, 181, 189–91; Wilcox's complaints against, 260–67

Crazy Horse, 3, 111, 431

Crook, Charles, 454, 456

Crook, George, *124*, *336*, *403*, *432*; assignment to Arizona, 124–25; on assimilation, 28, 164, 256, 271, 384, 425; attempts to earn outside income, 78, 113–18, 406, 418; autobiography and journal of, 294–96, 400, 403–4, 405–6, 449, 452; Bannocks and, 12–13, 14, 15–16; on Cibicue mutiny, 146; civilian law enforcement and, 100–102; Civil War and, 404, 449–50, 450; consolidation policy and, 150–51; criticism of, 4, 232, 283–84, 355; criticism of, Crook response to, 372–76; death of, 397, 452–53; on dual control of San Carlos, 284–85; financial estate of, 461–62; funeral of, 454–57; as hunter, 19–20, 317–18, 401–3, 446–48; illnesses, 327, 405, 445–46, 451–52; Indian policy and, letter on, 73–76; Indian policy and, use of press in publicizing, 48; Indian Rights Association and, 380–81; on Indian Ring, 56; on Indian scout strategy, 374–75; interview with Thomas Tibbles, 15, 47; Miles and, 309–15, 376, 396; Military Division of the Missouri and, 389; on Mount Vernon Barracks' condition, 393; on Nez Perce War, 11; Northern Cheyenne and, 20–21, 44; pension, 112–13; Ponca Commission and, 82–83, 88; Ponca court case and, 62, 64, 66, 69; Poncas and, 47, 50–51, 55–57; promotion efforts, 118–22; promotion to major general, 389–91, 414–15; public opinion of, 356–57; reform movement and, 377; on reservation management, 27–29, 31, 130; respect for individual Indians, 111; *Resumé of Operations against the Apache Indians, 1882 to 1886*, 375–76; on sabotage of Chiricahua resettlement, 221–22; on scouts' loyalty, 344; in Soldier Lodge, 48; on temperance, 448; Utes and, 110–11; visit to Havasupai,

Crook, George (*continued*)
272–75; on voting rights for Indians, 381–82; on white usurpation of Indian lands, 424

Crook, Mary, 4–5, 18, 92, 93, 94, 96, 227, 294, 317, 329, 356, 380, 400, 405, 414, 416, 418–19, 452, 454, 456, 461–62

Crook, Oliver, 114, 118

Crook, Walter, 454, 456

Crook Crest, *456*, 462

Crook House, 89–96, *91*

Crook's gravesite, 458–59, *459*

Crook's Monument, 338, 456–58

Crow Creek Reservation, 429, 437

Crows, 13, 80

Cruse, Thomas, 142, 144

Curley, 210

Custer, George Armstrong, 309

Dailey, James, 456

Dakota statehood, 429

Daly, Henry, 296, 320, 324, 334–35, 341, 342, 509n24

Dandy Jim, 142

Danilson, William, 9, 10, 11

Darlington Reservation, 20–22

Darrow, Ruey, 492n39

Davis, Britton, *154*, 237, 239, 240, 357; annuity issue and, 268–69; on Apache scouts, 290; on Apache unrest, 278–79; assassination attempt on, 282, 286, 503n23; background, 152–54; confrontation with Ka-ya-ten-nae, 248–50; Dutchy and, 251; employment of Indians and, 244; on Geronimo, 277; Peaches and, 176, 177; in rations issue, 158–59; resignation of, 301; role at San Carlos, 231; second breakout and, 287, 296, 298, 299, 300–301; tiswin-drunk response, 279, 280–81; *The Truth about Geronimo*, 153–54; at Turkey Creek, 248–49, 277, 285

Davis, Jefferson C., 319

Davis, Thomas, 319, 325

Davis, Wirt, 291–92, 293, 298, 302, 303, 308, 316, 320, 329

Dawes, Henry L., 82, 87, 88, 394, 426, 443, 450–51

Dawes Act of 1889, 88, 426–27, 435, 442

Day, Mathias W., 298, 302

Deadshot, 142, 487n17

Debo, Angie, 197

Deer Creek affair, 245

Denver Tribune, 150

Department of Arizona, 119, 125, 355

Department of the Columbia, 8, 13, 17

Department of the Missouri, 22, 310

Department of the Platte, 8, 20, 26, 89, *98*, 353, 400, 408–10

detribalized Indians, 65, 71–72, 427

Dickey, J. J., 5

Division of the Missouri, 7, 389

Division of the Pacific, 266, 310

Dji-li-kine, 210

Dorst, Joseph H., 365

Dougherty, William E., 250

Douglas County Historical Society, 92

Drake, John S., 453

Drum, Richard C., 225

due process, 60–70

Dull Knife, 20, 22, 24, 26, 30–31, 32, 33, 34, 36, 41, 42–43, 46

Dull Knife, Guy, Jr., 43

Dundy, Elmer, 61–62, 64, 65, 67, 69, 71, 415

Dutchy (scout), 251–52, 263, 320, 321, 331, 509n24

"Duties of Guards and Sentinels" (Kennon), 406

Early, Jubal, 449, 451

Edmonds, Newton, 425–26

Egan, 14

Elliott, Charles P., 300

Empire-State Mines, 483n7

Endicott, William C., 271, 285, 308, 364, 365, 375, 385, 390, 391

Eskiminzin, 111

Evans, Andrew W., 39

Faison, Samson L., 319, 345

Fiebeger, Gustav J., 178, 185, 202, 203

Field, George W., 91

Field, Marshall, 416–17, 417, 455

Fly, Camillis Sydney, 333–34, 337–38, 456–58

Ford, Charles D., 268–70, 277, 284–85

Forsyth, George A., 448

Forsyth, William W., 185

Fort Apache, 123, 127–28, 140, 145, 231, 302, 359, 366

Fort Bayard, 289

Fort Bliss, 301

Fort Bowie, 140, 237, 293, 302, 329, 341, 347, 368

Fort Bridger, 410–11

fort closures, 408

Fort Crook, 459, 526n42

Fort Douglas, 9

Fort Duchesne, 409–11

Fort Hall, 8, 9, 10, 469n34

Fort Keogh, 43, 50

Fort Laramie Treaty, 52, 422, 425, 427–28

Fort Leavenworth, 307, 366

Fort Marion, 307, 346, 365, 366, 368, 382, 384–87

Fort McDowell, 127

Fort Niobrara, 379

Fort Omaha, 55, 57, 93, 96

Fort Pickens, 370, 385, 387–88

Fort Robinson, 32, 33, 35–36, 38, 39, 40, 42, 43, 445, 446

Fort Russell, 107

Fort Sill, 391, 392, 394, 397–98, 451

Fort Steele, 23, 25–26, 104, 408

Fort Terwaw, 114

Fort Thomas, 220, 224

Fort Thornburgh, 408

Fort Union, 253

Fort Verde, 152

Fort Washaki, 403

Fort Whipple, 272, 356

Fort Yates, 439

Foster, Charles, 430, 431, 432, 455

Fountain, Samuel, 318

Frazer, Robert, 381

Free, Mickey, 162, 163, 183, 204, 207, 238, 280, 282, 296, 486n66. See also Ward, John

Fuller, Melville, 390

Garfield, James A., 81, 121, 226

Garnier, Baptiste, 447

Gatewood, Charles (son), 458

Gatewood, Charles B., 152, 155, 156, 161, 184, 189, 190, 231, 268–69, 282–83, 297, 303, 361–62, 368, 371, 386–87, 458, 516n73

General Allotment Act, 426

General Order No. 13, 230

George (scout), 486n74

Geronimo, 171, 336; attitude toward agricultural work, 277; Crook on, 393, 395; delay in returning to San Carlos, 213–15, 217, 223, 231–40, 236–37, 239; depiction of on Crook's Monument, 458; description of, 197; early life, 197–200; factors in second breakout, 279–80; in first breakout from San Carlos, 141, 142; in later life, 398–99; Mexicans and, enmity toward, 198; at Mount Vernon Barracks, 392–93; murder of chief of police by, 224; mystical powers of, 199–200; rescue of family members as focus of, 301–2; return to San Carlos, 240–41; reward offered for, 361; rise of as military leader, 196–97; in second breakout from San Carlos, 289, 298–99, 304, 336–37; strategy in Sierra Madre, 170–71; surrender negotiations with, 201–3, 209, 211, 325, 335–38, 338, 339, 362–63, 367–68, 370; surrender of, 340; in tiswin-drunk incident, 279, 281–82; at Turkey Creek, 248

Geronimo campaign, first. See Sierra Madre expedition

Geronimo campaign, second: Apache scouts in, 290, 293–94, 308, 320;

Geronimo campaign, second (*continued*) bounty on hostile Chiricahuas, 303, 305; Crawford in, 291–92, 293, 296–99, 301, 303, 316, 319, 320–24; Crook strategy for, 285–89, 316–17; cross-border agreements and, 290–91; Miles's assumption of command of, 351, 355–56; Miles's peace offer in, 361–62; Miles's strategy for, 357–58; negotiation of surrender terms in, 306–8, 325, 327–28, 367–69; removal to Florida as option in, 307–9; Sheridan strategy for, 360. *See also* Cañon de los Embudos peace talks; San Carlos breakout, second

Geronimo campaign map, *182*

Ghost Dance movement, 138–39

Gibbon, John G., 11

Gibbs, Barnett, 259

Gilson (reservation employee), 267

Goodwin, Grenville, 203, 210

Gould, Jay, 119, 484n29

government policy. *See* Indian policy

Goyakla, 198. *See also* Geronimo

Grand Army of the Republic, 430

Grand Pacific Hotel, 416

Grant, Jesse, 402

Grant, Ulysses S., 27, 83, 94, 119, 122, 186, 309, 405; peace policy, 27, 130, 164, 377

Grass, John, 439, 440

Great Sioux Reservation, 27, 41, 88, 379, 422; ration system on, 441–42

Green (aide-de-camp), 415, 417

Greene, Jerome, 324

Grijalva, Merejildo, 176–77

Hamilton, John M., 39

Hare, William Hobart, 379

Harmer, Alexander, 272

Harrison, Benjamin, 392, 394, 420, 429, 442, 448

Havasupai, 272

Hay, John, 120

Hayes, Lucy, 95, 437

Hayes, Rutherford B., 14, 15, 16, 38, 80; civilian law enforcement and, 100–101; on Crook, 460; Crook's death and, 455, 456; Crook's friendship with, 18–19, 390, 402, 404; Crook's promotion efforts and, 119, 120; Ponca Commission and, 82–83, 87; Standing Bear meeting with, 54; visit to Crook House, 95

Hayes, Webb, 18–20, 23, 25, 78–79, 119, 401, 402, *403*, 417, 447, 456, 458

Haynes, William P., 334

Hayt, Ezra, 27, 44, 62–63, 70, 103–4, 476n56

Head (army colonel), 329

heliographic coordinate system, 358

Herbert, George, 396

Hoar, George Frisbie, 81, 82

Hoddentin pollen, 183

Homestead Act, 427, 442

Hopis, 380

Horbach, Mary, 228

Horn, Tom, 162, 207–8, 210, 319, 321, 322–23, 490n1

hot-pursuit doctrine, 166–67, 170, 177, 180, 290–91

House Committee on Indian Affairs, 395

Howard, Oliver O., 9, 13, 135, 165, 186, 312, 315, 353, 368–69, 387–88, 389, 396–97, 460

Hualapai, 186

Hualapai Reservation, 380

Hualapai scouts, 380

Huera, 279, 280, 282

Hump, 438–39

Hurlbut, Vincent L., 453

Hyde, George C., 438

Indian agents: Apache complaints concerning, 131–32, 139; congressional investigation of, 28–29; corruption of, 15, 133, 262–63; at San Carlos, 136–37

Indian Bureau, 27, 29, 44, 53, 59, 80, 104, 132, 149, 156, 158, 256, 271. *See also* Interior Department

Indian courts, 278

Indian police force, 164

Indian policy: buffalo slaughter and, 470n16; civilian/military rivalry for control of Indian policy, 150–51, 156–57, 219–22, 253, 258, 261, 264, 268, 284–85; Crook on policy toward Bannock, 14, 15–16; Crook's open letter on, 73–76; Crook's use of press to publicize, 48; due process rights and, 60–70; officers' objections to, 14–15; reservation management and, 27–30, 59–60, 132–33. *See also* judicial issues

Indian reservations: congressional hearings on management of, 27–30; consolidation of tribes on, 132–34, 148–49; Crook's attitude toward, 130, 148, 243–44; headcounts, 151, 157, 165; identification tags, 151, 157, 165, 247; post trader, 159; rations issue on, 158–59, 380; reservation system, 59–60, 63. *See also specific reservations*

Indian Rights Association, 126, 365, 378, 380–81, 382–83, 426, 460–61, 465–66

Indian rights movement, 377, 424

Indian Ring, 56, 133, 255, 313

Indians: assimilationist theory and, 75–76; detribalized, 65, 71–72, 427; legal status of, 61, 64–65, 67, 69, 75, 87. *See also specific groups*

Indian scouts: in Arizona, 127; Bannocks, 8–9; Cheyenne, 24; civilian distrust of, 174; clothing and equipment, 183; in Ghost Dance movement, 138–39; Hualapai, 380; as intelligence gatherers, 164; Navajo, 318; in tracking Fort Robinson escapees, 39–40; Yuma, 358, 359–60. *See also* Apache scouts; Cibicue mutiny

Indian Territory: Poncas and, 52–53, 55, 57, 80, 84–88; as relocation option for Cheyenne, 20–21, 24, 29, 30, 32, 41, 43–44; as relocation option for Chiricahuas, 141, 158, 206, 217, 284, 364–65, 394–96, 451

Indian voting rights, 381–82

Interior Department, 13, 15, 20, 21; allotment system and, 427; consolidation policy and, 132–34, 148–49; Northern Cheyenne and, 32, 34, 43; Poncas and, 53, 62, 70; public opinion and, 41; ration system and, 441–42; reservation management and, 27–30, 130, 132, 220, 226, 255, 261, 264; resistance to Chiricahua resettlement, 258–59; rivalry with military for control of reservations, 150–51, 156–57, 219–22, 253, 258, 261, 264, 268, 284–85; Utes and, 103. *See also* Indian Bureau

Iron Eye, 47, 50, 51, 55

Irwin, James, 39, 40

Jackson, Helen Hunt, 71, 84

Johnson, Barry C., 376

Josslyn, Merritt L., 221

Journal of the Military Service Institution of the United States, 374, 406

judicial process: Indian courts, 278; introduction to San Carlos Indians, 264–65; trial of Cibicue mutineers, 147–48. *See also* law enforcement, civilian

Juh, 141, 169–70, 196, 197, 199, 212, 213, 215, 223, 234, 236

Kautz, August, 129–30

Ka-ya-ten-nae, 214, 237, 238, 241, 244, 246, 248–50, 249–51, 287, 332, 333, 334, 338, 339, 365

Kayitah, 361–62, 369, 371, 516n67

Kelley, Benjamin, 404

Kelton, John C., 375

Kemble, Edward, 52–53

Kennon, Lyman W.V., 373, 383, 396, 406–8, *407*, 415, 417, 419, 420, 442, 449–50, 456, 462

King, Charles, 114–15, 452

King, Jonathan, 51

La Fleshe, Joseph, 51. *See also* Iron Eye

La Fleshe, Susette, 55. *See also* Bright Eyes

Lamar, Lucius Q. C., 271, 285, 364, 365

Lambertson, Genio Madison, 64, 65, 67, 71

land reform and ownership: allotment system and, 422–24; Apaches and, 425; Crook on, 381, 425; as factor in assimilation, 379–80, 424; impact on tribal leadership, 432, 434, 443; Sioux reaction to, 426, 432–33. *See also* Sioux Land Commission

land rush, 442–43

Laurie, Clayton, 102

law enforcement, civilian: Army's intervention in, 98–99; attempt to arrest Apache scout for murder, 251–52, 321; posse comitatus and, 98–99, 412. *See also* judicial process

Lawton, Henry, 358–60, 362, 369, 419, 515n57

Lee (cook), 356, 415, 521n3

Leland Hotel, 416

Lemhi agency, 9, 13

Letter from General Crook on Giving the Ballot to the Indians, 381–82

Lincoln, Robert, 120, 220–21, 223, 224, 226, 227, 259, 260, 268, 270

Little Bat, 447

Little Chief, 24–25, 25

Little Wolf, 20, 22, 24, 30–31, 32, 42, 43, 46, 50

Llewellyn, William H. H., 313–14

Lockwood, Frank, 167

Loco, 142, 170, 212, 215, 219, 223, 224, 232, 246, 253, 287, 458

Los Angeles Daily Times, 348–49

Lower Brulé Reservation, 429, 437

Loyal Legion, 460

Lummis, Charles Fletcher, 324, 348–51, 353

MacArthur, Arthur, 421

Mackenzie, Ranald S., 14, 21, 29, 140–41, 175

Malheur Reservation, 13

Mangas, 171, 246, 253, 279, 286, 289–90, 332, 340–41, 493n14

Mangas Coloradas, 171, 196, 198–99, 202, 339

Martin, James P., 220

Martine, 361–62, 369, 371, 386, 516n67

Martine, George, 361

Maus, Marion, 319, 320, 322, 323, 325, 326, 327, 331–32, 333, 341, 342, 343, 351

Maynard, George W., 116–18

McClellan, Ely, 452, 454

McClelland, Jennie, 401, 415

McComas, Charlie, 171, 174, 191, 193, 194, 211, 223, 235–36, 238–39, 241, 492n39

McComas killings, 176

McCrary, George W., 70, 72, 101

McDowell, Irvin, 119, 122, 140, 146

McIntosh, Archie, 162, 253–54

McKinley, William, 119, 449

McKinn (captive), 302

McLaughlin, James, 440–41

Meeker, Nathan, 104–7, 108, 109

Merritt, Wesley, 108–9, 122

Mescalero Reservation, 301, 314, 398

Mexican forces: animosity toward U.S. forces, 300–301; attack on Juh's camp, 169–70; combat with Apaches, 189, 215; in Crawford's death, 320–24

Mexico: Apache captives held by, 253, 287–88, 304; Apache enmity toward, 297; Chiricahua raiding in, 135–36, 234–35; on Chiricahua relocation, 397; complaints concerning Apache scouts, 327; cross-border agreements with, 166–67, 170, 177–79, 179–80, 290–91, 300–301; Geronimo's enmity toward, 198

Miguel, 128

Miles, John, 470n15

Miles, Mary, 355, 390

Miles, Nelson A., 8, 14, *311*; Bannocks and, 13; Cheyenne and, 24, 43; on Chiricahua relocation, 395–97; criti-

cism of, 390; Crook on, 314, 354–55,
376; on Crook's death, 459; distrust
of Chiricahuas, 363; on Indian scouts,
312, 354, 357–58; opposition to
Crook's promotion, 122; in peace talks
with Geronimo, 367–68; on "plot"
to discredit, 370–71, 516n65; Ponca
Commission and, 83; rivalry with
Crook, 309–15, 396; second breakout
and, 307; in second Geronimo cam-
paign, 351, 355–56; in Sioux War, 314
Miller, Samuel, 71
mining operations: Crook's investment
in, 78, 113–18, 406; incursion on res-
ervation lands, 245, 499n10; officers'
investment in, 113–18; Utes perceived
as threat to, 103–4
Modocs, 206, 328
Mojaves, 225, 308
Monthly Weather Review, 3
Moore, Tom, 79, 127, 332, 333
Morgan, Thomas J., 429, 441–42
Mormon settlers, 244–45
Mose, 132, 145
Mount Vernon Barracks, 388–89, 391–93,
397, 451
Murchie mine, 113–18, 483n7
My-klitz-so, 251–52

Naiche, 135, 170, 171, *171*, 237, 282, 302,
321, 322, 370, 392, 398; in peace
negotiations, 335, 338, 341, 342, 343,
368; raiding in Arizona, 359, 360; in
second breakout, 286, 289; surrender
of, 340
Nana, 212, 215, 223, 280–81, 287, 298,
325, 340, 343
Nance, Albinus, 99–100
Natches, 223, 248
National Indian Defense Association, 435
National Park Service, 77
Navajo (Supai chief), 274
Navajos, 129, 318, 380
Navajo scouts, 318

Nebraska State Historical Society, 92
New York City, 418–19
New York Daily Tribune, 216
New York Herald, 36, 37, 38, 39, 186, 211,
227, 395
New York Times, 232, 259, 313, 460
New York Tribune, 385
Nez Perce, 24
Nez Perce War, 8–9, 9, 11
Nicaagat, 103, 111, 482n57
Nickerson, Azor, 16–17, 373–74
Noble, John W., 429, 430, 442
Noch-ay-del-klinne, 138–40, 145
Noche, 320, 361, 386
Norris, Philatus, 79, 80
Northern Pacific Railroads, 89
Northwestern Railroad, 431

Oakland, MD, 105, 227, 228, 401, 416,
454–57, 462
Offutt Field, 526n42
Old Crow, 22, 42
Olive, Isom Prentice "Print," 99–103,
412, 480n3, 481n10
Omaha, Neb., 90, 94, 400–402
Omaha Barracks, 89–91
Omaha Bee, 462
Omaha Daily Herald, 15, 47, 59
Omaha Daily World, 373
Omaha Gun Club, 402
Omaha Ponca Relief Committee, 73
Omaha Republican, 5–6
Omaha Reservation, 63
Omahas, 48, 55, 63. *See also* Poncas
Omaha Soldier Society. *See* Soldier Lodge
Omaha Union Club, 415
On the Border with Crook (Bourke), 131, 421
Ord, Edward, 310
Otis, Harrison Gray, 348, 349
Ouray, 109
Outing Magazine, 180

Paiutes, 13, 14
Payne, John S., 108

Peaches (scout), 176–77, 188, 190, 202, 458, 490n48. *See also* Tzoe

Pedro, 128, 129, 131, 137, 144

Peison, Andrew, 356, 415

Pettigrew, Richard, 422–24

Phoenix Herald, 174

Pierce, Francis E., 270, 276, 277, 278–79, 281, 285, 303, 360

Pierre, S.Dak., 438

Pimas, 358

Pine Ridge agency, 39, 42, 429, 434, 435

Pitkin, Frederick, 103

Ponca Chiefs (Tibbles), 474n2

Ponca Commission, 77–96; appointment of, 81; circumvention of recommendations of, 88; findings of, 86–87; Indians' testimony to, 84–86; members, 82–84; mission of, 82

Ponca Reservation, 52

Poncas: breakout of, 54–55; court case on due process rights of, 60–70; in Crook House construction, 92; Crook's advocacy for, 47, 50–51, 55–57, 62; Crook's meeting with, 57, 59; as detribalized Indians, 71–72; disease and death rate, 53–54; financial support for, 72–73; public opinion on, 59, 62, 70; relations with whites, 51–52; relocation of, 52–53, 55, 72; Schurz on removal of, 80–81; treaties with, 52

Pope, John, 14, 106, 122, 264, 265–66, 285, 310, 482n50

Poppleton, Andrew J., 60–61, 62, 64–65, 67

Porter Joseph C., 17

Posse Comitatus Act, 98–99, 412

Powell, William H., 449

Pratt, Richard H., 428

Prescott Weekly Courier, 396, 454

Price, Hiram, 262

Proctor, Redfield, 392

Pullman Building, 416

Quanah Parker, 398–99

Quapaw Reservation, 53

Rafferty, William A., 236–40

railroads, 89, 97, 125, 415; accommodation of Crook's hunting parties by, 401–2; in Sioux Commission transport, 431

Randall, A. Franklin, 188, 439

Randall, George M., 438

range wars, 97–98

ration system, 158–59, 262–63, 266–67, 380; ration insufficiency, 468n11; reduction of entitlements on Sioux Reservation, 441–42

Reconstruction, 27

Red Cloud, 30, 32, 39–40, 43, 111; on Crook's death, 444; land reform and, 429, 430–31, 434–35, 436

Red Cloud agency, 21, 25, 30, 31

Red River War, 351

Reid, Fanny, 356, 452, 453, 454, 456, 462

Resumé of Operations against the Apache Indians, 1882 to 1886 (Crook), 375–76, 386

Riley, Sinew, 487n17

Roberts, Charlie, 298, 333, 335–36, 336, 341, 351, 401, 510n22

Roberts, Cyrus Swan, 78, 84, 86, 178, 272, 303, 327, 333, 336, 351, 356, 375, 391, 414, 419, 420, 421, 431, 442, 450, 453, 455, 513n10

Roberts, Laura, 391, 455

Robinson, Charles, 25

Robinson, Levi, 472n46

Roosevelt, Theodore, 398–99

Rope, John, 191, 193, 203–4, 210, 225, 491n11

Rosebud agency, 429, 431, 434

Ross, Edmond, 313–14

Ross Fork agency, 11, 14

Royall, William B., 10–11, 122, 373–74

Sackett, Delos, 114, 116–17

San Carlos breakout, first. *See* Cibicue mutiny; Sierra Madre expedition

San Carlos breakout, second: Crook on reasons for, 284–85; cross-border agreements and, 300–301; Geronimo's motivations in, 279–80; initial pursuit following, 282–83; leaders of, 286–87; non participants, 287; press accounts of, 283–84; tiswin-drunk as factor in, 279–82; tribe's transfer to Fort Leavenworth following, 307; unrest preceding, 276–78; use of scouts in pursuit, 290. *See also* Geronimo campaign

San Carlos Reservation: annuity issue, 268–69; civilian versus military control on, 150–51, 156–57, 219–22, 253, 258, 261, 264, 268, 284–85; consolidation policy impact on, 133–34; corruption of employees, 253; Crook on dual control of, 284–85; foraging parties and, 266–67; headcounts and identification tags, 151, 157, 165, 247; Indian agents at, 136–37; judicial process introduction at, 264–65; mining operations on, 499n10; police force on, 164, 248; rationing system, 158–59, 262–63, 266–67; reforms on, 158–60; scouting force, 127; tiswin ban on, 157, 247, 279. *See also* Apache Reservation

Sand Creek Massacre, 471n37, 482n32

Sandoz, Mari, 471n37

San Franciscan, 313

San Francisco Tribune, 217

Saunders, Alvin, 119

scalp taking, 493n12

Schenck, Robert C., 450

Schmitt, Martin, 114, 118

Schofield, John, 175, 186, 216, 221, 222, 311, 392, 456

Schurz, Carl, 27, 32–33, 50, 55, 59–60, 71, 77, 78–81, 82, 85, 87, 476n56

Schuyler, Walter S., 11, 23, 25, 38, 39, 40, 61, 113–18, *115*

scouts. *See* Apache scouts; Indian scouts

Seguridad Pública, 324

severalty, 379, 381, 424, 426, 435. *See also* land reform and ownership

Severiano, 128, 183, 193

Sheepeaters, 80

She-gha, 302

Shenandoah campaign, 374, 449–50

Sheridan, Philip H., 15, 19, 27, *121*; on buffalo slaughter, 470n16; in Chicago, 417; on Chiricahua relocation, 364; Chiricahua second breakout and, 293, 306–7, 318; civilian law enforcement and, 101; Civil War and, 449, 450; at Civil War reunion, 404–5; fear of general uprising, 26–27; on foraging parties, 267; Fort Duchesne and, 409–10; Fort Marion investigation and, 385, 387; on Geronimo campaign strategy, 360; on Geronimo's escape, 343–44; on Indian policy, 70; on Indian scouts, 40, 309, 318, 374, 507n55; Miles and, 309, 310, 311, 358; mining investment, 114, 116–18; Northern Cheyenne and, 20–21, 22–23, 24–25, 30, 32, 33, 37–38, 38; on peace talks with Geronimo, 330–31, 338; Sierra Madre expedition and, 186; Sioux and, 7, 39

Sherman, John, 309

Sherman, William T., 27, 38, 40, 43, 83, 96, 309, 390; Apaches and, 140, 175; Cibicue mutiny and, 147; in Crook's assignment to Arizona, 125; Omaha Barracks and, 90; Ponca court case and, 70–71; Sierra Madre expedition and, 179–80

Sherman Barracks, 89

Shipp, William E., 319, 320, 322, 323, 343

Shoshones, 7, 8, 10, 14, 20, 80

Showalter, John A., 150, 159

Sidney Barracks, 23, 24

Sieber, Al, 161, 184, 208, 209–10, 213, 224, 267, 281, 296, 297, 299, 319, 458, 491n11

Sierra Madre expedition: amnesty offer, 208–9; Apache scouts in, 148, 161–64, 181, 183; army regulars in, 185; Chiricahua leadership's delay in returning to

Sierra Madre expedition (*continued*)
San Carlos, 213–15, 217, 223, 231–40, 236–40; Chiricahua resettlement following, 219–28; Crook's "capture" during, 204–6, 259–60; Crook's meeting with scouts prior to, 181–85; Crook's Monument depiction of, 458; Crook's strategy for, 165–66, 169; cross-border agreements and, 166–67, 170, 177–80; McComas incident as factor in, 171, 174, 235; mule train in, 185; press reports on, 216–17; public opinion concerning, 174–75; rancheria battle, 191–92; rules of engagement in, 190; Sherman disapproval of, 179–80; surrender negotiations, 168, 192–94, 201–3, 207–9, 211; terrain as factor in, 167. *See also* Cibicue mutiny

Sioux, 13, 14, 24, 30, 103; Cheyenne and, 20–21, 39, 41–42; Crook reputation with, 430–31, 523n26; ration entitlements and, 441–42, 448–49

Sioux, Blackfeet, 438

Sioux, Brulé, 30, 48, 72, 85, 469n38; Sioux Commission and, 431–34

Sioux, Hunkpapa, 428–29, 439–41

Sioux, Lakota, 3, 22, 26, 30, 40; reservations, *423*

Sioux, Miniconjou, 438

Sioux, Northern, 3–4

Sioux, Oglala, 20, 39–40, 429, 469n38; Sioux Commission and, 434–37

Sioux, Sans Arc, 438

Sioux, Two Kettle, 438

Sioux Land Act, 427

Sioux Land Commission: background to, 422–24; Bourke and, 421; Brulés and, 431–34; Crook on, 428, 430; Crook's death impact on, 443; Hunkpapas and, 439–41; mandate of, 425; Oglalas and, 434–37. *See also* land reform and ownership

Sioux Reservation. *See* Great Sioux Reservation

Sioux War, 3–4, 103, 310, 314, 354, 429

Sitting Bull, 3, 7, 439, 440–41

Skinner, John O., 128

Skippy (scout), 142

Smith, Allen, 282–83

Smith, John E., 9–10, 11–12

Snider, Andrew, 114

Society of Arizona Pioneers, 356

Society of the Army of West Virginia, 18, 404, 456

Soldier Lodge, 48, 50, 57, 438

Southern Pacific Railway, 181, 292, 293

Spees, Everett K., 524n3

Spencer, Charlie, 272

Spotted Tail, 48, 72, 111, 431

Spotted Tail agency, 30

Standing Bear, 50, *58*, 72, 82, 111, 384; Crook's meeting with, 59; death of family members, 53, 54, 55; "I am a man" speech, 68–69; physical description, 57; Ponca Commission and, 85–86, Ponca court case and, 63, 64, 65–68; on resettlement, 52; Tibbles's meeting with, 57

Standing Rock Reservation, 428, 439

Stanley, David S., 370

Stanton, Thaddeus H., 79, *403*, 406, 414, 455, 456, 462

Starvation March, 4

Stickney, William, 83

Strauss, Charles, 333

Studebaker, Peter, 417, 455

Supai. *See* Havasupai

Sweeney, Edwin, 233

Swing, David, 455, 461

Tambiago, 9–10, 12, 468n13

Tarahumaras, 169–70, 324

Taza, 135

Tecumseh, 138

telegraph system, 293

telephones, 5, 94

Teller, Henry M., 150, 160, 217, 220–21, 222, 227, 245, 252, 255, 258–60, 268

Telles, Felix, 162. *See also* Free, Mickey

Terry, Alfred, 312, 315, 389–90

Tesorabibi Ranch, 187–88

Thirty-Sixth Ohio Volunteer Infantry, 18, 404–5

Thornburgh, Thomas T., 23, 25, 104–8, 481n27

Thrapp, Dan, 180, 204–6

Thurston, John, 101–2

Tibbles, Thomas Henry, 15; advocacy for Poncas, 72–73; background, 49–50; Crook interview with, 47, 55–57; Indian rights movement and, 383, 384, 386; physical description, 48–49, *49*; *Ponca Chiefs*, 474n2; Ponca court case and, 62, 68, 71; report on Apache prisoners at Fort Marion, 386; in Soldier Lodge, 48, 50, 57

Tidball, Zan L., 251–52

Tiffany, Joseph C., 137, 139, 141, 142, 150, 230, 245, 486n61

tiswin-drunk incidents, 249, 279–82

tiswin homebrew, 157, 247

Tokio, 11

Tombstone Epitaph, 174, 217, 356–57, 395

Topete, Bonafacio, 177–78, 178

Torres, Felizardo, 178–79

Torres, Luis, 300, 327

Touzalin, Albert, 402, *403*, 447, 524n7

tribalism, 76, 424

Tribolet (trader in alcohol), 334–35, 343, 511n38, 512n4

Tritle, Frederick, 316–17

Truth about Geronimo, The (Davis), 153–54

Tsitsistas, 20. *See also* Cheyenne, Northern

Tucson Weekly Citizen, 233

Turkey Creek: Chiricahua relocation to, 246, 363–64; Davis at, 248–49, 277, 285; Geronimo at, 248

Tuzzone, 214

Tzoe, 176, 490n48. *See also* Peaches

Ulzana, 297, 307–8, 317, 343

Ulzana's raid, 304–5, 316, 318, 337

Umatillas, 13, 14

Uncompahgre agency, 409

Union Pacific Railroad, 89

United States ex rel. Ma-chu-nah-zha (Standing Bear) v. George Crook, a Brigadier General of the Army of the United States and Commander of the Department of the Platte, 62

U.S. Army: civilian law enforcement and, 98–99; officer finances, 112–13; officer promotion, 119; officer retirement age, 120; officer self-promotion in, 312–15; reservation management and, 27–30, 130, 149–50; weapons training, 408–9

U.S. Army Heritage and Education Center, 294

U.S. Congress, 90; on Chiricahua relocation, 394–97; civilian law enforcement and, 98; on Indian voting rights, 381–82; military retirement age and, 120; on Ponca relocation, 80–81; recognition of Indian War veterans, 482n56; reservation management hearings, 27–30

U.S. Constitution, Fourteenth Amendment, 60, 64–65

U.S. Fifth Cavalry, 471n25

U.S. Fourteenth Infantry, 471n25

U.S. Fourth Cavalry, 294

U.S. Ninth Cavalry Buffalo Soldiers, 410

U.S. Ninth Infantry, 471n25

U.S. Ninth Infantry orchestra, 94

U.S. Seventh Cavalry, 471n25

U.S. Sixth Cavalry, 185, 296

U.S. Third Cavalry, 122, 230, 471n25

Ute John. *See* Nicaagat

Ute Reservation, 77–78

Utes, 77–78, 482n50; departure from White River on annual hunt, 104–6; in Milk River battle, 107–9, 110; perceived unrest among, 409–13; public

Utes (*continued*)
   opinion on, 102–3; as threat to mining operations, 103–4
Utley, Robert, 153–54, 197, 200

Victorio, 136, 141, 196, 237, 339
Vore, Jacob, 55
voting rights, 381–82

Wade, James, 361
Wanamaker, John, 417
Ward, John, 162. *See also* Free, Mickey
War Department: Apaches and, 135, 225, 244, 251, 266, 267, 348, 389; Bannocks and, 15; Bourke's effort to obtain transfer in, 419–20; Cheyenne and, 41, 43; on Chiricahua resettlement at San Carlos, 225; Crook honored by after death, 459; Crook's promotion efforts and, 313; Poncas and, 50; rivalry with Interior Department for control of Indian policy, 150–51, 156–57, 219–22, 226, 228, 253, 258, 261, 264, 268, 284–85; role in conflict between Crawford and Wilcox, 267–68, 270; Sioux and, 28, 41; in Yellowstone Park management, 77
Ware, Eugene, 236
Warner, William, 430, 431, *432*, 436
Washakie, 8
Washington, George, centennial of inauguration of, 418
Washington Post, 393, 395
weapons training, 408–9
Webster, John L., 60–61, 62, 65, 66–67
Welsh, Herbert, 126, 365, 377, *378*, 391; background, 378–79; Bourke and, 382–83; on Chiricahua relocation site, 397; Crook and, 380; on Fort Marion conditions, 385–86; on Indian land use, 424, 426; Indian Rights Association and, 380; on social structures, 379–80
Wessells, Henry, 33–39, 43
West, Frank, 185
Whipple Barracks, 127, 161
White Eagle, 84–85
White Mountain Reservation, 125, 133, 149, 381
White River agency, 104, 105, 108
Wilcox, Philip P.: assertions of authority by, 219–22, 255, 257–59; on Chiricahuas' disruptive influence, 223, 224, 227; complaints against Emmet Crawford, 260–67; Crawford's complaints against, 261–62; Crook on, 227–28, 257; initial cooperation with Crook, 150–51, 156, 160, 256–57; profiteering by, 150, 159; resignation of, 268
Wild Hog, 22, 35, 42
Willcox, Orlando O., 125, 130, 140, 143
Williams, Robert, 26, 106, 108, 327, 417
Wind River agency, 9
Woman's Christian Temperance Union, 448
Wood, Leonard, 359, 369
Wratten, George, 361–62
Wright, John M., 236
writ of habeas corpus, 60–61, 67

Yantonai, 428–29
Yavapai, 130, 134–35, 181, 231, 246
Yellow Coyote, 251–52
Yellowstone National Park, 77, 79–80
Young Man Afraid of His Horse, 415
Yumas, 225, 308, 358, 359–60
Yuma scouts, 358, 359–60

Zulick, Conrad M., 348